Houghton
Mifflin
Harcourt

Integrated Mathematics 2

Volume 1

TIMOTHY D. KANOLD

EDWARD B. BURGER

JULI K. DIXON

MATTHEW R. LARSON

STEVEN J. LEINWAND

Printed in the U.S.A.

ISBN 978-0-544-38983-0

10 1026 24 23 22 21 20 19 18 17

4500658076 D E F G H

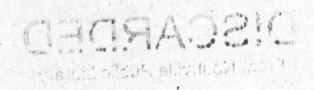

Timothy D. Kanold, Ph.D., is an award-winning international educator, author, and consultant. He is a former superintendent and director of mathematics and science at Adlai E. Stevenson High School District 125 in Lincolnshire, Illinois. He is a past president of the National Council of Supervisors of Mathematics (NCSM) and the Council for the Presidential Awardees of Mathematics (CPAM). He has served on several writing and leadership commissions for NCTM during the past decade. He presents motivational professional development seminars with a focus on developing professional learning communities (PLC's) to improve the teaching, assessing, and learning of students. He has recently authored nationally recognized articles, books, and textbooks for mathematics education and school leadership, including *What Every Principal Needs to Know about the Teaching and Learning of Mathematics*.

Edward B. Burger, Ph.D., is the President of Southwestern University, a former Francis Christopher Oakley Third Century Professor of Mathematics at Williams College, and a former vice provost at Baylor University. He has authored or coauthored more than sixty-five articles, books, and video series; delivered over five hundred addresses and workshops throughout the world; and made more than fifty radio and television appearances. He is a Fellow of the American Mathematical Society as well as having earned many national honors, including the Robert Foster Cherry Award for Great Teaching in 2010. In 2012, Microsoft Education named him a "Global Hero in Education."

Juli K. Dixon, Ph.D., is a Professor of Mathematics Education at the University of Central Florida. She has taught mathematics in urban schools at the elementary, middle, secondary, and post-secondary levels. She is an active researcher and speaker with numerous publications and conference presentations. Key areas of focus are deepening teachers' content knowledge and communicating and justifying mathematical ideas. She is a past chair of the NCTM Student Explorations in Mathematics Editorial Panel and member of the Board of Directors for the Association of Mathematics Teacher Educators.

Matthew R. Larson, Ph.D., is the K-12 mathematics curriculum specialist for the Lincoln Public Schools and served on the Board of Directors for the National Council of Teachers of Mathematics from 2010 to 2013. He is a past chair of NCTM's Research Committee and was a member of NCTM's Task Force on Linking Research and Practice. He is the author of several books on implementing the Common Core Standards for Mathematics. He has taught mathematics at the secondary and college levels and held an appointment as an honorary visiting associate professor at Teachers College, Columbia University.

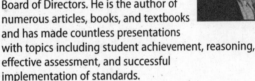

Steven J. Leinwand is a Principal Research Analyst at the American Institutes for Research (AIR) in Washington, D.C., and has over 30 years in leadership positions in mathematics education. He is past president of the National Council of Supervisors of Mathematics and served on the NCTM Board of Directors. He is the author of numerous articles, books, and textbooks and has made countless presentations with topics including student achievement, reasoning, effective assessment, and successful implementation of standards.

Performance Task Consultant

Robert Kaplinsky
Teacher Specialist, Mathematics
Downey Unified School District
Downey, California

STEM Consultants

Science, Technology, Engineering, and Mathematics

Michael A. DiSpezio
Global Educator
North Falmouth, Massachusetts

Michael R. Heithaus
Executive Director, School of Environment, Arts, and Society
Professor, Department of Biological Sciences
Florida International University
North Miami, Florida

Reviewers

Mindy Eden
Richwoods High School
Peoria School District
Peoria, IL

Dustin Johnson
Badger High School Math Teacher
Department Chair
Lake Geneva-Genoa City Union High School District
Lake Geneva, WI

Ashley D. McSwain
Murray High School
Murray City School District
Salt Lake City, UT

Rebecca Quinn
Doherty Memorial High School
Worcester Public Schools District
Worcester, MA

Ted Ryan
Madison LaFollette High School
Madison Metropolitan School District
Madison, WI

Tony Scoles
Fort Zumwalt School District
O'Fallon, MO

Cynthia L. Smith
Higley Unified School District
Gilbert, AZ

Phillip E. Spellane
Doherty Memorial High School
Worcester Public Schools District
Worcester, MA

Mona Toncheff
Math Content Specialist
Phoenix Union High School District
Phoenix, AZ

Characteristics of Functions

UNIT 1

Volume 1

MODULE 1

Analyzing Functions

MODULE 2

Absolute Value Functions, Equations, and Inequalities

UNIT 2

Volume 1

Polynomial Operations

MODULE 3

Rational Exponents and Radicals

MODULE 4

Adding and Subtracting Polynomials

MODULE 5

Multiplying Polynomials

UNIT 3

Volume 1

Quadratic Functions

MODULE 6

Graphing Quadratic Functions

MODULE 7

Connecting Intercepts, Zeros, and Factors

Quadratic Equations and Models

UNIT 4

Volume 1

MODULE 8 Using Factors to Solve Quadratic Equations

MODULE 9 Using Square Roots to Solve Quadratic Equations

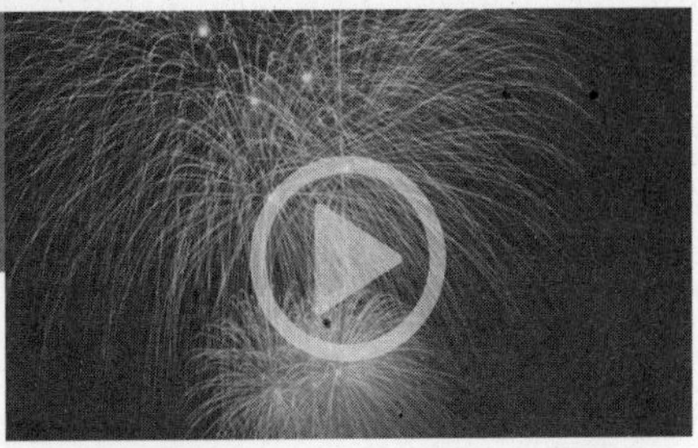

MODULE 10

Linear, Exponential, and Quadratic Models

Extending Quadratic Equations

UNIT 5

Volume 1

MODULE 11 Quadratic Equations and Complex Numbers

MODULE 12 Quadratic Relations and Systems of Equations

MODULE 13

Functions and Inverses

Geometric Proof

UNIT 6

Volume 2

MODULE 14 Proofs with Lines and Angles

MODULE 15

Proofs with Triangles and Quadrilaterals

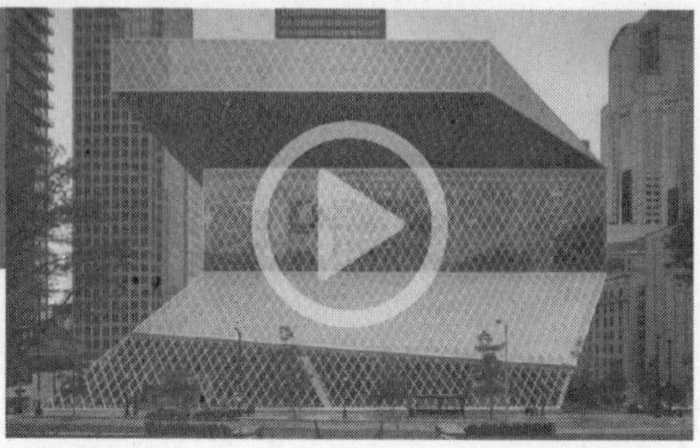

Similarity and Right Triangles

UNIT 7

Volume 2

MODULE 16 Similarity and Transformations

MODULE 17 Using Similar Triangles

MODULE 18 Trigonometry with Right Triangles

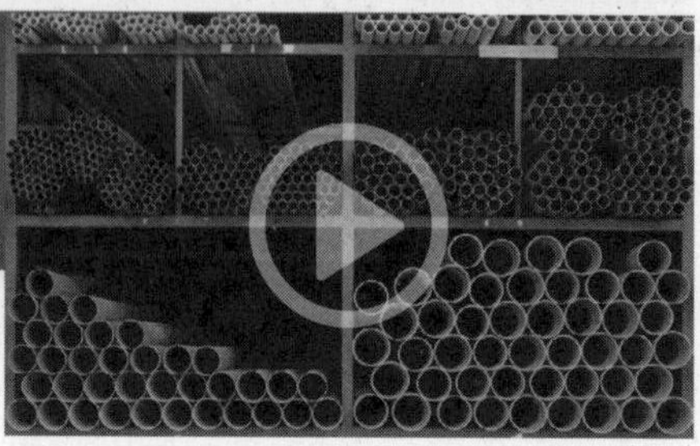

Properties of Circles

UNIT 8

Volume 2

MODULE 19

Angles and Segments in Circles

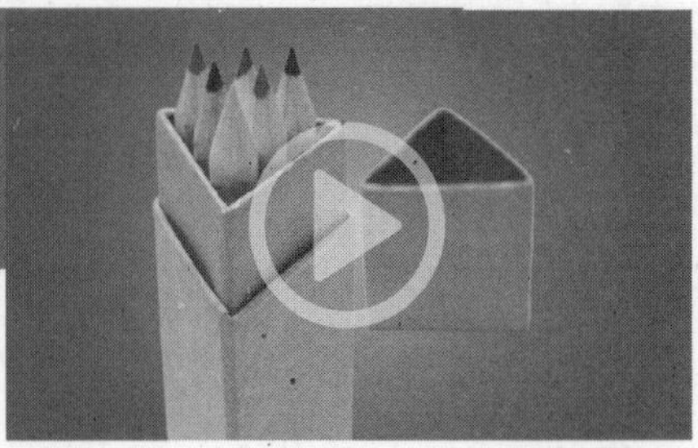

MODULE 20

Arc Length and Sector Area

UNIT 9

Volume 2

Volume

MODULE 21

Volume Formulas

Understanding Probability

UNIT 10

Volume 2

MODULE 22 Introduction to Probability

MODULE 23 Conditional Probability and Independence of Events

MODULE 24

Probability and Decision Making

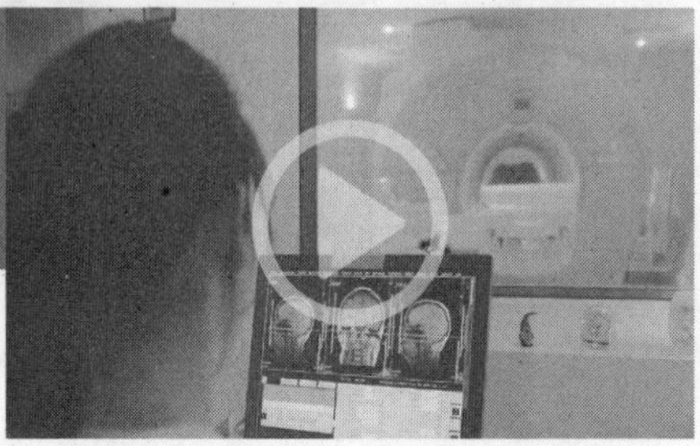

HMH Integrated Math 2
Online State Resources

Scan the QR code or visit:
my.hrw.com/nsmedia/osp/2015/ma/hs/tempint
for correlations and other state-specific resources.

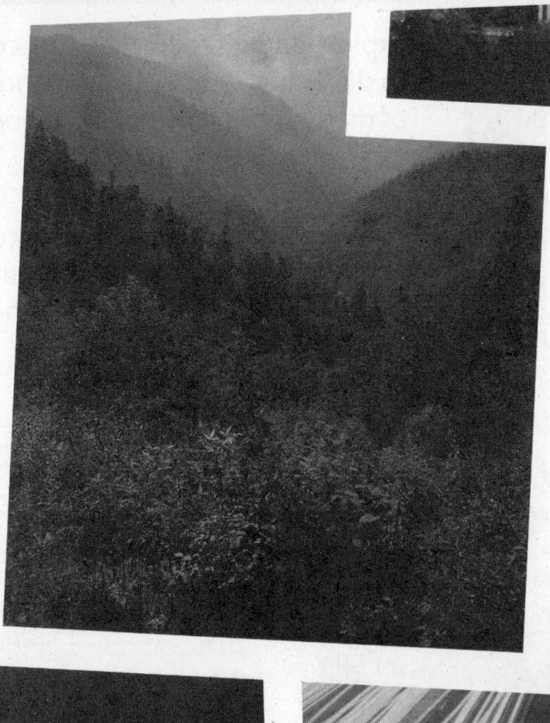

HMH Integrated Math 2 is built on the 5E instructional model--Engage, Explore, Explain, Elaborate, Evaluate--to develop strong conceptual understanding and mastery of key mathematics standards.

ENGAGE

Preview the Lesson Performance Task in the Interactive Student Edition.

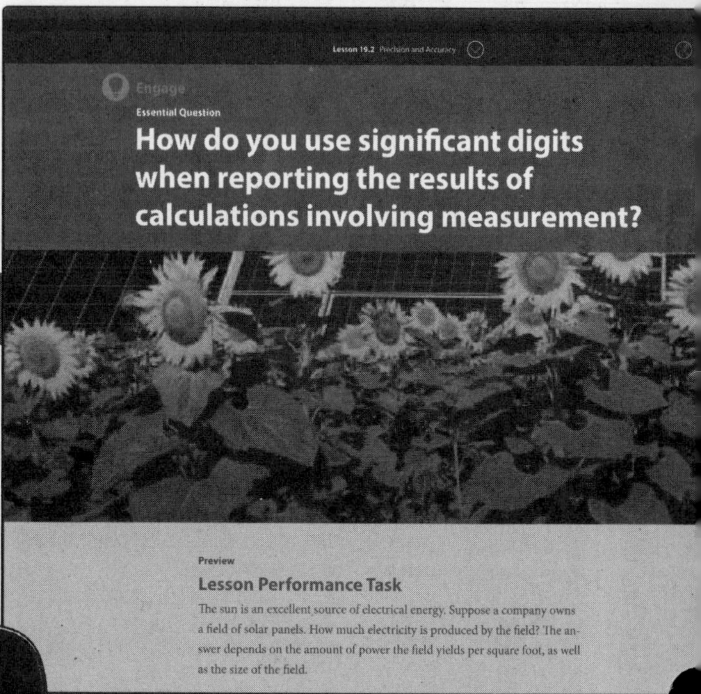

Lesson 19.2 Precision and Accuracy
Engage
Essential Question
How do you use significant digits when reporting the results of calculations involving measurement?
Preview
Lesson Performance Task
The sun is an excellent source of electrical energy. Suppose a company owns a field of solar panels. How much electricity is produced by the field? The answer depends on the amount of power the field yields per square foot, as well as the size of the field.

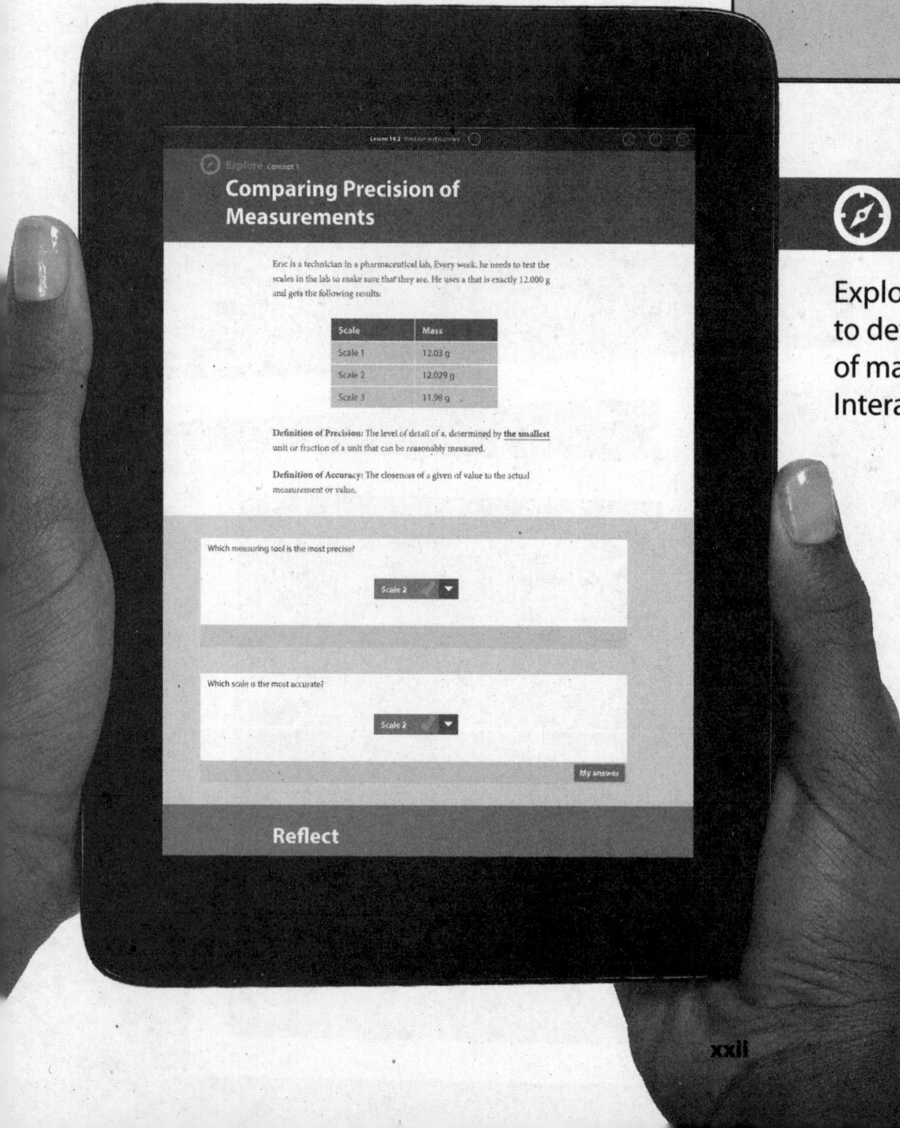

Lesson 19.2 Precision and Accuracy
Explore Concept 1
Comparing Precision of Measurements
Eric is a technician in a pharmaceutical lab. Every week, he needs to test the scales in the lab to make sure that they are. He uses a that is exactly 12.000 g and gets the following results:
Scale | Mass
Scale 1 | 12.03 g
Scale 2 | 12.029 g
Scale 3 | 11.98 g
Definition of Precision: The level of detail of a, determined by the smallest unit or fraction of a unit that can be reasonably measured.
Definition of Accuracy: The closeness of a given of value to the actual measurement or value.
Which measuring tool is the most precise?
Scale 2
Which scale is the most accurate?
Scale 2
My answer
Reflect

EXPLORE

Explore and interact with new concepts to develop a deeper understanding of mathematics in your book and the Interactive Student Edition.

Scan the QR code to access engaging videos, activities, and more in the Resource Locker for each lesson.

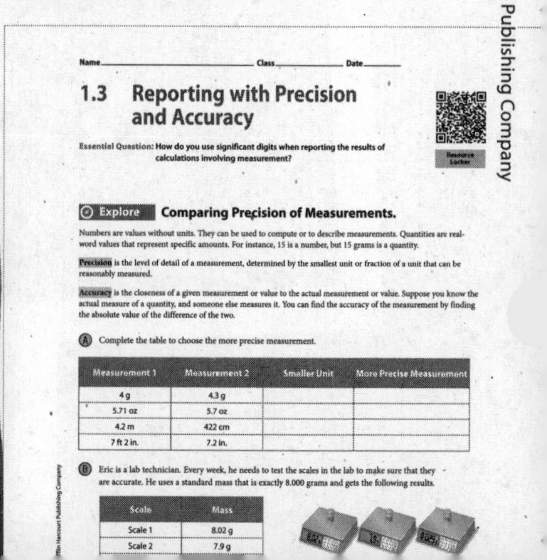

Name_____ Class_____ Date_____

1.3 Reporting with Precision and Accuracy

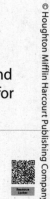

Essential Question: How do you use significant digits when reporting the results of calculations involving measurement?

Resource Locker

Explore Comparing Precision of Measurements.

Numbers are values without units. They can be used to compute or to describe measurements. Quantities are real-word values that represent specific amounts. For instance, 15 is a number, but 15 grams is a quantity.

Precision is the level of detail of a measurement, determined by the smallest unit or fraction of a unit that can be reasonably measured.

Accuracy is the closeness of a given measurement or value to the actual measurement or value. Suppose you know the actual measure of a quantity, and someone else measures it. You can find the accuracy of the measurement by finding the absolute value of the difference of the two.

(A) Complete the table to choose the more precise measurement.

Measurement 1	Measurement 2	Smaller Unit	More Precise Measurement
4 g	4.3 g		
5.71 oz	5.7 oz		
4.2 m	422 cm		
7 ft 2 in.	7.2 in.		

(B) Eric is a lab technician. Every week, he needs to test the scales in the lab to make sure that they are accurate. He uses a standard mass that is exactly 8.000 grams and gets the following results.

Scale	Mass
Scale 1	8.02 g
Scale 2	7.9 g

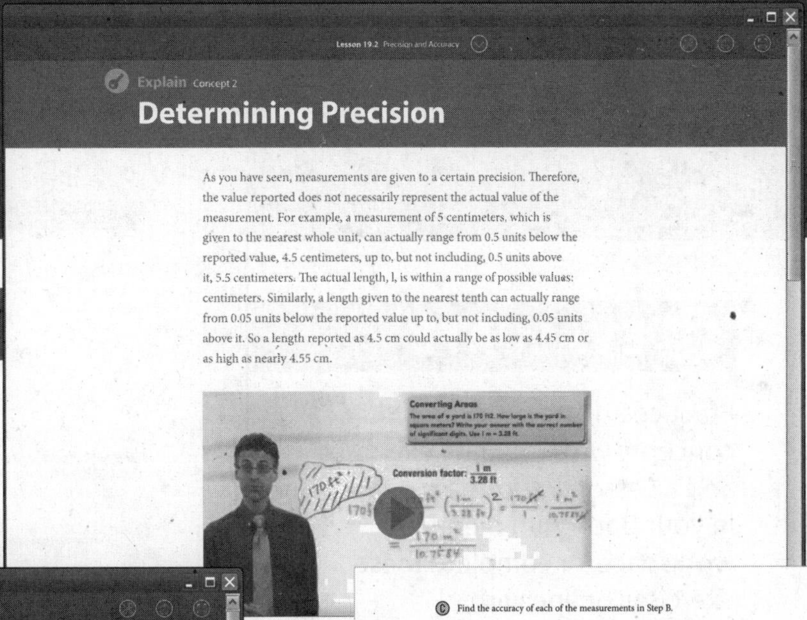

Lesson 19.2 Precision and Accuracy
1 2 3 4 5 6 7 8 9 10 11 - 17
Question 3 of 17
Explain Concept 2
Determining Precision
As you have seen, measurements are given to a certain precision. Therefore, the value reported does not necessarily represent the actual value of the measurement. For example, a measurement of 5 centimeters, which is given to the nearest whole unit, can actually range from 0.5 units below the reported value, 4.5 centimeters, up to, but not including, 0.5 units above it, 5.5 centimeters. The actual length, l, is within a range of possible values: centimeters. Similarly, a length given to the nearest tenth can actually range from 0.05 units below the reported value up to, but not including, 0.05 units above it. So a length reported as 4.5 cm could actually be as low as 4.45 cm or as high as nearly 4.55 cm.
Converting Areas
Conversion factor: 1 m / 3.28 ft

Save & Close
Turn It In
EXPLAIN

Learn concepts with step-by-step interactive examples. Every example is also supported by a Math On the Spot video tutorial.

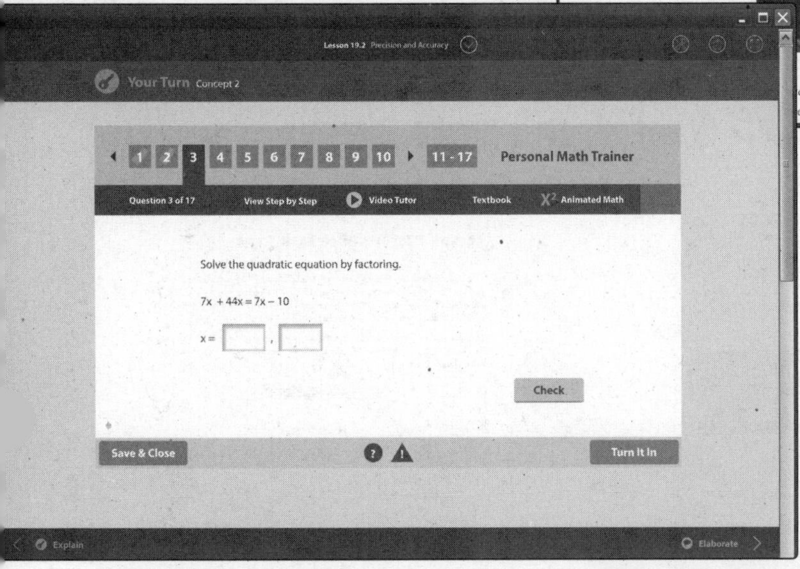

Animated Math

7x + 44x = 7x − 10

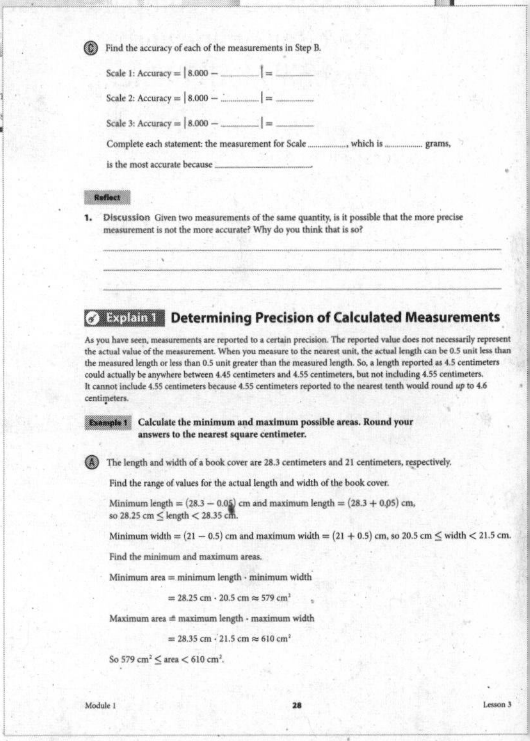

Scale 1: Accuracy = |8.000 − ____| = ____
Scale 2: Accuracy = |8.000 − ____| = ____
Scale 3: Accuracy = |8.000 − ____| = ____

1. Discussion Given two measurements of the same quantity, is it possible that the more precise measurement is not the more accurate? Why do you think that is so?

Example 1 Calculate the minimum and maximum possible areas. Round your answers to the nearest square centimeter.
A The length and width of a book cover are 28.3 centimeters and 21 centimeters, respectively.
Find the range of values for the actual length and width of the book cover.
Minimum length = (28.3 − 0.05) cm and maximum length = (28.3 + 0.05) cm, so 28.25 cm ≤ length < 28.35 cm.
Minimum width = (21 − 0.5) cm and maximum width = (21 + 0.5) cm, so 20.5 cm ≤ width < 21.5 cm.
Find the minimum and maximum areas.
Minimum area = minimum length · minimum width

Maximum area = maximum length · maximum width

So 579 cm² ≤ area < 610 cm².

Check your understanding of new concepts and skills with Your Turn exercises in your book or online with Personal Math Trainer.

ELABORATE
17. Given two measurements, is it possible that the more accurate measurement is not the more precise? Justify your answer.
© Houghton Mifflin Harcourt Publishing Company • Image Credits: ©Michael Freeman/Corbis
Send to Notebook

Show your understanding and reasoning with Reflect and Elaborate questions.

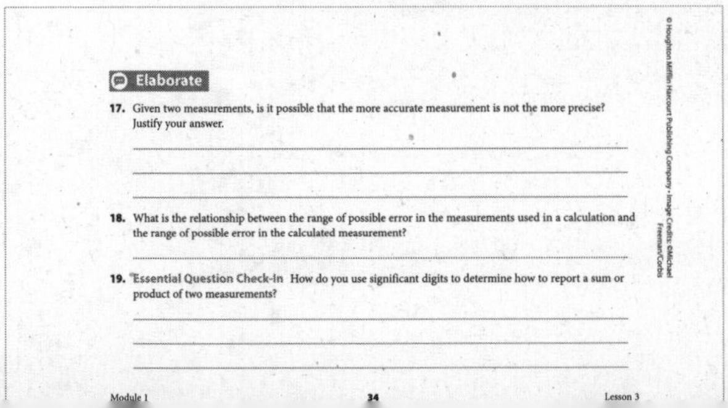

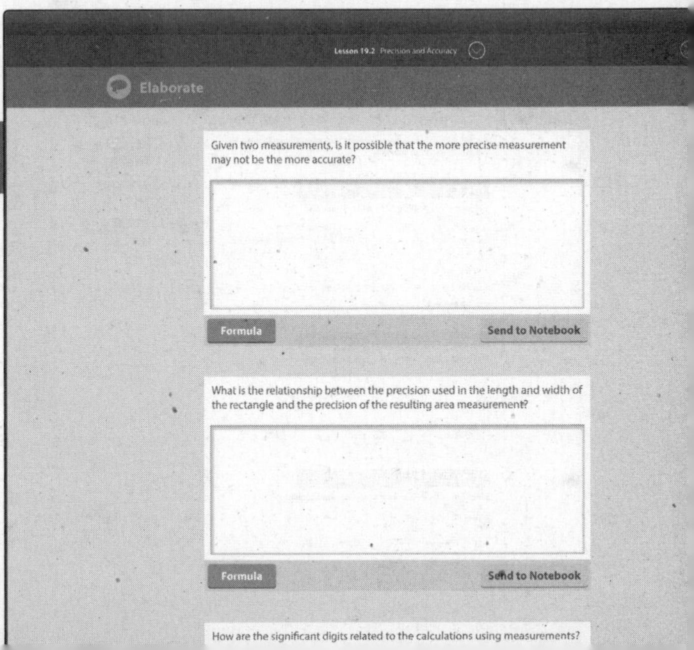

Send to Notebook

EVALUATE

Practice and apply skills and concepts with Evaluate exercises and a Lesson Performance Task in your book with plenty of workspace, or complete these exercises online with Personal Math Trainer.

Personal
Math
Trainer

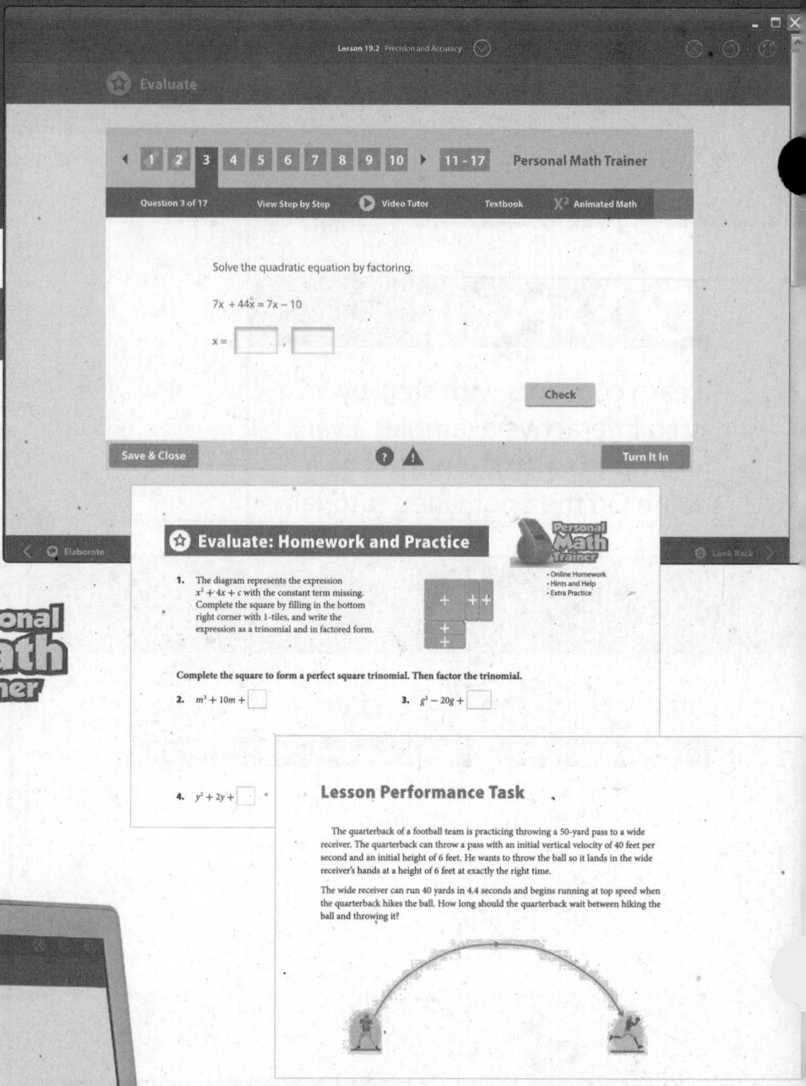

Lesson 19.2 Precision and Accuracy
Evaluate
Personal Math Trainer
Question 3 of 17
View Step by Step
Video Tutor
Textbook
Animated Math
Solve the quadratic equation by factoring.
7x + 44x = 7x − 10
x =
Check
Save & Close
Turn It In
Evaluate: Homework and Practice
• Online Homework
• Hints and Help
• Extra Practice
1. The diagram represents the expression x² + 4x + c with the constant term missing. Complete the square by filling in the bottom right corner with 1-tiles, and write the expression as a trinomial and in factored form.
Complete the square to form a perfect square trinomial. Then factor the trinomial.
2. m² + 10m +
3. g² − 20g +
4. y² + 2y +
Lesson Performance Task
The quarterback of a football team is practicing throwing a 50-yard pass to a wide receiver. The quarterback can throw a pass with an initial vertical velocity of 40 feet per second and an initial height of 6 feet. He wants to throw the ball so it lands in the wide receiver's hands at a height of 6 feet at exactly the right time.
The wide receiver can run 40 yards in 4.4 seconds and begins running at top speed when the quarterback hikes the ball. How long should the quarterback wait between hiking the ball and throwing it?

LOOK BACK

Review what you have learned and prepare for high-stakes tests with a variety of resources, including Study Guide Reviews, Performance Tasks, and Assessment Readiness test preparation.

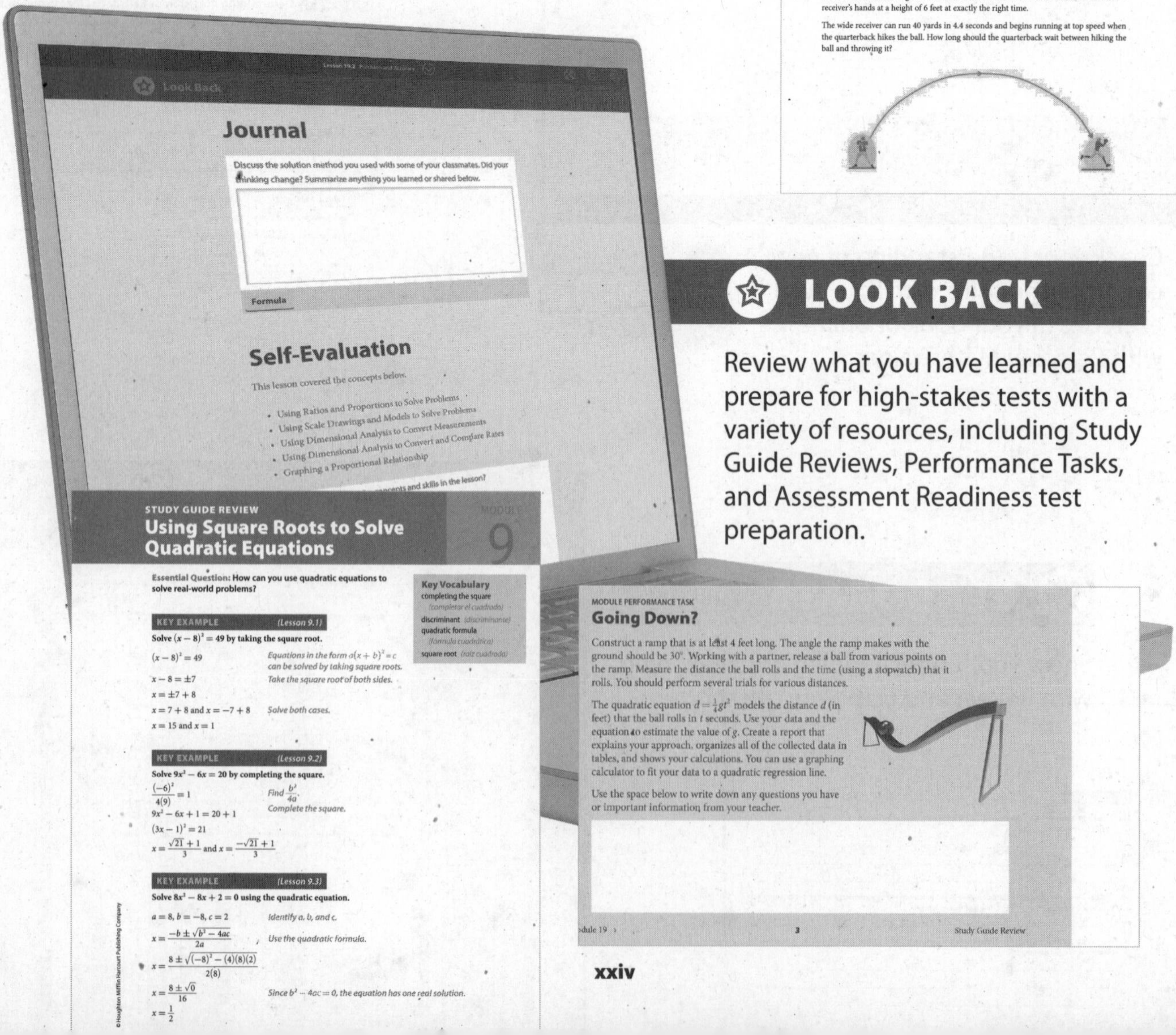

Look Back
Journal
Discuss the solution method you used with some of your classmates. Did your thinking change? Summarize anything you learned or shared below.
Formula
Self-Evaluation
This lesson covered the concepts below.
• Using Ratios and Proportions to Solve Problems
• Using Scale Drawings and Models to Solve Problems
• Using Dimensional Analysis to Convert Measurements
• Using Dimensional Analysis to Convert and Compare Rates
• Graphing a Proportional Relationship
STUDY GUIDE REVIEW
Using Square Roots to Solve Quadratic Equations
MODULE 9
Essential Question: How can you use quadratic equations to solve real-world problems?
Key Vocabulary
completing the square
discriminant
quadratic formula
square root
KEY EXAMPLE (Lesson 9.1)
Solve (x − 8)² = 49 by taking the square root.
KEY EXAMPLE (Lesson 9.2)
Solve 9x² − 6x = 20 by completing the square.
KEY EXAMPLE (Lesson 9.3)
Solve 8x² − 8x + 2 = 0 using the quadratic equation.
MODULE PERFORMANCE TASK
Going Down?
Construct a ramp that is at least 4 feet long. The angle the ramp makes with the ground should be 30°. Working with a partner, release a ball from various points on the ramp. Measure the distance the ball rolls and the time (using a stopwatch) that it rolls. You should perform several trials for various distances.
Use the space below to write down any questions you have or important information from your teacher.
Study Guide Review

UNIT 1

Characteristics of Functions

MODULE 1

Analyzing Functions

MODULE 2

Absolute Value Functions, Equations, and Inequalities

MATH IN CAREERS

Community Theater Owner
A community theater owner uses math to determine revenue, profit, and expenses related to operating the theater. Probability and statistical methods are useful for determining the types of performances that will appeal to the public and attract patrons. Community theater owners should also understand the geometry of stage sets, and algebraic formulas for stage lighting, including those used to calculate light beam spread, throw distance, angle, and overall length.

If you are interested in a career as a community theater owner, you should study these mathematical subjects:

- Algebra
- Geometry
- Trigonometry
- Business Math
- Probability
- Statistics

Research other careers that require determining revenue, profit, and expenses. Check out the career activity at the end of the unit to find out how **Community Theater Owners** use math.

Visualize Vocabulary

Use the ✔ words to complete the graphic. You can put more than one word on each spoke of the information wheel.

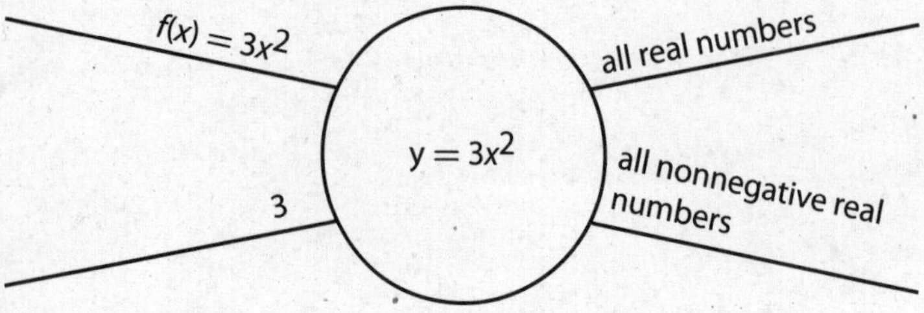

Vocabulary

Review Words

- ✔ coefficient *(coeficiente)*
- ✔ domain *(dominio)*
- ✔ function *(función)*
- ✔ inequality *(desigualdad)*
- ✔ interval *(intervalo)*
- ✔ quadratic function *(función cuadrática)*
- ✔ range *(rango)*

Preview Words

- conjunction *(conjunción)*
- disjunction *(disyunción)*
- even function *(función par)*
- inverse function *(función inversa)*
- odd function *(función impar)*
- parameter *(parámetro)*

Understand Vocabulary

To become familiar with some of the vocabulary terms in the module, consider the following. You may refer to the module, the glossary, or a dictionary.

1. A ______________________ is a constant in the equation of a curve that yields a family of similar curves as it changes.

2. A function $f(x)$ such that $f(x) = f(-x)$ is an ______________________.

3. A compound statement that uses the word *or* is a ______________________.

Active Reading

Three-Panel Flip Chart Before beginning each lesson, create a three-panel flip chart to help you summarize important aspects of the lesson. As you study each lesson, record algebraic examples of functions on the first flap, their graphs on the second flap, and analyses of the functions on the third flap. Add to flip charts from previous lessons by extending the analyses of the functions when possible. For equations and inequalities, record an example on the first flap, a worked out solution on the second flap, and a graph on the third flap.

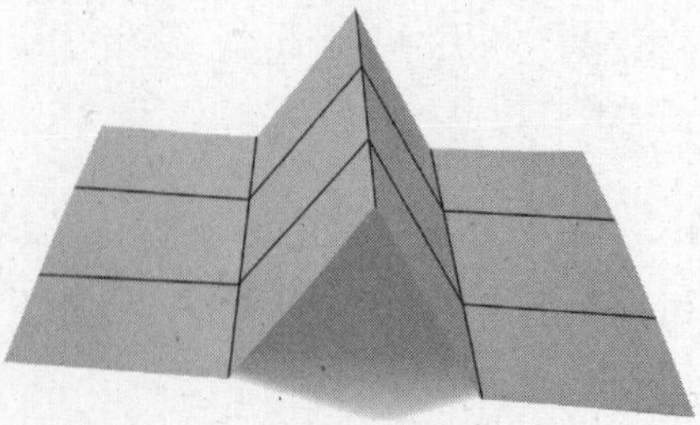

Analyzing Functions

MODULE 1

Essential Question: How can you analyze functions to solve real-world problems?

REAL WORLD VIDEO
Pole vaulting is just one of many track-and-field events that feature a person or object flying through the air. The path of a pole vaulter or of a shot put can be modeled using a quadratic function.

MODULE PERFORMANCE TASK PREVIEW

How High Does a Pole Vaulter Go?

In pole vaulting, a person jumps over a horizontal bar with the assistance of a long fiberglass or carbon-fiber pole. The flexible pole makes it possible for vaulters to achieve much greater heights than jumping without a pole. The goal is to clear the bar without knocking it down. How can mathematics be used to compare the heights of a pole vaulter for two different vaults? Let's jump in and find out!

Are YOU Ready?

Complete these exercises to review skills you will need for this module.

Personal Math Trainer

- Online Homework
- Hints and Help
- Extra Practice

Algebraic Representations of Transformations

Example 1

Rotate $A(-6,3)$ 90° clockwise.
$(-6(-1), 3) = (6, 3)$ **Multiply.**
$A(-6, 3) \rightarrow A'(3, 6)$ **Switch.**

Translate $B(4,7)$ 5 units down.
$(4, 7 - 5) = (4, 2)$ **Subtract.**
$B(4, 7) \rightarrow B'(4,2)$

Find the location of A' given that A is $(1, 5)$.

1. Rotate 90° clockwise. __________

2. Translate 1 unit left. __________

3. Reflect across the x-axis. __________

Linear Functions

Example 2

Name the x- and y-intercepts for $y = -2x + 1$.
x-intercept: $0 = -2x + 1$, so $x = 0.5$.
y-intercept: $y = -2(0) + 1 = 1$

Find the x- and y-intercepts for each equation.

4. $y = 8x - 4$ __________

5. $y = -x + 12$ __________

6. $y = 1.2x + 4.8$ __________

7. $3x + 4y = -60$ __________

Rate of Change and Slope

Example 3

Two points on a line are $(-3, 3)$ and $(4, 1)$. Find the slope.

$$\frac{y_1 - y_2}{x_1 - x_2} = \frac{3 - 1}{-3 - 4} = -\frac{2}{7}$$

The slope is $-\frac{2}{7}$.

Find the slope of the line that passes through the two points.

8. $(0, 5)$ and $(-9, -4)$ __________

9. $(6, -2)$ and $(1, -1)$ __________

10. $(-7, 3)$ and $(-4, -12)$ __________

11. $(-0.5, 10)$ and $(1.5, 30)$ __________

Name______________________ Class______________ Date__________

1.1 Domain, Range, and End Behavior

Essential Question: How can you determine the domain, range, and end behavior of a function?

Resource Locker

Explore Representing an Interval on a Number Line

An **interval** is a part of a number line without any breaks. A *finite interval* has two endpoints, which may or may not be included in the interval. An *infinite interval* is unbounded at one or both ends.

Suppose an interval consists of all real numbers greater than or equal to 1. You can use the inequality $x \geq 1$ to represent the interval. You can also use *set notation* and *interval notation*, as shown in the table.

Description of Interval	Type of Interval	Inequality	Set Notation	Interval notation
All real numbers from a to b, including a and b	Finite	$a \leq x \leq b$	$\{x \mid a \leq x \leq b\}$	$[a, b]$
All real numbers greater than a	Infinite	$x > a$	$\{x \mid x > a\}$	$(a, +\infty)$
All real numbers less than or equal to a	Infinite	$x \leq a$	$\{x \mid x \leq a\}$	$(-\infty, a]$

For set notation, the vertical bar means "such that," so you read $\{x \mid x \geq 1\}$ as "the set of real numbers x such that x is greater than or equal to 1."

For interval notation, do the following:

- Use a square bracket to indicate that an interval includes an endpoint and a parenthesis to indicate that an interval doesn't include an endpoint.
- For an interval that is unbounded at its positive end, use the symbol for positive infinity, $+\infty$. For an interval that unbounded at its negative end, use the symbol for negative infinity, $-\infty$. Always use a parenthesis with positive or negative infinity.

So, you can write the interval $x \geq 1$ as $[1, +\infty)$.

(A) Complete the table by writing the finite interval shown on each number line as an inequality, using set notation, and using interval notation.

Finite Interval	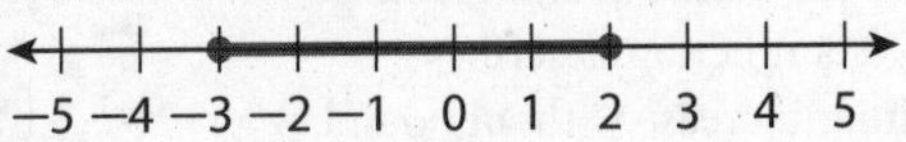	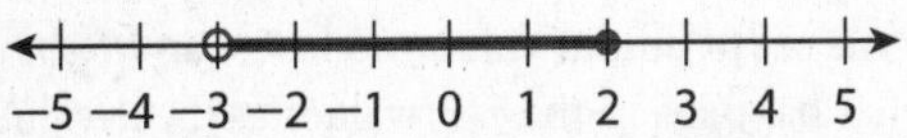
Inequality		
Set Notation		
Interval Notation		

(B) Complete the table by writing the infinite interval shown on each number line as an inequality, using set notation, and using interval notation.

Infinite Interval	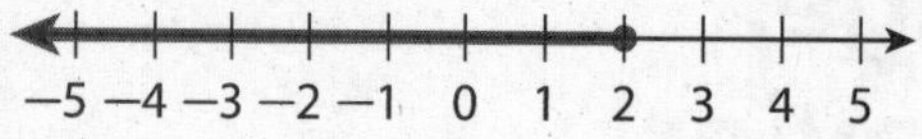	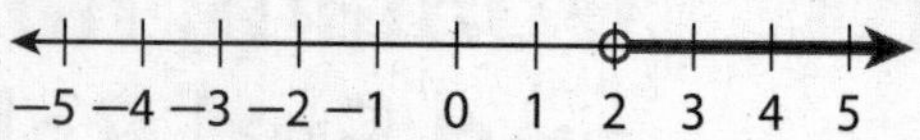
Inequality		
Set Notation		
Interval Notation		

Reflect

1. Consider the interval shown on the number line.

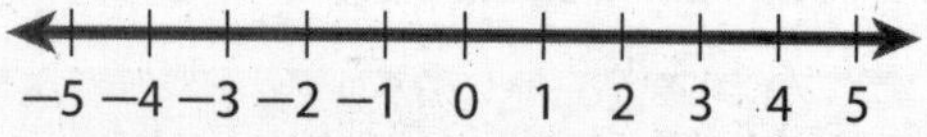

a. Represent the interval using interval notation. ______

b. What numbers are in this interval? ______

2. What do the intervals [0, 5], [0, 5), and (0, 5) have in common? What makes them different?

3. **Discussion** The symbol ∪ represents the *union* of two sets. What do you think the notation $(-\infty, 0) \cup (0, +\infty)$ represents?

Explain 1 Identifying a Function's Domain, Range and End Behavior from its Graph

Recall that the *domain* of a function f is the set of input values x, and the *range* is the set of output values $f(x)$. The **end behavior** of a function describes what happens to the $f(x)$-values as the x-values either increase without bound (approach positive infinity) or decrease without bound (approach negative infinity). For instance, consider the graph of a linear function shown. From the graph, you can make the following observations.

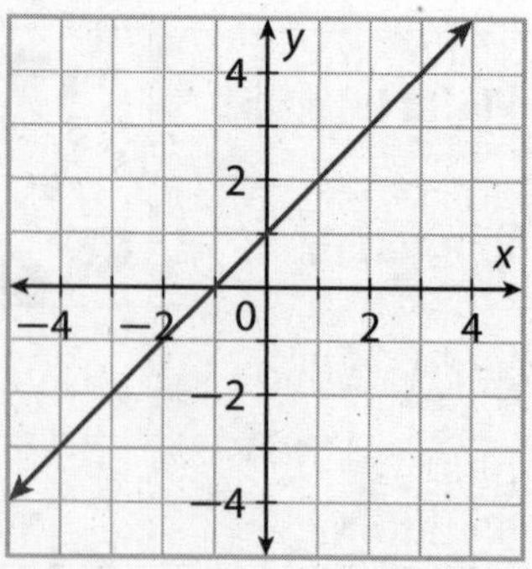

Statement of End Behavior	Symbolic Form of Statement
As the *x*-values increase without bound, the *f*(*x*)-values also increase without bound.	As $x \to +\infty$, $f(x) \to +\infty$.
As the *x*-values decrease without bound, the *f*(*x*)-values also decrease without bound.	As $x \to -\infty$, $f(x) \to -\infty$.

Example 1 **Write the domain and the range of the function as an inequality, using set notation, and using interval notation. Also describe the end behavior of the function.**

(A) The graph of the quadratic function $f(x) = x^2$ is shown.

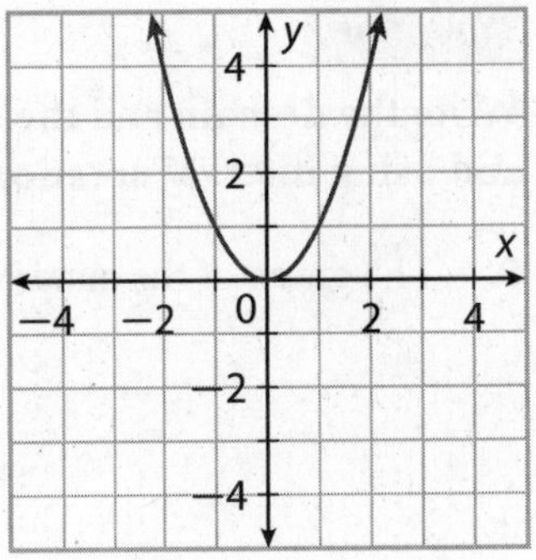

Domain:

Inequality: $-\infty < x < +\infty$

Set notation: $\{x \mid -\infty < x < +\infty\}$

Interval notation: $(-\infty, +\infty)$

Range:

Inequality: $y \geq 0$

Set notation: $\{y \mid y \geq 0\}$

Interval notation: $[0, +\infty)$

End behavior:

As $x \to +\infty$, $f(x) \to +\infty$.

As $x \to -\infty$, $f(x) \to +\infty$.

(B) The graph of the exponential function $f(x) = 2^x$ is shown.

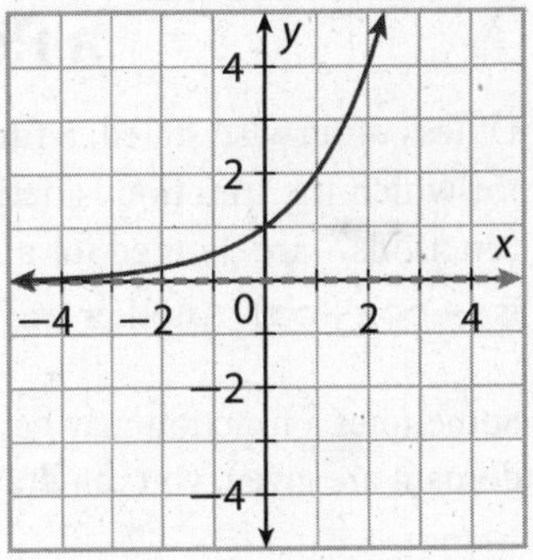

Domain:

Inequality: ______________________

Set notation: ______________________

Interval notation: ______________________

Range:

Inequality: ______________________

Set notation: ______________________

Interval notation: ______________________

End behavior:

As $x \to +\infty$, ______________________.

As $x \to -\infty$, ______________________.

Reflect

4. Why is the end behavior of a quadratic function different from the end behavior of a linear function?

5. In Part B, the $f(x)$-values decrease as the x-values decrease. So, why can't you say that $f(x) \to -\infty$ as $x \to -\infty$?

Your Turn

Write the domain and the range of the function as an inequality, using set notation, and using interval notation. Also describe the end behavior of the function.

6. The graph of the quadratic function $f(x) = -x^2$ is shown.

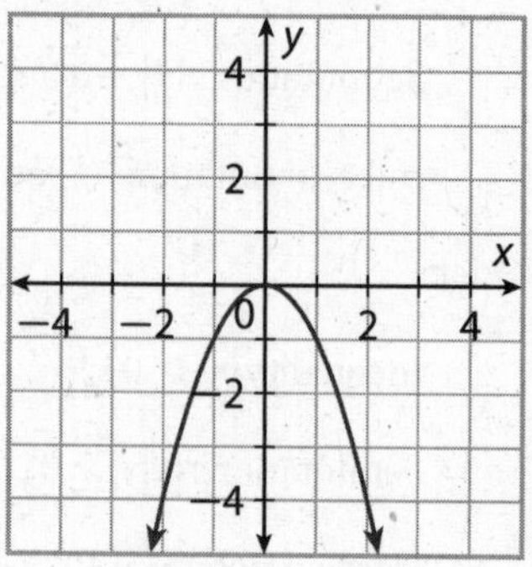

Explain 2 Graphing a Linear Function on a Restricted Domain

Unless otherwise stated, a function is assumed to have a domain consisting of all real numbers for which the function is defined. Many functions—such as linear, quadratic, and exponential functions—are defined for all real numbers, so their domain, when written in interval notation, is $(-\infty, +\infty)$. Another way to write the set of real numbers is $\mathbb{R}$.

Sometimes a function may have a restricted domain. If the rule for a function and its restricted domain are given, you can draw its graph and then identify its range.

Example 2 **For the given function and domain, draw the graph and identify the range using the same notation as the given domain.**

Ⓐ $f(x) = \frac{3}{4}x + 2$ with domain $[-4, 4]$

Since $f(x) = \frac{3}{4}x + 2$ is a linear function, the graph is a line segment with endpoints at $(-4, f(-4))$, or $(-4, -1)$, and $(4, f(4))$, or $(4, 5)$. The endpoints are included in the graph.

The range is $[-1, 5]$.

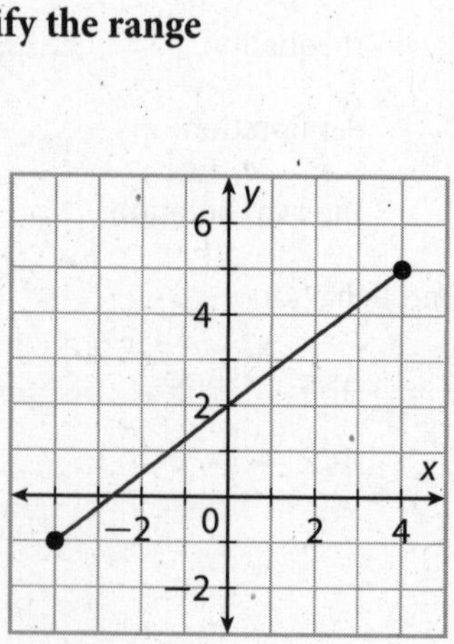

Ⓑ $f(x) = -x - 2$ with domain $\{x|x > -3\}$

Since $f(x) = -x - 2$ is a linear function, the graph is a ray with its endpoint at $(-3, f(-3))$, or ____________. The endpoint ____________ included in the graph. The range is ____________.

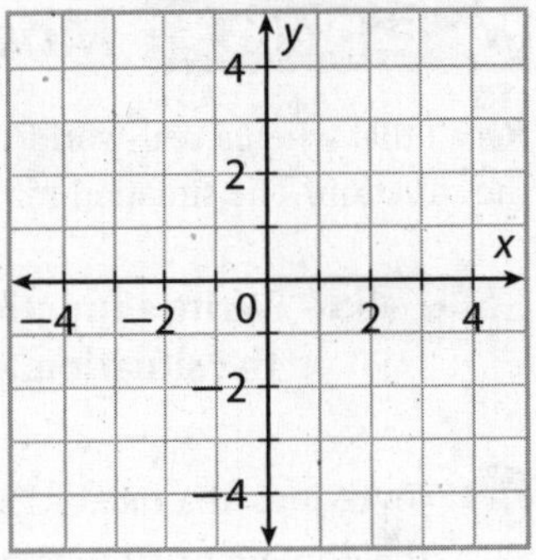

Reflect

7. In Part A, how does the graph change if the domain is $(-4, 4)$ instead of $[-4, 4]$?

____

8. In Part B, what is the end behavior as x increases without bound? Why can't you talk about the end behavior as x decreases without bound?

____

____

Your Turn

For the given function and domain, draw the graph and identify the range using the same notation as the given domain.

9. $f(x) = -\frac{1}{2}x + 2$ with domain $-6 \leq x < 2$

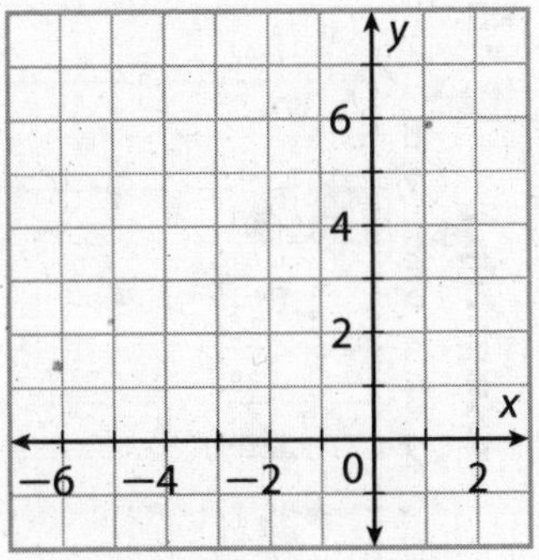

10. $f(x) = \frac{2}{3}x - 1$ with domain $(-\infty, 3]$

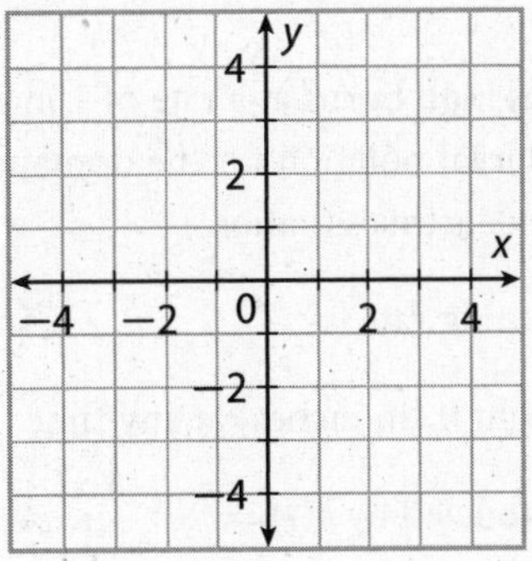

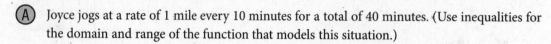

Explain 3 Modeling with a Linear Function

Recall that when a real-world situation involves a constant rate of change, a linear function is a reasonable model for the situation. The situation may require restricting the function's domain.

Example 3 **Write a function that models the given situation. Determine a domain from the situation, graph the function using that domain, and identify the range.**

(A) Joyce jogs at a rate of 1 mile every 10 minutes for a total of 40 minutes. (Use inequalities for the domain and range of the function that models this situation.)

Joyce's jogging rate is 0.1 mi/min. Her jogging distance d (in miles) at any time t (in minutes) is modeled by $d(t) = 0.1t$. Since she jogs for 40 minutes, the domain is restricted to the interval $0 \leq t \leq 40$.

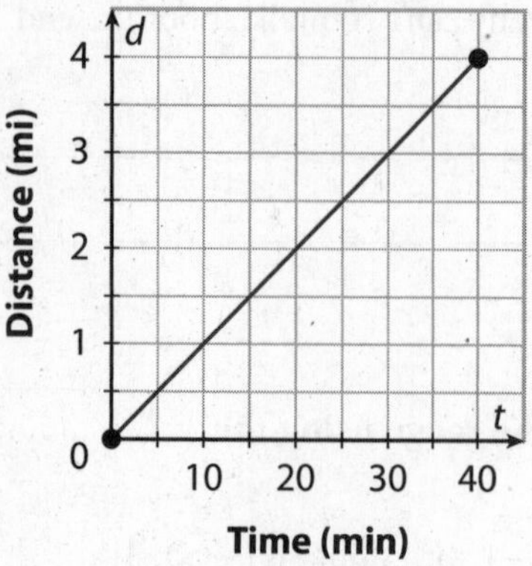

The range is $0 \leq d \leq 4$.

(B) A candle 6 inches high burns at a rate of 1 inch every 2 hours for 5 hours. (Use interval notation for the domain and range of the function that models this situation.)

The candle's burning rate is ____________ in./h.

The candle's height h (in inches) at any time t (in hours) is modeled by $h(t) =$ ____________.

Since the candle burns for 5 hours, the domain is restricted to the interval $[0, \square]$.

The range is ____________.

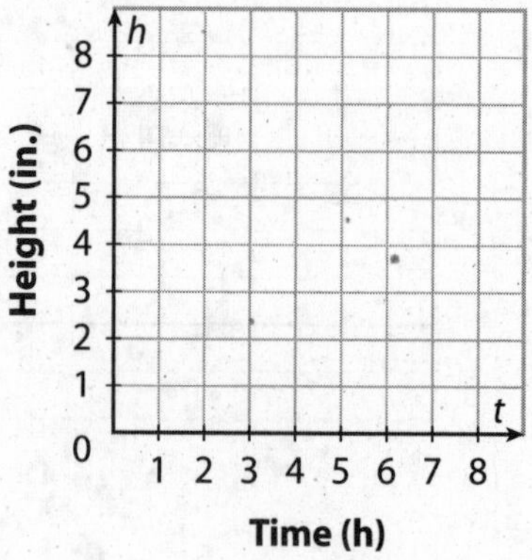

Reflect

11. In Part A, suppose Joyce jogs for only 30 minutes.

A. How does the domain change? ______

B. How does the graph change? ______

C. How does the range change? ______

Your Turn

12. While standing on a moving walkway at an airport, you are carried forward 25 feet every 15 seconds for 1 minute. Write a function that models this situation. Determine the domain from the situation, graph the function, and identify the range. Use set notation for the domain and range.

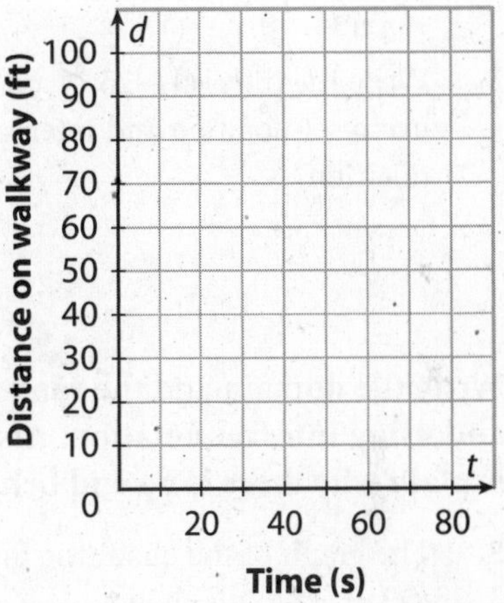

Elaborate

13. If a and b are real numbers such that $a < b$, use interval notation to write four different intervals having a and b as endpoints. Describe what numbers each interval includes.

______

14. What impact does restricting the domain of a linear function have on the graph of the function?

______

15. **Essential Question Check-In** How does slope determine the end behavior of a linear function with an unrestricted domain?

______

Evaluate: Homework and Practice

- Online Homework
- Hints and Help
- Extra Practice

1. Write the interval shown on the number line as an inequality, using set notation, and using interval notation.

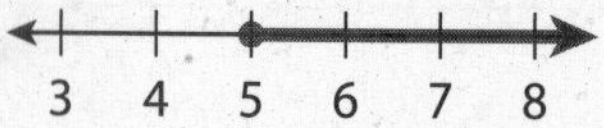

2. Write the interval (5, 100] as an inequality and using set notation.

3. Write the interval $-25 \leq x < 30$ using set notation and interval notation.

4. Write the interval $\{x \mid -3 < x < 5\}$ as an inequality and using interval notation.

Write the domain and the range of the function as an inequality, using set notation, and using interval notation. Also describe the end behavior of the function or explain why there is no end behavior.

5. The graph of the quadratic function $f(x) = x^2 + 2$ is shown.

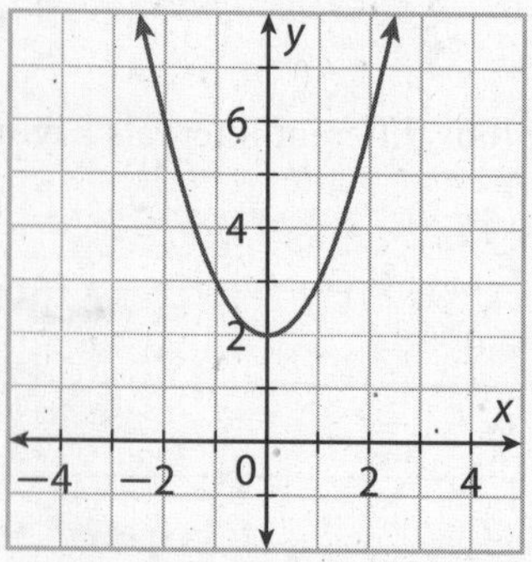

6. The graph of the exponential function $f(x) = 3^x$ is shown.

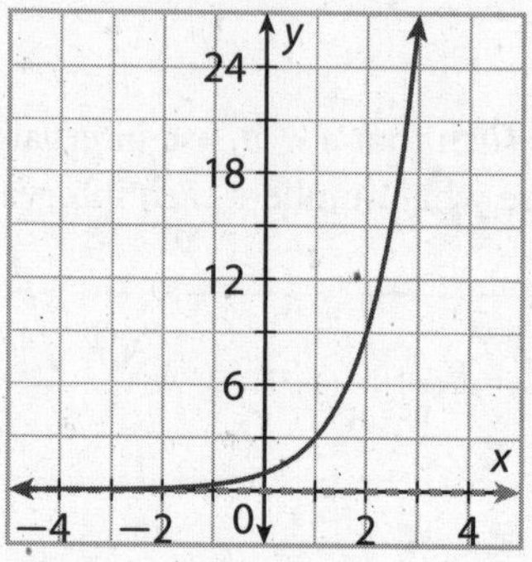

7. The graph of the linear function $g(x) = 2x - 2$ is shown.

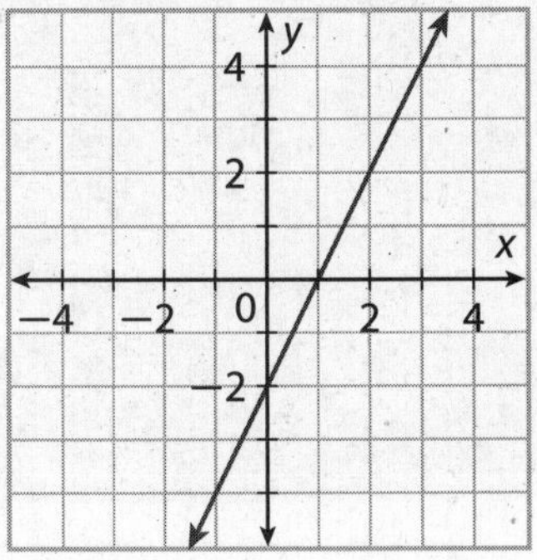

8. The graph of a function is shown.

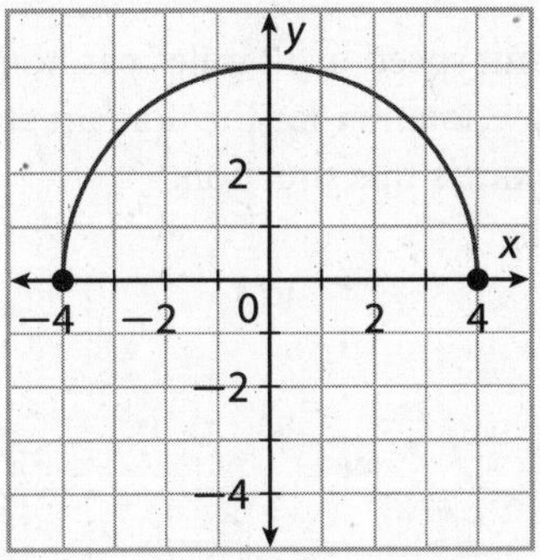

For the given function and domain, draw the graph and identify the range using the same notation as the given domain.

9. $f(x) = -x + 5$ with domain $[-3, 2]$

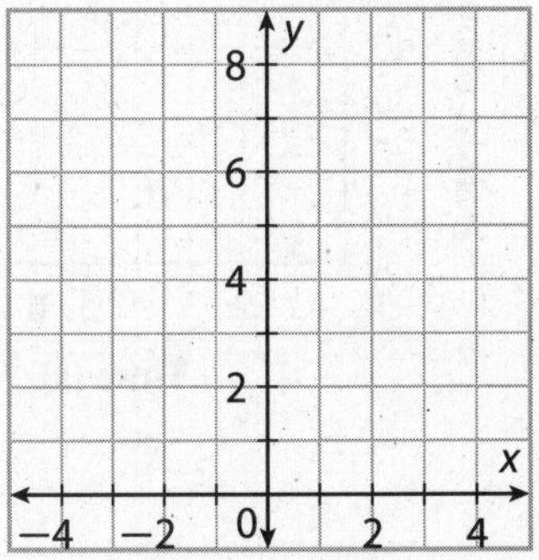

10. $f(x) = \frac{3}{2}x + 1$ with domain $\{x \mid x > -2\}$

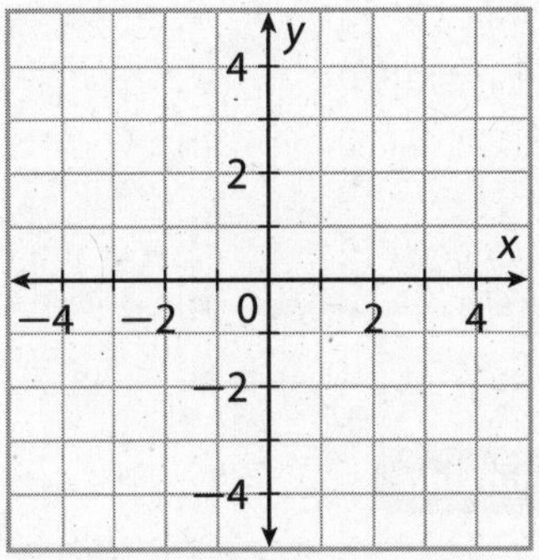

Write a function that models the given situation. Determine the domain from the situation, graph the function using that domain, and identify the range.

11. A bicyclist travels at a constant speed of 12 miles per hour for a total of 45 minutes. (Use set notation for the domain and range of the function that models this situation.)

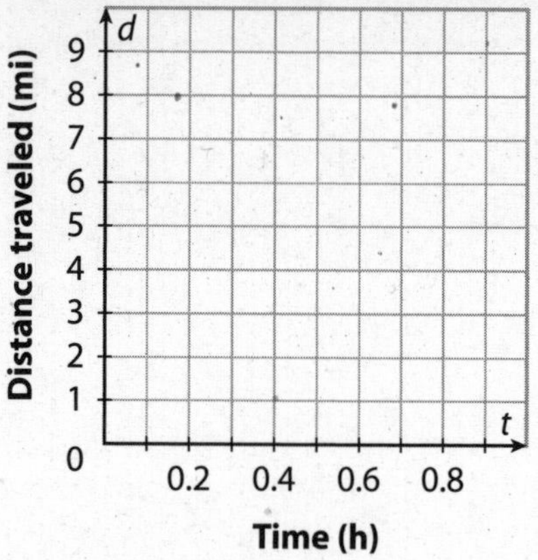

12. An elevator in a tall building starts at a floor of the building that is 90 meters above the ground. The elevator descends 2 meters every 0.5 second for 6 seconds. (Use an inequality for the domain and range of the function that models this situation.)

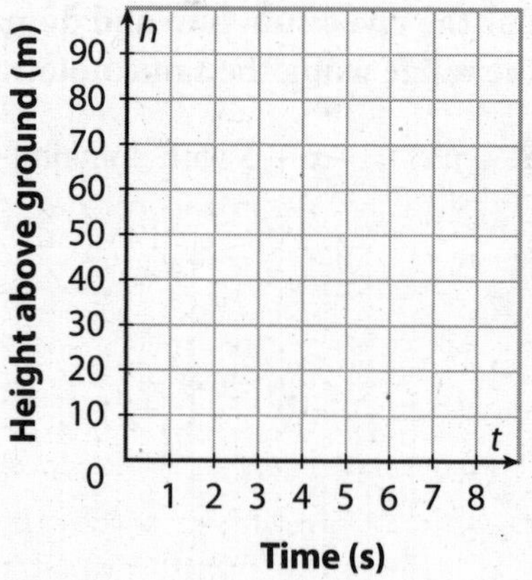

H.O.T. Focus on Higher Order Thinking

13. Explain the Error Cameron sells tickets at a movie theater. On Friday night, she worked from 4 p.m. to 10 p.m. and sold about 25 tickets every hour. Cameron says that the number of tickets, n, she has sold at any time t (in hours) can be modeled by the function $n(t) = 25t$, where the domain is $0 \leq t \leq 1$ and the range is $0 \leq n \leq 25$. Is Cameron's function, along with the domain and range, correct? Explain.

14. Multi-Step The graph of the cubic function $f(x) = x^3$ is shown.

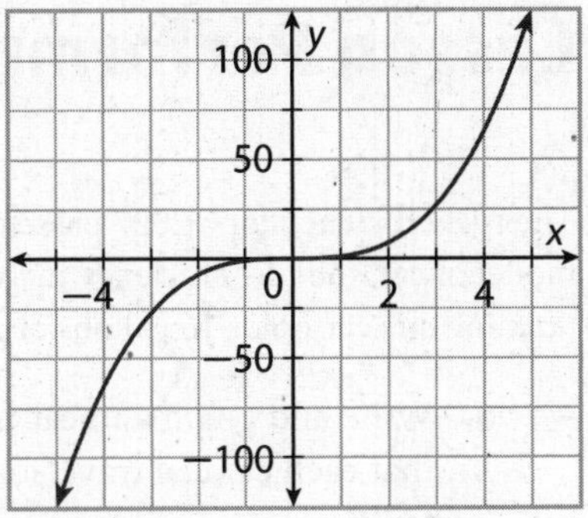

a. What are the domain, range, and end behavior of the function? (Write the domain and range as an inequality, using set notation, and using interval notation.)

b. How is the range of the function affected if the domain is restricted to [−4, 4]? (Write the range as an inequality, using set notation, and using interval notation.)

c. Graph the function with the restricted domain.

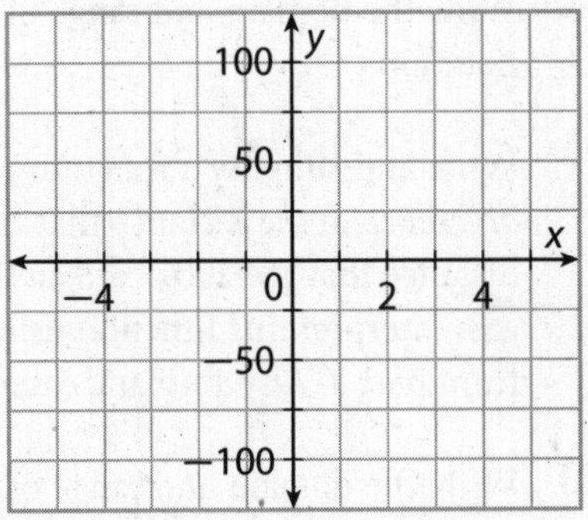

15. Represent Real-World Situations The John James Audubon Bridge is a cable-stayed bridge in Louisiana that opened in 2011. The height from the bridge deck to the top of the tower where a particular cable is anchored is about 500 feet, and the length of that cable is about 1200 feet. Draw the cable on a coordinate plane, letting the x-axis represent the bridge deck and the y-axis represent the tower. (Only use positive values of x and y.) Write a linear function whose graph models the cable. Identify the domain and range, writing each as an inequality, using set notation, and using interval notation.

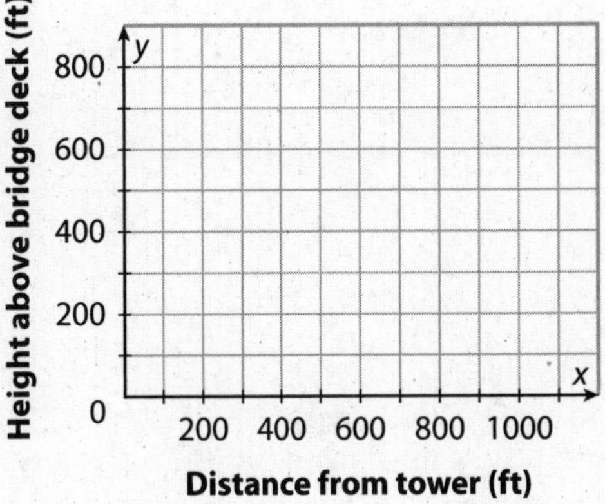

Lesson Performance Task

The fuel efficiency for a 2007 passenger car was 31.2 mi/gal. For the same model of car, the fuel efficiency increased to 35.6 mi/gal in 2012. The gas tank for this car holds 16 gallons of gas.

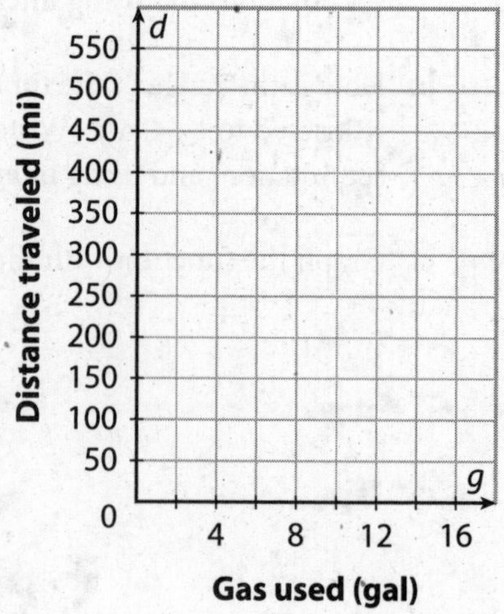

a. Write and graph a linear function that models the distance that each car can travel for a given amount of gas (up to one tankful).

b. Write the domain and range of each function using interval notation.

c. Write and simplify a function $f(g)$ that represents the *difference* in the distance that the 2012 car can travel and the distance that the 2007 car can travel on the same amount of gas. Interpret this function using the graphs of the functions from part a. Also find and interpret $f(16)$.

d. Write the domain and range of the difference function using set notation.

Name______________________ Class______________ Date__________

1.2 Characteristics of Function Graphs

Resource Locker

Essential Question: What are some of the attributes of a function, and how are they related to the function's graph?

Explore Identifying Attributes of a Function from Its Graph

You can identify several attributes of a function by analyzing its graph. For instance, for the graph shown, you can see that the function's domain is $\{x|0 \leq x \leq 11\}$ and its range is $\{y| -1 \leq y \leq 1\}$. Use the graph to explore the function's other attributes.

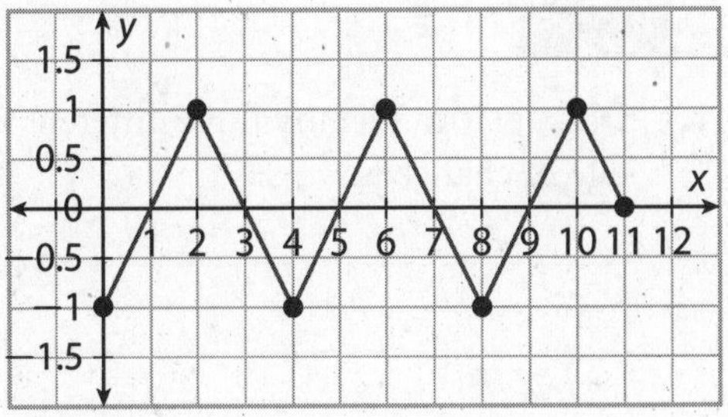

(A) The values of the function on the interval $\{x|1 < x < 3\}$ are positive/negative.

(B) The values of the function on the interval $\{x|8 < x < 9\}$ are positive/negative.

A function is **increasing** on an interval if $f(x_1) < f(x_2)$ when $x_1 < x_2$ for any x-values x_1 and x_2 from the interval. The graph of a function that is increasing on an interval rises from left to right on that interval. Similarly, a function is **decreasing** on an interval if $f(x_1) > f(x_2)$ when $x_1 < x_2$ for any x-values x_1 and x_2 from the interval. The graph of a function that is decreasing on an interval falls from left to right on that interval.

(C) The given function is increasing/decreasing on the interval $\{x|2 \leq x \leq 4\}$.

(D) The given function is increasing/decreasing on the interval $\{x|4 \leq x \leq 6\}$.

For the two points $(x_1, f(x_1))$ and $(x_2, f(x_2))$ on the graph of a function, the **average rate of change** of the function is the ratio of the change in the function values, $f(x_2) - f(x_1)$, to the change in the x-values, $x_2 - x_1$. For a linear function, the rate of change is constant and represents the slope of the function's graph.

(E) What is the given function's average rate of change on the interval $\{x|0 \leq x \leq 2\}$?

____

A function may change from increasing to decreasing or from decreasing to increasing at *turning points*. The value of $f(x)$ at a point where a function changes from increasing to decreasing is a **maximum value**. A maximum value occurs at a point that appears higher than all nearby points on the graph of the function. Similarly, the value of $f(x)$ at a point where a function changes from decreasing to increasing is a **minimum value**. A minimum value occurs at a point that appears lower than all nearby points on the graph of the function. If the graph of a function has an endpoint, the value of $f(x)$ at that point is considered a maximum or minimum value of the function if the point is higher or lower, respectively, than all nearby points.

(F) At how many points does the given function change from increasing to decreasing? __________

Ⓖ What is the function's value at these points? ______

Ⓗ At how many points does the given function change from decreasing to increasing? ______

Ⓘ What is the function's value at these points? ______

A **zero** of a function is a value of x for which $f(x) = 0$. On a graph of the function, the zeros are the x-intercepts.

Ⓙ How many x-intercepts does the given function's graph have? ______

Ⓚ Identify the zeros of the function. ______

Reflect

1. **Discussion** Identify three different intervals that have the same average rate of change, and state what the rate of change is.

2. **Discussion** If a function is increasing on an interval $\{x | a \leq x \leq b\}$, what can you say about its average rate of change on the interval? Explain.

Explain 1 Sketching a Function's Graph from a Verbal Description

By understanding the attributes of a function, you can sketch a graph from a verbal description.

Example 1 **Sketch a graph of the following verbal descriptions.**

Ⓐ Lyme disease is a bacterial infection transmitted to humans by ticks. When an infected tick bites a human, the probability of transmission is a function of the time since the tick attached itself to the skin. During the first 24 hours, the probability is 0%. During the next three 24-hour periods, the rate of change in the probability is always positive, but it is much greater for the middle period than the other two periods. After 96 hours, the probability is almost 100%. Sketch a graph of the function for the probability of transmission.

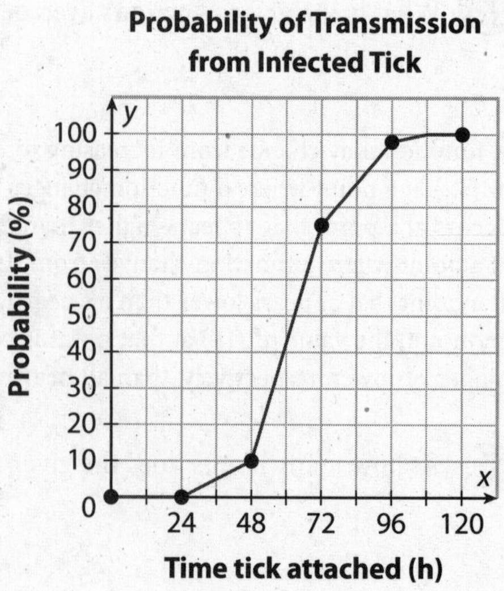

Identify the axes and scales.

The x-axis will be time (in hours) and will run from 0 to at least 96. The y-axis will be the probability of infection (as a percent) from 0 to 100.

Identify key intervals.

The intervals are in increments of 24 hours: 0 to 24, 24 to 48, 48 to 72, 72 to 96, and 96 to 120.

Sketch the graph of the function.

Draw a horizontal segment at $y = 0$ for the first 24-hour interval. The function increases over the next three 24-hour intervals with the middle interval having the greatest increase (the steepest slope). After 96 hours, the graph is nearly horizontal at 100%.

(B) The incidence of a disease is the rate at which a disease occurs in a population. It is calculated by dividing the number of new cases of a disease in a given time period (typically a year) by the size of the population. **To avoid small decimal numbers, the rate is often expressed in terms of a large number of people rather than a single person.** For instance, the incidence of measles in the United States in 1974 was about 10 cases per 100,000 people.

From 1974 to 1980, there were drastic fluctuations in the incidence of measles in the United States. In 1975, there was a slight increase in incidence from 1974. The next two years saw a substantial increase in the incidence, which reached a maximum in 1977 of about 26 cases per 100,000 people. From 1977 to 1979, the incidence fell to about 5 cases per 100,000 people. The incidence fell much faster from 1977 to 1978 than from 1978 to 1979. Finally, from 1979 to 1980, the incidence stayed about the same. **Sketch a graph of the function for the incidence of measles.**

Incidence of Measles in the U.S.

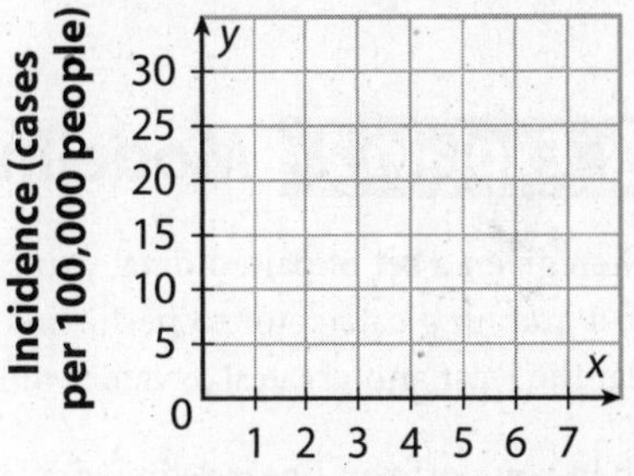

Identify the axes and scales.

The x-axis will represent time given by years and will run from 0 to ________. The y-axis will represent ________________, measured in cases per 100,000 people, and will run from 0 to 30.

Identify key intervals.

The intervals are one-year increments from ________ to ________.

Sketch the graph of the function.

The first point on the graph is ________. The graph slightly rises/falls from $x = 0$ to $x = 1$.

From $x = 1$ to $x = 3$, the graph rises/falls to a maximum y-value of ________. The graph rises/falls steeply from $x = 3$ to $x = 4$ and then rises/falls less steeply from $x = 4$ to $x = 5$. The graph is horizontal from $x = 5$ to $x = 6$.

Reflect

3. In Part B, the graph is horizontal from 1979 to 1980. What can you say about the rate of change for the function on this interval?

____

____

Your Turn

4. A grocery store stocks shelves with 100 cartons of strawberries before the store opens. For the first 3 hours the store is open, the store sells 20 cartons per hour. Over the next 2 hours, no cartons of strawberries are sold. The store then restocks 10 cartons each hour for the next 2 hours. In the final hour that the store is open, 30 cartons are sold. Sketch a graph of the function.

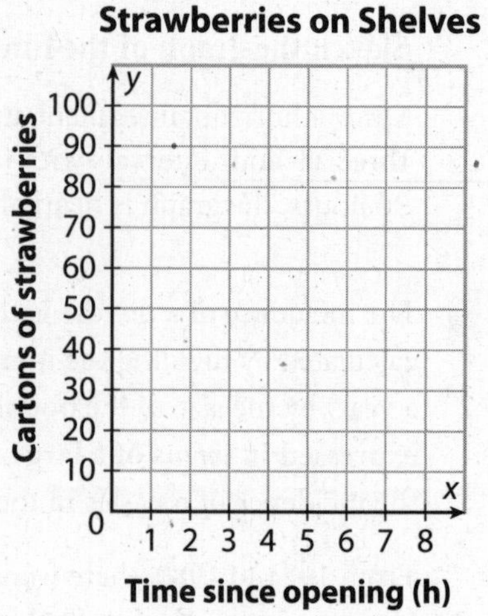

Explain 2 Modeling with a Linear Function

When given a set of paired data, you can use a scatter plot to see whether the data show a linear trend. If so, you can use a graphing calculator to perform linear regression and obtain a linear function that models the data. You should treat the least and greatest x-values of the data as the boundaries of the domain of the linear model.

When you perform linear regression, a graphing calculator will report the value of the *correlation coefficient r*. This variable can have a value from -1 to 1. It measures the direction and strength of the relationship between the variables x and y. If the value of r is negative, the y-values tend to decrease as the x-values increase. If the value of r is positive, the y-values tend to increase as the x-values increase. The more linear the relationship between x and y is, the closer the value of r is to -1 or 1 (or the closer the value of r^2 is to 1).

You can use the linear model to make predictions and decisions based on the data. Making a prediction within the domain of the linear model is called *interpolation*. Making a prediction outside the domain is called *extrapolation*.

Example 2 **Perform a linear regression for the given situation and make predictions.**

Ⓐ A photographer hiked through the Grand Canyon. Each day she stored photos on a memory card for her digital camera. When she returned from the trip, she deleted some photos from each memory card, saving only the best. The table shows the number of photos she kept from all those stored on each memory card. Use a graphing calculator to create a scatter plot of the data, find a linear regression model, and graph the model. Then use the model to predict the number of photos the photographer will keep if she takes 150 photos.

Grand Canyon Photos

Photos Taken	Photos Kept
117	25
128	31
140	39
157	52
110	21
188	45
170	42

Step 1: Create a scatter plot of the data.

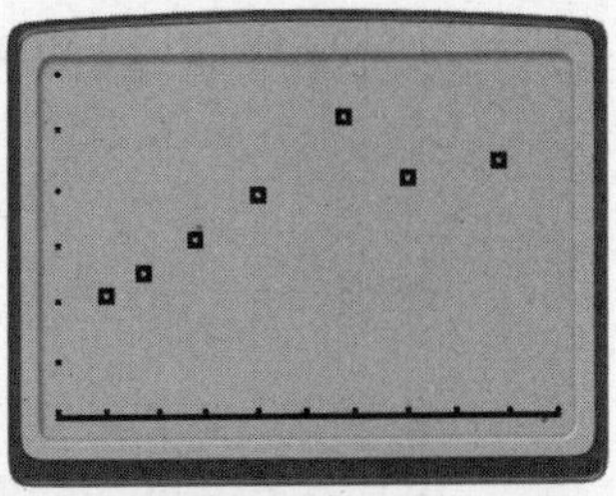

Let x represent the number of photos taken, and let y represent the number of photos kept. Use a viewing window that shows x-values from 100 to 200 and y-values from 0 to 60.

Notice that the trend in the data appears to be roughly linear, with y-values generally increasing as x-values increase.

Step 2: Perform linear regression. Write the linear model and its domain.

The linear regression model is $y = 0.33x - 11.33$. Its domain is $\{x | 110 \leq x \leq 188\}$.

Step 3: Graph the model along with the data to obtain a visual check on the goodness of fit.

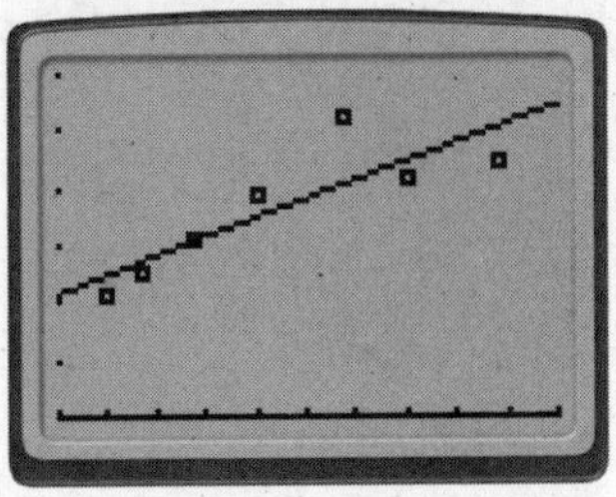

Notice that one of the data points is much farther from the line than the other data points are. The value of the correlation coefficient r would be closer to 1 without this data point.

Step 4: Predict the number of photos this photographer will keep if she takes 150 photos.

Evaluate the linear function when $x = 150$: $y = 0.33(150) - 11.33 \approx 38$. So, she will keep about 38 photos if she takes 150 photos.

(B) As a science project, Shelley is studying the relationship of car mileage (in miles per gallon) and speed (in miles per hour). The table shows the data Shelley gathered using her family's vehicle. Use a graphing calculator to create a scatter plot of the data, find a linear regression model, and graph the model. Then use the model to predict the gas mileage of the car at a speed of 20 miles per hour.

Speed (mi/h)	30	40	50	60	70
Mileage (mi/gal)	34.0	33.5	31.5	29.0	27.5

Step 1: Create a scatter plot of the data.

What do x and y represent?

____

____

What viewing window will you use?

____

____

What trend do you observe?

____

____

Step 2: Perform linear regression. Write the linear model and its domain.

Step 3: Graph the model along with the data to obtain a visual check on the goodness of fit.

What can you say about the goodness of fit?

Step 4: Predict the gas mileage of the car at a speed of 20 miles per hour.

Reflect

5. Identify whether each prediction in Parts A and B is an interpolation or an extrapolation.

Your Turn

6. Vern created a website for his school's sports teams. He has a hit counter on his site that lets him know how many people have visited the site. The table shows the number of hits the site received each day for the first two weeks. Use a graphing calculator to find the linear regression model. Then predict how many hits there will be on day 15.

Day	1	2	3	4	5	6	7	8	9	10	11	12	13	14
Hits	5	10	21	24	28	36	33	21	27	40	46	50	31	38

Elaborate

7. How are the attributes of increasing and decreasing related to average rate of change? How are the attributes of maximum and minimum values related to the attributes of increasing and decreasing?

8. How can line segments be used to sketch graphs of functions that model real-world situations?

9. When making predictions based on a linear model, would you expect interpolated or extrapolated values to be more accurate? Justify your answer.

10. Essential Question Check-In What are some of the attributes of a function?

☆ Evaluate: Homework and Practice

Personal Math Trainer

- Online Homework
- Hints and Help
- Extra Practice

The graph shows a function that models the value *V* (in millions of dollars) of a stock portfolio as a function of time *t* (in months) over an 18-month period.

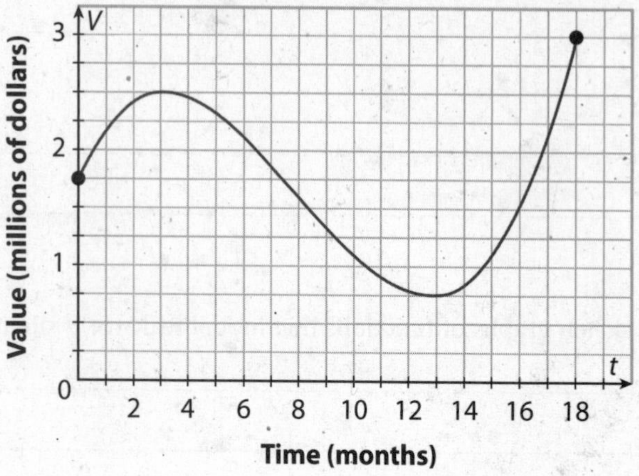

1. On what interval is the function decreasing?

On what intervals is the function increasing?

2. Identify any maximum values and minimum values.

3. What are the function's domain and range?

The table of values gives the probability *P*(*n*) for getting all 5's when rolling a number cube *n* times.

n	1	2	3	4	5
$P(n)$	$\frac{1}{6}$	$\frac{1}{36}$	$\frac{1}{216}$	$\frac{1}{1296}$	$\frac{1}{7776}$

4. Is $P(n)$ increasing or decreasing? Explain the significance of this.

5. What is the end behavior of $P(n)$? Explain the significance of this.

6. The table shows some values of a function. On which intervals is the function's average rate of change positive? Select all that apply.

x	0	1	2	3
$f(x)$	50	75	40	65

a. From $x = 0$ to $x = 1$

b. From $x = 0$ to $x = 2$

c. From $x = 0$ to $x = 3$

d. From $x = 1$ to $x = 2$

e. From $x = 1$ to $x = 3$

f. From $x = 2$ to $x = 3$

Use the graph of the function $f(x)$ to identify the function's specified attributes.

7. Find the function's average rate of change over each interval.

a. From $x = -3$ to $x = -2$

b. From $x = -2$ to $x = 1$

c. From $x = 0$ to $x = 1$

d. From $x = 1$ to $x = 2$

e. From $x = -1$ to $x = 0$

f. From $x = -1$ to $x = 2$

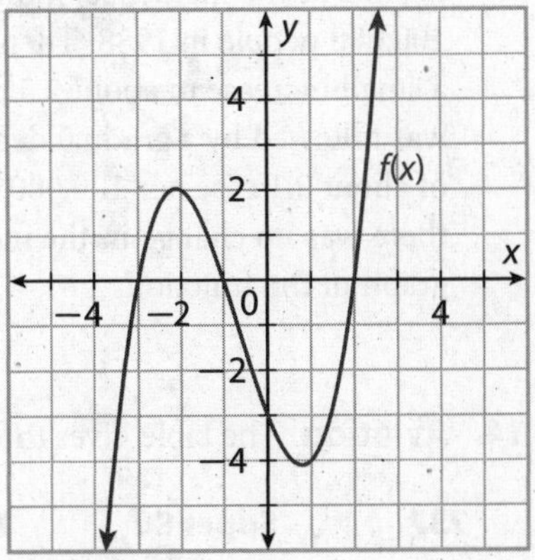

8. On what intervals are the function's values positive?

9. On what intervals are the function's values negative?

10. What are the zeros of the function?

11. The following describes the United States nuclear stockpile from 1944 to 1974. From 1944 to 1958, there was a gradual increase in the number of warheads from 0 to about 5000. From 1958 to 1966, there was a rapid increase in the number of warheads to a maximum of about 32,000. From 1966 to 1970, there was a decrease in the number of warheads to about 26,000. Finally, from 1970 to 1974, there was a small increase to about 28,000 warheads. Sketch a graph of the function.

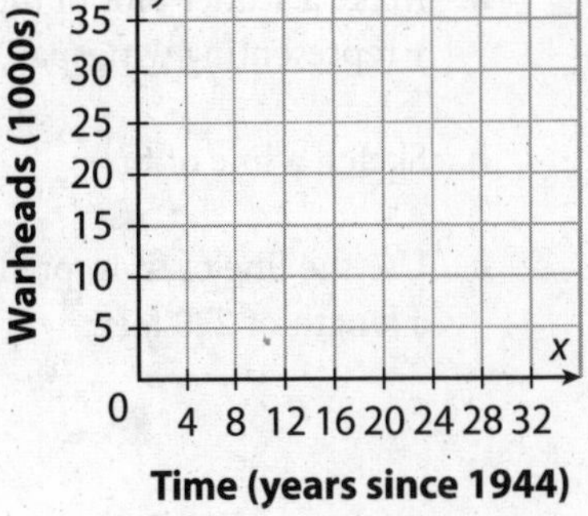

12. The following describes the unemployment rate in the United States from 2003 to 2013. In 2003, the unemployment rate was at 6.3%. The unemployment rate began to fall over the years and reached a minimum of about 4.4% in 2007. A recession that began in 2007 caused the unemployment rate to increase over a two-year period and reach a maximum of about 10% in 2009. The unemployment rate then decreased over the next four years to about 7.0% in 2013. Sketch a graph of the function.

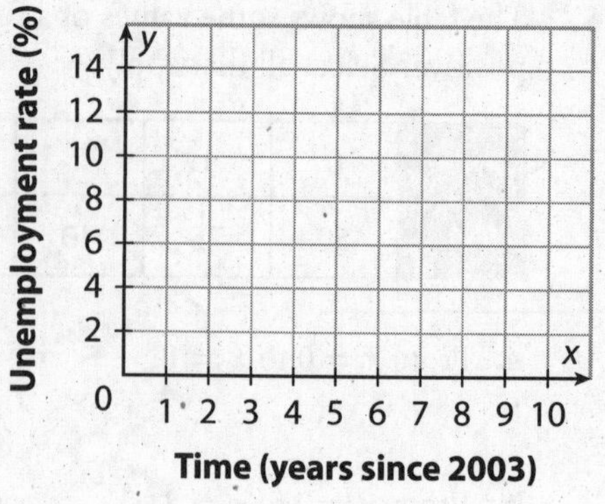

13. The following describes the incidence of mumps in the United States from 1984 to 2004. From 1984 to 1985, there was no change in the incidence of mumps, staying at about 1 case per 100,000 people. Then there was a spike in the incidence of mumps, which reached a peak of about 5.5 cases per 100,000 in 1987. Over the next year, there was a sharp decline in the incidence of mumps, to about 2 cases per 100,000 people in 1988. Then, from 1988 to 1989, there was a small increase to about 2.5 cases per 100,000 people. This was followed by a gradual decline, which reached a minimum of about 0.1 case per 100,000 in 1999. For the next five years, there was no change in the incidence of mumps. Sketch a graph of the function.

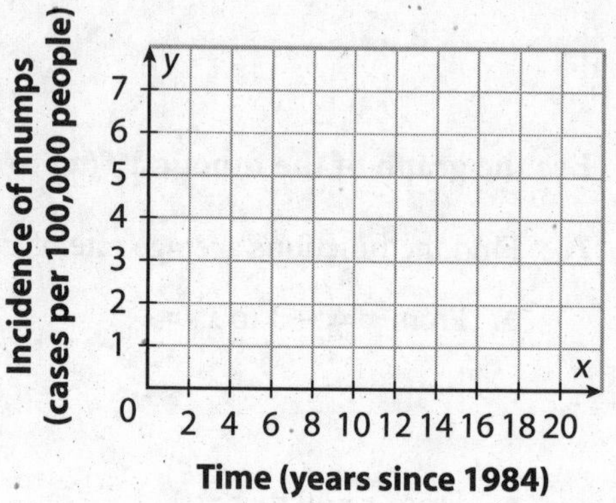

14. **Aviation** The table gives the lengths and wingspans of airplanes in an airline's fleet.

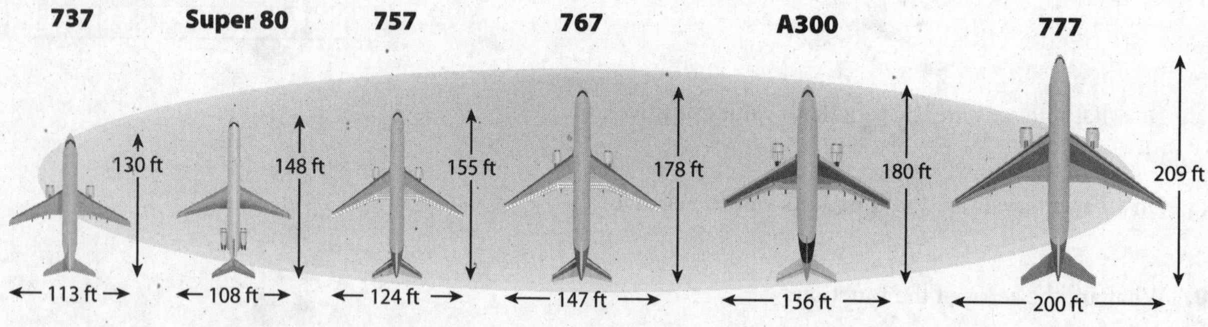

a. Make a scatter plot of the data with x representing length and y representing wingspan.

b. Sketch a line of fit.

c. Use the line of fit to predict the wingspan of an airplane with a length of 220 feet.

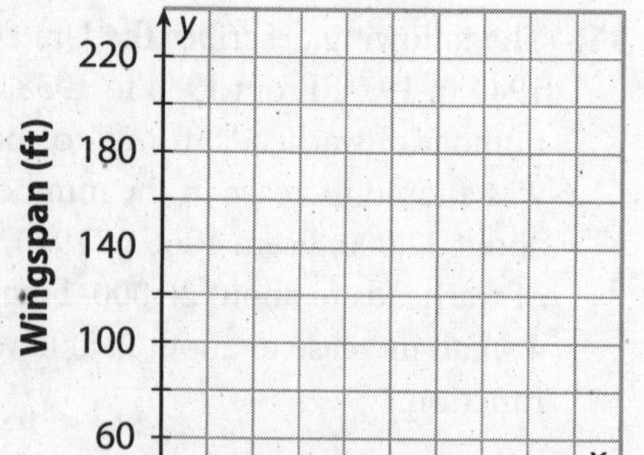

15. Golf The table shows the height (in feet) of a golf ball at various times (in seconds) after a golfer hits the ball into the air.

Time (s)	0	0.5	1	1.5	2	2.5	3	3.5	4
Height (ft)	0	28	48	60	64	60	48	28	0

a. Graph the data in the table. Then draw a smooth curve through the data points. (Because the golf ball is a projectile, its height h at time t can be modeled by a quadratic function whose graph is a parabola.)

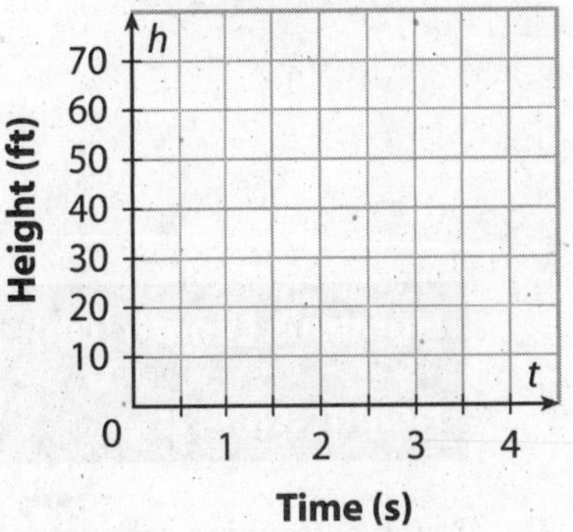

b. What is the maximum height that the golf ball reaches?

c. On what interval is the golf ball's height increasing?

d. On what interval is the golf ball's height decreasing?

16. The model $a = 0.25t + 29$ represents the median age a of females in the United States as a function of time t (in years since 1970).

a. Predict the median age of females in 1995.

b. Predict the median age of females in 2015 to the nearest tenth.

H.O.T. Focus on Higher Order Thinking

17. Make a Prediction Anthropologists who study skeletal remains can predict a woman's height just from the length of her humerus, the bone between the elbow and the shoulder. The table gives data for humerus length and overall height for various women.

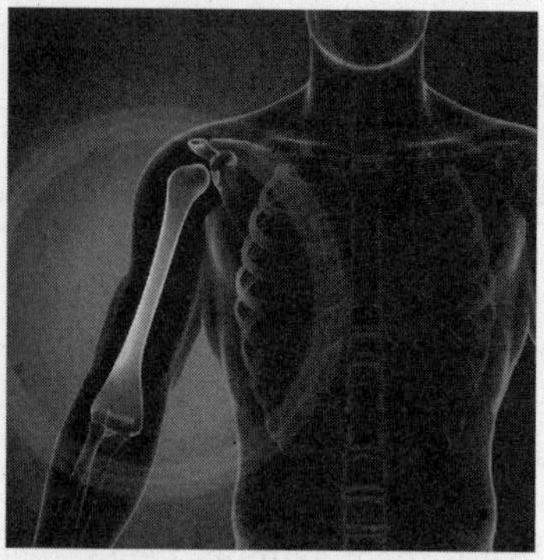

Humerus Length (cm)	35	27	30	33	25	39	27	31
Height (cm)	167	146	154	165	140	180	149	155

Using a graphing calculator, find the linear regression model and state its domain. Then predict a woman's height from a humerus that is 32 cm long, and tell whether the prediction is an interpolation or an extrapolation.

18. Make a Prediction Hummingbird wing beat rates are much higher than those in other birds. The table gives data about the mass and the frequency of wing beats for various species of hummingbirds.

Mass (g)	3.1	2.0	3.2	4.0	3.7	1.9	4.5
Frequency of Wing Beats (beats per second)	60	85	50	45	55	90	40

a. Using a graphing calculator, find the linear regression model and state its domain.

b. Predict the frequency of wing beats for a Giant Hummingbird with a mass of 19 grams.

c. Comment on the reasonableness of the prediction and what, if anything, is wrong with the model.

19. Explain the Error A student calculates a function's average rate of change on an interval and finds that it is 0. The student concludes that the function is constant on the interval. Explain the student's error, and give an example to support your explanation.

20. Communicate Mathematical Ideas Describe a way to obtain a linear model for a set of data without using a graphing calculator.

Lesson Performance Task

Since 1980 scientists have used data from satellite sensors to calculate a daily measure of Arctic sea ice extent. Sea ice extent is calculated as the sum of the areas of sea ice covering the ocean where the ice concentration is greater than 15%. The graph here shows seasonal variations in sea ice extent for 2012, 2013, and the average values for the 1980s.

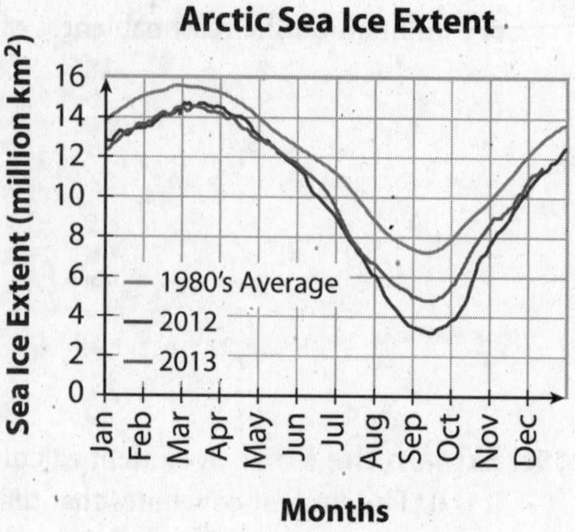

a. According to the graph, during which month does sea ice extent usually reach its maximum? During which month does the minimum extent generally occur? What can you infer about the reason for this pattern?

b. Sea ice extent reached its lowest level to date in 2012. About how much less was the minimum extent in 2012 compared with the average minimum for the 1980s? About what percentage of the 1980s average minimum was the 2012 minimum?

c. How does the maximum extent in 2012 compare with the average maximum for the 1980s? About what percentage of the 1980s average maximum was the 2012 maximum?

d. What do the patterns in the maximum and minimum values suggest about how climate change may be affecting sea ice extent?

e. How do the 2013 maximum and minimum values compare with those for 2012? What possible explanation can you suggest for the differences?

Name______________________ Class______________ Date__________

1.3 Inverses of Functions

Essential Question: What is an inverse function, and how do you know it's an inverse function?

Resource Locker

Explore Understanding Inverses of Functions

Recall that a *relation* is any pairing of the elements of one set (the domain) with the elements of a second set (the range). The elements of the domain are called inputs, while the elements of the range are called outputs. A function is a special type of relation that pairs every input with exactly one output. In a *one-to-one function,* no output is ever used more than once in the function's pairings. In a *many-to-one function,* at least one output is used more than once.

An **inverse relation** reverses the pairings of a relation. If a relation pairs an input x with an output y, then the inverse relation pairs an input y with an output x. The inverse of a function may or may not be another function. If the inverse of a function $f(x)$ is also a function, it is called the **inverse function** and is written $f^{-1}(x)$. If the inverse of a function is not a function, then it is simply an inverse relation.

(A) The mapping diagrams show a function and its inverse. Complete the diagram for the inverse of the function.

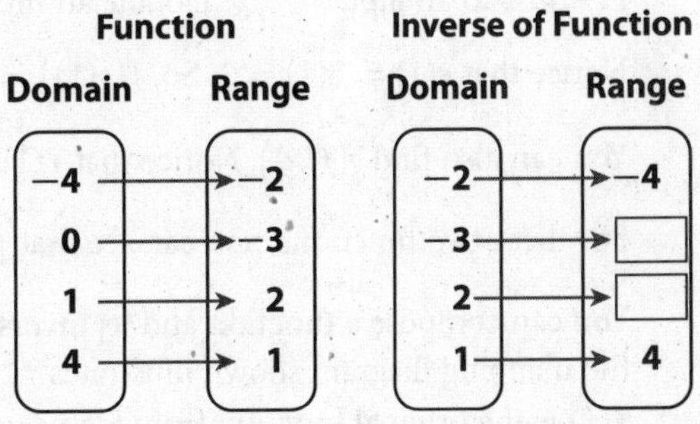

Is the function one-to-one or many-to-one? Explain.

____

____

Is the inverse of the function also a function? Explain.

____

(B) The mapping diagrams show a function and its inverse. Complete the diagram for the inverse of the function.

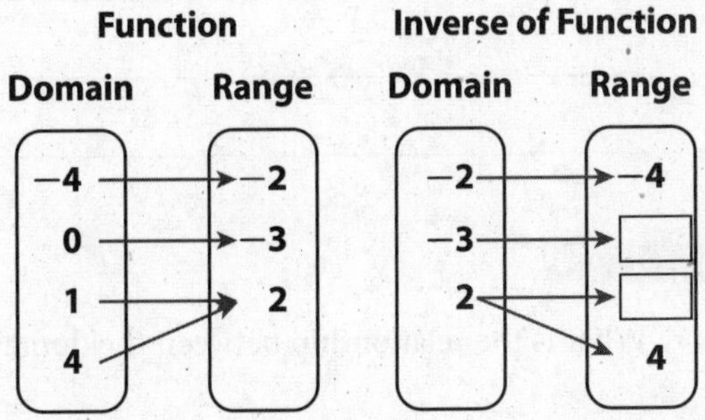

Is the function one-to-one or many-to-one? Explain.

____

____

Is the inverse of the function also a function? Explain.

____

Ⓒ The graph of the original function in Step A is shown. Note that the graph shows the dashed line $y = x$. Write the inverse of the function as a set of ordered pairs and graph them.

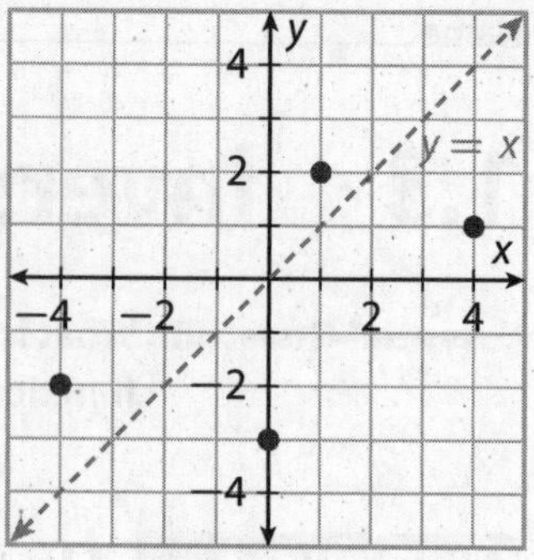

Function: $\{(-4, -2), (0, -3), (1, 2), (4, 1)\}$

Inverse of function:

$\{(\square, \square), (\square, \square), (\square, \square), (\square, \square)\}$

What do you observe about the graphs of the function and its inverse in relationship to the line $y = x$? Why does this make sense?

Ⓓ The **composition of two functions** $f(x)$ and $g(x)$, written $f(g(x))$ and read as "f of g of x," is a new function that uses the output of $g(x)$ as the input of $f(x)$. For example, consider the functions f and g with the following rules.

f: Add 1 to an input. g: Double an input.

Notice that $g(1) = 2(1) = 2$. So, $f(g(1)) = f(2) = 2 + 1 = 3$.

You can also find $g(f(x))$. Notice that $f(1) = 1 + 1 = 2$. So, $g(f(1)) = g(2) = 2(2) = 4$.

For these two functions, you can see that $f(g(1)) \neq g(f(1))$.

You can compose a function and its inverse. For instance, the mapping diagram shown illustrates $f^{-1}(f(x))$ where $f(x)$ is the original function from Step A and $f^{-1}(x)$ is its inverse. Notice that the range of $f(x)$ serves as the domain of $f^{-1}(x)$. Complete the diagram. What do you notice about the outputs of $f^{-1}(f(x))$? Explain why this makes sense.

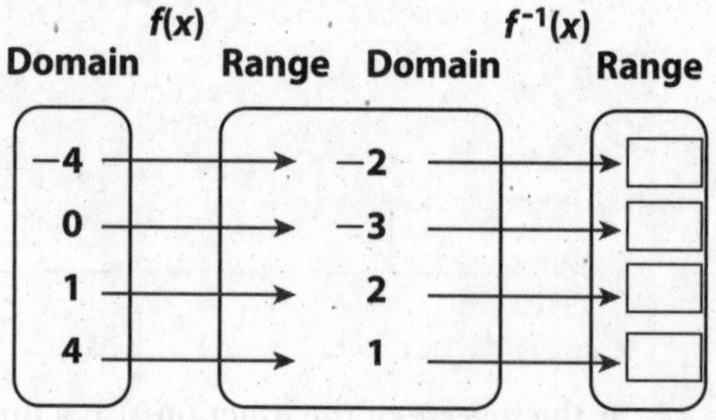

Reflect

1. What is the relationship between the domain and range of a relation and its inverse?

---

2. **Discussion** In Step D, you saw that for inverse functions, $f^{-1}(f(x)) = x$. What do you expect $f(f^{-1}(x))$ to equal? Explain.

Explain 1 Finding the Inverse of a Linear Function

Every linear function $f(x) = mx + b$ where $m \neq 0$ is a one-to-one function. So, its inverse is also a function. To find the equation of the inverse function, use the fact that inverse functions undo each other's pairings.

To find the inverse of a function $f(x)$:

1. Substitute y for $f(x)$.
2. Solve for x in terms of y.
3. Switch x and y (since the inverse switches inputs and outputs).
4. Replace y with $f^{-1}(x)$.

To check your work and verify that the functions are inverses, show that $f\left(f^{-1}(x)\right) = x$ and that $f^{-1}\left(f(x)\right) = x$.

Example 1 **Find the inverse function $f^{-1}(x)$ for the given function $f(x)$. Use composition to verify that the functions are inverses. Then graph the function and its inverse.**

(A) $f(x) = 3x + 4$

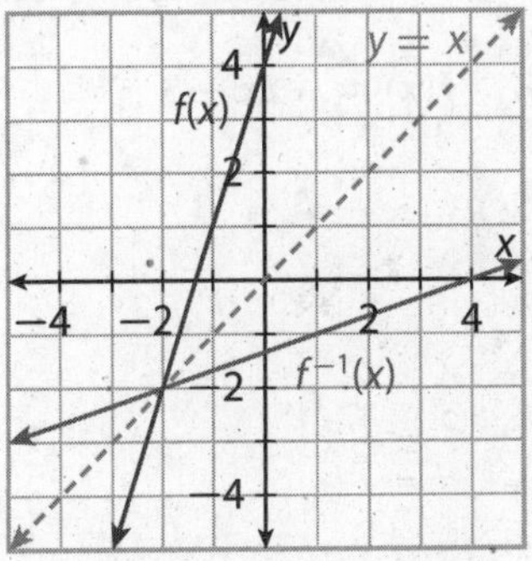

Replace $f(x)$ with y. $\quad y = 3x + 4$

Solve for x. $\quad y - 4 = 3x$

$$\frac{y-4}{3} = x$$

Interchange x and y. $\quad y = \frac{x-4}{3}$

Replace y with $f^{-1}(x)$. $\quad f^{-1}(x) = \frac{x-4}{3}$

Check: Verify that $f^{-1}\left(f(x)\right) = x$ and $f\left(f^{-1}(x)\right) = x$.

$$f^{-1}\left(f(x)\right) = f^{-1}(3x+4) = \frac{(3x+4)-4}{3} = \frac{3x}{3} = x$$

$$f\left(f^{-1}(x)\right) = f\left(\frac{x-4}{3}\right) = 3\left(\frac{x-4}{3}\right) + 4 = (x-4) + 4 = x$$

(B) $f(x) = 2x - 2$

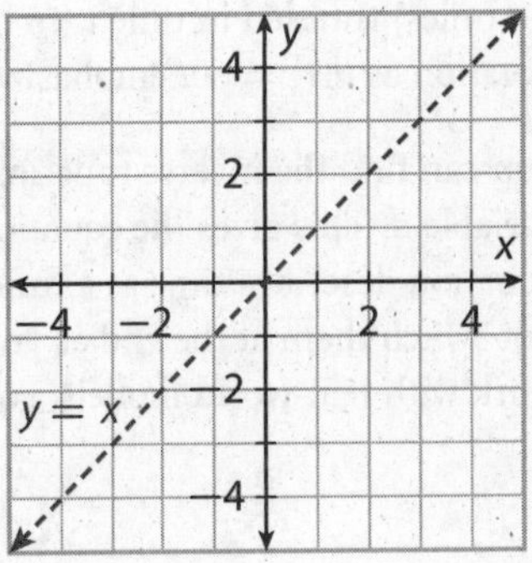

Replace $f(x)$ with y. $\quad y = \square$

Solve for x. $\quad y\ \square = 2x$

$$\frac{y+2}{2} = x$$

Interchange x and y. $\quad y = \square$

Replace y with $f^{-1}(x)$. $\quad \square = \frac{x+2}{2}$

Check: Verify that $f^{-1}\left(f(x)\right) = x$ and $f\left(f^{-1}(x)\right) = x$.

$$f^{-1}\left(f(x)\right) = f^{-1}\left(\square\right) = \frac{(2x-2)+\square}{\square} = \frac{\square}{2} = \square$$

$$f\left(f^{-1}(x)\right) = f\left(\square\right) = \square\left(\frac{x+2}{2}\right) - \square = \left(\square\right) - 2 = \square$$

Reflect

3. What is the significance of the point where the graph of a linear function and its inverse intersect?

4. The graph of a constant function $f(x) = c$ for any constant c is a horizontal line through the point $(0, c)$. Does a constant function have an inverse? Does it have an inverse function? Explain.

Your Turn

Find the inverse function $f^{-1}(x)$ for the given function $f(x)$. Use composition to verify that the functions are inverses. Then graph the function and its inverse.

5. $f(x) = -2x + 3$

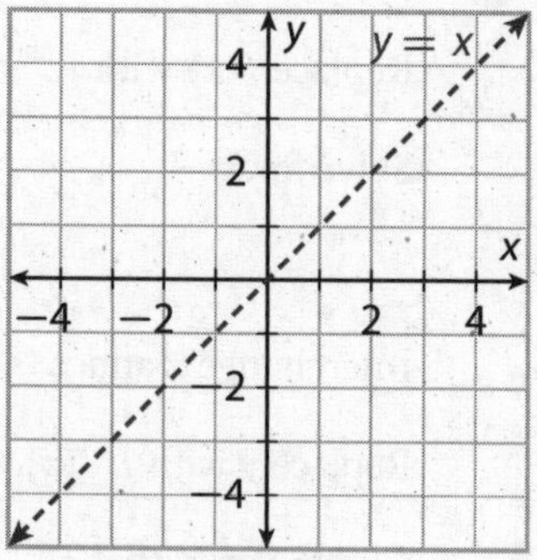

Explain 2 Modeling with the Inverse of a Linear Function

In a model for a real-world situation, the variables have specific real-world meanings. For example, the distance d (in miles) traveled in time t (in hours) at a constant speed of 60 miles per hour is $d = 60t$. Writing this in function notation as $d(t) = 60t$ emphasizes that this equation describes distance as a function of time.

You can find the inverse function for $d = 60t$ by solving for the independent variable t in terms of the dependent variable d. This gives the equation $t = \frac{d}{60}$. Writing this in function notation as $t(d) = \frac{d}{60}$ emphasizes that this equation describes time as a function of distance. Because the meanings of the variables can't be interchanged, you do not switch them at the end as you would switch x and y when working with purely mathematical functions. As you work with real-world models, you may have to restrict the domain and range.

Example 2 **For the given function, state the domain of the inverse function using set notation. Then find an equation for the inverse function, and graph it. Interpret the meaning of the inverse function.**

(A) The equation $C = 3.5g$ gives the cost C (in dollars) as a function of the number of gallons of gasoline g when the price is \$3.50 per gallon.

The domain of the function $C = 3.5g$ is restricted to nonnegative numbers to make real-world sense, so the range of the function also consists of nonnegative numbers. This means that the domain of the inverse function is $\{C \mid C \geq 0\}$

Solve the given equation for g to find the inverse function.

Write the equation. $C = 3.5g$

Divide both sides by 3.5. $\frac{C}{3.5} = g$

So, the inverse function is $g = \frac{C}{3.5}$.

Graph the inverse function.

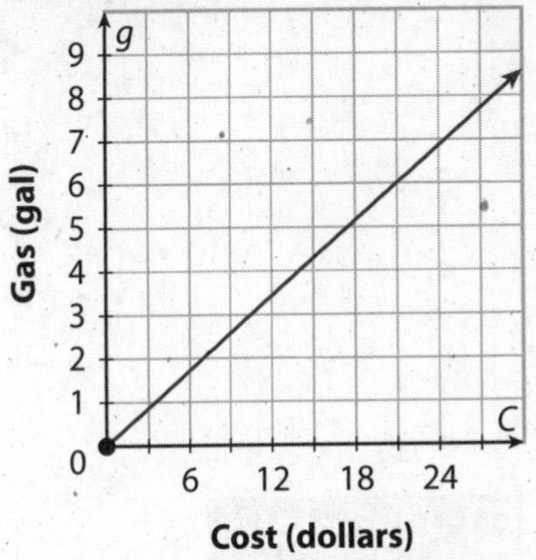

The inverse function gives the number of gallons of gasoline as a function of the cost (in dollars) when the price of gas is \$3.50 per gallon.

(B) A car's gas tank, which can hold 14 gallons of gas, contains 4 gallons of gas when the driver stops at a gas station to fill the tank. The gas pump dispenses gas at a rate of 5 gallons per minute. The equation $g = 5t + 4$ gives the number of gallons of gasoline g in the tank as a function of the pumping time t(in minutes).

The range of the function $g = 5t + 4$ is the number of gallons of gas in the tank, which varies from ______ gallons to ______ gallons. So, the domain of the inverse function is $\left\{g \mid \square \leq g \leq \square\right\}$.

Solve the given equation for g to find the inverse function.

Write the equation. $g = \square t + \square$

Solve for t. $\frac{\square}{5} = t$

So, the inverse function is $t = \square$.

Graph the inverse function.

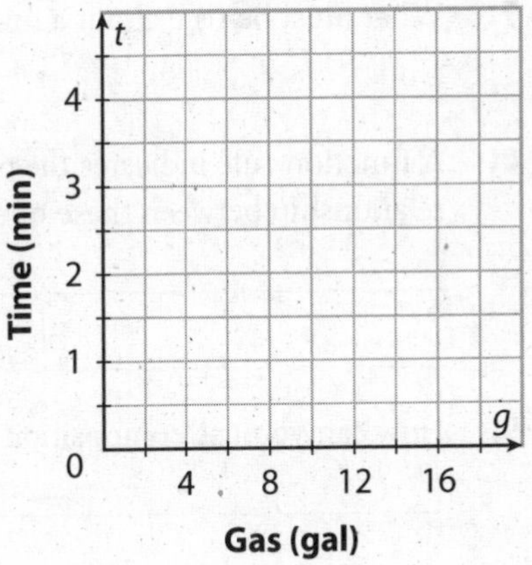

The inverse function gives ______________________________ as a function of ______________________________.

Your Turn

For the given function, determine the domain of the inverse function. Then find an equation for the inverse function, and graph it. Interpret the meaning of the inverse function.

6. A municipal swimming pool containing 600,000 gallons of water is drained. The amount of water w (in thousands of gallons) remaining in the pool at time t (in hours) after the draining begins is $w = 600 - 20t$.

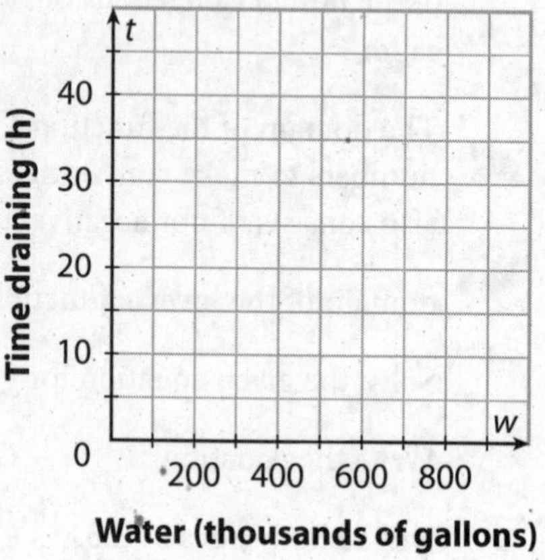

Elaborate

7. What must be true about a function for its inverse to be a function?

8. A function rule indicates the operations to perform on an input to produce an output. What is the relationship between these operations and the operations indicated by the inverse function?

9. How can you use composition to verify that two functions $f(x)$ and $g(x)$ are inverse functions?

10. Describe a real-world situation modeled by a linear function for which it makes sense to find an inverse function. Give an example of how the inverse function might also be useful.

11. Essential Question Check-In What is an inverse relation?

Evaluate: Homework and Practice

Personal Math Trainer

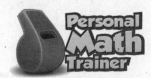

- Online Homework
- Hints and Help
- Extra Practice

The mapping diagrams show a function and its inverse. Complete the diagram for the inverse of the function. Then tell whether the inverse is a function, and explain your reasoning.

1.

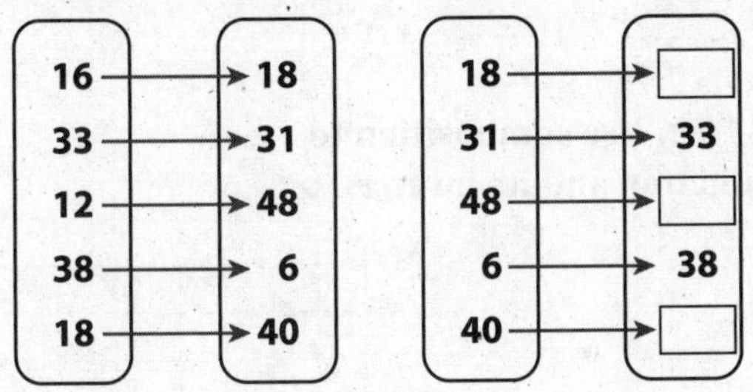

2.

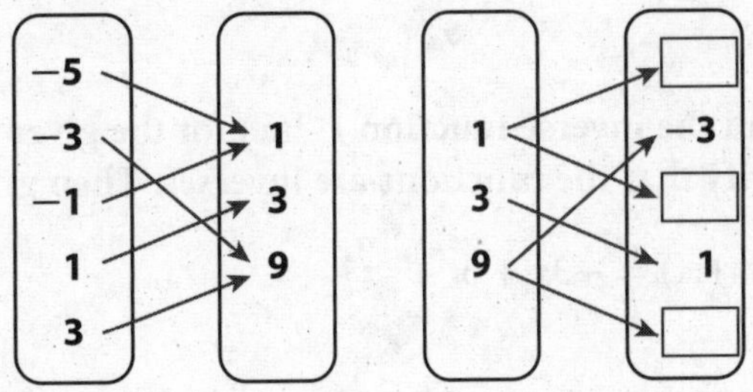

Write the inverse of the given function as a set of ordered pairs and then graph the inverse on the coordinate plane.

3. Function:

$\{(-4, -3), (-2, -4), (0, -2), (1, 0), (2, 3)\}$

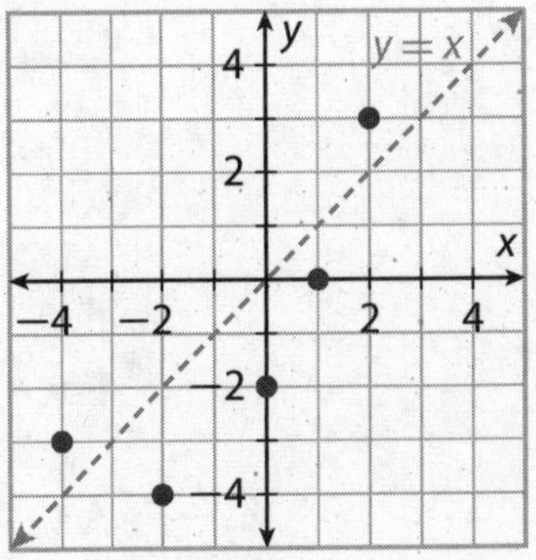

4. Function:

$\{(-3, -4), (-2, -3), (-1, 2), (1, 2), (2, 4), (3, 4)\}$

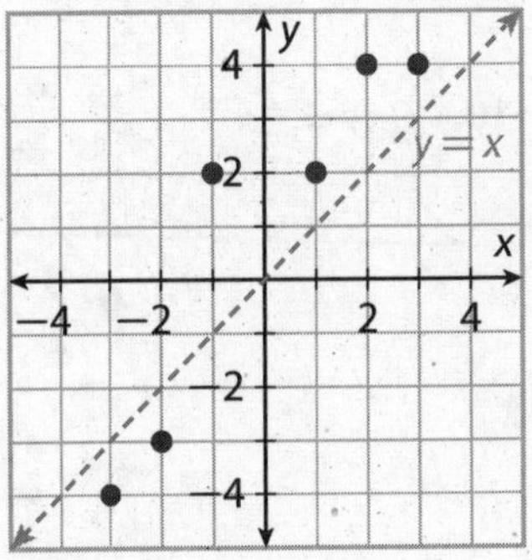

Find the inverse function $f^{-1}(x)$ for the given function $f(x)$.

5. $f(x) = 4x - 8$

6. $f(x) = \frac{x}{3}$

7. $f(x) = \frac{x+1}{6}$

8. $f(x) = -0.75x$

Find the inverse function $f^{-1}(x)$ for the given function $f(x)$. Use composition to verify that the functions are inverses. Then graph the function and its inverse.

9. $f(x) = -3x + 3$

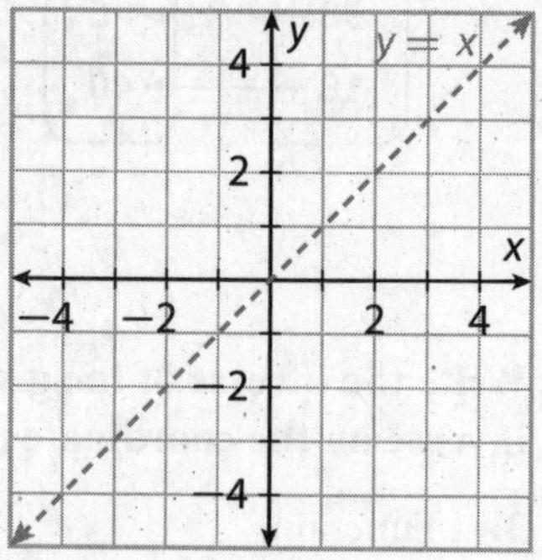

10. $f(x) = \frac{2}{5}x - 2$

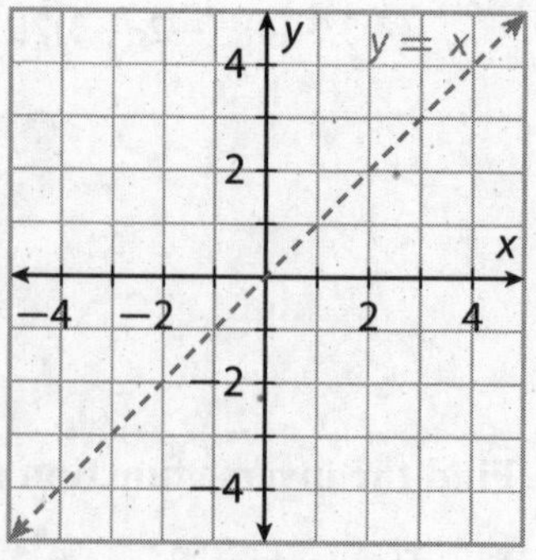

For the given function, determine the domain of the inverse function. Then find an equation for the inverse function, and graph it. Interpret the meaning of the inverse function.

11. **Geometry** The equation $A = \frac{1}{2}(20)h$ gives the area A (in square inches) of a triangle with a base of 20 inches as a function of its height h (in inches).

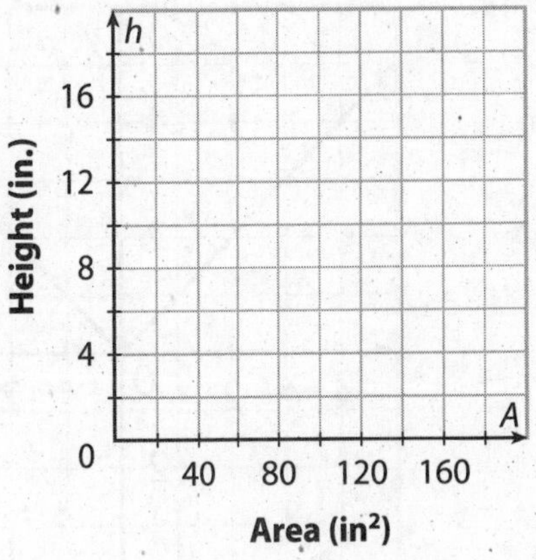

12. The label on a gallon of paint says that it will cover from 250 square feet to 450 square feet depending on the surface that is being painted. A painter has 12 gallons of paint on hand. The equation $A = 12c$ gives the area A (in square feet) that the 12 gallons of paint will cover if applied at a coverage rate c (in square feet per gallon).

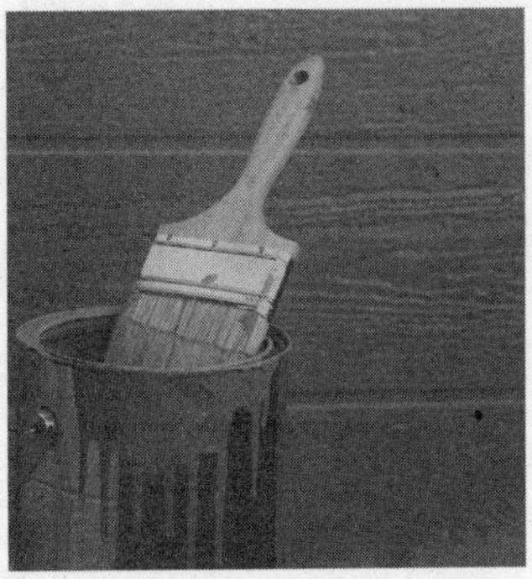

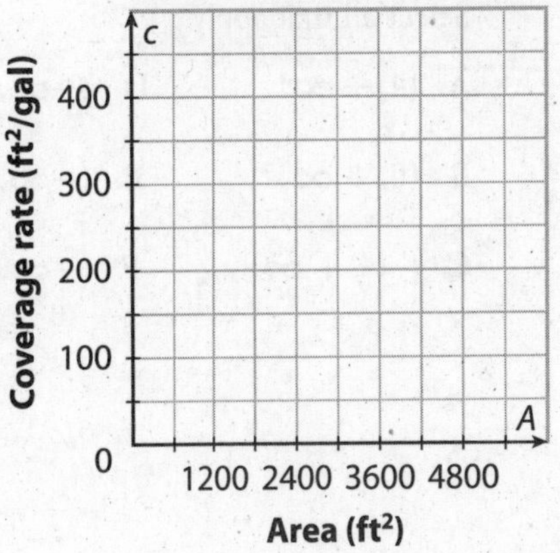

The graph of a function is given. Tell whether the function's inverse is a function, and explain your reasoning. If the inverse is not a function, tell how can you restrict the domain of the function so that its inverse is a function.

13.

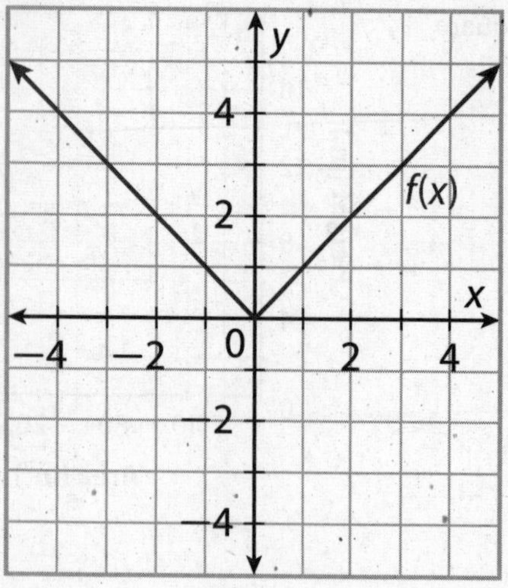

14.

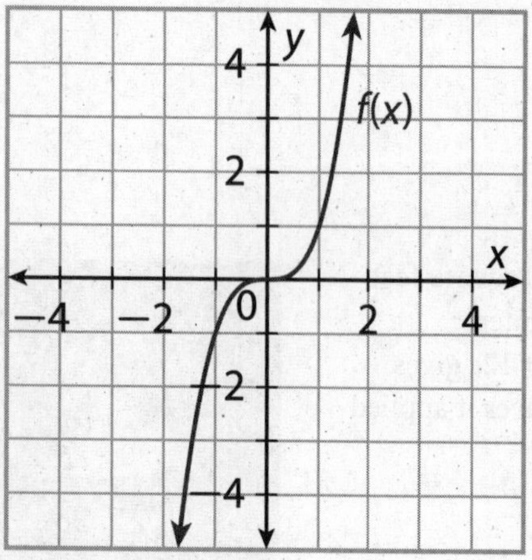

15. Multiple Response Identify the domain intervals over which the inverse of the graphed function is also a function. Select all that apply.

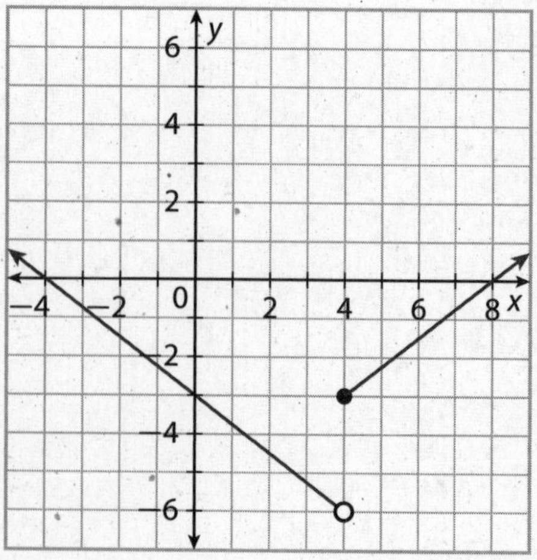

A. $[4, +\infty)$

B. $(0, +\infty)$

C. $[-4, +\infty)$

D. $(-\infty, +\infty)$

E. $(-\infty, 4]$

F. $(-\infty, 4)$

G. $(4, 8)$

H. $(8, +\infty)$

I. $(0, 8]$

H.O.T. Focus on Higher Order Thinking

16. Draw Conclusions Identify all linear functions that are their own inverse.

17. Make a Conjecture Among linear functions (excluding constant functions), quadratic functions, absolute value functions, and exponential functions, which types of function do you have to restrict the domain for the inverse to be a function? Explain.

18. Find the Error A student was asked to find the inverse of $f(x) = 2x + 1$. The student's work is shown. Explain why the student is incorrect and what the student should have done to get the correct answer.

> The function $f(x) = 2x + 1$ involves two operations: multiplying by 2 and adding 1. The inverse operations are dividing by 2 and subtracting 1. So, the inverse function is $f^{-1}(x) = \frac{x}{2} - 1$.

Lesson Performance Task

In an anatomy class, a student measures the femur of an adult male and finds the length of the femur to be 50.0 cm. The student is then asked to estimate the height of the male that the femur came from.

The table shows the femur lengths and heights of some adult males and females. Using a graphing calculator, perform linear regression on the data to obtain femur length as a function of height (one function for adult males, one for adult females). Then find the inverse of each function. Use the appropriate inverse function to find the height of the adult male and explain how the inverse functions would be helpful to a forensic scientist.

Femur Length (cm)	30	38	46	54	62
Male Height (cm)	138	153	168	183	198
Female Height (cm)	132	147	163	179	194

STUDY GUIDE REVIEW

MODULE 1

Analyzing Functions

Essential Question: How can you analyze functions to solve real-world problems?

Key Vocabulary

finite interval *(intervalo finito)*

infinite interval *(intervalo infinito)*

domain *(dominio)*

range *(rango)*

end behavior *(comportamiento final)*

KEY EXAMPLE *(Lesson 1.1)*

Write the domain and range of $f(x) = 3^x$ as an inequality, using set notation, and using interval notation. Then describe the end behavior of the function.

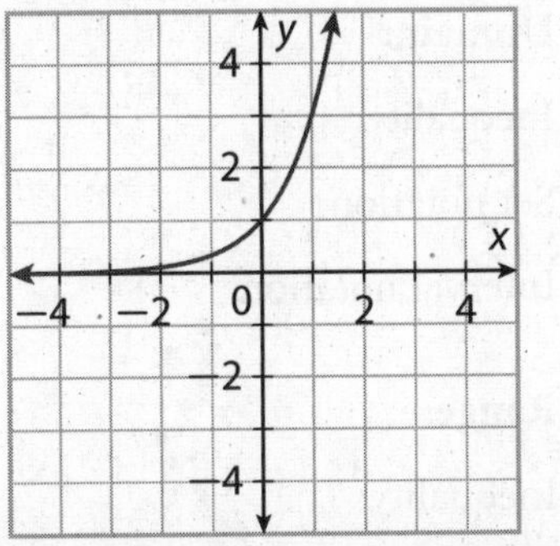

	Domain	Range
Inequality	$\{-\infty < x < +\infty\}$	$y > 0$
Set notation	$\{x \mid -\infty < x < +\infty\}$	$y \mid y > 0$
Interval notation	$(-\infty, +\infty)$	$(0, +\infty)$

End behavior: As $x \to +\infty$, $f(x) \to +\infty$, and as $x \to -\infty$, $f(x) \to 0$.

KEY EXAMPLE *(Lesson 1.3)*

Find the inverse function $f^{-1}(x)$ for $f(x) = -2x + 3$.

$y = -2x + 3$ Replace **f(x)** with **y**.

$\frac{y-3}{-2} = x$ Solve for **x**.

$y = \frac{x-3}{-2}$ Switch **x** and **y**.

$f^{-1}(x) = \frac{x-3}{-2}$ Replace **y** with $f^{-1}(x)$.

Find the inverse function $g^{-1}(x)$ for $g(x) = \frac{(x-3)}{2}$.

$y = \frac{(x-3)}{2}$

$2y + 3 = x$

$g^{-1}(x) = 2x + 3$

EXERCISES

Write the domain and range of the function as an inequality, using set notation, and using interval notation. *(Lesson 1.1)*

1.

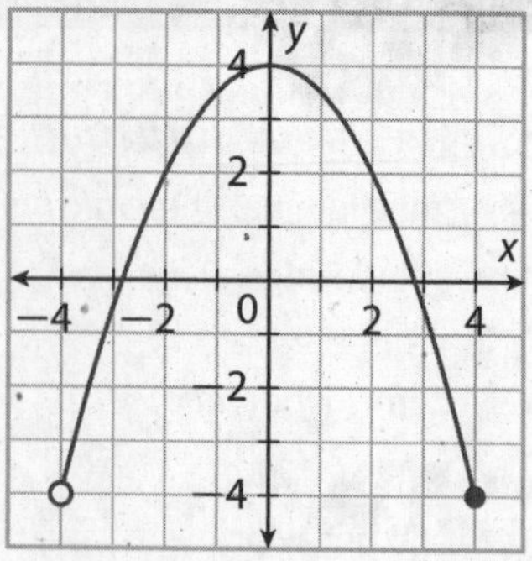

Domain:

Inequality:

Set notation:

Interval notation:

Range:

Inequality:

Set Notation:

Interval Notation:

2.

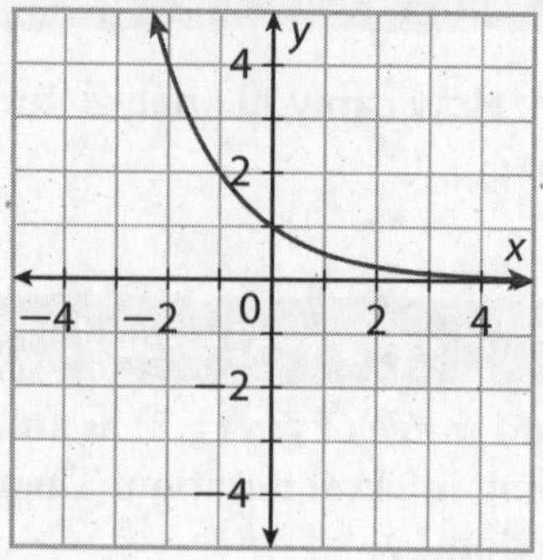

Domain:

Inequality:

Set notation:

Interval notation:

Range:

Inequality:

Set Notation:

Interval Notation:

Find the inverse function $f^{-1}(x)$ for the given function $f(x)$. *(Lesson 1.3)*

3. $f(x) = \frac{x+3}{5}$

4. $f(x) = 2x + 6$

MODULE PERFORMANCE TASK

How High Does a Pole-Vaulter Go?

A pole-vaulter performs two vaults, which can be modeled using the functions $h_1(t) = 9.8t - 4.9t^2$ and $h_2(t) = 8.82t - 4.9t^2$ where h is the height in meters at time t in seconds. How do the two vaults compare graphically in terms of the vertices and intercepts, and what do these represent? Which was the higher vault? How do you know?

Use your own paper to complete the task. Be sure to write down all your data and assumptions. Then use graphs, numbers, words, or algebra to explain how you reached your conclusions.

Ready to Go On?

1.1–1.3 Analyzing Functions

Personal Math Trainer
- Online Homework
- Hints and Help
- Extra Practice

Write the domain and range of the function $g(x) = 3x^2 - 4$ as an inequality, using set notation, and using interval notation. *(Lesson 1.1)*

1.	Domain	Range
Inequality		
Set notation		
Interval notation		

Find the inverse for each linear function. *(Lesson 1.3)*

2. $f(x) = -2x + 4$

3. $g(x) = \frac{x}{4} - 3$

4. $h(x) = \frac{3}{4}x + 1$

5. $j(x) = 5x - 6$

ESSENTIAL QUESTION

6. What are two ways the graphed function could be used to solve real-world problems? *(Lesson 1.2)*

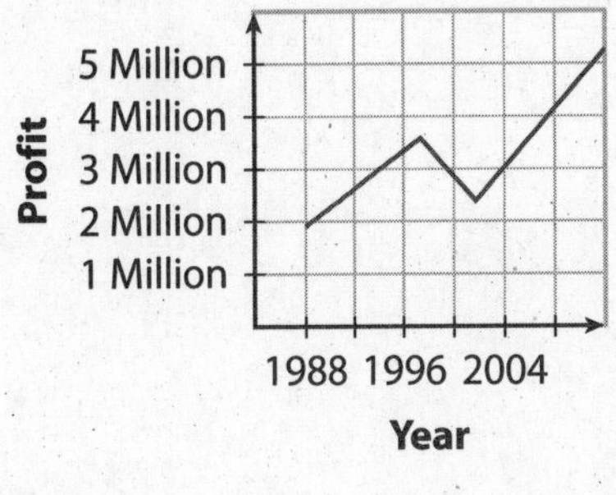

MODULE 1
MIXED REVIEW

Assessment Readiness

1. Look at each equation. Does the graph of the equation have an end behavior that approaches infinity (∞) as $x \rightarrow -\infty$?
Select Yes or No for A–C.

A. $y = -2x - 5$ ○ Yes ○ No

B. $y = 5(x + 2)^2 - 3$ ○ Yes ○ No

C. $y = -3^x$ ○ Yes ○ No

2. Consider the function $y = x^2 - 4$. Choose True or False for each statement.

A. The function has a domain of $(-\infty, \infty)$. ○ True ○ False

B. The function has a range of $(-\infty, \infty)$. ○ True ○ False

C. As $x \rightarrow -\infty, y \rightarrow -\infty$. ○ True ○ False

3. A bike rider starts at a fast pace and rides 40 miles in 2 hours. He gets tired, and slows down, traveling only 20 miles in the next 3 hours. He takes a rest for an hour, then rides back to where he started at a steady pace without stopping for 4 hours. Draw a graph to match the real world situation. Explain your choices.

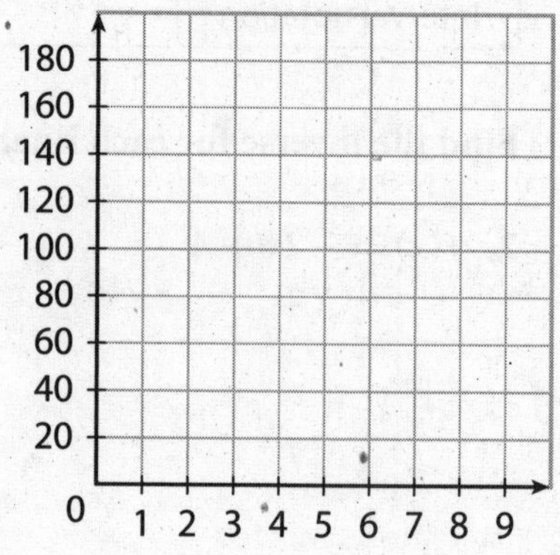

4. The function to convert Fahrenheit to Celsius is $°C = f(°F) = \frac{5(°F - 32)}{9}$. The inverse function will convert Celsius to Fahrenheit. What is the inverse function? Explain how determining this inverse is different than determining the previous inverses.

MODULE 2

Absolute Value Functions, Equations, and Inequalities

Essential Question: How can you use absolute value functions to solve real-world problems?

REAL WORLD VIDEO
Gold jewelry is sold with a rating for purity. For instance, 18-karat gold is 75% pure by weight. The purity level has to meet tolerances that can be expressed using absolute value inequalities.

MODULE PERFORMANCE TASK PREVIEW

What Is the Purity of Gold?

Because gold is such a soft metal, it is usually mixed with another metal such as copper or silver. Pure gold is 24 karat, and 18 karat indicates a mixture of 18 parts gold and 6 parts of another metal or metals. Imagine someone wants to sell you a ring and claims it is 18 karat. How can you use math to be sure the gold is indeed 18 karat? Let's find out!

Are YOU Ready?

Complete these exercises to review skills you will need for this module.

Personal Math Trainer
- Online Homework
- Hints and Help
- Extra Practice

One-Step Equations

Example 1 Solve $x - 6.8 = 2$ for x.

$x - 6.8 + 6.8 = 2 + 6.8$ Add.

$x = 8.8$ Combine like terms.

Solve each equation.

1. $r + 9 = 7$ ________ **2.** $\frac{w}{4} = -3$ ________ **3.** $10b = 14$ ________

Slope and Slope-Intercept Form

Example 2 Find the slope and y-intercept of $3x - y = 6$.

$-3x + 3x - y = -3x + 6$ Write the equation in $y = mx + b$ form.

$-y(-1) = (-3x + 6)(-1)$

$y = 3x - 6$ The slope is 3 and the y-intercept is -6.

Find the slope and y-intercept for each equation.

4. $y - 8 = 2x + 9$ ________

5. $3y = 2(x - 3)$ ________

6. $2y + 8x = 1$ ________

Linear Inequalities in Two Variables

Example 3 Graph $y < 2x - 3$.

Graph the y-intercept of $(0, -3)$.

Use the slope of 2 to plot a second point, and draw a dashed line connecting the points. Shade below the line.

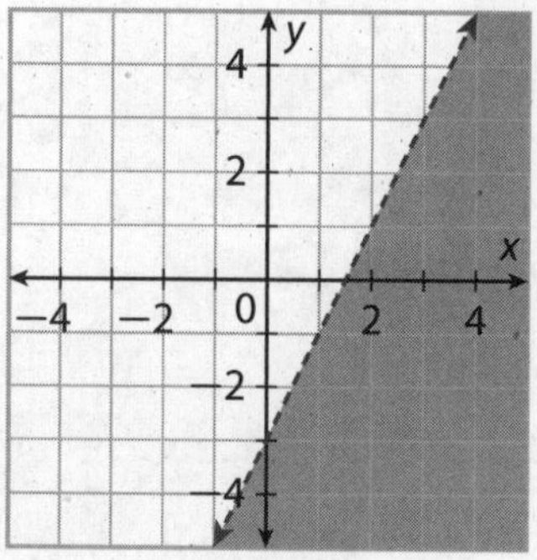

Graph and label each inequality on the coordinate plane.

7. $y \geq -x + 2$

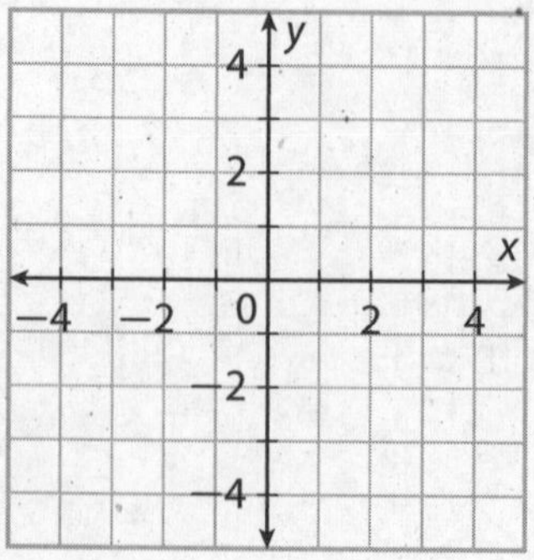

8. $y < x - 1$

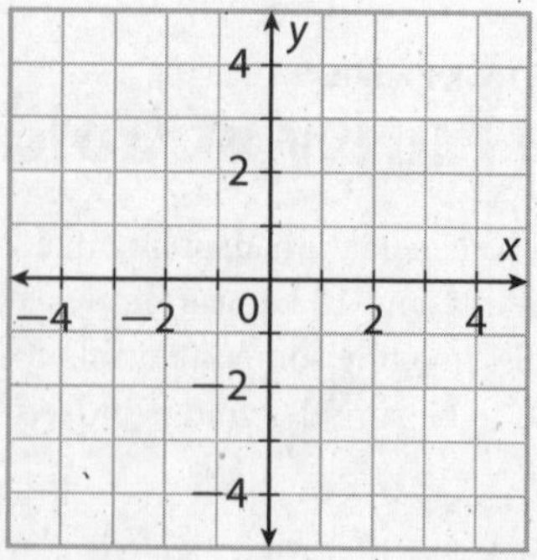

Name ______________________ Class ______________ Date ________

2.1 Graphing Absolute Value Functions

Essential Question: How can you identify the features of the graph of an absolute value function?

Resource Locker

Explore Graphing and Analyzing the Parent Absolute Value Function

Absolute value, written as $|x|$, represents the distance between x and 0 on a number line. As a distance, absolute value is always nonnegative. For every point on a number line (except at 0), there is another point on the opposite side of 0 that is the same distance from 0. For example, both 5 and –5 are five units away from 0. Thus, $|-5| = 5$ and $|5| = 5$.

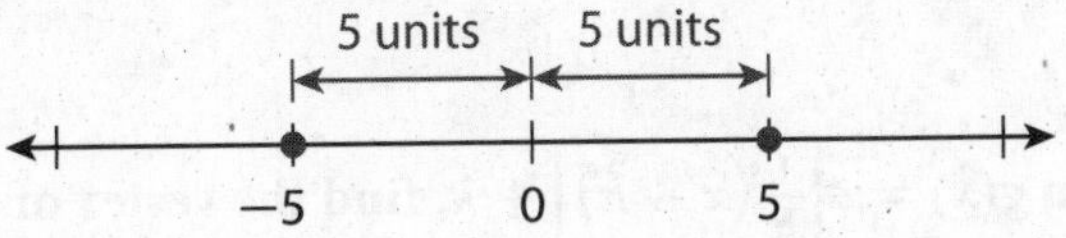

The absolute value function $|x|$, can be defined piecewise as $|x| = \begin{cases} x & x \geq 0 \\ -x & x < 0 \end{cases}$. When x is nonnegative, the function simply returns the number. When x is negative, the function returns the opposite of x.

(A) Complete the input-output table for $f(x)$.

$$f(x) = |x| = \begin{cases} x & x \geq 0 \\ -x & x < 0 \end{cases}$$

x	f(x)
–8	
–4	
0	
4	
8	

(B) Plot the points you found on the coordinate grid. Use the points to complete the graph of the function.

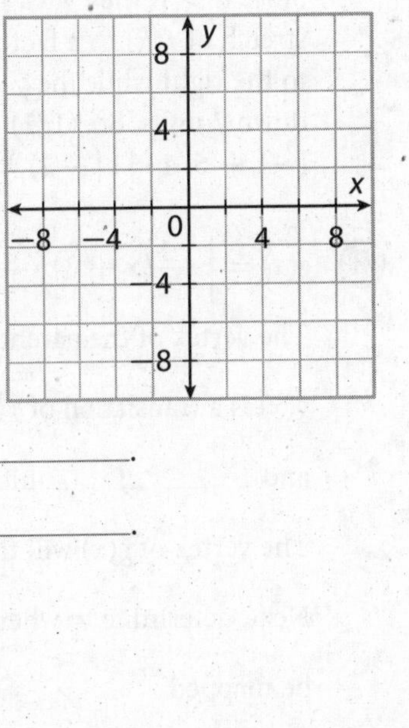

(C) Now, examine your graph of $f(x) = |x|$ and complete the following statements about the function.

$f(x) = |x|$ is symmetric about the ____________ and therefore is a(n) ____________ function.

The domain of $f(x) = |x|$ is ______________________.

The range of $f(x) = |x|$ is ______________________.

Reflect

1. Use the definition of the absolute value function to show that $f(x) = |x|$ is an even function.

____

____

____

____

____

____

Explain 1 Graphing Absolute Value Functions

You can apply general transformations to absolute value functions by changing parameters in the equation $g(x) = a\left|\frac{1}{b}(x - h)\right| + k$.

Example 1 **Given the function $g(x) = a\left|\frac{1}{b}(x - h)\right| + k$, find the vertex of the function. Use the vertex and two other points to help you graph $g(x)$.**

Ⓐ $g(x) = 4|x - 5| - 2$

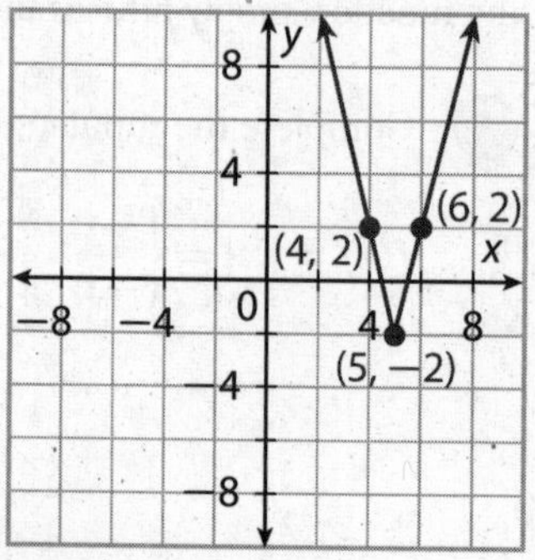

The vertex of the parent absolute value function is at (0, 0).

The vertex of $g(x)$ will be the point to which (0, 0) is mapped by $g(x)$.

$g(x)$ involves a translation of $f(x)$ 5 units to the right and 2 units down.

The vertex of $g(x)$ will therefore be at (5, −2).

Next, determine the location to which each of the points (1, 1) and (−1, 1) on $f(x)$ will be mapped.

Since $a > 1$, then $g(x)$, in addition to being a translation, is also a vertical stretch of $f(x)$ by a factor of 4. The x-coordinate of each point will be shifted 5 units to the right while the y-coordinate will be stretched by a factor of 4 and then moved down 2 units. So, (1, 1) moves to $(1 + 5, 4 \cdot |1| - 2) = (6, 2)$, and (−1, 1) moves to $(-1 + 5, 4 \cdot |1| - 2) = (4, 2)$. Now plot the three points and graph $g(x)$.

Ⓑ $g(x) = \left|-\frac{1}{2}(x + 3)\right| + 1$

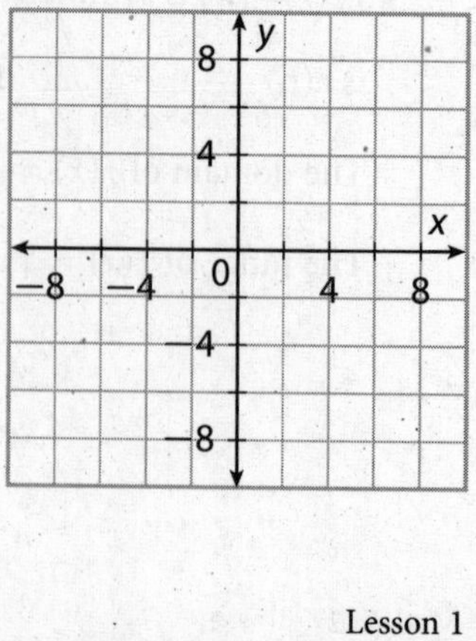

The vertex of the parent absolute value function is at (0, 0).

$g(x)$ is a translation of $f(x)$ __________ units to the __________

and __________ unit __________.

The vertex of $g(x)$ will therefore be at (☐ , ☐).

Next, determine to where the points (2, 2) and (−2, 2) on $f(x)$ will be mapped.

Since $|b| = 2$, $g(x)$ is also a ________________________ of $f(x)$ and since b is negative,

a ________________________.

The x-coordinate will be reflected in the y-axis and ____________ by a factor of ____________, then moved ____________ units to the ____________.

The y-coordinate will move ____________ unit.

So, (2, 2) becomes $\left(\boxed{}, \boxed{}\right) = \left(\boxed{}, \boxed{}\right)$, and (−2, 2) becomes $\left(\boxed{}, \boxed{}\right)$. Now plot the three points and use them to sketch $g(x)$.

Your Turn

2. Given $g(x) = -\frac{1}{5}\left|(x + 6)\right| + 4$, find the vertex and two other points and use them to help you graph $g(x)$.

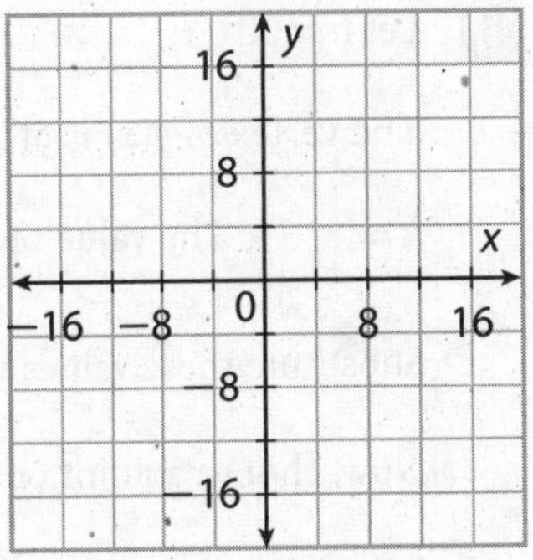

Explain 2 Writing Absolute Value Functions from a Graph

If an absolute value function in the form $g(x) = a\left|\frac{1}{b}(x - h)\right| + k$ has values other than 1 for both a and b, you can rewrite that function so that the value of at least one of a or b is 1.

When a and b are positive: $a\left|\frac{1}{b}(x - h)\right| = \left|\frac{a}{b}(x - h)\right| = \frac{a}{b}\left|(x - h)\right|$.

When a is negative and b is positive, you can move the opposite of a inside the absolute value expression. This leaves −1 outside the absolute value symbol: $-2\left|\frac{1}{b}\right| = -1(2)\left|\frac{1}{b}\right| = -1\left|\frac{2}{b}\right|$.

When b is negative, you can rewrite the equation without a negative sign, because of the properties of absolute value: $a\left|\frac{1}{b}(x - h)\right| = a\left|\frac{1}{-b}(x - h)\right|$. This case has now been reduced to one of the other two cases.

Example 2 **Given the graph of an absolute value function, write the function in the form $g(x) = a\left|\frac{1}{b}(x - h)\right| + k$.**

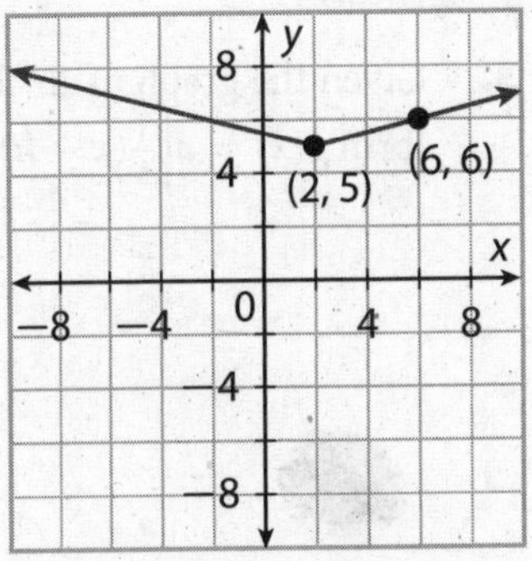

Ⓐ Let $a = 1$.

The vertex of $g(x)$ is at (2, 5). This means that $h = 2$ and $k = 5$.

The value of a is given: $a = 1$.

Substitute these values into $g(x)$, giving $g(x) = \left|\frac{1}{b}(x - 2)\right| + 5$.

Choose a point on $g(x)$ like (6, 6), Substitute these values into $g(x)$, and solve for b.

Substitute. $6 = \left|\frac{1}{b}(6-2)\right| + 5$

Simplify. $6 = \left|\frac{1}{b}(4)\right| + 5$

Subtract 5 from each side. $1 = \left|\frac{4}{b}\right|$

Rewrite the absolute value as two equations. $1 = \frac{4}{b}$ or $1 = -\frac{4}{b}$

Solve for b. $b = 4$ or $b = -4$

Based on the problem conditions, only consider $b = 4$. Substitute into $g(x)$ to find the equation for the graph.

$g(x) = \left|\frac{1}{4}(x-2)\right| + 5$

(B) Let $b = 1$.

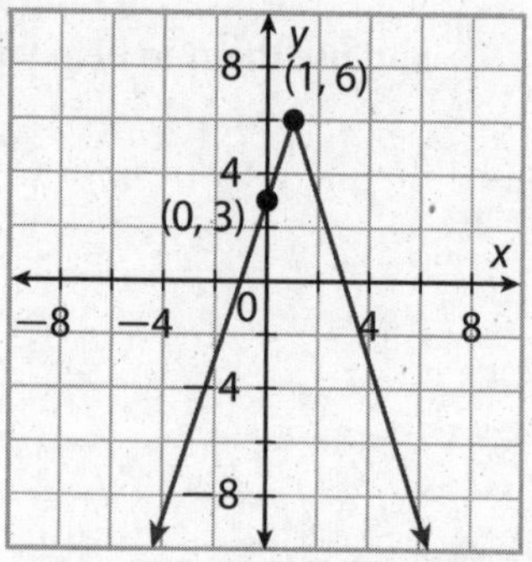

The vertex of $g(x)$ is at ____________. This means that $h =$ ☐ and $k =$ ☐. The value of b is given: $b = 1$.

Substitute these values into $g(x)$, giving $g(x) = a\left|x - \square\right| + \square$.

Now, choose a point on $g(x)$ with integer coordinates, $(0, \square)$.

Substitute these values into $g(x)$ and solve for a.

$g(x) = a\left|x - \square\right| + \square$

Substitute. $\square = a|0 - 1| + 6$

Simplify. $\square = a|-1| + 6$

Solve for a. $\square = a$

Therefore $g(x) =$ ☐.

Your Turn

3. Given the graph of an absolute value function, write the function in the form $g(x) = a\left|\frac{1}{b}(x - h)\right| + k$.

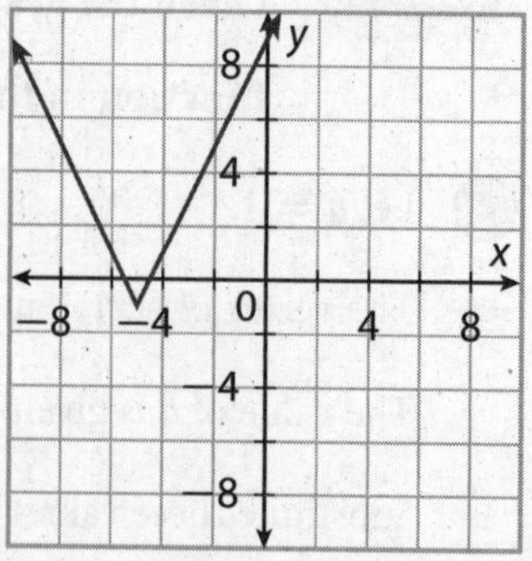

Explain 3 Modeling with Absolute Value Functions

Light travels in a straight line and can be modeled by a linear function. When light is reflected off a mirror, it travels in a straight line in a different direction. From physics, the angle at which the light ray comes in is equal to the angle at which it is reflected away: the angle of incidence is equal to the angle of reflection. You can use an absolute value function to model this situation.

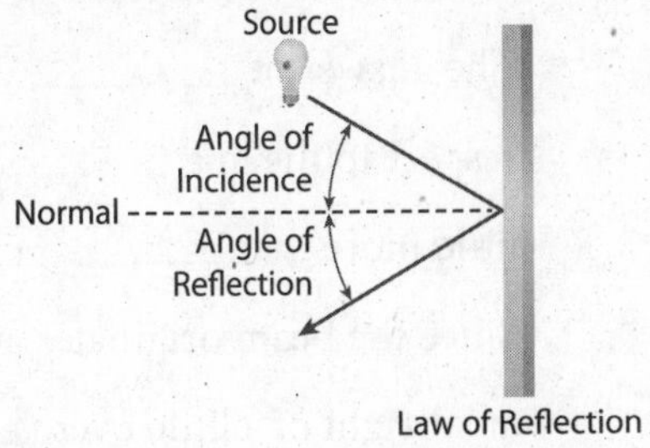

Example 3 **Solve the problem by modeling the situation with an absolute value function.**

At a science museum exhibit, a beam of light originates at a point 10 feet off the floor. It is reflected off a mirror on the floor that is 15 feet from the wall the light originates from. How high off the floor on the opposite wall does the light hit if the other wall is 8.5 feet from the mirror?

Analyze Information

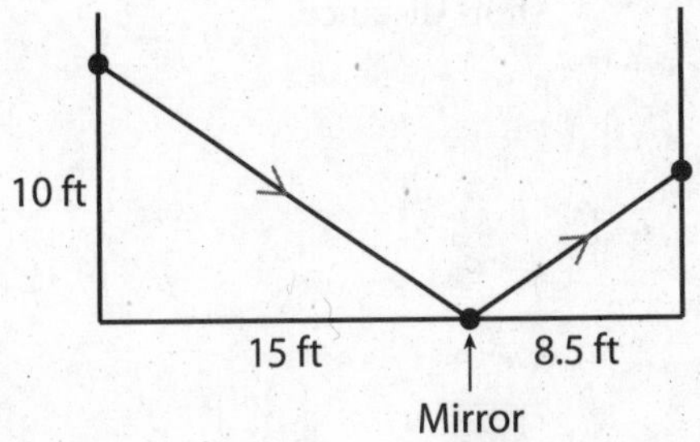

Identify the important information.

- The model will be of the form $g(x) =$ ________.
- The vertex of $g(x)$ is ________.
- Another point on $g(x)$ is ________.
- The opposite wall is ________ feet from the first wall.

Formulate a Plan

Let the base of the first wall be the origin. You want to find the value of $g(x)$ at $x = \square$, which will give the height of the beam on the opposite wall. To do so, find the value of the parameters in the transformation of the parent function.

In this situation, let $b = 1$. The vertex of $g(x)$ will give you the values of ________.

Use a second point to solve for a. Evaluate $g(\square)$.

Solve

The vertex of $g(x)$ is at $(\square, 0)$. Substitute, giving $g(x) = a|x - \square| + \square$.

Evaluate $g(x)$ at ________ and solve for a.

Substitute. $10 = a|\square - 15| + \square$

Simplify. $\square = a|\square|$

Simplify. $10 = \square a$

Solve for a. $a = \square$

Therefore $g(x) =$ ________. Find $g(\square)$. $g(23.5) = \square$

Justify and Evaluate

The answer of __________ makes sense because the function is symmetric with respect to the line __________. The distance from this line to the second wall is a little more than __________ the distance from the line to the beam's origin. Since the beam originates at a height of __________, it should hit the second wall at a height of a little over __________.

Your Turn

4. Two students are passing a ball back and forth, allowing it to bounce once between them. If one student bounce-passes the ball from a height of 1.4 m and it bounces 3 m away from the student, where should the second student stand to catch the ball at a height of 1.2 m? Assume the path of the ball is linear over this short distance.

Elaborate

5. In the general form of the absolute value function, what does each parameter represent?

6. **Discussion** Explain why the vertex of $f(x) = |x|$ remains the same when $f(x)$ is stretched or compressed but not when it is translated.

7. **Essential Question Check-In** What are the features of the graph of an absolute value function?

Evaluate: Homework and Practice

Personal Math Trainer
- Online Homework
- Hints and Help
- Extra Practice

Predict what the graph of each given function will look like. Verify your prediction using a graphing calculator. Then sketch the graph of the function.

1. $g(x) = 5|x - 3|$

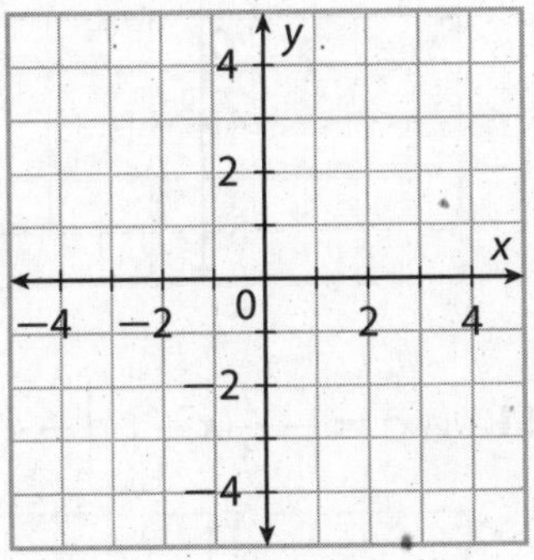

2. $g(x) = -4|x + 2| + 5$

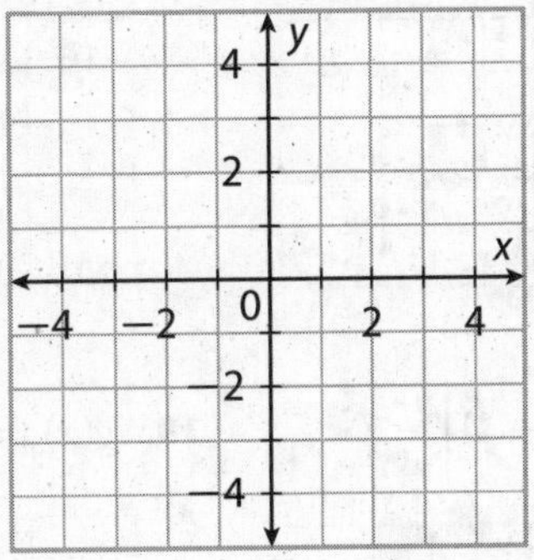

3. $g(x) = \left|\frac{7}{5}(x - 6)\right| + 4$

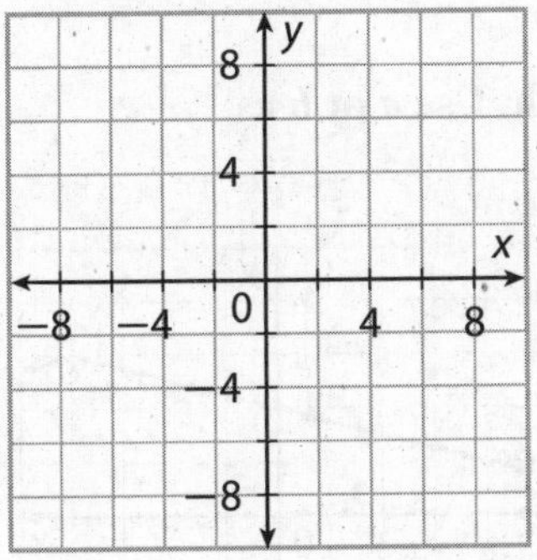

4. $g(x) = \left|\frac{3}{7}(x - 4)\right| + 2$

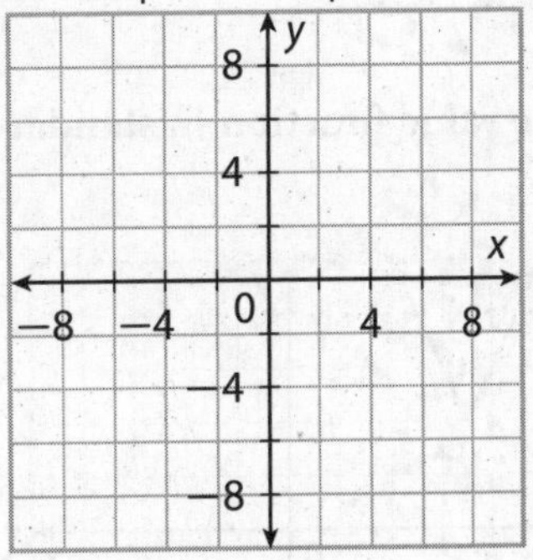

5. $g(x) = \frac{7}{4}\left|(x - 2)\right| - 3$

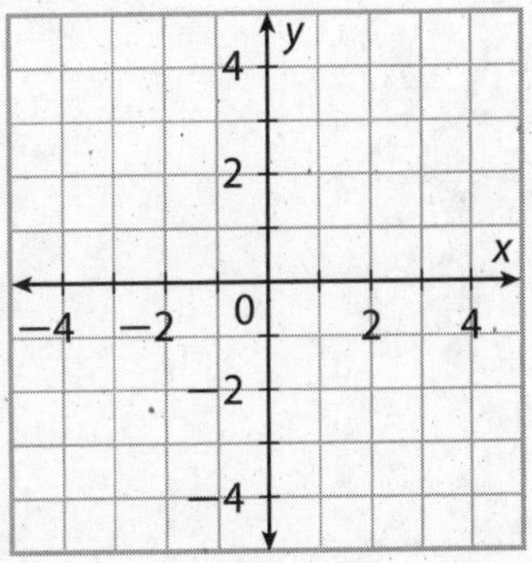

Graph the given function and identify the domain and range.

6. $g(x) = |x|$

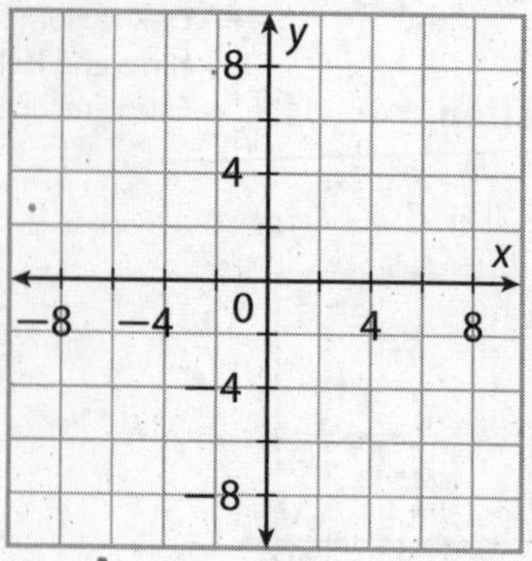

7. $g(x) = \frac{4}{3}\left|(x - 5)\right| + 7$

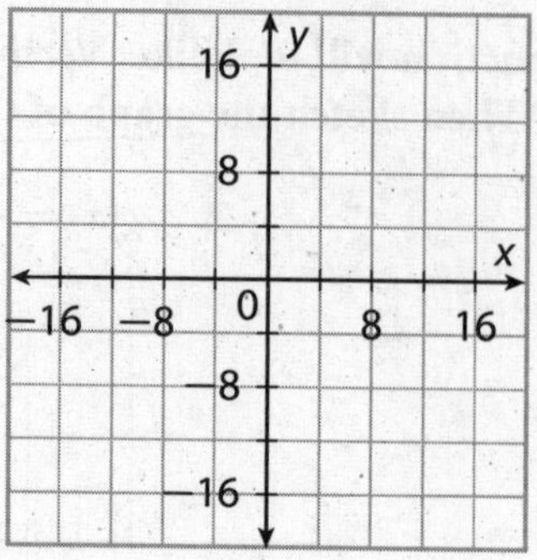

8. $g(x) = -\frac{7}{6}\left|(x - 2)\right|$

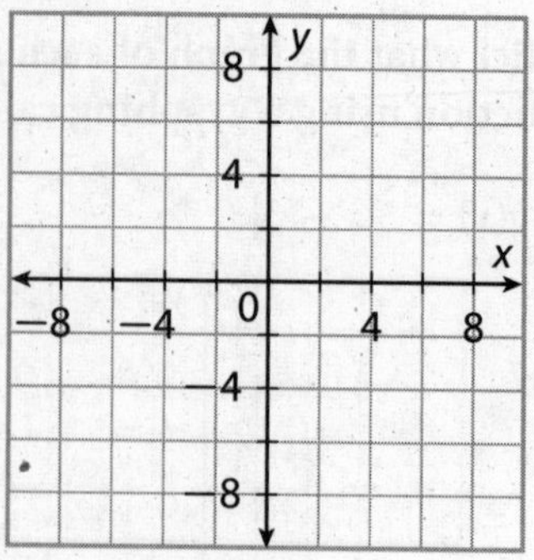

9. $g(x) = \left|\frac{3}{4}(x - 2)\right| - 7$

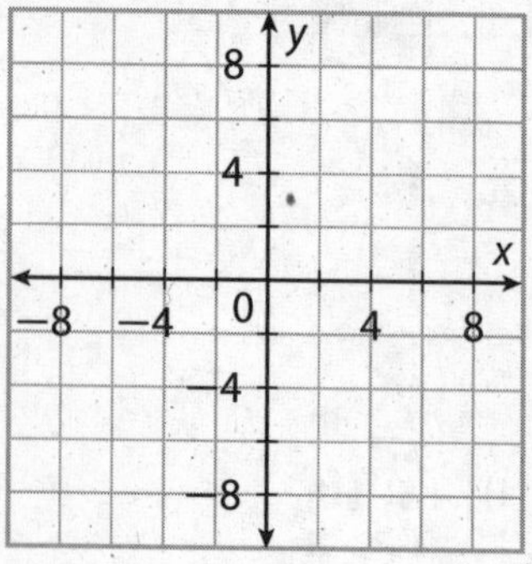

10. $g(x) = \left|\frac{5}{7}(x - 4)\right|$

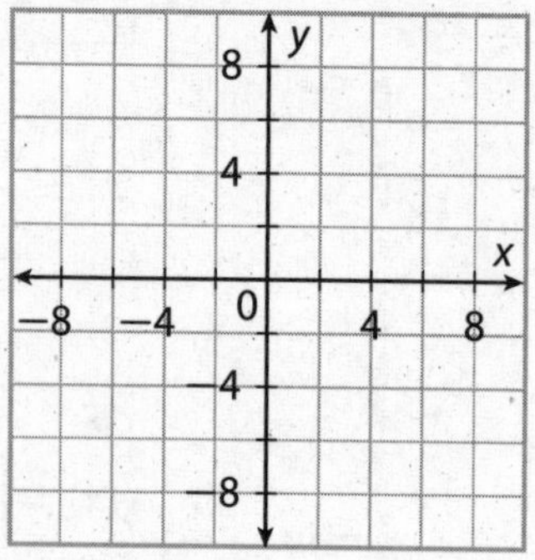

11. $g(x) = \left|-\frac{7}{3}(x + 5)\right| - 4$

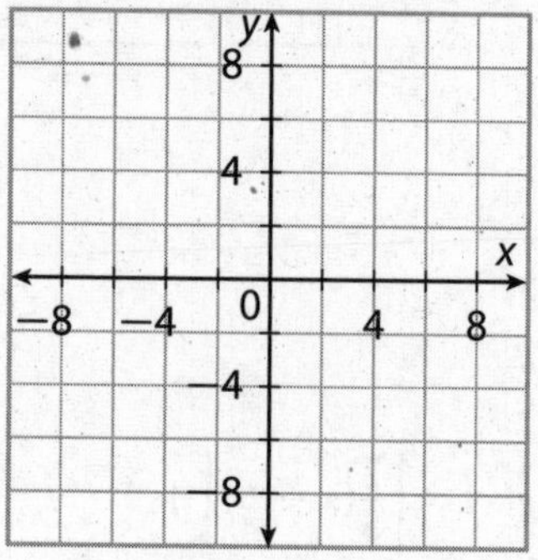

Write the absolute value function in standard form for the given graph. Use *a* or *b* as directed, $b > 0$.

12. Let $a = 1$.

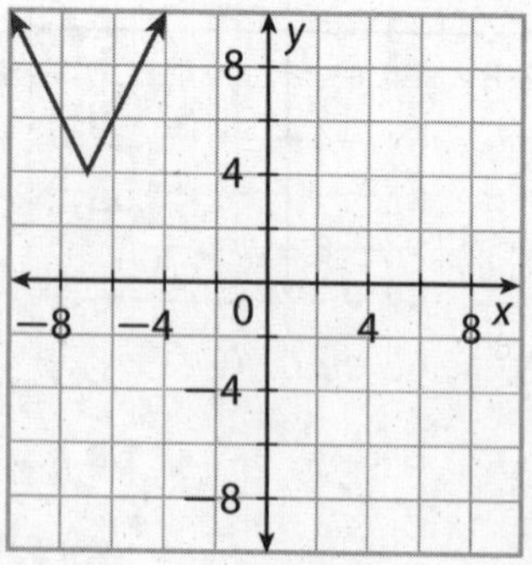

13. Let $b = 1$.

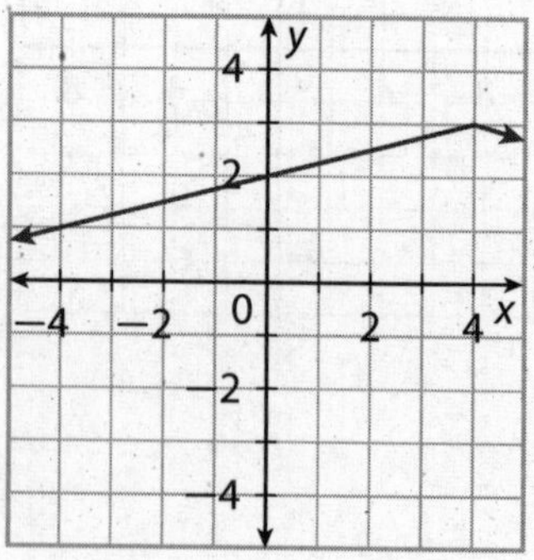

14. A rainstorm begins as a drizzle, builds up to a heavy rain, and then drops back to a drizzle. The rate r (in inches per hour) at which it rains is given by the function $r = -0.5|t - 1| + 0.5$, where t is the time (in hours). Graph the function. Determine for how long it rains and when it rains the hardest.

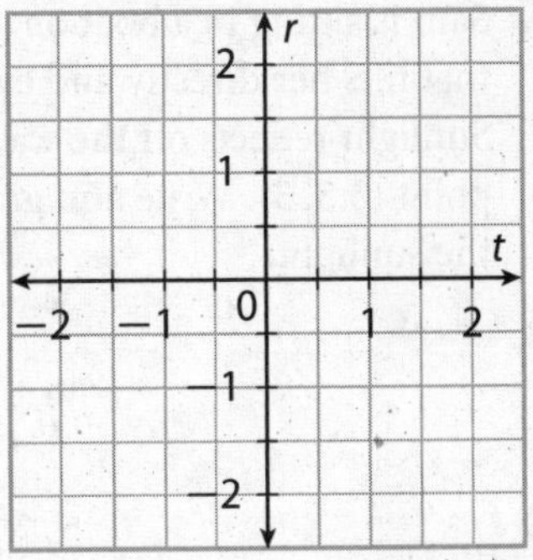

15. While playing pool, a player tries to shoot the eight ball into the corner pocket as shown. Imagine that a coordinate plane is placed over the pool table. The eight ball is at $\left(5, \frac{5}{4}\right)$ and the pocket they are aiming for is at (10, 5). The player is going to bank the ball off the side at (6, 0).

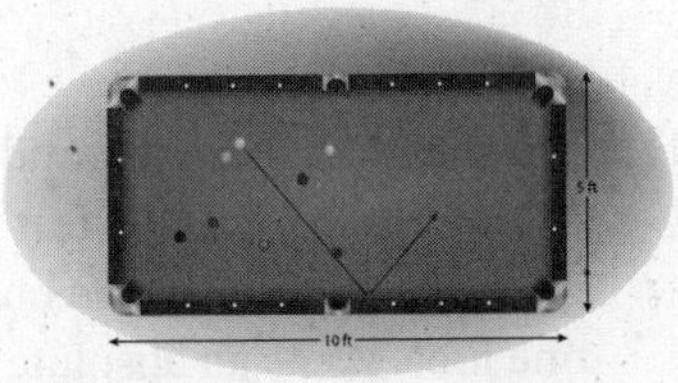

a. Write an equation for the path of the ball.

b. Did the player make the shot? How do you know?

16. Sam is sitting in a boat on a lake. She can get burned by the sunlight that hits her directly and by sunlight that reflects off the water. Sunlight reflects off the water at the point (2, 0) and hits Sam at the point (3.5, 3). Write and graph the function that shows the path of the sunlight.

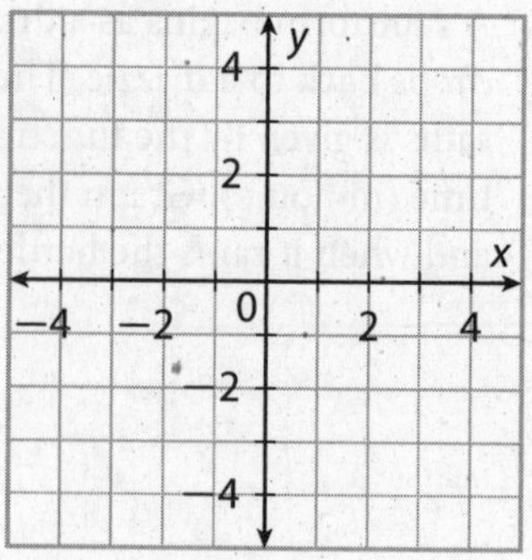

17. The Transamerica Pyramid is an office building in San Francisco. It stands 853 feet tall and is 145 feet wide at its base. Imagine that a coordinate plane is placed over a side of the building. In the coordinate plane, each unit represents one foot. Write an absolute value function whose graph is the V-shaped outline of the sides of the building, ignoring the "shoulders" of the building.

18. Match each graph with its function.

__________ $y = |x + 6| - 4$ __________ $y = |x - 6| - 4$ __________ $y = |x - 6| + 4$

A

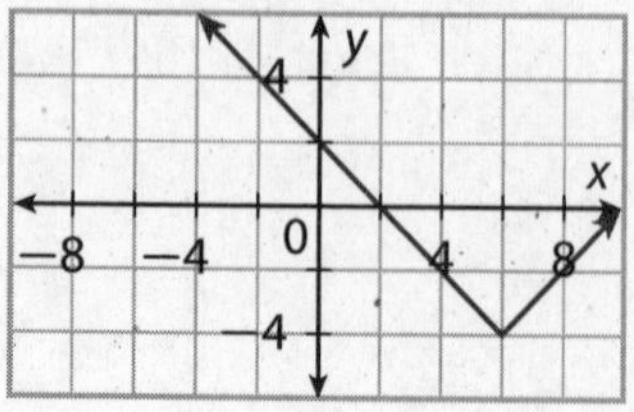

B

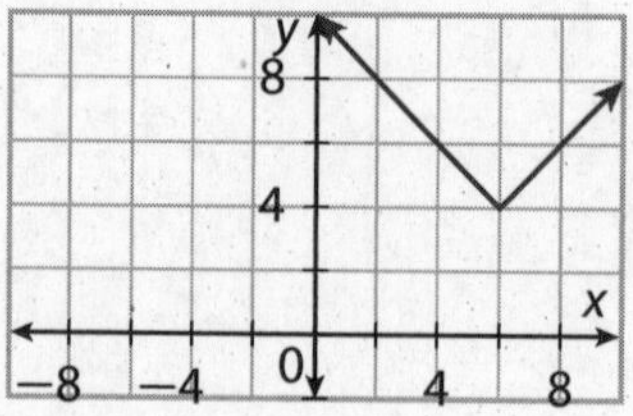

C

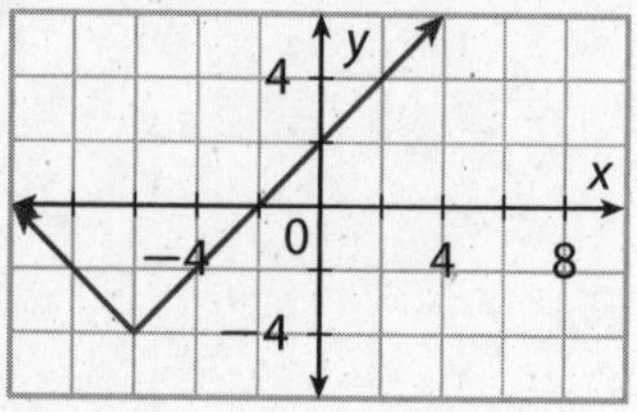

H.O.T. Focus on Higher Order Thinking

19. Explain the Error Explain why the graph shown is not the graph of $y = |x + 3| + 2$. What is the correct equation shown in the graph?

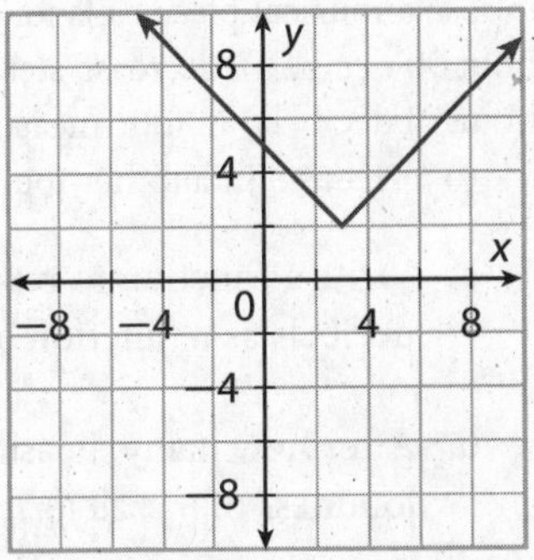

20. Multi-Step A golf player is trying to make a hole-in-one on the miniature golf green shown. Imagine that a coordinate plane is placed over the golf green. The golf ball is at (2.5, 2) and the hole is at (9.5, 2). The player is going to bank the ball off the side wall of the green at (6, 8).

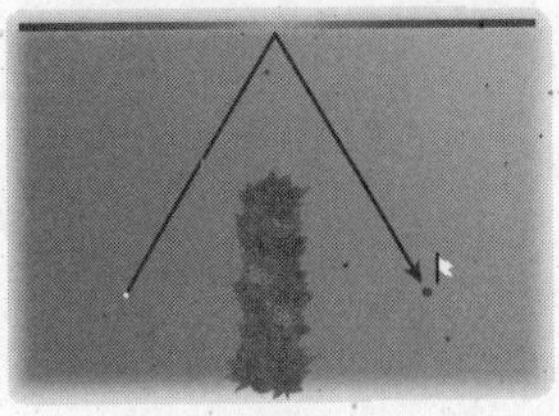

a. Write an equation for the path of the ball.

b. Use the equation in part a to determine if the player makes the shot.

Lesson Performance Task

Suppose a musical piece calls for an orchestra to start at *fortissimo* (about 90 decibels), decrease steadily in loudness to *pianissimo* (about 50 decibels) in four measures, and then increase steadily back to *fortissimo* in another four measures.

a. Write a function to represent the sound level s in decibels as a function of the number of measures m.

b. After how many measures should the orchestra be at the loudness of *mezzo forte* (about 70 decibels)?

c. Describe what the graph of this function would look like.

Name ______________________ Class __________ Date __________

2.2 Solving Absolute Value Equations

Essential Question: How can you solve an absolute value equation?

Resource Locker

Explore Solving Absolute Value Equations Graphically

Absolute value equations differ from linear equations in that they may have two solutions. This is indicated with a **disjunction**, a mathematical statement created by a connecting two other statements with the word "or." To see why there can be two solutions, you can solve an absolute value equation using graphs.

(A) Solve the equation $2|x - 5| - 4 = 2$.

Plot the function $f(x) = 2|x - 5| - 4$ on the grid. Then plot the function $g(x) = 2$ as a horizontal line on the same grid, and mark the points where the graphs intersect.

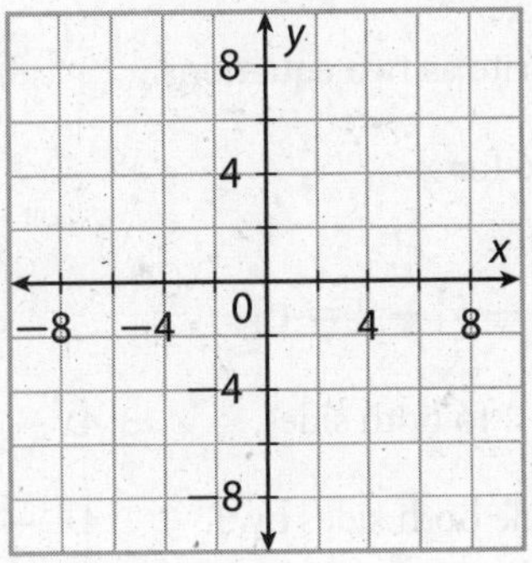

(B) Write the solution to this equation as a disjunction:

$x =$ ______ or $x =$ ______

Reflect

1. Why might you expect most absolute value equations to have two solutions? Why not three or four?

____

____

____

____

2. Is it possible for an absolute value equation to have no solutions? one solution? If so, what would each look like graphically?

____

____

____

____

Explain 1 Solving Absolute Value Equations Algebraically

To solve absolute value equations algebraically, first isolate the absolute value expression on one side of the equation the same way you would isolate a variable. Then use the rule:

If $|x| = a$ (where a is a positive number), then $x = a$ OR $x = -a$.

Notice the use of a **disjunction** here in the rule for values of x. You cannot know from the original equation whether the expression inside the absolute value bars is positive or negative, so you must work through both possibilities to finish isolating x.

Example 1 **Solve each absolute value equation algebraically. Graph the solutions on a number line.**

(A) $|3x| + 2 = 8$

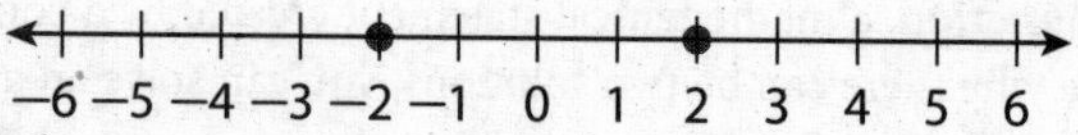

Subtract 2 from both sides. $|3x| = 6$

Rewrite as two equations. $3x = 6$ or $3x = -6$

Solve for x. $x = 2$ or $x = -2$

(B) $3|4x - 5| - 2 = 19$

Add 2 to both sides. $3|4x - 5| = \square$

Divide both sides by 3. $|4x - 5| = \square$

Rewrite as two equations. $4x - 5 = \square$ or $4x - 5 = \square$

Add 5 to all four sides. $4x = \square$ or $4x = \square$

Solve for x. $x = \square$ or $x = -\frac{\square}{\square}$

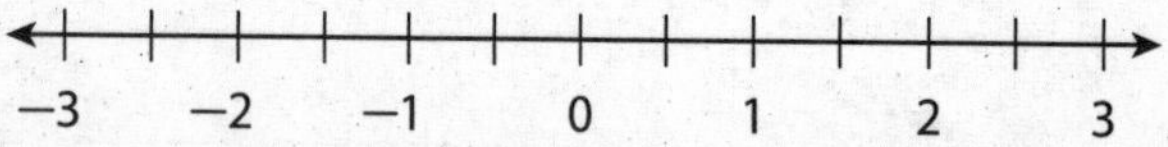

Your Turn

Solve each absolute value equation algebraically. Graph the solutions on a number line.

3. $\frac{1}{2}|x + 2| = 10$

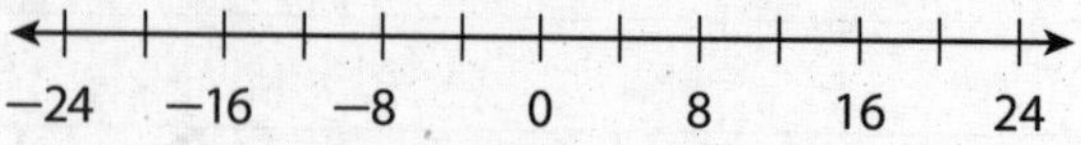

4. $-2|3x - 6| + 5 = 1$

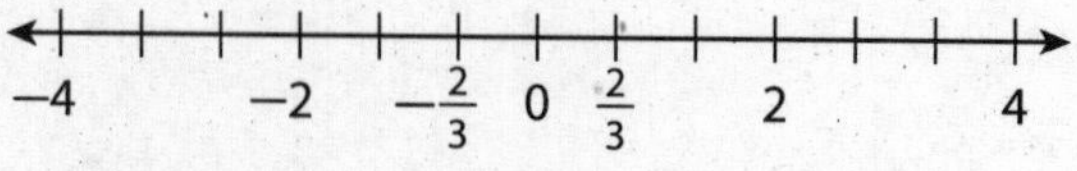

Explain 2 Absolute Value Equations with Fewer than Two Solutions

You have seen that absolute value equations have two solutions when the isolated absolute value expression is equal to a positive number. When the absolute value expression is equal to zero, there is a single solution because zero is its own opposite. When the absolute value is equal to a negative number, there is no solution because absolute value is never negative.

Example 2 **Isolate the absolute value expression in each equation to determine if the equation can be solved. If so, finish the solution. If not, write "no solution."**

(A) $-5|x+1|+2=12$

Subtract 2 from both sides. $-5|x+1|=10$

Divide both sides by -5. $|x+1|=-2$

Absolute values are never negative. No Solution

(B) $\frac{3}{5}|2x-4|-3=-3$

Add 3 to both sides. $\frac{3}{5}|2x-4|=$ ☐

Multiply both sides by $\frac{5}{3}$. $|2x-4|=$ ☐

Rewrite as one equation. $2x-4=$ ☐

Add 4 to both sides. $2x=$ ☐

Divide both sides by 2. $x=$ ☐

Your Turn

Isolate the absolute value expression in each equation to determine if the equation can be solved. If so, finish the solution. If not, write "no solution."

5. $3\left|\frac{1}{2}x+5\right|+7=5$

6. $9\left|\frac{4}{3}x-2\right|+7=7$

Elaborate

7. Why is important to solve both equations in the disjunction arising from an absolute value equation? Why not just pick one and solve it, knowing the solution for the variable will work when plugged backed into the equation?

8. **Discussion** Discuss how the range of the absolute value function differs from the range of a linear function. Graphically, how does this explain why a linear equation always has exactly one solution while an absolute value equation can have one, two, or no solutions?

9. **Essential Question Check-In** Describe, in your own words, the basic steps to solving absolute value equations and how many solutions to expect.

☆ Evaluate: Homework and Practice

Personal Math Trainer

- Online Homework
- Hints and Help
- Extra Practice

Solve the following absolute value equations by graphing.

1. $|x-3|+2=5$

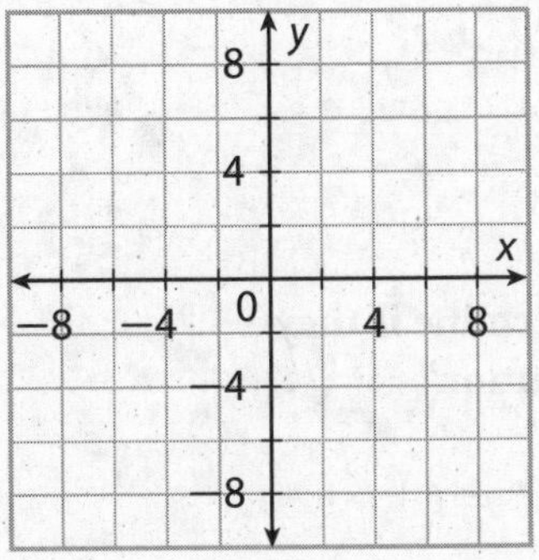

2. $2|x+1|+5=9$

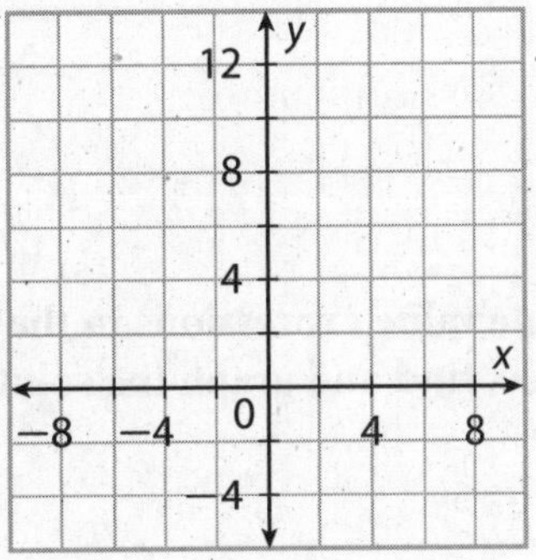

3. $-2|x+5|+4=2$

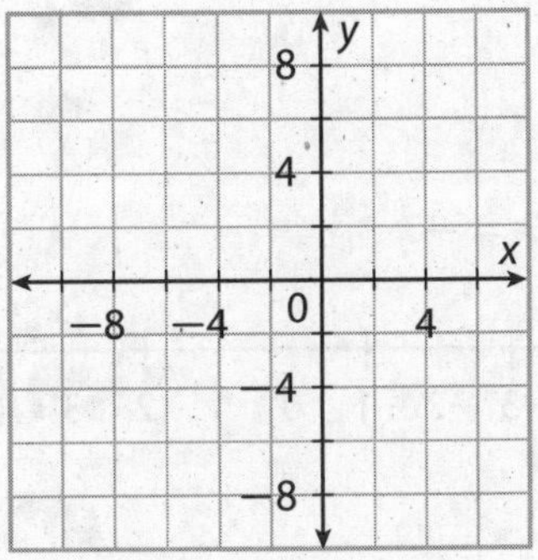

4. $\left|\frac{3}{2}(x-2)\right|+3=2$

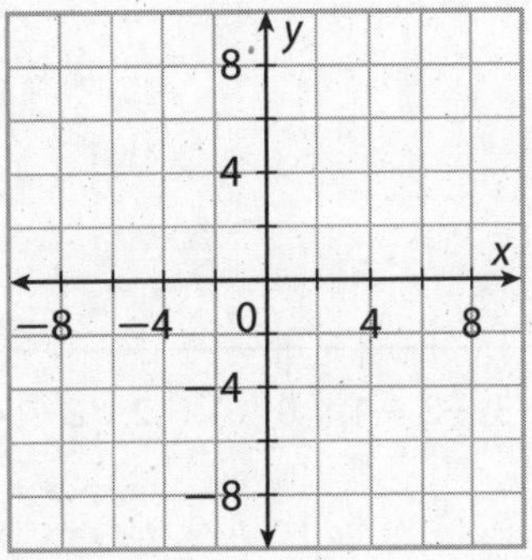

Solve each absolute value equation algebraically. Graph the solutions on a number line.

5. $|2x|=3$

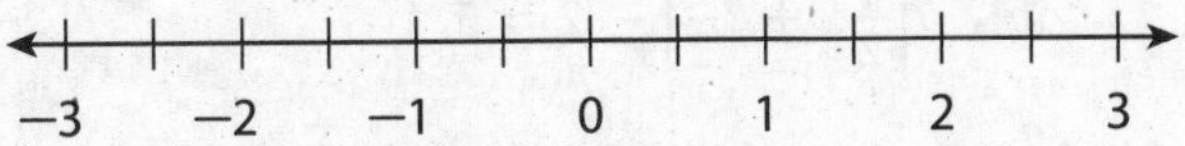

6. $\left|\frac{1}{3}x+4\right|=3$

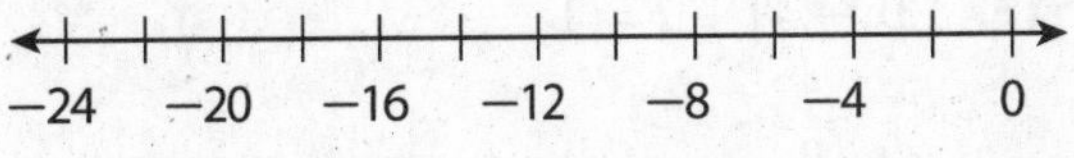

7. $3|2x - 3| + 2 = 3$

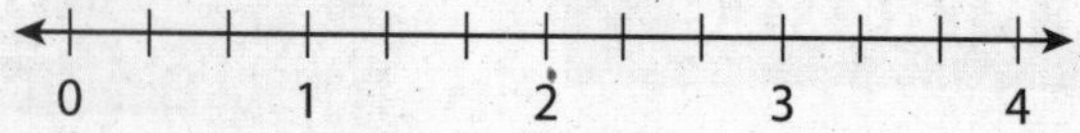

8. $-8|-x - 6| + 10 = 2$

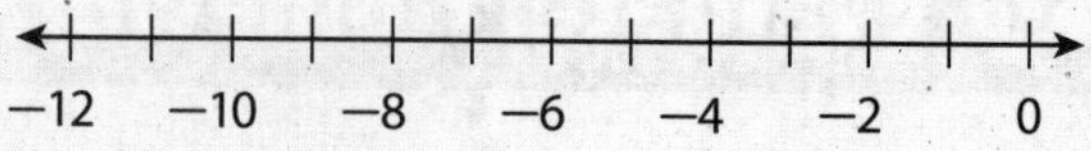

Isolate the absolute value expressions in the following equations to determine if they can be solved. If so, find and graph the solution(s). If not, write "no solution".

9. $\frac{1}{4}|x + 2| + 7 = 5$

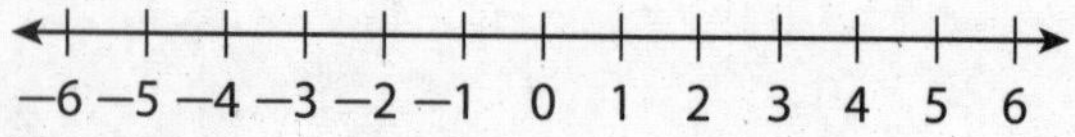

10. $-3|x - 3| + 3 = 6$

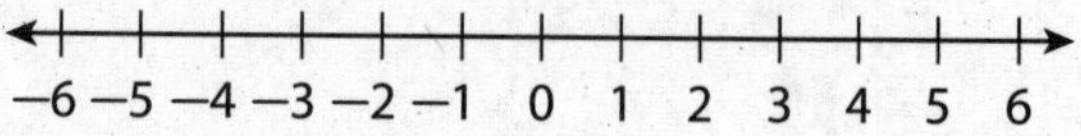

11. $2\left(|x + 4| + 3\right) = 6$

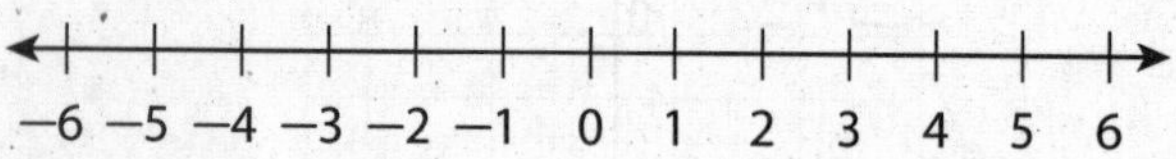

12. $5|2x + 4| - 3 = -3$

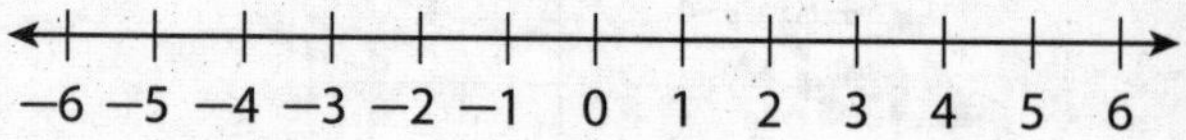

Solve the absolute value equations.

13. $|3x - 4| + 2 = 1$

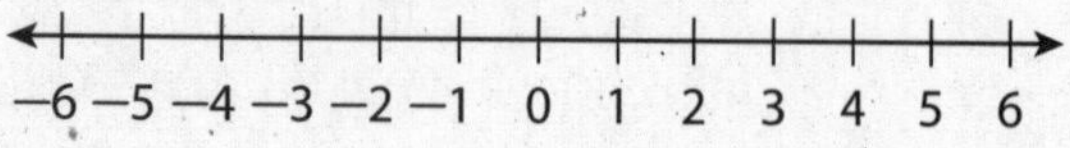

14. $7\left|\frac{1}{2}x + 3\frac{1}{2}\right| - 2 = 5$

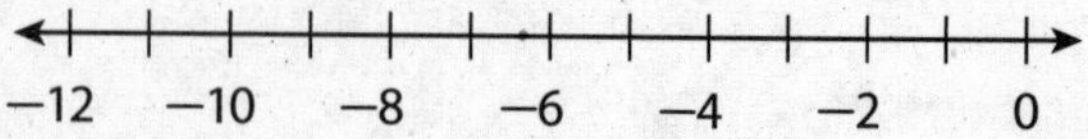

15. $|2(x+5)-3|+2=6$

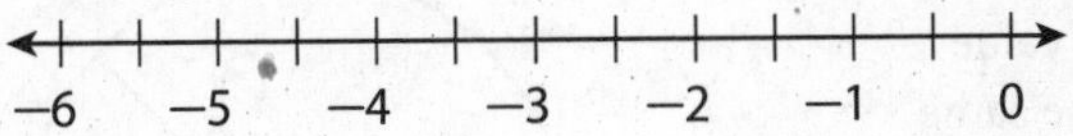

16. $-5|-3x+2|-2=-2$

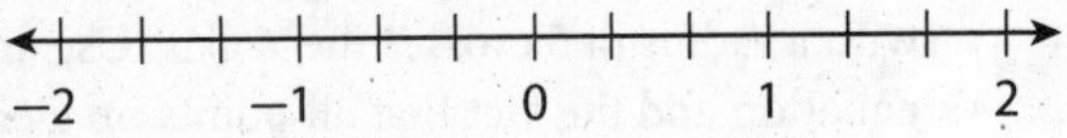

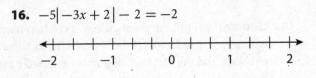

17. The bottom of a river makes a V-shape that can be modeled with the absolute value function, $d(h)=\frac{1}{5}|h-240|-48$, where d is the depth of the river bottom (in feet) and h is the horizontal distance to the left-hand shore (in feet).

A ship risks running aground if the bottom of its keel (its lowest point under the water) reaches down to the river bottom. Suppose you are the harbormaster and you want to place buoys where the river bottom is 30 feet below the surface. How far from the left-hand shore should you place the buoys?

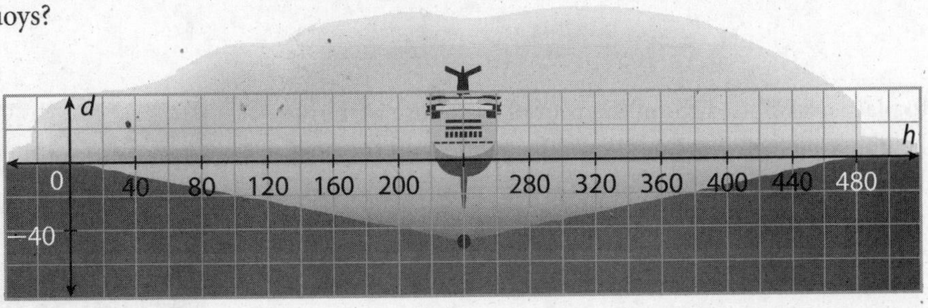

18. A flock of geese is approaching a photographer, flying in formation. The photographer starts taking photographs when the lead goose is 300 feet horizontally from her, and continues taking photographs until it is 100 feet past. The flock is flying at a steady 30 feet per second. Write and solve an equation to find the times after the photographing begins that the lead goose is at a horizontal distance of 75 feet from the photographer.

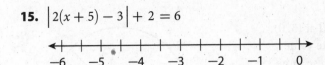

19. Geometry Find the points where a circle centered at (3, 0) with a radius of 5 crosses the x-axis. Use an absolute value equation and the fact that all points on a circle are the same distance (the radius) from the center.

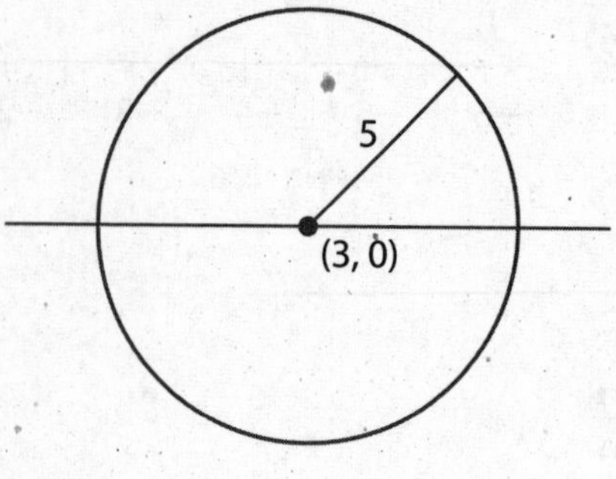

20. Select the value or values of x that satisfy the equation $-\frac{1}{2}|3x - 3| + 2 = 1$.

A. $x = \frac{5}{3}$ B. $x = -\frac{5}{3}$

C. $x = \frac{1}{3}$ D. $x = -\frac{1}{3}$

E. $x = 3$ F. $x = -3$

G. $x = 1$ H. $x = -1$

21. Terry is trying to place a satellite dish on the roof of his house at the recommended height of 30 feet. His house is 32 feet wide, and the height of the roof can be described by the function $h(x) = -\frac{3}{2}|x - 16| + 24$, where x is the distance along the width of the house. Where should Terry place the dish?

H.O.T. Focus on Higher Order Thinking

22. Explain the Error While attempting to solve the equation $-3|x - 4| - 4 = 3$, a student came up with the following results. Explain the error and find the correct solution:

$$-3|x - 4| - 4 = 3$$

$$-3|x - 4| = 7$$

$$|x - 4| = -\frac{7}{3}$$

$$x - 4 = -\frac{7}{3} \quad \text{or} \quad x - 4 = \frac{7}{3}$$

$$x = \frac{5}{3} \quad \text{or} \quad x = \frac{19}{3}$$

23. Communicate Mathematical Ideas Solve this absolute value equation and explain what algebraic properties make it possible to do so.

$3|x - 2| = 5|x - 2| - 7$

24. Justify Your Reasoning This absolute value equation has nested absolute values. Use your knowledge of solving absolute value equations to solve this equation. Justify the number of possible solutions.

$||2x + 5| - 3| = 10$

25. Check for Reasonableness For what type of real-world quantities would the negative answer for an absolute value equation not make sense?

Lesson Performance Task

A snowball comes apart as a child throws it north, resulting in two halves traveling away from the child. The child is standing 12 feet south and 6 feet east of the school door, along an east-west wall. One fragment flies off to the northeast, moving 2 feet east for every 5 feet north of travel, and the other moves 2 feet west for every 5 feet north of travel. Write an absolute value function that describes the northward position, $n(e)$, of both fragments as a function of how far east of the school door they are. How far apart are the fragments when they strike the wall?

Name________________________________ Class__________________ Date__________

2.3 Solving Absolute Value Inequalities

Essential Question: What are two ways to solve an absolute value inequality?

Resource Locker

Explore — Visualizing the Solution Set of an Absolute Value Inequality

You know that when solving an absolute value equation, it's possible to get two solutions. Here, you will explore what happens when you solve absolute value inequalities.

(A) Determine whether each of the integers from -5 to 5 is a solution of the inequality $|x| + 2 < 5$. Write *yes* or *no* for each number in the table. If a number is a solution, plot it on the number line.

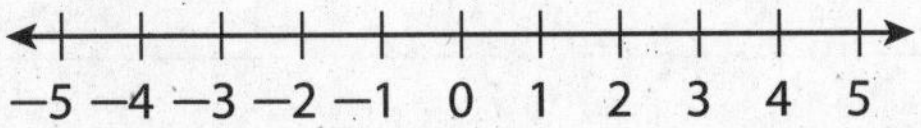

Number	Solution?
$x = -5$	
$x = -4$	
$x = -3$	
$x = -2$	
$x = -1$	
$x = 0$	
$x = 1$	
$x = 2$	
$x = 3$	
$x = 4$	
$x = 5$	

(B) Determine whether each of the integers from -5 to 5 is a solution of the inequality $|x| + 2 > 5$. Write *yes* or *no* for each number in the table. If a number is a solution, plot it on the number line.

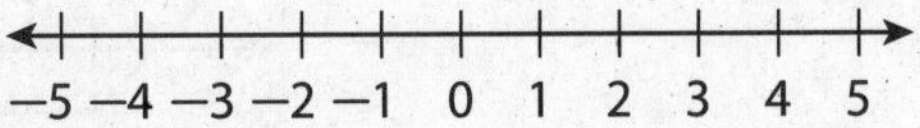

Number	Solution?
$x = -5$	
$x = -4$	
$x = -3$	
$x = -2$	
$x = -1$	
$x = 0$	
$x = 1$	
$x = 2$	
$x = 3$	
$x = 4$	
$x = 5$	

(C) State the solutions of the equation $|x| + 2 = 5$ and relate them to the solutions you found for the inequalities in Steps A and B.

(D) If x is any real number and not just an integer, graph the solutions of $|x| + 2 < 5$ and $|x| + 2 > 5$.

Graph of all real solutions of $|x| + 2 < 5$:

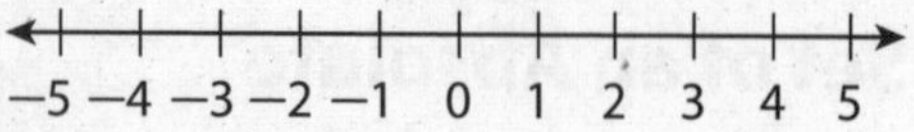

Graph of all real solutions of $|x| + 2 > 5$:

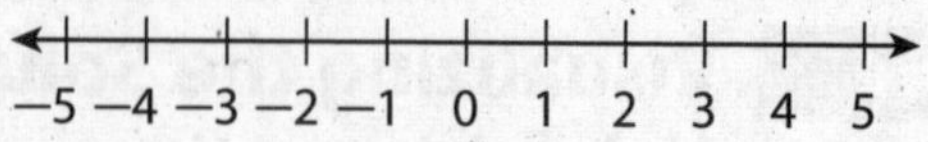

Reflect

1. It's possible to describe the solutions of $|x| + 2 < 5$ and $|x| + 2 > 5$ using inequalities that don't involve absolute value. For instance, you can write the solutions of $|x| + 2 < 5$ as $x > -3$ and $x < 3$. Notice that the word *and* is used because x must be both greater than −3 and less than 3. How would you write the solutions of $|x| + 2 > 5$? Explain.

2. Describe the solutions of $|x| + 2 \leq 5$ and $|x| + 2 \geq 5$ using inequalities that don't involve absolute value.

Explain 1 Solving Absolute Value Inequalities Graphically

You can use a graph to solve an absolute value inequality of the form $f(x) > g(x)$ or $f(x) < g(x)$, where $f(x)$ is an absolute value function and $g(x)$ is a constant function. Graph each function separately on the same coordinate plane and determine the intervals on the x-axis where one graph lies above or below the other. For $f(x) > g(x)$, you want to find the x-values for which the graph $f(x)$ is above the graph of $g(x)$. For $f(x) < g(x)$, you want to find the x-values for which the graph of $f(x)$ is below the graph of $g(x)$.

Example 1 **Solve the inequality graphically.**

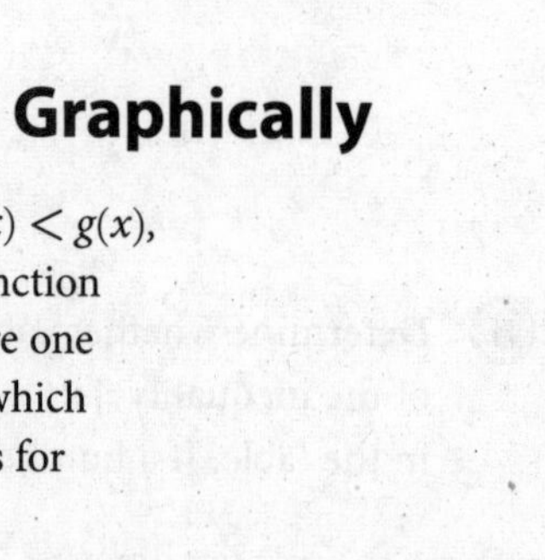

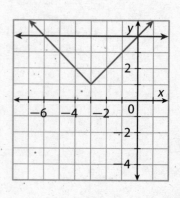

(A) $|x + 3| + 1 > 4$

The inequality is of the form $f(x) > g(x)$, so determine the intervals on the x-axis where the graph of $f(x) = |x + 3| + 1$ lies above the graph of $g(x) = 4$.

The graph of $f(x) = |x + 3| + 1$ lies above the graph of $g(x) = 4$ to the left of $x = -6$ and to the right of $x = 0$, so the solution of $|x + 3| + 1 > 4$ is $x < -6$ or $x > 0$.

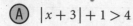

(B) $|x-2|-3<1$

The inequality is of the form $f(x) < g(x)$, so determine the intervals on the x-axis where the graph of $f(x) = |x-2|-3$ lies ________ the graph of $g(x) = 1$.

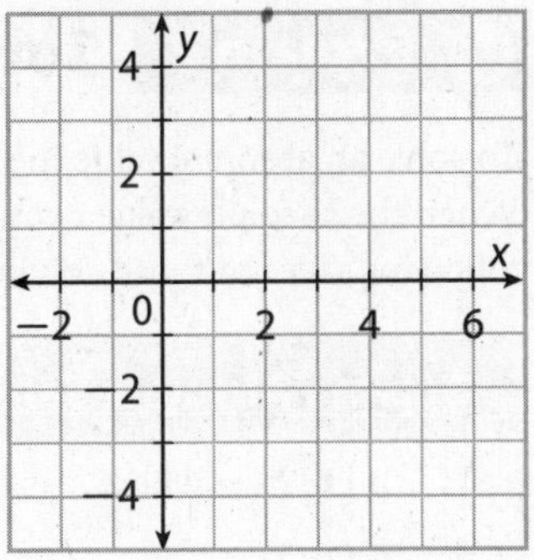

The graph of $f(x) = |x-2|-3$ lies ________ the graph of $g(x) = 1$ between $x =$ ☐ and $x =$ ☐, so the solution of $|x-2|-3<1$ is $x >$ ☐ *and* $x <$ ☐.

Reflect

3. Suppose the inequality in Part A is $|x+3|+1 \geq 4$ instead of $|x+3|+1>4$. How does the solution change?

4. In Part B, what is another way to write the solution $x>-2$ and $x<6$?

5. **Discussion** Suppose the graph of an absolute value function $f(x)$ lies entirely above the graph of the constant function $g(x)$. What is the solution of the inequality $f(x) > g(x)$? What is the solution of the inequality $f(x) < g(x)$?

Your Turn

6. Solve $|x+1|-4 \leq -2$ graphically.

Explain 2 Solving Absolute Value Inequalities Algebraically

To solve an absolute value inequality algebraically, start by isolating the absolute value expression. When the absolute value expression is by itself on one side of the inequality, apply one of the following rules to finish solving the inequality for the variable.

Solving Absolute Value Inequalities Algebraically

1. If $|x| > a$ where a is a positive number, then $x < -a$ or $x > a$.
2. If $|x| < a$ where a is a positive number, then $-a < x < a$.

Example 2 **Solve the inequality algebraically. Graph the solution on a number line.**

(A) $|4 - x| + 15 > 21$

$|4 - x| > 6$

$4 - x < -6$ or $4 - x > 6$

$-x < -10$ or $-x > 2$

$x > 10$ or $x < -2$

The solution is $x > 10$ or $x < -2$.

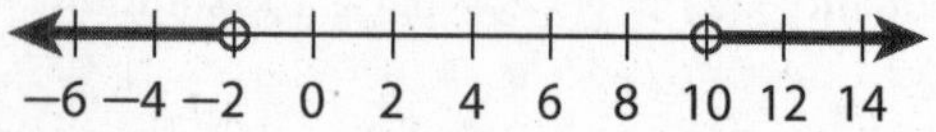

(B) $|x + 4| - 10 \leq -2$

$|x + 4| \leq \square$

$x + 4 \geq \square$ and $x + 4 \leq \square$

$x \geq \square$ and $x \leq \square$

The solution is $x \geq \square$ and $x \leq \square$,

or $\square \leq x \leq \square$.

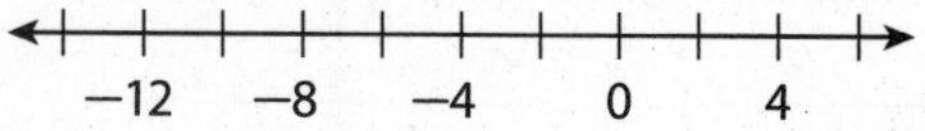

Reflect

7. In Part A, suppose the inequality were $|4 - x| + 15 > 14$ instead of $|4 - x| + 15 > 21$. How would the solution change? Explain.

8. In Part B, suppose the inequality were $|x + 4| - 10 \leq -11$ instead of $|x + 4| - 10 \leq -2$. How would the solution change? Explain.

Your Turn

Solve the inequality algebraically. Graph the solution on a number line.

9. $3|x-7| \geq 9$

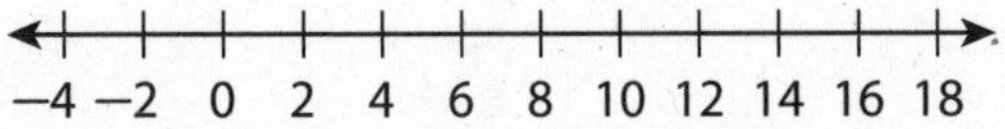

10. $|2x+3| < 5$

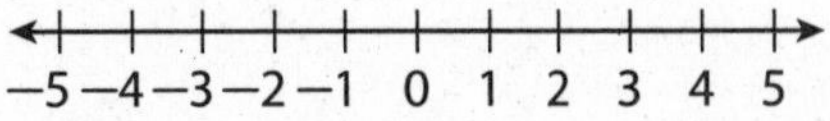

Explain 3 Solving a Real-World Problem with Absolute Value Inequalities

Absolute value inequalities are often used to model real-world situations involving a margin of error or *tolerance*. Tolerance is the allowable amount of variation in a quantity.

Example 3

A machine at a lumber mill cuts boards that are 3.25 meters long. It is acceptable for the length to differ from this value by at most 0.02 meters. Write and solve an absolute value inequality to find the range of acceptable lengths.

Analyze Information

Identify the important information.

- The boards being cut are ____ meters long.
- The length can differ by at most 0.02 meters.

Formulate a Plan

Let the length of a board be ℓ. Since the sign of the difference between ℓ and 3.25 doesn't matter, take the absolute value of the difference. Since the absolute value of the difference can be at most 0.02, the inequality that models the situation is

$|\ell - \square| \leq \square$.

Solve

$|\ell - 3.25| \leq 0.02$

$\ell - 3.25 \geq -0.02$ and $\ell - 3.25 \leq 0.02$

$\ell \geq \square$ and $\ell \leq \square$

So, the range of acceptable lengths is $\square \leq \ell \leq \square$.

Justify and Evaluate

The bounds of the range are positive and close to ☐, so this is a reasonable answer.

The answer is correct since ☐ $+ 0.02 = 3.25$ and ☐ $- 0.02 = 3.25$.

Your Turn

11. A box of cereal is supposed to weigh 13.8 oz, but it's acceptable for the weight to vary as much as 0.1 oz. Write and solve an absolute value inequality to find the range of acceptable weights.

Elaborate

12. Describe the values of x that satisfy the inequalities $|x| < a$ and $|x| > a$ where a is a positive constant.

13. How do you algebraically solve an absolute value inequality?

14. Explain why the solution of $|x| > a$ is all real numbers if a is a negative number.

15. Essential Question Check-In How do you solve an absolute value inequality graphically?

☆ Evaluate: Homework and Practice

Personal Math Trainer

• Online Homework
• Hints and Help
• Extra Practice

1. Determine whether each of the integers from −5 to 5 is a solution of the inequality $|x-1|+3 \geq 5$. If a number is a solution, plot it on the number line.

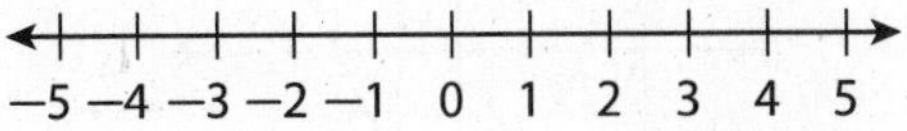

2. Determine whether each of the integers from −5 to 5 is a solution of the inequality $|x+1|-2 \leq 1$. If a number is a solution, plot it on the number line.

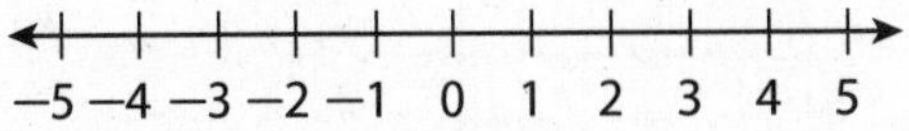

Solve each inequality graphically.

3. $2|x| \leq 6$

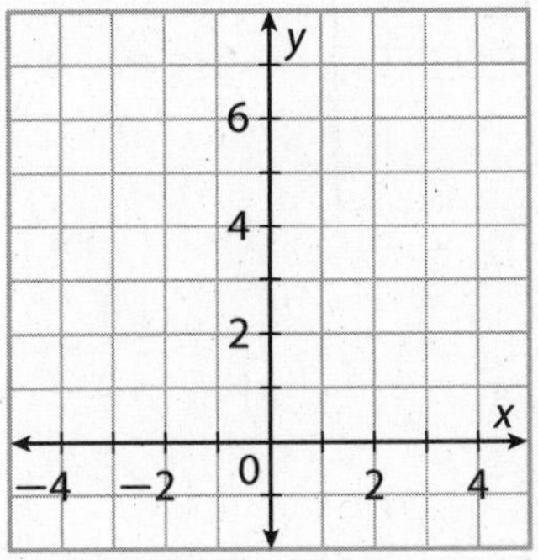

4. $|x-3|-2 > -1$

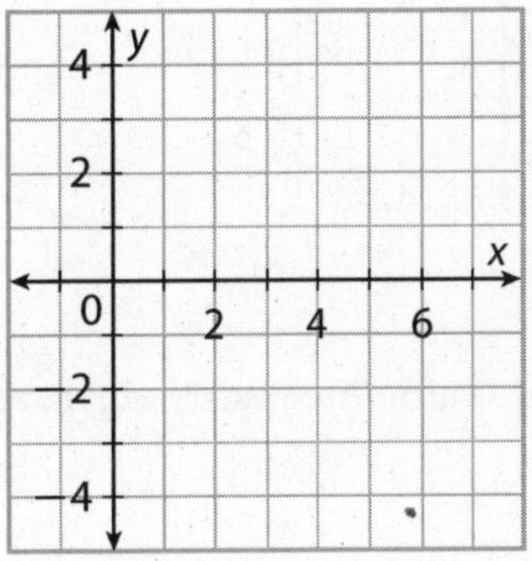

5. $\frac{1}{2}|x|+2 < 3$

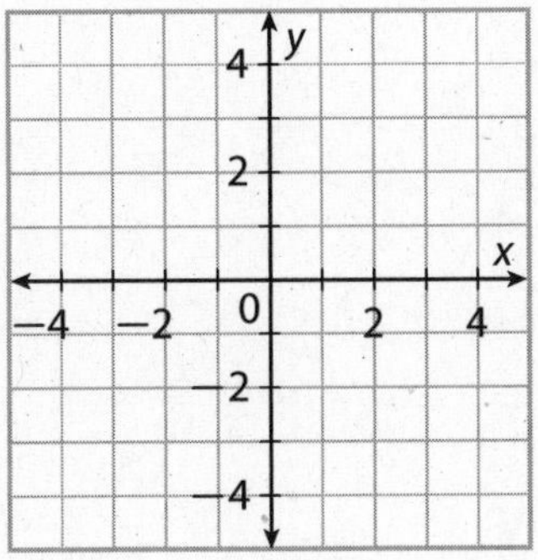

6. $|x+2|-4 \geq -2$

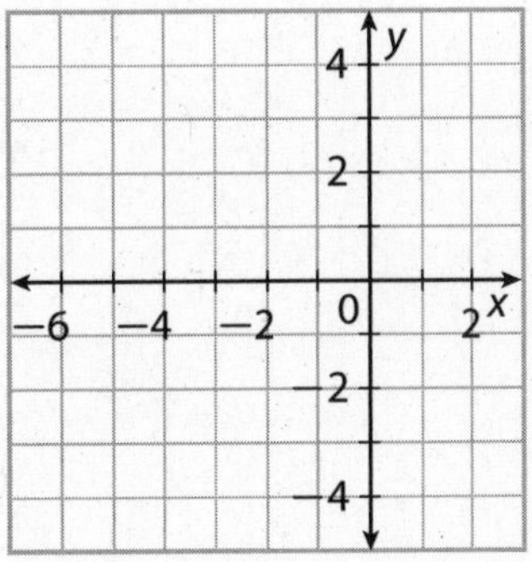

Match each graph with the corresponding absolute value inequality. Then give the solution of the inequality.

A. $2|x| + 1 > 3$ **B.** $2|x + 1| < 3$ **C.** $2|x| - 1 > 3$ **D.** $2|x - 1| < 3$

7.

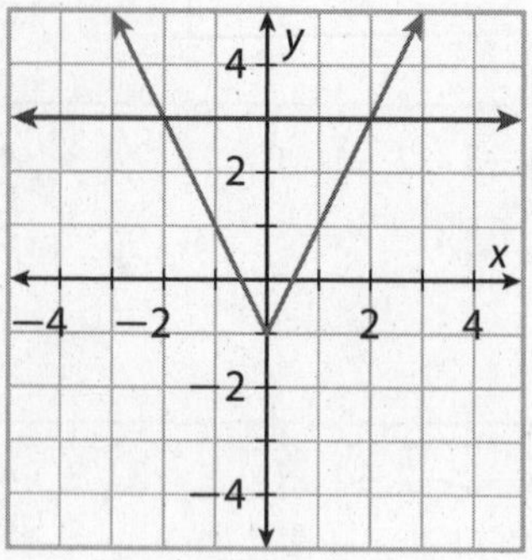

8.

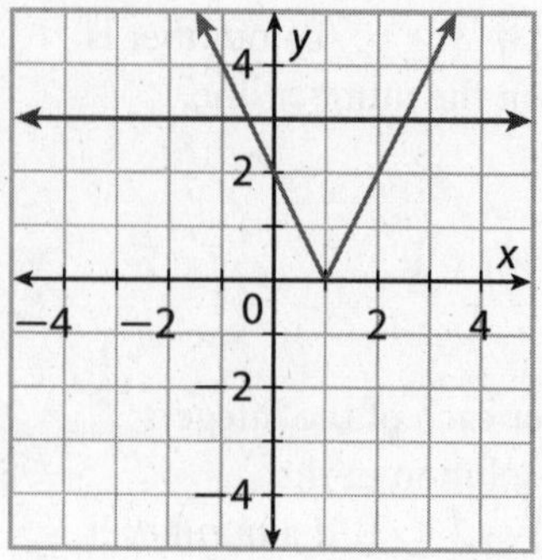

9.

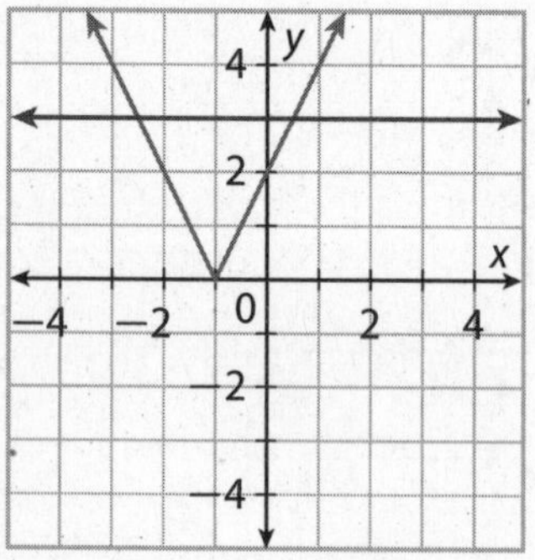

10.

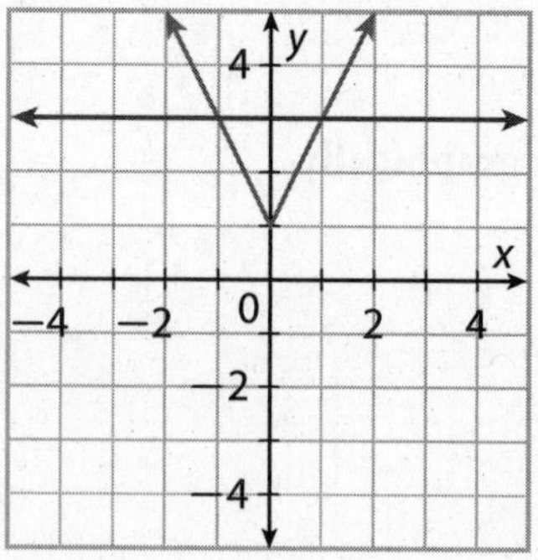

Solve each absolute value inequality algebraically. Graph the solution on a number line.

11. $2\left|x - \frac{7}{2}\right| + 3 > 4$

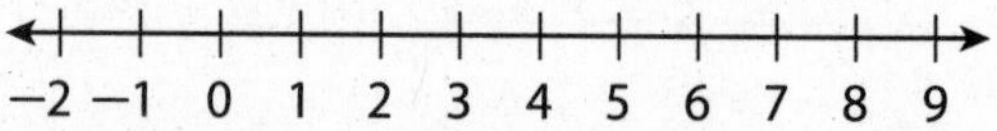

12. $|2x+1|-4<5$

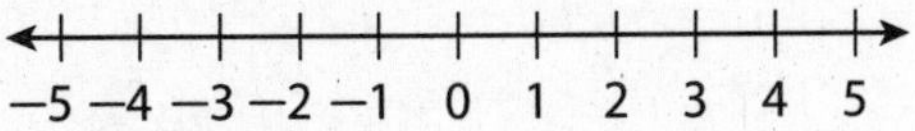

13. $3|x+4|+2\geq 5$

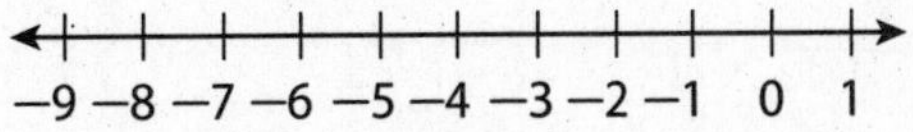

14. $|x+11|-8\leq -3$

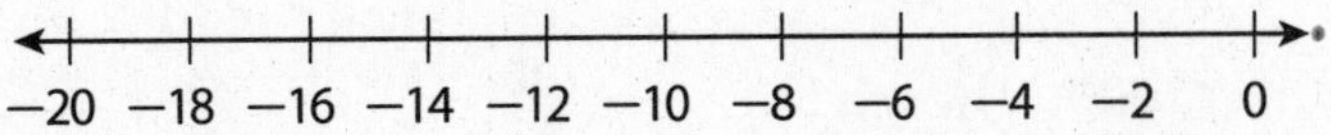

15. $-5|x-3|-5<15$

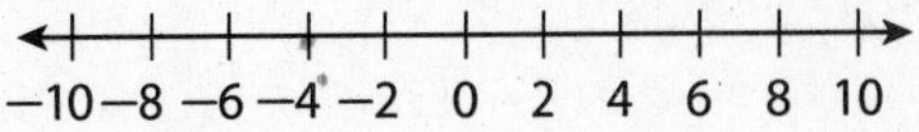

16. $8|x+4|+10<2$

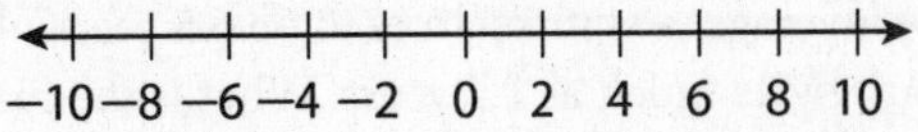

Solve each problem using an absolute value inequality.

17. The thermostat for a house is set to 68 °F, but the actual temperature may vary by as much as 2 °F. What is the range of possible temperatures?

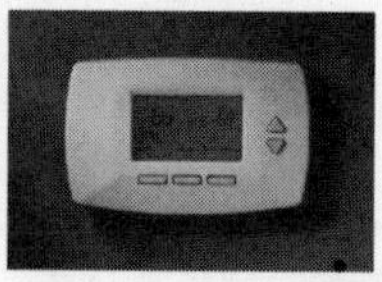

18. The balance of Jason's checking account is \$320. The balance varies by as much as \$80 each week. What are the possible balances of Jason's account?

19. On average, a squirrel lives to be 6.5 years old. The lifespan of a squirrel may vary by as much as 1.5 years. What is the range of ages that a squirrel lives?

20. You are playing a history quiz game where you must give the years of historical events. In order to score any points at all for a question about the year in which a man first stepped on the moon, your answer must be no more than 3 years away from the correct answer, 1969. What is the range of answers that allow you to score points?

21. The speed limit on a road is 30 miles per hour. Drivers on this road typically vary their speed around the limit by as much as 5 miles per hour. What is the range of typical speeds on this road?

H.O.T. Focus on Higher Order Thinking

22. Represent Real-World Problems A poll of likely voters shows that the incumbent will get 51% of the vote in an upcoming election. Based on the number of voters polled, the results of the poll could be off by as much as 3 percentage points. What does this mean for the incumbent?

23. Explain the Error A student solved the inequality $|x - 1| - 3 > 1$ graphically. Identify and correct the student's error.

I graphed the functions $f(x) = |x - 1| - 3$ and $g(x) = 1$. Because the graph of $g(x)$ lies above the graph of $f(x)$ between $x = -3$ and $x = 5$, the solution of the inequality is $-3 < x < 5$.

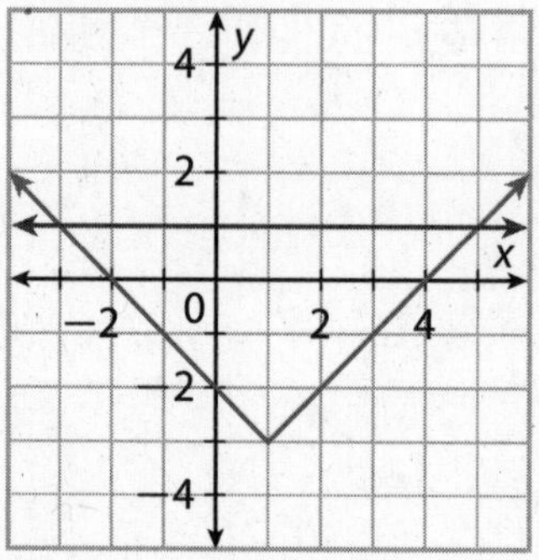

24. Multi-Step Recall that a literal equation or inequality is one in which the constants have been replaced by letters.

a. Solve $|ax + b| > c$ for x. Write the solution in terms of a, b, and c. Assume that $a > 0$ and $c \geq 0$.

b. Use the solution of the literal inequality to find the solution of $|10x + 21| > 14$.

c. In Part a, explain how the restrictions $a > 0$ and $c \geq 0$ affect finding the solutions of the inequality.

Lesson Performance Task

The distance between the Sun and each planet in our solar system varies because the planets travel in elliptical orbits around the Sun. Here is a table of the average distance and the variation in the distance for the five innermost planets in our solar system.

	Average Distance	Variation
Mercury	36.0 million miles	7.39 million miles
Venus	67.2 million miles	0.43 million miles
Earth	93.0 million miles	1.55 million miles
Mars	142 million miles	13.2 million miles
Jupiter	484 million miles	23.2 million miles

a. Write and solve an inequality to represent the range of distances that can occur between the Sun and each planet.

b. Calculate the percentage variation (variation divided by average distance) in the orbit of each of the planets. Based on these percentages, which planet has the most elliptical orbit?

STUDY GUIDE REVIEW

Absolute Value Functions, Equations, and Inequalities

MODULE 2

Essential Question: How can you use absolute value functions to solve real-world problems?

Key Vocabulary

absolute value *(valor absoluto)*
absolute-value equation *(ecuación de valor absoluto)*
coefficient *(coeficiente)*
disjunction *(disyunción)*
domain *(dominio)*
function *(función)*
inequality *(desigualdad)*
parameter *(parámetro)*
range *(rango)*
symmetry *(simetría)*
vertex *(vértice)*

KEY EXAMPLE (Lesson 2.1)

Given the function $g(x) = \left|\frac{1}{3}(x+6)\right| - 1$, predict what the graph will look like compared to the parent function, $f(x) = |x|$.

The graph of $g(x)$ will be the graph of $f(x)$ translated down 1 unit and left 6 units. There will also be a horizontal stretch of $f(x)$ by a factor of 3.

KEY EXAMPLE (Lesson 2.2)

Solve $6|2x + 3| + 1 = 25$ algebraically.

$6|2x+3| = 24$		Subtract 1 from both sides.
$|2x+3| = 4$		Divide both sides by 6.
$2x + 3 = 4$	or $2x + 3 = -4$	Rewrite as two equations.
$2x = 1$	or $2x = -7$	Subtract 3 from both sides.
$x = \frac{1}{2}$	or $x = -\frac{7}{2}$	Solve for x.
So, $x = \frac{1}{2}$	or $-\frac{7}{2}$.	

KEY EXAMPLE (Lesson 2.3)

Solve $|x + 2| - 4 < 4$ algebraically, then graph the solution on a number line.

$|x+2| - 4 < 4$		
$|x+2| < 8$		Add 4 to both sides.
$x + 2 < 8$	and $x + 2 > -8$	Rewrite as two inequalities.
$x < 6$	and $x > -10$	Subtract 2 from both sides.

The solution is $x < 6$ and $x > -10$.

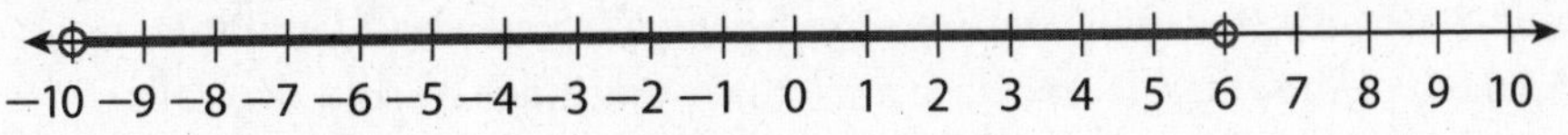

EXERCISES

Solve. *(Lessons 2.2, 2.3)*

1. $-10|x + 2| = -70$

2. $|3x + 7| = 27$

3. $\frac{1}{7}|8 + x| \leq 5$

4. $|x - 2| - 5 > 10$

5. Explain how the graph of $g(x) = \left|\frac{3}{7}(x - 4)\right| + 2$ compares to the graph of $h(x) = \frac{3}{7}|x - 4| + 2$. *(Lesson 2.1)*

6. Leroy wants to place a chimney on his roof. It is recommended that the chimney be set at a height of at least 25 feet. The height of the roof is described by the function $r(x) = -\frac{4}{3}|x - 10| + 35$, where x is the width of the roof. Where should Leroy place the chimney if the house is 40 feet wide? *(Lesson 2.3)*

MODULE PERFORMANCE TASK

What Is the Purity of Gold?

The purity of gold in jewelry is measured in "karats," with 24-karat gold the highest purity (100% pure gold). You have three gold rings labeled 10 karat, 14 karat, and 18 karat, and would like to know if the rings are correctly labeled. The table shows the results of an analysis of the rings.

Ring Label	Actual Percentage of Gold
10-karat	40.6%
14-karat	59.5%
18-karat	71.2%

In the United States, jewelry manufacturers are legally allowed a half karat tolerance. Determine which of the rings, if any, have an actual percentage of gold that falls outside this tolerance.

Use your own paper to list any additional information you will need and then complete the task. Be sure to write down all your data and assumptions. Then use graphs, numbers, words, or algebra to explain how you reached your conclusion.

Ready to Go On?

2.1–2.3 Absolute Value Functions, Equations, and Inequalities

Personal Math Trainer

- Online Homework
- Hints and Help
- Extra Practice

Solve. *(Lesson 2.1)*

1. $|-2x - 3| = 6$

2. $\frac{1}{4}|-4 - 3x| = 2$

3. $|3x + 8| = 2$

4. $4|x + 7| + 3 = 59$

Solve each inequality using the method indicated. *(Lesson 2.2)*

5. $|5x + 2| \leq 13$ (algebraically)

6. $|x - 2| + 1 \leq 5$ (graphically)

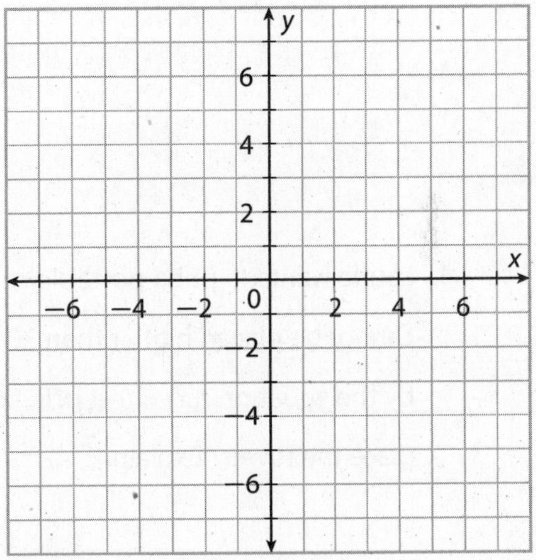

ESSENTIAL QUESTION

7. Write a real world situation that could be modeled by $|x - 14| = 3$. *(Lesson 2.1)*

MODULE 2
MIXED REVIEW

Assessment Readiness

1. Look at each function. Is the point $(-2, -1)$ on the graph of the function? Select Yes or No for A–C.

A. $g(x) = 3|x - 4|$ ○ Yes ○ No

B. $h(x) = -\frac{1}{2}|x|$ ○ Yes ○ No

C. $j(x) = |x + 3| - 2$ ○ Yes ○ No

2. Consider the absolute value equation $\frac{2}{3}|x - 4| + 2 = 5$. Choose True or False for each statement.

A. Solving $\frac{2}{3}|x - 4| + 2 = 5$ gives the same x-values as solving $\left|\frac{2}{3}(x - 4)\right| + 2 = 5$. ○ True ○ False

B. To solve the equation for x, the first step is to add 4 to both sides. ○ True ○ False

C. Before the step to rewrite as two equations, the equation looks like: $|x - 4| = 3$. ○ True ○ False

3. Describe the domain, range, and vertex of the function $f(x) = 3|x - 4| + 2$. Explain your answers.

4. Laurie wants to put a portable cellular phone mini-tower on her roof. The tower cannot be placed higher than 30 feet. The slant of her roof can be represented by the equation $r(x) = -\frac{1}{4}|x| + 60$. If her house is 40 feet wide, where could she place the tower? Explain.

Assessment Readiness

Personal Math Trainer

- Online Homework
- Hints and Help
- Extra Practice

1. Consider the function $f(x) = 2(x - 1)^2 + 5$. Choose True or False for each statement.

A. The range is $y \geq 5$. ○ True ○ False

B. The range is $y \geq 7$. ○ True ○ False

C. The domain is $-\infty < x < \infty$. ○ True ○ False

2. Consider the function $g(x) = x^3 + 7$. Choose True or False for each statement.

A. As $x \to \infty, y \to \infty$. ○ True ○ False

B. As $x \to -\infty, y \to \infty$. ○ True ○ False

C. The range is $y \geq 7$. ○ True ○ False

3. Consider the equation $f(x) = \frac{1}{2}x - 5$. Is the given equation the inverse of $f(x)$? Select Yes or No for A–C.

A. $f^{-1}(x) = 2x - 10$ ○ Yes ○ No

B. $f^{-1}(x) = -\frac{1}{2}x + 5$ ○ Yes ○ No

C. $f^{-1}(x) = 2x + 10$ ○ Yes ○ No

4. Consider the equation $3|x - 2| + 6 = 12$. Choose True or False for each statement.

A. The equation can be solved using the Pythagorean Theorem. ○ True ○ False

B. The solutions of the equation are $x = 4$ and $x = 0$. ○ True ○ False

C. The first step to solving the equation could be subtracting 6 from both sides of the equation. ○ True ○ False

5. Consider the inequality $|2x - 3| + 1 < 7$. Is the number a solution to the inequality? Select Yes or No for A–C.

A. 0 ○ Yes ○ No

B. 6 ○ Yes ○ No

C. −1.5 ○ Yes ○ No

6. A triathlete is training for her next race and starts by swimming 2 miles in 1 hour. She rests for 1 hour and then rides her bike 100 miles in 5 hours. She rests another hour and runs 20 miles in 5 hours. Draw a graph showing the distance she travels over time. Explain your choice.

7. The maximum number of oranges in a box of volume one cubic foot can be modeled by the inequality $|x - 17| \leq 5$, depending on the size of the oranges. Solve the inequality to find the greatest and least numbers of oranges that could be in a box. Explain your answer.

8. How does the end behavior of $f(x) = (x - 2)^2 + 3$ differ from that of $g(x) = -(3x + 7)^2 - 8$ as $x \to -\infty$? Explain your answer.

Performance Tasks

★ 9. The revenue from an amusement park ride is given by the admission price of $3 times the number of riders. As part of a promotion, the first 10 riders ride for free.

A. Write a function for the revenue, *R*, in terms of the number of riders, *n*.

B. Find the inverse of the function found in part A and use it to determine how many riders are needed for the revenue to be $240.

★★10. A purified water dispenser can be used to fill 5-gallon containers. If the dispenser is functioning properly, the amount of water dispensed is within 4 ounces of 5 gallons.

A. Write and solve an absolute-value equation to find the maximum and minimum volumes of water the machine disperses if it is functioning properly. Your answer should be in terms of ounces. Recall that one gallon is 128 ounces.

B. A technician fills her 5-gallon container using the dispenser and later measures the volume of water to be 2% less than 5 gallons. Is the dispenser working properly? Explain.

★★★11. **Diving** Scuba divers must know that the deeper the dive, the greater the water pressure in pounds per square inch (psi) for fresh water diving, as shown in the table.

Depth (feet)	Pressure (psi)
34	29.4
68	44.1
102	58.8

A. Write the pressure as a function of depth, and identify a reasonable domain and range for this function.

B. Find the inverse of the function from part **A**. What does the inverse function represent?

C. The point (25.9, 25.9) is an approximate solution to both the function from part **A** and its inverse. What does this point mean in the context of the problem?

MATH IN CAREERS

Community Theater Owner A community theater currently sells 200 season tickets at $50 each. In order to increase its season-ticket revenue, the theater surveys its season-ticket holders to see if they would be willing to pay more. The survey finds that for every $5 increase in the price of a season ticket, the theater would lose 10 season-ticket holders. What action, if any, should the theater owner take to increase revenue?

a. Let n be the number of $5 price increases in the cost of a season ticket. Write an expression for the cost of a season ticket after n price increases, and an expression for the number of season-ticket holders after n price increases.

b. Use the expressions from part **a** to create a revenue function, $R(n)$, from the survey information.

c. Determine a constraint on the value of n. That is, write and solve an inequality that represents an upper bound on the value of n, then state a reasonable domain for the revenue function.

d. Graph the revenue function. Be sure to label the axes with the quantities they represent and indicate the axis scales by showing numbers for some grid lines.

e. Write a brief paragraph describing what actions the theater owner should take to maximize revenue. Include what happens to the number of season-ticket holders as well as the season-ticket prices.

UNIT 2

Polynomial Operations

MATH IN CAREERS

Camp Director A camp director is in charge of organizing activities, hiring and supervising staff, and overseeing maintenance of the camp facilities. Camp directors use math for bookkeeping, creating budgets, negotiating vendor contracts, and planning new construction of camp buildings and outdoor spaces.

If you are interested in a career as a camp director, you should study these mathematical subjects:

- Algebra
- Geometry
- Business math

Research other careers that require keeping financial books. Check out the career activity at the end of the unit to find out how **camp directors** use math.

Reading Start-Up

Vocabulary

Review Words

✔ Associative Property (*Propiedad asociativa*)

✔ closure (*cerradura*)

✔ Commutative Property (*Propiedad conmutativa*)

✔ Distributive Property (*Propiedad distributiva*)

✔ like terms (*términos semejantes*)

✔ simplify (*simplificar*)

✔ rational number (*número racional*)

Preview Words

binomial (*binomio*)
FOIL (*FOIL*)
monomial (*monomio*)
perfect-square trinomial (*trinomio cuadrado perfecto*)
polynomial (*polinomio*)
trinomial (*trinomio*)
rational exponent (*exponente racional*)

Visualize Vocabulary

Use the ✔ words to complete the chart.

Properties

The property that states that the sum or product of any two real numbers will equal another real number	The property that states that for all real numbers, the sum is always the same, regardless of their grouping
The property that states that for all real numbers, the sum is always the same, regardless of their ordering	The property that states that if you multiply a sum by a number, you will get the same result if you multiply each addend by that number and then add the products

Understand Vocabulary

To become familiar with some of the vocabulary terms in this unit, consider the following. You may refer to the module, the glossary, or a dictionary.

1. The prefix *tri-* is used to identify an item that has three parts, such as a *triangle*. What do you think a **trinomial** might be?

____

2. The prefix *poly-* is used to identify an item with many elements, such as a *polygon*. What do you think a **polynomial** might be?

____

Active Reading

Four-Corner Fold Before beginning the unit, create a four-corner fold to help you organize what you learn. Label the flaps "Adding Polynomials," "Subtracting Polynomials," "Multiplying Polynomials," and "Special Products of Binomials." As you study this unit note important ideas and concepts used when performing operations with polynomials under the appropriate flap. You can use your FoldNote later to study for tests and complete assignments.

MODULE 3

Rational Exponents and Radicals

Essential Question: How can you use rational exponents and radicals to solve real-world problems?

REAL WORLD VIDEO
Zoo managers must determine the amount of food needed for a healthy diet for the animals.

How Much Should We Feed the Animals?

You have been selected to be the next reptile chef at the local zoo. This means you are in charge of feeding the reptiles. Reptiles get much of their moisture from the foods they eat, so they need food to stay hydrated as well as to keep from starving. Of course, if they don't get enough food, they starve. If they get too much food, however, they can develop serious health issues that may cause death. So, how much food is enough? How much is too much? Let's find out!

Are YOU Ready?

Complete these exercises to review skills you will need for this module.

Personal Math Trainer
- Online Homework
- Hints and Help
- Extra Practice

Exponents

Example 1 Write $(-4)^3$ as a multiplication of factors. Then find its value.

$(-4)^3 = (-4)(-4)(-4)$ **Write the base −4 multiplied by itself 3 times.**

$(-4)(-4)(-4) = -64$ **Multiply.**

Write each expression as a multiplication of factors. Then find its value.

1. 13^2 ________

2. $(-5)^4$ ________

3. 9^3 ________

4. 2^5 ________

Algebraic Expressions

Example 2 Evaluate $x^2 + 4$ for $x = -2$.

$x^2 + 4$

$(-2)^2 + 4$ **Substitute −2 for *x*.**

$4 + 4$ **Evaluate the exponent.**

8 **Add.**

Evaluate each expression for the given value of the variables.

5. $p^3 - 2$ for $p = 3$ ________

6. $5a + b^2$ for $a = -3$ and $b = 4$ ________

7. $6m - n^2$ for $m = 5$ and $n = -7$ ________

8. $x^2 - y^3$ for $x = 6$ and $y = -2$ ________

Real Numbers

Example 3 Tell if 13 is a rational number or an irrational number.

13 can be written as $\frac{13}{1}$, so 13 is a rational number.

A rational number can be expressed in the form $\frac{p}{q}$, where *p* and *q* are integers and $q \neq 0$.

An irrational number cannot be written as the quotient of two integers.

Tell if the number is a rational number or irrational number.

9. -23 ________

10. $\sqrt{8}$ ________

11. $\frac{3}{8}$ ________

Name ____________________ Class ____________ Date ________

3.1 Understanding Rational Exponents and Radicals

Essential Question: How are radicals and rational exponents related?

Resource Locker

Explore 1 Understanding Integer Exponents

Recall that powers like 3^2 are evaluated by repeating the base (3) as a factor a number of times equal to the exponent (2). So $3^2 = 3 \cdot 3 = 9$. What about a negative exponent, or an exponent of 0? You cannot write a product with a negative number of factors, but a pattern emerges if you start from a positive exponent and divide repeatedly by the base.

(A) Starting with powers of 3:

$3^3 = \square$

$3^2 = \square$

$3^1 = \square$

(B) Dividing a power of 3 by 3 is equivalent to ________ the exponent by __.

(C) Complete the pattern:

$3^3 \xrightarrow[\div 3]{} 3^2 \xrightarrow[\div 3]{} 3^1 \xrightarrow[\div 3]{} 3^0 \xrightarrow[\div 3]{} 3^{-1} \xrightarrow[\div 3]{} 3^{-2}$

$27 \xrightarrow[\div 3]{} 9 \xrightarrow[\div 3]{} 3 \xrightarrow[\div 3]{} \square \xrightarrow[\div 3]{} \square \xrightarrow[\div 3]{} \square$

(D) $3^{-1} = \frac{1}{3}, 3^{-2} = \frac{1}{9} = \frac{1}{3^{\square}}$

Integer exponents less than 1 can be summarized as follows:

Words	Numbers	Variables
Any non-zero number raised to the power of 0 is; 0° is undefined.	$3^0 = 1$ $(2.4)^0 = 1$	$x^0 = 1$ for $x \neq 0$
Any non-zero number raised to a negative power is equal to 1 divided by the same number raised to the opposite, positive power.	$3^{-2} = \frac{1}{3^2} = \frac{1}{9}$	$x^{-n} = \frac{1}{x^n}$ for $x \neq 0$, and integer n.

Reflect

1. **Discussion** Why does there need to be an exception in in the second rule for the case of $x = 0$?

____

____

Explore 2 Exploring Rational Exponents

A radical expression is an expression that contains the radical symbol, $\sqrt{\ }$.

For $\sqrt[n]{a}$, n is called the **index** and a is called the **radicand**. n must be an integer greater than 1. a can be any real number when n is odd, but must be non-negative when n is even. When $n = 2$, the radical is a square root and the index 2 is usually not shown.

You can write a radical expression as a power. First, note what happens when you raise a power to a power.

$(2^3)^2 = (2 \cdot 2 \cdot 2)^2 = (2 \cdot 2 \cdot 2)(2 \cdot 2 \cdot 2) = 2^6$, so $(2^3)^2 = 2^{3 \cdot 2}$.

In fact, for all real numbers a and all rational numbers m and n, $(a^m)^n = a^{m \cdot n}$. This is called the **Power of a Power Property**.

A radical expression can be written as an exponential expression: $\sqrt[n]{a} = a^k$. Find the value for k when $n = 2$.

(A) Start with the equation. $\sqrt{a} = a^k$

Square both sides. $(\sqrt{a})^{\square} = (a^k)^{\square}$

(B) Definition of square root $\square = (a^k)^2$

(C) Power of a power property $a^1 = a^{\square}$

(D) Equate exponents. $1 = \square$

(E) Solve for k. $k = \square$

Reflect

2. What do you think will be the rule for other values of the radical index n?

____

Explain 1 Simplifying Numerical Expressions with nth Roots

For any integer $n > 1$, the nth root of a is a number that, when multiplied by itself n times, is equal to a.

$$x = \sqrt[n]{a} \Rightarrow x^n = a$$

The nth root can be written as a radical with an index of n, or as a power with an exponent of $\frac{1}{n}$.
An exponent in the form of a fraction is a **rational exponent**.

$$\sqrt[n]{a} = a^{\frac{1}{n}}$$

The expressions are interchangeable, and to evaluate the nth root, it is necessary to find the number, x, that satisfies the equation $x^n = a$.

Example 1 **Find the root and simplify the expression.**

(A) $64^{\frac{1}{3}}$

Convert to radical. $64^{\frac{1}{3}} = \sqrt[3]{64}$

Rewrite radicand as a power. $= \sqrt[3]{4^3}$

Definition of nth root $= 4$

(B) $81^{\frac{1}{4}} + 9^{\frac{1}{2}}$

Convert to radicals. $81^{\frac{1}{4}} + 9^{\frac{1}{2}} = \sqrt[\square]{\square} + \sqrt{\square}$

Rewrite radicands as powers. $= \sqrt[4]{\square^4} + \sqrt{\square^2}$

Apply definition of nth root. $= \square + \square$

Simplify. $= \square$

Your Turn

3. $8^{\frac{1}{3}}$

4. $16^{\frac{1}{2}} + 27^{\frac{1}{3}}$

Explain 2 Simplifying Numerical Expressions with Rational Exponents

Given that for an integer n greater than 1, $\sqrt[n]{a} = a^{\frac{1}{n}}$, you can use the Power of a Power Property to define $a^{\frac{m}{n}}$ for any positive integer m.

$a^{\frac{m}{n}} = a^{\frac{1}{n} \cdot m}$		$a^{\frac{m}{n}} = a^{m \cdot \frac{1}{n}}$
$= \left(a^{\frac{1}{n}}\right)^m$	Power of a Power Property	$= (a^m)^{\frac{1}{n}}$
$= \left(\sqrt[n]{a}\right)^m$	Definition of $a^{\frac{1}{n}}$	$= \sqrt[n]{a^m}$

The definition of a number raised to the power of $\frac{m}{n}$ is the nth root of the number raised to the mth power. The power of m and the nth root can be evaluated in either order to obtain the same answer, although it is generally easier to find the nth root first when working without a calculator.

Example 2 **Simplify expressions with fractional exponents.**

Ⓐ $27^{\frac{2}{3}}$

Definition of $a^{\frac{m}{n}}$ $\quad 27^{\frac{2}{3}} = \left(\sqrt[3]{27}\right)^2$

Rewrite radicand as a power. $\quad = \left(\sqrt[3]{3^3}\right)^2$

Definition of cube root $\quad = 3^2$

$= 9$

Ⓑ $25^{\frac{3}{2}}$

Definition of $a^{\frac{m}{n}}$ $\quad 25^{\frac{3}{2}} = \left(\sqrt{25}\right)^{\square}$

Rewrite radicand as a power. $\quad = \left(\sqrt{\square^{\square}}\right)^{\square}$

Definition of ☐ root $\quad = 5^3$

$= \square$

YourTurn

5. $32^{\frac{3}{5}}$

6. $4^{\frac{5}{2}} - 4^{\frac{3}{2}}$

Elaborate

7. Why can you evaluate an odd root for any radicand, but even roots require non-negative radicands?

8. In evaluating powers with rational exponents with values like $\frac{2}{3}$, why is it usually better to find the root before the power? Would it change the answer to switch the order?

9. **Essential Question Check-In** How can radicals and rational exponents be used to simplify expressions involving one or the other?

Evaluate: Homework and Practice

Personal Math Trainer

- Online Homework
- Hints and Help
- Extra Practice

Evaluate the expressions.

1. 10^{-2}

2. 56^{-1}

3. 2^{-4}

4. $\left(\frac{1}{3}\right)^{-2}$

5. $(-2)^0$

6. $3 \cdot 6^{-2}$

Find the root(s) and simplify the expression.

7. $81^{\frac{1}{2}}$

8. $125^{\frac{1}{3}}$

9. $49^{\frac{1}{2}} - 4^{\frac{1}{2}}$

10. $16^{\frac{1}{4}} + 32^{\frac{1}{5}}$

Simplify the expressions with rational exponents.

11. $49^{\frac{3}{2}}$

12. $8^{\frac{5}{3}}$

13. $27^{\frac{4}{3}} + 4^{\frac{3}{2}}$

14. $25^{\frac{3}{2}} + 16^{\frac{3}{2}}$

Simplify the expressions.

15. $25^{-\frac{1}{2}}$

16. $8^{-\frac{1}{3}}$

17. $1^{-\frac{2}{3}}$

18. $8^{\frac{2}{3}} + 8^{-\frac{2}{3}}$

19. $\dfrac{25^{\frac{1}{2}}}{27^{\frac{1}{3}}}$

20. $7 \cdot 10^{-3}$

21. $\left(\dfrac{1}{4}\right)^{-\frac{3}{2}}$

22. $2 \cdot 36^{-\frac{1}{2}} + 6^{-1}$

23. Geometry The volume of a cube is related to the area of a face by the formula $V = A^{\frac{3}{2}}$.

What is the volume of a cube whose face has an area of 100 cm^2?

24. Biology The approximate number of Calories, C, that an animal needs each day is given by $C = 72m^{\frac{3}{4}}$, where m is the animal's mass in kilograms. Find the number of Calories that a 16 kilogram dog needs each day.

25. Rocket Science Escape velocity is a measure of how fast an object must be moving to escape the gravitational pull of a planet or moon with no further thrust. The escape velocity for the moon is given approximately by the equation $V = 5600 \cdot \left(\frac{d}{1000}\right)^{-\frac{1}{2}}$, where v is the escape velocity in miles per hour and d is the distance from the center of the moon (in miles). If a lunar lander thrusts upwards until it reaches a distance of 16,000 miles from the center of the moon, about how fast must it be going to escape the moon's gravity?

26. Multiple Response Which of the following expressions cannot be evaluated?

a. $4^{\frac{1}{2}}$

b. $(-4)^{-\frac{1}{2}}$

c. 4^{-2}

d. $(-4)^{-2}$

e. $0^{-\frac{1}{2}}$

f. 0^{-2}

H.O.T. Focus on Higher Order Thinking

27. Explain the Error Yuan is asked to evaluate the expression $(-8)^{\frac{2}{3}}$ on his exam, and writes that it is unsolvable because you cannot evaluate a negative number to an even fractional power. Is he correct, and if so, why? If he is not correct, what is the correct answer?

28. Communicate Mathematical Ideas Show that the *n*th root of a number *a* can be expressed with an exponent of $\frac{1}{n}$ for any positive integer *n*.

29. Explain the Error Xia, Yen, and Zane are working on homework together, and come to the problem "Find $\left(-\frac{1}{64}\right)^{-\frac{2}{3}}$." Xia says "It's undefined because you can't find a square root of a negative number." Yen says "No, it's $1365\frac{1}{3}$ because I entered $(-\frac{1}{64})^{\frac{(-2)}{3}}$ on a scientific calculator and got 1365.333333." Zane says "No, it's −512, look…" and shows this work:

$$\left(-\frac{1}{64}\right)^{-\frac{2}{3}} = \frac{1}{-\left(\frac{1}{64}\right)^{\frac{3}{2}}} = \frac{1}{-\left(\sqrt{\frac{1}{64}}\right)^{3}} = \frac{1}{-\left(\frac{1}{8}\right)^{3}} = \frac{1}{-\frac{1}{512}} = -512.$$

Who's right, if anyone? Explain.

Lesson Performance Task

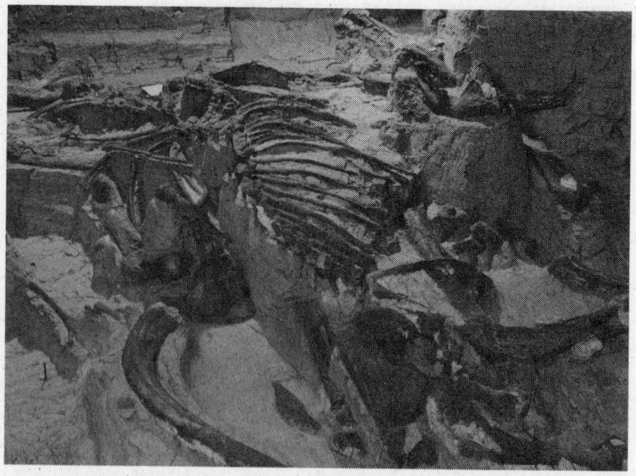

Carbon-14 dating is used to determine the age of archeological artifacts of biological (plant or animal) origin. Items that are dated using carbon-14 include objects made from bone, wood, or plant fibers. This method works by measuring the fraction of carbon-14 remaining in an object. The fraction of the original carbon-14 remaining can be expressed by the function, $f = 2^{\left(-\frac{t}{5700}\right)}$,

where t is the length of time since the organism died.

a. Fill in the following table to see what fraction of the original carbon-14 still remains after the passage of time.

t	$\frac{t}{5700}$	Fraction of Carbon-14 Remaining
0		
5700		
11,400		
17,100		

b. The duration of 5700 years is referred to as the "half-life" of carbon-14 because the amount of carbon-14 drops in half 5700 years after any starting point (not just $t = 0$ years). Verify this property by comparing the amount of remaining carbon-14 after 11,400 years and 17,100 years.

c. Write the corresponding expression for the remaining fraction of uranium-234, which has a half-life of about 80,000 years.

Name ______________________ Class ____________ Date ________

3.2 Simplifying Expressions with Rational Exponents and Radicals

Resource Locker

Essential Question: How can you write a radical expression as an expression with a rational exponent?

Explore Exploring Operations with Rational and Irrational Numbers

What happens when you add two rational numbers? Is the result always another rational number or can it be irrational? Will the sum of two irrational numbers always be rational, always be irrational, or can it be either? What about the product of two irrational numbers?

These questions are all used to determine whether a set of numbers is closed under an operation. If the sum of two rational numbers is always rational, the set of rational numbers would be said to be closed under addition. The following tables will combine rational and irrational numbers in various ways. The various sums and products should provide a general idea of which sets are closed under the different operations.

(A) Define rational and irrational numbers.

____

____

(B) Complete the following addition table. Note that there are both rational and irrational addends.

$+$	$-\pi$	7	$\frac{1}{4}$	0	$\sqrt{3}$	$-\sqrt{3}$
$-\pi$	-2π					$-\sqrt{3}-\pi$
7						
$\frac{1}{4}$						
0						
$\sqrt{3}$						
$-\sqrt{3}$						

(C) Based on the results in the table, will the sum of two rational numbers sometimes, always, or never be a rational number?

____

Ⓓ What about the sum of two irrational numbers?

Ⓔ And finally, the sum of a rational number and an irrational number?

Ⓕ Now complete the following multiplication table. Similarly, it has both rational and irrational factors.

$\times$	$-\pi$	7	$\frac{1}{4}$	0	$\sqrt{3}$	$\frac{1}{\sqrt{3}}$
$-\pi$	π^2					
7						
$\frac{1}{4}$						
0						
$\sqrt{3}$	$-\pi\sqrt{3}$					
$\frac{1}{\sqrt{3}}$						

Ⓖ Based on the results in the table, will the product of two rational numbers sometimes, always, or never be a rational number?

Ⓗ What about the product of two irrational numbers?

Ⓘ And finally, the product of a rational number and an irrational number?

Reflect

1. Prove that the product of two rational numbers is a rational number by confirming the general case.

2. Discussion Consider the following statement: The product of two rational numbers is an irrational number. Is it a true statement? Justify your answer.

Explain 1 Simplifying Multivariable Expressions Containing Radicals

As you have seen, to simplify expressions containing radicals, you can rewrite the expressions as powers with rational exponents. You can use properties of exponents. You have already seen the Power of a Power Property of exponents. There are additional properties of exponents that are suggested by the following examples.

$$2^2 \cdot 2^3 = (2 \cdot 2)(2 \cdot 2 \cdot 2) = 2^5 = 2^{2+3}$$

$$\frac{2^3}{2^2} = \frac{2 \cdot 2 \cdot 2}{2 \cdot 2} = 2^1 = 2^{3-2}$$

$$(2 \cdot 3)^2 = (2 \cdot 3)(2 \cdot 3) = (2 \cdot 2)(3 \cdot 3) = 2^3 \cdot 3^2$$

$$\left(\frac{2}{3}\right)^2 = \frac{2}{3} \cdot \frac{2}{3} = \frac{2 \cdot 2}{3 \cdot 3} = \frac{2^2}{3^2}$$

$$(2^3)^2 = (2 \cdot 2 \cdot 2)^2 = (2 \cdot 2 \cdot 2)(2 \cdot 2 \cdot 2) = 2^6 = 2^{3 \cdot 2}$$

These relationships are formalized in the table on the following page.

In the previous lesson, $a^{\frac{1}{n}}$ was defined as $a^{\frac{1}{n}} = \sqrt[n]{a}$ for an integer $n > 1$ and a real number a ($a \geq 0$ for even n) in order to demonstrate that $a^{\frac{m}{n}} = (\sqrt[n]{a})^m$ where m is an integer:

$$a^{\frac{m}{n}} = a^{\frac{1}{n} \cdot m} = \left(a^{\frac{1}{n}}\right)^m = (\sqrt[n]{a})^m$$

The properties of integer exponents now extend to rational exponents.

Properties of Exponents	
Let *a* and *b* be real numbers and *m* and *n* be rational numbers.	
Product of Powers Property	$a^m \cdot a^n = a^{m+n}$
Quotient of Powers Property	$\frac{a^m}{a^n} = a^{m-n},\ a \neq 0$
Power of a Product Property	$(a \cdot b)^n = a^n \cdot b^n$
Power of a Quotient Property	$\left(\frac{a}{b}\right)^n = \frac{a^n}{b^n},\ b \neq 0$
Power of a Power Property	$(a^m)^n = a^{mn}$

Example 1 **Simplify each expression. Assume all variables are positive.**

(A) $\sqrt[3]{(xy)^9}$

$\sqrt[3]{(xy)^9} = (xy)^{\frac{9}{3}}$ Rewrite using rational exponent.

$= (xy)^3$ Simplify the fraction in the exponent.

$= x^3y^3$ Power of a Product Property

(B) $\sqrt[5]{x}\sqrt{x}$

$\sqrt[5]{x}\sqrt{x} = x^{\square} x^{\frac{1}{2}}$ Rewrite using rational exponents.

$= x^{\square}$ Product of Powers Property

$= x^{\square}$ Simplify the exponent.

$= \sqrt[\square]{x^{\square}}$ Rewrite the expression in radical form.

Reflect

3. **Discussion** Why is $\sqrt[n]{a}$ not defined when n is even and $a < 0$?

____

____

____

4. Kris says that $\frac{1}{\sqrt[n]{a}} = \frac{1}{a^{\frac{1}{n}}} = a^{-\frac{1}{n}} = a^{\frac{1}{-n}} = \sqrt[-n]{a}$. Is this true? If not, explain the mistake in reasoning.

____

____

Your Turn

Simplify each expression. Assume all variables are positive.

5. $(x^2y)^2\sqrt[4]{y^4}$

6. $\dfrac{\sqrt[4]{x^8}}{\sqrt[4]{x^6}}$

Explain 2 Simplifying Multivariable Expressions Containing Rational Exponents

Use properties of rational exponents to simplify expressions.

Example 2 **Simplify each expression. Assume all variables are positive.**

Ⓐ $(8x^9)^{\frac{2}{3}}$

$(8x^9)^{\frac{2}{3}} = (2^3)^{\frac{2}{3}}(x^9)^{\frac{2}{3}}$ Power of a Product Property

$= 2^{\left(3 \cdot \frac{2}{3}\right)}x^{\left(9 \cdot \frac{2}{3}\right)}$ Power of a Power Property

$= 2^2x^6$ Simplify within the parentheses.

$= 4x^6$ Simplify.

Ⓑ $(64x^{12})^{\frac{1}{6}}$

$(64x^{12})^{\frac{1}{6}} = \left(2^{\square}\right)^{\square}(x^{12})^{\square}$ Power of a Product Property

$= 2^{\left(\square\right)}x^{\left(\square\right)}$ Power of a Power Property

$= 2^{\square}x^{\square}$ Simplify within the parentheses.

$= \square x^{\square}$ Simplify.

Reflect

7. Simplify $(8x^9)^{-\frac{2}{3}}$. How is it related to the simplified form of $(8x^9)^{\frac{2}{3}}$ found in example 2A? Verify the relationship if one exists.

Your Turn

Simplify each expression. Assume all variables are positive.

8. $\left(\frac{1}{4x^4} \cdot x^{12}\right)^{-\frac{1}{2}}$

9. $\left(\frac{1}{9x^{12}} \cdot x^4\right)^{\frac{1}{2}}$

Explain 3 Simplifying Real-World Expressions with Rational Exponents

The relationship between some real-world quantities can be more complicated than a linear or quadratic model can accurately represent. Sometimes, in the most accurate model, the dependent variable is a function of the independent variable raised to a rational exponent. Use the properties of rational exponents to solve the following real-world scenarios.

Example 3 **Biology Application** **The approximate number of Calories C that an animal needs each day is given by $C = 72m^{\frac{3}{4}}$, where m is the animal's mass in kilograms.**

(A) Find the number of Calories that a 625 kg bear needs each day.
To solve this, evaluate the equation when $m = 625$.

$C = 72m^{\frac{3}{4}}$

$= 72(625)^{\frac{3}{4}}$ Substitute 625 for m.

$= 72\left(\sqrt[4]{625}\right)^3$ Definition of $a^{\frac{m}{n}}$

$= 72\left(\sqrt[4]{5^4}\right)^3$

$= 72(5)^3$

$= 72(125) = 9000$

A 625 kilogram bear needs 9000 Calories each day.

(B) A particular panda consumes 1944 Calories each day. How much does this panda weigh?

Substitute ☐ for C in the original equation and solve for m.

$C = 72m^{\frac{3}{4}}$	Original equation
$\square = 72m^{\frac{3}{4}}$	Substitute for C.
$\frac{\square}{72} = m^{\frac{3}{4}}$	Divide each side by 72.
$\square = m^{\frac{3}{4}}$	Simplify.
$3^3 = m^{\frac{3}{4}}$	Rewrite the left side as a power.
$(3^3)^{\square} = \left(m^{\frac{3}{4}}\right)^{\square}$	Raise both sides to the ☐ power.
$3^{(3 \cdot \square)} = m^{\left(\frac{3}{4} \cdot \square\right)}$	Power of a Power Property
$3^4 = m$	Simplify inside the parentheses.
$m = \square$	Simplify.

The panda weighs ☐ kilograms.

Your Turn

Solve each real-world scenario.

10. The speed of light is the product of its frequency f and its wavelength w. In air, the speed of light is 3×10^8 m/s.

a. Write an equation for the relationship described above, and then solve this equation for frequency.

b. Rewrite this equation with w raised to a negative exponent.

c. What is the frequency of violet light when its wavelength is approximately 400 nanometers $\left(1 \text{ nm} = 10^{-9} \text{ m}\right)$?

11. **Geometry** The formula for the surface area S of a sphere in terms of its volume V is $S = (4\pi)^{\frac{1}{3}}(3V)^{\frac{2}{3}}$. What is the surface area of a sphere that has a volume of 36π cubic centimeters? Leave the answer in terms of π. What do you notice?

Elaborate

12. A set of elements is said to be closed under some operation if performance of that operation on elements of the set always produces an element of the set. Examine the set of integers and the set of rational numbers. Is each set closed under each of the following operations: addition, multiplication, division, and subtraction? Provide a counterexample if the set is not closed under an operation.

13. Why are integers closed under multiplication?

14. Is the set of all numbers of the form a^x, where a is a positive constant and x is a rational number, closed under multiplication? Justify your answer.

15. **Essential Question Check-In** How can you write a radical expression as a power with a rational exponent?

Evaluate: Homework and Practice

Personal Math Trainer

- Online Homework
- Hints and Help
- Extra Practice

1. Why are the tables symmetric about the diagonal from the upper-left corner to the lower-right? For example, why is the entry in the third row of the second column equal to the entry in the second row of the third column? Would a subtraction table be symmetric about the same diagonal?

2. Prove that the rational numbers are closed under addition.

Simplify the given expression.

3. $\sqrt[3]{\left(27x^3\right)^4}$

4. $\sqrt[3]{\left(8x^3\right)^2}$

5. $\sqrt[3]{\left(8y^3\right)^4}\ \sqrt[6]{\left(8y^3\right)^4}$

6. $\sqrt[10]{0x}$

7. $\sqrt{(2x)^2\sqrt{2y}}$

8. $\dfrac{\sqrt{8x}}{\sqrt[3]{16x}}$

9. $(0x)^{\frac{1}{3}}$

10. $10,000^{\frac{1}{4}} \cdot z + 10,000^{\frac{1}{2}} \cdot z$

11. $\left(\frac{1}{25x} \cdot x^9\right)^{-\frac{1}{2}}$

12. $\left(\frac{1}{125x^3}\right)^{-\frac{1}{3}}$

13. $\left[(2x)^x(2x)^{2x}\right]^{\frac{1}{x}}$

14. $\left[\left(1{,}000{,}000x^6\right)^{-\frac{1}{3}}\right]^{-\frac{1}{2}}$

15. $\left(x^2y\right)^3\sqrt[2]{y^4}$

16. $\frac{\left[\left(x^2y\right)^4\right]^{\frac{1}{2}}}{\left[\left(x^2y\right)^{\frac{1}{2}}\right]^4}$

17. $\left(x^{\frac{1}{8}}y^{\frac{1}{4}}z^{\frac{1}{2}}\right)^8$

18. $\left(\sqrt{z\sqrt{y\sqrt{x}}}\right)^8$

19. $\frac{\left(x^{10}\right)^{\frac{1}{5}}}{\sqrt[2]{x^8}}$

20. $\frac{\left[\left(x^{-8}\right)^{\frac{1}{4}}\right]^{-1}\sqrt[3]{x^2}}{\sqrt[6]{x^4}}$

21. $(x^2y)^4\left(\sqrt{y^{\frac{1}{2}}}\right)$

22. $\left(\sqrt{y^{\frac{1}{4}}}\right)^8$

23. Biology Biologists use a formula to estimate the mass of a mammal's brain. For a mammal with a mass of m grams, the approximate mass B of the brain, also in grams, is given by $B = \frac{1}{8}m^{\frac{2}{3}}$. Find the approximate mass of the brain of a mouse that has a mass of 64 grams.

24. Multi-Step Scientists have found that the life span of a mammal living in captivity is related to the mammal's mass. The life span in years L can be approximated by the formula $L = 12m^{\frac{1}{5}}$, where m is the mammal's mass in kilograms. How much longer is the life span of a lion compared with that of a wolf?

Typical Mass of Mammals

Mammal	Mass (kg)
Koala	8
Wolf	32
Lion	243
Giraffe	1024

Tim and Tom are painters. Use the given information to provide the desired estimate.

25. Tim and Tom use a liters of paint on a building. If the next building they need to paint has a similar shape but twice the volume, how much paint should they plan on buying?

26. Tim and Tom are painting a building. Tom paints 10 square feet per minute. They painted a particular building in 1 day. Tim uses a sprayer and is 4.7 times as fast as Tom. How long would it take them to paint a building with twice the volume and a similar shape?

27. Determine whether each of the following is rational or irrational. Select the correct answer for each lettered part.

a. The product of $\sqrt{2}$ and $\sqrt{50}$ ○ Rational ○ Irrational

b. The product of $\sqrt{2}$ and $\sqrt{25}$ ○ Rational ○ Irrational

c. $C = 2\pi r$ evaluated for $r = \pi^{-1}$ ○ Rational ○ Irrational

d. $C = 2\pi r$ evaluated for $r = 1$ ○ Rational ○ Irrational

e. $A = \pi r^2$ evaluated for $r = \pi^{\frac{1}{2}}$ ○ Rational ○ Irrational

f. The product of $\sqrt{\frac{2}{\pi}}$ and $\sqrt{50\pi}$ ○ Rational ○ Irrational

g. The product of $\sqrt{2}$ and $\sqrt{\frac{9}{2}}$ ○ Rational ○ Irrational

H.O.T. Focus on Higher Order Thinking

28. Explain the Error Jim tried to show how to write a radical expression as a power with a rational exponent.

Suppose that $\sqrt[n]{a} = a^k$.

$\left(\sqrt[n]{a}\right)^n = \left(a^k\right)^n$	Raise each side to the nth power.
$a = \left(a^k\right)^n$	Definition of nth root.
$a = a^{\frac{n}{k}}$	Power of a Power Property
$a^1 = a^{\frac{n}{k}}$	
$1 = \frac{n}{k}$	Equate exponents.
$k = n$	Solve for k.

Jim claimed to have shown that $\sqrt[n]{a} = a^n$. Explain and correct his error.

29. Communicate Mathematical Ideas Given that the set of rational numbers is closed under multiplication, prove by contradiction that the product of a nonzero rational number and an irrational number is an irrational number. To do this, assume the negation of what you are trying to prove and show how it will logically lead to something contradicting a given statement. Let $a \neq 0$ be rational, let b be irrational, and let $a \bullet b = c$. Assume that a nonzero rational number times an irrational number is rational, so c is rational.

$a \bullet b = c$	Given
$\left(\frac{1}{a}\right) \bullet a \bullet b = \left(\frac{1}{a}\right) \bullet c$	Multiply both sides by $\frac{1}{a}$.
$b = \left(\frac{1}{a}\right) \bullet c$	Simplify.

Provide the contradiction statement to finish the proof.

30. Communicate Mathematical Ideas Prove by contradiction that a rational number plus an irrational number is irrational. To do this assume the negation of what you are trying to prove and show how it will logically lead to something contradicting the given. Assume that a rational number plus an irrational number is rational.

$r_1 + i_1 = r_2$	Given
$r_1 + i_1 - r_1 = r_2 - r_1$	Subtract r_1 from both sides.
$i_1 = r_2 - r_1$	Simplify left side.

Provide the contradiction statement to finish the proof.

31. Critical Thinking Show that a number raised to the $\frac{1}{3}$ power is the same as the cube root of that number.

Lesson Performance Task

The balls used in soccer, baseball, basketball, and golf are spheres. How much material is needed to make each of the balls in the table?

The formula for the surface area of a sphere is $S_A = 4\pi r^2$, and the formula for the volume of a sphere is $V = \frac{4}{3}\pi r^3$. Use algebra to find the formula for the surface area of a sphere given its volume.

Complete the table with the surface area of each ball.

Ball	Volume (in cubic inches)	Surface Area (in square inches)
soccer ball	356.8	
baseball	12.8	
basketball	455.9	
golf ball	2.48	

STUDY GUIDE REVIEW

Rational Exponents and Radicals

MODULE 3

Essential Question: How can you use rational exponents and radicals to solve real-world problems?

Key Vocabulary
index *(índice)*
radical expression *(expresión radical)*
radicand *(radicando)*
rational exponent *(exponente racional)*

KEY EXAMPLE *(Lesson 3.1)*

Evaluate the expression 3^{-4}.

$3^{-4} = \frac{1}{3^4}$ *Definition of negative exponent*

$= \frac{1}{81}$ *Evaluate.*

KEY EXAMPLE *(Lesson 3.1)*

Simplify $64^{\frac{2}{3}}$.

$64^{\frac{2}{3}} = \left(\sqrt[3]{64}\right)^2$ *Definition of $b^{\frac{m}{n}}$*

$= \left(\sqrt[3]{4^3}\right)^2$ *Rewrite radicand as a power.*

$= 4^2$ *Definition of cube root*

$= 16$

Simplify $128^{-\frac{8}{7}}$.

$128^{-\frac{8}{7}} = \frac{1}{\left(\sqrt[7]{128}\right)^8}$ *Definition of negative exponent and $b^{\frac{m}{n}}$*

$= \frac{1}{\left(\sqrt[7]{2^7}\right)^8}$ *Rewrite radicand as a power.*

$= \frac{1}{2^8}$ *Definition of nth root*

$= \frac{1}{256}$

KEY EXAMPLE *(Lesson 3.2)*

Simplify $\frac{\sqrt[3]{x^8}}{\sqrt[3]{x^6}}$. Assume x is positive.

$\frac{\sqrt[3]{x^8}}{\sqrt[3]{x^6}} = \frac{x^{\frac{8}{3}}}{x^{\frac{6}{3}}}$

$= x^{\frac{8}{3} - \frac{6}{3}}$

$= x^{\frac{2}{3}}$

$= \sqrt[3]{x^2}$

EXERCISES

Simplify each expression. *(Lesson 3.1)*

1. $25^{\frac{3}{2}}$

2. $81^{\frac{1}{2}} - 16^{\frac{1}{2}}$

3. $27^{\frac{4}{3}}$

4. $8^{\frac{5}{3}} + 4^{\frac{5}{2}}$

Simplify each expression. *(Lesson 3.2)*

5. $1{,}000{,}000^{\frac{1}{3}} \cdot d + 1{,}000{,}000^{\frac{1}{2}} \cdot d$

6. $\sqrt[3]{(64x^3)^4}$

7. $\sqrt[3]{(27x^3)^2}$

8. $\left(\frac{1}{216x^3}\right)^{-\frac{1}{3}}$

MODULE PERFORMANCE TASK

How Much Should We Feed the Reptiles?

The zoo is expecting a new alligator to arrive in a few days. The previous Reptile Chef fed other species of reptiles currently at the zoo according to the information in the table. You speak with the Mammal Chef, who uses the formula $y = 72m^{\frac{3}{4}}$ to determine the daily calorie intake for mammals, where y is the number of Calories eaten and m is the mammal's mass in kilograms. You wonder if a similar formula might help determine the number of calories for the new alligator. Substitute data pairs from the table into the formula to find a number a so that the expression $y = am^{\frac{3}{4}}$ gives the daily number of Calories required by a reptile with a mass of m kilograms.

Reptile Type	Mass	Daily Calories
Bearded Dragon	0.4 kg	5.0
Spur-thighed Tortoise	4.2 kg	29.3
Spectacled Caiman	34 kg	141
Rhinoceros Iguana	7.4 kg	44.9
Giant Tortoise	250 kg	629

If the alligator has a mass of 400 kilograms, how many calories will it require per day?

Complete the task on your own paper. Use graphs, numbers, words, or algebra to support your conclusion.

Ready to Go On?

3.1–3.2 Rational Exponents and Radicals

Personal Math Trainer

- Online Homework
- Hints and Help
- Extra Practice

Simplify each expression. *(Lesson 3.1)*

1. $216^{\frac{1}{3}} - 125^{\frac{1}{3}}$

2. $3 \cdot 49^{-\frac{1}{2}} + 7^{-1}$

Simplify each expression. *(Lesson 3.2)*

3. $\left(\frac{1}{16x} \cdot x^7\right)^{-\frac{1}{2}}$

4. $(xy^2)^2 \sqrt[2]{y^8}$

5. The volume of a cube is related to the area of a face by the formula $V = A^{\frac{3}{2}}$. What is the volume of a cube whose face has an area of 25 mm^2? *(Lesson 3.1)*

6. Biologists use a formula to estimate the mass of a mammal's brain. For a mammal with a mass of m grams, the approximate mass B of the brain, also in grams, is given by $B = \frac{1}{8}m^{\frac{2}{3}}$. Find the approximate mass of the brain of a shrew that has a mass of 27 grams. *(Lesson 3.2)*

ESSENTIAL QUESTION

7. How are rational exponents and radicals related?

MODULE 3
MIXED REVIEW

Assessment Readiness

1. Consider each expression. Is the expression equivalent to $\frac{512^{\frac{1}{3}}}{64^{\frac{2}{3}}}$? Select Yes or No for each.

A. $\left(\frac{64^{\frac{2}{3}}}{512^{\frac{1}{3}}}\right)^{-1}$ ○ Yes ○ No

B. $\left(64^{\frac{2}{3}} \times 512^{-\frac{1}{3}}\right)^{-1}$ ○ Yes ○ No

C. $\frac{64^{-\frac{2}{3}}}{512^{-\frac{1}{3}}}$ ○ Yes ○ No

2. Consider each set. Does the set represent a function? Select Yes or No for each.

A. $\{(5, -2), (5, 0), (5, 2), (5, 4),\}$ ○ Yes ○ No

B. $\{(3, 4), (4, 4), (5, 2), (6, 4),\}$ ○ Yes ○ No

C. $\{(-4, 1), (-2, 3), (0, 4), (2, 3),\}$ ○ Yes ○ No

3. Consider the graph of $y = \left(\sqrt[3]{8x^3}\right) + 8$. Determine if each of the following statements is True or False.

A. The slope is 8. ○ Yes ○ No

B. The y-intercept is 8. ○ Yes ○ No

C. The x-intercept is -4. ○ Yes ○ No

4. Simplify $216^{\frac{2}{3}}$.

5. Jasmine believes that the sum of two positive irrational numbers can be a rational number. She gives the following example: $\sqrt{2} + \sqrt{2}$. Do you agree with Jasmine? Explain why or why not.

MODULE 4

Adding and Subtracting Polynomials

Essential Question: How can you use adding and subtracting polynomials to solve real-world problems?

REAL WORLD VIDEO
Vehicles, such as planes and cars, are aerodynamically tested in a wind tunnel. The complex factors involved in wind tunnel testing can be modeled with polynomial functions.

MODULE PERFORMANCE TASK PREVIEW

Ozone Levels in the Los Angeles Basin

Ozone in the upper atmosphere helps protect living things from the harmful effects of ultraviolet radiation. However, ozone near the ground is harmful and a major component of air pollution. Suppose you have some data on ozone levels in a community for an entire year. How would you find out the trend in ozone levels for that community? Let's find out!

Are YOU Ready?

Complete these exercises to review skills you will need for this module.

Personal Math Trainer
- Online Homework
- Hints and Help
- Extra Practice

Add and Subtract Integers

Example 1 Add or subtract.

$-9 + (-6)$ Think: Find the sum of 9 and 6.
-15 Same sign, so use the sign of the integers.

$14 + (-17)$ Think: Find the difference of 14 and
-3 17. $17 > 14$, so use the sign of 17.

$3 - (-11)$
$3 + 11$ Think: Add the opposite of −11.
14 Same sign, so use the sign of the integers.

Add or subtract.

1. $-16 + 21$ **2.** $-13 - 12$ **3.** $-23 - (-8)$

Algebraic Expressions

Example 2 Simplify $15 + 9x - 6 - 5x$ by combining like terms.

$15 + 9x - 6 - 5x$
$9x - 5x + 15 - 6$ Reorder, grouping like terms together.
$9x - 5x + 9$ Subtract the integers.
$4x + 9$ Combine the like terms.

Simplify by combining like terms.

4. $8a + 5 - 10a - 11$ **5.** $-7 + d - 6 + 2d$

6. $19z + 14y - y - 3z$ **7.** $21 - 13p + 12q - 5 + 2p - 15q$

Exponents

Example 3 Find the value of $x^3 + x^2$ when $x = 2$.

$x^3 + x^2$
$2^3 + 2^2$ Substitute 2 for x.
$8 + 4$ Evaluate the exponents.
12 Add.

Find the value.

8. $x^3 + x^2$ when $x = -2$ **9.** $x^3 - 4$ when $x = 3$ **10.** $x^3 - 4$ when $x = -3$

Name ______________________ Class ____________ Date ________

4.1 Understanding Polynomial Expressions

Essential Question: What are polynomial expressions, and how do you simplify them?

Resource Locker

Explore Identifying Monomials

A **monomial** is an expression consisting of a number, variable, or product of numbers and variables that have whole number exponents. *Terms* of an expression are parts of the expression separated by plus signs. (Remember that $x - y$ can be written as $x + (-y)$.) A monomial cannot have more than one term, and it cannot have a variable in its denominator. Here are some examples of monomials and expressions that are not monomials.

Monomials					Not Monomials				
4	x	$-4xy$	$0.25x^3$	$\frac{xy}{4}$	$4 + x$	$x - 1$	$0.7x^{-2}$	$0.25x^{-1}$	$\frac{y}{x^3}$

Use the following process to determine if $5ab^2$ is a monomial.

(A) $5ab^2$ has ________ term(s), so it ________ be a monomial.

(B) Does $5ab^2$ have a denominator?

____

(C) If possible, split it into a product of numbers and variables.

$5ab^2 = 5 \cdot \square \cdot \square$

(D) List the numbers and variables in the product.

Numbers: $\square$ Variables: $\square$

(E) Check the exponent of each variable. Complete the following table.

Variable	Exponent
a	
b	

(F) The exponents of the variables in $5ab^2$ are all ________________.
Therefore, $5ab^2$ ____ a monomial.

(G) Is $\frac{5}{k^2}$ a monomial?

____

Ⓗ Complete the table below.

Term	Is this a monomial?	Explain your reasoning.
$5ab^2$	yes	$5ab^2$ is the product of a number, 5, and the variables *a* and *b*.
x^2		
$\sqrt{y}$	no	
2^2		
$\frac{5}{k^2}$	no	
$5x + 7$		
$x^2 + 4ab$		
$\frac{k^2}{4}$		

Reflect

1. **Discussion** Explain why $16^{\frac{1}{3}}$ is a monomial but $x^{\frac{1}{3}}$ is not a monomial.

2. **Discussion** Is x^0 a monomial? Justify your answer in two ways.

Explain 1 Classifying Polynomials

A **polynomial** can be a monomial or the sum of monomials. Polynomials are classified by the number of terms they contain. A monomial has one term, a **binomial** has two terms, and a **trinomial** has three terms. $8xy^2 - 5x^3y^3z$, for example, is a binomial.

Polynomials are also classified by their degree. The **degree of a polynomial** is the greatest value among the sums of the exponents on the variables in each term.

The binomial $8xy^2 - 5x^3y^3z$ has two terms. The variables in the first term are *x* and *y*. The exponent on *x* is 1, and the exponent on *y* is 2. The number 8 is not a variable, so it has a degree of 0. The first term has a degree of $0 + 1 + 2 = 3$. The degree of the second term is $0 + 3 + 3 + 1 = 7$. Therefore, $8xy^2 - 5x^3y^3z$ is a 7th degree binomial.

Example 1 **Classify each polynomial by its degree and the number of terms.**

(A) $7x^2 - 5x^3y^3$

Find the degree of each term by adding the exponents of the variables in that term. The greatest degree is the degree of the polynomial. The degree of the term $-5x^3y^3$ is 6, which you obtain by adding the exponents of x and y: $6 = 3 + 3$. Numbers have degree 0.

$7x^2 - 5x^3y^3$

Degree : 6 — $7x^2$ has degree 2, and $-5x^3y^3$ has degree $6 = 3 + 3$.

Binomial — There are two terms.

(B) $3^2 + 2n^3 + 8n$

$3^2 + 2n^3 + 8n$

Degree: ☐ — 3^2 has degree ☐, $2n^3$ has degree ☐, and $8n$ has degree ☐.

Trinomial — There are ☐ terms.

Reflect

3. What is the degree of $5x^0y^0 + 5$?

____

4. Is $5x^0y^{0.5} + 5$ a polynomial? Justify your answer.

____

Your Turn

Classify each polynomial by its degree and the number of terms.

5. $3x^2y^2 + 3xy^2 + 5xy$

6. $8ab^2 - 3a^2b$

Explain 2 Writing Polynomials in Standard Form

The terms of a polynomial may be written in any order, but when a polynomial contains only one variable there is a standard form in which it can be written.

The **standard form of a polynomial** containing only one variable is written with the terms in order of decreasing degree. The first term will have the greatest degree, the next term will have the next greatest degree, and so on, until the final term, which will have the lowest degree.

When written in this form, the coefficient of the first term is called **the leading coefficient**.

$5x^4 + 4x^2 + x - 2$ is a 4th degree polynomial written in standard form. It consists of one variable, and its first term is $5x^4$. The leading coefficient is 5 because it is in front of the highest-degree term.

Example 2 **Write each polynomial in standard form. Then give the leading coefficient.**

(A) $20x - 4x^3 + 1 - 2x^2$

Find the degree of each term and then arrange them in descending order of their degree.

$$\underbrace{20x}_{1}\ \underbrace{-4x^3}_{3}\ \underbrace{+1}_{0}\ \underbrace{-2x^2}_{2} = \underbrace{-4x^3}_{3}\ \underbrace{-2x^2}_{2}\ \underbrace{+20x}_{1}\ \underbrace{+1}_{0}$$

Degree: 1 3 0 2 = 3 2 1 0

The standard form is $-4x^3 - 2x^2 + 20x + 1$. The leading coefficient is -4.

(B) $z^3 - z^6 + 4z$

Find the degree of each term and then arrange them in descending order of their degree.

$$\underbrace{z^3}\ \underbrace{-z^6}\ \underbrace{+4z} = \square\ \square\ \square$$

Degree: $\square\ \square\ \square$ $\square\ \square\ \square$

The standard form is ________. The leading coefficient is $\square$.

Your Turn

Write each polynomial in standard form. Then give the leading coefficient.

7. $10 - 3x^2 + x^5 + 4x^3$

8. $18y^5 - 3y^8 + 10y$

9. $10x + 13 - 15x^2$

10. $-3b^2 + 2b - 7 + 6b^3 + 12b^4 + 7$

Explain 3 Simplifying Polynomials

Polynomials are simplified by combining like terms. Like terms are monomials that have the same variables raised to the same powers. Unlike terms have different powers.

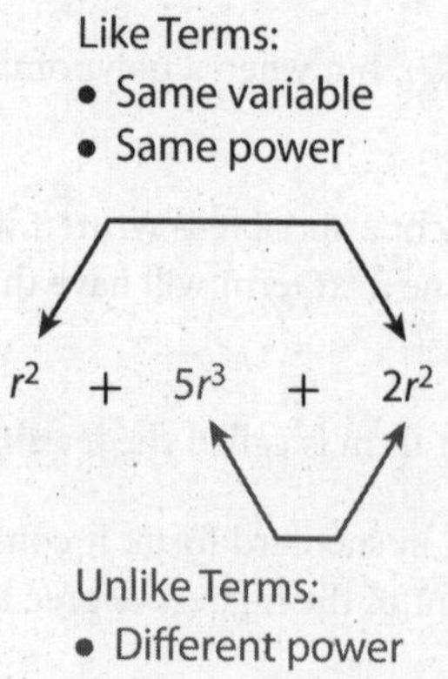

Identify like terms and combine them using the Distributive Property. Simplify.

$r^2 + 5r^3 + 2r^2$

$(r^2 + 2r^2) + 5r^3$ Identify like terms by grouping them together in parentheses.

$r^2(1 + 2) + 5r^3$ Combine using the Distributive Property.

$3r^2 + 5r^3$ Simplify.

Example 3 **Combine like terms to simplify each polynomial.**

(A) $-2y^3 - 8y^2 + y^2 + 2y^3$

$-2y^3 + 2y^3 - 8y^2 + y^2$ Rearrange in descending order of exponents.

$(-2y^3 + 2y^3) + (-8y^2 + y^2)$ Group like terms.

$y^3(-2 + 2) + y^2(-8 + 1)$ Combine using the Distributive Property.

$y^3(0) + y^2(-7)$ Simplify.

$-7y^2$

(B) $p^2q^3 - 4p^5q^4 - 4p^2q^3 + 3p^5q^4$

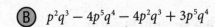

____________________ Rearrange in descending order of exponents.

____________________ Group like terms.

$p^5q^4(\boxed{}) + p^2q^3(\boxed{})$ Combine using the Distributive Property.

$p^5q^4(\boxed{}) + p^2q^3(\boxed{})$ Simplify.

____

Reflect

11. Can you combine like terms without formally showing the Distributive Property? Explain.

____

Your Turn

Simplify.

12. $3p^2q^2 - 3p^2q^3 + 4p^2q^3 - 3p^2q^2 + pq$

13. $3(a + b) - 6(b + c) + 8(a - c)$

14. $ab - a^2 + 4^2 - 5ab + 3a^2 + 10$

Explain 4 Evaluating Polynomials

Given a polynomial expression describing a real-world situation and a specific value for the variable(s), evaluate the polynomial by substituting for the variable(s). Then interpret the result.

Example 4 **Evaluate the given polynomial to find the solution in each real-world scenario.**

(A) A skyrocket is launched from a 6-foot-high platform with an initial speed of 200 feet per second. The polynomial $-16t^2 + 200t + 6$ gives the height in feet that the skyrocket will rise in t seconds. How high will the rocket rise if it has a 5-second fuse?

$-16t^2 + 200t + 6$	Write the expression.
$-16(5)^2 + 200(5) + 6$	Substitute 5 for t.
$-16(25) + 200(5) + 6$	Simplify using the order of operations.
$-400 + 1000 + 6$	
606	

The rocket will rise 606 feet.

(B) Lisa wants to measure the depth of an empty well. She drops a ball from a height of 3 feet into the well and measures how long it takes the ball to hit the bottom of the well. She uses a stopwatch, starting when she lets go of the ball and ending when she hears the ball hit the bottom of the well. The polynomial $-16t^2 + 0t + 3$ gives the height of the ball after t seconds where 0 is the initial speed of the ball and 3 is the initial height the ball was dropped from. Her stopwatch measured a time of 2.2 seconds. How deep is the well? (Neglect the speed of sound and air resistance).

__________	Write the expression.
__________	Substitute ______ for t.
__________	Simplify using order of operations.
__________	

The ball goes [ ] feet below the ground. The well is [ ] feet deep.

Your Turn

Solve each real-world scenario.

15. Nate's architectural client said she wanted the width of every room in her house increased by 2 feet and the length decreased by 5 feet. Before the changes, the length of every room is twice the width. The polynomial $2w^2 - w - 10$ gives the area of any room in the house with w representing the room's width. The width of the kitchen is 16 feet. What is the area of the kitchen?

16. A skyrocket is launched from a 20-foot-high platform, with an initial speed of 200 feet per second. If the polynomial $-16t^2 + 200t + 20$ gives the height that the rocket will rise in t seconds, how high will a rocket with a 4-second fuse rise?

Elaborate

17. What is the degree of the expression $-16t^2 + 200t + 20$, where t is a variable? What is the degree of the expression if $t = 1$? Are the expressions monomials, binomials, or trinomials?

18. Two cars drive toward each other along a straight road at a constant speed. The distance between the cars is $l - (r_1 + r_2)t$, where r_1 and r_2 are their speeds, l is the length of their original separation, and t is a variable representing time. Write the expression in standard form. What is its degree? What is its leading coefficient?

19. The polynomial $-16t^2 + 200t + 20$ gives the height of a projectile launched with an initial speed of 200 feet per second in feet t seconds after launch. A second projectile is launched at the same time but with an initial speed of 300 feet per second, with its height given by the polynomial $-16t^2 + 300t + 20$. How much higher will the second projectile be than the first after 10 seconds?

20. Essential Question Check-In What do you have to do to simplify sums of polynomials? What property do you use to accomplish this?

Evaluate: Homework and Practice

Personal Math Trainer
- Online Homework
- Hints and Help
- Extra Practice

1. Is $(5 + 4x^0)2x$ a monomial? What about $(5 + 4x^2)2x$?

2. Is the sum of two monomials always a monomial? Is their product always a monomial?

Classify each polynomial by its degree and the number of terms.

3. $x^2 - 5x^3$

4. $x^2 - x^4 + y^2x^3$

5. $a^4b^3 - a^3b^2 + a^2b$

6. $15 + x\sqrt{2}$

7. $x + y + z$

8. $a^5 + b^2 + a^2b^2$

Write each polynomial in standard form. Then give the leading coefficient.

9. $2x - 40x^3 - 2x^2$

10. $3 + c - c^2$

11. $3b^2 - 2b + b^2$

12. $4a - 3a + 21 + 6$

Simplify each polynomial.

13. $-2y^3 - y^2 + y^2 + y^3$

14. $-y^3x - y^2x + y^2 + y^3x + y^2$

15. $xyz\sqrt[3]{2} + 2^5xyz + 2^{10}xy$

16. $a^3 + a^2 + ab$

Use the information to solve the problem.

17. Persevere in Problem Solving Lisa is measuring the depth of a well. She drops a ball from a height of h feet into the well and measures how long it takes the ball to hit the bottom of the well. The polynomial $-16t^2 + 0t + h$ models this situation, where 0 is the initial speed of the ball and h is the height it was dropped from. (This is a different well from the problem you solved before.) She raises her arm very high and drops the ball from a height of 6.0 feet. Her stopwatch measured a time of 3.5 seconds. How deep is the well?

18. Multi-Step Claire and Richard are both artists who use square canvases. Claire uses the polynomial $50x^2 + 250$ to decide how much to charge for her paintings, and Richard uses the polynomial $40x^2 + 350$ to decide how much to charge for his paintings. In each polynomial, x is the height of the painting in feet.

a. How much does Claire charge for a 6-foot painting?

b. How much does Richard charge for a 5-foot painting?

c. To the nearest tenth, for what height will both Claire and Richard charge the same amount for a painting? Explain how to find the answer.

d. When both Claire and Richard charge the same amount for a painting, how much does each charge?

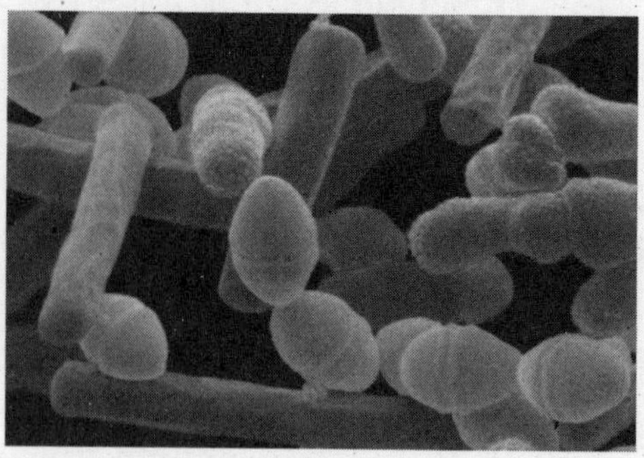

19. Make a Prediction The number of cells in a bacteria colony increases according to a polynomial expression that depends on the temperature. The expression for the number of bacteria is $t^2 + 4t + 4$ when the temperature of the colony is 20°C and $t^2 + 3t + 4$ when the colony grows at 30 °C. t represents the time in seconds that the colony grows at the given temperature.

a. After 1 minute, will the population be greater in a colony at 20 °C or 30 °C? Explain.

b. After 10 minutes, how will the colonies compare in size? Explain.

c. After 1000 minutes, how will the colonies compare in size? Will one colony always have more bacteria? Explain.

20. Two cars are driving toward each other along a straight road. Their separation distance is $\ell - (r_1 + r_2)t$, where ℓ is their original separation distance and r_1 and r_2 are their speeds. Will the cars meet? When? What if they are going in the same direction and not driving toward one another? Will they meet then?

H.O.T. Focus on Higher Order Thinking

21. Explain the Error Enrique thinks that the polynomial $2^2x^2 + 2^3x + 2^4$ has a degree of 4 since $2 + 2 = 3 + 1 = 4$. Explain his error and determine the correct degree.

22. Analyze Relationships Sewell is doing a problem regarding the area of pairs of squares. Sewell says that the expression $(x + 1)^2$ will be greater than $(x - 1)^2$ for all values of x because $x + 1$ will always be greater than $x - 1$. Why is he correct when the expressions are areas of squares? Is he correct for any real x outside this model?

23. Counterexamples Prove by counterexample that the sum of monomials is not necessarily a monomial.

24. Communicate Mathematical Ideas Polynomials are simplified by combining like terms. When combining like terms, you use the Distributive Property. Prove that the Distributive Property, $a \cdot (b + c) = a \cdot b + a \cdot c$, holds over the positive integers $a, b, c > 0$ from the definition of multiplication: $a \cdot b = \underbrace{a + a + \ldots + a}_{b \text{ times}}$.

25. Analyze Relationships A right triangle has height h and base $h + 8$. Write an expression that represents the area of the triangle. Then calculate the area of a triangle with a height of 16 cm.

Lesson Performance Task

A pyrotechnics specialist is designing a firework spectacular for a company's 75th anniversary celebration. She can vary the launch speed to 200, 250, 300, or 400 feet per second, and can set the fuse on each firework for 3, 4, 5, or 6 seconds. Create a table of the various heights the fireworks can explode at if the height of the firework is modeled by the function $h(t) = -16t^2 + v_0 t$, where t is the time in seconds and v_0 is the initial speed of the firework.

Design a fireworks show using 3 firing heights and at least 30 fireworks. Have some fireworks go off simultaneously at different heights. Describe your display so you will know what needs to be launched and when they will go off.

Name ______________ Class ______________ Date ______________

4.2 Adding Polynomial Expressions

Essential Question: How do you add polynomials?

Resource Locker

Explore Modeling Polynomial Addition Using Algebra Tiles

You have added numbers and variables, which is the same as adding polynomials of degree 0 and degree 1. Adding polynomials of higher degree is similar, but there are more possible like terms to consider.

You can use algebra tiles to model polynomial addition.

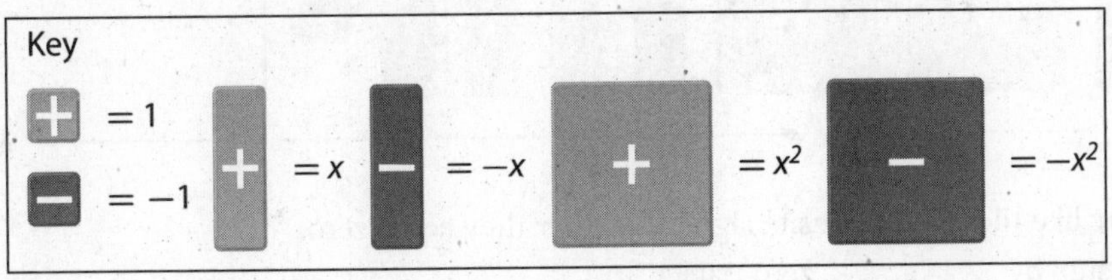

As the Key shows, a different-sized tile represents each monomial. Like terms have the same shape and size, but if they are positive, they have a + (plus) sign. If they are negative, they have a − (minus) sign. Use these visual aids to add polynomials.

To add polynomials, start by representing each addend with tiles. Add them by placing the tiles for each polynomial next to each other. Cancel out opposite tiles that are of the same size but have a different symbol. Count the remaining tiles of each size and note the symbol. Translate the tiles to a polynomial. This polynomial represents the simplified sum.

Use algebra tiles to find $(2x^2 - x) + (x^2 + 3x - 1)$.

(A) Which of the two polynomials in the addition expression do these algebra tiles represent?

Model	Algebra

(B) Which polynomial do these algebra tiles represent?

Model	Algebra
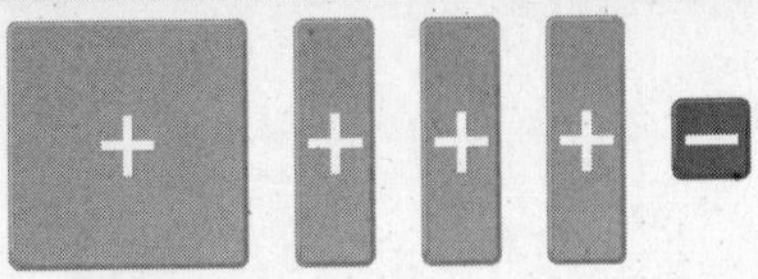	

Ⓒ Place the algebra tiles representing each expression next to each other. This represents addition/subtraction.

Model	Algebra
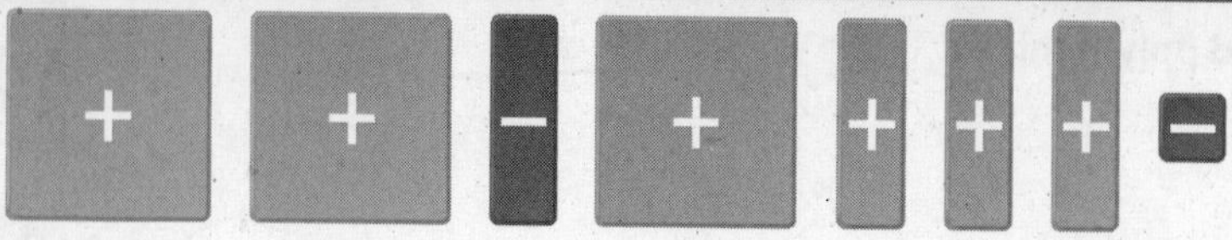	

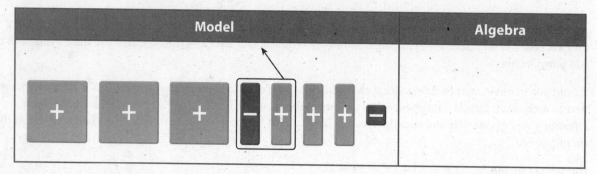

Ⓓ Rearrange tiles so that like tiles are together. ***Like tiles*** are the same size and shape.

Model	Algebra

Ⓔ ***Zero pairs*** are like tiles with opposite signs. Together they equal zero.
Simplify the sum by __________ zero pairs.

Model	Algebra

Reflect

1. **Discussion** What properties of addition allow you to rearrange the tiles?

____

____

Explain 1 Adding Polynomials Using a Vertical Format

To add polynomials vertically, add like terms in columns. Write the first polynomial in standard form; then write the second polynomial below the first, aligning like terms. Use a monomial with a zero coefficient as a placeholder for missing terms. Add the coefficients of each group and write the sum aligned with the like terms above. Simplify if necessary.

Example 1 **Use the vertical format to find the sum.**

Ⓐ $5x^2 + 2x - 1$ and $4x^2 - x + 2$

$(5x^2 + 2x - 1) + (4x^2 - x + 2)$

Rewrite the problem, vertically aligning the terms.

$$\begin{array}{r} 5x^2 + 2x - 1 \\ +4x^2 - 1x + 2 \\ \hline 9x^2 + 1x + 1 \end{array}$$

Simplify.

$9x^2 + x + 1$

Ⓑ $3y^3 + 2y + 1$ and $y^2 - 1$

$(3y^3 + 2y + 1) + (y^2 - 1)$

Rewrite the problem, vertically aligning the terms.

$$\begin{array}{rrrr} 3y^3 + & \square\, y^2 + & 2y + & \square \\ +0y^3 + & 1y^2 + & \square\, y + & \square \\ \hline 3y^3 + & \square + & 2y + & \square \end{array}$$

Simplify.

____

Reflect

2. Is the sum of two polynomials always another polynomial? Explain.

____

____

____

Your Turn

Add the given polynomials using the vertical format.

3. $-x^2 - 1$ and $4x^2 - x$

4. $-z^3 - 2z - 1$ and $2z^3 - z^2 + 2z$

5. $x - 1$ and $4x - 6$

Explain 2 Adding Polynomials Using a Horizontal Format

To add polynomials horizontally, combine like terms: Use the Associative and Commutative Properties to regroup. Place all like terms within the same parentheses. Combine like terms by adding their coefficients, simplifying if necessary.

Example 2 **Add the polynomials using the horizontal format.**

(A) $5x^2 + 2x + 1$ and $-4x^2 - x - 2$

$(5x^2 + 2x + 1) + (-4x^2 - x - 2)$ — Add.

$= (5x^2 - 4x^2) + (2x - x) + (1 - 2)$ — Group like terms by using the Commutative and Associative Properties.

$= x^2 + x - 1$ — Combine like terms.

(B) $-ab + b$ and $ab - a$

$(-ab + b) + (ab - a)$ — Add.

$= \left(-ab + \boxed{}\right) + b + \left(\boxed{}\right)$ — Group like terms together.

$= \boxed{}$ — Combine like terms.

Your Turn

Use the horizontal format to find the sum.

6. $(-6x^2 + 2)$ and $(-4x^2)$

7. $(-x^3 + 2)$ and $(-4x^3 + y + x)$

8. $(y - 7)$ and $(3y + 18)$

Explain 3 Modeling with Polynomials

You can model many situations using polynomials. Sometimes you can model a new situation by adding two or more polynomials.

For example, a company offers two services. The number of people using each service at a given time can be modeled by polynomials that use the same variable. The total number of people using both services can be modeled by adding the two polynomials.

Example 3 **A box company owns two factories in different parts of the country. The profit for each factory is modeled by a polynomial with x representing the number of boxes each produces. Solve by adding the polynomials. The models needed in each situation are provided.**

(A) The first factory makes a profit of $-0.03x^2 + 20x - 500$, and the second makes $-0.04x^2 + 25x - 1000$. What is the polynomial modeling the box company's total profit if both factories make the same number of boxes?

$\left(-0.03x^2 + 20x - 500\right) + \left(-0.04x^2 + 25x - 1000\right)$ Add.

$= \left(-0.03x^2 - 0.04x^2\right) + (20x + 25x) + (-500 - 1000)$ Group like terms together.

$= -0.07x^2 + 45x - 1{,}500$ Simplify.

The factories make a total profit of $-0.07x^2 + 45x - 1500$.

(B) The company plans to open a third factory with a projected profit of $-0.03x^2 + 50x - 100$. What will be the total profit of the box company, written as a polynomial, if the projected profit is correct?

The total profit from the first two factories mentioned is $-0.07x^2 + 45x - 1500$. The projected profit from the new factory is $-0.03x^2 + 50x - 100$. Add to solve.

________________________________ Add.

= ________________________________ Group like terms together.

= ________________________________ Simplify.

The total projected profit is ____________.

Reflect

9. **Discussion** How could the polynomials be added if the first factory produced x boxes, the second factory produce y boxes, and the third company z boxes? What kind of polynomial would it be?

Your Turn

Model various situations with the sum of polynomials. Simplify their sum.

10. A scientist is growing cell cultures and examining the effects of various substances on them as part of his research. The culture in one petri dish increases according to the expression $t^2 + 4t + 4$ for time t in minutes. Another increases according to $t^2 + 2t + 4$. He needs to feed all the cells equally, so he needs to know the expression for the total number of cells in both dishes because the food is proportional to the total number of cells. Find the expression.

11. A farmer must add the areas of two plots of land to determine the amount of seed to plant. The area of Plot A can be represented by $3x^2 + 7x - 5$, and the area of Plot B can be represented by $5x^2 - 4x + 11$. Write a polynomial that represents the total area of both plots of land.

Elaborate

12. Is adding polynomials horizontally or vertically equivalent? Explain, describing how the steps are similar or different.

13. A car company is analyzing the profits of two car manufacturing plants. The profit of each plant is modeled by a polynomial. What operation would it use to compute the total profit of both plants? The amount of success of one plant versus the other? The total profit of both plants if the polynomials modeling each plant's profits are the same? Will the results be polynomials?

14. **Essential Question Check-In** What do you have to do to simplify sums of polynomials? What property do you use to accomplish this?

Evaluate: Homework and Practice

Personal Math Trainer
- Online Homework
- Hints and Help
- Extra Practice

1. In adding with tiles, one step corresponds to grouping like terms. Do you think this is more similar to the horizontal or vertical method? Explain your reasoning.

2. Show how to add $(x^2 + x)$ and $(-x^2 - 2x)$ with tiles.

Model	Algebra
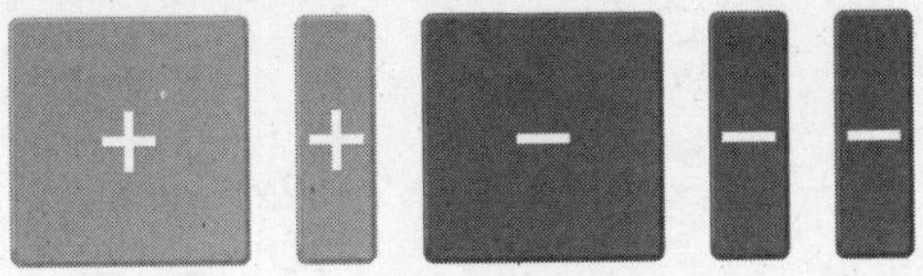	______________________
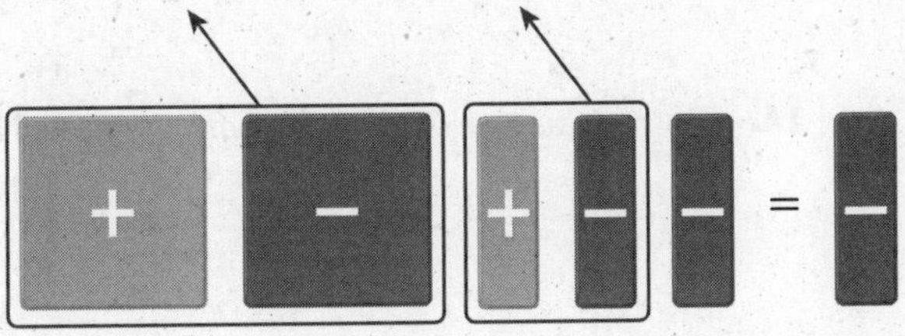	______________________ = ______

Find each sum vertically.

3. $(x^2 - x^4) + (x^4 - x^2)$

4. $(y^2 - x^4) + (x^4 - x^2)$

5. Add $0.5x + 2$ and $x^2 + 1.5x$.

6. $(2x + y + z) + (-x + y - z)$

7. $(x^2 + y + z) + (-x + y - z) + x - y$

8. $-a^5 + (b^2 + a^2b^2) + (a^5 + b^2 - a^2b^2)$

Find each sum horizontally.

9. $(-x^2 + x) + (x^2 - x - 1)$

10. $(a + b - c^2) + (a + b)$

11. $(ab^2 + b^2) + (-2cab^2 + b^2)$

12. $(2x - x^3 - 2x^2) + (-x^3 - 2x)$

13. $(2^{10}a + ab) + (ab\sqrt[3]{2} + ab - 2^{10}a)$

14. $(7q^3r^2 + 6qr^2 + 21q) + (-6qr^2 - qr^2 - 11q - 3q^3r^2)$

Model various situations using the sum of polynomials. Simplify their sum.

15. A pool is being filled with a large water hose. The height of the water in a pool is determined by $8g^2 + 3g - 4$. Previously, the pool had been filled with a different hose. Then, the height was determined by $6g^2 + 2g - 1$. Write an expression that determines the height of the water in the pool if both hoses are on at the same time. Simplify the expression.

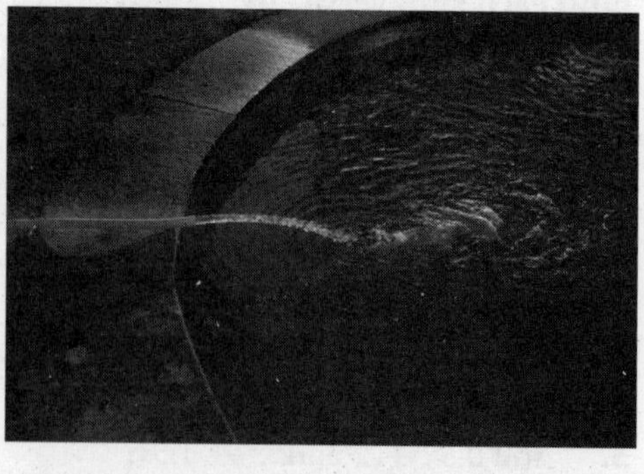

16. The polynomial $-2x^2 + 500x$ represents the budget surplus of the town of Alphaville. Betaville's surplus is represented by $x^2 - 100x + 10,000$. If x represents the tax revenue in thousands from both towns, which expression represents the total surplus of both towns together?

17. Geometry The length of a rectangle is represented by $4a + 3b$, and its width is represented by $3a - 2b$. Write a polynomial for the perimeter of the rectangle. What is the minimum perimeter of the rectangle if $a = 12$ and b is a non-zero whole number?

18. Multi-Step Tara plans to put wallpaper on the walls of her room. She will not put the wallpaper across the doorway, which is 3 feet wide and 7 feet tall.

a. Write an expression that represents the number of square feet of wallpaper she will need if the height of her room is x feet, with a length and width that are each 3 times the height of the room. Assume that the walls are four rectangles.

b. Write the expression for the amount of wallpaper in square feet Tara needs for the living room, which is the same height and width as her bedroom, but has a length that is 5 times the height of the room. The living room has 2 doors that are the same size as the door in her bedroom.

c. Tara decides to get the same wallpaper for both rooms. Write the expression for the total amount of wallpaper she needs.

d. If $x = 8$, how much more wallpaper will Tara need for the living room than for the bedroom?

H.O.T. Focus on Higher Order Thinking

19. Critical Thinking Subtracting one polynomial from another is the same as adding the opposite of the polynomial by distributing a -1.
Substitute $n = -1$ in $(x^2 + x) + n(x^2 + 2x)$ and simplify.

20. Multiple Representations Two polynomials model different financial information for a company. The first polynomial, $40{,}000 + 3x^2$ represents the gross monthly income from selling x units, while the second one, $0.05x + 100$ represents the monthly production cost of x units.
Which of the following expressions models gross income less production costs?

a. $40{,}000 + 3x^2 - 0.05x + 100$

b. $(40{,}000 - 100) + 3x^2 - 0.05x$

c. $3x^2 - 0.05x + 39{,}900$

d. $3x^2 - 0.05x + 40{,}100$

e. a and b

f. b and c

21. Explain the Error Jane and Jill were simplifying the expression $(2x^2 + x) + 2(-x^2 + x)$ and obtained different answers. Who is correct and why?

Jane

$= (2x^2 + x) + 2(-x^2 + x)$
$= (2x^2 + x) + (-x^2 + x) + (-x^2 + x)$
$= (2x^2 - x^2 - x^2) + (x + x + x)$
$= 3x$

Jill

$= (2x^2 + x) + 2(-x^2 + x)$
$= (2x^2 + x) - 2x^2 + x$
$= 2x$

22. Critical Thinking A set is **closed** under an operation if performing that operation on two members of the set results in another member of the set. Is the set of polynomials closed under addition? Is the set of polynomials closed under multiplication by a constant? Explain.

23. Counterexamples You can prove that a statement isn't true by finding a single example that contradicts the statement, which is called a *counterexample*. Show that the set of polynomials is not closed under division by finding a counterexample of division of a polynomial by a polynomial that does not result in a polynomial.

24. Communicate Mathematical Ideas Simplify $(x^2 + x) + n(x^2 + 2x)$ by distributing the n. Show that it is equivalent for $n = 2$ to $(x^2 + x) + (x^2 + 2x) + (x^2 + 2x)$.

25. Multiple Representations Write two polynomials whose sum is $4m^2 + 2m$. Write two polynomials whose difference is $4m^2 + 2m$.

Lesson Performance Task

Swimming pools offer a wide range of activities for both health and leisure. They typically service everyone in the community, from the very young to the elderly. In community pools, the water temperature is often a much debated topic. If the water is too cold, children and older individuals may not be able to use the pool for the length of time they wish. On the other hand, if the pool is too warm, people swimming laps can get overheated.

An architect is working with a health club to design a multi-use aquatics facility that will have two pools. One pool will be primarily used by lap swimmers and local school swim teams. A second pool will be more of a mixed usage pool and have regions of various depths to service the remainder of the community.

Design two swimming pools for the aquatics center and calculate the volume of each pool. The lap pool should be 25 yards long, between 4 and 6 feet deep, and should consist of x lanes, with the width of each lane between 6 and 8 feet. The multi-use pool should have 3 sections. The first section should be a shallow end, where the depth begins between 2.5 and 3.5 feet, and slopes down to a depth equal to one-sixth the width of the pool over about one-third of the pool's length. The last section should slope down to the maximum depth of the pool which should be between 9 and 12 feet. Both pools should have approximately the same width and the multi-use pool should be between 2 and 3 times as long as it is wide.

Produce polynomials representing the volume of each pool and the total volume of water needed by the facility.

Name________________________ Class________________ Date____________

4.3 Subtracting Polynomial Expressions

Essential Question: How do you subtract polynomials?

Resource Locker

Explore Modeling Polynomial Subtraction Using Algebra Tiles

You can also use algebra tiles to model polynomial subtraction.

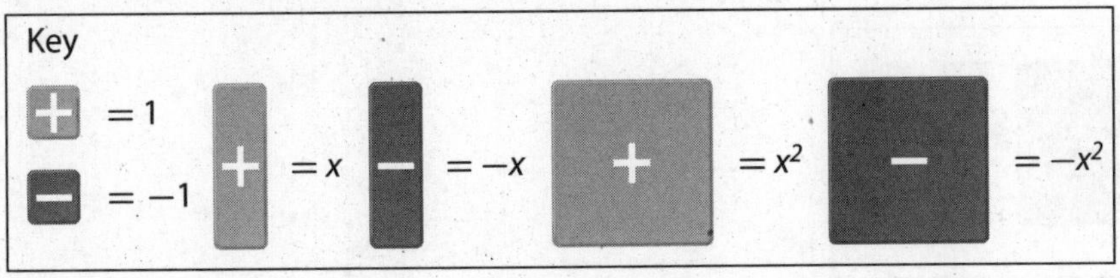

To subtract polynomials, recall that subtraction is equivalent to addition of the opposite.

$5 - 6 = 5 + (-6)$

Polynomial subtraction is the same. To subtract polynomial B from polynomial A, create a new polynomial C that consists of the opposite of each monomial in polynomial B. Add polynomial A and polynomial C.

When using tiles, switch every tile in the polynomial being subtracted for its opposite, the tile of the same size but the opposite sign. Once this is done, place the tiles representing the first polynomial and the new set of tiles next to each other and add like you have done previously. (The opposite of a polynomial is the negative of it. When you add a polynomial to its opposite you get 0.)

(A) Use algebra tiles to find $(2x^2 + 4) - (4x^2)$. Write the polynomial expression for each set of algebra tiles.

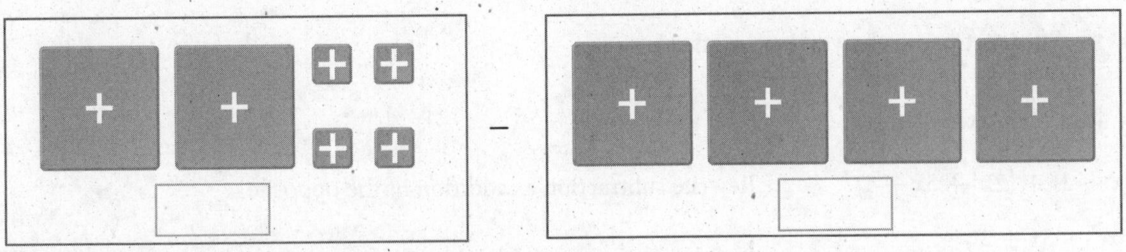

(B) Write the opposite of $4x^2$.

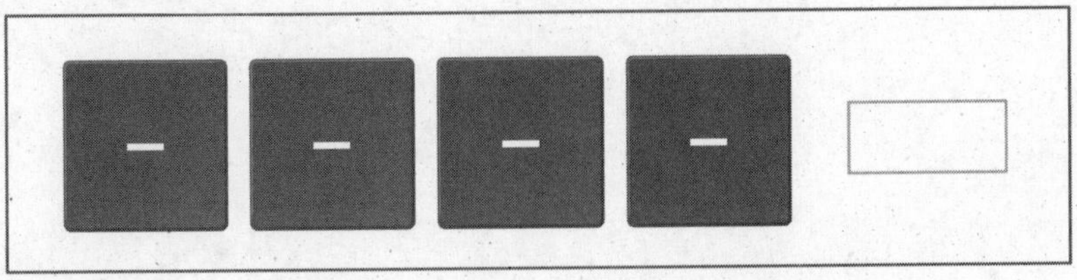

Ⓒ Write the subtraction as addition of the opposite.

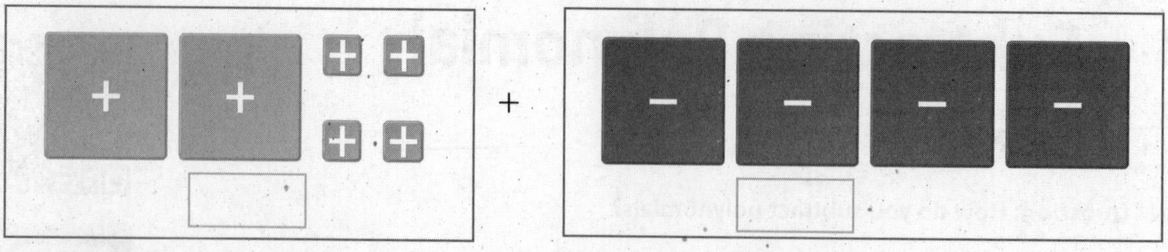

Ⓓ Group like terms and remove zero pairs. Write the resulting expression.

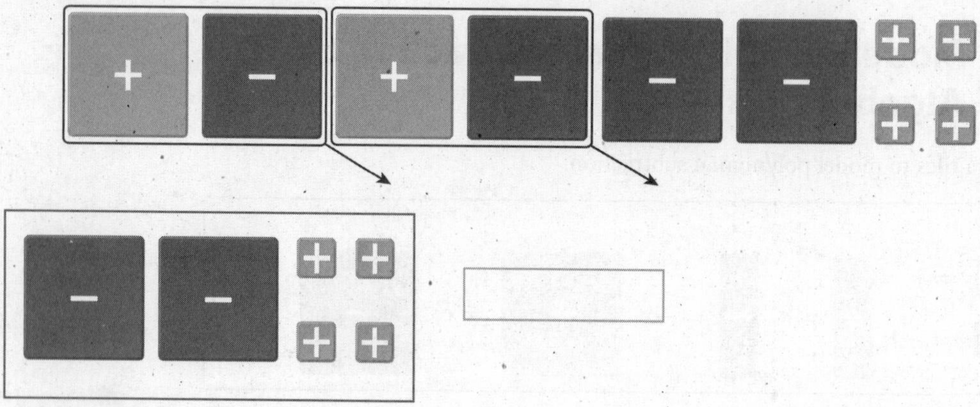

Reflect

1. Discussion Explain how removing zero pairs is an application of the additive inverse and the Identity Property of Addition.

Explain 1 Subtracting Polynomials Using a Vertical Format

To subtract polynomials, rewrite the subtraction as addition of the opposite.

Example 1 **Subtract using the vertical method.**

Ⓐ $(5x + 2) - (-2x^2 - 3x + 4)$

$(5x + 2) + (2x^2 + 3x - 4)$ Rewrite subtraction as addition of the opposite.

$$\begin{array}{r} 0x^2 + 5x + 2 \\ + \; 2x^2 + 3x - 4 \\ \hline 2x^2 + 8x - 2 \end{array}$$

Use the vertical method. Write $0x^2$ as a placeholder.

Combine like terms.

Ⓑ $(y^2 + y - 1) - (-2y^2 + y + 1)$

$(y^2 + y - 1) + (\square\ 2y^2\ \square\ y\ \square\ 1)$ Rewrite subtraction as addition of the opposite.

Use the vertical method.

$+$

Combine like terms and simplify.

Simplify.

Reflect

2. Is the difference of two polynomials always another polynomial? Explain.

Your Turn

Find the difference using a vertical format.

3. $(4x^2 - x) - (-x^2 - 1)$ **4.** $(-z^3 - 2z - 1) - (-z^3 + 2z + 1)$ **5.** $(8y - 7) - (1 - 3y)$

Explain 2 Subtracting Polynomials Using a Horizontal Format

Once the subtraction problem has been rewritten as a sum, the polynomials can be added using the horizontal method. Recall that this method uses the Associative, Commutative, and Distributive properties to group and combine like terms.

Example 2 **Find the difference of the polynomials horizontally.**

Ⓐ $(2q^2 - q - 8) - (2q^2 + q - 4)$

$= (2q^2 - q - 8) + (-2q^2 - q + 4)$ Rewrite subtraction as addition of the opposite.

$= (2q^2 - 2q^2) + (-q - q) + (-8 + 4)$ Group like terms together.

$= -2q - 4$ Simplify.

(B) $(2ab - b + a) - (2b^2 + b + a + 4)$

$= (2ab - b + a) + $ ________________ Rewrite subtraction as addition of the opposite.

$=$ ________________________ Group like terms together.

$=$ ________________ Simplify.

Your Turn

Find each difference.

6. $(-x^3 + y^2 + y - x) - (-x^3 + y + x)$

7. $(18z + 12) - (11z - 5)$

Explain 3 Modeling with Polynomials

Some scenarios can be modeled by the difference of two polynomials.

Example 3 Find the difference between two polynomials to solve a real-world problem.

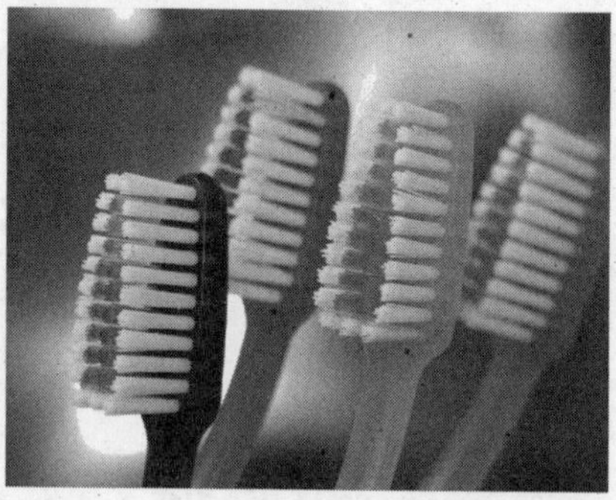

(A) The cost in dollars of producing x toothbrushes is given by the polynomial $400{,}000 + 3x$, and the revenue generated from sales is given by the polynomial $20x - 0.00004x^2$. Write a polynomial expression for the profit from making and selling x toothbrushes. Then find the profit for selling 200,000 toothbrushes.

Use the formula: Profit = revenue − cost

$(20x - 0.00004x^2) - (400{,}000 + 3x)$

$= (20x - 0.00004x^2) + (-400{,}000 - 3x)$ Add the opposite.

$= -0.00004x^2 + 17x - 400{,}000$ Combine like terms.

To find the profit for selling 200,000 toothbrushes, evaluate the polynomial when $x = 200{,}000$.

$-0.00004x^2 + 17x - 400{,}000$

$= -0.00004(200{,}000)^2 + 17(200{,}000) - 400{,}000 = 1{,}400{,}000$

The company will make $1.4 million from the sale of 200,000 toothbrushes.

B The revenue made by a car company from the sale of y cars is given by $0.005y^2 + 10y$. The cost to produce y cars is given by the polynomial $20y + 1{,}000{,}000$. Write a polynomial expression for the profit from making and selling y cars. Find the profit the company will make if it sells 30,000 cars.

$(0.005y^2 + 10y) -$ ________	Profit = revenue − cost
$= (0.005y^2 + 10y) +$ ________	Add the opposite.
$= 0.005y^2$ [ ] ________ $- 1{,}000{,}000$	Combine like terms.

To find the profit for selling 30,000 cars, evaluate the polynomial when $x = 30{,}000$.

$0.005y^2 -$ [ ] $- 1{,}000{,}000$

$= 0.005(30{,}000)^2 -$ [ ] $- 1{,}000{,}000 =$ [ ]

The company will make ________ million from the sale of 30,000 cars.

Reflect

8. What is the addition problem corresponding to profit = revenue − cost? How do you find revenue if you know profit and cost?

Your Turn

Find the difference between two polynomials to solve a real-world problem.

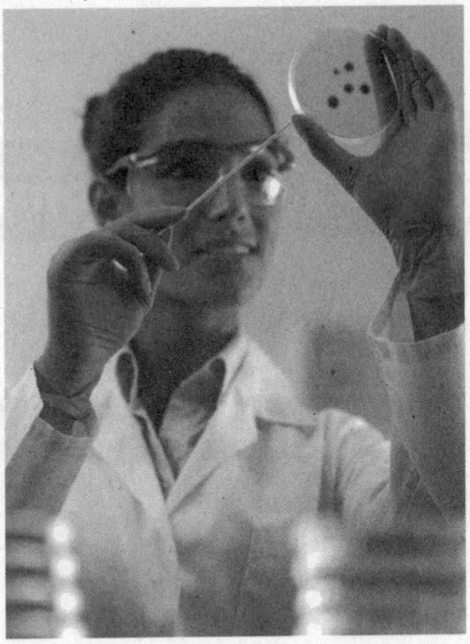

9. Jen, a biologist, is growing bacterial cultures at different temperatures as part of her research. The number of cells in the culture growing at 25 °C is given by the polynomial $t^2 + 4t + 4$, where t is the time elapsed in minutes. The number of cells in the second culture growing at 35 °C is modeled by the polynomial $t^2 + 4$. She needs to measure the success of the 25 °C culture over the 35 °C culture. Find the polynomial representing how many more cells are in the 25 °C culture for time t. How many more cells are there after 15 minutes?

10. The number of gallons of water in a leaking pool is determined by the rate that the water is filling, $8g^2 + 3g - 4$, and the rate that water leaks from the pool, $9g^2 - 2g - 5$, where g represents the number of gallons entering or leaving the pool per minute. Write an expression for the net change in gallons per minute of the water in the pool. Find the change in the amount when the rate, g, is 5 gallons per minute.

Elaborate

11. You can turn a polynomial subtraction problem into an addition problem. Can you turn a polynomial addition problem into a subtraction problem?

12. Discussion Write a pair of polynomials whose sum is $3m^2 + 1$. Write a pair of polynomials whose difference is $3m^2 + 1$. Write a pair of polynomials whose sum and difference are both $3m^2 + 1$.

13. Essential Question Check-In What do you have to do to simplify differences of polynomials? What properties do you use to accomplish this?

Evaluate: Homework and Practice

Personal Math Trainer

- Online Homework
- Hints and Help
- Extra Practice

1. Use algebra tiles to model the difference: $(x^2 + x - 3) - (x^2 + 2x + 1)$.

Model	Algebra

2. James was solving a subtraction problem using algebra tiles, and he ended with 1 x^2-tile, $2x^2$-tiles, 3 1-tiles, and 1 −1-tile. Model these results with algebra tiles. Assuming James' steps were correct up to that point, explain his mistake. Write the algebraic expression and draw the tiles that should be his result.

Model	Algebra

Find each difference vertically.

3. $\left(2x^2 - 2x^4\right) - \left(x^4 - x^2\right)$

4. $\left(y^2 - x^4\right) - \left(-x^4 - x^2\right)$

5. $\left(0.75x + 2\right) - \left(2.75x + x^2\right)$

6. $\left(x^2 + y^2x + z\right) - \left(-x + xy^2 - z\right)$

7. $\left(m + x + 2z\right) - \left(x - y\right)$

8. $-a^5 - \left(b^2 + a^2b^2\right) - \left(-a^5 - a^2b^2\right)$

Find each difference horizontally.

9. $\left(-2x^2 + x + 1\right) - \left(2x^2 - x - 1\right)$

10. $\left(a + b - 2c\right) - \left(a + b + 2c\right)$

11. $\left(-2cab^2 + ab^2 + b^2\right) - \left(-b^2\right)$

12. $\left(-2cab^2 + ab^2 + b^2\right) - \left[-\left(-b^2\right)\right]$

13. $\left(4^{10}a + ab\sqrt[3]{2}\right) - \left(ab\sqrt[3]{2} + ab + 4^{10}a\right)$

14. $\left(q^3r^2 - 6qr^2 - 21q\right) - \left(-qr^2 - 6qr^2 - 11q - 3q^3r^2\right)$

Model various situations with the difference of polynomials. Simplify.

15. A bicycle company produces y bicycles at a cost represented by the polynomial $y^2 + 10y + 100,000$. The revenue for y bicycles is represented by $2y^2 + 10y + 500$. Find a polynomial that represents the company's profit. If the company only has enough materials to make 300 bicycles, should it make the bicycles?

16. The polynomial $-2x^2 + 500x$ represents the budget surplus of the town of Alphaville for the year 2010. Alphaville's surplus in 2011 can be modeled by $-1.5x^2 + 400x$. If x represents the yearly tax revenue in thousands, by how much did Alphaville's budget surplus increase from 2010 to 2011? If Alphaville took in \$750,000 in tax revenue in 2011, what was the budget surplus that year?

Geometry **Mrs. Isabelle is making paper and plastic foam animals for her first-grade class. She is calculating the amount of wasted materials for environmental and financial reasons.**

17. Mrs. Isabelle is cutting circles out of square pieces of paper to make paper animals in her class. Write a polynomial that represents the amount of paper wasted if the class cuts out the biggest circles possible in squares of length ℓ.

18. Mrs. Isabelle's class is making spheres out of plastic foam cubes. Write a polynomial that represents the amount of plastic foam wasted if the class cuts out the biggest spheres possible from cubes with side lengths of l. The volume of a sphere of radius r is $\frac{4}{3}\pi r^3$.

Persevere in Problem Solving **John has yellow, green, and red cubes, each with side length c. Eight yellow cubes are glued together to make a larger cube. An even larger cube is made by gluing on green cubes until no yellow cubes can be seen. After that, John covers the green cubes with red ones so that green also cannot be seen, making an even larger cube. The minimum number of green and red cubes were used to cover previous colors. Use this information for Exercises 19 and 20.**

19. What is the volume of the final big red cube?

20. Write an expression for the volume of the final cube after performing this procedure with n colors of cubes.

21. Suppose you have two polynomials regarding the financial situation of a bicycle company. The first polynomial, $20{,}000 + x^2$, represents revenue from selling x units, and the second, $0.05x + 300$, represents the cost to produce x units.

Which of the following can be the net profit for the company if x units are produced and x units are sold?

a. $20{,}000 + x^2 - (0.05x + 300)$

b. $(20{,}000 + x^2) - (0.05x + 300)$

c. $(20{,}000 + x^2) - 0.05x + 300$

d. $(20{,}000 + x^2) - 0.05x - 300$

e. $(20{,}000 + x^2) + 0.05x + 300$

H.O.T. Focus on Higher Order Thinking

22. Explain the Error Kate performed the following subtraction problem. Explain her error and correct it.

$(5x^2 + x) - (x^3 + 2x)$

$= 5x^2 + x - x^3 + 2x$

$= 5x^2 - x^3 + (1 + 2)x$

$= -x^3 + 5x^2 + 3x$

23. Communicate Mathematical Ideas Hallie subtracted a quantity from the polynomial $3y^2 + 8y - 16$ and produced the expression $y^2 - 4$. What quantity did Hallie subtract? Explain how you got your answer.

24. Counterexamples The Associative Property works for polynomial addition. Does it work for polynomial subtraction? If not, provide a counterexample. Remember, the Associative Property for addition is $(a + b) + c = a + (b + c)$.

25. Draw Conclusions Finish a standard proof that the Associative Property does not work for polynomial subtraction.

To show $(a - b) - c \neq a - (b - c)$, take the right side of the Associative Property and simplify it:

$a - (b - c) = a + \left(\square + \square\right) = a - \square + \square$, which is not generally the same as $a - b - c$ unless $c = 0$.

Lesson Performance Task

The profits of two different manufacturing plants can be modeled as shown, where x is the number of units produced at each plant.

Plant 1: $P_1(x) = -0.03x^2 + 25x - 1500$

Plant 2: $P_2(x) = -0.02x^2 + 21x - 1700$

Find polynomials representing the difference in profits between the companies. Find $P_1(x) - P_2(x)$ and $P_2(x) - P_1(x)$. Compare the two differences and draw conclusions.

Adding and Subtracting Polynomials

Essential Question: How can you use adding and subtracting polynomials to solve real-world problems?

Key Vocabulary

binomial *(binomio)*
degree of a polynomial *(grado de un polinomio)*
leading coefficient *(coeficiente principal)*
monomial *(monomio)*
polynomial *(polinomio)*
standard form of a polynomial *(forma estándar de un polinomio)*
trinomial *(trinomio)*

KEY EXAMPLE (Lesson 4.1)

Combine like terms to simplify the polynomial.

$5y^2 + 12xy + 10 - y^2 + 6xy - 20$

$5y^2 - y^2 + 12xy + 6xy + 10 - 20$ *Rearrange in descending order of exponents.*

$(5y^2 - y^2) + (12xy + 6xy) + (10 - 20)$ *Group like terms.*

$y^2(5 - 1) + xy(12 + 6) + (10 - 20)$ *Distributive Property*

$y^2(4) + xy(18) + (-10)$ *Simplify.*

$4y^2 + 18xy - 10$

KEY EXAMPLE (Lesson 4.2)

A city planner must add the area of 2 lots to determine the total area of a new park. The area of lot A can be represented by $(2x^2 + 6x + 4)$ ft². The area of lot B can be represented by $(5x^2 - 5x + 10)$ ft². Write an expression that represents the total area of the park.

$(2x^2 + 6x + 4) + (5x^2 - 5x + 10)$ *Add.*

$= (2x^2 + 5x^2) + (6x - 5x) + (4 + 10)$ *Group like terms.*

$= 7x^2 + x + 14$ *Simplify.*

The area of the park is $(7x^2 + x + 14)$ ft².

KEY EXAMPLE (Lesson 4.3)

Find the difference.

$(b^2 + 9ab + 15a) - (3b^2 - 25ab + 1)$

$= (b^2 + 9ab + 15a) + (-3b^2 + 25ab - 1)$ *Rewrite subtraction as addition of the opposite.*

$= (b^2 - 3b^2) + (9ab + 25ab) + 15a - 1$ *Group like terms.*

$= -2b^2 + 34ab + 15a - 1$ *Simplify.*

EXERCISES

Classify each polynomial by degree and number of terms. *(Lesson 4.1)*

1. $z^2 - 12$

2. $r^2 + 8 - 7r^3s$

Combine like terms. *(Lesson 4.1)*

3. $5y - 7y^2 + 10 - 10y^2 + y$

4. $4b(a + b) - 8b^2 + 9ab$

Add or subtract. *(Lessons 4.2, 4.3)*

5. $(7p^2 - 5p + 10) + (p^2 - 8)$

6. $(4r^2 + 9r - 4) - (-2r^2 + 7r + 6)$

7. A student is cutting a square out of a piece of poster board. The area of the poster board can be represented as $(4x^2 + 14x - 8)$ in^2. The area of the square can be represented as $(x^2 + 8x + 16)$ in^2. Write an expression to represent the area of the poster board left after the student cuts out the square. *(Lesson 4.3)*

MODULE PERFORMANCE TASK

Ozone Levels in the Los Angeles Basin

You probably know that ozone in the upper atmosphere protects Earth from ultraviolet radiation, but ozone near the ground is harmful and a major component of air pollution. The table below provides maximum and minimum surface-level ozone concentrations in per parts million (ppm) in the Los Angeles Basin area for several months during 2012.

	Jan	Mar	May	June	Aug	Oct	Dec
Max	0.049	0.078	0.097	0.123	0.098	0.076	0.049
Min	0.020	0.040	0.048	0.054	0.053	0.041	0.038

Use the data to find an equation that models the average ozone level by month and use it to predict the average level for the months of February, April, September, and November of 2012.

Use your own paper to complete the task. Be sure to write down all your data and assumptions. Then use numbers, tables, graphs, or algebra to explain how you reached your conclusion.

Ready to Go On?

4.1–4.3 Adding and Subtracting Polynomials

Personal Math Trainer
- Online Homework
- Hints and Help
- Extra Practice

Simplify each expression by combining like terms. Classify the simplified expression by degree and number of terms. *(Lesson 4.1)*

1. $16 - 5x^2 + 6x - 2x^2 + 10$

2. $p^4 - 5p + 3p(p^3 + 4)$

Add or subtract. Write the expression in standard form. *(Lessons 4.1, 4.2, 4.3)*

3. $(9z^2 + 28) - (z^2 + 8z - 8)$

4. $(12y - 8 + 6y^2) + (9 - 4y)$

5. A community swimming pool has a deep end and a shallow end. The volume of water in the deep end can be represented by $(2x^3 + 12x^2 + 10x)$ ft^3, and the volume of water in the shallow end can be represented by $(4x^3 - 100x)$ ft^3. Write an expression that represents the total volume of water in the pool in ft^3. *(Lesson 4.2)*

ESSENTIAL QUESTION

6. What is one way that adding and subtracting polynomials is similar to adding and subtracting whole numbers and integers?

MODULE 4
MIXED REVIEW

Assessment Readiness

1. Is the given polynomial in standard form? Select Yes or No for each polynomial.

   A. $-10r^3 + 3r - 18$ ○ Yes ○ No

   B. $-35t^3 - 13t + t^2$ ○ Yes ○ No

   C. $12x^4 - 12x^2 - 5$ ○ Yes ○ No

2. Consider the sum of $6m^2n + mn - 15$ and $-10mn^2 + mn + 12$. Choose True or False for each statement.

   A. The constant of the sum is -3. ○ True ○ False

   B. $6m^2n$ and $-10mn^2$ are like terms. ○ True ○ False

   C. In simplest form, the sum has 4 terms. ○ True ○ False

3. A clothing store sells t-shirts and jeans. The store charges customers \$15 per t-shirt and \$35 per pair of jeans. The store pays \$4.50 per t-shirt and \$5.00 per pair of jeans, plus a flat fee of \$150 per order. Write an expression that represents the store's profit for an order if they sell t t-shirts and j pairs of jeans. Show your work.

4. The value of a company, in millions of dollars, during its first 10 years increased by 2% each year. The original valuation of the company was 2.1 million dollars. Write a function to represent the value of the company x years after being founded. How much more was the company worth, in millions of dollars, after 6 years than after 2 years? Explain how you solved this problem.

Multiplying Polynomials

MODULE 5

Essential Question: How can you use multiplying polynomials to solve real-world problems?

LESSON 5.1
Multiplying Polynomial Expressions by Monomials

LESSON 5.2
Multiplying Polynomial Expressions

LESSON 5.3
Special Products of Binomials

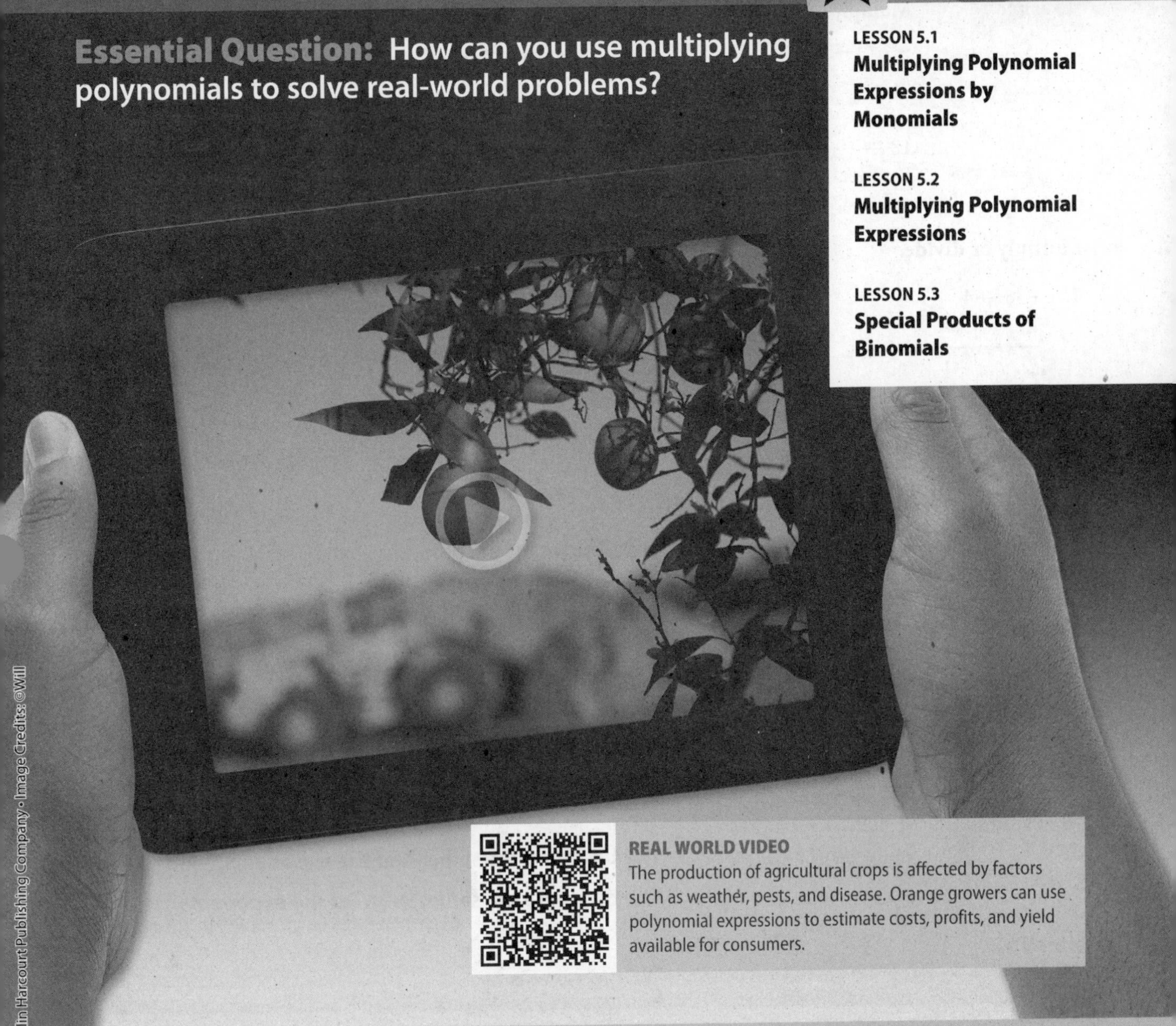

REAL WORLD VIDEO
The production of agricultural crops is affected by factors such as weather, pests, and disease. Orange growers can use polynomial expressions to estimate costs, profits, and yield available for consumers.

MODULE PERFORMANCE TASK PREVIEW

Orange Consumption

Do you eat oranges? You probably already know they are high in vitamin C, but they are also good for your skin, eyes, heart, and immune system. Each year the price of oranges increases while the amount consumed varies. In this module, you will explore polynomial operations that will help you model the per capita spending on oranges. So, about how much do Americans spend on oranges each year? Let's find out!

Are YOU Ready?

Complete these exercises to review skills you will need for this module.

- Online Homework
- Hints and Help
- Extra Practice

Multiply and Divide Integers

Example 1 Multiply or divide.

$-7 \cdot (-3)$ — Think: Multiply 7 and 3.

21 — Same signs, so the product is positive.

$18 \div (-9)$ — Think: Divide 18 by 9.

-2 — Different signs, so the quotient is negative.

Multiply or divide.

1. $-36 \div 4$ ______

2. $13 \cdot (-5)$ ______

3. $-56 \div -8$ ______

Algebraic Expressions

Example 2 Multiply $3(2x - 5)$.

$3(2x - 5)$

$3(2x) - 3(5)$ — Distributive Property

$6x - 15$ — Multiply.

Multiply.

4. $8(3a + 5)$ ______

5. $4(6 - 2d)$ ______

6. $9(2x - 7y)$ ______

Exponents

Example 3 Simplify.

$x^4 \cdot x^2 = x^{4+2} = x^6$ — The bases are the same. Add the exponents.

$\frac{x^7}{x^3} = x^{7-3} = x^4$ — The bases are the same. Subtract the exponents.

Simplify.

7. $y^3 \cdot y^6$ ______

8. $\frac{n^{10}}{n^2}$ ______

9. $\frac{a^3 \cdot a^9}{a^4}$ ______

10. $m^2 \cdot m^5 \cdot m^3$ ______

Name________________________ Class____________ Date__________

5.1 Multiplying Polynomial Expressions by Monomials

Essential Question: How can you multiply polynomials by monomials?

Resource Locker

Explore Modeling Polynomial Multiplication

Algebra tiles can be used to model the multiplication of a polynomial by a monomial.

Rules
1. The first factor goes on the left side of the grid, the second factor on the top.
2. Fill in the grid with tiles that have the same height as tiles on the left and the same length as tiles on the top.
3. Follow the key. The product of two tiles of the same color is positive; the product of two tiles of different colors is negative.

(A) Use algebra tiles to find $2(x + 1)$. Then recount the tiles in the grid and write the expression.

First, fill in the factors.

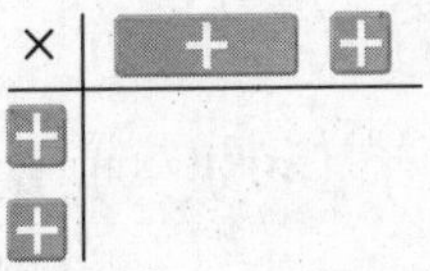

Key

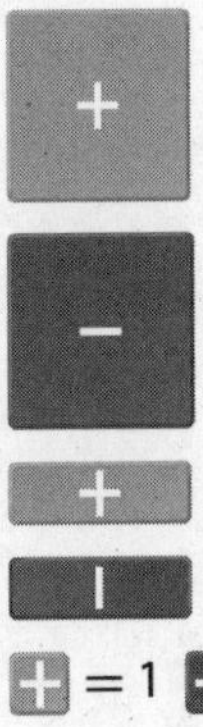

Now fill in the table.

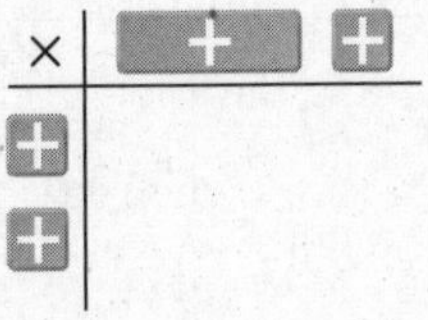

The simplified expression for $2(x + 1) =$ ☐ $x +$ ☐.

Ⓑ Use algebra tiles to model $2x(x - 3)$. Then write the expression.

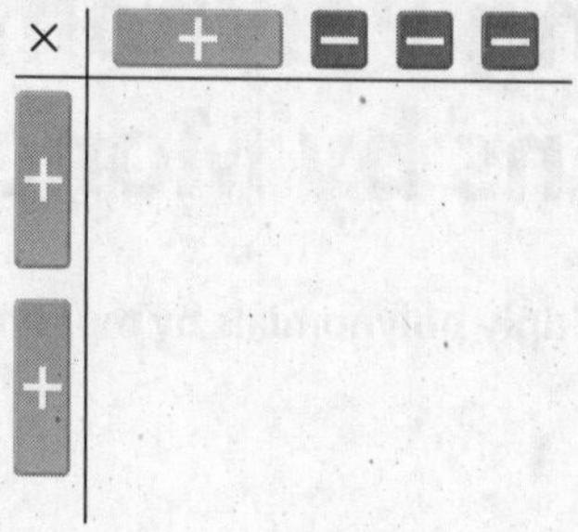

The simplified expression for

$2x(x - 3) =$ ____ $x^2 -$ ____ x.

Reflect

1. Discussion How do the tiles illustrate the idea of x^2 geometrically?

____

____

2. Discussion How does the grid illustrate the Distributive Property?

____

____

____

Explain 1 Multiplying Monomials

When multiplying monomials, variables with exponents may need to be multiplied. Recall the Product of Powers Property, which states that $a^m \cdot a^n = a^{(m+n)}$.

Example 1 **Find each product.**

Ⓐ $(6x^3)(-4x^4)$

$(6x^3)(-4x^4)$

$= (6 \cdot -4)(x^3 \cdot x^4)$

$= (6 \cdot -4)(x^{3+4})$

$= -24x^7$

Ⓑ $(5xy^2)(7xy)$

$(5xy^2)(7xy)$

$= (5 \cdot \square)(x \cdot \square)(\square \cdot y)$

$= (5 \cdot \square)(x^{1+\square})(y^{\square+1})$

$= \square \cdot x^{\square}y^{\square}$

Reflect

3. In the Product of Powers Property, do the bases need to be the same or can they be different?

____

Your Turn

4. $(18y^2x^3z)(3x^8y^6z^4)$

Explain 2 Multiplying a Polynomial by a Monomial

Remember that the Distributive Property states that multiplying a term by a sum is the same thing as multiplying the term by each part of the sum then adding the results.

Example 2 **Find each product.**

Ⓐ $3x(3x^2 + 6x - 5)$

$3x(3x^2 + 6x - 5)$ — Distribute and simplify.

$= 3x(3x^2) + 3x(6x) + 3x(-5)$

$= 9x^{1+2} + 18x^{1+1} - 15x^1$

$= 9x^3 + 18x^2 - 15x$

Ⓑ $2xy(5x^2y + 3xy^2 + 7xy)$

$2xy(5x^2y + 3xy^2 + 7xy)$ — Distribute and simplify.

$= 2xy(5x^2y) + 2xy(\square) + 2xy(\square)$

$= 10x^{1+2}y^{1+1} + \square x^{1+\square}y^{1+\square} + \square x^{1+\square}y^{1+\square}$

$= 10x^3y^2 + \square x^{\square}y^{\square} + \square x^{\square}y^{\square}$

Reflect

5. Is the product of a monomial and a polynomial always a polynomial? Explain. If so, how many terms does it have?

____

____

____

Your Turn

6. $2a^2(5b^2 + 3ab + 6a + 1)$

Explain 3 Multiplying a Polynomial by a Monomial to Solve a Real-World Problem

Knowing how to multiply polynomials and monomials is useful when solving real-world problems.

Example 3 **Write a polynomial equation and solve the problem.**

Design Harry is building a fish tank that is a rectangular prism. He wants the height of the tank to be 6 inches longer than the length and width. If he needs the volume to be as close as possible to 3500 in^3, what should be the length of the tank? Round to the nearest inch.

Analyze Information

Identify the important information

- Since the bases are squares, the length and width are ________.
- The height of the tank is ________ more inches than the length.
- The total volume of the model should be as close as possible to ________ in^3.

Formulate a Plan

Since the desired volume of the model is given, the volume formula should be used to find the answer. The volume formula for a rectangular prism is

$V =$ ☐. Use this formula and the given information to write and solve an equation.

Solve

Build the equation.

Since the length and width are equal, let s represent these measurements. The volume will be $V = (s \cdot s)(\square) = s^{\square}(\square) = s^{\square} + \square s^{\square}$.

s	$s^{\square} + \square s^{\square}$
11	
12	
13	
14	

Justify and Evaluate

________ is closer to ________ than any of the other results, so the length of the fish tank to the nearest whole inch should be ________ inches.

Your Turn

7. **Engineering** Diane needs a piece of paper whose length is 4 more inches than the width, and the area is as close as possible to 50 in^2. To the nearest whole inch, what should the dimensions of the paper be?

Elaborate

8. What is the power if a monomial is multiplied by a constant?

9. **Essential Question Check-In** What properties and rules are used to multiply a multi-term polynomial by a monomial?

Evaluate: Homework and Practice

Personal Math Trainer
- Online Homework
- Hints and Help
- Extra Practice

Find each product.

1. $(3x)(2x^2)$
2. $(19x^5)(8x^3)$
3. $(6x^7)(3x^3)$
4. $(3x^2)(2x^3)$
5. $7xy(3x^2y^3)$
6. $(6xyz^4)(5xy^3)$
7. $(8xy^3)(4y^4z^2)$
8. $(11xy)(x^3y^2)$
9. $(x^2 + x)(x^3)$

10. $(x^3 + 2x^2)(x^4)$

11. $(x^2 + 2x + 5)(x^3)$

12. $(x^4 + 3x^3 + 2x^2 + 11x + 4)(x^2)$

13. $(x^3 + 2y^2 + 3xy)(4x^2y)$

14. $(2x^3 + 5y)(3xy)$

15. $(x^4 + 3x^3y + 3xy^3)(6xy^2)$

16. $(x^4 + 3x^3y^2 + 4x^2y + 8xy + 12x)(11x^2y^3)$

Write a polynomial equation for each situation and then solve the problem.

17. Design A bedroom has a length of $x + 3$ feet and a width of x feet. Find the area when $x = 10$.

18. Engineering A flat-screen television has a length that is 1 more inch than its width. The area of the television's screen is 1500 in^2. To the nearest whole inch, what are the dimensions of the television?

19. Construction Zach is building a new shed shaped like a square prism. He wants the height of the shed to be 2 feet less than the length and width. If he needs the volume to be as close as possible to 3174 ft^3, what should the length be? Round to the nearest foot.

20. State whether each expression is or can be written as a monomial.

a. x^3	◯ Yes	◯ No
b. $a^2 + 2a^b + b^c$	◯ Yes	◯ No
c. $x^3 + 4x^3$	◯ Yes	◯ No
d. $y^{2^{x^3}}$	◯ Yes	◯ No
e. $xyz + txy + tyz + txz$	◯ Yes	◯ No

21. Draw the algebra tiles that model the factors in the multiplication shown. Then determine the simplified product.

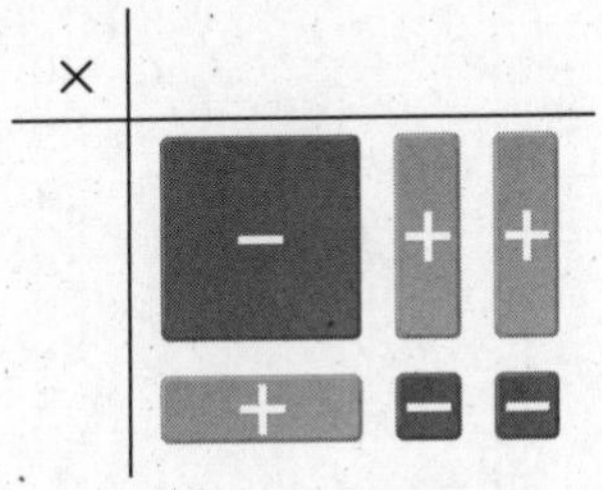

H.O.T. Focus on Higher Order Thinking

22. Critical Thinking When finding the product of a monomial and a binomial, how is the degree of the product related to the degree of the monomial and the degree of the binomial?

23. Explain the Error Sandy says that the product of x^2 and $x^3 + 5x^2 + 1$ is $x^6 + 5x^4 + x^2$. Explain the error that Sandy made.

24. Communicate Mathematical Ideas What is the lowest degree that a polynomial can have? Explain.

Lesson Performance Task

A craftsman is making a dulcimer with the same dimensions as the one shown. The surface shown requires a special, more durable type of finish. Write a polynomial that represents the area to be finished on the dulcimer shown.

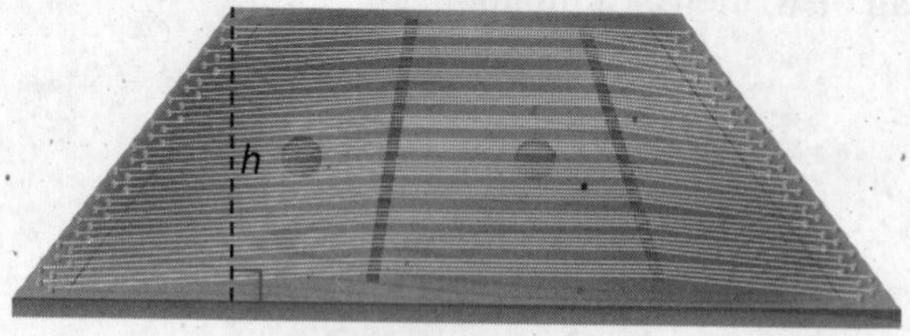

Name _______________ Class _______________ Date _______________

5.2 Multiplying Polynomial Expressions

Resource Locker

Essential Question: How do you multiply binomials and polynomials?

Explore Modeling Binomial Multiplication

Using algebra tiles to model the product of two binomials is very similar to using algebra tiles to model the product of a monomial and a polynomial.

Rules

1. The first factor goes on the left side of the grid, and the second factor goes on the top.
2. Fill in the grid with tiles that have the same height as tiles on the left and the same length as tiles on the top.
3. Follow the key. The product of two tiles of the same color is positive; the product of two tiles of different colors is negative.

Use algebra tiles to model $(x + 1)(x - 2)$. Then write the product. First fill in the factors and mat.

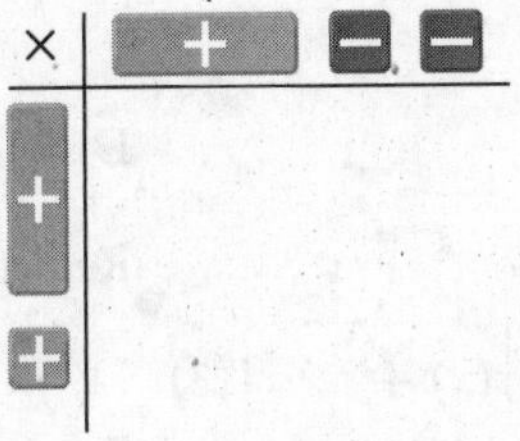

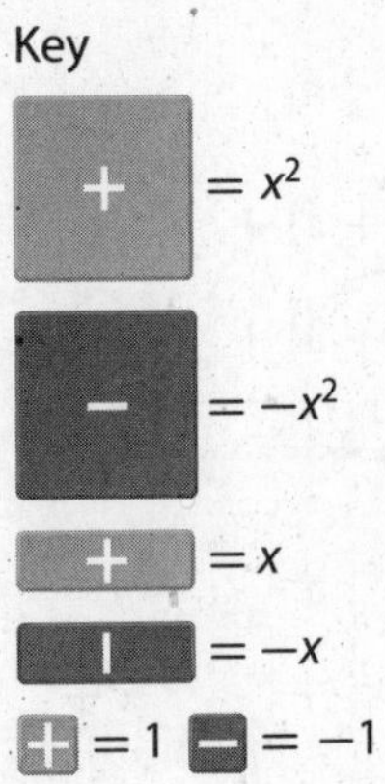

Now remove any zero pairs.

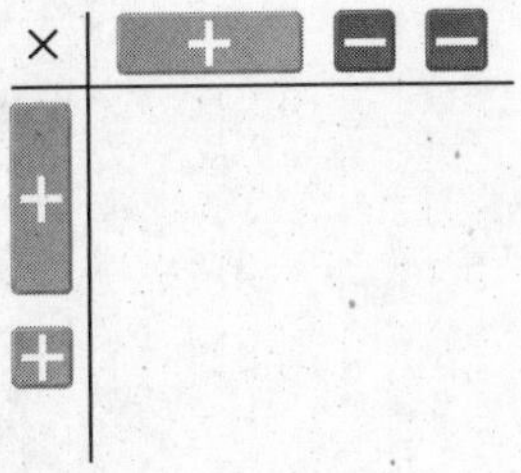

The product $(x + 1)(x - 2)$ in simplest form is $\square x^2 - \square x - \square$.

Reflect

1. **Discussion** Why can zero pairs be removed from the product?

____

____

2. **Discussion** Is it possible for more than one pair of tiles to form a zero pair?

____

____

Explain 1 Multiplying Binomials Using the Distributive Property

To multiply a binomial by a binomial, the Distributive Property must be applied more than once.

Example 1 **Multiply by using the Distributive Property.**

(A) $(x + 5)(x + 2)$

$(x + 5)(x + 2) = x(x + 2) + 5(x + 2)$ Distribute.

$= x(x + 2) + 5(x + 2)$ Redistribute and simplify.

$= x(x) + x(2) + 5(x) + 5(2)$

$= x^2 + 2x + 5x + 10$

$= x^2 + 7x + 10$

(B) $(2x + 4)(x + 3)$

$(2x + 4)(x + 3) = 2x(x + 3) + \square(x + 3)$ Distribute.

$= 2x(x + 3) + \square(x + 3)$ Redistribute and simplify.

$= 2x(x) + \square(3) + \square(x) + \square(3)$

$= \square x^{\square} + \square x + \square x + \square$

$= \square x^{\square} + \square x + \square$

Your Turn

3. $(x + 1)(x - 2)$

Explain 2 Multiplying Binomials Using FOIL

Another way to use the Distributive Property is the *FOIL* method. The **FOIL** method uses the Distributive Property to multiply terms of binomials in this order: First terms, Outer terms, Inner terms, and Last terms.

Example 2 **Multiply by using the FOIL method.**

(A) $(x^2 + 3)(x + 2)$

Use the FOIL method.

$(x^2 + 3)(x + 2) = (x^2 + 3)(x + 2)$	F	Multiply the first terms. Result: x^3
$= (x^2 + 3)(x + 2)$	O	Multiply the outer terms. Result: $2x^2$
$= (x^2 + 3)(x + 2)$	I	Multiply the inner terms. Result: $3x$
$= (x^2 + 3)(x + 2)$	L	Multiply the last terms. Result: 6

Add the result.

$(x^2 + 3)(x + 2) = x^3 + 2x^2 + 3x + 6$

(B) $(3x^2 - 2x)(x + 5)$

Use the FOIL method.

$(3x^2 - 2x)(x + 5) = (3x^2 - 2x)(x + 5)$	F	Multiply the first terms. Result: ☐
$= (3x^2 - 2x)(x + 5)$	O	Multiply the outer terms. Result: ☐
$= (3x^2 - 2x)(x + 5)$	I	Multiply the inner terms. Result: ☐
$= (3x^2 - 2x)(x + 5)$	L	Multiply the last terms. Result: ☐

Add the result.

$(3x^2 - 2x)(x + 5) = \square x^3 + \square x^2 - \square x$

Reflect

4. The FOIL method finds the sum of four partial products. Why does the result from part B only have three terms?

____

5. Can the FOIL method be used for numeric expressions? Give an example.

____

____

____

____

Your Turn

6. $(x^2 + 3)(x + 6)$

Explain 3 Multiplying Polynomials

To multiply polynomials with more than two terms, the Distributive Property must be used several times.

Example 3 **Multiply the polynomials.**

(A) $(x+2)(x^2-5x+4)$

$$\begin{aligned}(x+2)(x^2-5x+4) &= x(x^2-5x+4)+2(x^2-5x+4) && \text{Distribute.}\\ &= x(x^2-5x+4)+2(x^2-5x+4) && \text{Redistribute.}\\ &= x(x^2)+x(-5x)+x(4)+2(x^2)+2(-5x)+2(4) && \text{Simplify.}\\ &= x^3-5x^2+4x+2x^2-10x+8\\ &= x^3-3x^2-6x+8\end{aligned}$$

(B) $(3x-4)(-2x^2+5x-6)$

$$\begin{aligned}(3x-4)(-2x^2+5x-6) &= 3x(-2x^2+5x-6)-\square(-2x^2+5x-6) && \text{Distribute.}\\ &= 3x(-2x^2+5x-6)-\square(-2x^2+5x-6) && \text{Redistribute.}\\ &= 3x(-2x^2)+3x(\square)+3x(\square)-4(\square)-4(\square)-4\square\end{aligned}$$

Simplify.

$$\begin{aligned}&= \square x^{\square}+\square x^{\square}-\square x+\square x^{\square}-\square x+\square\\ &= \square x^{\square}+\square x^{\square}-\square x+\square\end{aligned}$$

Reflect

7. **Discussion** Is the product of two polynomials always another polynomial?

____

____

8. Can the Distributive Property be used to multiply two trinomials?

____

9. $(3x+1)(x^3+4x^2-7)$

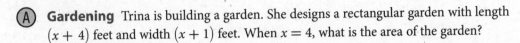

Explain 4 Modeling with Polynomial Multiplication

Polynomial multiplication is sometimes necessary in problem solving.

Example 4

(A) **Gardening** Trina is building a garden. She designs a rectangular garden with length $(x + 4)$ feet and width $(x + 1)$ feet. When $x = 4$, what is the area of the garden?

Let y represent the area of Trina's garden. Then the equation for this situation is $y = (x + 4)(x + 1)$.

$y = (x + 4)(x + 1)$

Use FOIL.

$y = x^2 + x + 4x + 4$

$y = x^2 + 5x + 4$

Now substitute 4 for x to finish the problem.

$y = x^2 + 5x + 4$

$y = (4)^2 + 5(4) + 4$

$y = 16 + 20 + 4$

$y = 40$

The area of Trina's garden is 40 ft^2.

(B) **Design** Orik has designed a rectangular mural that measures 20 feet in width and 30 feet in length. Laura has also designed a rectangular mural, but it measures x feet shorter on each side. When $x = 6$, what is the area of Laura's mural?

Let y represent the area of Laura's mural. Then the equation for this situation is $y = (20 - x)(30 - x)$.

$y = (20 - x)(30 - x)$

Use FOIL.

$y = \square - \square x - \square x + \square x^2$

$y = \square x^2 - \square x + \square$

Now substitute $\square$ for x to finish the problem.

$y = \square^2 - \square \cdot \square + \square$

$y = \square - \square + \square$

$y = \square$

The area of Laura's mural is $\square$ ft^2.

Your Turn

10. **Landscaping** A landscape architect is designing a rectangular garden in a local park. The garden will be 20 feet long and 15 feet wide. The architect wants to place a walkway with a uniform width all the way around the garden. What will be the area of the garden, including the walkway?

Elaborate

11. How is the FOIL method different from the Distributive Property? Explain.

12. Why can FOIL not be used for polynomials with three or more terms?

13. **Essential Question Check-In** How do you multiply two binomials?

Evaluate: Homework and Practice

Personal Math Trainer

- Online Homework
- Hints and Help
- Extra Practice

Multiply by using the Distributive Property.

1. $(x + 6)(x - 4)$

2. $(2x + 5)(x - 3)$

3. $(x - 6)(x + 1)$

4. $(x^2 + 3)(x - 4)$

5. $(x^2 + 11)(x + 6)$

6. $(x^2 + 8)(x - 5)$

Multiply by using the FOIL method.

7. $(x + 3)(x + 7)$

8. $(4x + 2)(x - 2)$

9. $(3x + 2)(2x + 5)$

10. $(x^2 - 6)(x - 4)$

11. $(x^2 + 9)(x - 3)$

12. $(4x^2 - 4)(2x + 1)$

Multiply the polynomials.

13. $(x - 3)(x^2 + 2x + 1)$

14. $(x + 5)(x^3 + 6x^2 + 18x)$

15. $(x + 4)(x^4 + x^2 + 1)$

16. $(x - 6)(x^5 + 4x^3 + 6x^2 + 2x)$

17. $(x^2 + x + 3)(x^3 - x^2 + 4)$

18. $(x^3 + x^2 + 2x)(x^4 - x^3 + x^2)$

Write a polynomial equation for each situation.

19. Gardening Cameron is creating a garden. He designs a rectangular garden with a length of $(x + 6)$ feet and a width of $(x + 2)$ feet. When $x = 5$, what is the area of the garden?

20. Design Sabrina has designed a rectangular painting that measures 50 feet in length and 40 feet in width. Alfred has also designed a rectangular painting, but it measures x feet shorter on each side. When $x = 3$, what is the area of Alfred's painting?

21. Photography Karl is putting a frame around a rectangular photograph. The photograph is 12 inches long and 10 inches wide, and the frame is the same width all the way around. What will be the area of the framed photograph?

22. **Sports** A tennis court is surrounded by a fence so that the distance from each boundary of the tennis court to the fence is the same. If the tennis court is 78 feet long and 36 feet wide, what is the area of the entire surface inside the fence?

23. State the first term of each product.

a. $(2x + 1)(3x + 4)$

b. $(x^4 + x^2)(3x^8 + x^{11})$

c. $x(x + 9)$

d. $(x^2 + 9)(3x + 4)(2x + 6)$

e. $(x^3 + 4)(x^2 + 6)(x + 5)$

24. Draw algebra tiles to model the factors in the polynomial multiplication modeled on the mat. Then write the factors and the product in simplest form.

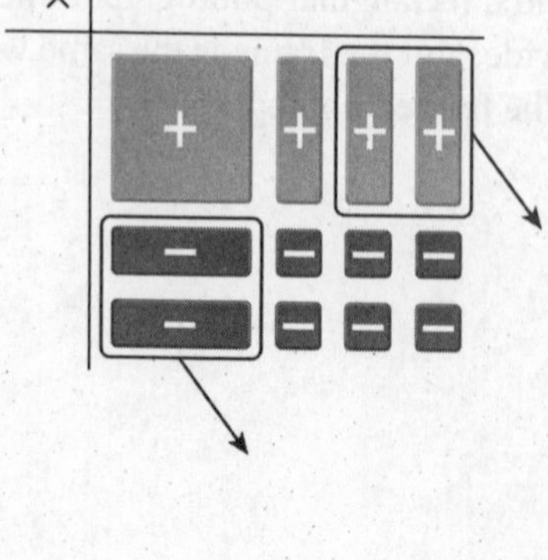

H.O.T. Focus on Higher Order Thinking

25. Critical Thinking The product of 3 consecutive odd numbers is 2145. Write an expression for finding the numbers.

26. Represent Real-World Problems The town swimming pool is d feet deep. The width of the pool is 10 feet greater than 5 times its depth. The length of the pool is 35 feet greater than 5 times its depth. Write and simplify an expression to represent the volume of the pool.

27. Explain the Error Bill argues that $(x + 1)(x + 19)$ simplifies to $x^2 + 20x + 20$. Explain his error.

Lesson Performance Task

Roan is planning a large vegetable garden in her yard. She plans to have at least six x by x regions for rotating crops and some 2 or 3 feet by x strips for fruit bushes like blueberries and raspberries.

Design a rectangular garden for Roan and write a polynomial that will give its area.

Name________________________ Class________________ Date__________

5.3 Special Products of Binomials

Essential Question: How can you find special products of binomials?

Resource Locker

Explore Modeling Special Products

Use algebra tiles to model the special products of binomials.

(A) Use algebra tiles to model $(2x + 3)^2$. Then write the product in simplest form.

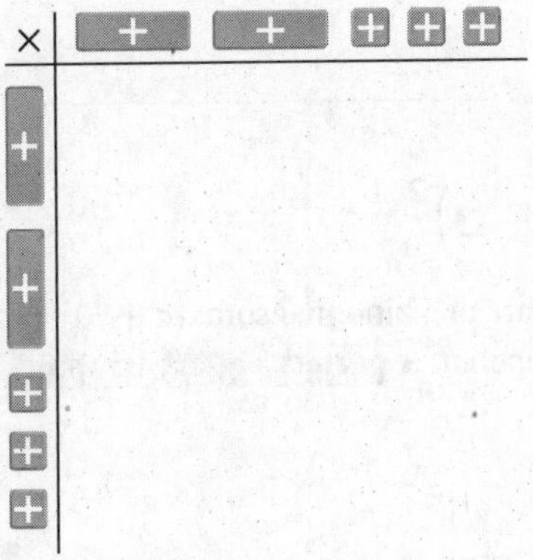

$(2x + 3)^2 = \square x^2 + \square x + \square$.

(B) Use algebra tiles to model $(2x - 3)^2$. Then write the product in simplest form.

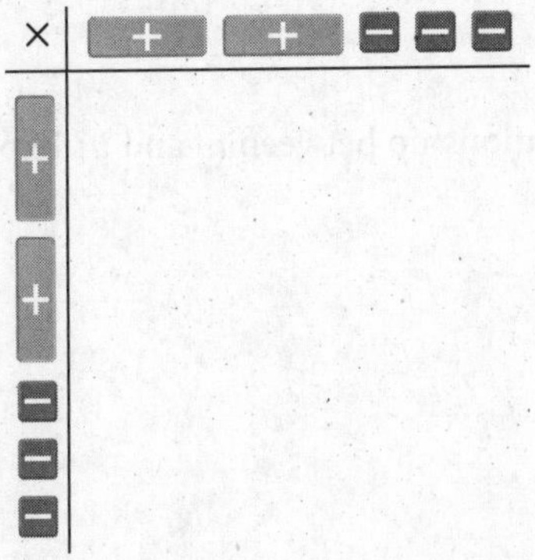

$(2x - 3)^2 = \square x^2 - \square x + \square$.

(C) Use algebra tiles to model $(2x + 3)(2x - 3)$. Then recount the tiles in the grid and write the expression.

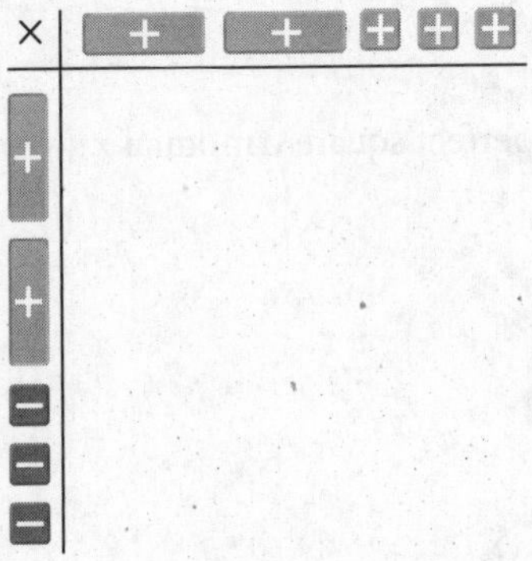

$(2x + 3)(2x - 3) = \square x^2 + \square x - \square$.

Reflect

1. **Discussion** In Step A, which terms of the trinomial are perfect squares? What is the coefficient of x in the product? How can you use the values of a and b in the expression $(2x + 3)^2$ to produce the coefficient of each term in the trinomial? How can you generalize these results to write a rule for the product $(a + b)^2$?

2. **Discussion** In Step B, which terms of the trinomial are perfect squares? What is the coefficient of x in the trinomial? How can you use the values of a and b in the expression $(2x - 3)^2$ to produce the coefficient of each term in the trinomial? How can you generalize these results to write a rule for the product $(a - b)^2$?

3. **Discussion** In Step C, which terms of the product are perfect squares? What is the coefficient of x in the product? How can you use the values of a and b in the expression $(2x + 3)(2x - 3)$ to produce the coefficient of each term in the product? How can you generalize these results to write a rule for the product $(a + b)(a - b)$?

Explain 1 Multiplying $(a + b)^2$

In the Explore, you determined a formula for the square of a binomial sum, $(a + b)^2 = a^2 + 2ab + b^2$. A trinomial of the form $a^2 + 2ab + b^2$ is called a *perfect-square trinomial.* A **perfect-square trinomial** is a trinomial that is the result of squaring a binomial.

Example 1 Multiply.

(A) $(x + 4)^2$

$a + b = a^2 + 2ab + b^2$

$(x + 4)^2 = x^2 + 2(x)(4) + 4^2$

$= x^2 + 8x + 16$

(B) $(3x + 2y)^2$

$(a + b)^2 = a^2 + 2ab + b^2$

$(3x + 2y)^2 = (3x)^2 + 2(\square x)(\square y) + (\square y)^2$

$= 9x^2 + \square xy + \square y^2$

Reflect

4. In the perfect square trinomial $x^2 + mx + n$, what is the relationship between m and n? Explain.

Your Turn

Multiply.

5. $(4 + x^2)^2$

6. $(-x + 3)^2$

Explain 2 Multiplying $(a - b)^2$

In the Explore, you determined the square of a binomial difference, $(a - b)^2 = a^2 - 2ab + b^2$. Because $a^2 - 2ab + b^2$ is the result of squaring the binomial $(a - b)$, $a^2 - 2ab + b^2$ is also a perfect-square trinomial.

Example 2 **Multiply.**

(A) $(x - 5)^2$

$$(a - b)^2 = a^2 - 2ab + b^2$$
$$(x - 5)^2 = x^2 - 2(x)(5) + 5^2$$
$$= x^2 - 10x + 25$$

(B) $(6x - 1)^2$

$$(a - b)^2 = a^2 - 2ab + b^2$$
$$(6x - 1)^2 = (\square x)^2 - 2(\square x)(\square) + \square^2$$
$$= \square x^2 - \square x + \square$$

Reflect

7. Why is the last term of a perfect square trinomial always positive?

____

____

Your Turn

Multiply.

8. $(4x - 3y)^2$

9. $(3 - x^2)^2$

Explain 3 Multiplying $(a + b)(a - b)$

In the Explore, you determined the formula $(a + b)(a - b) = a^2 - b^2$. A binomial of the form $a^2 - b^2$ is called a **difference of two squares.**

Example 3 **Multiply.**

(A) $(x + 6)(x - 6)$

$$(a + b)(a - b) = a^2 - b^2$$
$$(x + 6)(x - 6) = x^2 - 6^2$$
$$= x^2 - 36$$

(B) $(x^2 + 2y)(x^2 - 2y)$

$$(a + b)(a - b) = a^2 - b^2$$
$$(x^2 + 2y)(x^2 - 2y) = (\square)^2 - (\square)^2$$
$$= \square x^{\square} - \square y^{\square}$$

Reflect

10. Why does the product of $a + b$ and $a - b$ always include a minus sign?

____

Your Turn

11. $(7 + x)(7 - x)$

Explain 4 Modeling with Special Products

Example 4 **Write and simplify an expression to represent the situation.**

Design A designer adds a border with a uniform width to a square rug. The original side length of the rug is $(x - 5)$ feet. The side length of the entire rug including the original rug and the border is $(x + 5)$ feet. What is the area of the border? Evaluate the area of the border if $x = 10$ feet.

Analyze Information

Identify the important information.

The answer will be an expression that represents the area of the border.

List the important information:

- The rug is a square with a side length of $\square$ feet.
- The side length of the entire square area including the original rug and the border is $\square$ feet.

Formulate a Plan

The area of the rug in square feet is $(\square)^2$. The total area of the rug plus the border in square feet is $(\square)^2$. The area of the rug can be subtracted from the total area to find the area of the border.

Solve

Find the total area:

$(x + 5)^2 = \square x^2 + 2(\square)(\square) + \square^2$

$= \square x^2 + \square x + \square$

Find the area of the rug:

$(x - 5)^2 = \square x^2 - 2(\square)(\square) + (\square)^2$

$= \square x^2 - \square x + \square$

Find the area of the border:

Area of border = total area – area of rug

Area $= \square x^2 + \square x + \square - (\square x^2 - \square x + \square)$

$= \square x^2 + \square x + \square - \square x^2 + \square x - \square$

$= (\square x^2 - \square x^2) + (\square x + \square x) + (\square - \square)$

$= \square x^2 + \square x + \square$

$= \square x$

The area of the border is $\square x^2 + \square x + \square = \square$ square feet.

Justify and Evaluate

Suppose that $x = 10$. The rug is $\square$ feet by $\square$ feet, so its area is $\square$ square feet. The total area is $(\square + \square)^2 = \square$ square feet, so the area of the border is $\square - \square = \square$ square feet, which is $\square(10)$ when $x = 10$. So the answer makes sense.

Reflect

12. Critique Reasoning Estelle solved a problem just like the example, except that the value of b in the two expressions was 8. Her expression for the area of the border was $-32x$. How do you know that she made an error? What do you think her error might have been?

Your Turn

Write and simplify an expression.

13. A square patio has a side length of $(x - 3)$ feet. It is surrounded by a flower garden with a uniform width. The side length of the entire square area including the patio and the flower garden is $(x + 3)$ feet. Write an expression for the area of the flower garden.

Elaborate

14. How can you use the formula for the square of a binomial sum to write a formula for the square of a binomial difference?

15. Can you use the formula for the square of a binomial sum to write a formula for a difference of squares?

16. Essential Question Check-In Use one of the special product rules to describe in words how to find the coefficient of xy in the product $(5x - 3y)^2$.

Evaluate: Homework and Practice

Personal Math Trainer

- Online Homework
- Hints and Help
- Extra Practice

Multiply.

1. $(x+8)^2$

2. $(4x+6y)^2$

3. $(6+x^2)^2$

4. $(-x+5)^2$

5. $(x+11)^2$

6. $(8x+9y)^2$

7. $(x-3)^2$

8. $(5x-2)^2$

9. $(6x-7y)^2$

10. $(5-x^2)^2$

11. $(5x-4y)^2$

12. $(7-2x^2)^2$

13. $(x + 4)(x - 4)$

14. $(x^2 + 6y)(x^2 - 6y)$

15. $(9 + x)(9 - x)$

16. $(2x + 5)(2x - 5)$

17. $(3x^2 + 8y)(3x^2 - 8y)$

18. $(7 + 3x)(7 - 3x)$

Write and simplify an expression to represent the situation.

19. Design A square swimming pool is surrounded by a cement walkway with a uniform width. The swimming pool has a side length of $(x - 2)$ feet. The side length of the entire square area including the pool and the walkway is $(x + 1)$ feet. Write an expression for the area of the walkway. Then find the area of the cement walkway when $x = 7$ feet.

20. This week Leo worked $(x + 4)$ hours at a pizzeria. He is paid $(x - 4)$ dollars per hour. Leo's friend Frankie worked the same number of hours, but he is paid $(x - 2)$ dollars per hour. Write an expression for the total amount paid to the two workers. Then find the total amount if $x = 12$ dollars.

21. Kyra is framing a square painting with side lengths of $(x + 8)$ inches. The total area of the painting and the frame has a side length of $(2x - 6)$ inches. The material for the frame will cost \$0.08 per square inch. Write an expression for the area of the frame. Then find the cost of the material for the frame if $x = 16$.

22. Geometry Circle A has a radius of $(x + 4)$ units. A larger circle, B, has a radius of $(x + 5)$ units. Use the formula $A = \pi r^2$ to write an expression for the difference in the areas of the circles. Leave your answer in terms of π. Then use 3.14 for π to approximate to the nearest whole number the difference in the areas when $x = 10$.

23. A square has sides with lengths of $(x - 1)$ units. A rectangle has a length of x units and a width of $(x - 2)$ units. Which statements about the situation are true? Select all that apply.

a. The area of the square is $(x^2 - 1)$ square units.

b. The area of the rectangle is $x^2 - 2x$ square units.

c. The area of the square is greater than the area of the rectangle.

d. The value of x must be greater than 2.

e. The difference in the areas is $2x - 1$.

24. Explain the Error Marco wrote the expression $(2x - 7y)^2 = 4x^2 - 49b^2$. Explain and correct his error.

H.O.T. Focus on Higher Order Thinking

25. Critical Thinking Use the FOIL method to justify each special product rule that $(a + b)^2 = a^2 + 2ab + b^2$.

a. $(a + b)^2$

b. $(a - b)^2$

c. $(a + b)(a - b)$

26. Communicate Mathematical Ideas Explain how you can use the special product rules and the Distributive Property to write a general rule for $(a - b)^3$. Then write the rule.

Lesson Performance Task

When building a square-shaped outdoor fireplace, the ground needs to be replaced with stone for an additional two feet on each side. Write a polynomial for the area that needs to be excavated to create an x by x fireplace.

Design your ideal space for sitting around a fire pit and relaxing. Add furniture, flowerbeds, rock gardens, and any other desired features.

Evaluate the polynomial for the size fireplace you are including.

STUDY GUIDE REVIEW

Multiplying Polynomials

MODULE 5

Essential Question: How can you use multiplying polynomials to solve real-world problems?

Key Vocabulary
difference of two squares *(diferencia de dos cuadrados)*
FOIL *(FOIL)*
perfect-square trinomial *(trinomio cuadrado perfecto)*

KEY EXAMPLE (Lesson 5.1)

Multiply.

$\left(-3x^2y^4\right)\left(-6x^3y\right)$

$\left(-3 \cdot -6\right)\left(x^2 \cdot x^3\right)\left(y^4 \cdot y\right)$ *Gather terms with the same base.*

$\left(-3 \cdot -6\right)\left(x^{2+3}\right)\left(y^{4+1}\right)$ *Apply the product of powers rule: $a^m \cdot a^n = a^{m+n}$.*

$18x^5y^5$

KEY EXAMPLE (Lesson 5.2)

Multiply.

$(3x + 7)(x - 1)$

$= 3x^2 - 3x + 7x - 7$

$= 3x^2 + 4x - 7$

Multiply using FOIL.

First terms $(3x \cdot x)$ Outer terms $(3x \cdot -1)$ Inner terms $(7 \cdot x)$ and Last terms $(7 \cdot -1)$

$(4x - 2)(-2x - 9)$

$= (4x)(-2x) + (4x)(-9) + (-2)(-2x) + (-2)(-9)$

$= -8x^2 - 36x + 4x + 18$

$= -8x^2 - 32x + 18$

KEY EXAMPLE (Lesson 5.3)

Multiply

$(x - 7)(x + 7)$

$= x^2 - 7^2$

$= x^2 - 49$

The product will be the difference of two squares.

$(a + b) = (a - b) = a^2 - b^2$

$(2x + 5)^2$

$= (2x)^2 + 2(2x)(5) + 5^2$

$= 4x^2 + 20x + 25$

The product will be a perfect-square trinomial.

$(a + b)^2 = a^2 + 2ab + b^2$

EXERCISES

Multiply. *(Lessons 5.1, 5.2)*

1. $(7y^5)(-4y^2)$

2. $(3p^4q)(12p^3q^2)$

3. $(x-4)(x+8)$

4. $(4x-1)(2x+6)$

Multiply. Identify each product as a perfect-square trinomial or a difference of squares. *(Lesson 5.3)*

5. $(3x+9)(3x-9)$

6. $(x-8)^2$

MODULE PERFORMANCE TASK

Orange Consumption

About how much do Americans spend per capita on oranges each year? The average price of oranges was $0.57 per pound in 2004 and has been increasing at a rate of $0.02 per year. The table below shows the per capita orange consumption (in pounds) in the United States from 2004–2012.

Year	2004	2005	2006	2007	2008	2009	2010	2011	2012
Pounds Consumed	83.6	80.3	72.8	65.2	62.3	62.7	61.8	62.3	54.9

How can you use this data to find a model and use it to predict how much money the average American spent on oranges in 2014?

Use your own paper to complete the task. Be sure to write down all your data and assumptions. Then use graphs, numbers, words, or algebra to explain how you reached your conclusion.

Ready to Go On?

5.1–5.3 Multiplying Polynomials

Personal Math Trainer
- Online Homework
- Hints and Help
- Extra Practice

Multiply. Identify each product as a perfect-square trinomial, a difference of squares, or neither. ***(Lessons 5.1, 5.2, 5.3)***

1. $(2y - 5)(2y + 5)$

2. $(9r^3s^3)(10r^3s^2)$

3. $(4x + 1)^2$

4. $(3x - 4)(x + 8)$

Use the model of the rectangular prism to answer 5 and 6. The width of the prism is $(2x - 2)$ ft, and its height is $(x + 6)$ ft. The area of the base of the prism is $(3x^2 + 2x - 4)$ ft².

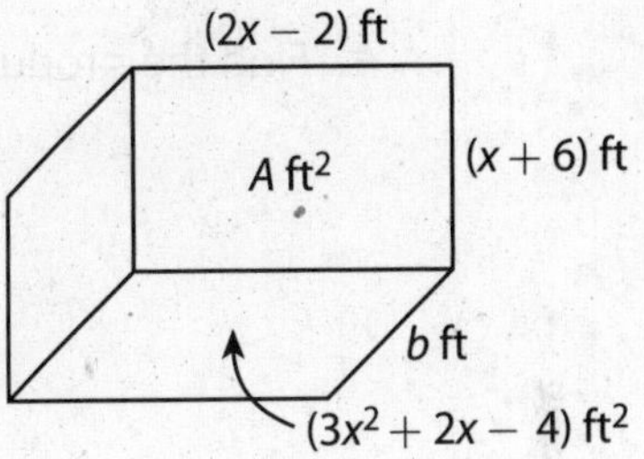

5. Write an expression to represent the area of side A. ***(Lesson 5.3)***

6. Could the length of b be $(3x - 1)$ ft? Explain why or why not. ***(Lesson 5.3)***

ESSENTIAL QUESTION

7. Is it necessary to use the formulas for special products of binomials to multiply these binomials? Explain.

MODULE 5
MIXED REVIEW

Assessment Readiness

1. Find the standard form for the product of $(x^2 + 8)$ and $(x^2 - 2)$. Choose True or False for each statement about the product.

   A. It is a 4th degree polynomial. ○ True ○ False

   B. The constant term is -16. ○ True ○ False

   C. It has 3 terms. ○ True ○ False

2. Multiply $(5x - 9)^2$. Choose True or False for each statement about the product.

   A. The coefficient of the x-term is -45. ○ True ○ False

   B. The leading term is $25x^2$. ○ True ○ False

   C. The constant term is 81. ○ True ○ False

3. Find the product $(3x + 6)(3x - 6)$. Show your work.

4. Find the product $(x + 10)(4x + 5)$. Show your work.

5. A rectangle has a length $(x + 6)$ m and a width of 7 m. Write expressions to represent the perimeter and area of the rectangle. Explain how you determined your answers.

UNIT 2 MIXED REVIEW

Assessment Readiness

Personal Math Trainer

- Online Homework
- Hints and Help
- Extra Practice

1. Solve each equation. Is the correct solution given?

A. $-4(p+3) = -3p - 7; p = -5$ ○ Yes ○ No

B. $8r - 18 = -14; r = \frac{1}{2}$ ○ Yes ○ No

C. $\frac{t}{5} - 2 = -5; t = 15$ ○ Yes ○ No

2. Simplify $5x^2\left(\frac{2}{5} - x\right)$. Determine if each statement is True or False.

A. The expression is a trinomial. ○ True ○ False

B. The expression has a degree of 3. ○ True ○ False

C. The expression has a constant of -2. ○ True ○ False

3. Is the given polynomial in standard form?

A. $-5y^2 + 5y + 24$ ○ Yes ○ No

B. $7x^5 - 19 + x$ ○ Yes ○ No

C. $15z - 3$ ○ Yes ○ No

4. Simplify $(3x - 8)(x + 2)$. Is the given statement True or False?

A. The coefficient of the x-term is -2. ○ Yes ○ No

B. The leading term is $3x^2$. ○ Yes ○ No

C. The constant is -16. ○ Yes ○ No

5. Is the product of each of the following factors a difference of squares?

A. $3(x - 3)$ ○ Yes ○ No

B. $4(4x^2 - 1)$ ○ Yes ○ No

C. $(5x - 2)(5x + 2)$ ○ Yes ○ No

6. Write the difference of the following polynomials in standard form: $(11 - 8y + 2y^2) - (y^2 - 15)$. Classify the difference by its degree and the number of terms.

7. Sandra has been offered two jobs. Job A pays \$25,000 a year with an 8% raise each year. Job B pays \$28,000 a year with a \$2,500 raise each year. Write a function to represent each salary t years after being hired. Use a graphing calculator to compare the two salary plans. Will Job A ever have a higher salary than Job B? If so, after how many years will this occur? Explain how you solved this problem.

8.

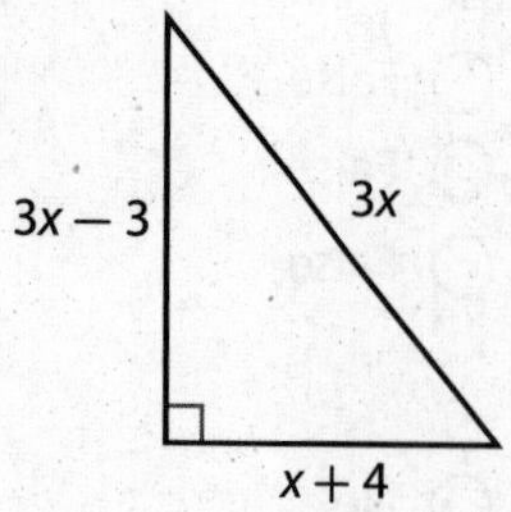

Write an expression that represents the perimeter of the triangle in terms of x and an expression that represents the area of the triangle in terms of x. If the perimeter is 36 cm, what is the area of the triangle? Explain how you solved this problem.

Performance Tasks

★ **9.** The profits of two different manufacturing plants can be modeled as shown.

Eastern: $-0.03x^2 + 25x - 1500$

Southern: $-0.02x^2 + 21x - 1700$

A. Write a polynomial that represents the difference of the profits at the Eastern plant and the profits at the Southern plant.

B. Write a polynomial that represents the total profits from both plants.

★★10. A rectangular swimming pool is 25 feet long and 10 feet wide. It is surrounded by a fence that is x feet from each side of the pool.

A. Draw a diagram of the situation.

B. Write expressions for the length, width, and area of the fenced region.

★★★11. Tammy plans to put a wallpaper border around the perimeter of her room. She will not put the border across the doorway, which is 3 feet wide.

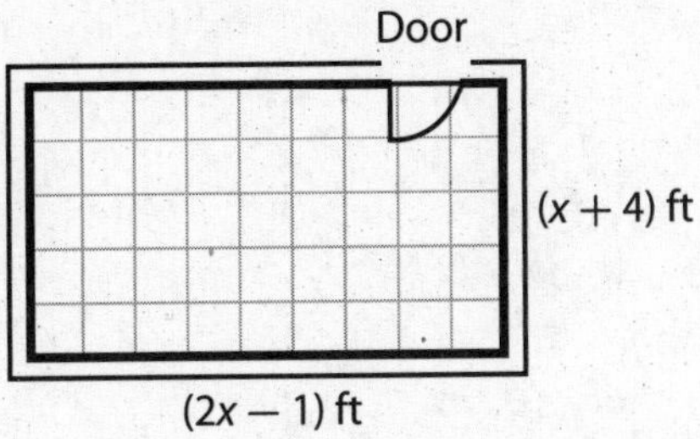

A. Write a polynomial that represents the number of feet of wallpaper border that Tammy will need.

B. A local store has 50 feet of the border that Tammy has chosen. What is the greatest whole-number value of x for which this amount would be enough for Tammy's room? Justify your answer.

C. Determine the dimensions of Tammy's room for the value of x that you found in part **B**.

MATH IN CAREERS

Camp Director For the initial year of a summer camp, 44 girls and 56 boys enrolled. Each year thereafter, 5 more girls and 8 more boys enrolled in the camp.

a. Let t be the time (in years) since the camp opened. Write a rule for each of the following functions:

- $g(t)$, the number of girls enrolled as a function of time t
- $b(t)$, the number of boys enrolled as a function of time t
- $T(t)$, the total enrollment as a function of time t

b. The cost per child each year was $200. Write a rule for each of the following functions:

- $C(t)$, the cost per child as a function of time t
- $R(t)$, the revenue generated by the total enrollment as a function of time t

c. Explain why $C(t)$ is a constant function.

d. What was the initial revenue for the camp? What was the annual rate of change in the revenue?

e. The camp director had initial expenses of $18,000, which increased each year by $2,500. Write a rule for the expenses function $E(t)$. Then write a rule for the profit function $P(t)$ based on the fact that profit is the difference between revenue and expenses.

UNIT 3

Quadratic Functions

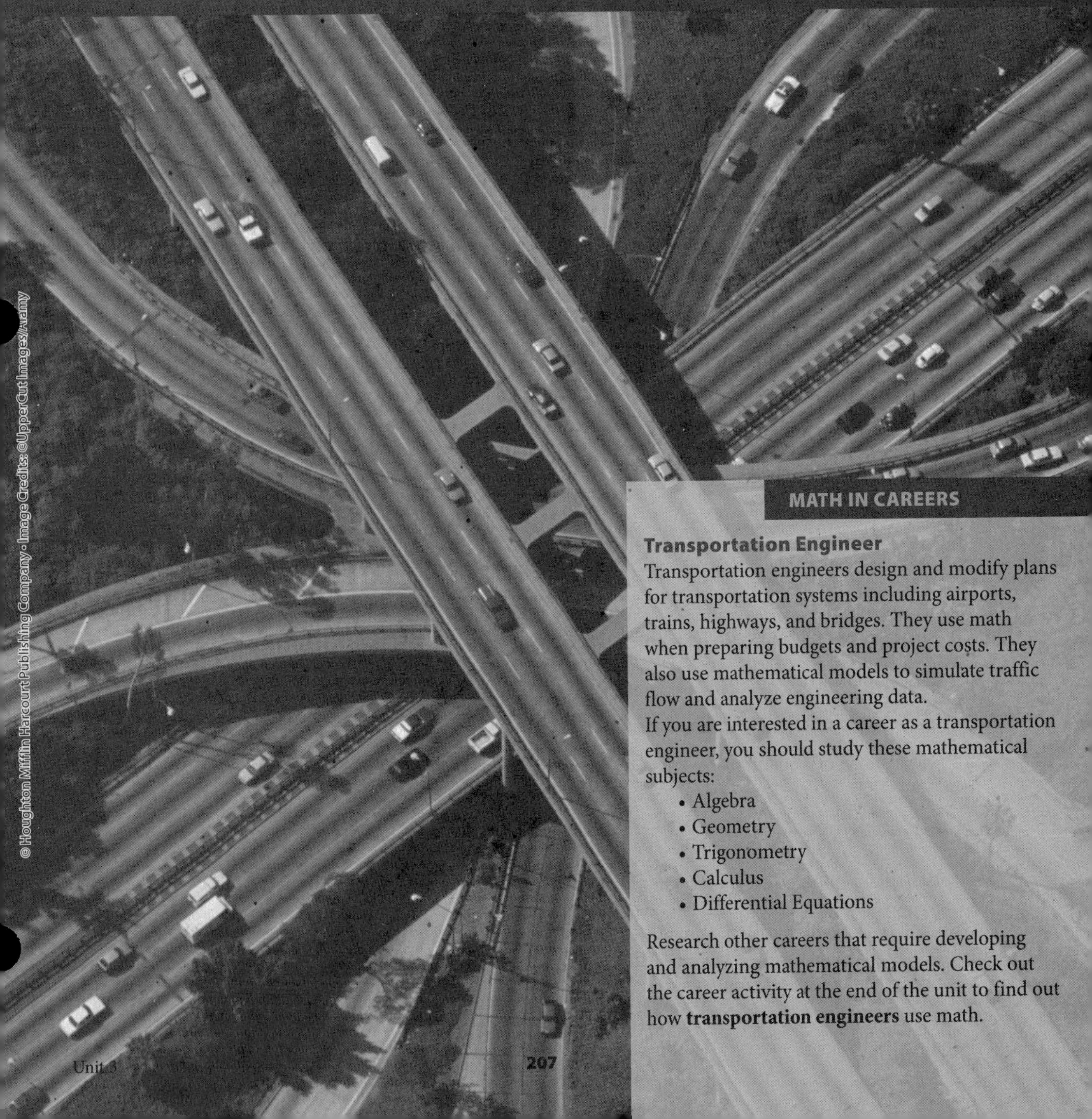

MATH IN CAREERS

Transportation Engineer
Transportation engineers design and modify plans for transportation systems including airports, trains, highways, and bridges. They use math when preparing budgets and project costs. They also use mathematical models to simulate traffic flow and analyze engineering data.

If you are interested in a career as a transportation engineer, you should study these mathematical subjects:

- Algebra
- Geometry
- Trigonometry
- Calculus
- Differential Equations

Research other careers that require developing and analyzing mathematical models. Check out the career activity at the end of the unit to find out how **transportation engineers** use math.

Reading Start-Up

Visualize Vocabulary

Use the ✔ words to complete the graphic. Write the name of a form of linear equation that best fits each equation.

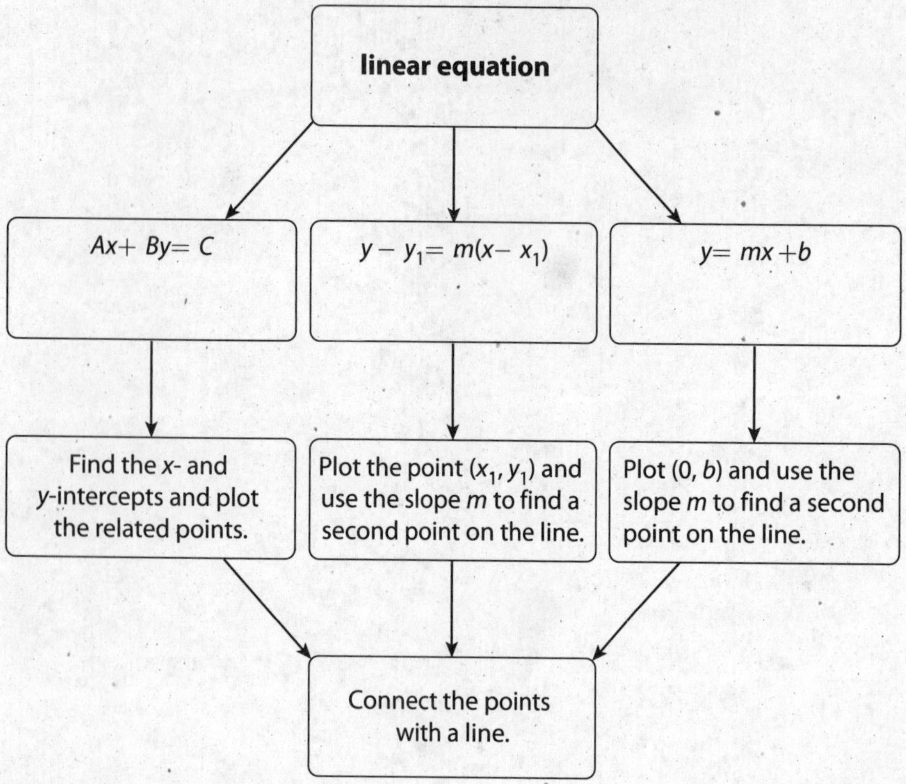

linear equation
Ax+ By= C
y − y1= m(x− x1)
y= mx +b
Find the x- and y-intercepts and plot the related points.
Plot the point (x1, y1) and use the slope m to find a second point on the line.
Plot (0, b) and use the slope m to find a second point on the line.
Connect the points with a line.

Vocabulary

Review Words

✔ point-slope form *(forma de punto y pendiente)*

✔ slope-intercept form *(forma de pendiente-intersección)*

✔ standard form *(forma estándar)*

x-intercept *(intersección con el eje x)*

y-intercept *(intersección con el eje y)*

Preview Words

intercept form of a quadratic equation *(forma en intersección de una función cuadrática)*

standard form of a quadratic equation *(forma estándar de una ecuación cuadrática)*

vertex form of a quadratic function *(forma en vértice de una función cuadrática)*

Understand Vocabulary

Match the term on the left to the example on the right.

1. ___ standard form of a quadratic equation A. $y = -(x - 2)^2 + 9$

2. ___ intercept form of a quadratic equation B. $y = -(x + 1)(x - 5)$

3. ___ vertex form of a quadratic function C. $y = -x^2 + 4x + 5$

Active Reading

Tri-Fold Before beginning the unit, create a tri-fold to help you learn the concepts and vocabulary in this unit. Fold the paper into three sections. Label the columns "What I Know, "What I Need to Know," and "What I Learned." Complete the first two columns before you read. After studying the unit, complete the third column.

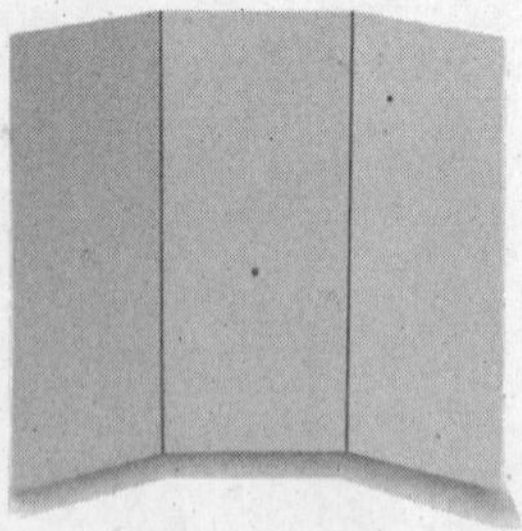

Graphing Quadratic Functions

MODULE 6

Essential Question: How can you use the graph of a quadratic function to solve real-world problems?

REAL WORLD VIDEO
Projectile motion describes the height of an object thrown or fired into the air. The height of a football, volleyball, or any projectile can be modeled by a quadratic equation.

MODULE PERFORMANCE TASK PREVIEW

Throwing for a Completion

Do you wonder how fast a football leaves the hands of a quarterback or how high up it goes? Some professionals can throw approximately 45 miles per hour or faster. The height the ball reaches depends on the initial velocity as well as the angle at which it was thrown. You can use a mathematical model to see how high a football is at different times.

Are YOU Ready?

Complete these exercises to review skills you will need for this module.

Personal Math Trainer

- Online Homework
- Hints and Help
- Extra Practice

Linear Functions

Example 1 Tell whether $6x - 2y = 9$ represents a linear function.

When a linear equation is written in standard form, the following are true.

- *x* and *y* both have exponents of 1.
- *x* and *y* are not multiplied together.
- *x* and *y* do not appear in denominators, exponents, or radicands.

$6x - 2y = 9$ represents a linear function.

Tell whether the equation represents a linear function.

1. $y = 3x^2 + 4x + 1$ ______ **2.** $3y = 12 - \frac{1}{2}x$ ______ **3.** $y = 2x + 5$ ______

Algebraic Representations of Transformations

Example 2 The vertices of a triangle are $A(-3, 1)$, $B(0, -2)$, and $C(-4, 2)$. Find the vertices if the figure is translated by the rule $(x, y) \rightarrow (x + 4, y - 3)$.

A $(-3, 1) \rightarrow A'(-3 + 4, 1 - 3)$, so $A'(1, -2)$

B $(0, -2) \rightarrow B'(0 + 4, -2 - 3)$, so $B'(4, -5)$

C $(-4, 2) \rightarrow C'(-4 + 4, 2 - 3)$, so $C'(0, -1)$

Add 4 to each *x*-coordinate and subtract 3 from each *y*-coordinate.

The vertices of a triangle are $A(0, 3)$, $B(-2, -4)$, and $C(1, 5)$. Find the new vertices.

4. Use the rule $(x, y) \rightarrow (x - 2, y + 4)$ to translate each vertex.

______

5. Use the rule $(x, y) \rightarrow (x + 1, y - 2)$ to translate each vertex.

______

Algebraic Expressions

Example 3 Find the value of $x^2 + 5x - 3$ when $x = 2$.

$x^2 + 5x - 3$

$(2)^2 + 5(2) - 3$ Substitute 2 for *x*.

$4 + 10 - 3$ Follow the order of operations.

11

Find the value.

6. $x^2 - 7x + 9$ when $x = 6$ ______ **7.** $2x^2 + 4x - 7$ when $x = -3$ ______

Name______________________ Class______________ Date______________

6.1 Understanding Quadratic Functions

Essential Question: What is the effect of the constant a on the graph of $f(x) = ax^2$?

Resource Locker

Explore Understanding the Parent Quadratic Function

A function that can be represented in the form of $f(x) = ax^2 + bx + c$ is called a **quadratic function**. The terms a, b, and c, are constants where $a \neq 0$. The greatest exponent of the variable x is 2. The most basic quadratic function is $f(x) = x^2$, which is the parent quadratic function.

(A) Here is an incomplete table of values for the parent quadratic function. Complete it.

x	$f(x) = x^2$
−3	$f(x) = x^2 = (-3)^2 = 9$
	4
−1	
0	0
1	1
2	
3	

(B) Plot the ordered pairs as points on the graph, and connect the points to sketch a curve.

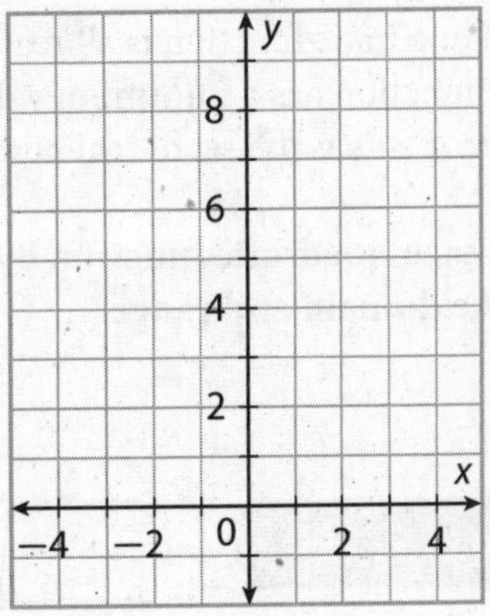

The curve is called a **parabola**. The point through which the parabola turns direction is called its **vertex**. The vertex occurs at $(0, 0)$ for this function. A vertical line that passes through the vertex and divides the parabola into two symmetrical halves is called the **axis of symmetry**. For this function, the axis of symmetry is the y-axis.

Reflect

1. **Discussion** What is the domain of $f(x) = x^2$?

____

2. **Discussion** What is the range of $f(x) = x^2$?

____

Explain 1 Graphing $g(x) = ax^2$ when $a > 0$

The graph $g(x) = ax^2$, is a vertical stretch or compression of its parent function $f(x) = x^2$. The graph opens upward when $a > 0$.

Vertical Stretch

$g(x) = ax^2$ with $|a| > 1$.

The graph of $g(x)$ is narrower than the parent function $f(x)$.

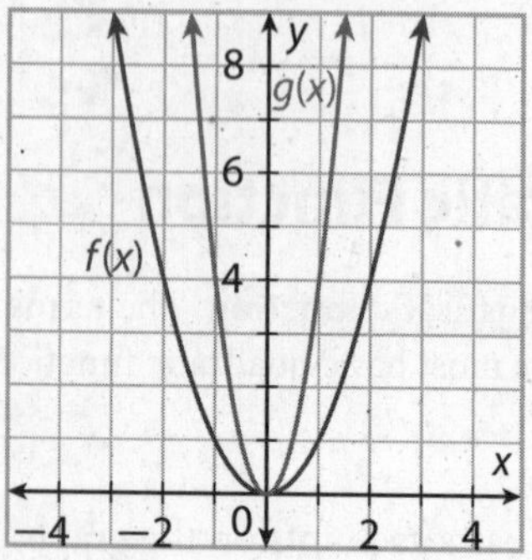

Vertical Compression

$g(x) = ax^2$ with $0 < |a| < 1$.

The graph of $g(x)$ is wider than the parent function $f(x)$.

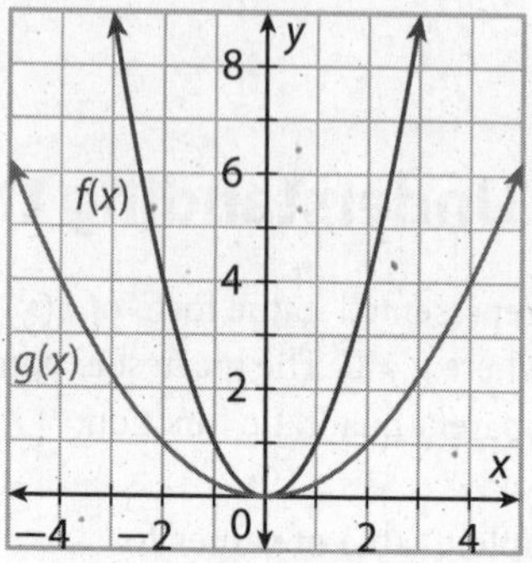

The domain of a quadratic function is all real numbers. When $a > 0$, the graph of $g(x) = ax^2$ opens upward, and the function has a **minimum value** that occurs at the vertex of the parabola. So, the range of $g(x) = ax^2$, where $a > 0$, is the set of real numbers greater than or equal to the minimum value.

Example 1 **Graph each quadratic function by plotting points and sketching the curve. State the domain and range.**

(A) $g(x) = 2x^2$

x	$g(x) = 2x^2$
−3	18
−2	8
−1	2
0	0
1	2
2	8
3	18

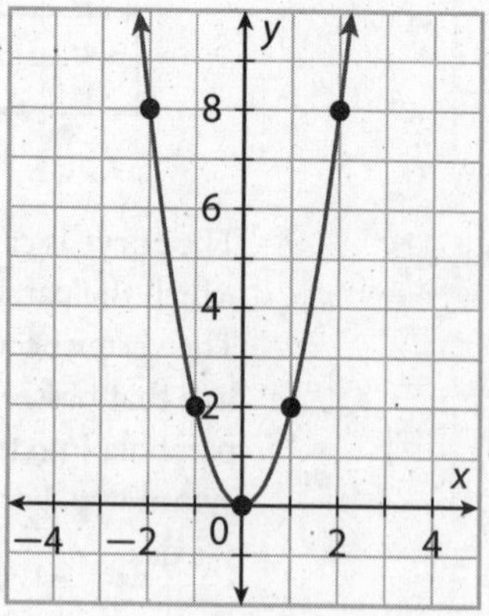

Domain: all real numbers x

Range: $y \geq 0$

(B) $g(x) = \frac{1}{2}x^2$

x	$g(x) = \frac{1}{2}x^2$
−3	
−2	
0	
2	
3	

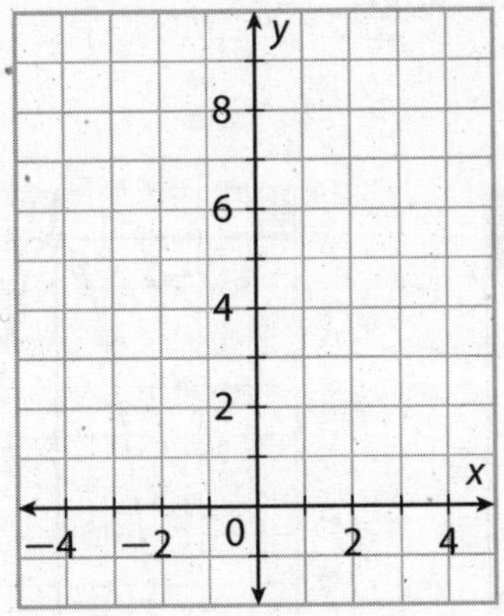

Domain: ______

Range: ______

Reflect

3. For a graph that has a vertical compression or stretch, does the axis of symmetry change?

______

Your Turn

Graph each quadratic function. State the domain and range.

4. $g(x) = 3x^2$

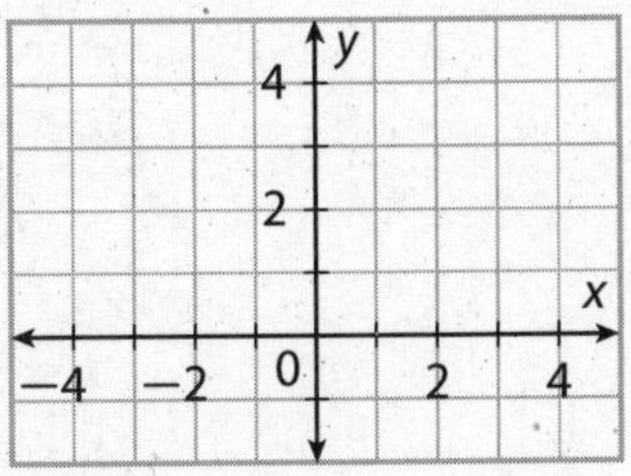

5. $g(x) = \frac{1}{3}x^2$

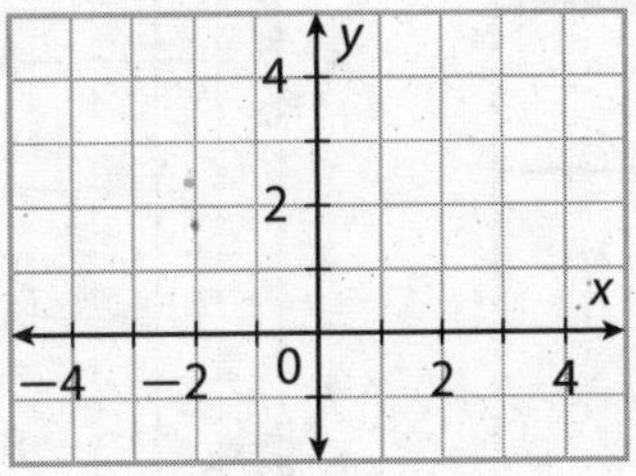

Explain 2 Graphing $g(x) = ax^2$ when $a < 0$

The graph of $y = -x^2$ opens downward. It is a reflection of the graph of $y = x^2$ across the x-axis. So, When $a < 0$, the graph of $g(x) = ax^2$ opens downward, and the function has a **maximum value** that occurs at the vertex of the parabola. In this case, the range is the set of real numbers less than or equal to the maximum value.

Vertical Stretch

$g(x) = ax^2$ with $|a| > 1$.

The graph of $g(x)$ is narrower than the parent function $f(x)$.

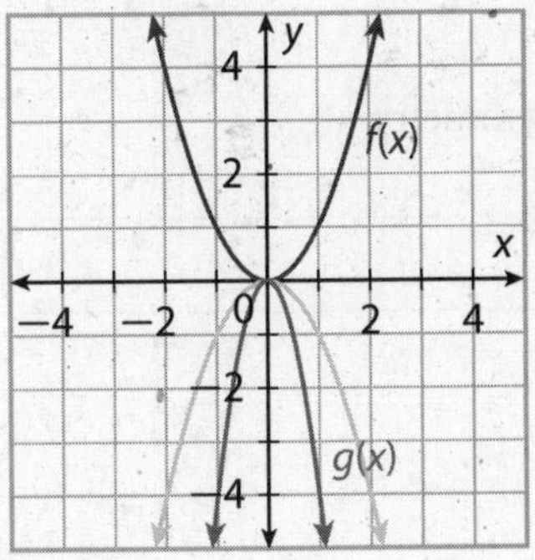

Vertical Compression

$g(x) = ax^2$ with $0 < |a| < 1$.

The graph of $g(x)$ is wider than the parent function $f(x)$.

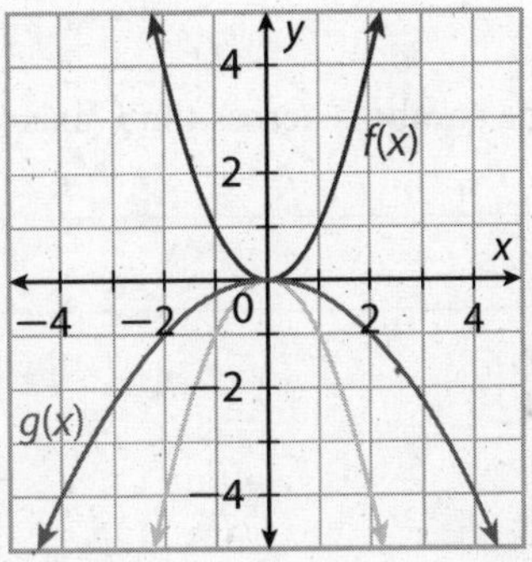

Example 2 **Graph each quadratic function by plotting points and sketching the curve. State the domain and range.**

(A) $g(x) = -2x^2$

x	$g(x) = 2x^2$
−3	−18
−2	−8
−1	−2
0	0
1	−2
2	−8
3	−18

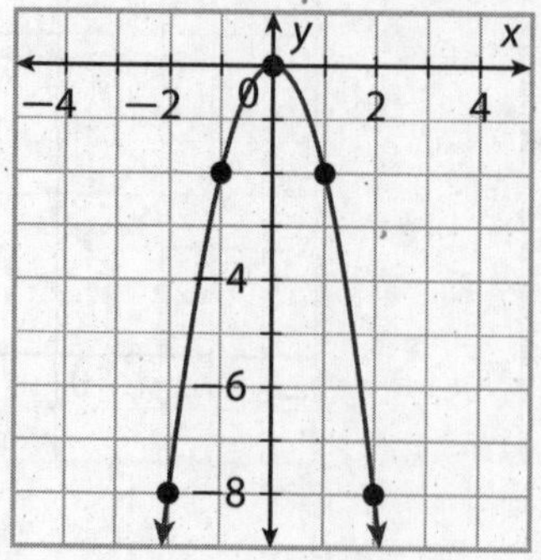

Domain: all real numbers

Range: $y \leq 0$

(B) $g(x) = -\frac{1}{2}x^2$

x	$g(x) = -\frac{1}{2}x^2$
−3	
−2	
−1	
0	
1	
2	
3	

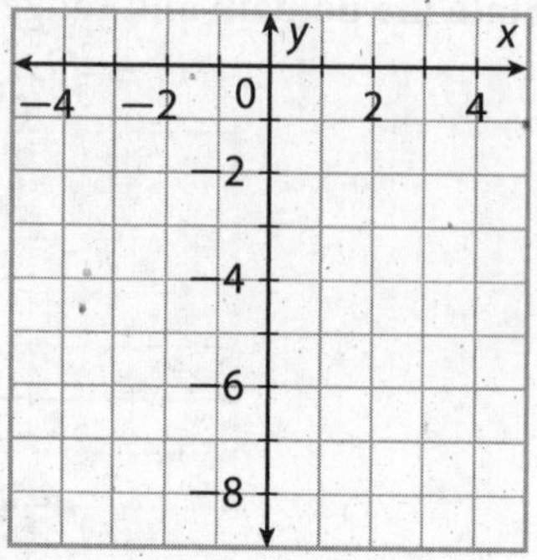

Domain: ______________

Range: ______________

Reflect

6. Does reflecting the parabola across the x-axis ($a < 0$) change the axis of symmetry?

____

____

Your Turn

Graph each function. State the domain and range.

7. $g(x) = -3x^2$

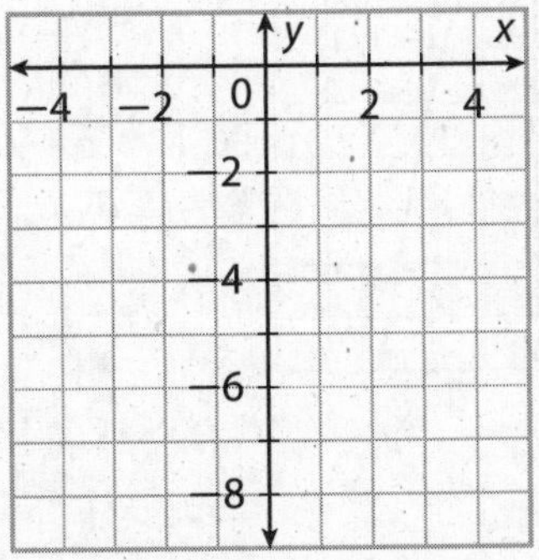

8. $g(x) = -\frac{1}{3}x^2$

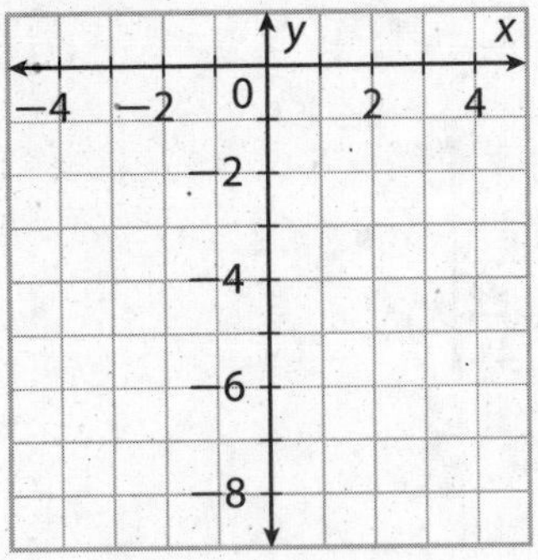

Explain 3 Writing a Quadratic Function Given a Graph

You can determine a function rule for a parabola with its vertex at the origin by substituting x and y values for any other point on the parabola into $g(x) = ax^2$ and solving for a.

Example 3 **Write the rule for the quadratic functions shown on the graph.**

(A)

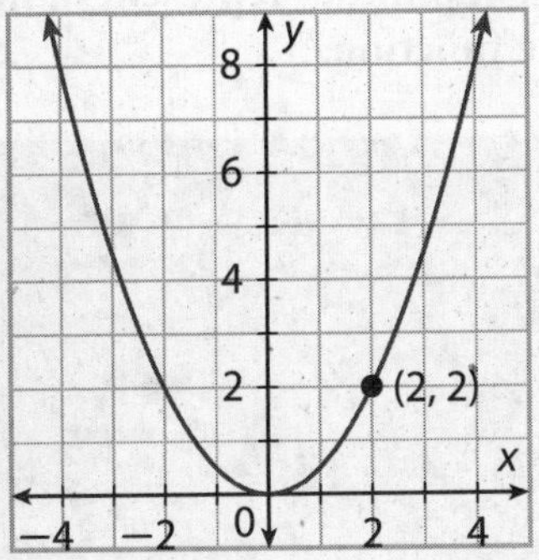

Use the point (2, 2).

Start with the functional form.	$g(x) = ax^2$
Replace x and $g(x)$ with point values.	$2 = a(2)^2$
Evaluate x^2.	$2 = 4a$
Divide both sides by 4 to isolate a.	$\frac{1}{2} = a$
Write the function rule.	$g(x) = \frac{1}{2}x^2$

(B)

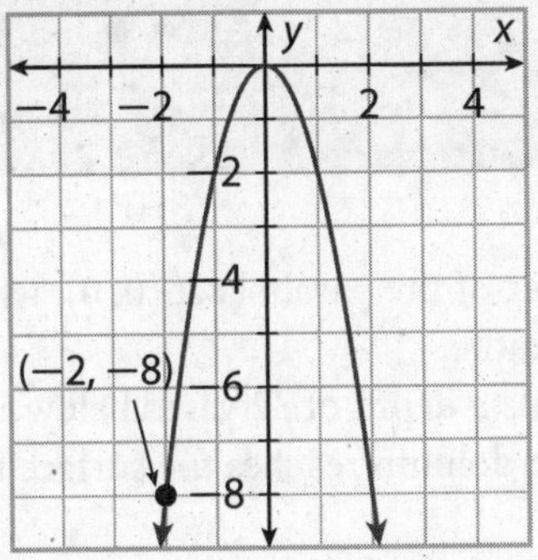

Use the point $\left(-2, \square\right)$.

Start with the functional form.	$g(x) = ax^2$
Replace x and $g(x)$ with point values.	$\square = a\left(\square\right)^2$
Evaluate x^2.	$-8 = \square a$
Divide both sides by $\square$ to isolate a.	$\square = a$
Write the function rule.	$g(x) = \square$

Your Turn

9.

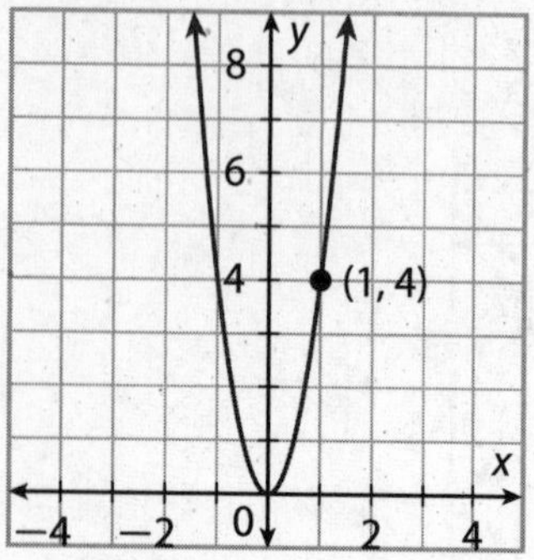

10.

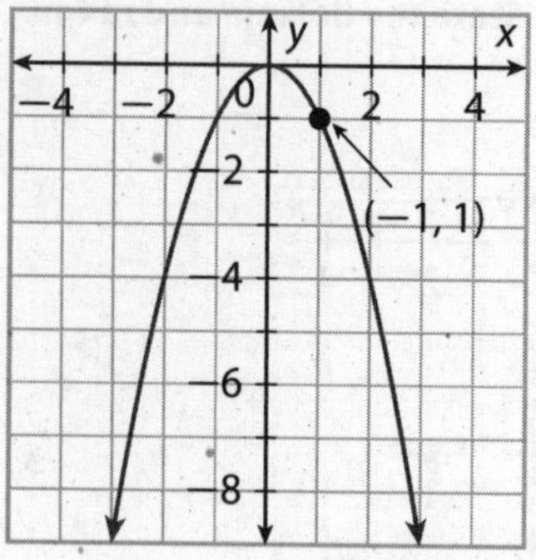

Explain 4 Modeling with a Quadratic Function

Real-world situations can be modeled by parabolas.

Example 4 **For each model, describe what the vertex, y-intercept, and endpoint(s) represent in the situation it models, and then determine the equation of the function.**

(A) This graph models the depth in yards below the water's surface of a dolphin before and after it rises to take a breath and descends again. The depth d is relative to time t, in seconds, and $t = 0$ is when dolphin reaches a depth of 0 yards at the surface.

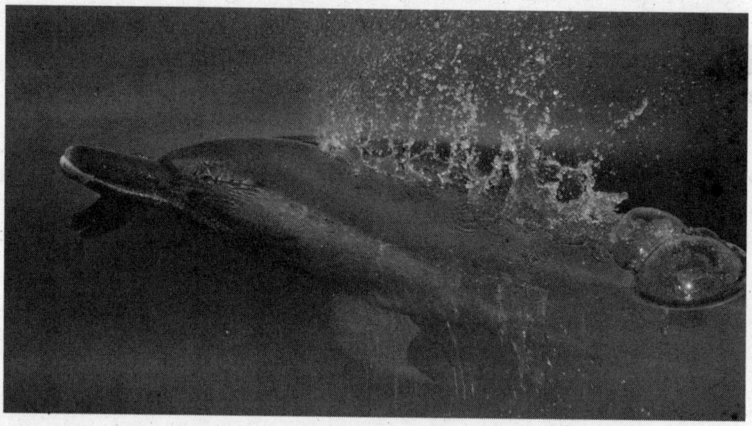

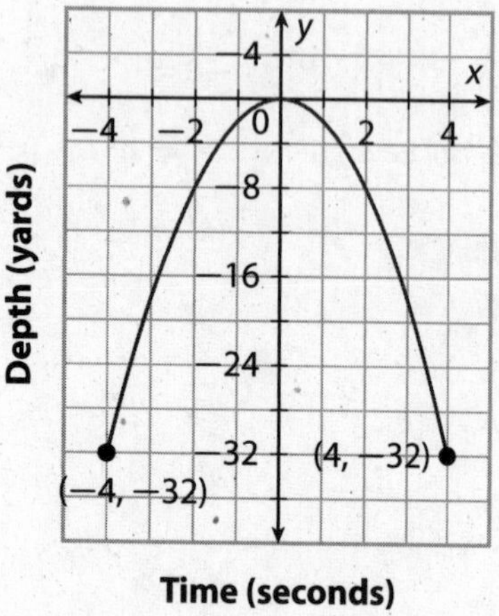

The y-intercept occurs at the vertex of the parabola at $(0, 0)$, where the dolphin is at the surface to breathe.

The endpoint $(-4, -32)$ represents a depth of 32 yards below the surface at 4 seconds before the dolphin reaches the surface to breathe.

The endpoint $(4, -32)$ represents a depth of 32 yards below the surface at 4 seconds after the dolphin reaches the surface to breathe.

The graph is symmetric about the y-axis with the vertex at the origin, so the function will be of the form $y = ax^2$, or $d(t) = at^2$.

Use a point to determine the equation.

$d(t) = at^2$

$-32 = a(4)^2$

$-32 = a \cdot 16$

$-2 = a$

The function is $d(t) = -2t^2$.

B) Satellite dishes reflect radio waves onto a collector by using a reflector (the dish) shaped like a parabola. The graph shows the height h in feet of the reflector relative to the distance x in feet from the center of the satellite dish.

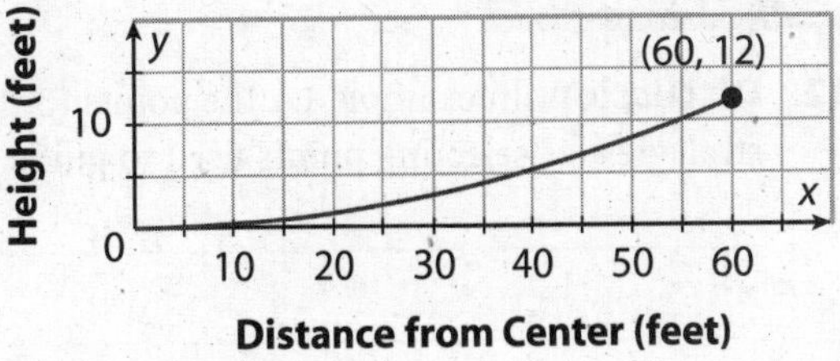

The y-intercept occurs at the vertex, which represents the distance $x =$ ___ feet from the center of the dish.
The left endpoint represents the height $h =$ ___ feet at the center of the dish.
The right endpoint represents the height $h =$ ___ feet at the distance $x =$ ___ feet from the center of the dish.
The function will be of the form __________. Use (☐ , ☐) to determine the equation.

$h(x) = ax^2$

$\square = a\left(\square\right)^2$

$12 = \square\, a$

$\square = \frac{1}{300}$

$h(x) = \square\, x^2$

Your Turn

11. The graph shows the height h in feet of a rock dropped down a deep well as a function of time t in seconds.

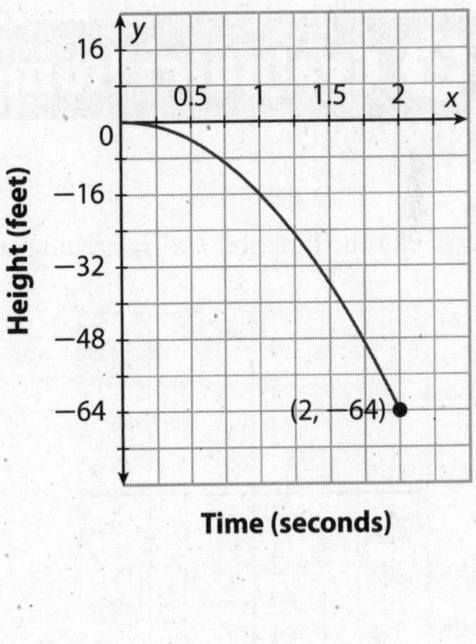

Elaborate

12. Discussion In example 1A the points (3, 18) and (−3, 18) did not fit on the grid. Describe some strategies for selecting points used to guide the shape of the curve.

13. Describe how the axis of symmetry of the parabola sitting on the y-axis can be used to help plot the graph of $f(x) = ax^2$.

14. Essential Question Check-In How can you use the value of a to predict the shape of $f(x) = ax^2$ without plotting points?

Evaluate: Homework and Practice

Personal Math Trainer

- Online Homework
- Hints and Help
- Extra Practice

1. Plot the function $f(x) = x^2$ and $g(x) = -x^2$ on the grid.

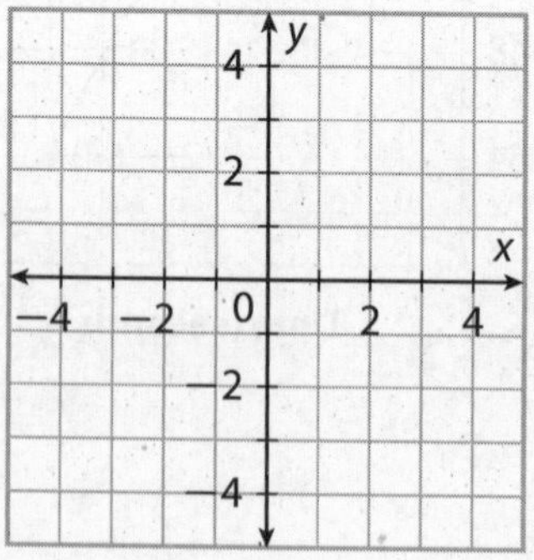

Which of the following features are the same and which are different for the two functions?

a. Domain

b. Range

c. Vertex

d. Axis of symmetry

e. Minimum

f. Maximum

Graph each quadratic function. State the domain and range.

2. $g(x) = 4x^2$

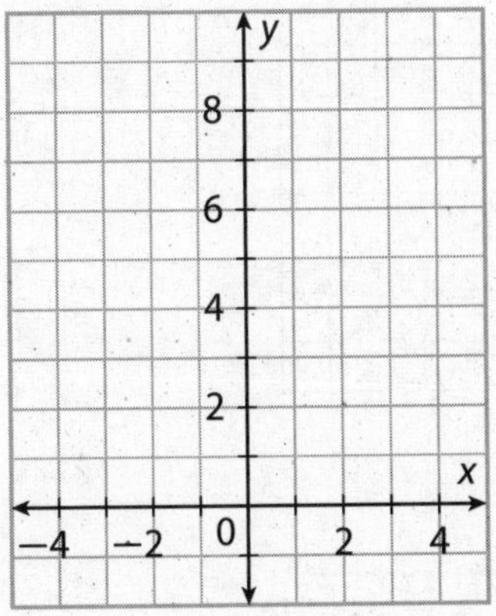

3. $g(x) = \frac{1}{4}x^2$

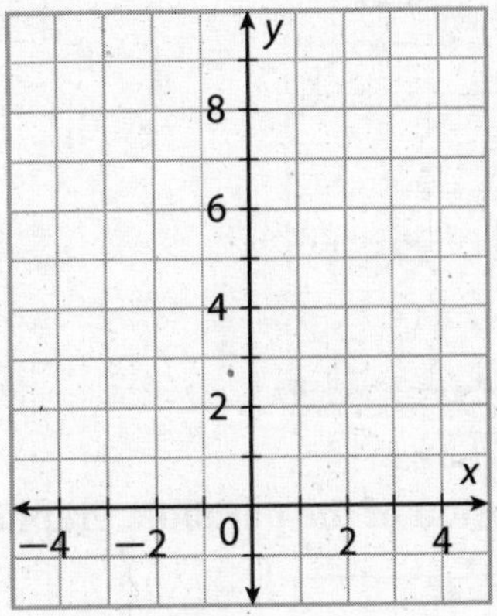

4. $g(x) = \frac{3}{2}x^2$

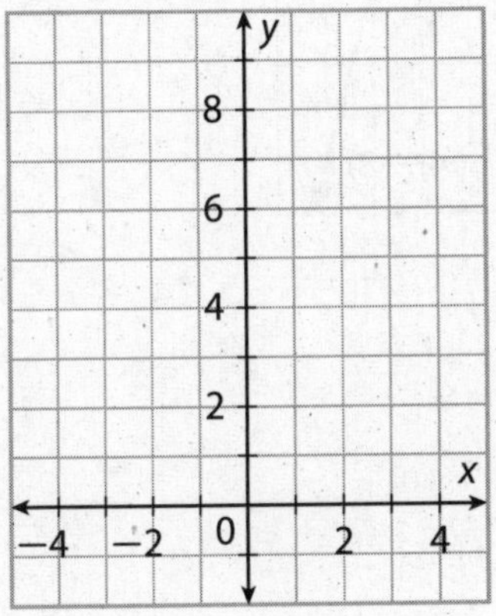

5. $g(x) = 5x^2$

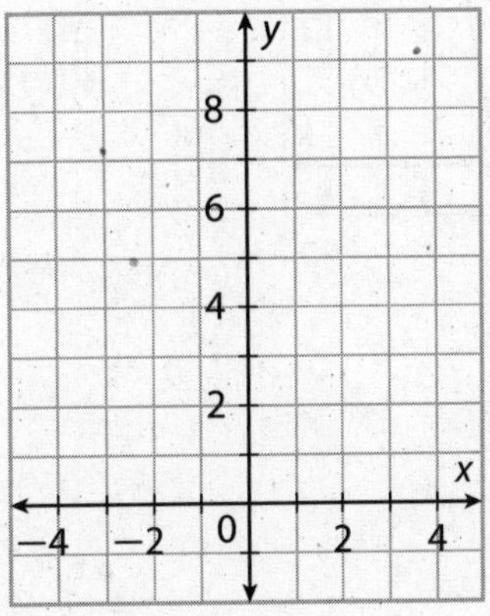

6. $g(x) = -\frac{1}{4}x^2$

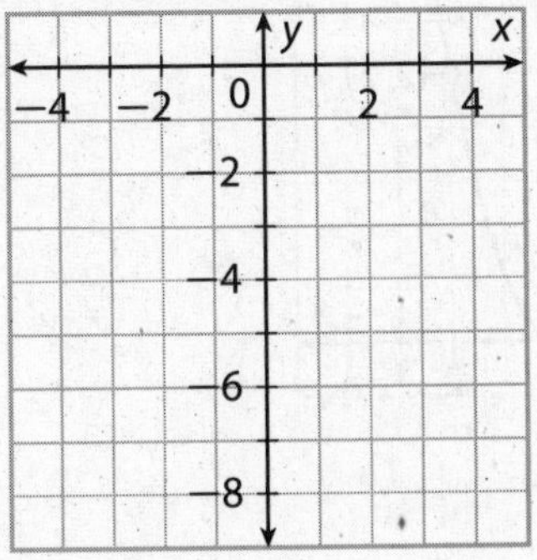

7. $g(x) = -4x^2$

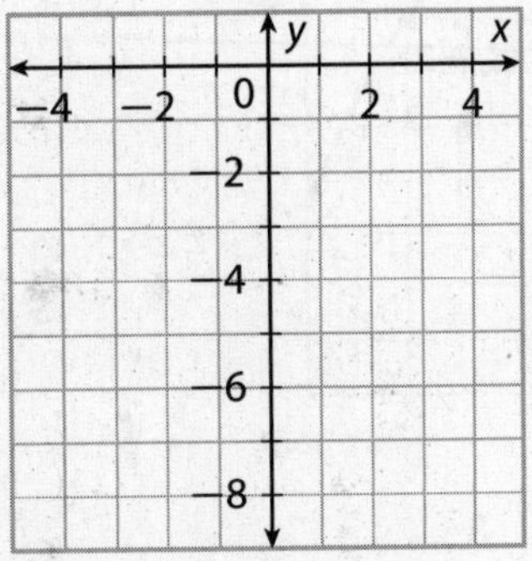

8. $g(x) = -\frac{3}{2}x^2$

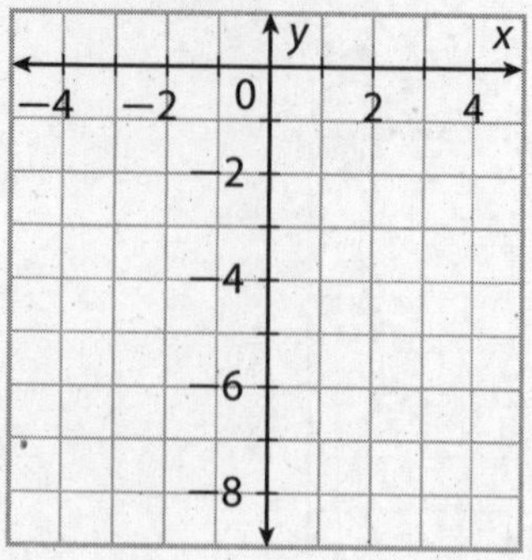

9. $g(x) = -5x^2$

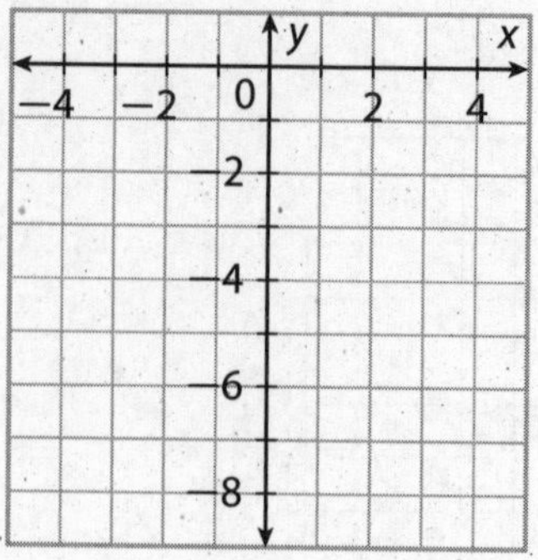

Determine the equation of the parabola graphed.

10.

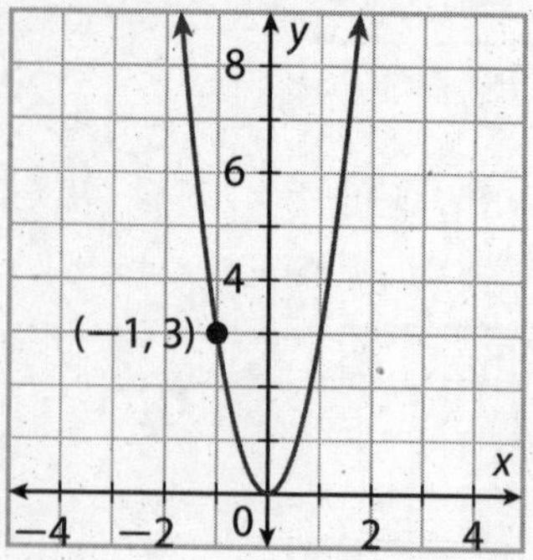

11.

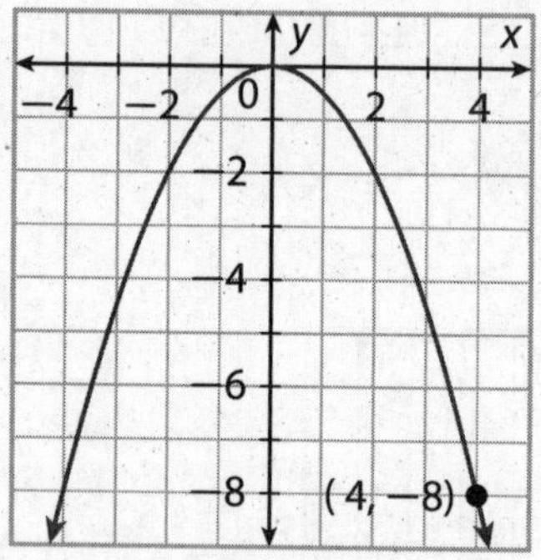

12.

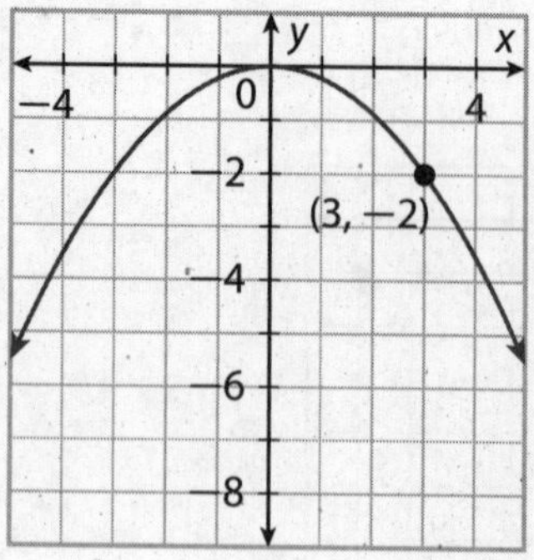

13.

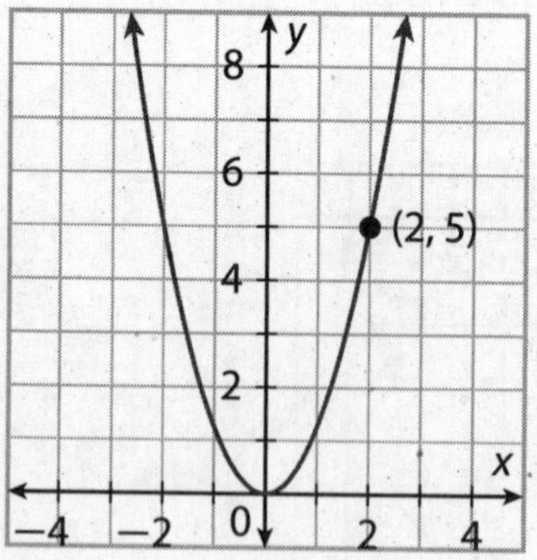

A cannonball fired horizontally appears to travel in a straight line, but drops to earth due to gravity, just like any other object in freefall. The height of the cannonball in freefall is parabolic. The graph shows the change in height of the cannonball (in meters) as a function of distance traveled (in kilometers). Refer to this graph for questions 14 and 15.

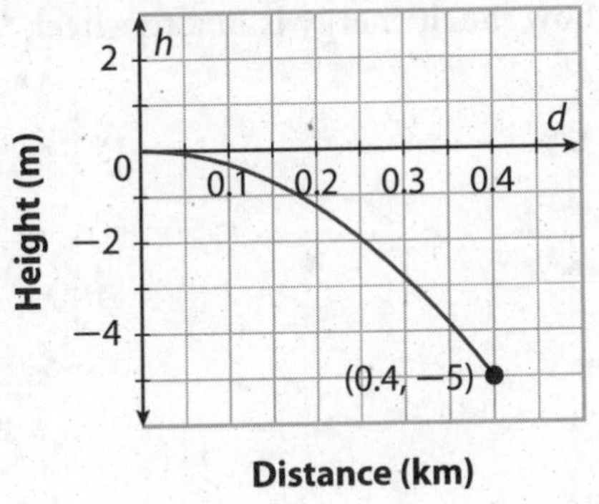

14. Describe what the vertex, y-intercept, and endpoint represent.

15. Find the function $h(d)$ that describes these coordinates.

A slingshot stores energy in the stretched elastic band when it is pulled back. The amount of stored energy versus the pull length is approximately parabolic. Questions 16 and 17 refer to this graph of the stored energy in millijoules versus pull length in centimeters.

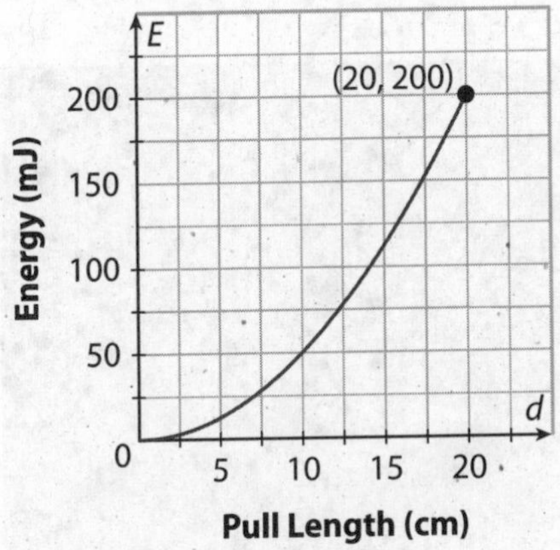

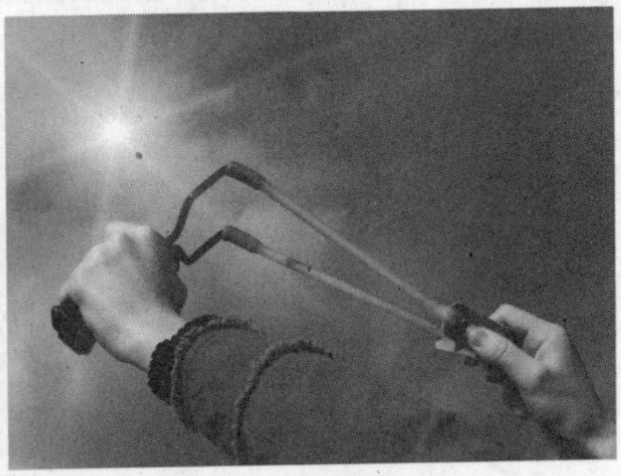

16. Describe what the vertex, y-intercept, and endpoint represent.

17. Determine the function, $E(d)$, that describes this plot.

Newer clean energy sources like solar and wind suffer from unsteady availability of energy. This makes it impractical to eliminate more traditional nuclear and fossil fuel plants without finding a way to store extra energy when it is not available.

One solution being investigated is storing energy in mechanical flywheels. Mechanical flywheels are heavy disks that store energy by spinning rapidly. The graph shows how much energy is in a flywheel, as a function of revolution speed.

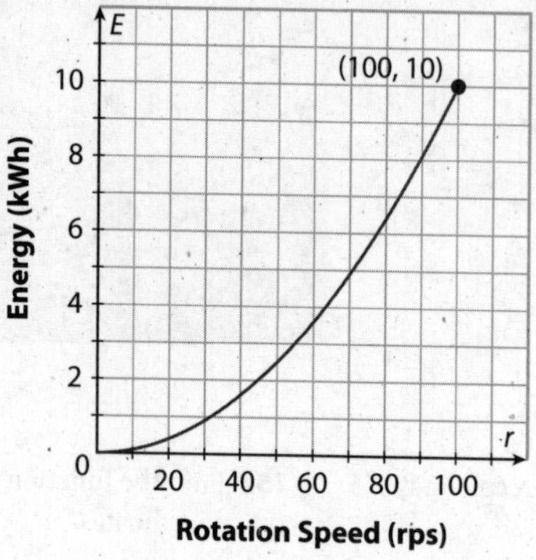

18. Describe what the vertex, y-intercept, and endpoint represent.

19. Determine the function, $E(r)$, that describes this plot.

Phineas is building a homemade skate ramp and wants to model the shape as a parabola. He sketches out a cross section shown in the graph.

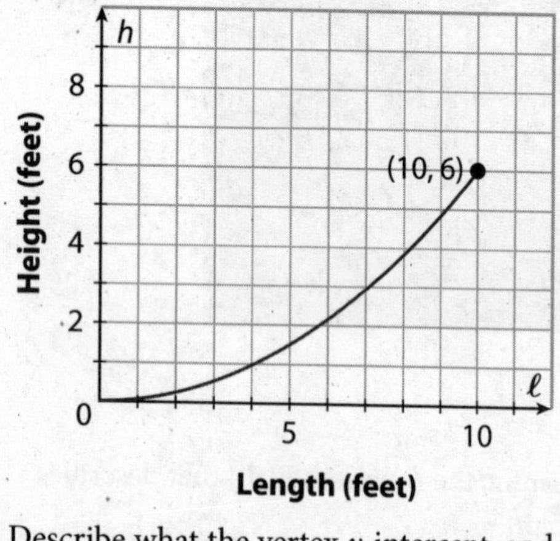

20. Describe what the vertex y-intercept, and endpoint represent.

21. Determine the function, $h(\ell)$, that describes this plot.

H.O.T. Focus on Higher Order Thinking

22. Multipart Classification

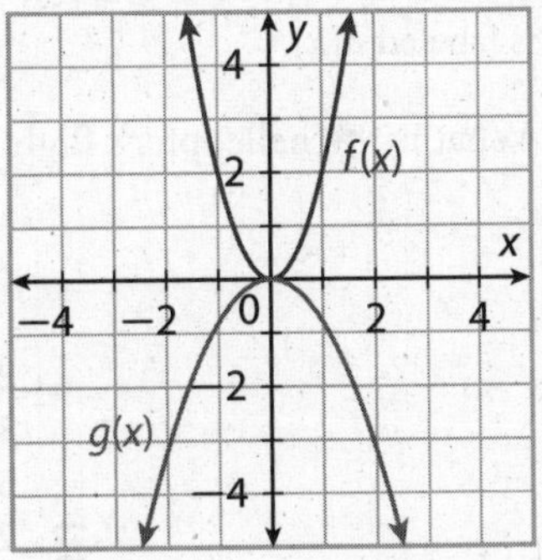

Mark the following statements about $f(x) = x^2$ and $g(x) = ax^2$ as true or false.

a. $a > 1$

b. $a < 0$

c. $a > 0$

d. $|a| < 0$

e. $|a| < 1$

f. The graphs of $f(x)$ and $g(x)$ share a vertex.

g. The graphs share an axis of symmetry.

h. The graphs share a minimum.

i. The graphs share a maximum.

23. Check for Reasonableness The graph of $g(x) = ax^2$ is a parabola that passes through the point $(-2, 2)$. Kyle says the value of a must be $-\frac{1}{2}$. Explain why this value of a is not reasonable.

24. Communicate Mathematical Ideas Explain how you know, without graphing, what the graph of $g(x) = \frac{1}{10}x^2$ looks like.

25. Critical Thinking A quadratic function has a minimum value when the function's graph opens upward, and it has a maximum value when the function's graph opens downward. In each case, the minimum or maximum value is the y-coordinate of the vertex of the function's graph. What can you say about a when the function $f(x) = ax^2$ has a minimum value? A maximum value? What is the minimum or maximum value in each case?

Lesson Performance Task

Kylie made a paper helicopter and is testing its flight time from two different heights. The graph compares the height of the helicopter during the two drops. The graph of the first drop is labeled $g(x)$ and the graph of the second drop is labeled $h(x)$.

a. At what heights did Kylie drop the helicopter? What is the helicopter's flight time during each drop?

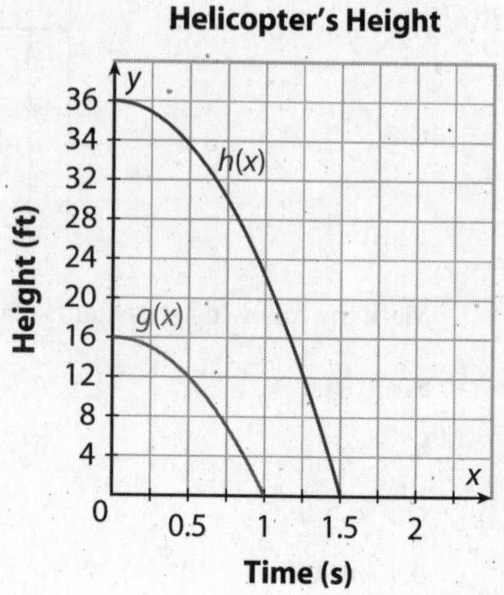

b. If each graph is represented by a function of the form $f(x) = ax^2$, are the coefficients positive or negative? Explain.

c. Estimate the functions for each graph.

Name______________________ Class______________ Date________

6.2 Transforming Quadratic Functions

Essential Question: How can you obtain the graph of $g(x) = a(x - h)^2 + k$ from the graph of $f(x) = x^2$?

Resource Locker

Explore Understanding Quadratic Functions of the Form $g(x) = a(x - h)^2 + k$

Every quadratic function can be represented by an equation of the form $g(x) = a(x - h)^2 + k$. The values of the parameters a, h, and k determine how the graph of the function compares to the graph of the parent function, $y = x^2$. Use the method shown to graph $g(x) = 2(x - 3)^2 + 1$ by transforming the graph of $f(x) = x^2$.

(A) Graph $f(x) = x^2$.

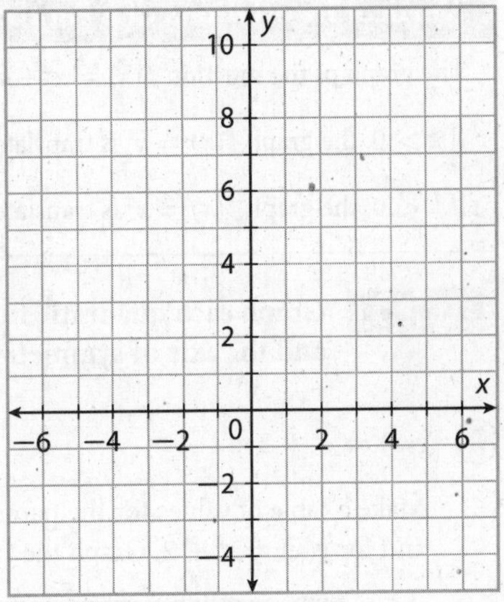

(B) Stretch the graph vertically by a factor of ____ to obtain the graph of $y = 2x^2$. Graph $y = 2x^2$.

Notice that point $(2, 4)$ moves to point [ ].

(C) Translate the graph of $y = 2x^2$ right 3 units and up 1 unit to obtain the graph of $g(x) = 2(x - 3)^2 + 1$. Graph $g(x) = 2(x - 3)^2 + 1$.

Notice that point $(2, 8)$ moves to point [ ].

(D) The vertex of the graph of $f(x) = x^2$ is ______ while the vertex of the graph of $g(x) = 2(x - 3)^2 + 1$ is ______.

Reflect

1. **Discussion** Compare the minimum values of $f(x) = x^2$ and $g(x) = 2(x - 3)^2 + 1$. How is the minimum value related to the vertex?

2. **Discussion** What is the axis of symmetry of the function $g(x) = 2(x - 3)^2 + 1$? How is the axis of symmetry related to the vertex?

Explain 1 Understanding Vertical Translations

A **vertical translation** of a parabola is a shift of the parabola up or down, with no change in the shape of the parabola.

Vertical Translations of a Parabola

The graph of the function $f(x) = x^2 + k$ is the graph of $f(x) = x^2$ translated vertically.

If $k > 0$, the graph $f(x) = x^2$ is translated k units up.

If $k < 0$, the graph $f(x) = x^2$ is translated $|k|$ units down.

Example 1 **Graph each quadratic function. Give the minimum or maximum value and the axis of symmetry.**

(A) $g(x) = x^2 + 2$

Make a table of values for the parent function $f(x) = x^2$ and for $g(x) = x^2 + 2$. Graph the functions together.

x	$f(x) = x^2$	$g(x) = x^2 + 2$
−3	9	11
−2	4	6
−1	1	3
0	0	2
1	1	3
2	4	6
3	9	11

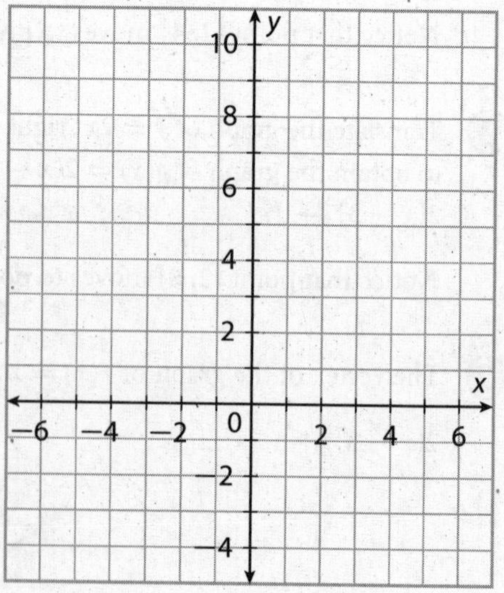

The function $g(x) = x^2 + 2$ has a minimum value of 2.

The axis of symmetry of $g(x) = x^2 + 2$ is $x = 0$.

(B) $g(x) = x^2 - 5$

Make a table of values for the parent function $f(x) = x^2$ and for $g(x) = x^2 - 5$. Graph the functions together.

x	$f(x) = x^2$	$g(x) = x^2 - 5$
−3		
−2		
−1		
0		
1		
2		
3		

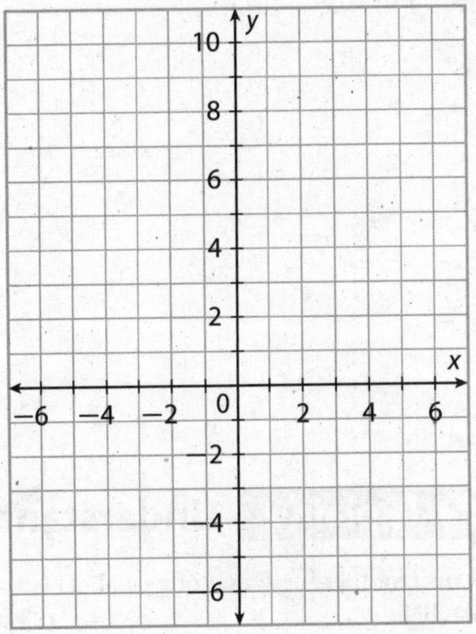

The function $g(x) = x^2 - 5$ has a minimum value of ____.

The axis of symmetry of $g(x) = x^2 - 5$ is ________.

Reflect

3. How do the values in the table for $g(x) = x^2 + 2$ compare with the values in the table for the parent function $f(x) = x^2$?

____

4. How do the values in the table for $g(x) = x^2 - 5$ compare with the values in the table for the parent function $f(x) = x^2$?

____

Your Turn

Graph each quadratic function. Give the minimum or maximum value and the axis of symmetry.

5. $g(x) = x^2 + 4$

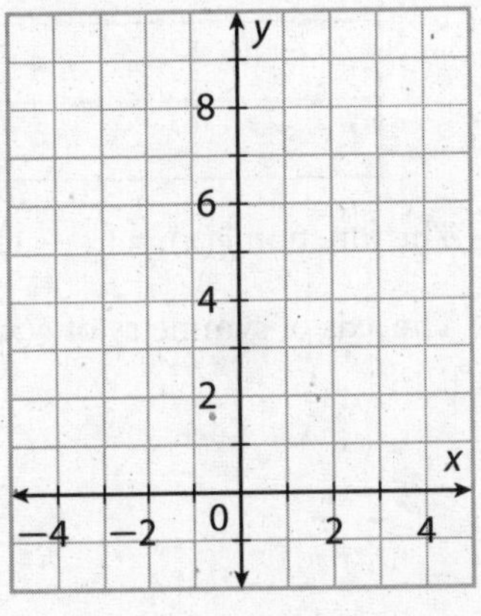

6. $g(x) = x^2 - 7$

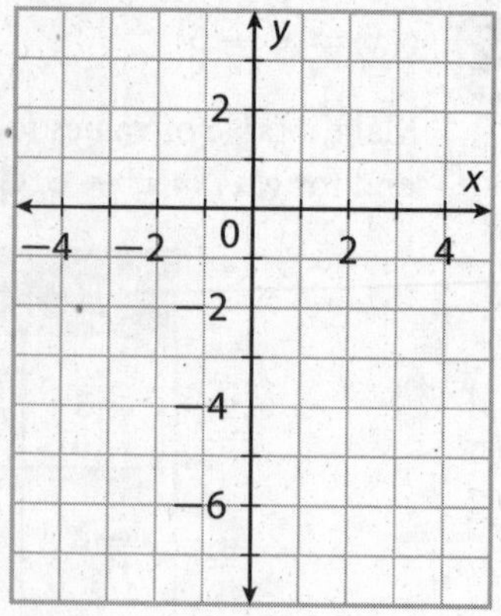

Explain 2 Understanding Horizontal Translations

A **horizontal translation** of a parabola is a shift of the parabola left or right, with no change in the shape of the parabola.

Horizontal Translations of a Parabola

The graph of the function $f(x) = (x - h)^2$ is the graph of $f(x) = x^2$ translated horizontally.

If $h > 0$, the graph $f(x) = x^2$ is translated h units right.

If $h < 0$, the graph $f(x) = x^2$ is translated h units left.

Example 2 **Graph each quadratic function. Give the minimum or maximum value and the axis of symmetry.**

(A) $g(x) = (x - 1)^2$

Make a table of values for the parent function $f(x) = x^2$ and for $g(x) = (x - 1)^2$. Graph the functions together.

x	$f(x) = x^2$	$g(x) = (x - 1)^2$
−3	9	16
−2	4	9
−1	1	4
0	0	1
1	1	0
2	4	1
3	9	4

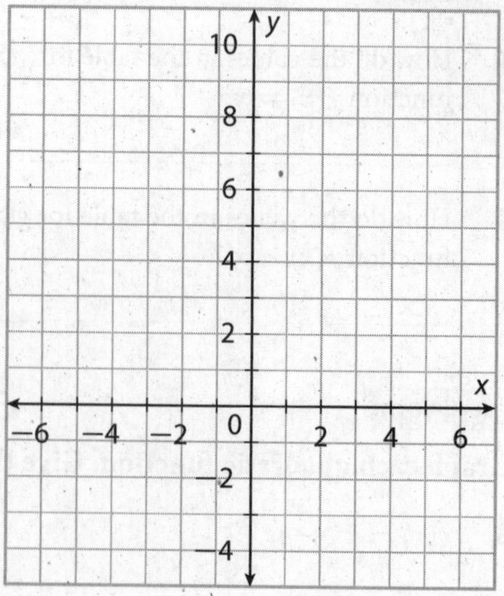

The function $g(x) = (x - 1)^2$ has a minimum value of 0.

The axis of symmetry of $g(x) = (x - 1)^2$ is $x = 1$.

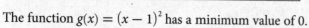

(B) $g(x) = (x + 1)^2$

Make a table of values and graph the functions together.

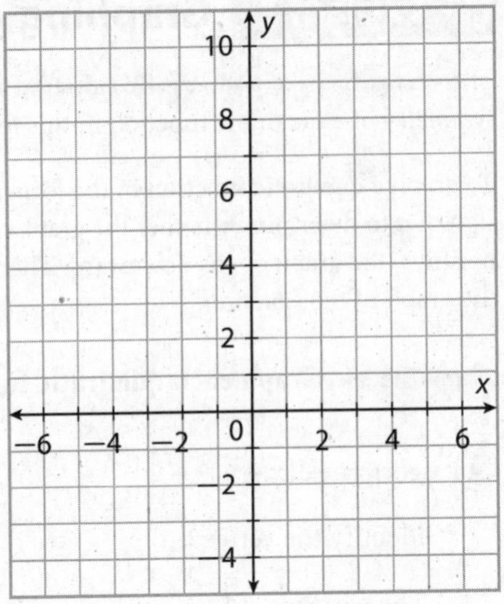

x	$f(x) = x^2$	$g(x) = (x + 1)^2$
−3	9	
−2	4	
−1	1	
0	0	
1	1	
2	4	
3	9	

The function $g(x) = (x + 1)^2$ has a minimum value of ____.

The axis of symmetry of $g(x) = (x + 1)^2$ is ________.

Reflect

7. How do the values in the table for $g(x) = (x - 1)^2$ compare with the values in the table for the parent function $f(x) = x^2$?

____

8. How do the values in the table for $g(x) = (x + 1)^2$ compare with the values in the table for the parent function $f(x) = x^2$?

____

Your Turn

Graph each quadratic function. Give the minimum or maximum value and the axis of symmetry.

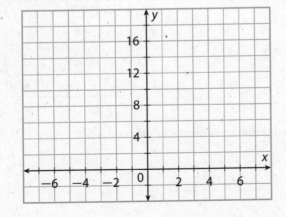

9. $g(x) = (x - 2)^2$

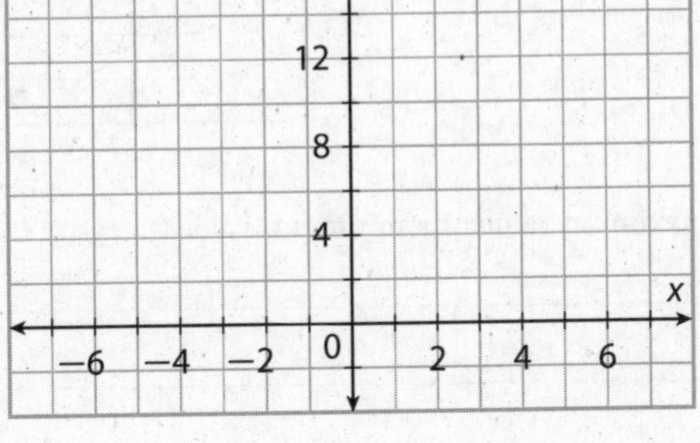

10. $g(x) = (x + 3)^2$

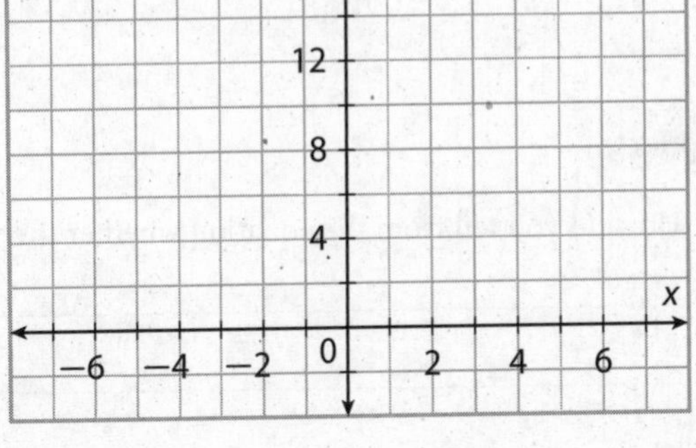

Explain 3 Graphing $g(x) = a(x - h)^2 + k$

The **vertex form of a quadratic function** is $g(x) = a(x - h)^2 + k$, where the point (h, k) is the vertex. The *axis of symmetry* of a quadratic function in this form is the vertical line $x = h$.

To graph a quadratic function in the form $g(x) = a(x - h)^2 + k$, first identify the vertex (h, k). Next, consider the sign of a to determine whether the graph opens upward or downward. If a is positive, the graph opens upward. If a is negative, the graph opens downward. Then generate two points on each side of the vertex. Using those points, sketch the graph of the function.

Example 3 **Graph each quadratic function.**

(A) $g(x) = -3(x + 1)^2 - 2$

Identify the vertex.

The vertex is at $(-1, -2)$.

Make a table for the function. Find two points on each side of the vertex.

x	-3	-2	-1	0	1
$g(x)$	-14	-5	-2	-5	-14

Plot the points and draw a parabola through them.

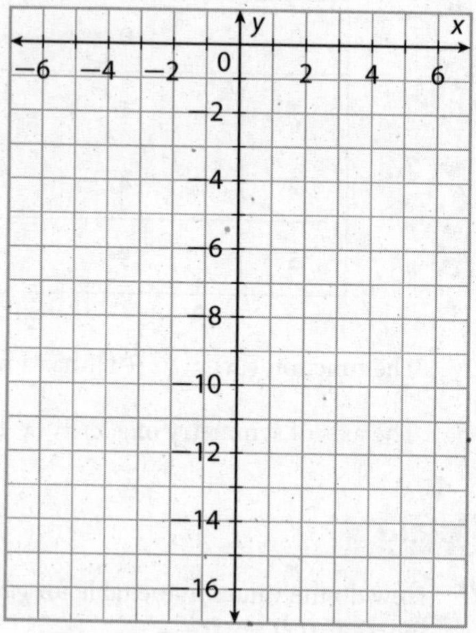

(B) $g(x) = 2(x - 1)^2 - 7$

Identify the vertex.

The vertex is at ______.

Make a table for the function. Find two points on each side of the vertex.

x	-2	0	1	2	4
$g(x)$					

Plot the points and draw a parabola through them.

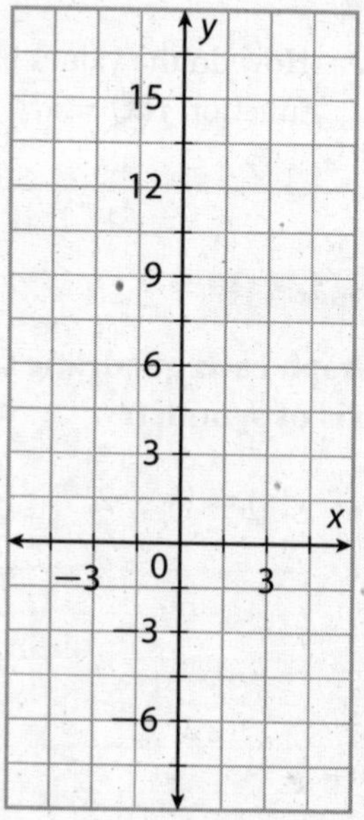

Reflect

11. How do you tell from the equation whether the vertex is a maximum value or a minimum value?

____

____

Your Turn

Graph each quadratic function.

12. $g(x) = -(x - 2)^2 + 4$

x					
$g(x)$					

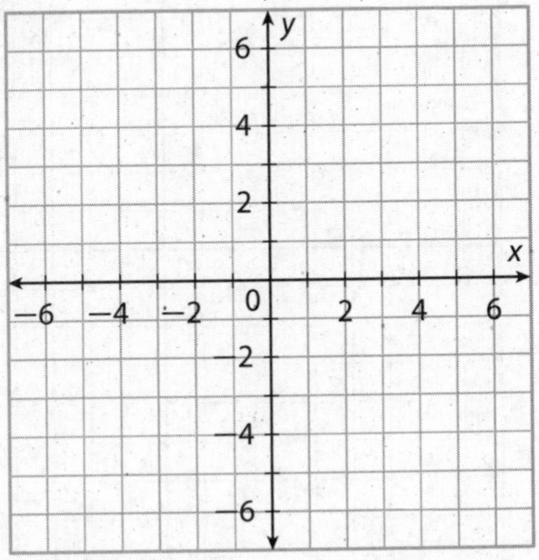

13. $g(x) = 2(x + 3)^2 - 1$

x					
$g(x)$					

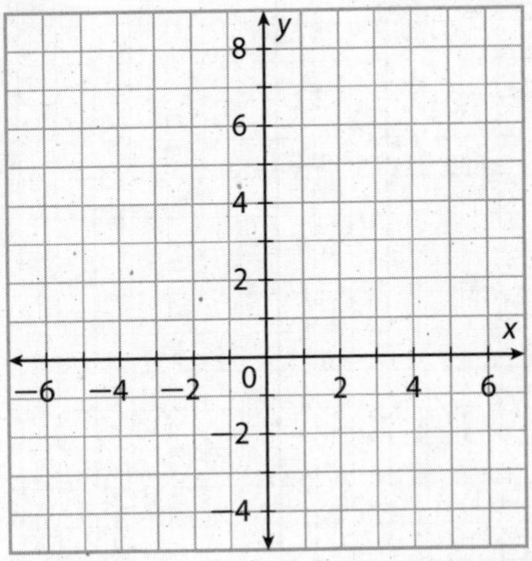

Elaborate

14. How does the value of k in $g(x) = x^2 + k$ affect the translation of $f(x) = x^2$?

---

15. How does the value of h in $g(x) = (x - h)^2$ affect the translation of $f(x) = x^2$?

---

16. In $g(x) = a(x - h)^2 + k$, what are the coordinates of the vertex?

---

17. **Essential Question Check-In** How can you use the values of a, h, and k, to obtain the graph of $g(x) = a(x - h)^2 + k$ from the graph $f(x) = x^2$?

Evaluate: Homework and Practice

Personal Math Trainer

- Online Homework
- Hints and Help
- Extra Practice

Graph each quadratic function by transforming the graph of $f(x) = x^2$. Describe the transformations.

1. $g(x) = 2(x - 2)^2 + 5$

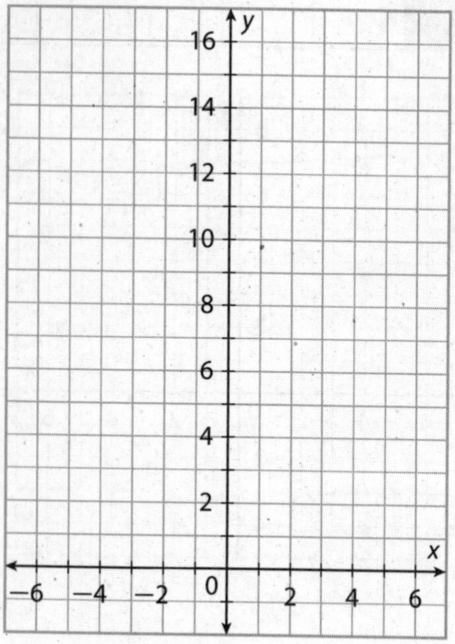

2. $g(x) = 2(x + 3)^2 - 6$

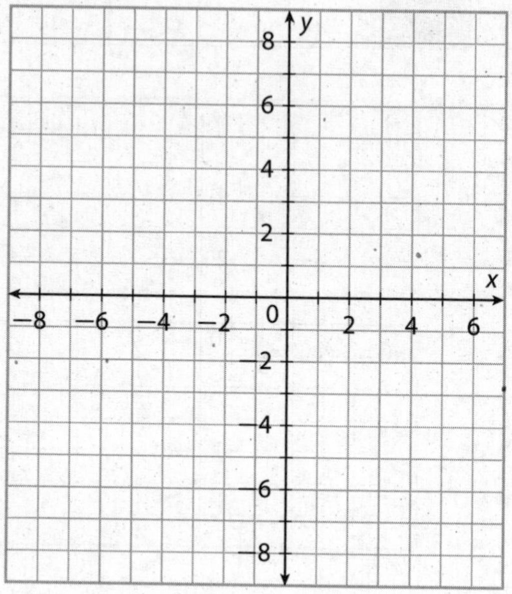

3. $g(x) = \frac{1}{2}(x - 3)^2 - 4$

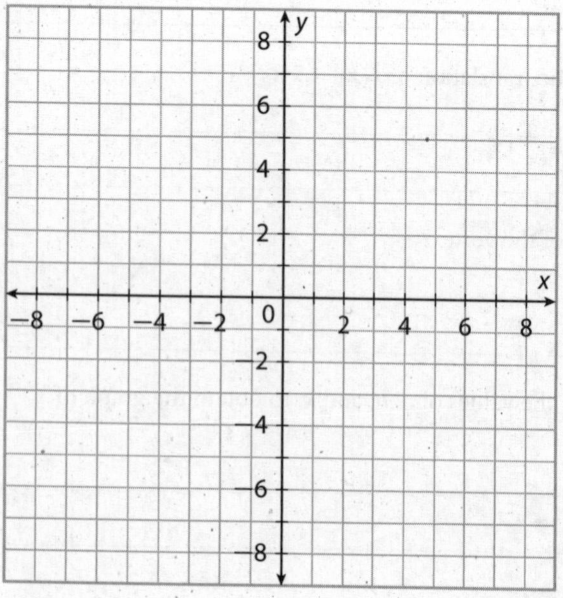

4. $g(x) = 3(x - 4)^2 - 2$

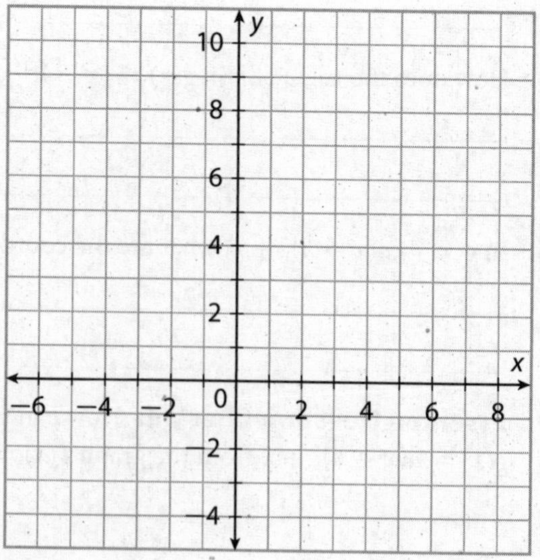

Graph each quadratic function.

5. $g(x) = x^2 - 2$

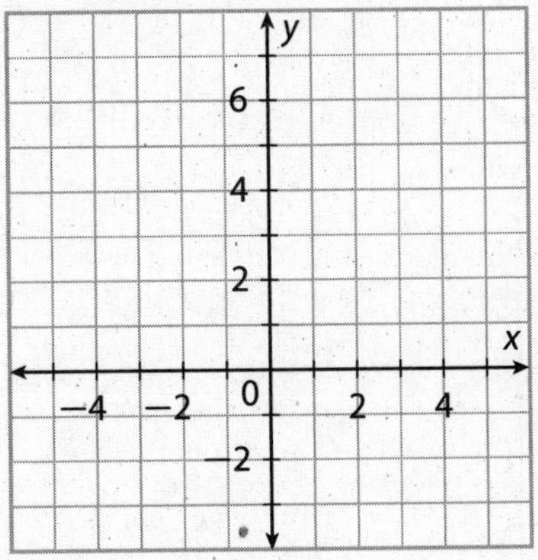

6. $g(x) = x^2 + 5$

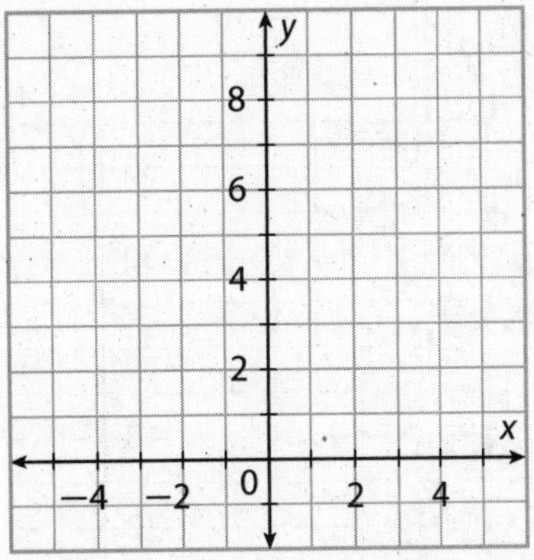

7. $g(x) = x^2 - 6$

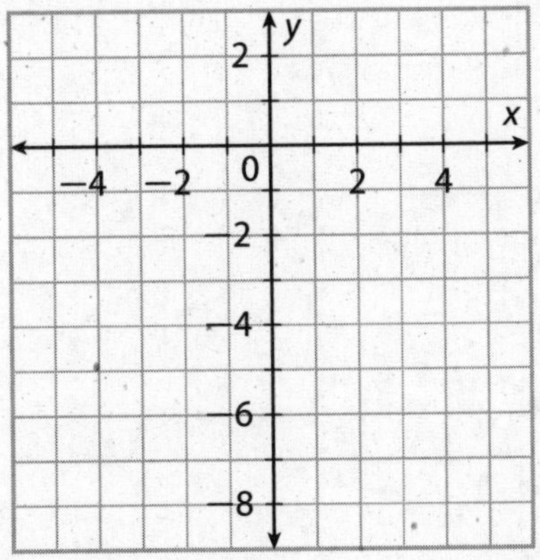

8. $g(x) = x^2 + 3$

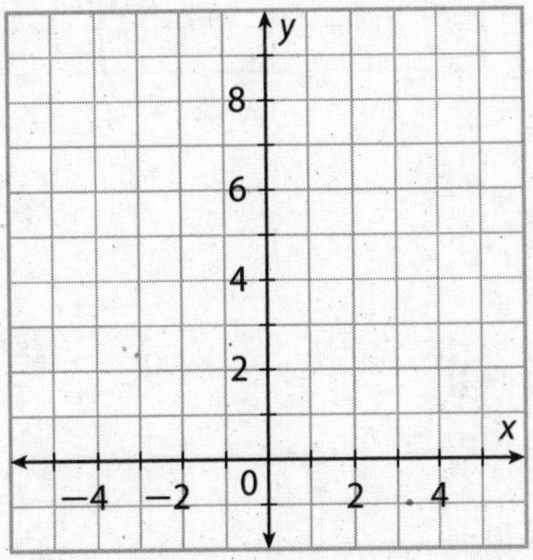

9. Graph $g(x) = x^2 - 9$. Give the minimum or maximum value and the axis of symmetry.

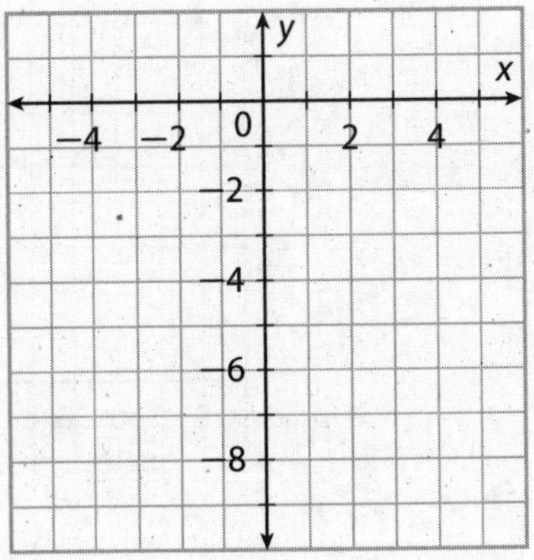

10. How is the graph of $g(x) = x^2 + 12$ related to the graph of $f(x) = x^2$?

Graph each quadratic function. Give the minimum or maximum value and the axis of symmetry.

11. $g(x) = (x - 3)^2$

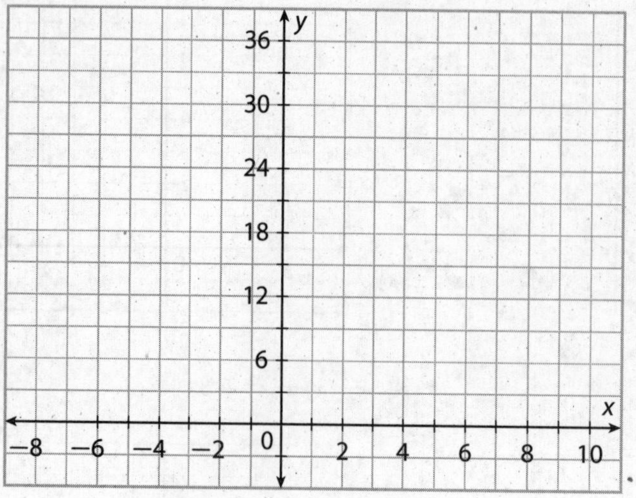

12. $g(x) = (x + 2)^2$

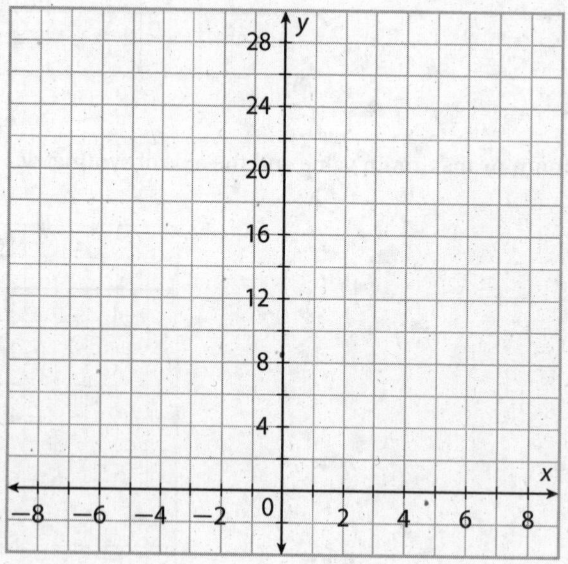

13. How is the graph of $g(x) = (x + 12)^2$ related to the graph of $f(x) = x^2$?

14. How is the graph of $g(x) = (x - 10)^2$ related to the graph of $f(x) = x^2$?

15. Compare the given graph to the graph of the parent function $f(x) = x^2$. Describe how the parent function must be translated to get the graph shown here.

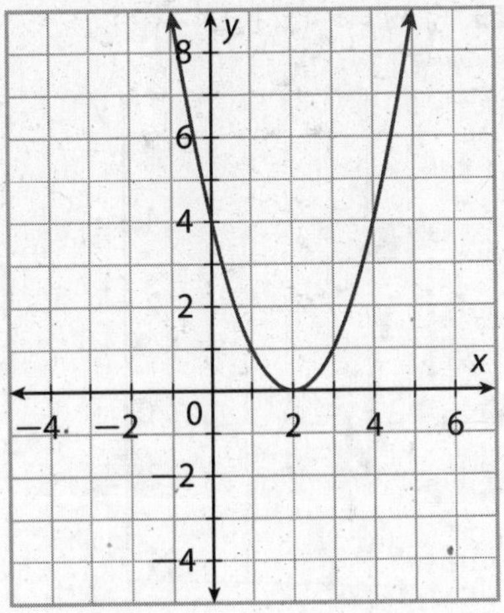

16. For the function $g(x) = (x - 9)^2$ give the minimum or maximum value and the axis of symmetry.

Graph each quadratic function. Give the minimum or maximum value and the axis of symmetry.

17. $g(x) = (x - 1)^2 - 5$

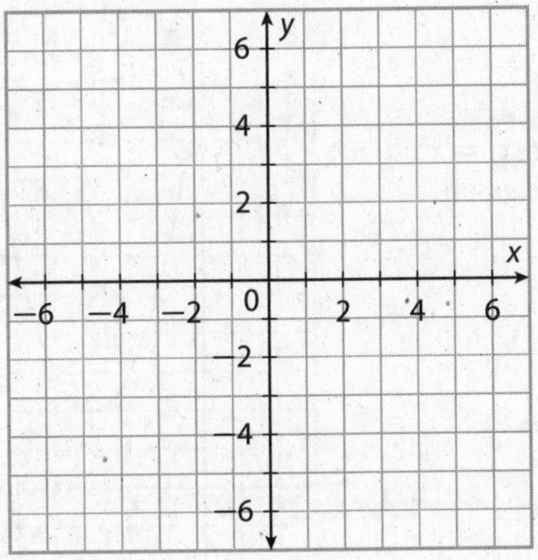

18. $g(x) = -(x + 2)^2 + 5$

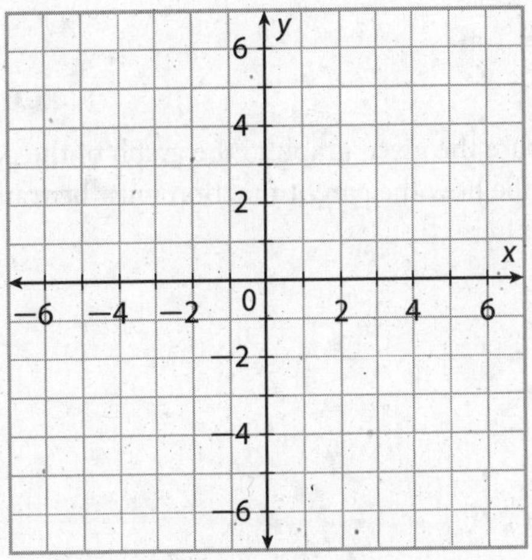

19. $g(x) = \frac{1}{4}(x+1)^2 - 7$

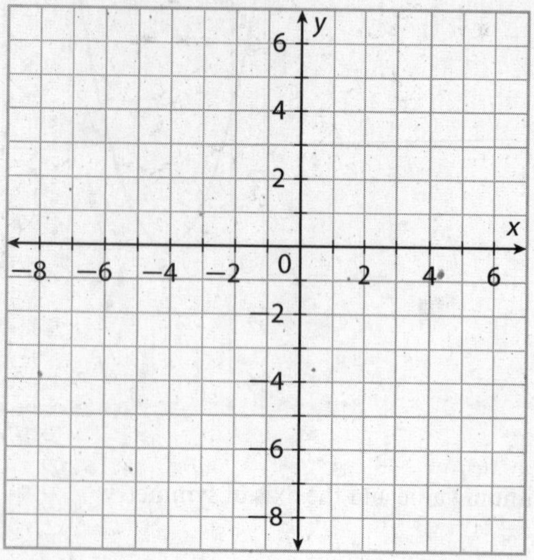

20. $g(x) = -\frac{1}{3}(x+3)^2 + 8$

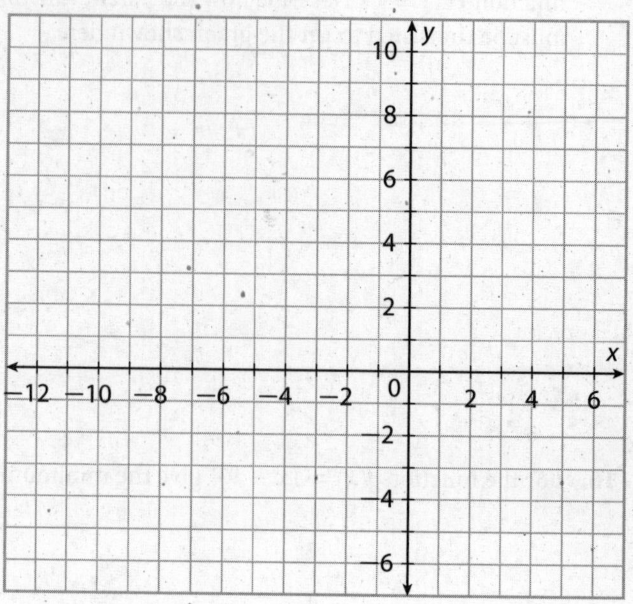

21. Compare the given graph to the graph of the parent function $f(x) = x^2$. Describe how the parent function must be translated to get the graph shown here.

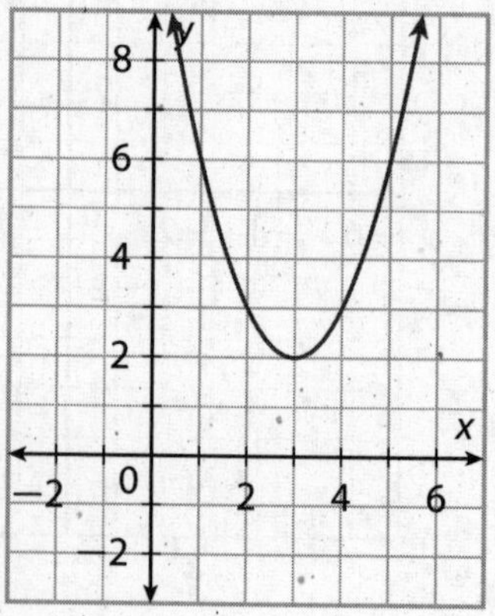

22. Multiple Representations If the graph of $f(x) = x^2$ is translated 11 units to the left and 5 units down, which function is represented by the translated graph?

a. $g(x) = (x - 11)^2 - 5$
b. $g(x) = (x + 11)^2 - 5$
c. $g(x) = (x + 11)^2 + 5$
d. $g(x) = (x - 11)^2 + 5$
e. $g(x) = (x - 5)^2 - 11$
f. $g(x) = (x - 5)^2 + 11$
g. $g(x) = (x + 5)^2 - 11$
h. $g(x) = (x + 5)^2 + 11$

H.O.T. Focus on Higher Order Thinking

Critical Thinking Use a graphing calculator to compare the graphs of $y = (2x)^2$, $y = (3x)^2$, and $y = (4x)^2$ with the graph of the parent function $y = x^2$. Then compare the graphs of $y = \left(\frac{1}{2}x\right)^2$, $y = \left(\frac{1}{3}x\right)^2$, and $y = \left(\frac{1}{4}x\right)^2$ with the graph of the parent function $y = x^2$.

23. Explain how the parameter b horizontally stretches or compresses the graph of $y = (bx)^2$ when $b > 1$.

24. Explain how the parameter b horizontally stretches or compresses the graph of $y = (bx)^2$ when $0 < b < 1$.

25. **Explain the Error** Nina is trying to write an equation for the function represented by the graph of a parabola that is a translation of $f(x) = x^2$. The graph has been translated 4 units to the right and 2 units up. She writes the function as $g(x) = (x + 4)^2 + 2$. Explain the error.

26. **Multiple Representations** A group of engineers drop an experimental tennis ball from a catwalk and let it fall to the ground. The tennis ball's height above the ground (in feet) is given by a function of the form $f(t) = a(t - h)^2 + k$ where t is the time (in seconds) after the tennis ball was dropped. Use the graph to find the equation for $f(t)$.

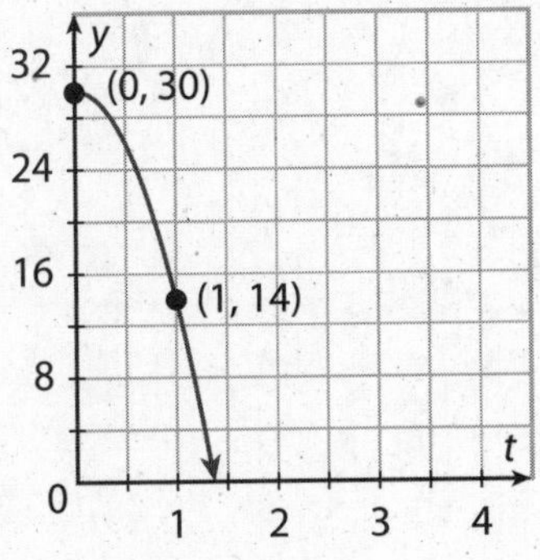

27. **Make a Prediction** For what values of a and c will the graph of $f(x) = ax^2 + c$ have one x-intercept?

Lesson Performance Task

The path a baseball takes after it has been hit is modeled by the graph. The baseball's height above the ground is given by a function of the form $f(t) = a(t - h)^2 + k$, where t is the time in seconds since the baseball was hit.

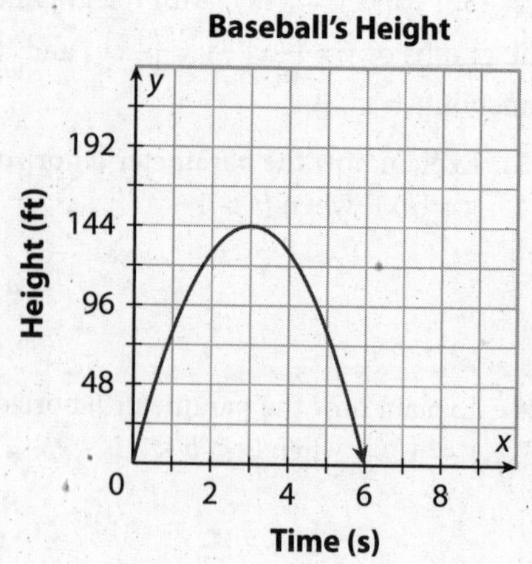

a. What is the baseball's maximum height? At what time was the baseball at its maximum height?

b. When does the baseball hit the ground?

c. Find an equation for $f(t)$.

d. A player hits a second baseball. The second baseball's path is modeled by the function $g(t) = -16(t - 4)^2 + 256$. Which baseball has a greater maximum height? Which baseball is in the air for the longest?

Name ______________________ Class ______________ Date ________

6.3 Interpreting Vertex Form and Standard Form

Resource Locker

Essential Question: How can you change the vertex form of a quadratic function to standard form?

Explore Identifying Quadratic Functions from Their Graphs

Determine whether a function is a quadratic function by looking at its graph. If the graph of a function is a parabola, then the function is a quadratic function. If the graph of a function is not a parabola, then the function is not a quadratic function.

Use a graphing calculator to graph each of the functions. Set the viewing window to show −10 to 10 on both axes. Determine whether each function is a quadratic function.

(A) Use a graphing calculator to graph $f(x) = x + 1$.

(B) Determine whether the function $f(x) = x + 1$ is a quadratic function.

The function $f(x) = x + 1$ ________ a quadratic function.

(C) Use a graphing calculator to graph $f(x) = x^2 + 2x - 6$.

(D) Determine whether the function $f(x) = x^2 + 2x - 6$ is a quadratic function.

The function $f(x) = x^2 + 2x - 6$ ________ a quadratic function.

(E) Use a graphing calculator to graph $f(x) = 2^x$.

(F) Determine whether the function $f(x) = 2^x$ is a quadratic function.

The function $f(x) = 2^x$ ________ a quadratic function.

Ⓖ Use a graphing calculator to graph $f(x) = 2x^2 - 3$.

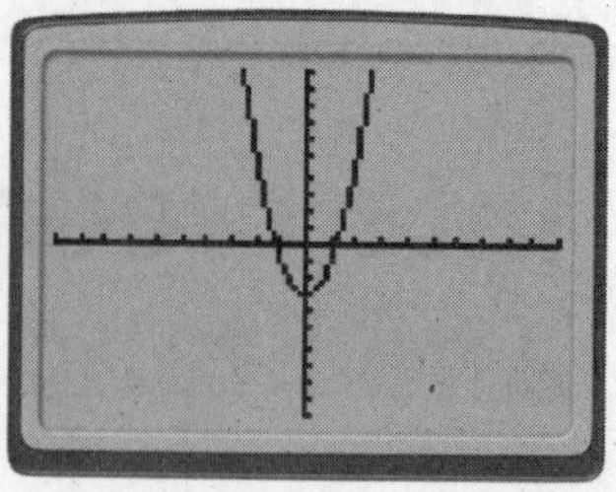

Ⓗ Determine whether the function $f(x) = 2x^2 - 3$ is a quadratic function.

The function $f(x) = 2x^2 - 3$ ________ a quadratic function.

Ⓘ Use a graphing calculator to graph $f(x) = -(x - 3)^2 + 7$.

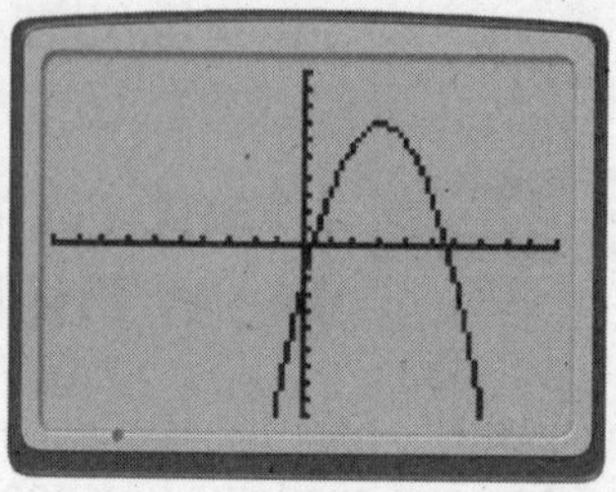

Ⓙ Determine whether the function $f(x) = -(x - 3)^2 + 7$ is a quadratic function.

The function $f(x) = -(x - 3)^2 + 7$ ________ a quadratic function.

Ⓚ Use a graphing calculator to graph $f(x) = \sqrt{x}$.

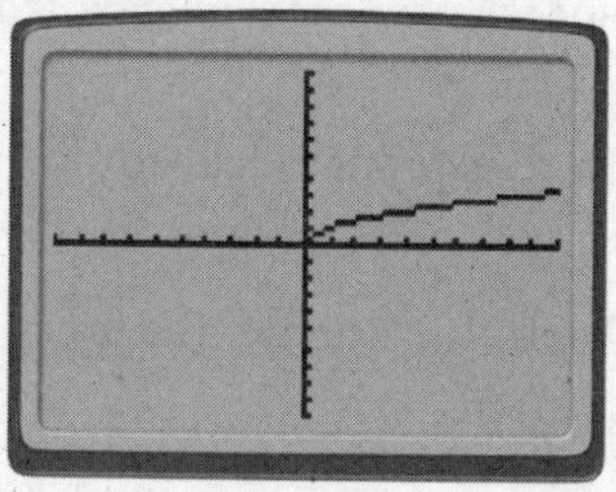

Ⓛ Determine whether the function $f(x) = \sqrt{x}$ is a quadratic function.

The function $f(x) = \sqrt{x}$ ________ a quadratic function.

Reflect

1. How can you determine whether a function is quadratic or not by looking at its graph?

____

____

____

2. **Discussion** How can you tell if a function is a quadratic function by looking at the equation?

____

Explain 1 Identifying Quadratic Functions in Standard Form

If a function is quadratic, it can be represented by an equation of the form $y = ax^2 + bx + c$, where a, b, and c are real numbers and $a \neq 0$. This is called the **standard form of a quadratic equation**.

The axis of symmetry for a quadratic equation in standard form is given by the equation $x = -\frac{b}{2a}$. The vertex of a quadratic equation in standard form is given by the coordinates $\left(-\frac{b}{2a}, f\left(-\frac{b}{2a}\right)\right)$.

Example 1 **Determine whether the function represented by each equation is quadratic. If so, give the axis of symmetry and the coordinates of the vertex.**

(A) $y = -2x + 20$

$y = -2x + 20$ Compare to $y = ax^2 + bx + c$.

This is not a quadratic function because $a = 0$.

(B) $y + 3x^2 = -4$

Rewrite the function in the form $y = ax^2 + bx + c$.

$y =$ ______

Compare to $y = ax^2 + bx + c$.

This ______ a quadratic function.

If $y + 3x^2 = -4$ is a quadratic function, give the axis of symmetry. ______

If $y + 3x^2 = -4$ is a quadratic function, give the coordinates of the vertex. ______

Reflect

3. Explain why the function represented by the equation $y = ax^2 + bx + c$ is quadratic only when $a \neq 0$.

______

______

4. Why might it be easier to determine whether a function is quadratic when it is expressed in function notation?

______

______

5. How is the axis of symmetry related to standard form?

______

______

Your Turn

Determine whether the function represented by each equation is quadratic.

6. $y - 4x + x^2 = 0$

7. $x + 2y = 14x + 6$

Explain 2 Changing from Vertex Form to Standard Form

It is possible to write quadratic equations in various forms.

Example 2 **Rewrite a quadratic function from vertex form, $y = a(x - h)^2 + k$, to standard form, $y = ax^2 + bx + c$.**

(A) $y = 4(x - 6)^2 + 3$

$y = 4(x^2 - 12x + 36) + 3$ Expand $(x - 6)^2$.

$y = 4x^2 - 48x + 144 + 3$ Multiply.

$y = 4x^2 - 48x + 147$ Simplify.

The standard form of $y = 4(x - 6)^2 + 3$ is $y = 4x^2 - 48x + 147$.

(B) $y = -3(x + 2)^2 - 1$

$y = -3(\square) - 1$ Expand $(x + 2)^2$.

$y = \square - 1$ Multiply.

$y = \square$ Simplify.

The standard form of $y = -3(x + 2)^2 - 1$ is $y = \square$.

Reflect

8. If in $y = a(x - h)^2 + k$, $a = 1$, what is the simplified form of the standard form, $y = ax^2 + bx + c$?

Your Turn

Rewrite a quadratic function from vertex form, $y = a(x - h)^2 + k$, to standard form, $y = ax^2 + bx + c$.

9. $y = 2(x + 5)^2 + 3$

10. $y = -3(x - 7)^2 + 2$

Explain 3 Writing a Quadratic Function Given a Table of Values

You can write a quadratic function from a table of values.

Example 3 **Use each table to write a quadratic function in vertex form, $y = a(x - h)^2 + k$. Then rewrite the function in standard form, $y = ax^2 + bx + c$.**

(A) The minimum value of the function occurs at $x = -3$.

x	y
−6	9
−4	1
−3	0
−2	1
0	9

The vertex of the parabola is $(-3, 0)$.

Substitute the values for h and k into $y = a(x - h)^2 + k$.

$y = a(x - (-3))^2 + 0$, or $y = a(x + 3)^2$

Use any point from the table to find a.

$y = a(x + 3)^2$

$1 = a(-2 + 3)^2 = a$

The vertex form of the function is $y = 1(x - (-3))^2 + 0$ or $y = (x + 3)^2$.

Rewrite the function $y = (x + 3)^2$ in standard form, $y = ax^2 + bx + c$.

$y = (x + 3)^2 = x^2 + 6x + 9$

The standard form of the function is $y = x^2 + 6x + 9$.

(B) The minimum value of the function occurs at $x = -2$.

x	y
0	13
−1	1
−2	−3
−3	1
−4	13

The vertex of the parabola is is $(-2, -3)$.

Substitute the values for h and k into $y = a(x - h)^2 + k$.

$y =$ [ ]

Use any point from the table to find a. $a =$ [ ]

The vertex form of the function is $y =$ [ ].

Rewrite the resulting function in standard form, $y = ax^2 + bx + c$.

$y =$ [ ]

Reflect

11. How many points are needed to find an equation of a quadratic function?

Your Turn

Use each table to write a quadratic function in vertex form, $y = a(x - h)^2 + k$. Then rewrite the function in standard form, $y = ax^2 + bx + c$.

12. The vertex of the parabola is (2, 5).

x	y
−1	59
1	11
2	5
3	11
5	59

13. The vertex of the parabola is (−2, −7).

x	y
0	−27
−1	−12
−2	−7
−3	−12
−4	−27

Explain 4 Writing a Quadratic Function Given a Graph

The graph of a parabola can be used to determine the corresponding function.

Example 4 **Use each graph to find an equation for $f(t)$.**

(A) A house painter standing on a ladder drops a paintbrush, which falls to the ground. The paintbrush's height above the ground (in feet) is given by a function of the form $f(t) = a(t - h)^2$ where t is the time (in seconds) after the paintbrush is dropped.

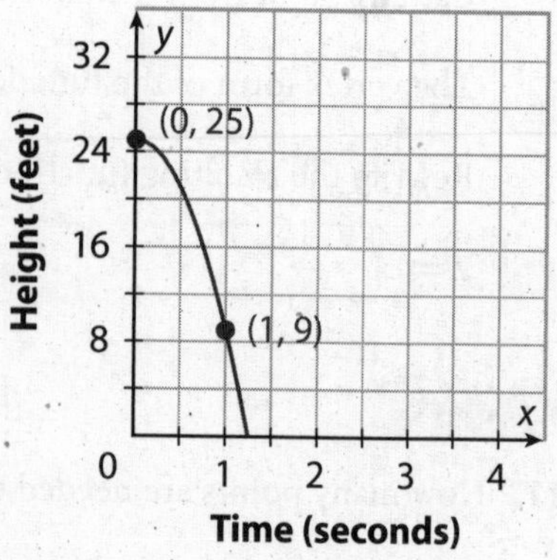

The vertex of the parabola is $(h, k) = (0, 25)$.

$f(t) = a(x - h)^2 + k$

$f(t) = a(t - 0)^2 + 25$

$f(t) = at^2 + 25$

Use the point (1, 9) to find a.

$f(t) = at^2 + 25$

$9 = a(1)^2 + 25$

$-16 = a$

The equation for the function is $f(t) = -16t^2 + 25$.

(B) A rock is knocked off a cliff into the water far below. The falling rock's height above the water (in feet) is given by a function of the form $f(t) = a(t - h)^2 + k$ where t is the time (in seconds) after the rock begins to fall.

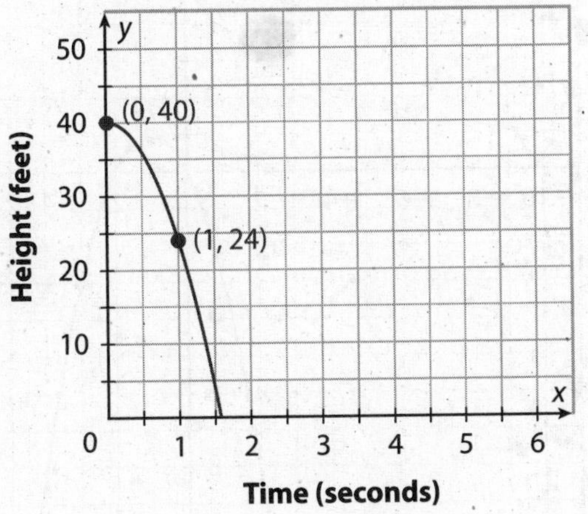

The vertex of the parabola is $(h, k) =$ ☐.

$f(t) = a(t - h)^2 + k$

$f(t) = a(t - ☐)^2 + ☐$

$f(t) =$ ☐

Use the point ______ to find a.

$f(t) = at^2 +$ ☐

☐ $= a$ ☐^{2} $+$ ☐

$a =$ ☐

The equation for the function is $f(t) =$ ☐.

Reflect

14. Identify the domain and explain why it makes sense for this problem.

____

____

15. Identify the range and explain why it makes sense for this problem.

____

____

Your Turn

16. The graph of a function in the form $f(x) = a(x - h)^2 + k$, is shown. Use the graph to find an equation for $f(x)$.

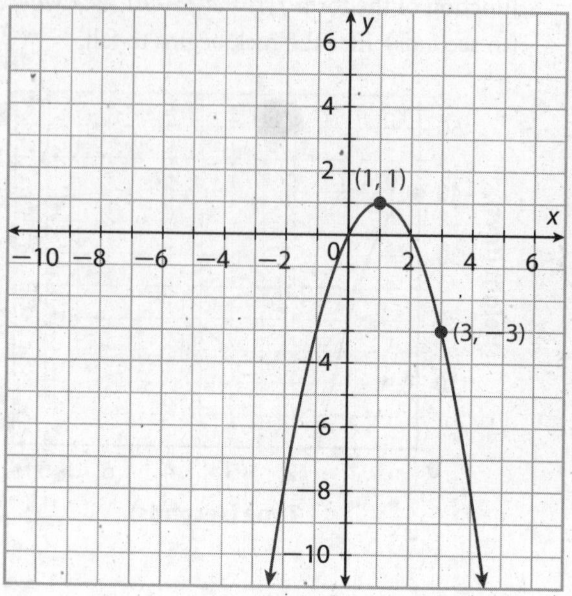

17. A roofer accidentally drops a nail, which falls to the ground. The nail's height above the ground (in feet) is given by a function of the form $f(t) = a(t - h)^2 + k$, where t is the time (in seconds) after the nail drops. Use the graph to find an equation for $f(t)$.

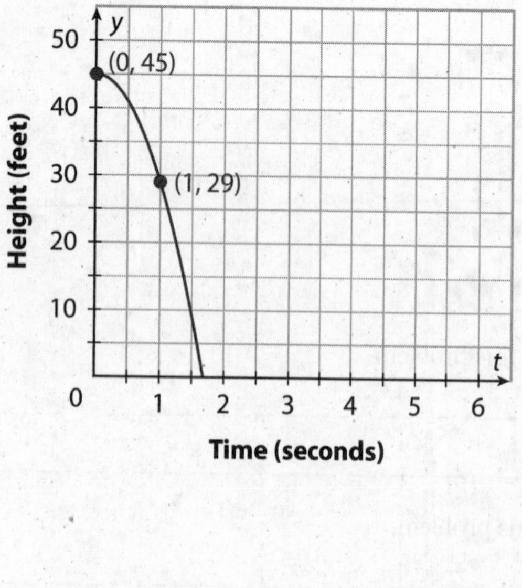

Elaborate

18. Describe the graph of a quadratic function.

19. What is the standard form of the quadratic function?

20. Can any quadratic function in vertex form be written in standard form?

21. How many points are needed to write a quadratic function in vertex form, given the table of values?

22. If a graph of the quadratic function is given, how do you find the vertex?

23. **Essential Question Check-In** What can you do to change the vertex form of a quadratic function to standard form?

Evaluate: Homework and Practice

Personal Math Trainer

- Online Homework
- Hints and Help
- Extra Practice

Determine whether each function is a quadratic function by graphing.

1. $f(x) = 0.01 - 0.2x + x^2$

2. $f(x) = \frac{1}{2}x - 4$

3. $f(x) = -4x^2 - 2$

4. $f(x) = 2^{x-3}$

Determine whether the function represented by each equation is quadratic.

5. $y = -3x + 15$

6. $y - 6 = 2x^2$

7. $3 + y + 5x^2 = 6x$

8. $y + 6x = 14$

9. Which of the following functions is a quadratic function? Select all that apply.

a. $2x = y + 3$

b. $2x^2 + y = 3x - 1$

c. $5 = -6x + y$

d. $6x^2 + y = 0$

e. $y - x = 4$

10. For $f(x) = x^2 + 8x - 14$, give the axis of symmetry and the coordinates of the vertex.

11. Describe the axis of symmetry of the graph of the quadratic function represented by the equation $y = ax^2 + bx + c$. when $b = 0$.

Rewrite each quadratic function from vertex form, $y = a(x - h)^2 + k$, to standard form, $y = ax^2 + bx + c$.

12. $y = 5(x - 2)^2 + 7$

13. $y = -2(x + 4)^2 - 11$

14. $y = 3(x + 1)^2 + 12$

15. $y = -4(x - 3)^2 - 9$

16. Explain the Error Tim wrote $y = -6(x + 2)^2 - 10$ in standard form as $y = 6x^2 + 24x + 14$. Find his error.

17. How do you change from vertex form, $f(x) = a(x - h)^2 + k$, to standard form, $y = ax^2 + bx + c$?

Use each table to write a quadratic function in vertex form, $y = a(x - h)^2 + k$. Then rewrite the function in standard form, $y = ax^2 + bx + c$.

18. The vertex of the function is (6, −8).

x	y
10	24
8	0
6	−8
4	0
2	24

19. The vertex of the function is (4, 7).

x	y
0	−1
2	5
4	7
6	5
8	−1

20. The vertex of the function is (−2, −12).

x	y
2	52
0	4
−2	−12
−4	4
−6	52

21. The vertex of the function is (−3, 10).

x	y
−1	−6
−2	6
−3	10
−4	6
−5	−6

H.O.T. Focus on Higher Order Thinking

22. Make a Prediction A ball was thrown off a bridge. The table relates the height of the ball above the ground in feet to the time in seconds after it was thrown. Use the data to write a quadratic model in vertex form and convert it to standard form. Use the model to find the height of the ball at 1.5 seconds.

Time (seconds)	Height (feet)
0	128
1	144
2	128
3	80
4	0

23. Multiple Representations A performer slips and falls into a safety net below. The function $f(t) = a(t - h)^2 + k$, where t represents time (in seconds), gives the performer's height above the ground (in feet) as he falls. Use the graph to find an equation for $f(t)$.

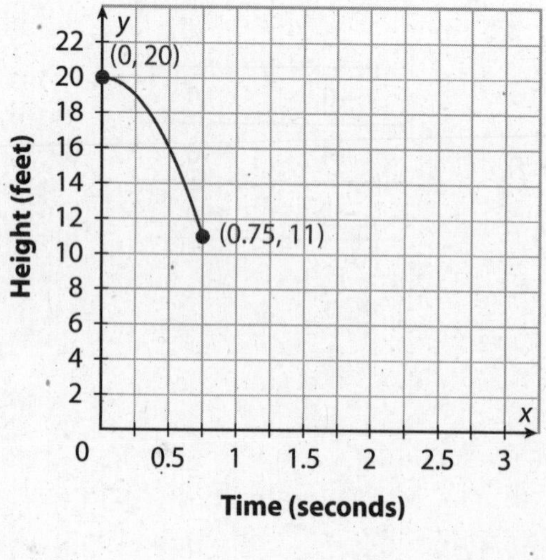

24. Represent Real-World Problems After a heavy snowfall, Ken and Karin made an igloo. The dome of the igloo is in the shape of a parabola, and the height of the igloo in inches is given by the function $f(x) = a(x - h)^2 + k$. Use the graph to find an equation for $f(x)$.

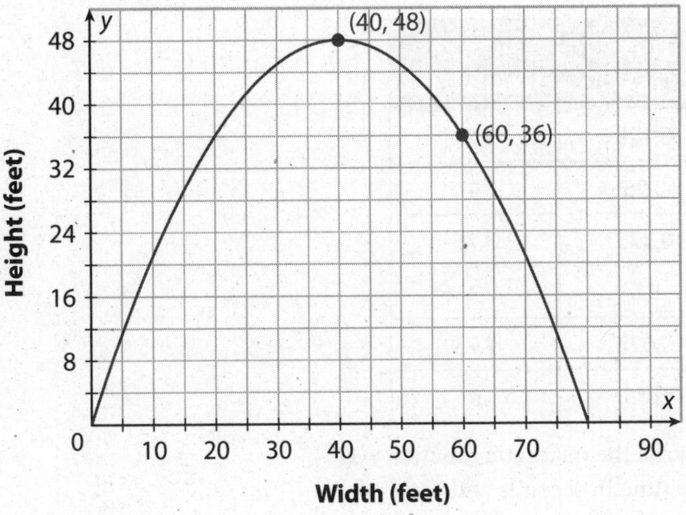

25. Check for Reasonableness Tim hits a softball. The function $f(t) = a(t - h)^2 + k$ describes the height (in feet) of the softball, and t is the time (in seconds). Use the graph to find an equation for $f(t)$. Estimate how much time elapses before the ball hits the ground. Use the equation for the function and your estimate to explain whether the equation is reasonable.

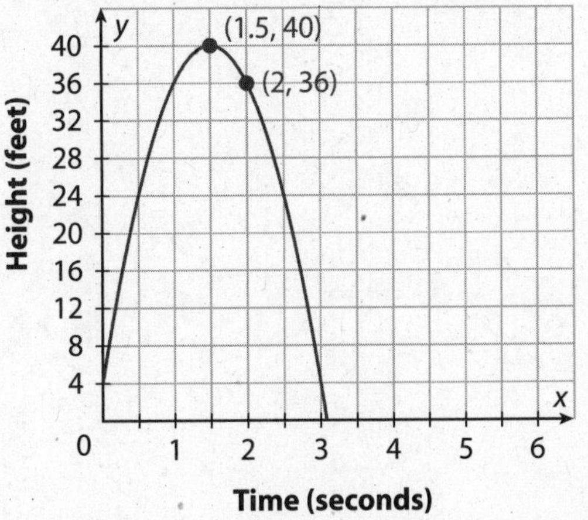

Lesson Performance Task

The table gives the height of a tennis ball t seconds after it has been hit, where the maximum height is 4 feet.

Time (s)	Height (ft)
0.125	3.75
0.25	4
0.375	3.75
0.5	3
0.625	1.75
0.75	0

a. Use the data in the table to write the quadratic function $f(t)$ in vertex form, where t is the time in seconds and $f(t)$ is the height of the tennis ball in feet.

b. Rewrite the function found in part a in standard form.

c. At what height was the ball originally hit? Explain.

Graphing Quadratic Functions

Essential Question: How can you use the graph of a quadratic function to solve real-world problems?

Key Vocabulary

axis of symmetry *(eje de simetría)*
parabola *(parábola)*
quadratic function *(función cuadrática)*
standard form of a quadratic equation *(forma estándar de una ecuación cuadrática)*
vertex *(vértice)*

KEY EXAMPLE *(Lesson 6.3)*

The graph of a function in the form $f(x) = a(x - h)^2 + k$ is shown. Use the graph to find an equation for $f(x)$.

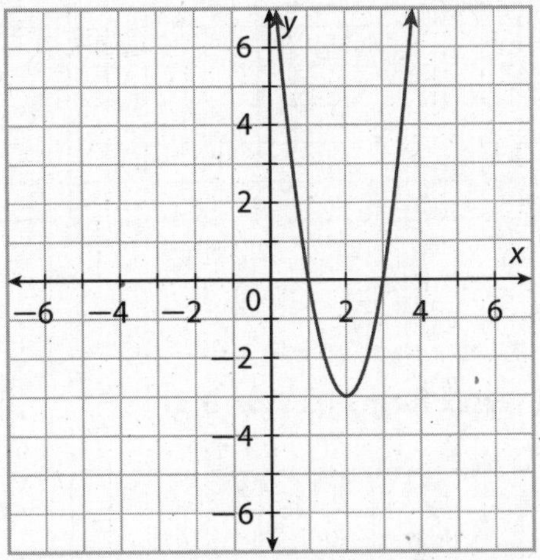

The vertex of the parabola is $(h, k) = (2, -3)$.

$f(x) = a(x - 2)^2 - 3$

From the graph, $f(3) = 0$. Substitute 3 for x and 0 for $f(x)$ and solve for a.

$0 = a(3 - 2)^2 - 3$

$3 = a$

The equation for the function is $f(x) = 3(x - 2)^2 - 3$.

KEY EXAMPLE *(Lesson 6.2)*

Graph $g(x) = -2(x + 2)^2 + 2$.

The vertex is at $(-2, 2)$.

Make a table for the function. Find two points on each side of the vertex.

x	−4	−3	−2	−1	0
$g(x)$	−6	0	2	0	−6

Plot the points and draw a parabola through them.

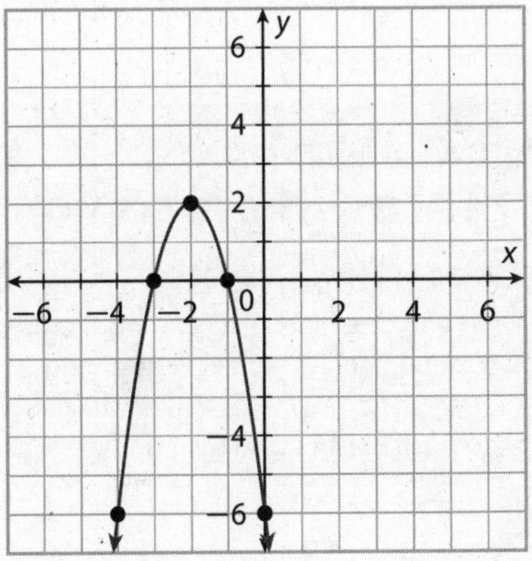

EXERCISES

Graph each quadratic function. Give the minimum or maximum value and the axis of symmetry. *(Lessons 6.1, 6.2)*

1. $f(x) = 2x^2$

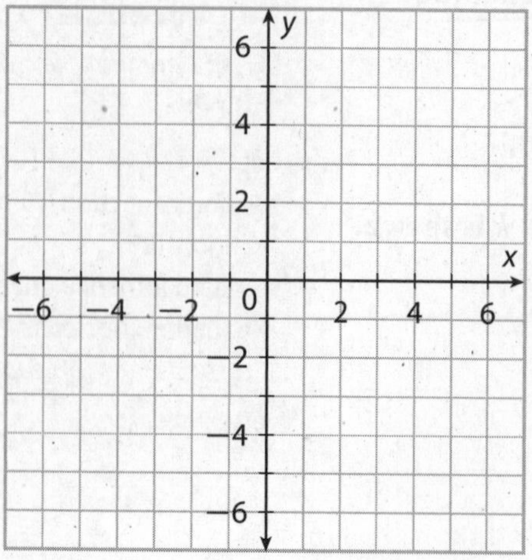

2. $g(x) = -(x + 2)^2 + 4$

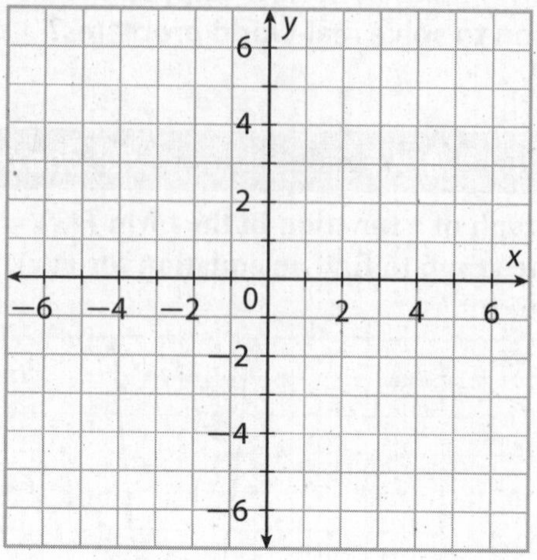

Write the equation for the function in each graph, in vertex form. *(Lesson 6.3)*

3.

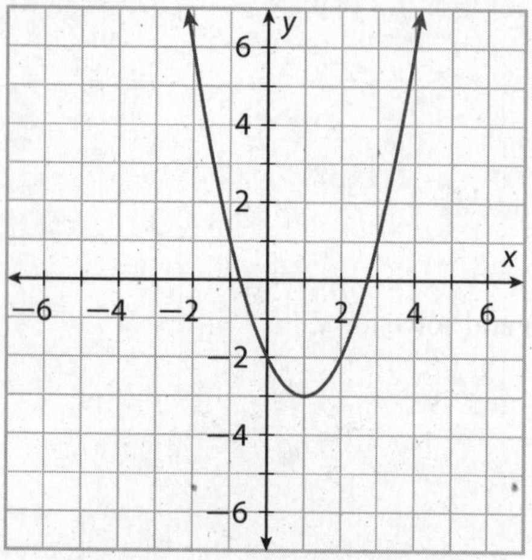

4.

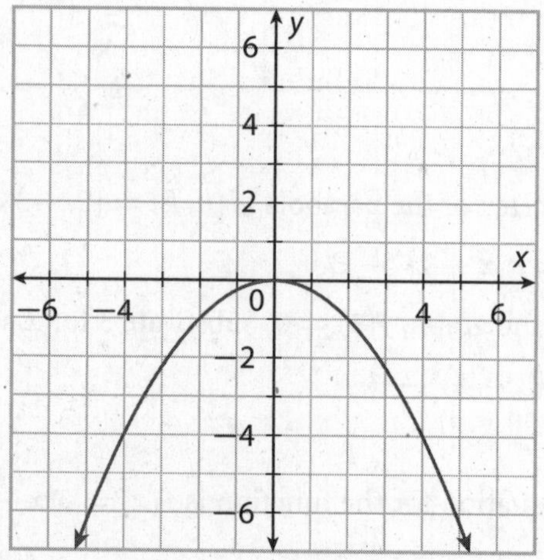

MODULE PERFORMANCE TASK

Throwing for a Completion

Professional quarterbacks can throw a football to a receiver with a velocity of 66 feet per second or greater. If a quarterback throws a pass with that velocity at a 30° angle with the ground, then the initial vertical velocity is 33 feet per second. How can you use the formula $h = -16t^2 + vt + h_0$ to describe the quarterback's pass? Find the maximum height that the football reaches, and then find the total amount of time that the pass is in the air.

Ready to Go On?

6.1–6.3 Graphing Quadratic Functions

Personal Math Trainer
- Online Homework
- Hints and Help
- Extra Practice

Graph each quadratic function. *(Lesson 6.1)*

1. $f(x) = -4x^2$

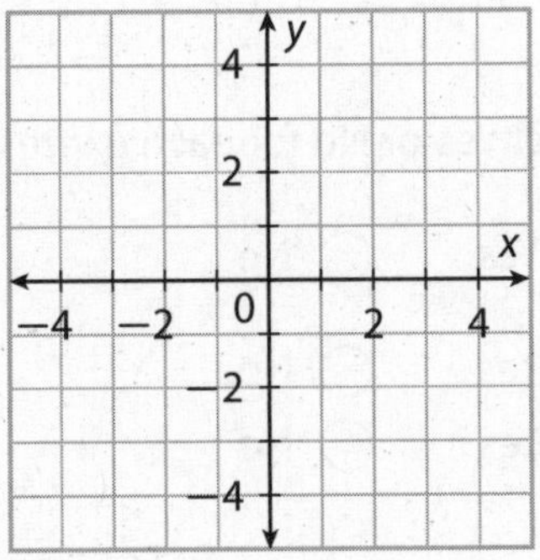

2. $g(x) = \frac{1}{2}x^2$

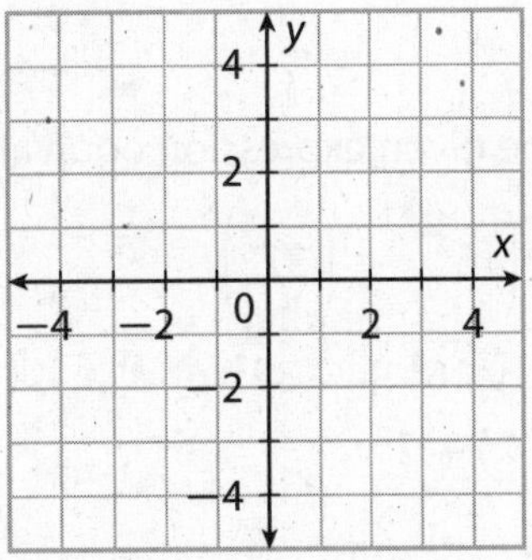

Describe the transformations necessary to get from the graph of the parent function $f(x) = x^2$ to the graph of each of the given functions. *(Lesson 6.2)*

3. $g(x) = (x + 4)^2 - 7$

4. $g(x) = 5(x - 6)^2 + 9$

Rewrite each function in standard form. *(Lesson 6.3)*

5. $f(x) = 2(x + 3)^2 - 6$

6. $f(x) = 3(x - 2)^2 + 3$

ESSENTIAL QUESTION

7. If the only information you have about a parabola is the location of its vertex, what other characteristics of the graph do you know?

MODULE 6
MIXED REVIEW

Assessment Readiness

1. Consider the graph of $f(x) = \frac{2}{3}(x - 3)^2$.

Choose True or False for each statement about the graph.

A. The vertex is $(3, 0)$. ○ True ○ False

B. The minimum value is 0. ○ True ○ False

C. The axis of symmetry is $x = \frac{2}{3}$. ○ True ○ False

2. Is the given expression equivalent to $16^{\frac{3}{4}} + 32^{\frac{2}{5}}$? Select Yes or No for each expression.

A. $\left(16^{\frac{1}{4}}\right)^3 + \left(32^{\frac{1}{5}}\right)^2$ ○ Yes ○ No

B. $\sqrt[4]{16^3} + \sqrt[5]{32^2}$ ○ Yes ○ No

C. $2^3 + 2^2$ ○ Yes ○ No

3. Write the slope-intercept equation of the line that has the same slope as $y - 3 = \frac{1}{2}(x + 3)$ and contains the point $(8, 4)$. Explain how you wrote the equation.

4. Write $f(x) = -2(x - 5)^2 + 3$ in standard form. In which form is it easier to determine the maximum value of the graph? Explain.

Connecting Intercepts, Zeros, and Factors

Essential Question: How can you use intercepts of a quadratic function to solve real-world problems?

REAL WORLD VIDEO
Skateboard ramps come in many shapes and sizes. The iconic half-pipe ramp has a flat section in the middle and curved, raised sides. Skateboarders can use a half-pipe ramp to perform tricks, turns, and flips.

MODULE PERFORMANCE TASK PREVIEW

Skateboard Ramp

Skateboard riders often use curved ramps to perform difficult tricks and have fun. In this module, you will imagine that you are a design engineer hired by the local government to help construct a new skateboard ramp for the skateboard riders in the area. How do you model the curve of the ramp? Let's find out!

Are YOU Ready?

Complete these exercises to review skills you will need for this module.

Personal Math Trainer

- Online Homework
- Hints and Help
- Extra Practice

Exponents

Example 1 Simplify.

$x^5 \cdot x^3 = x^{5+3} = x^8$ The bases are the same. Add the exponents.

$\frac{x^9}{x^4} = x^{9-4} = x^5$ The bases are the same. Subtract the exponents.

Simplify.

1. $b^2 \cdot b^6$ ______

2. $\frac{a^{12}}{a^7}$ ______

3. $\frac{n^4 \cdot n^7}{n^5}$ ______

Algebraic Expressions

Example 2 Find the value of $3x - 6$ when $x = 2$.

$3x - 6$

$3(2) - 6$ Substitute 2 for *x*.

$6 - 6$ Follow the order of operations.

0

Find the value.

4. $6x + 3$ when $x = -\frac{1}{2}$ ______

5. $2x - 5$ when $x = \frac{5}{2}$ ______

6. $9x + 6$ when $x = -\frac{2}{3}$ ______

Linear Functions

Example 3 Tell whether $y = x^2 - 7$ represents a linear function.

$y = x^2 - 7$ does not represent a linear function because x has an exponent of 2.

When a linear equation is written in standard form, the following are true.

- *x* and *y* both have exponents of 1.
- *x* and *y* are not multiplied together.
- *x* and *y* do not appear in denominators, exponents, or radicands.

Tell whether the equation represents a linear function.

7. $y = 3^x + 1$ ______

8. $3x - 2y = 6$ ______

9. $xy + 5 = 8$ ______

Name _______________ Class _______________ Date _______________

7.1 Connecting Intercepts and Zeros

Essential Question: How can you use the graph of a quadratic function to solve its related quadratic equation?

Resource Locker

Explore Graphing Quadratic Functions in Standard Form

A parabola can be graphed using its vertex and axis of symmetry. Use these characteristics, the y-intercept, and symmetry to graph a quadratic function.

Graph $y = x^2 - 4x - 5$ by completing the steps.

(A) Find the axis of symmetry.

$x = -\frac{b}{2a}$

$= -\frac{\square}{2 \cdot \square}$

$= \square$

The axis of symmetry is $x = \square$.

(B) Find the vertex.

$y = x^2 - 4x - 5$

$= \square^2 - 4 \cdot \square - 5$

$= \square - \square - 5$

$= \square$

The vertex is $(\square, \square)$.

(C) Find the y-intercept.

$y = x^2 - 4x - 5$

$y = \square^2 - 4\square + (\square)$

The y-intercept is $\square$; the graph passes through $(0, \square)$.

(D) Find two more points on the same side of the axis of symmetry as the y-intercept.

a. Find y when $x = 1$.

$y = x^2 - 4x - 5$

$= \square^2 - 4 \cdot \square - 5$

$= \square - \square - 5$

$= \square$

The first point is $(\square, \square)$.

b. Find y when $x = -1$.

$y = x^2 - 4x - 5$

$= \square^2 - 4(\square) - 5$

$= \square - (\square) - 5$

$= \square$

The second point is $(\square, \square)$.

(E) Graph the axis of symmetry, the vertex, the y-intercept, and the two extra points on the same coordinate plane. Then reflect the graphed points over the axis of symmetry to create three more points, and sketch the graph.

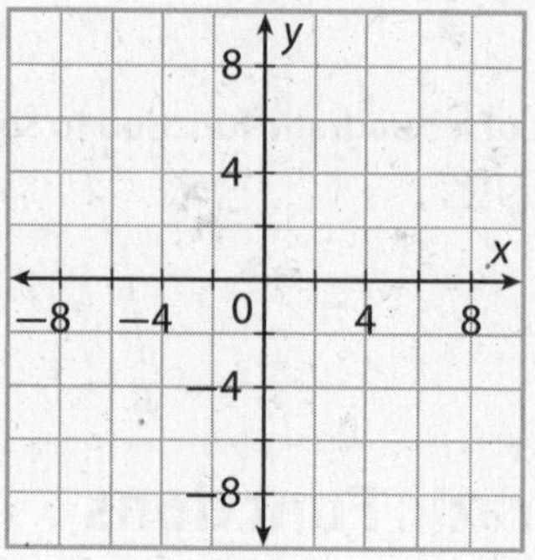

Reflect

1. **Discussion** Why is it important to find additional points before graphing a quadratic function?

____

____

Explain 1 Using Zeros to Solve Quadratic Equations Graphically

A **zero of a function** is an x-value that makes the value of the function 0. The zeros of a function are the x-intercepts of the graph of the function. A quadratic function may have one, two, or no zeros.

Quadratic equations can be solved by graphing the related function of the equation. To write the related function, rewrite the quadratic equation so that it equals zero on one side. Replace the zero with y.

Graph the related function. Find the x-intercepts of the graph, which are the zeros of the function. The zeros of the function are the solutions to the original equation.

Example 1 **Solve by graphing the related function.**

(A) $2x^2 - 5 = -3$

a. Write the related function. Add 3 to both sides to get $2x^2 - 2 = 0$. The related function is $y = 2x^2 - 2$.

b. Make a table of values for the related function.

x	−2	−1	0	1	2
y	6	0	−2	0	6

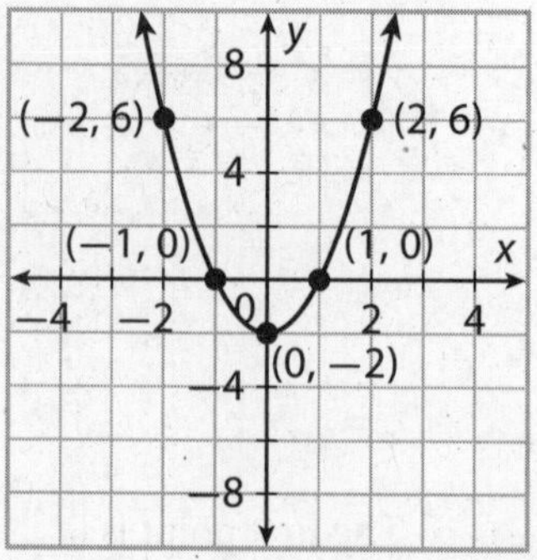

c. Graph the points represented by the table and connect the points.

d. The zeros of the function are −1 and 1, so the solutions of the equation $2x^2 - 5 = -3$ are $x = -1$ and $x = 1$.

(B) $6x + 8 = -x^2$

a. Write the related function. Add x^2 to both sides to get ☐ $+ 6x + 8 =$ ☐.

The related function is ☐ $=$ ☐ $+ 6x + 8$.

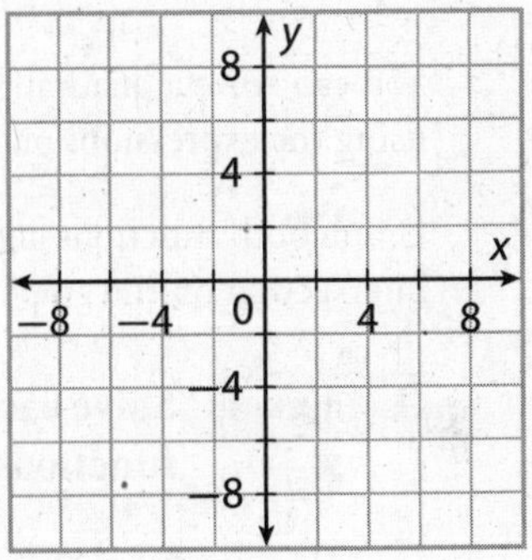

b. Make a table of values for the related function.

x	−5	−4	−3	−2	−1
y					

c. Graph the points represented by the table and connect the points.

d. The zeros of the function are ☐ and ☐, so the solutions of the equation

$6x + 8 = -x^2$ are $x =$ ☐ and $x =$ ☐.

Reflect

2. How would the graph of a quadratic equation look if the equation has one zero?

____

Your Turn

3. $x^2 - 4 = -3$

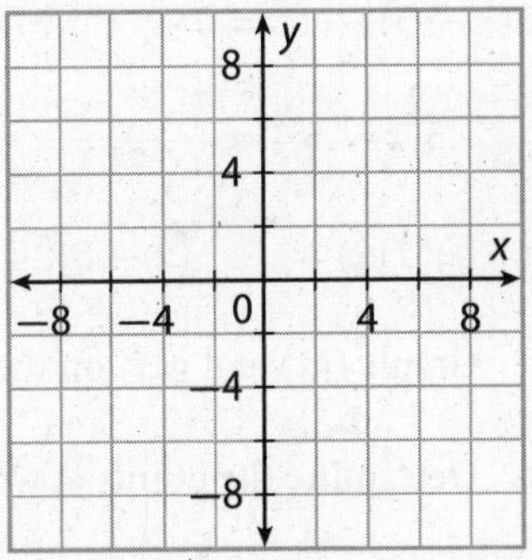

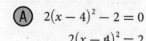

Explain 2 Using Points of Intersection to Solve Quadratic Equations Graphically

You can solve a quadratic equation by rewriting the equation in the form $ax^2 + bx = c$ or $a(x - h)^2 = k$ and then using the expressions on each side of the equal sign to define a function.

Graph both functions and find the points of intersection. The solutions are the x-coordinates of the points of intersection on the graph. As with using zeros, there may be two, one, or no points of intersection.

Example 2 **Solve each equation by finding points of intersection of two related functions.**

(A) $2(x - 4)^2 - 2 = 0$

$2(x - 4)^2 = 2$ Rewrite as $a(x - h)^2 = k$. Graph each side as related function.

a. Let $f(x) = 2(x - 4)^2$. Let $g(x) = 2$.

b. Graph $f(x)$ and $g(x)$ on the same graph.

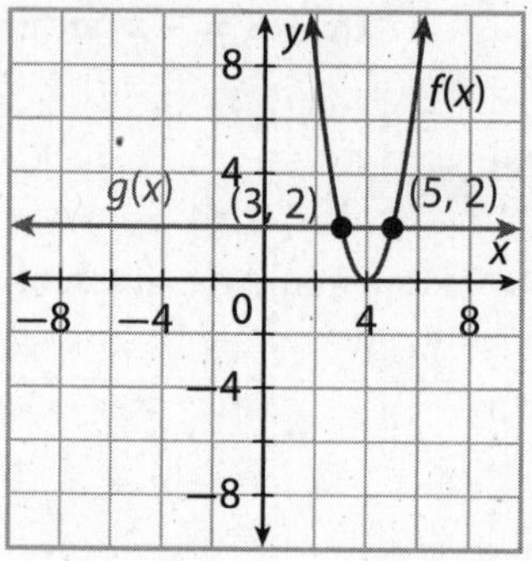

c. Determine the points at which the graphs of $f(x)$ and $g(x)$ intersect.

The graphs intersect at two locations: $(3, 2)$ and $(5, 2)$.

This means $f(x) = g(x)$ when $x = 3$ and $x = 5$.

So the solutions of $2(x - 4)^2 - 2 = 0$ are $x = 3$ and $x = 5$.

(B) $3(x - 5)^2 - 12 = 0$

$3(x - 5)^2 = \square$

a. Let $f(x) = \square(x - 5)^2$. Let $g(x) = \square$.

b. Graph $f(x)$ and $g(x)$ on the same graph.

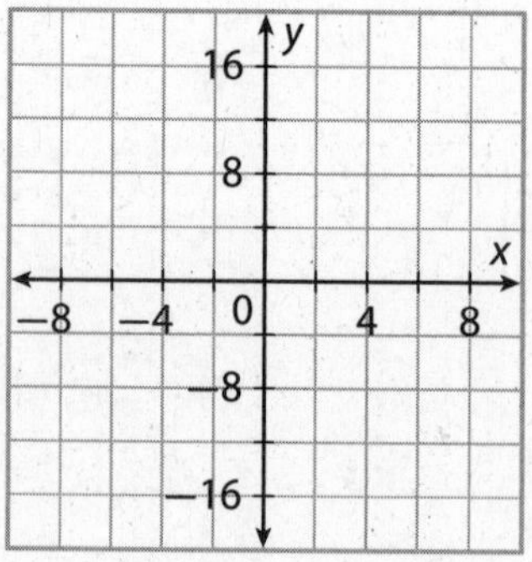

c. Determine the points at which the graphs of $f(x)$ and $g(x)$ intersect.

The graphs intersect at two locations:

$(\square, \square)$ and $(\square, \square)$.

This means $f(x) = g(x)$ when $x = \square$ and $x = \square$.

Therefore, the solutions of the equation $f(x) = g(x)$ are $\square$ and $\square$.

So the solutions of $3(x - 5)^2 - 12 = 0$ are $x = \square$ and $x = \square$.

Reflect

4. In Part B above, why is the x-coordinates the answer to the equation and not the y-coordinates?

____

____

____

____

Your Turn

5. Solve $3(x-2)^2 - 3 = 0$ by finding the points of intersection of the two related functions.

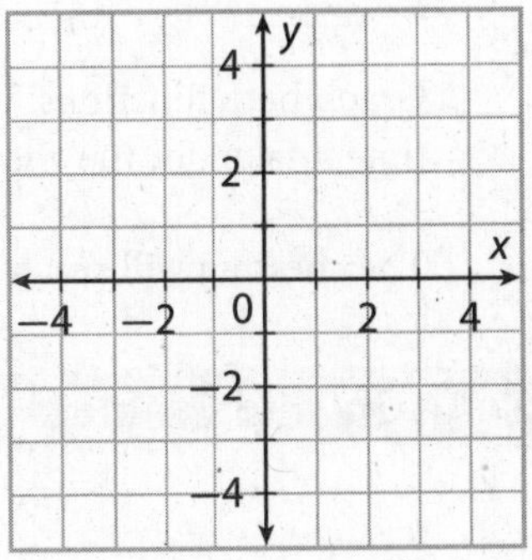

Explain 3 Modeling a Real-World Problem

Many real-world problems can be modeled by quadratic functions.

Example 3 **Create a quadratic function for each problem and then solve it by using a graphing calculator.**

Nature A squirrel is in a tree holding a chestnut at a height of 46 feet above the ground. It drops the chestnut, which lands on top of a bush that is 36 feet below the squirrel. The function $h(t) = -16t^2 + 46$ gives the height in feet of the chestnut as it falls, where t represents time. When will the chestnut reach the top of the bush?

Analyze Information

Identify the important information.

- The chestnut is ☐ feet above the ground, and the top of the bush is ☐ feet below the chestnut.
- The chestnut's height as a function of time can be represented by $h(t) =$ ☐ $t^2 +$ ☐, where $(h)t$ is the height of the chestnut in feet as it is falling.

Formulate a Plan

Create a related quadratic equation to find the height of the chestnut in relation to time. Use $h(t) = -16t^2 + 46$ and insert the known value for h.

Solve

Write the equation that needs to be solved. Since the top of the bush is 36 feet below the squirrel, it is 10 feet above the ground.

$-16t^2 + 46 = 10$

Separate the function into $y = f(t)$ and $y = g(t)$. $f(t) = \square t^{\square} + \square$ and $g(t) = \square$.

To graph each function on a graphing calculator, rewrite them in terms of x and y.

$y = \square x^{\square} + \square$ and $y = \square$

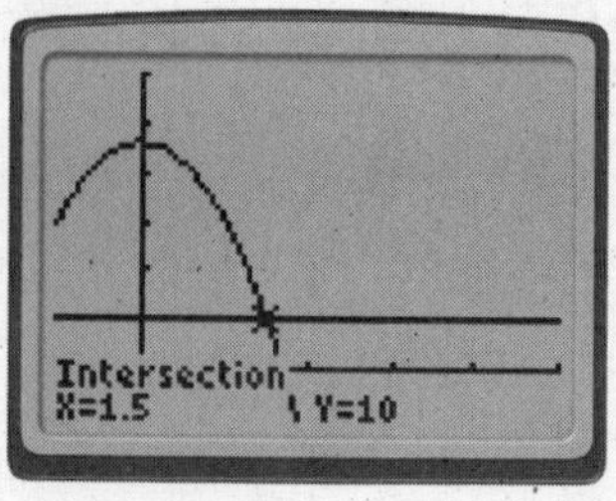

Graph both functions. Use the intersect feature to find the amount of time it takes for the chestnut to hit the top of the bush.

The chestnut will reach the top of the bush in $\square$ seconds.

Justify and Evaluate

$-16\left(\square\right)^2 + 46 = 10$

$\square + 46 = 10$

$\square = \square$

When t is replaced by ________ in the original equation, $-16t^2 + 46 = 10$ is true.

Reflect

6. In Example 3 above, the graphs also intersect to the left of the y-axis. Why is that point irrelevant to the problem?

____

Your Turn

7. **Nature** An egg falls from a nest in a tree 25 feet off the ground and lands on a potted plant that is 20 feet below the nest. The function $h(t) = -16t^2 + 25$ gives the height in feet of the egg as it drops, where t represents time. When will the egg land on the plant?

Explain 4 Interpreting a Quadratic Model

The solutions of a quadratic equation can be used to find other information about the situation modeled by the related function.

Example 4 **Use the given quadratic function model to answer questions about the situation it models.**

(A) **Nature** A dolphin jumps out of the water. The quadratic function $h(t) = -16t^2 + 20t$ models the dolphin's height above the water in feet after t seconds. How long is the dolphin out of the water?

Use the level of the water as a height of 0 feet. $h(0) = 0$, so the dolphin leaves the water at $t = 0$. When the dolphin reenters the water again, its height is 0 feet.

Solve $0 = -16t^2 + 20t$ to find the time when the dolphin reenters the water.

Graph the function on a graphing calculator, and find the other zero that occurs at $x > 0$.

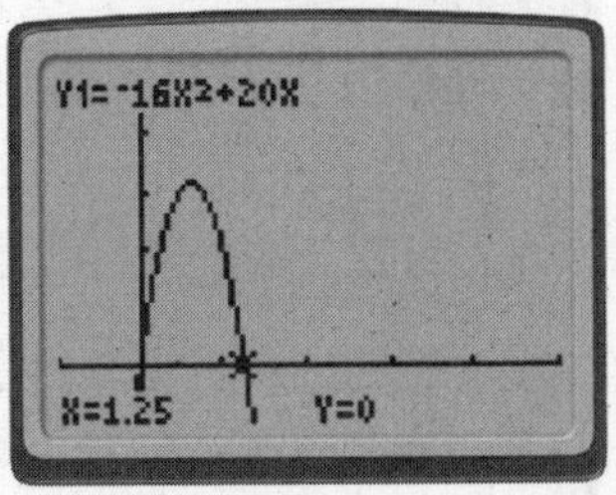

The zeros appear to be 0 and 1.25.

Check $x = 1.25$.

$-16(1.25)^2 + 20(1.25) = 0$ so 1.25 is a solution.

The dolphin is out of the water for 1.25 seconds.

(B) **Sports** A baseball coach uses a pitching machine to simulate pop flies during practice. The quadratic function $h(t) = -16t^2 + 80t + 5$ models the height in feet of the baseball after t seconds. The ball leaves the pitching machine and is caught at a height of 5 feet. How long is the baseball in the air?

To find when the ball is caught at a height of 5 feet, you need to solve $5 = -16t^2 + 80t + 5$.

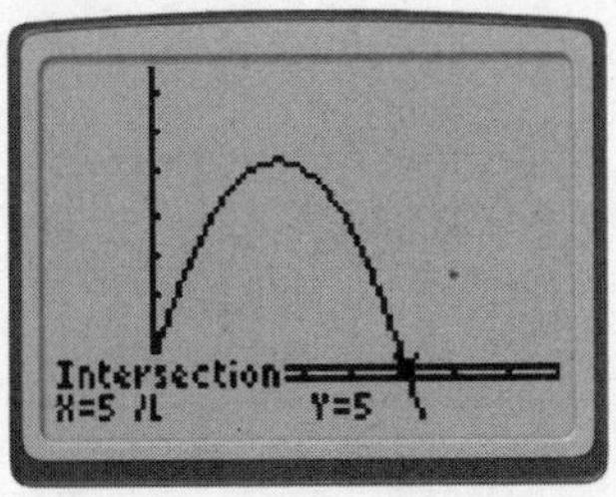

Graph Y1 = ☐ and Y2 = ☐, and use the intersection feature to find x-values when $y = 5$.

From the graph, it appears that the ball is 5 feet above the ground when

$y =$ ☐ or $y =$ ☐.

Therefore, the ball is in the air for ☐ − 0 = ☐ seconds.

Your Turn

8. **Nature** The quadratic function $y = -16x^2 + 5x$ models the height, in feet, of a flying fish above the water after x seconds. How long is the flying fish out of the water?

Elaborate

9. How is graphing quadratic functions in standard form similar to using zeros to solve quadratic equations graphically?

10. How can graphing calculators be used to solve real-world problems represented by quadratic equations?

11. **Essential Question Check-In** How can you use the graph of a quadratic function to solve a related quadratic equation by way of intersection?

Evaluate: Homework and Practice

Personal Math Trainer

- Online Homework
- Hints and Help
- Extra Practice

Solve each equation by graphing the related function and finding its zeros.

1. $3x^2 - 9 = -6$

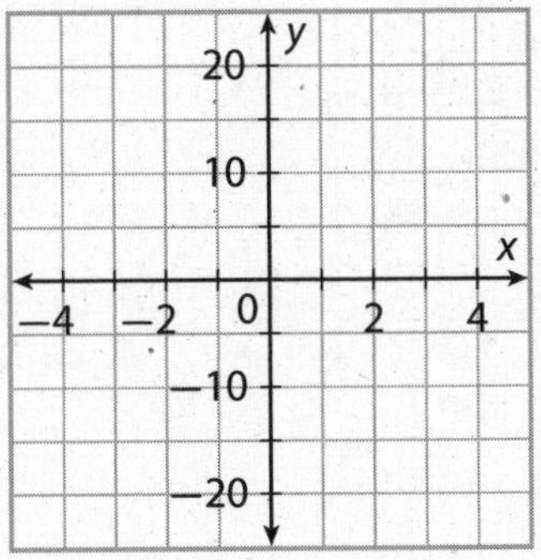

2. $2x^2 - 9 = -1$

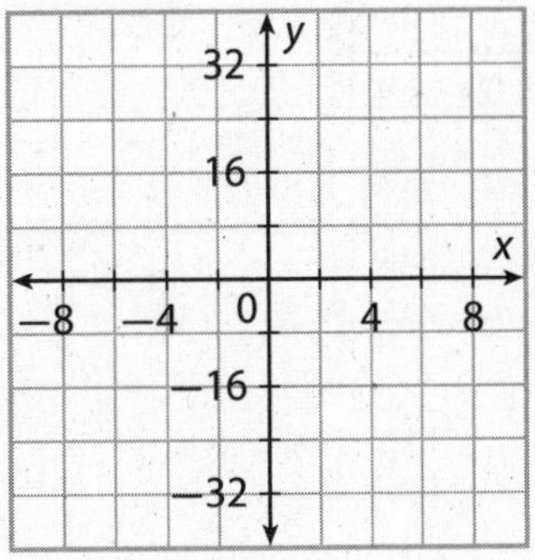

3. $4x^2 - 7 = -3$

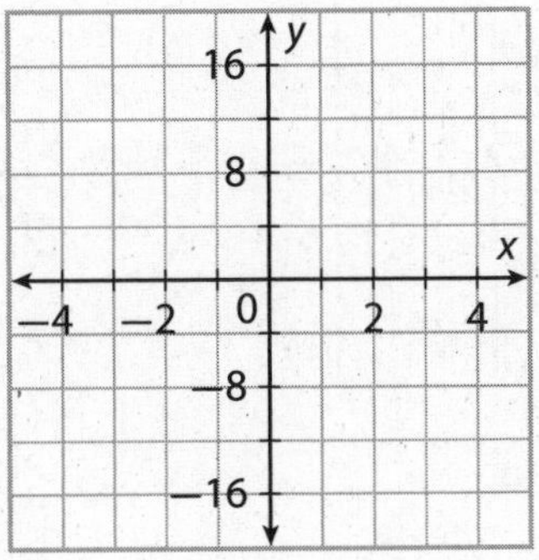

4. $7x + 10 = -x^2$

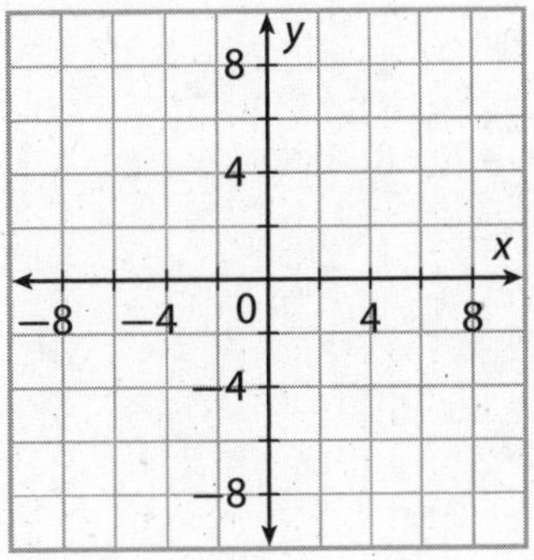

5. $2x - 3 = -x^2$

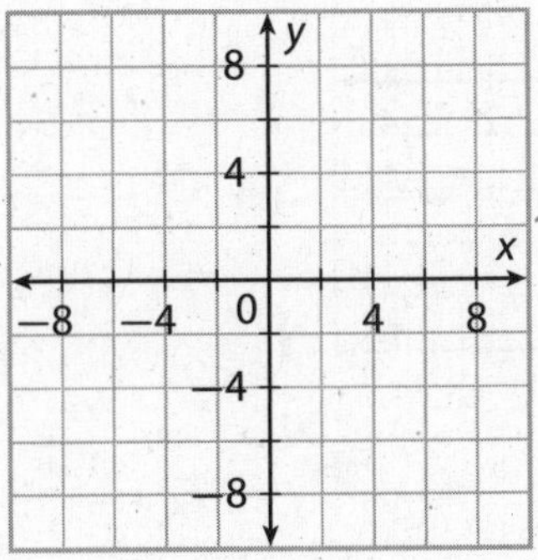

6. $-1 = -x^2$

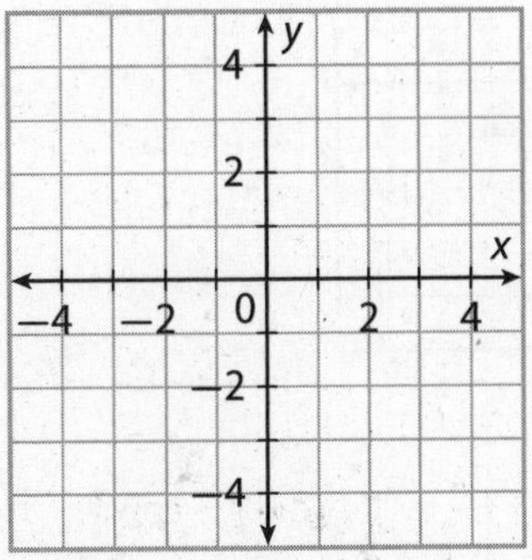

Solve each equation by finding points of intersection of two functions.

7. $2(x - 3)^2 - 4 = 0$

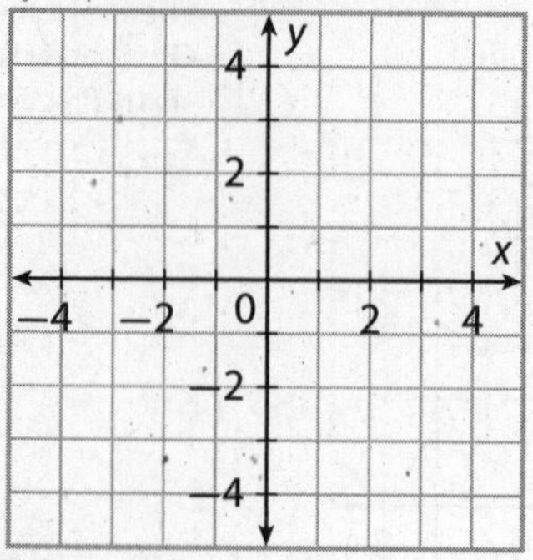

8. $(x + 2)^2 - 4 = 0$

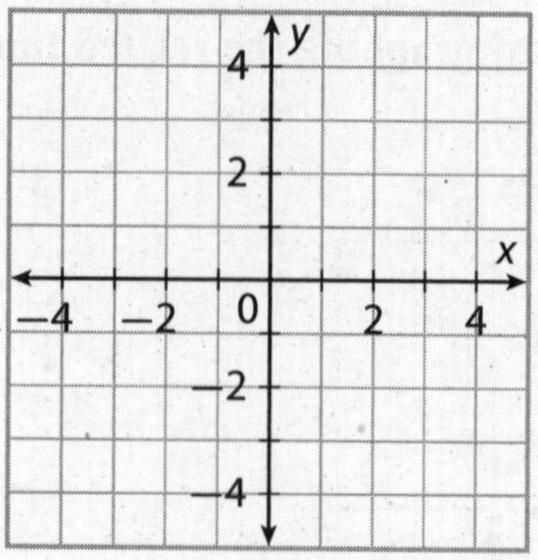

9. $-(x - 3)^2 + 4 = 0$

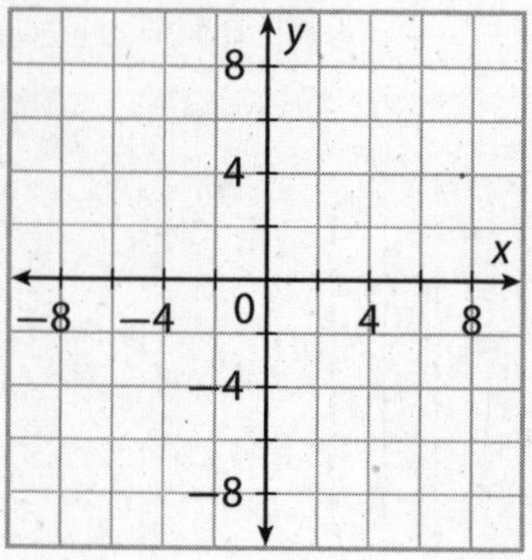

10. $-(x + 2)^2 - 2 = 0$

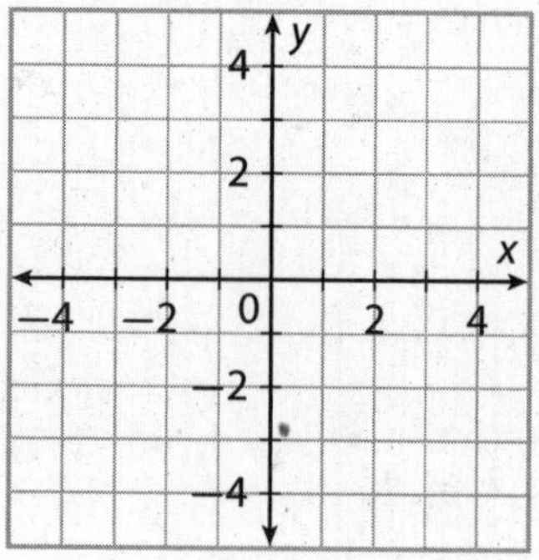

11. $(x + 1)^2 - 1 = 0$

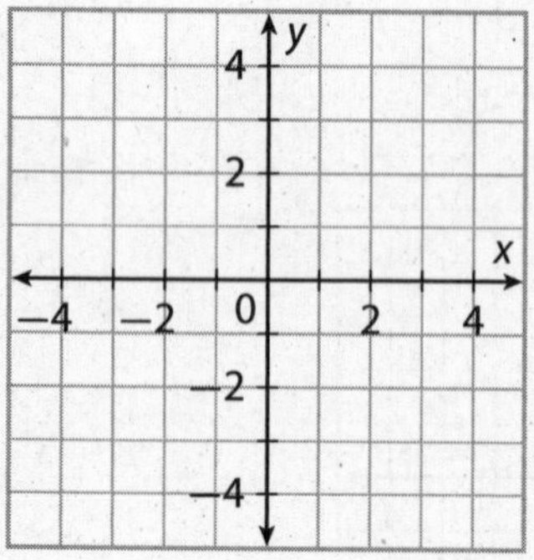

12. $(x + 2)^2 - 2 = 0$

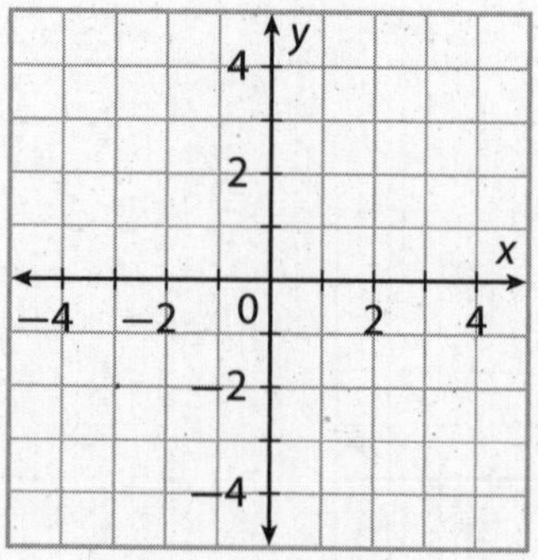

Create a quadratic equation for each problem and then solve the equation with a related function using a graphing calculator.

13. **Nature** A bird is in a tree 30 feet off the ground and drops a twig that lands on a rosebush 25 feet below. The function $h(t) = -16t^2 + 30$, where t represents the time in seconds, gives the height h, in feet, of the twig above the ground as it falls. When will the twig land on the bush?

14. **Nature** A monkey is in a tree 50 feet off the ground and drops a banana, which lands on a shrub 30 feet below. The function $h(t) = -16t^2 + 50$, where t represents the time in seconds, gives the height h, in feet, of the banana above the ground as it falls. When will the banana land on the shrub?

15. **Sports** A trampolinist steps off from 15 feet above ground to a trampoline 13 feet below. The function $h(t) = -16t^2 + 15$, where t represents the time in seconds, gives the height h, in feet, of the trampolinist above the ground as he falls. When will the trampolinist land on the trampoline?

16. **Physics** A ball is dropped from 10 feet above the ground. The function $h(t) = -16t^2 + 10$, where t represents the time in seconds, gives the height h, in feet, of the ball above the ground. When will the ball be 4 feet above the ground?

Use the given quadratic function model to answer questions about the situation it models.

17. **Nature** A shark jumps out of the water. The quadratic function $f(x) = -16x^2 + 18x$ models the shark's height, in feet, above the water after x seconds. How long is the shark out of the water?

18. **Sports** A baseball coach uses a pitching machine to simulate pop flies during practice. The quadratic function $f(x) = -16x^2 + 70x + 10$ models the height in feet of the baseball after x seconds. How long is the baseball in the air if the ball is not caught?

19. The quadratic function $f(x) = -16x^2 + 11x$ models the height, in feet, of a flying fish above the water after x seconds. How long is the flying fish out of the water?

20. A football coach uses a passing machine to simulate 50-yard passes during practice. The quadratic function $f(x) = -16x^2 + 60x + 5$ models the height in feet of the football after x seconds. How long is the football in the air if the ball is not caught?

21. In each polynomial function in standard form, identify a, b, and c.

a. $y = 3x^2 + 2x + 4$

b. $y = 2x + 1$

c. $y = x^2$

d. $y = 5$

e. $y = 3x^2 + 8x + 11$

22. Identify the axis of symmetry, y-intercept, and vertex of the quadratic function $y = x^2 + x - 6$ and then graph the function on a graphing calculator to confirm.

H.O.T. Focus on Higher Order Thinking

23. Counterexamples Pamela says that if the graph of a function opens upward, then the related quadratic equation has two solutions. Provide a counterexample to refute Pamela's claim.

24. Explain the Error Rodney was given the function $h(t) = -16t^2 + 50$ representing the height above the ground (in feet) of a water balloon t seconds after being dropped from a roof 50 feet above the ground. He was asked to find how long it took the balloon to fall 20 feet. Rodney used the equation $-16t^2 + 50 = 20$ to solve the problem. What was his error?

25. Critical Thinking If Jamie is given the graph of a quadratic function with only the x-intercepts and a random point labeled, can she determine an equation for the function? Explain.

Lesson Performance Task

Stella is competing in a diving competition. Her height in feet above the water is modeled by the function $f(x) = -16x^2 + 8x + 48$, where x is the time in seconds after she jumps from the diving board. Graph the function and solve the related equation $0 = -16x^2 + 8x + 48$. What do the solutions mean in the context of the problem? Are there solutions that do not make sense? Explain.

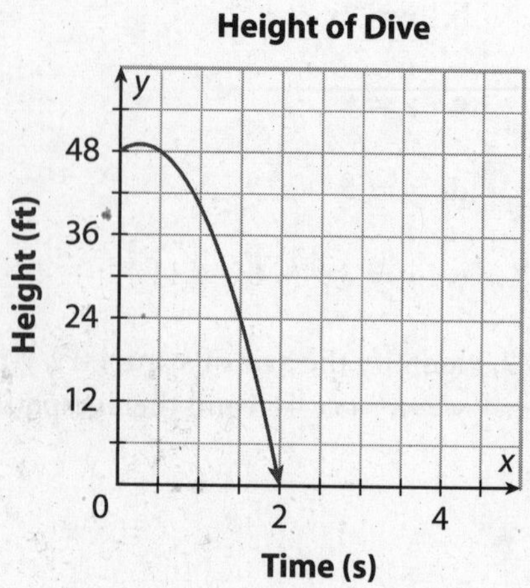

Name________________ Class________________ Date________________

7.2 Connecting Intercepts and Linear Factors

Essential Question: How are x-intercepts of a quadratic function and its linear factors related?

Resource Locker

Explore Connecting Factors and x–Intercepts

Use graphs and linear factors to find the x–intercepts of a parabola.

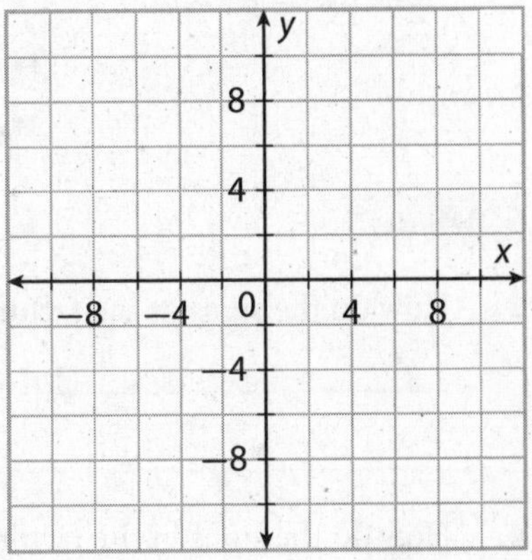

(A) Graph $y = x + 4$ and $y = x - 2$ using a graphing calculator. Then sketch the graphs on the grid.

(B) Identify the x-intercept of each line.

The x-intercepts are ____ and ____.

(C) The quadratic function $y = (x + 4)(x - 2)$ is the product of the two linear factors that have been graphed. Use a graphing calculator to graph the function $y = (x + 4)(x - 2)$. Then sketch a graph of the quadratic function on the same grid with the linear factors that have been graphed.

(D) Identify the x-intercepts of the parabola.

The x-intercepts are ____ and ____.

(E) What do you notice about the x–intercepts of the parabola?

____

Reflect

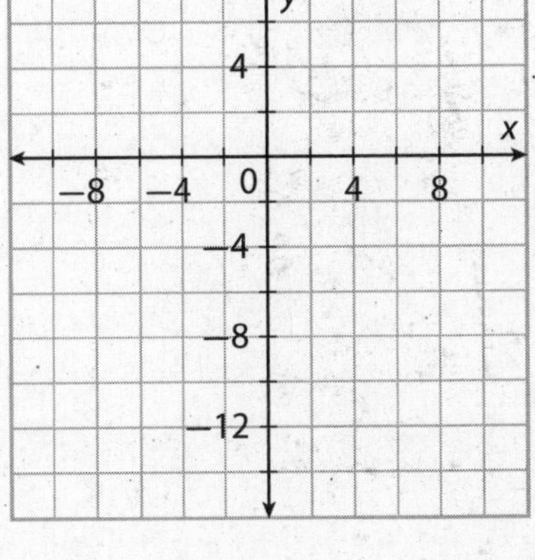

1. Use a graph to determine whether $2x^2 + 5x - 12$ is the product of the linear factors $2x - 3$ and $x + 4$.

____

____

2. **Discussion** Make a conjecture about the linear factors and x-intercepts of a quadratic function.

____

____

Explain 1 Rewriting from Factored Form to Standard Form

A quadratic function is in **factored form** when it is written as $y = k(x - a)(x - b)$ where $k \neq 0$.

Example 1 Write each function in standard form.

Ⓐ $y = 2(x + 1)(x - 4)$

Multiply the two linear factors.

$y = 2(x^2 - 4x + x - 4)$

$y = 2(x^2 - 3x - 4)$

Multiply the resulting trinomial by 2.

$y = 2x^2 - 6x - 8$

The standard form of $y = 2(x + 1)(x - 4)$ is $y = 2x^2 - 6x - 8$.

Ⓑ $y = 3(x - 5)(x - 2)$

Multiply the two linear factors.

$y = 3(\square)(\square)$

$y = 3(\square)$

Multiply the resulting trinomial by 3.

$y = \square$

The standard form of $y = 3(x - 5)(x - 2)$ is

______.

Reflect

3. How do the signs in the factors affect the sign of the x–term in the resulting trinomial?

______

______

4. How do the signs in the factors affect the sign of the constant term in the resulting trinomial?

______

______

Your Turn

Write each function in standard form.

5. $y = (x - 7)(x - 1)$

6. $y = 4(x - 1)(x + 3)$

Explain 2 Connecting Factors and Zeros

In the Explore you learned that the factors in factored form indicate the x-intercepts of a function. In a previous lesson you learned that the x-intercepts of a graph are the zeros of the function.

Example 2 **Write each function in standard form. Determine x-intercepts and zeros of each function.**

(A) $y = 2(x - 1)(x - 3)$

Write the function in standard form.

$y = 2(x^2 - 3x - x + 3)$

$y = 2(x^2 - 4x + 3)$

$y = 2x^2 - 8x + 6$

The factors indicate the x–intercepts.

* Factor $(x - 1)$ indicates an x–intercept of 1.
* Factor $(x - 3)$ indicates an x–intercept of 3.

The x-intercepts of a graph are the zeros of the function.

* An x–intercept of 1 indicates that the function has a zero of 1.
* An x–intercept of 3 indicates that the function has a zero of 3.

(B) $y = 2(x + 4)(x + 2)$

Write the function in standard form.

$y = 2(\square)(\square)$

$y = 2\square$

$y = \square$

The factors indicate the x–intercepts.

* Factor $(x + 4)$ indicates an x–intercept of ____.
* Factor ________ indicates an x–intercept of –2.

The x–intercepts of a graph are the zeros of the function.

* An x–intercept of –4 indicates that the function has a zero of ____.
* An x–intercept of ____ indicates that the function has a zero of –2.

Reflect

7. **Discussion** What are the zeros of a function?

____

____

8. How many x-intercepts can quadratic functions have?

____

Your Turn

Write each function in standard form. Determine x–intercepts and zeros of each function.

9. $y = -2(x + 5)(x + 1)$

10. $y = 5(x - 3)(x - 1)$

Explain 3 Writing Quadratic Functions Given x-Intercepts

Given two quadratic functions $f(x) = (x - a)(x - b)$ and $g(x) = k(x - a)(x - b)$, where k is any non-zero real constant, examine the x–intercepts for each quadratic function.

$f(x) = (x - a)(x - b)$ $0 = (x - a)(x - b)$ $x - a = 0$ or $x - b = 0$ $x = a$ $x = b$	$g(x) = k(x - a)(x - b)$ $0 = k(x - a)(x - b)$ $0 = (x - a)(x - b)$ $x - a = 0$ or $x - b = 0$ $x = a$ $x = b$

Notice that $f(x) = (x - a)(x - b)$ and $g(x) = k(x - a)(x - b)$ have the same x-intercepts. You can use the factored form to construct a quadratic function given the x–intercepts and the value of k.

Example 3 **For the two given intercepts, use the factored form to generate a quadratic function for each given constant k. Write the function in standard form.**

(A) x-intercepts: 2 and 5; $k = 1$, $k = -2$, $k = 3$

Write the quadratic function with $k = 1$.

$f(x) = k(x - a)(x - b)$

$f(x) = 1(x - 2)(x - 5)$

$f(x) = (x - 2)(x - 5)$

$f(x) = x^2 - 7x + 10$

Write the quadratic function with $k = -2$.

$f(x) = -2(x - 2)(x - 5)$

$f(x) = -2(x^2 - 7x + 10)$

$f(x) = -2x^2 + 14x - 20$

Write the quadratic function with $k = 3$.

$f(x) = 3(x - 2)(x - 5)$

$f(x) = 3(x^2 - 7x + 10)$

$f(x) = 3x^2 - 21x + 30$

(B) x-intercepts: -3 and 4; $k = 1$, $k = -3$, $k = 2$

Write the quadratic function with $k = 1$.

$f(x) =$

$f(x) =$

Write the quadratic function with $k = -3$.

$f(x) =$

$f(x) =$

Write the quadratic function with $k = 2$.

$f(x) =$

$f(x) =$

Reflect

11. How are the functions with same intercepts but different constant factors the same? How are they different?

Your Turn

For the given two intercepts and three values of k generate three quadratic functions. Write the functions in factored form and standard form.

12. x-intercepts: 1 and 8; $k = 1$, $k = -4$, $k = 5$

13. x-intercepts: -7 and 3; $k = 1$, $k = -5$, $k = 7$

Elaborate

14. If the x–intercepts of a quadratic function are 3 and 8, what can be said about the x–intercepts of its linear factors?

15. If a quadratic function has only one zero, it has to occur at the vertex of the parabola. Using the graph of a quadratic function, explain why.

16. How are x–intercepts and zeros related?

17. What would the factored form look like if there were only one x–intercept?

18. **Essential Question Check-In** How can you find x–intercepts of a quadratic function if its linear factors are known?

Evaluate: Homework and Practice

Personal Math Trainer
- Online Homework
- Hints and Help
- Extra Practice

Graph each quadratic function and each of its linear factors. Then identify the x-intercepts and the axis of symmetry of each parabola.

1. $y = (x - 2)(x - 6)$

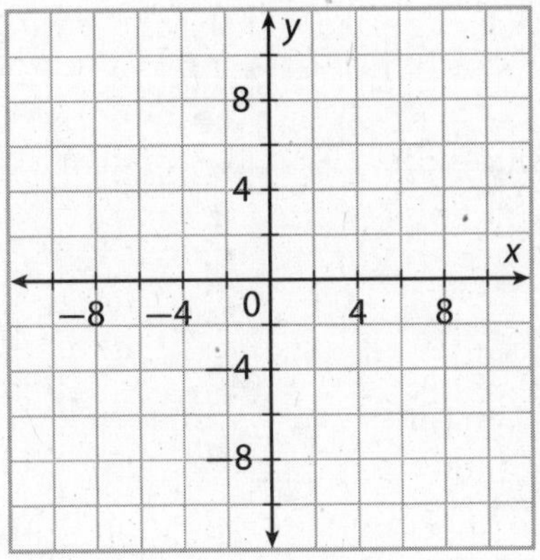

2. $y = (x + 3)(x - 1)$

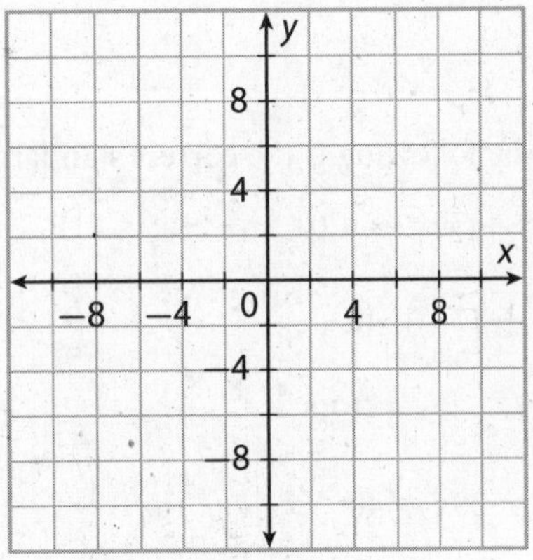

3. $y = (x - 5)(x + 2)$

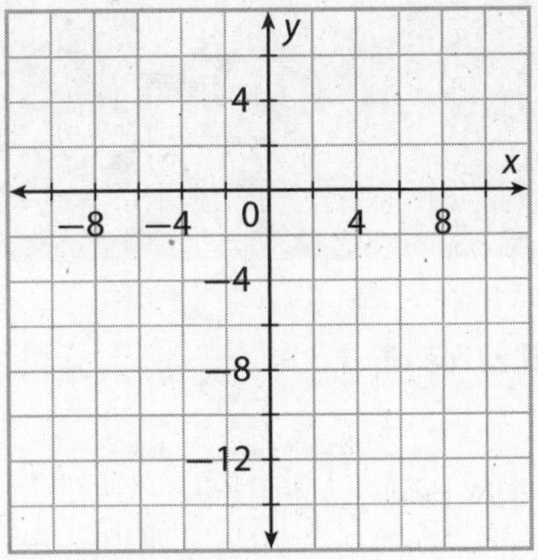

4. $y = (x - 5)(x - 5)$

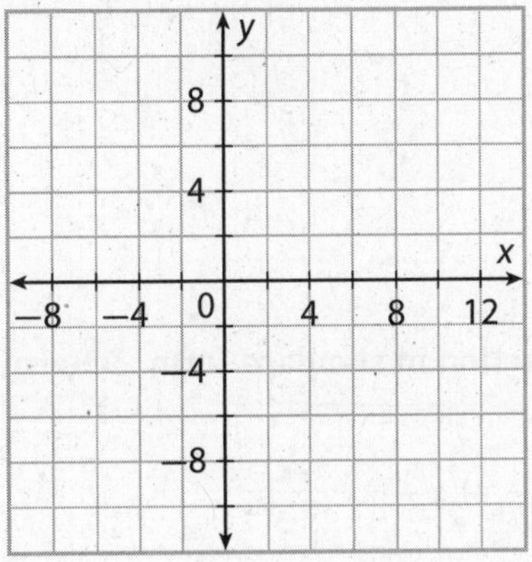

Write each function in standard form.

5. $y = 5(x - 2)(x + 1)$

6. $y = 2(x + 6)(x + 3)$

7. $y = -2(x + 4)(x - 5)$

8. $y = -4(x + 2)(x + 3)$

9. Which of the following is the correct standard form of $y = 3(x - 8)(x - 5)$?

a. $y = 3x^2 + 39x - 120$

b. $y = x^2 - 13x + 40$

c. $y = 3x^2 - 39x + 120$

d. $y = x^2 - 39x + 40$

e. $y = 3x^2 + 13x + 120$

10. The area of a Japanese rock garden is $y = 7(x - 3)(x + 1)$. Write $y = 7(x - 3)(x + 1)$ in standard form.

Write each function in standard form. Determine x–intercepts and zeros of each function.

11. $y = -2(x - 4)(x - 2)$

12. $y = 2(x + 4)(x - 2)$

13. $y = -3(x + 1)(x - 3)$

14. $y = 2(x + 2)(x - 1)$

15. A soccer ball is kicked from ground level. The function $y = -16x(x - 2)$ gives the height (in feet) of the ball, where x is time (in seconds). After how many seconds will the ball hit the ground? Use a graphing calculator to verify your answer.

16. A tennis ball is tossed upward from a balcony. The height of the ball in feet can be modeled by the function $y = -4(2x + 1)(2x - 3)$ where x is the time in seconds after the ball is released. Find the maximum height of the ball and the time it takes the ball to reach this height. Determine how long it takes the ball to hit the ground.

For the two given intercepts, use the factored form to generate a quadratic function for each given constant *k*. Write the function in standard form.

17. x-intercepts: -5 and 3; $k = 1$, $k = -2$, $k = 5$

18. x-intercepts: 4 and 7; $k = 1$, $k = -3$, $k = 5$

H.O.T. Focus on Higher Order Thinking

19. Explain the Error For the given two intercepts, 3 and 9, $k = 4$, Kelly wrote a quadratic function in factored form, $f(x) = 4(x + 3)(x + 9)$, and in standard form, $f(x) = 4x^2 + 48x + 108$. What error did she make?

20. Critical Thinking How is the graph of $f(x) = 7(x + 3)(x - 2)$ similar to and different from the graph of $f(x) = -7x^2 - 7x + 42$?

21. Make a Prediction How could you find an equation of a quadratic function with zeros at -3 and at 1?

Lesson Performance Task

The cross-sectional shape of the archway of a bridge (measured in feet) is modeled by the function $f(x) = -0.5x^2 + 6x$ where $f(x)$ is the height of the arch and x is the horizontal distance from one side of the base of the arch. How wide is the arch at its base? Will a box truck that is 8 feet wide and 13.5 feet tall fit under the arch? If not, what is the maximum height a truck that is 8 feet wide and is passing under the bridge can be?

Name ______________________ Class ______________ Date ____________

7.3 Applying the Zero Product Property to Solve Equations

Resource Locker

Essential Question: How can you use the Zero Product Property to solve quadratic equations in factored form?

Explore Understanding the Zero Product Property

For all real numbers a and b, if the product of the two quantities equals zero, then at least one of the quantities equals zero.

Zero Product Property		
For all real numbers a and b, the following is true.		
Words	**Sample Numbers**	**Algebra**
If the product of two quantities equals zero, at least one of the quantities equals zero.	$9(\square) = 0$ $0(4) = \square$	If $ab = 0$, then $\square = 0$ or $b = \square$.

(A) Consider the equation $(x - 3)(x + 8) = 0$. Let $a = x - 3$ and $b = \square$.

(B) Since $ab = 0$, you know that $a = 0$ or $b = 0$. $\square = 0$ or $x + 8 = 0$

(C) Solve for x.

$x - 3 = 0$ or $x + 8 = 0$

$x = \square$ $\qquad$ $x = \square$

(D) So, the solutions of the equation $(x - 3)(x + 8) = 0$ are $x = \square$ and $x = \square$.

(E) Recall that the solutions of an equation are the zeros of the related function. So, the solutions of the equation $(x - 3)(x + 8) = 0$ are the zeros of the related function $f(x) =$ ______________ because they satisfy the equation $f(x) = 0$. The solutions of the related function $f(x) =$ ______________ are __________ and __________.

Reflect

1. Describe how you can find the solutions of the equation $(x - a)(x - b) = 0$ using the Zero Product Property.

____

____

Explain 1 Applying the Zero Product Property to Functions

When given a function of the form $f(x) = (x + a)(x + b)$, you can use the Zero Product Property to find the zeros of the function.

Example 1 **Find the zeros of each function.**

(A) $f(x) = (x - 15)(x + 7)$

Set $f(x)$ equal to zero. $(x - 15)(x + 7) = 0$

Apply the Zero Product Property. $x - 15 = 0$ or $x + 7 = 0$

Solve each equation for x. $x = 15$ $x = -7$

The zeros are 15 and −7.

(B) $f(x) = (x + 1)(x + 23)$

Set $f(x)$ equal to zero. $(x + 1)(x + 23) = \square$

Apply the Zero Product Property. $x + \square = 0$ or $x + 23 = \square$

Solve for x. $x = \square$ $x = \square$

The zeros are $\square$ and $\square$.

Reflect

2. **Discussion** Jordie was asked to identify the zeros of the function $f(x) = (x - 5)(x + 3)$. Her answers were $x = -5$ and $x = 3$. Do you agree or disagree? Explain.

3. How would you find the zeros of the function $f(x) = -4(x - 8)$?

4. What are the zeros of the function $f(x) = x(x - 12)$? Explain.

Your Turn

Find the zeros of each function.

5. $f(x) = (x - 10)(x - 6)$

6. $f(x) = 7(x - 13)(x + 12)$

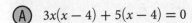

Explain 2 Solving Quadratic Equations Using the Distributive Property and the Zero Product Property

The Distributive Property states that, for real numbers a, b, and c, $a(b + c) = ab + ac$ and $ab + ac = a(b + c)$. The Distributive Property applies to polynomials, as well. For instance, $3x(x - 4) + 5(x - 4) = (3x + 5)(x - 4)$. You can use the Distributive Property along with the Zero Product Property to solve certain equations.

Example 2 **Solve each equation using the Distributive Property and the Zero Product Property.**

(A) $3x(x - 4) + 5(x - 4) = 0$

Use the Distributive Property to rewrite the expression $3x(x - 4) + 5(x - 4)$ as a product. $3x(x - 4) + 5(x - 4) = (3x + 5)(x - 4)$

Rewrite the equation. $(3x + 5)(x - 4) = 0$

Apply the Zero Product Property. $3x + 5 = 0$ or $x - 4 = 0$

Solve each equation for x. $3x = -5$ $x = 4$

$x = -\frac{5}{3}$

The solutions are $x = -\frac{5}{3}$ and $x = 4$.

(B) $-9(x + 2) + 3x(x + 2) = 0$

Use the Distributive Property to rewrite the expression $-9(x + 2) + 3x(x + 2)$ as a product. $-9(x + 2) + 3x(x + 2) = (\square + 3x)(x + \square)$

Rewrite the equation. $(\square + 3x)(x + \square) = 0$

Apply the Zero Product Property. $\square + 3x = 0$ or $x + \square = 0$

Solve each equation for x. $3x = \square$ $x = \square$

$x = \square$

The solutions are $x = \square$ and $x = \square$.

Reflect

7. How can you solve the equation $5x(x - 3) + 4x - 12 = 0$ using the Distributive Property?

Your Turn

Solve each equation using the Distributive Property and the Zero Product Property.

8. $7x(x - 11) - 2(x - 11) = 0$

9. $-8x(x + 6) + 3x + 18 = 0$

Explain 3 Solving Real-World Problems Using the Zero Product Property

Example 3

The height of one diver above the water during a dive can be modeled by the equation $h = -4(4t + 5)(t - 3)$, where h is height in feet and t is time in seconds. Find the time it takes for the diver to reach the water.

Analyze Information

Identify the important information.

- The height of the diver is given by the equation $h = -4(4t + 5)(t - 3)$.
- The diver reaches the water when $h = \square$.

Formulate a Plan

To find the time it takes for the diver to reach the water, set the equation equal to $\square$ and use the ______________ Property to solve for t.

Solve

Set the equation equal to zero. $\quad -4(4t + 5)(t - 3) = 0$

Apply the Zero Product Property. Since $-4 \neq 0$, set the other factors equal to 0. $\quad 4t + 5 = 0$ or $t - 3 = 0$

Solve each equation for x.

$4t + 5 = 0$ or $t - 3 = 0$

$4t = \square \qquad t = \square$

$t = \square$

The zeros are $t = \square$ and $t = \square$. Since time cannot be negative, the time it takes for the diver to reach the the water is $\square$ seconds.

Justify and Evaluate

Check to see that the answer is reasonable by substituting 3 for t in the equation $-4(4t + 5)(t - 3) = 0$.

$$-4(4(3) + 5)(3 - 3) = -4(\square + 5)(\square - 3)$$

$$= -4(\square)(\square)$$

$$= \square$$

Since the equation is equal to $\square$ for $t = 3$, the solution is reasonable. The diver will reach the water after $\square$ seconds.

Reflect

10. If you were to graph the function $f(t) = -4(4t + 5)(t - 3)$, what points would be associated with the zeros of the function?

Your Turn

11. The height of a golf ball after it has been hit from the top of a hill can be modeled by the equation $h = -8(2t - 4)(t + 1)$, where h is height in feet and t is time in seconds. How long is the ball in the air?

Elaborate

12. Can you use the Zero Product Property to find the zeros of the function $f(x) = (x - 1) + (2 - 9x)$? Explain.

13. Suppose a and b are the zeros of a function. Name two points on the graph of the function and explain how you know they are on the graph. What are the x-coordinates of the points called?

14. Essential Question Check-In Suppose you are given a quadratic function in factored form that is set equal to 0. Why can you solve it by setting each factor equal to 0?

Evaluate: Homework and Practice

Personal Math Trainer

- Online Homework
- Hints and Help
- Extra Practice

Find the solutions of each equation.

1. $(x - 15)(x - 22) = 0$

2. $(x + 2)(x - 18) = 0$

Find the zeros of each function.

3. $f(x) = (x + 15)(x + 17)$

4. $f(x) = \left(x - \frac{2}{9}\right)\left(x + \frac{1}{2}\right)$

5. $f(x) = -0.2(x - 1.9)(x - 3.5)$

6. $f(x) = x(x + 20)$

7. $f(x) = \frac{3}{4}\left(x - \frac{3}{4}\right)$

8. $f(x) = (x + 24)(x + 24)$

Solve each equation using the Distributive Property and the Zero Product Property.

9. $-6x(x + 12) - 15(x + 12) = 0$

10. $10(x - 3) - x(x - 3) = 0$

11. $5x\left(x + \frac{2}{3}\right) + \left(x + \frac{2}{3}\right) = 0$

12. $-(x + 4) + x(x + 4) = 0$

13. $7x(9 - x) + \frac{1}{3}(9 - x) = 0$

14. $-x(x - 3) + 6x - 18 = 0$

Solve using the Zero Product Property.

15. The height of a football after it has been kicked from the top of a hill can be modeled by the equation $h = 2(-2 - 4t)(2t - 5)$, where h is the height of the football in feet and t is the time in seconds. How long is the football in the air?

16. Football During football practice, a football player kicks a football. The height h in feet of the ball t seconds after it is kicked can be modeled by the function $h = -4t(4t - 11)$. How long is the football in the air?

17. Physics The height of a flare fired from a platform can be modeled by the equation $h = 8t(-2t + 10) + 4(-2t + 10)$, where h is the height of the flare in feet and t is the time in seconds. Find the time it takes for the flare to reach the ground.

18. Diving The depth of a scuba diver can be modeled by the equation $d = 0.5t(3.5t - 28.25)$, where d is the depth in meters of the diver and t is the time in minutes. Find the time it takes for the diver to reach the surface. Give your answer to the nearest minute.

19. A group of friends tries to keep a small beanbag from touching the ground by kicking it. On one kick, the beanbag's height can be modeled by the equation $h = -2(t - 1) - 16t(t - 1)$, where h is the height of the beanbag in feet and t is the time in seconds. Find the time it takes the beanbag to reach the ground.

20. Elizabeth and Markus are playing catch. Elizabeth throws the ball first. The height of the ball can be modeled by the equation $h = -16t(t - 5)$, where h is the height of the ball in feet and t is the time in seconds. Markus is distracted at the last minute and looks away. The ball lands at his feet. If the ball travels horizontally at an average rate of 3.5 feet per second, how far is Markus standing from Elizabeth when the ball hits the ground?

21. Match the function on the left with its zeros on the right. Indicate a match by writing the letter for a function on the line in front of the corresponding values of x.

A. $f(x) = 11(x - 9) + x(x - 9)$ ____ **a.** $x = -11$ and $x = -9$

B. $f(x) = (x + 9)(x - 11)$ ____ **b.** $x = 9$ and $x = -11$

C. $f(x) = 11(x - 9) - x(x - 9)$ ____ **c.** $x = 9$ and $x = 11$

D. $f(x) = (x - 9)(x + 11)$ ____ **d.** $x = -9$ and $x = 11$

E. $f(x) = -x(x + 9) - 11(x + 9)$

H.O.T. Focus on Higher Order Thinking

22. Explain the Error A student found the zeros of the function $f(x) = 2x(x - 5) + 6(x - 5)$. Explain what the student did wrong. Then give the correct answer.

$2x(x - 5) + 6(x - 5) = 0$

$2x(x - 5) = 0$, so $2x = 0$, and $x = 0$, or

$x - 5 = 0$, so $x = 5$, or

$6(x - 5) = 0$, so $x = 5$

Zeros: 0, 5 and 5

23. Draw Conclusions A ball is kicked into the air from ground level. The height h in meters that the ball reaches at a distance d in meters from the point where it was kicked is given by $h = -2d(d - 4)$. The graph of the equation is a parabola.

a. At what distance from the point where it is kicked does the ball reach its maximum height? Explain.

b. Find the maximum height. What is the point $(2, h)$ on the graph of the function called?

24. Justify Reasoning Can you solve $(x - 2)(x + 3) = 5$ by solving $x - 2 = 5$ and $x + 3 = 5$? Explain.

25. Persevere in Problem Solving Write an equation to find three numbers with the following properties. Let x be the first number. The second number is 3 more than the first number. The third number is 4 times the second number. The sum of the third number and the product of the first and second numbers is 0. Solve the equation and give the three numbers.

Lesson Performance Task

The height of a pole vaulter as she jumps over the bar is modeled by the function $f(t) = -1.75(t - 0)(t - 3.5)$, where t is the time in seconds at which the pole vaulter leaves the ground.

a. Find the solutions of the related equation when $f(t) = 0$ using the Zero Product Property. What do these solutions mean in the context of the problem?

b. If the bar is 6 feet high, will the pole vaulter make it over?

Connecting Intercepts, Zeros, and Factors

Essential Question: How can you use intercepts of a quadratic function to solve real-world problems?

Key Vocabulary
Zero Product Property
(Propiedad del producto cero)
zero of a function
(cero de una función)

KEY EXAMPLE *(Lesson 7.2)*

Generate the quadratic function with x-intercepts 3 and -2 and $k = 3$. Write the function in factored form and standard form.

Write the quadratic function with $k = 3$. Substitute the given values of the x-intercepts and k into $f(x) = k(x - a)(x - b)$ and simplify.

$f(x) = 3(x + 2)(x - 3)$

Write $f(x) = 3(x + 2)(x - 3)$ in standard form.

$$f(x) = 3(x + 2)(x - 3)$$
$$= 3x^2 - 3x - 18$$

KEY EXAMPLE *(Lesson 7.3)*

Solve $2x(x - 2) + 4(x - 2) = 0$ by using the Distributive Property and the Zero Product Property.

Use the Distributive Property to rewrite the expression $2x(x - 2) + 4(x - 2)$ as a product of binomials. $\quad 2x(x - 2) + 4(x - 2) = (2x + 4)(x - 2)$

Rewrite the equation. $\quad (2x + 4)(x - 2) = 0$

Apply the Zero Product Property. $\quad 2x + 4 = 0$ and $x - 2 = 0$

Solve each equation for x. $\quad 2x = -4$, $x = -2$ $\quad x = 2$

The solutions are $x = -2$ and $x = 2$.

EXERCISES

Solve each equation by graphing. *(Lesson 7.1)*

1. $x^2 - 2x - 1 = 2$

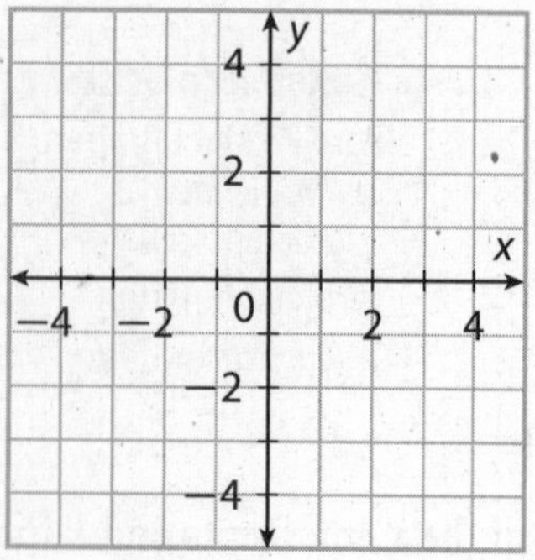

2. $(x + 2)^2 - 4 = 0$

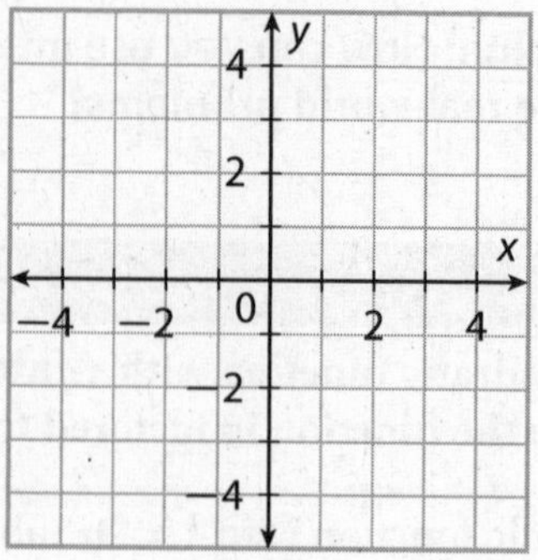

Write a function in factored and standard form for each *k* and set of *x*-intercepts. *(Lesson 7.2)*

3. x-intercepts: -3 and 4; $k = -2$

4. x-intercepts: 7 and 2; $k = 3$

Find the zeros of each function. *(Lesson 7.3)*

5. $f(x) = x(x + 17)$

6. $f(x) = -4(x - 2.3)(x - 4.6)$

MODULE PERFORMANCE TASK

Designing a Skateboard Ramp

The local government has made partial plans for the construction of a skateboard ramp, which are shown here. Your task is to complete the plans by modeling the parabolic curve of the ramp itself.

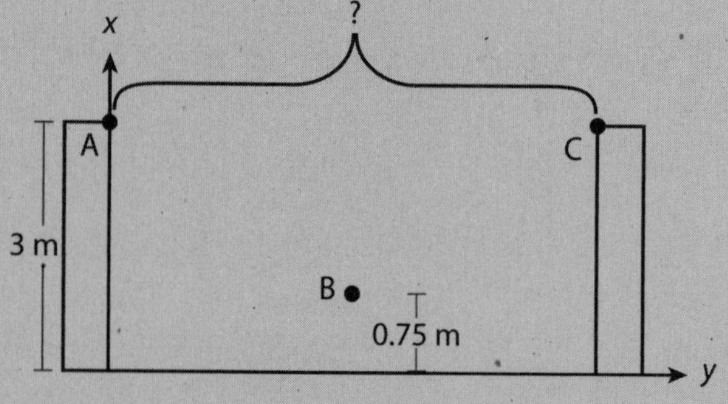

First, choose the total width of the parabola from point *A* to point *C*, which should be between 3 meters and 6 meters. Then, create an equation that models the parabola that starts at point *A*, reaches a minimum at point *B*, and ends at point *C*. Note that the *x*- and *y*-axes are marked in the diagram. Express your equation in standard form.

Use your own paper to complete the task, using graphs, numbers, or algebra to explain how you reached your conclusion.

Ready to Go On?

7.1–7.3 Connecting Intercepts, Zeros, and Factors

Personal Math Trainer

- Online Homework
- Hints and Help
- Extra Practice

Solve each equation by graphing. *(Lesson 7.1)*

1. $-4x + 4 = -x^2$

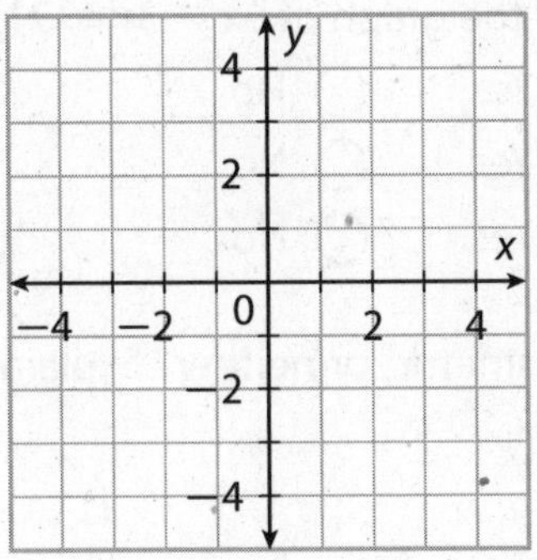

2. $-x^2 + 1 = 0$

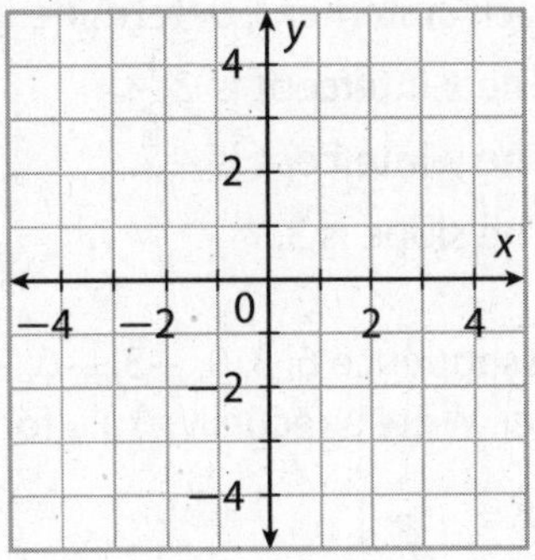

Write a function in factored and standard form for each k and set of x-intercepts. *(Lesson 7.2)*

3. x-intercepts: 5 and −7; $k = -3$

4. x-intercepts: −1 and −8; $k = 4$

Find the zeros of each function. *(Lesson 7.3)*

5. $f(x) = -8(x + 7)(x - 8.6)$

6. $f(x) = x(x - 42)$

7. $f(x) = 9x(x - 4) + 3(x - 4)$

8. $f(x) = -2x(x + 4) + 6x + 24$

ESSENTIAL QUESTION

9. How can you use factoring to solve quadratic equations in standard form?

MODULE 7
MIXED REVIEW

Assessment Readiness

1. Solve $8x(7 - x) + \frac{1}{5}(7 - x) = 0$.

A. $x = -7$ ○ Yes ○ No

B. $x = -\frac{8}{5}$ ○ Yes ○ No

C. $x = -\frac{1}{40}$ ○ Yes ○ No

2. For each statement, determine if it is True or False for the graph of $6x - 3y = 21$.

A. The *x*-intercept is $3\frac{1}{2}$. ○ Yes ○ No

B. The *y*-intercept is -7. ○ Yes ○ No

C. The slope is 3. ○ Yes ○ No

3. Is the sequence 6, 3, 0, −3, −6, −9, ... arithmetic, geometric, or neither? Explain your answer. Write a recursive rule for the sequence.

4. Graph $f(x) = (x - 2)^2 - 4$. Describe the relationship between the *x*-intercepts of the graph and the solutions of $(x - 2)^2 - 4 = 0$.

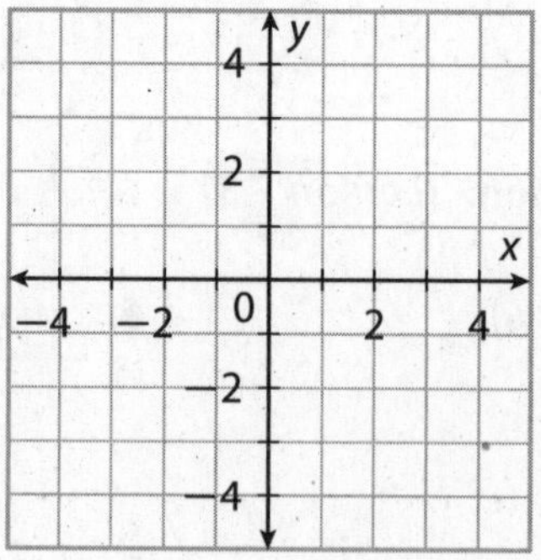

Assessment Readiness

Personal Math Trainer
- Online Homework
- Hints and Help
- Extra Practice

1. Consider the graph of $f(x) = -2x^2 - \frac{1}{2}$.
Determine if each statement is True or False.

A. The vertex is $\left(-2, \frac{1}{2}\right)$. ○ True ○ False
B. The maximum value is $-\frac{1}{2}$. ○ True ○ False
C. The axis of symmetry is $x = -2$. ○ True ○ False

2. Does the given statement describe a step in the transformation of the graph of $f(x) = x^2$ that would result in the graph of $g(x) = -5\,(x + 2)^2$?

A. The parent function is reflected across the x-axis. ○ Yes ○ No
B. The parent function is stretched by a factor of 5. ○ Yes ○ No
C. The parent function is translated 2 units up. ○ Yes ○ No

3. Use the graph of $f(x)$ to determine if each statement is True or False.

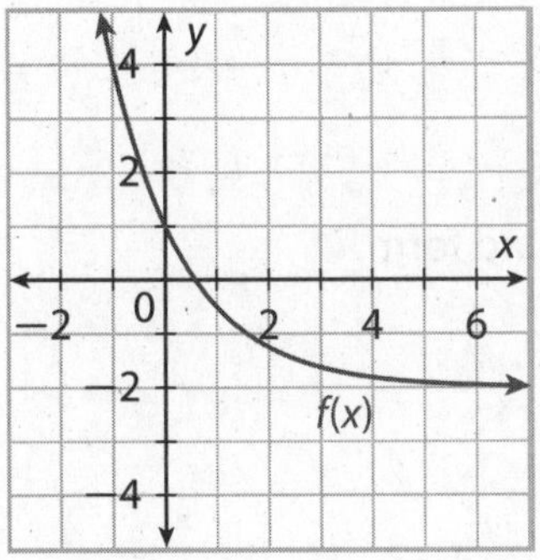

A. As $x \to \infty, y \to -2$. ○ True ○ False
B. The graph represents a quadratic function. ○ True ○ False
C. When $f(x) = 1, x = 0$. ○ True ○ False

4. Solve $\left(2x + \frac{2}{3}\right)(x + 5) = 0$. Is each of the following a solution of the equation?

A. $x = -\frac{1}{3}$ ○ Yes ○ No
B. $x = -5$ ○ Yes ○ No
C. $x = \frac{2}{3}$ ○ Yes ○ No

5. Use the table of values for $h(x)$ to determine if each statement is True or False.

x	−4	−2	0	2	4
$h(x)$	3	0	−3	0	3

A. A zero of the function is −3. ○ True ○ False

B. A zero of the function is −2. ○ True ○ False

C. A solution of the equation of the function $h(x) = 0$ is $x = 2$. ○ True ○ False

6. Graph $y = -2x^2 + 16x - 31$. What is the axis of symmetry of the graph? What is its vertex?

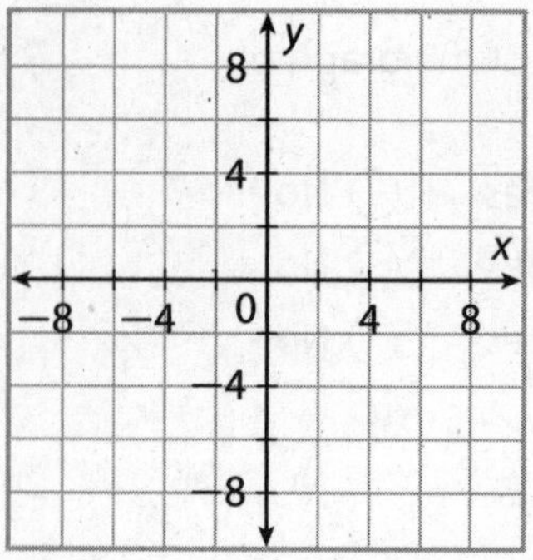

7. Graph $t(x) = \frac{1}{2}(x + 2)(x - 4)$, and write the function in standard form.

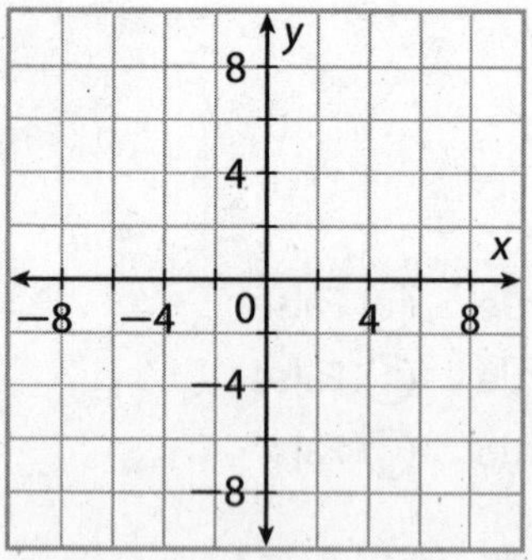

Performance Tasks

★ 8. A rectangular picture measuring 6 in. by 10 in. is surrounded by a frame with uniform width x.

A. Write a quadratic function to show the combined area of the picture and frame.

B. Write a quadratic function for the area of the frame.

★★ **9. Estimation** The graph shows the approximate height *y* in meters of a volleyball *x* seconds after it is served.

A. Estimate the time it takes for the volleyball to reach its greatest height.

B. Estimate the greatest height that the volleyball reaches.

C. If the domain of a quadratic function is all real numbers, why is the domain of this function limited to nonnegative numbers?

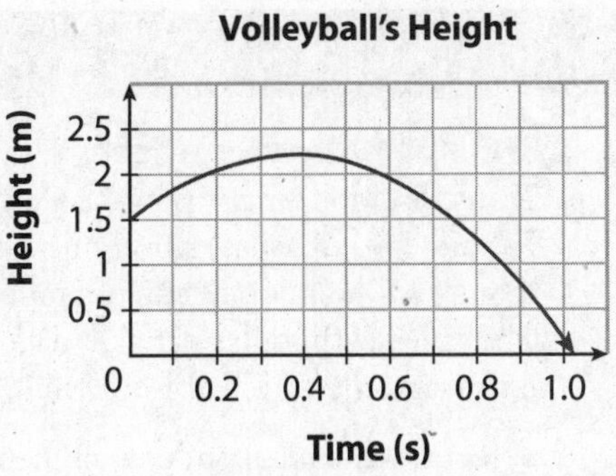

★★★**10.** A rocket team is using simulation software to create and study water bottle rockets. The team begins by simulating the launch of a rocket without a parachute. The table gives data for one rocket design.

A. Show that the data represent a quadratic function.

B. Graph the function.

C. The acceleration due to gravity is 9.8 m/s^2. How is this number related to the data for this water bottle rocket?

Time (s)	Height (m)
0	0
1	34.4
2	58.8
3	73.5
4	78.4
5	73.5
6	58.8
7	34.3
8	0

MATH IN CAREERS

Transportation Engineer The Center for Transportation Analysis in the Oak Ridge National Laboratory publishes data about the transportation industry. One study relates gas mileage and a car's speed. The mileage (in miles per gallon) for a particular year, make, and model of car is shown in the table.

Speed (miles per hour)	Gas Milage (miles per gallon)
40	23.0
50	27.3
55	29.1
60	28.2
70	22.9

a. Identify the independent and dependent variables in this situation. State the units associated with each variable.

b. Sketch a parabola that you think best fits the plotted points. (You will not be able to make the parabola pass through all the points. Instead, you should try to draw the parabola so that some points fall above it and some below it.) Explain why a parabola is a reasonable curve to fit to the data.

c. Write the equation for a function of the form $m(s) = -0.03(s - h)^2 + k$, where s is the speed and m is the gas mileage. Use the coordinates of the vertex of your parabola to determine h and k, and a point on your parabola other than the vertex to solve for the unknown a.

d. Suppose that when the car was driven at a steady speed, its gas mileage was 25 miles per gallon. Describe how you can use your model to find the car's speed. Is only one speed or more than one speed possible? Explain, and then find the speed(s).

UNIT 4

Quadratic Equations and Models

MATH IN CAREERS

Competitive Diver Diving is the sport of jumping into the water from a springboard or platform. Competitive divers should have a strong understanding of the mathematics of projectile motion, including the time spent in the air, the speed at which they hit the water, and the maximum height of a jump.

If you are interested in a career as a competitive diver, you should study these mathematical subjects:

- Algebra
- Business math

Research other careers that require understanding of the mathematics of projectile motion. Check out the career activity at the end of the unit to find out how **competitive divers** use math.

Reading Start-Up

Visualize Vocabulary

Use the review words to complete the chart.

	a square of a whole number
	one of two equal factors of a number
	the largest common factor of two or more given numbers
	a real number that cannot be expressed as the ratio of two integers
	a number that is multiplied by a variable

Understand Vocabulary

To become familiar with some of the vocabulary terms in this unit, consider the following. You may refer to the module, the glossary, or a dictionary.

1. The ________________ gives the solutions of a quadratic equation.

2. ________________ is a process that forms a perfect square trinomial.

3. By the ________________________, $\pm\sqrt{\frac{16}{9}} = \pm\frac{\sqrt{16}}{\sqrt{9}} = \pm\frac{4}{3}$.

Active Reading

Pyramid Before beginning this unit create a pyramid to help you organize what you learn. Label each side with one of the module titles from this unit: "Using Factors to Solve Quadratic Equations," "Using Square Roots to Solve Quadratic Equations," and "Linear, Exponential, and Quadratic Models." As you study each module, write important ideas like vocabulary, properties, and formulas on the appropriate side.

Vocabulary

Review Words

✔ coefficient *(coeficiente)*
✔ greatest common factor *(máximo común divisor (MCD)*
✔ irrational number *(número irracional)*
✔ perfect square *(cuadrado perfecto)*
✔ square root *(raíz cuadrada)*

Preview Words

completing the square *(completar el cuadrado)*
difference of two squares *(diferencia de dos cuadrados)*
Product Property of Square Roots *(Propiedad del producto de raíces cuadradas)*
quadratic formula *(fórmula cuadrática)*
Quotient Property of Square Roots *(Propiedad del cociente de raíces cuadradas)*

MODULE 8

Using Factors to Solve Quadratic Equations

Essential Question: How can you use factoring a quadratic equation to solve real-world problems?

REAL WORLD VIDEO
Ruling out common elements in a scientific experiment is similar to removing common factors in an equation; logically, whatever is common to two samples can't be the cause of differences between them.

MODULE PERFORMANCE TASK PREVIEW

Fitting Through the Arch

An arched doorway is a strong structure that can usually support more weight than a rectangular doorway. An arched opening is also far less likely than a rectangular opening to topple from vibrations of a train passing through it. However, many man-made objects are rectangular, not curved as an arch is curved. So, how big can a rectangular object be and still pass through an arched door? Let's find out!

Are YOU Ready?

Complete these exercises to review skills you will need for this module.

Personal Math Trainer

- Online Homework
- Hints and Help
- Extra Practice

Exponents

Example 1 Simplify $8^5 \cdot 8^{-2}$.

$8^5 \cdot 8^{-2} = 8^{5+(-2)}$ The bases are the same. Add the exponents.

$= 8^3$

$= 512$ Multiply.

Simplify.

1. $3^7 \cdot 3^{-3}$ ________

2. $7^7 \cdot 7^{-5}$ ________

3. $6^9 \cdot 6^{-4} \cdot 6^{-5}$ ________

Algebraic Expressions

Example 2 Simplify $13x + 5 - 9x^2 - 8$.

$13x + 5 - 9x^2 - 8$

$-9x^2 + 13x + 5 - 8$ Reorder in descending order of exponents.

$-9x^2 + 13x - 3$ Combine like terms.

Simplify.

4. $12x + 4x^2 - 3 - 7x$ ________

5. $7x^2 - 6 + 8x - 2x^2$ ________

6. $5 + 7x - 2x^2 - 6$ ________

7. $-4x + 6x^2 - 8 + 9x - 3x^2$ ________

Example 3 Multiply $(x + 7)(x - 3)$.

$(x + 7)(x - 3)$

$x(x) - 3(x) + 7(x) + 7(-3)$ Use FOIL.

$x^2 - 3x + 7x - 21$ Simplify.

$x^2 + 4x - 21$ Combine like terms.

Multiply.

8. $(x - 4)(x + 5)$ ________

9. $(x - 9)(x - 6)$ ________

10. $(2x - 3)(2x + 3)$ ________

11. $(3x - 2)(2x + 5)$ ________

Name _______________ Class _______________ Date _______________

8.1 Solving Equations by Factoring $x^2 + bx + c$

Resource Locker

Essential Question: How can you use factoring to solve quadratic equations in standard form for which $a = 1$?

Explore 1 Using Algebra Tiles to Factor $x^2 + bx + c$

In this lesson, multiplying binomials using the FOIL process will be reversed and trinomials will be factored into two binomials. To learn how to factor, let's start with the expression $x^2 + 7x + 6$.

(A) Identify and draw the tiles needed to model the expression $x^2 + 7x + 6$.

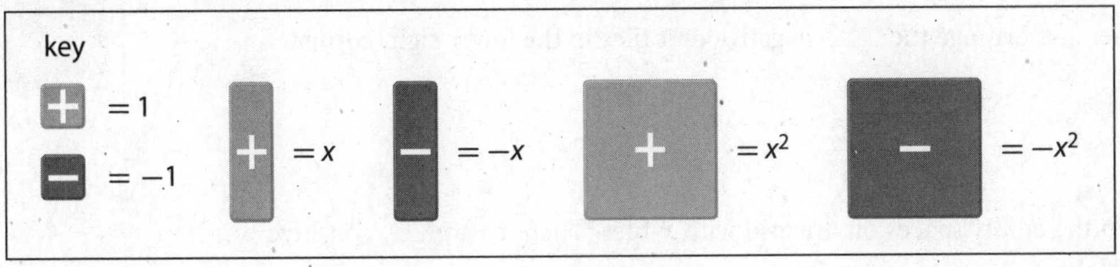

The tiles needed to model the expression $x^2 + 7x + 6$ are:

_____ x^2-tiles(s), _____ x-tile(s), and _____ unit tile(s).

(B) Arrange and draw the algebra tiles on the grid. Place the _____ x^2-tile(s) in the upper left corner and arrange the _____ unit tiles in two rows and three columns in the lower right corner.

×

(C) Try to complete the rectangle with the x-tiles. Notice that only _____ x-tiles fit on the grid, which leaves out _____ tile(s), so this arrangement is not correct.

×

(D) Rearrange the unit tiles so that all of the _____ x-tiles fit on the mat.

×

(E) Complete the multiplication grid by placing the factor tiles on the sides. Then write the factors modeled in this product.

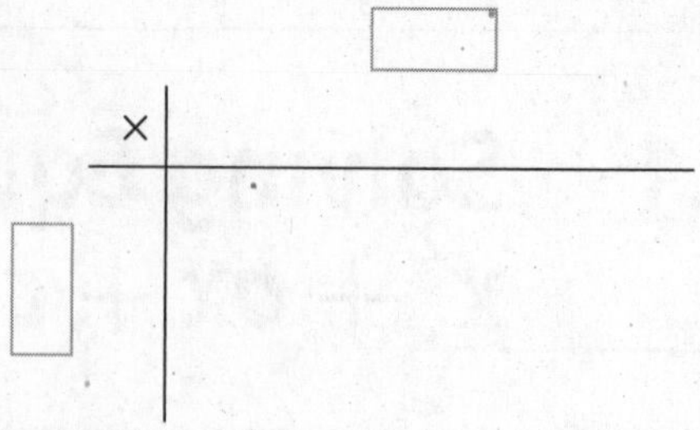

$x^2 + 7x + 6 = (x + \square)(x + \square)$

(F) Now let's look at how to factor a quadratic expression with a negative constant term. Use algebra tiles to factor $x^2 + x - 2$. Identify the tiles needed to model the expression.

____ positive x^2-tile(s), ____ positive x-tile(s), and ____ negative unit tile(s)

(G) Arrange the algebra tiles on the grid. Place the ____ positive x^2-tile(s) in the upper left

corner and arrange the ____ negative unit tiles in the lower right corner.

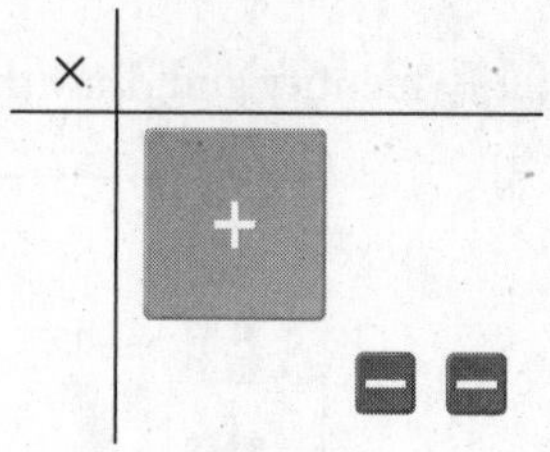

(H) Fill in the empty spaces on the grid with x-tiles. There is/are ____ positive x-tile(s) to

place on the grid, so there will be ____ empty places for x-tiles.

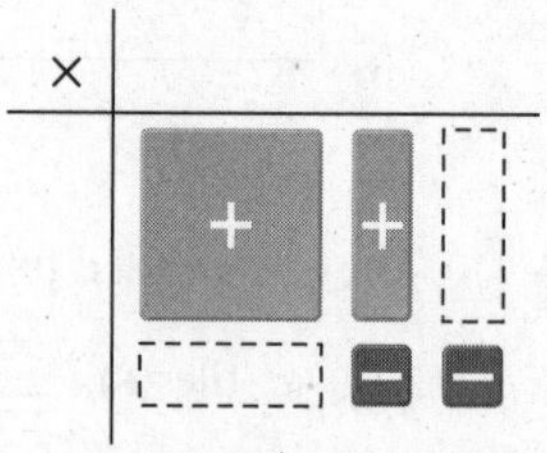

(I) Complete the rectangle on the mat by using *zero pairs*. Add ____ positive x-tile(s) and ____ negative x-tile(s) to the grid in such a way that the factors work with all the tiles on the mat. Circle the mat showing the correct position of zero pairs.

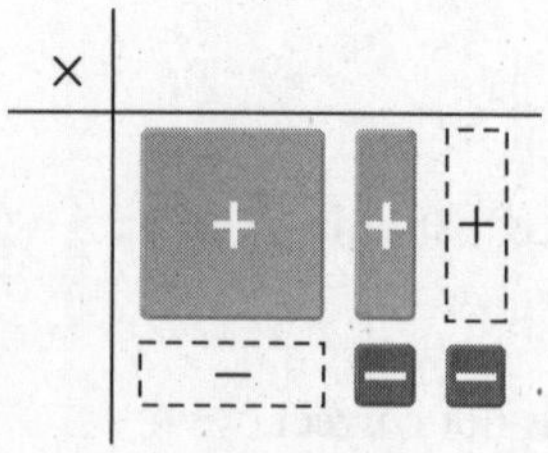

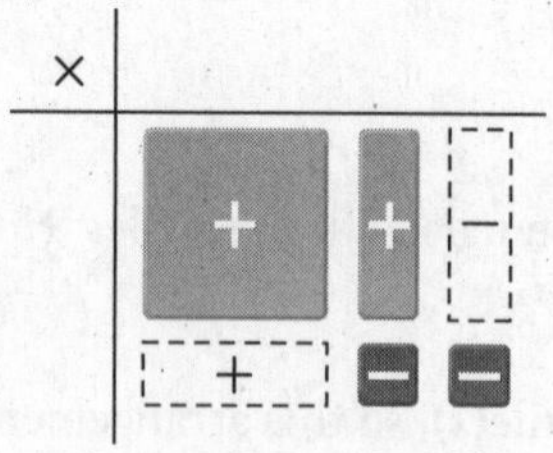

(J) Complete the multiplication grid by placing the factor tiles on the sides. Then write the factors modeled in this product.

$x^2 + x - 2 = (x + \square)(x - \square)$

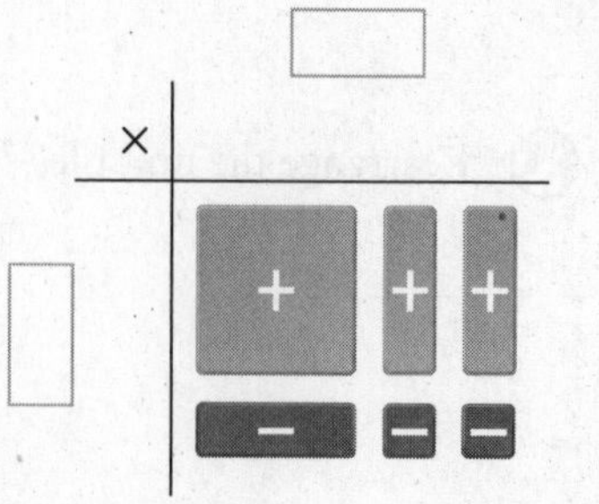

Reflect

1. Are there any other ways to factor the polynomial $x^2 + 7x + 6$ besides $(x + 6)(x + 1)$? Explain.

---

2. **Discussion** If c is positive in $x^2 + bx + c$, what sign can the constant terms of the factors have? What about when c is negative?

Explore 2 Factoring $x^2 + bx + c$

To factor $x^2 + bx + c$, you need to find two factors of c whose sum is b.

Factoring $x^2 + bx + c$	
WORDS	**EXAMPLE**
To factor a quadratic trinomial of the form $x^2 + bx + c$, find two factors of c whose sum is b. If no such integers exist, the trinomial is not factorable.	To factor $x^2 + 9x + 18$, look for factors of 18 whose sum is 9. Factors of 18 — Sum 1 and 18 — 19 — x 2 and 9 — 11 — x 3 and 6 — 9 — ✓ $x^2 + 9x + 18 = (x + 3)(x + 6)$

If c is positive, the constant terms of the factors have the same sign.

If c is negative, then one constant term of the factors is positive and one is negative.

(A) First, look at $x^2 + 11x + 30$. Find the values of b and c. $b =$ ☐ $c =$ ☐

(B) c is positive / negative. The sign of the factors will be the same / different.

(C) List the factor pairs of c, 30, and find the sum of each pair.

Factors of 30	Sum of Factors
1 and ☐	1 + ☐ = ☐
2 and ☐	2 + ☐ = ☐
3 and ☐	3 + ☐ = ☐
5 and ☐	5 + ☐ = ☐

(D) The factor pair whose sum equals b is ________.

Use this factor pair to factor the polynomial. $x^2 + 11x + 30 = (x + \square)(x + \square)$

Ⓔ Now, look at $x^2 + 13x - 30$. Find the values of b and c.

$b =$ ☐ $c =$ ☐

Ⓕ c is positive / negative. The sign of the factors will be the same / different.

Ⓖ List the factor pairs of c, –30, and find the sum of each pair.

Factors of –30	Sum of Factors
1 and ☐	1 + ☐ = ☐
2 and ☐	2 + ☐ = ☐
3 and ☐	3 + ☐ = ☐
5 and ☐	5 + ☐ = ☐
–1 and ☐	–1 + ☐ = ☐
–2 and ☐	–2 + ☐ = ☐
–3 and ☐	–3 + ☐ = ☐
–5 and ☐	–5 + ☐ = ☐

Ⓗ The factor pair whose sum equals b is ________.

Use this factor pair to factor the polynomial.

$x^2 + 13x - 30 = (x + \square)(x - \square)$

Reflect

3. **Discussion** When factoring a trinomial of the form $x^2 + bx + c$, where c is negative, one binomial factor contains a positive factor of c and one contains a negative factor of c. How do you know which factor of c should be positive and which should be negative?

____

____

Explain 1 Solving Equations of the Form $x^2 + bx + c = 0$ by Factoring

As you have learned, the Zero Product Property can be used to solve quadratic equations in factored form.

Example 1 **Solve each equation by factoring. Check your answer by graphing.**

(A) $x^2 - 8x = -12$

First, write the equation in the form $x^2 - bx + c = 0$.

$x^2 - 8x = -12$ Original equation

$x^2 - 8x + 12 = 0$ Add 12 to both sides.

The expression $x^2 - 8x + 12$ is in the form $ax^2 + bx + c$, with $b < 0$ and $c > 0$, so the factors will have the same sign and they both will be negative.

Factors of 12	Sum of Factors
−1 and −12	$-1 + (-12) = -13$
−2 and −6	$-2 + (-6) = -8$
−3 and −4	$-3 + (-4) = -7$

The factor pair whose sum equals −8 is −2 and −6. Factor the equation, and use the Zero Product Property.

$$x^2 - 8x + 12 = 0$$

$$(x - 2)(x - 6) = 0$$

$$x - 2 = 0 \quad \text{or} \quad x - 6 = 0$$

$$x = 2 \qquad\qquad x = 6$$

The zeros of the equation are 2 and 6. Check this by graphing the related function, $f(x) = x^2 - 8x + 12$.

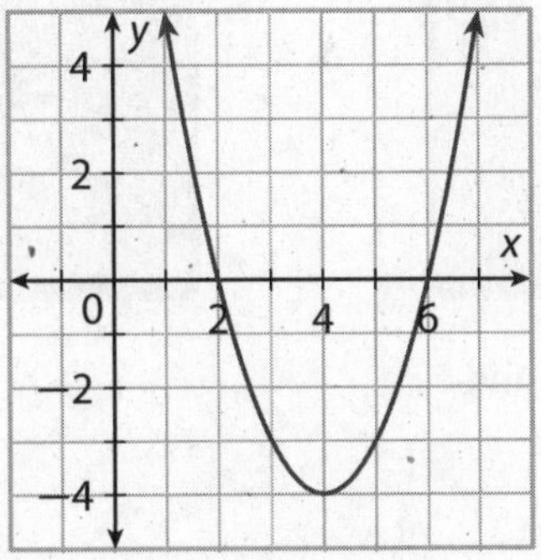

The x-intercepts of the graph are 2 and 6, which are the same as the zeros of the equation. The solutions of the equation are 2 and 6.

Ⓑ $x^2 - 2x = 15$

First, rewrite the expression in the form $x^2 + bx + c = 0$.

$x^2 - 2x = 15$	Original equation
$x^2 - 2x - \square = 0$	Subtract 15 both sides.

To find the zeros of the equation, start by factoring. List the factor pairs of c and find the sum of each pair. Since $c < 0$, the factors will have opposite signs. Since $c < 0$ and $b < 0$, the factor with the greater absolute value will be negative.

Factors of −15	Sum of Factors
1 and $\square$	$1 + \square = \square$
3 and $\square$	$3 + \square = \square$
−1 and $\square$	$-1 + \square = \square$
−3 and $\square$	$-3 + \square = \square$

The factor pair whose sum equals −2 is ________. Factor the equation, and use the Zero Product Property.

$$x^2 - 2x - 15 = 0$$

$$\left(x + \square\right)\left(x - \square\right) = 0$$

$$x + 3 = 0 \quad \text{or} \quad x - 5 = 0$$

$$x = \square \qquad\qquad x = \square$$

The zeros of the equation are $\square$ and $\square$. Check this by graphing the related function, $f(x) = x^2 - 2x = 15$.

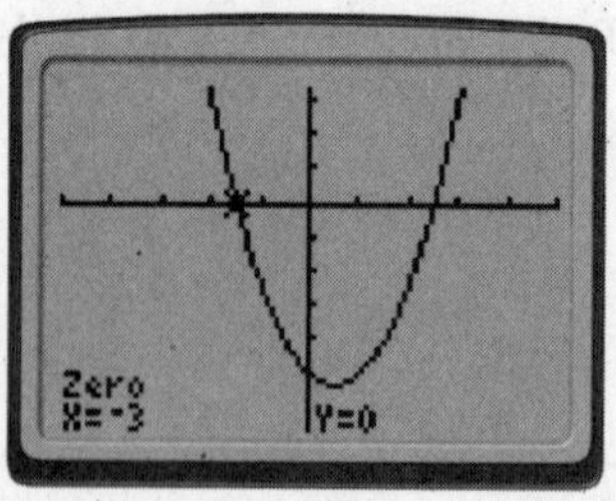

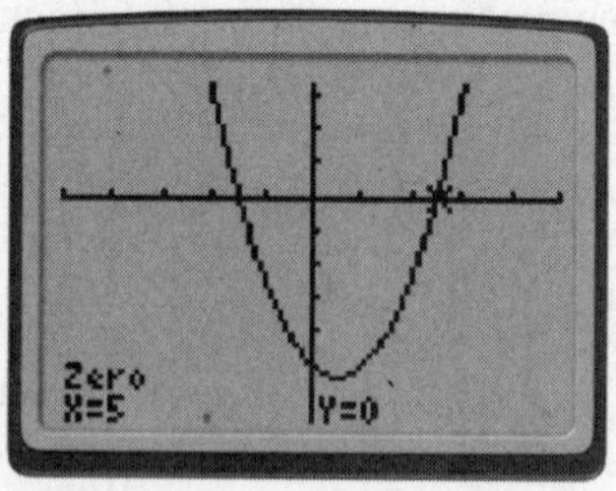

The solutions of the equation are −3 and 5.

Your Turn

Solve each equation.

4. $x^2 + 15x = -54$

5. $x^2 - 13x = -12$

6. $x^2 - x = 56$

Explain 2 Solving Equation Models of the Form $x^2 + bx + c = 0$ by Factoring

Some real-world problems can be solved by factoring a quadratic equation.

Example 2 **Solve each model by factoring.**

Architecture A rectangular porch has dimensions of $(x + 12)$ and $(x + 5)$ feet. If the area of the porch floor is 120 square feet, what are its length and width?

Write an equation for the problem. Substitute 120 for A for the area of the porch.

$$(x + 12)(x + 5) = A$$

$$x^2 + 17x + 60 = A$$

$$x^2 + 17 + 60 = 120$$

$$x^2 + 17x - 60 = 0$$

The factors of −60 that have a sum of 17 are 20 and −3. Use Zero Product Property to find x.

$$(x + 20)(x - 3) = 0$$

$$x + 20 = 0 \quad \text{or} \quad x - 3 = 0$$

$$x = -20 \qquad x = 3$$

Since the area cannot be negative, $x = 3$ feet.

Therefore, the dimensions of the porch are $3 + 12 =$ 15 feet long and $3 + 5 = 8$ feet wide.

Elaborate

7. How are the solutions of a quadratic equation related to the zeros of the related function?

____

____

8. **Essential Question Check-In** How can you solve a quadratic equation by factoring?

____

____

____

☆ Evaluate: Homework and Practice

Personal Math Trainer

- Online Homework
- Hints and Help
- Extra Practice

Use algebra tiles to model the factors of each expression.

1. $x^2 + 6x + 8$

$x^2 + 6x + 8 = (x \square)(x \square)$

2. $x^2 + 2x - 3$

$x^2 + 2x - 3 = (x \square)(x \square)$

Factor the expressions.

3. $x^2 - 15x + 44$

4. $x^2 + 22x + 120$

5. $x^2 + 14x - 32$

6. $x^2 - 12x - 45$

7. $x^2 + 10x + 24$

8. $x^2 + 7x - 8$

Solve each equation.

9. $x^2 + 19x = -84$

10. $x^2 - 18x = -56$

11. $x^2 - 12x + 27 = 0$

12. $x^2 - 9x - 10 = 0$

13. $x^2 + 6x = 135$

14. $x^2 + 13x = -40$

15. $x^2 + x - 132 = 0$

16. $x^2 - 14x = 32$

17. Construction The area of a rectangular fountain is $(x^2 + 12x + 20)$ square feet. A 2-foot walkway is built around the fountain. Find the dimensions of the outside border of the walkway.

18. The area of a room is 396 square feet. The length is $(x + 3)$, and the width is $(x + 7)$ feet. Find the dimensions of the room.

19. A rectangular Persian carpet has an area of $(x^2 + x - 20)$ square feet and a length of $(x + 5)$ feet. The Persian carpet is displayed on a wall. The wall has a width of $(x + 2)$ feet and an area of $(x^2 + 17x + 30)$ square feet. Find the dimensions of the rug and the wall if $x = 20$ feet.

20. The area of a poster board is $x^2 + 3x - 10$ square inches. Find the dimensions of the poster board if $x = 14$.

21. Match the equation to its solutions.

a. $x^2 - 3x - 18 = 0$ ________ 3 and 6

b. $x^2 - 9x + 18 = 0$ ________ −3 and −6

c. $x^2 + 3x - 18 = 0$ ________ 3 and −6

d. $x^2 + 9x + 18 = 0$ ________ −3 and 6

H.O.T. Focus on Higher Order Thinking

22. Explain the Error Amelie found the solutions of the equation $x^2 - x = 42$ to be 6 and −7. Explain why this answer is incorrect. Then, find the correct solutions.

23. Communicate Mathematical Ideas Rico says the expression $x^2 + bx + c$ is factorable when $b = c = 4$. Are there any other values where $b = c$ that make the expression factorable? Explain.

24. Multi-Step A homeowner wants to enlarge a rectangular closet that has an area of $(x^2 + 3x + 2)$ square feet. The length of the closet is greater than the width. After construction, the area will be $(x^2 + 8x + 15)$ square feet.

a. Find the dimensions of the closet before construction.

b. Find the dimensions of the closet after construction.

c. By how many feet will the length and width increase after construction?

25. Critical Thinking Given $x^2 + bx + 64$, find all the values of b for which the quadratic expression has factors $(x + p)$ and $(x + q)$, where p and q are integers.

Lesson Performance Task

Part of the the roof of a factory is devoted to mechanical support and part to green space. The area of the roof R of a large building can be modeled by the polynomial $2x^2 - 251x + 80{,}000$ and the area M roof that is devoted to mechanical support can be modeled by the polynomial $x^2 + 224x + 31{,}250$. The rest of the area is a rectangular green space. Given that the area G of the green space is 123,750 square feet, write and solve quadratic equations to find the dimensions of the green space.

Name________________________ Class________________ Date____________

8.2 Solving Equations by Factoring $ax^2 + bx + c$

Essential Question: How can you use factoring to solve quadratic equations in standard form for which $a \neq 1$?

Resource Locker

Explore Factoring $ax^2 + bx + c$ When $c > 0$

When you factor a quadratic expression in standard form $(ax^2 + bx + c)$, you are looking for two binomials, and possibly a constant numerical factor whose product is the original quadratic expression.

Recall that the product of two binomials is found by applying the Distributive Property, abbreviated sometimes as FOIL:

$$(2x + 5)(3x + 2) = \underbrace{6x^2}_{F} + \underbrace{4x}_{O} + \underbrace{15x}_{I} + \underbrace{10}_{L} = 6x^2 + 19x + 10$$

F The product of the coefficients of the first terms is *a*.

O, I } The sum of the coefficients of the outer and inner products is *b*.

L The product of the last terms is *c*.

Because the *a* and *c* coefficients each result from a single product of terms from the binomials, the coefficients in the binomial factors will be a combination of the factors of *a* and *c*. The trick is to find the combination of factors that results in the correct value of *b*.

Follow the steps to factor the quadratic $4x^2 + 26x + 42$.

(A) First, factor out the largest common factor of 4, 26, and 42 if it is anything other than 1.

$4x^2 + 26x + 42 = \square\left(2x^2 + 13x + 21\right)$

(B) Next, list the factor pairs of 2:

____

(C) List the factor pairs of 21:

____

(D) Make a table listing the combinations of the factors of *a* and *c*, and find the value of *b* that results from summing the outer and inner products of the factors.

Factors of 2	Factors of 21	Outer + inner
1 and 2	1 and 21	$(1)(21) + (2)(1) = 23$
1 and 2	____ and 7	____________
1 and 2	7 and 3	____________
1 and 2	____ and 1	____________

(E) Copy the pair of factors that resulted in an outer + inner sum of 13 into the binomial factors. Be careful to keep the inner and outer factors from the table as inner and outer coefficients in the binomials.

$2x^2 + 13x + 21 = (\square x + \square)(\square x + \square)$

(F) Replace the common factor of the original coefficients to complete the factorization of the original quadratic.

$4x^2 + 26x + 42 = \square(x + 3)(2x + 7)$

Reflect

1. **Critical Thinking** Explain why you should use negative factors of c when factoring a quadratic with $c > 0$ and $b < 0$.

2. **What If?** If none of the factor pairs for a and c result in the correct value for b, what do you know about the quadratic?

3. **Discussion** Why did you have to check each factor pair twice for the factors of c (3 and 7 versus 7 and 3) but only once for the factors of a (1 and 2, but not 2 and 1)? Hint: Compare the outer and inner sums of rows two and three in the table, and also check the outer and inner sums by switching the order of both pairs from row 2 (check 2 and 1 for a with 7 and 3 for c).

Explain 1 Factoring $ax^2 + bx + c$ When $c < 0$

Factoring $x^2 + bx + c$ when $c < 0$ requires one negative and one positive factor of c. The same applies for expressions of the form $ax^2 + bx + c$ as long as $a > 0$. When checking factor pairs, remember to consider factors of c in both orders, **and** consider factor pairs with the negative sign on either member of the pair of c factors.

When you find a combination of factors whose outer and inner product sum is equal to b, you have found the solution. Make sure you fill in the factor table systematically so that you do not skip any combinations.

If $a < 0$, factor out -1 from all three coefficients, or use a negative common factor, so that the factors of a can be left as positive numbers.

Example 1 **Factor the quadratic by checking factor pairs.**

Ⓐ $6x^2 - 21x - 45$

Find the largest common factor of 6, 21, and 45, and factor it out, keeping the coefficient of x^2 positive.

$6x^2 - 21x - 45 = 3(2x^2 - 7x - 15)$

Factors of *a*	Factors of *c*	Outer Product + Inner Product
1 and 2	1 and −15	$(1)(-15) + (2)(1) = -13$
1 and 2	3 and −5	$(1)(-5) + (2)(3) = 1$
1 and 2	5 and −3	$(1)(-3) + (2)(5) = 7$
1 and 2	15 and −1	$(1)(-1) + (2)(15) = 29$
1 and 2	−1 and 15	$(1)(15) + (2)(-1) = 13$
1 and 2	−3 and 5	$(1)(5) + (2)(-3) = -1$
1 and 2	−5 and 3	$(1)(3) + (2)(-5) = -7$
1 and 2	−15 and 1	$(1)(1) + (2)(-15) = -29$

Use the combination of factor pairs that results in a value of −7 for the *b* coefficient.

$2x^2 - 7x - 15 = (x - 5)(2x + 3)$

Replace the common factor of the original coefficients to factor the original quadratic.

$6x^2 - 21x - 45 = 3(x - 5)(2x + 3)$

Ⓑ $20x^2 - 40x - 25$

Factor out common factors of the terms.

$20x^2 - 40x - 25 =$ ___ $(4x^2 - 8x - 5)$

Factors of *a*	Factors of *c*	Outer Product + Inner Product
1 and 4	1 and − 5	$(1)(-5) + (4)(1) =$ ___
1 and 4	5 and −1	___ + ___ = ___
1 and 4	−1 and 5	___ + ___ = ___
1 and 4	−5 and 1	___ + ___ = ___
2 and 2	1 and −5	___ + ___ = ___
2 and 2	−1 and 5	___ + ___ = ___

Use the combination of factor pairs that results in a value of ___ for *b*.

$4x^2 - 8x - 5 =$ (___ $x +$ ___)(___ $x +$ ___)

Replace the common factor of the original coefficients to factor the original quadratic.

$20x^2 - 40x - 25 =$ ___ $(2x + 1)(2x - 5)$

Reflect

4. **What If?** Suppose a is a negative number. What would be the first step in factoring $ax^2 + bx + c$?

Your Turn

5. Factor. $-5x^2 + 8x + 4$

Explain 2 Solving Equations of the Form $ax^2 + bx + c = 0$ by Factoring

For a quadratic equation in standard form, $ax^2 + bx + c = 0$, factoring the quadratic expression into binomials lets you use the Zero Product Property to solve the equation, as you have done previously. If the equation is not in standard form, convert it to standard form by moving all terms to one side of the equation and combining like terms.

Example 2 **Change the quadratic equation to standard form if necessary and then solve by factoring.**

(A) $2x^2 + 7x - 2 = 4x^2 + 4$

Convert the equation to standard form:

Subtract $4x^2$ and 4 from both sides. $-2x^2 + 7x - 6 = 0$

Multiply both sides by -1. $2x^2 - 7x + 6 = 0$

Consider factor pairs for 2 and 6. Use negative factors of 6 to get a negative value for b.

Use the combination pair that results in a sum of -7 and write the equation in factored form. Then solve it using the Zero Product Property.

$$(x - 2)(2x - 3) = 0$$

$x - 2 = 0$ or $2x - 3 = 0$

$x = 2$ $\qquad 2x = 3$

$$x = \frac{3}{2} = 1.5$$

The solutions are 2 and $\frac{3}{2}$, or 1.5.

The solution can be checked by graphing the related function, $f(x) = 2x^2 - 7x + 6$, and finding the x-intercepts.

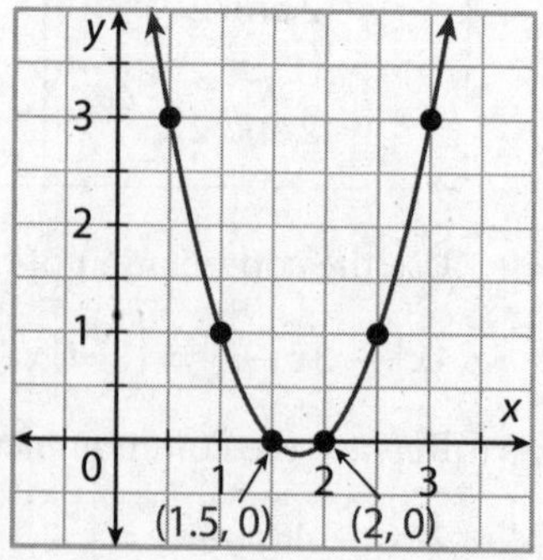

(B) $3(x^2 - 1) = -3x^2 + 2x + 5$

Write the equation in standard form and factor so you can apply the Zero Product Property.

$$\square x^2 - \square = -3x^2 + 2x + 5$$

$$\square x^2 - 2x - \square = 0$$

$$\square x^2 - x - 4 = 0$$

Use the combination pair that results in a sum of ____.

$$(x + 1)\left(\square x + \square\right) = 0$$

$x + 1 = \square$ or $3x - 4 = 0$

$x = \square$ $\quad\quad$ $\square x = 4$

$x = \square$

The solutions are -1 and $\frac{4}{3}$.

Use a graphing calculator to check the solutions.

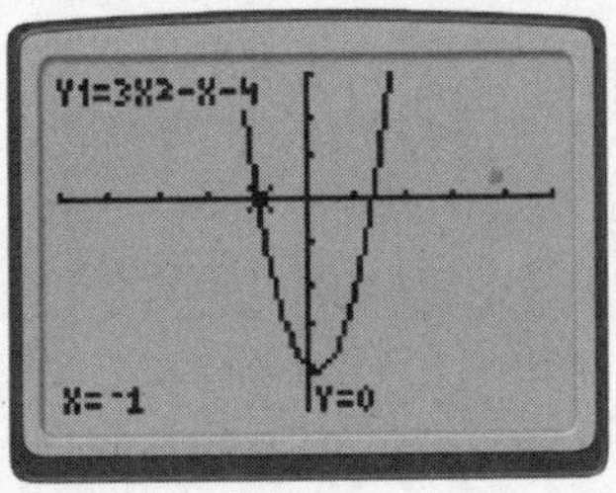

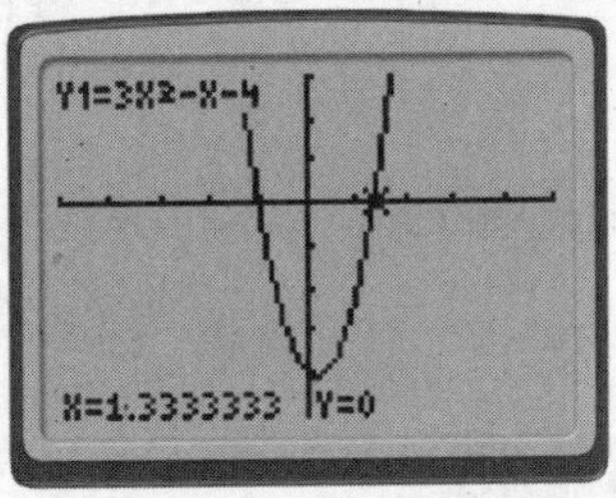

Reflect

6. In the two examples, a common factor was divided out at the beginning of the solution, and it was not used again. Why didn't you include the common term again when solving x for the original quadratic equation?

____

____

____

Your Turn

7. $12x^2 + 48x + 45 = 0$

Explain 3 Solving Equation Models of the Form $ax^2 + bx + c = 0$ by Factoring

A projectile is an object moving through the air without any forces other than gravity acting on it. The height of a projectile at a time in seconds can be found by using the formula $h = -16t^2 + vt + s$, where v is in the initial upwards velocity in feet per second (and can be a negative number if the projectile is launched downwards) and s is starting height in feet. The a term of -16 accounts for the effect of gravity accelerating the projectile downwards and is the only appropriate value when measuring distance with feet and time in seconds.

To use the model to make predictions about the behavior of a projectile, you need to read the description of the situation carefully and identify the initial velocity, the initial height, and the height at time t.

Example 3 **Read the real-world situation and substitute in values for the projectile motion formula. Then solve the resulting quadratic equation by factoring to answer the question.**

(A) When a baseball player hits a baseball into the air, the height of the ball at t seconds after the ball is hit can be modeled with the projectile motion formula. If the ball is hit at 3 feet off the ground with an upward velocity of 47 feet per second, how long will it take for the ball to hit the ground, assuming it is not caught?

Find the parameters v and s from the description of the problem.

$v = 47$ $s = 3$ $h = 0$

Substitute parameter values. $-16t^2 + 47t + 3 = 0$

Divide both sides by -1. $16t^2 - 47t - 3 = 0$

Use the combination pair that results in a sum of -47.

$$(t - 3)(16t + 1) = 0$$

$t - 3 = 0$ or $16t + 1 = 0$

$t = 3$ $16t = -1$

$t = -\frac{1}{16}$

The solutions are 3 and $-\frac{1}{16}$.

The negative time answer can be rejected because it is not a reasonable value for time in this situation. The correct answer is 3 seconds.

(B) A child standing on a river bank ten feet above the river throws a rock toward the river at a speed of 12 feet per second. How long does it take before the rock splashes into the river?

Find the parameters v and s from the description of the problem.

$\square = -12$ $\quad s = \square$ $\quad h = \square$

Substitute parameter values. $\square t^2 + \square t + \square = 0$

Divide both sides by $\square$. $8t^2 + \square t + \square = 0$

Use the combination pair that results in a sum of 6.

$$(\square t - 1)(\square t + 5) = 0$$

$2t - 1 = 0$ or $4t + 5 = 0$

$2t = \square$ $\quad 4t = \square$

$t = \square$ $\quad t = \square$

The solutions are $\square$ and $\square$.

The only correct solution to the time it takes the rock to hit the water is $\square$ second.

Your Turn

8. How long does it take a rock to hit the ground if thrown off the edge of a 72 foot tall building roof with an upward velocity of 24 feet per second?

Elaborate

9. Discussion What happens if you do not remove the common factor from the coefficients before trying to factor the quadratic equation?

10. Explain how you can know there are never more than two solutions to a quadratic equation, based on what you know about the graph of a quadratic function.

11. Essential Question Check-In Describe the steps it takes to solve a quadratic equation by factoring.

Evaluate: Homework and Practice

Personal Math Trainer

- Online Homework
- Hints and Help
- Extra Practice

Factor the following quadratic expressions.

1. $6x^2 + 5x + 1$

2. $9x^2 + 33x + 30$

3. $4x^2 - 8x + 3$

4. $24x^2 - 44x + 12$

5. $3x^2 - 2x - 5$

6. $-10x^2 + 3x + 4$

7. $12x^2 + 22x - 14$

8. $-15x^2 + 21x + 18$

Solve the following quadratic equations.

9. $5x^2 + 18x + 9 = 0$

10. $12x^2 - 36x + 15 = 0$

11. $6x^2 + 28x - 2 = 2x - 10$

12. $-100x^2 + 55x + 3 = 50x^2 - 55x + 23$

13. $8x^2 - 10x - 3 = 0$

14. $-12x^2 = 34x - 28$

15. $(8x + 7)(x + 1) = 9$

16. $3(4x - 1)(4x + 3) = 48x$

Read the real-world situation and substitute in values for the projectile motion formula. Then solve the resulting quadratic equation by factoring to answer the question.

17. A golfer takes a swing from a hill twenty feet above the cup with an initial upwards velocity of 32 feet per second. How long does it take the ball to land on the ground near the cup?

18. An airplane pilot jumps out of an airplane and has an initial velocity of 60 feet per second downwards. How long does it take to fall from 1000 feet to 900 feet before the parachute opens?

A race car driving under the caution flag at 80 feet per second begins to accelerate at a constant rate after the warning flag. The distance traveled since the warning flag in feet is characterized by $30t^2 + 80t$, where t is the time in seconds after the car starts accelerating again.

19. How long does it take the car to travel 30 feet after it begins accelerating?

20. How long will the car take to travel 160 feet?

Geometry **For each rectangle with area given, determine the binomial factors that describe the dimensions.**

21.

area = $6x^2 + 17x - 3$

22.

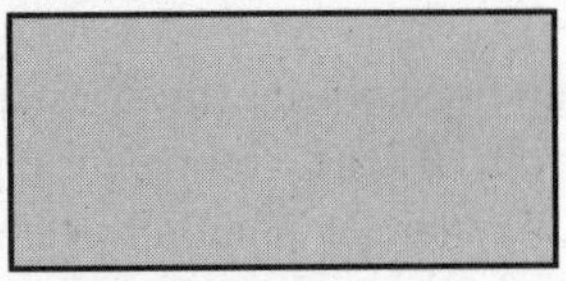

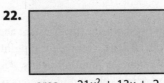

area = $21x^2 + 13x + 2$

23. Multiple Response Which of the following expressions in the list describes the complete factorization of the quadratic expression $15x^2 - 25x - 10$? Circle all that apply.

a. $(3x + 1)(5x - 10)$ **b.** $5(3x + 1)(x - 2)$ **c.** $5(x + 2)(3x - 1)$

d. $5(x - 2)(3x + 1)$ **e.** $5(3x - 1)(x + 2)$ **f.** $(5x - 10)(3x + 1)$

H.O.T. Focus on Higher Order Thinking

24. Multi-Part Response A basketball player shoots at the basket from a starting height of 6 feet and an upwards velocity of 20 feet per second. Determine how long it takes for the shot to drop through the basket, which is mounted at a height of 10 feet.

a. Set up the equation for projectile motion to solve for time and convert it to standard form.

b. Solve the equation by factoring.

c. Explain why you got two positive solutions to the equation, and determine how you can rule one of them out to find the answer to the question. Hint: Solving the equation graphically may give you a hint.

25. Critical Thinking Find the binomial factors of $4x^2 - 25$.

26. Communicate Mathematical Ideas Find all the values of b that make the expression $3x^2 + bx - 4$ factorable.

Lesson Performance Task

The equation for the motion of an object with constant acceleration is $d = d_0 + vt + \frac{1}{2}at^2$, where d is distance from a given point in meters, d_0 is the initial distance from the starting point in meters, v is the starting velocity in meters per second, a is acceleration in meters per second squared, and t is time in seconds.

A car is stopped at a traffic light. When the light turns green, the driver begins to drive, accelerating at a constant rate of 4 meters per second squared. A bus is traveling at a speed of 15 meters per second in another lane. The bus is 7 meters behind the car as it begins to accelerate.

Find when the bus passes the car, when the car passes the bus, and how far each has traveled each time they pass one another.

Name ____________ Class ____________ Date ____________

8.3 Using Special Factors to Solve Equations

Resource Locker

Essential Question: How can you use special products to aid in solving quadratic equations by factoring?

Explore Exploring Factors of Perfect Square Trinomials

When you use algebra tiles to factor a polynomial, you must arrange the unit tiles on the grid in a rectangle. Sometimes, you can arrange the unit tiles to form a square. Trinomials of this type are called perfect-square trinomials.

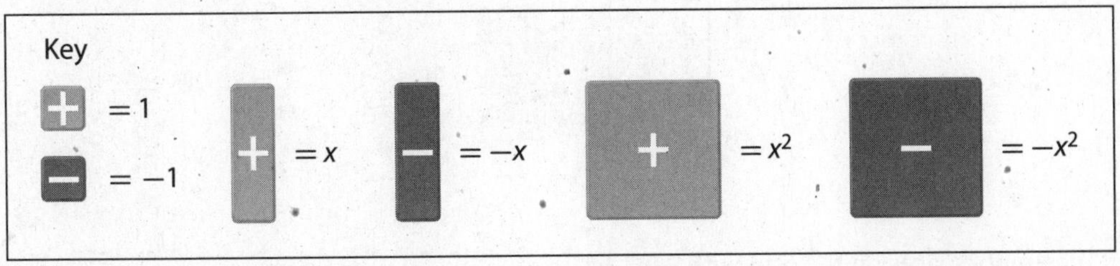

(A) Use algebra tiles to factor $x^2 + 6x + 9$.

Identify the number of tiles you need to model the expression. You need ☐ x^2-tiles, ☐ x-tiles, and ☐ unit tiles.

(B) Arrange the algebra tiles on the grid. Place the ☐ x^2-tile in the upper left corner, and arrange the ☐ unit tiles in the lower right corner.

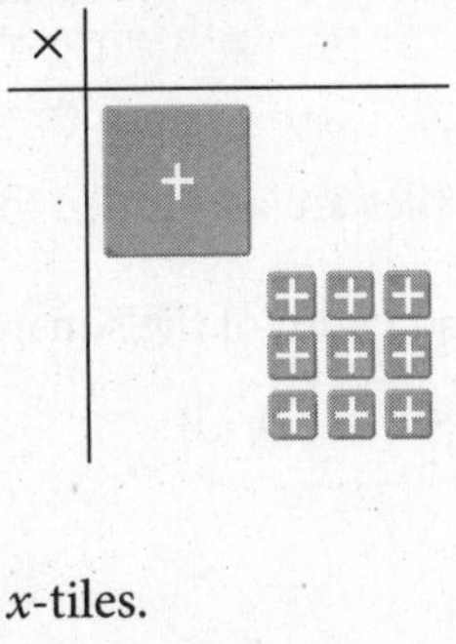

(C) Fill in the empty spaces on the grid with x-tiles.

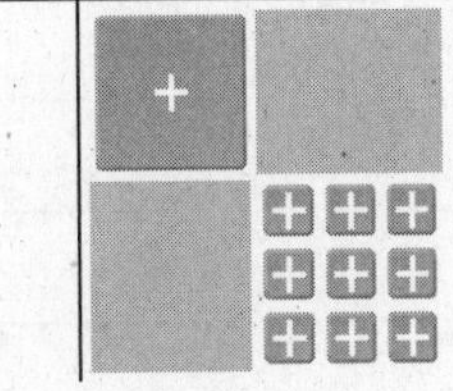

Ⓓ All ____ x-tiles were used, so all the tiles are accounted for and fit in the square with sides of length ________. Read the length and width of the square to get the factors of the trinomial $x^2 + 6x + 9 = (x + \square)(x + \square)$.

Ⓔ Now, use algebra tiles to factor $x^2 - 8x + 16$.

You need ____ x^2-tiles, ____ $-x$ -tiles, and ____ unit tiles to model the expression.

Ⓕ Arrange the algebra tiles on the grid. Place the ____ x^2-tile in the upper left corner, and arrange the ____ unit tiles in the lower right corner.

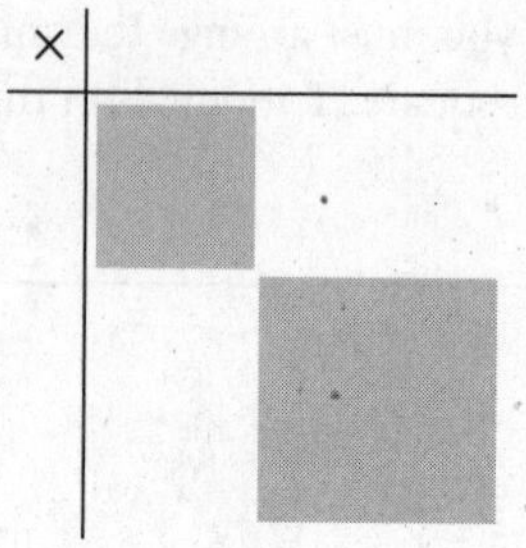

Ⓖ Fill in the empty spaces on the grid with $-x$-tiles.

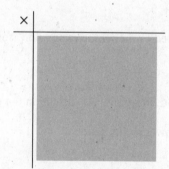

Ⓗ All ____ $-x$ -tiles were used, so all the tiles are accounted for and fit in a square with sides of length ________. Read the length and width of the square to get the factors of the trinomial $x^2 - 8x + 16 = (\square)(\square)$.

Reflect

1. **What If?** Suppose that the middle term in $x^2 + 6x + 9$ was changed from $6x$ to $10x$. How would this affect the way you factor the polynomial?

____

____

____

2. If the positive unit squares are arranged in a square of unit tiles when factoring with algebra tiles, what will be true about the binomial factors? (The coefficient of the x^2 term is 1 as in the previous problems.)

____

____

Explain 1 Factoring $a^2x^2 + 2abx + b^2$ and $a^2x^2 - 2abx + b^2$

Recall that a perfect-square trinomial can be represented algebraically in either the form $a^2 + 2ab + b^2$ or the form $a^2 - 2ab + b^2$.

Perfect-Square Trinomials

Perfect-Square Trinomials	
Perfect-Square Trinomial	**Examples**
$a^2 + 2ab + b^2 = (a + b)(a + b)$ $= (a + b)^2$	$x^2 + 6x + 9 = (x + 3)(x + 3)$ $= (x + 3)^2$
	$c^2x^2 + 2cdx + d^2 = (cx)^2 + 2cdx + d^2$ $= (cx + d)(cx + d)$ $= (cx + d)^2$
$a^2 - 2ab + b^2 = (a - b)(a - b)$ $= (a - b)^2$	$x^2 - 10x + 25 = (x - 5)(x - 5)$ $= (x - 5)^2$
	$c^2x^2 - 2cdx + d^2 = (cx)^2 - 2cdx + d^2$ $= (cx - d)(cx - d)$ $= (cx - d)^2$

Example 1 **Factor perfect-square trinomials.**

(A) $4x^3 - 24x^2 + 36x$

$4x^3 - 24x^2 + 36x = 4x(x^2 - 6x + 9)$ Factor out the common monomial factor $4x$.

$= 4x\,[x^2 - 2(1 \cdot 3)x + 3^2]$ Rewrite the perfect square trinomial in the form $a^2x^2 - 2abx + b^2$.

$= 4x(x - 3)(x - 3)$ Rewrite the perfect square trinomial in the form $(ax - b)(ax - b)$ to obtain factors.

The factored form of $4x^3 - 24x^2 + 36x$ is $4x(x - 3)(x - 3)$, or $4x(x - 3)^2$.

(B) $x^2 + 16x + 64$

$x^2 + 16x + 64 = x^2 + 2(\square \cdot \square)x + \square^2$ Rewrite in the form $a^2x^2 + 2abx + b^2$.

$= (x + \square)(x + \square)$ Rewrite in the form $(ax + b)(ax + b)$.

The factored form of $x^2 + 16x + 64$ is $(x + \square)(x + \square)$, or $(x + \square)^2$.

Your Turn

Factor perfect-square trinomials.

3. $2y^3 + 12y^2 + 18y$

4. $100z^2 - 20z + 1$

Explain 2 Factoring $a^2x^2 - b^2 = 0$

Recall that a difference of squares can be written algebraically as $a^2 - b^2$ and factored as $(a + b)(a - b)$.

Difference of Squares

Difference of Two Squares	
Perfect-Square Trinomial	**Examples**
$a^2 - b^2 = (a + b)(a - b)$	$x^2 - 9 = (x + 3)(x - 3)$ $4x^2 - 9 = (2x + 3)(2x - 3)$ $9x^2 - 1 = (3x + 1)(3x - 1)$ $c^2x^2 - d^2 = (cx)^2 - d^2$ $= (cx + d)(cx - d)$

Example 2 **Factor each difference of squares.**

(A) $x^2 - 49$

$x^2 - 49 = x^2 - 7^2$ Rewrite in the form $a^2x^2 - b^2$.

$= (x + 7)(x - 7)$ Rewrite in the form $(ax + b)(ax - b)$.

The factored form of $x^2 - 49$ is $(x + 7)(x - 7)$.

(B) $49q^2 - 4p^2$

$49q^2 - 4p^2 = \square^2 \square^2 - (\square)^2$ Rewrite in the form $a^2x^2 - b^2$.

$= (\square)(\square)$ Rewrite in the form $(ax + b)(ax - b)$.

The factored form of $49q^2 - 4p^2$ is $(\square)(\square)$.

Reflect

5. **Discussion** James was factoring a difference of squares but did not finish his work. What steps is he missing?

$$16x^4 - 1 = (4x^2)^2 - 1$$
$$= (4x^2 + 1)(4x^2 - 1)$$

Your Turn

Factor each difference of squares.

6. $x^2 - 144$

7. $81y^4 - 9y^2$

Explain 3 Solving Equations with Special Factors

Equations with special factors can be solved using the Zero Product Property. Remember, the Zero Product Property states that if the product of two factors is zero, then at least one of the factors must be zero. For example, if $(x + 1)(x + 9) = 0$ then $x + 1 = 0$ or $x + 9 = 0$. Consequently, the solutions for the equation are $x = -1$ or $x = -9$.

Example 3 **Solve the following equations with special factors.**

(A) $4x^2 + 12x + 9 = 0$

$4x^2 + 12x + 9 = 0$

$2^2x^2 + 2(2 \cdot 3)x + 3^2 = 0$ Rewrite in the form $a^2x^2 + 2abx + b^2$.

$(2x + 3)(2x + 3) = 0$ Rewrite in the form $(ax + b)(ax + b)$.

$2x + 3 = 0$ Set factors equal to 0 using Zero Product Property.

$x = -\frac{3}{2}$ Solve equation.

(B) $25x^2 - 1 = 0$

$25x^2 - 1 = 0$

$\square^2 x^2 - \square^2 = 0$ Rewrite in the form $a^2x^2 + 2abx + b^2$.

$(\square)(\square) = 0$ Rewrite in the form $(ax + b)(ax - b)$.

$\square = 0$ or $\square = 0$ Set factors equal to 0 using Zero Product Property.

$x = \square$ or $x = \square$ Solve equation.

Your Turn

Solve the following equations with special factors.

8. $25x^2 - 10x + 1 = 0$

9. $8x^4 - 2x^2 = 0$

Explain 4 Solving Equation Models with Special Factors

For each real-world scenario, solve the model which involves an equation with special factors.

Example 4 **Write the given information and manipulate into a familiar form. Solve the equation to answer a question about the situation.**

As a satellite falls from outer space onto Mars, its distance in miles from the planet is given by the formula $d = -9t^2 + 776$, where t is the number of hours it has fallen. Find when the satellite will be 200 miles away from Mars.

Analyze Information

Identify the important information

- The satellite's distance in miles is given by the formula ________.
- The satellite distance at some time t is $d = \square$.

Formulate a Plan

Substituting the value of the constant $d = \square$ into the equation ______________

you get the equation ______________. Simplify the new equation into a familiar form and solve it.

Solve

Rewrite the equation to be equal to 0.

$\square = -9t^2 + 776$ Subtract 200 from both sides.

$0 = -9t^2 + \square$ Divide both sides by -1.

$0 = 9t^2 - \square$ Factor out 9.

$0 = \square\left(t^2 - \square\right)$

The equation contains a ______________ that you can factor.

$0 = 9\left(\square\right)\left(\square\right)$

Use the ______________ Property to solve.

$0 = 9\left(t + \square\right)\left(t - \square\right)$

$\square = 0$ or $t - 8 = \square$

$t = \square$

The answer is $t = \square$ because time must be ______________. So, the satellite has fallen for $\square$ hours.

Justify and Evaluate

$t = \square$ makes sense because time must be ______________. Check by substituting this value of t into the original equation.

$-9 \cdot \square^2 + 776 = -9 \cdot \square + 776$

$= 776 - \square$

$= \square$

This is what is expected from the given information.

Your Turn

Write the given information and manipulate it into a familiar form. Solve the equation to answer a question about the situation.

10. A volleyball player sets the ball in the air, and the height of the ball after t seconds is given in feet by $h = -16t^2 + 12t + 6$. A teammate wants to wait until the ball is 8 feet in the air before she spikes it. When should the teammate spike the ball? How many reasonable solutions are there to this problem? Explain.

11. The height of a model rocket is given (in centimeters) by the formula $h = -490t^2$, where t is measured in seconds and $h = 0$ refers to its original height at the top of a mountain. It begins to fly down from the mountain-top at time $t = 0$. When has the rocket descended 490 centimeters?

Elaborate

12. Are the perfect square trinomials $a^2 + 2ab + b^2$ and $a^2 - 2ab + b^2$ very different? How can you get one from the other?

13. How would you go about factoring $a^2 - 2ab + b^2 - 1$?

14. Setting a perfect-square trinomial equal to zero, $a^2x^2 + 2abx + b^2 = 0$, produces how many solutions? How many solutions are produced setting a difference of squares equal to zero, $a^2x^2 - b^2 = 0$?

15. Physical problems involving projectile motion can be modeled using the general equation $h = -16t^2 + v_0t$. Here, h refers to the relative height of the projectile from its initial position, v_0 is its initial vertical velocity, and t is time elapsed from launch. If you are measuring the height of the projectile as it descends from a high place, and it was launched with $v_0 = 0$ (which means it was thrown horizontally or dropped), how would you find the solution using special factors? (Assume that the height the projectile has descended is a square number in this question, although this is not a requirement in real life).

16. Essential Question Check-In How can you use special products to solve quadratic equations?

Evaluate: Homework and Practice

Personal Math Trainer

- Online Homework
- Hints and Help
- Extra Practice

For each trinomial, draw algebra tiles to show the factored form. Then, write the factored form.

1. $x^2 - 10x + 25$

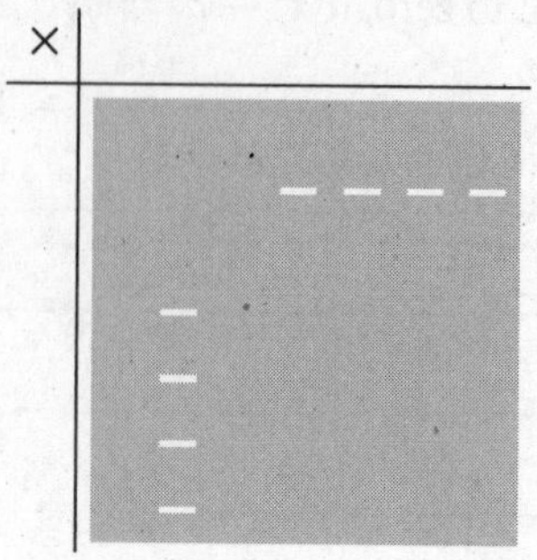

2. $x^2 + 8x + 16$

Factor.

3. $4x^2 + 4x + 1$

4. $9x^2 - 18x + 9$

5. $16x^3 + 8x^2 + x$

6. $32x^3 - 16x^2 + 2x$

7. $x^2 - 169$

8. $4p^2 - 9q^4$

9. $32x^4 - 8x^2$

10. $2y^5 - 32z^4y$

Solve the following equations with special factors.

11. $25x^2 + 20x + 4 = 0$

12. $x^3 - 10x^2 + 25x = 0$

13. $4x^4 + 8x^3 + 4x^2 = 0$

14. $4x^2 - 8x + 4 = 0$

15. $x^2 - 81 = 0$

16. $2x^3 - 2x = 0$

17. $16q^2 - 81 = 0$

18. $4p^4 - 25p^2 = -16p^2$

Jivesh is analyzing the flight of a few of his model rockets that he assembled with various equations. In each equation, h is the height of the rocket in centimeters, and the rocket was fired from the ground at time $t = 0$, where t is measured in seconds.

19. For Jivesh's Model A rocket, he uses the equation $h = -490t^2 + 1120t$. When is the height of the Model A rocket 640 centimeters?

20. Jivesh also has a more powerful Model B rocket. For this rocket, he uses the equation $h = -490t^2 + 1260t$. When is the height of the Model B rocket 810 centimeters?

21. Jivesh brought his Model B rocket on a camping trip near the top of a mountain. He wants to model how it descends down the mountain. Here, he uses the equation $h = -490t^2$. When has the rocket descended 1000 centimeters?

22. Geometry Claire is cutting a square out of a bigger square for an art project. She cuts out a square with an area of 9 cm^2. The leftover area is 16 cm^2. What is the length of one of the sides of the bigger square? The area of a square is $A = l^2$ where l is the length of one of its sides.

23. The height of a diver during a dive can be modeled by $h = -16t^2$, where h is height in feet relative to the diving platform and t is time in seconds. Find the time it takes for the diver to reach the water if the platform is 49 feet high.

24. Physics Consider a particular baseball player at bat. The height of the ball at time t can be modeled by $h = -16t^2 + v_0t + h_0$. Here, v_0 is the initial upward velocity of the ball, and h_0 is the height at which the ball is hit. If a ball is 4 feet off the ground when it is hit with a negligible upward velocity close to 0 feet per second, when will the ball hit the ground?

25. Explain the Error Jeremy factored $144x^2 - 100$ as follows:

$$144x^2 - 100 = (12x + 10)(12x - 10)$$

$$= 2(6x + 5)(6x - 5)$$

What was his error? Correct his work.

26. Which of the following are solutions to the equation $x^5 - 2x^3 + x = 0$? Select all that apply.

a. $x = -1$

b. $x = 2$

c. $x = 1$

d. $x = 0.5$

e. $x = 0$

H.O.T. Focus on Higher Order Thinking

27. Multi-Step An artist framed a picture. The picture is a square with a side length of 2y. It is surrounded by a square frame with a side length of 4x.

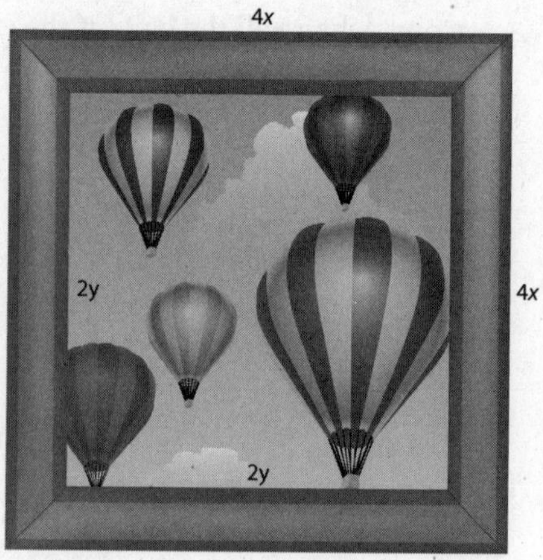

a. Find and completely factor the expression for the area of the frame.

b. The frame has an area of 11 square inches and the picture has an area of 25 square inches. Find the width of the frame.

28. Critical Thinking Sinea thinks that the fully factored form of the expression $x^4 - 1$ is $(x^2 - 1)(x^2 + 1)$. Is she correct? Explain.

29. Persevere in Problem Solving Samantha has the equation $x^3 + 2x^2 + x = x^3 - x$. Explain how she can find the solutions of the equation. Then solve the equation.

30. Communicate Mathematical Ideas Explain how to fully factor the expression $x^4 - 2x^2y^2 + y^4$.

Lesson Performance Task

A designer is planning to place a fountain in the lobby of an art museum. Four artists have each designed a fountain to fit the space. Some have designed rectangular fountains and the others designed square fountains. Given a quadratic equation representing the area of the fountain and the actual area of the fountain, find the dimensions of each fountain.

Artist	Artemis	Beatrice	Geoffrey	Daniel
Area equation	$A_A = 9x^2 - 25$	$A_B = 4x^2 - 25$	$A_G = 25x^2 + 80x + 64$	$A_D = 81x^2 + 198x + 121$
Fountain area	39 square feet	$28x - 74$ square feet	$160x$ square feet	$198x + 242$ square feet

Artemis:	Beatrice:

Geoffrey:	Daniel:

Using Factors to Solve Quadratic Equations

Essential Question: How can you use factoring a quadratic equation to solve real-world problems?

Key Vocabulary

difference of two squares *(diferencia de dos cuadrados)*

perfect-square trinomial *(trinomio cuadrado perfecto)*

KEY EXAMPLE (Lesson 8.1)

Factor $x^2 - 2x - 8$.

Find the factor pair of −8 whose sum is −2.

The factor pair is −4 and 2.

$x^2 - 2x - 8 = (x - 4)(x + 2)$

Factors of −8	Sum of Factors
−1 and 8	7
1 and −8	−7
−2 and 4	2
2 and −4	−2

KEY EXAMPLE (Lesson 8.2)

Solve $4x^2 + 8x + 3 = 0$.

Find the factor pairs of 4 and 3 that result in a sum of 8.

The factor pairs are 2 and 2 and 1 and 3.

Factors of 4	Factors of 3	Outer Product + Inner Product
1 and 4	1 and 3	$(1)(3) + (4)(1) = 7$
1 and 4	3 and 1	$(1)(1) + (4)(3) = 13$
2 and 2	1 and 3	$(2)(3) + (2)(1) = 8$

$$4x^2 + 8x + 3 = 0$$
$$(2x + 1)(2x + 3) = 0$$
$$2x + 1 = 0 \quad \text{and} \quad 2x + 3 = 0$$
$$x = -\frac{1}{2} \quad \text{and} \quad x = -\frac{3}{2}$$

KEY EXAMPLE (Lesson 8.3)

Solve $16x^2 - 25 = 0$.

$$4^2 \cdot x^2 - 5^2 = 0$$ *Rewrite in the form $a^2x^2 - b^2$.*

$$(4x + 5)(4x - 5) = 0$$ *Rewrite in the form $(ax + b)(ax - b)$.*

$$4x + 5 = 0 \quad \text{and} \quad 4x - 5 = 0$$ *Set factors equal to 0 using Zero Product Property.*

$$x = -\frac{5}{4} \quad \text{and} \quad x = \frac{5}{4}$$

EXERCISES

Solve each equation. *(Lessons 8.1, 8.2, 8.3)*

1. $x^2 - 81 = 0$

2. $2x^2 - 8x - 10 = 0$

3. $x^2 + 7x + 12 = 0$

4. $x^2 - 14x = -49$

5. $16 - 4x^2 = 0$

6. $6x^2 + 5x + 1 = 0$

7. The area of a rectangular pool is $(x^2 + 17x + 72)$ square meters. There is a 3-meter-wide concrete walkway around the pool. Write expressions to represent the dimensions of the outside border of the walkway. *(Lesson 8.1)*

MODULE PERFORMANCE TASK

Fitting Through the Arch

The Ship-Shape Shipping Company ships items in rectangular crates. At one shipping destination, each crate must be able to fit through an arched doorway. The shape of this arched doorway can be modeled by the quadratic equation $y = -x^2 + 16$, where x is the distance in feet from the center of the arch and y is the height of the arch. Find the width of the archway at its base.

The Ship-Shape Shipping Company just unloaded several crates outside the arch ranging in height from 2 feet to 6 feet. Choose a particular crate height. Then, find the maximum width the crate could have and still fit through the arched doorway.

Start by listing in the space below how you will tackle this problem. Then use your own paper to complete the task. Be sure to write down all your data and assumptions. Then use graphs, tables, or algebra to explain how you reached your conclusion.

Ready to Go On?

8.1–8.3 Using Factors to Solve Quadratic Equations

Personal Math Trainer

- Online Homework
- Hints and Help
- Extra Practice

Identify each expression as a perfect-square trinomial, a difference of squares, or neither. Factor each expression. *(Lessons 8.1, 8.2, 8.3)*

1. $4p^2 + 12p + 9$

2. $a^2 - 9a - 36$

Solve each equation. *(Lessons 8.1, 8.2, 8.3)*

3. $x^2 - 4x - 21 = 0$

4. $49x^2 - 100 = 0$

5. $5x^2 - 33x - 14 = 0$

6. $x^2 + 16x + 64 = 0$

7. A golfer hits a ball from a starting elevation of 4 feet with a vertical velocity of 70 feet per second down to a green with an elevation of −5 feet. The number of seconds t it takes the ball to hit the green can be represented by the equation $-16t^2 + 70t + 4 = -5$. How long does it take the ball to land on the green? *(Lesson 8.2)*

ESSENTIAL QUESTION

8. How can you use factoring to solve quadratic equations in standard form?

MODULE 8
MIXED REVIEW

Assessment Readiness

1. Consider the equation $5x(2x + 1) - 3(2x + 1) = 0$.

Choose True or False for each statement about the equation.

A. It is equivalent to $(5x - 3)(2x + 1) = 0$. ○ True ○ False

B. A solution of the equation is $x = \frac{1}{2}$. ○ True ○ False

C. A zero of the equation is $\frac{3}{5}$. ○ True ○ False

2. Factor to solve each equation. Does the equation have a solution of $x = 2$?

Select Yes or No for each.

A. $4x^2 - 16 = 0$ ○ Yes ○ No

B. $x^2 - 4x + 4 = 0$ ○ Yes ○ No

C. $4x^2 + 16x + 16 = 0$ ○ Yes ○ No

3. Larry thinks the quotient of $\frac{4x^2 + 7x - 15}{x + 3}$ is $4x - 5$. Explain how you can check his answer using multiplication. Then, check his answer. Is Larry correct?

4. Marcello is replacing a rectangular sliding glass door with dimensions of $(x + 7)$ and $(x + 3)$ feet. The area of the glass door is 45 square feet. What are the length and width of the door? Explain how you got your answer.

Using Square Roots to Solve Quadratic Equations

MODULE 9

Essential Question: How can you use quadratic equations to solve real-world problems?

REAL WORLD VIDEO
The designers of a fireworks display need to make precise timing calculations. An explosion too soon or too late could spell disaster!

MODULE PERFORMANCE TASK PREVIEW

Fireworks Display

As with any other projectile, the relationship between the time since a firework was launched and its height is quadratic. Fireworks must be carefully timed in order to ignite at the most impressive height. In this task, you will figure out how you can use math to launch fireworks that are safe and achieve the maximum possible effect.

Are YOU Ready?

Complete these exercises to review skills you will need for this module.

Personal Math Trainer

- Online Homework
- Hints and Help
- Extra Practice

Exponents

Example 1 Simplify $25^{\frac{1}{2}}$.

$25^{\frac{1}{2}} = \sqrt{25} = 5$ — A number raised to the $\frac{1}{2}$ power is equal to the square root of the number.

Simplify.

1. $100^{\frac{1}{2}}$ ________

2. $50^{\frac{1}{2}}$ ________

3. $\left(\frac{36}{81}\right)^{\frac{1}{2}}$ ________

Algebraic Expressions

Example 2 Evaluate $\left(\frac{b}{2}\right)^2$ when $b = 18$.

$\left(\frac{b}{2}\right)^2$

$\left(\frac{18}{2}\right)^2 = 9^2 = 81$ — Substitute 18 for *b* and evaluate the expression.

Evaluate $\left(\frac{b}{2}\right)^2$ for the given value of *b*.

4. $b = 24$ ________

5. $b = -10$ ________

6. $b = 3$ ________

Example 3 Factor $x^2 + 14x + 49$.

$x^2 + 14x + 49$ — $x^2 + 14x + 49$ is a perfect square.

$x^2 + 2(x)(7) + 7^2$ — Rewrite in the form $a^2 + 2ab + b^2$.

$(x + 7)(x + 7)$ — Rewrite in the form $(a + b)(a + b)$.

$(x + 7)^2$

Factor each perfect square trinomial.

7. $x^2 - 12x + 36$ ________

8. $x^2 + 22x + 121$ ________

9. $4x^2 + 12x + 9$ ________

10. $16x^2 - 40x + 25$ ________

Name ____________________ Class __________ Date __________

9.1 Solving Equations by Taking Square Roots

Essential Question: How can you solve quadratic equations using square roots?

Resource Locker

Explore Exploring Square Roots

Recall that the **square root** of a non-negative number a is the real number b such that $b^2 = a$. Since $4^2 = 16$ and $(-4)^2 = 16$, the square roots of 16 are 4 and −4. Thus, every positive real number has two square roots, one positive and one negative. The positive square root is given by $\sqrt{a}$ and the negative square root by $-\sqrt{a}$. These can be combined as $\pm\sqrt{a}$.

Properties of Radicals

Property	Symbols	Example
Product Property of Radicals	For $a \geq 0$ and $b \geq 0$, $\sqrt{ab} = \sqrt{a} \cdot \sqrt{b}$.	$\sqrt{36} = \sqrt{9 \cdot 4}$ $= \sqrt{9} \cdot \sqrt{4}$ $= 3 \cdot 2$ $= 6$
Quotient Property of Radicals	For $a \geq 0$ and $b > 0$, $\sqrt{\frac{a}{b}} = \frac{\sqrt{a}}{\sqrt{b}}$.	$-\sqrt{0.16} = -\sqrt{\frac{16}{100}}$ $= -\frac{\sqrt{16}}{\sqrt{100}}$ $= -\frac{4}{10}$ $= -0.4$

Find each square root.

(A) $\pm\sqrt{49} = +\square$ and $-\square$

(B) $\pm\sqrt{25} = +\square$ and $-\square$

(C) $\pm\sqrt{12} = \pm\sqrt{\square \cdot 3} = \pm\sqrt{\square} \cdot \sqrt{\square}$

$= \pm\square \cdot \sqrt{\square}$

(D) $\pm\sqrt{\frac{16}{9}} = \pm\frac{\sqrt{\square}}{\sqrt{\square}}$

$= \pm\frac{\square}{\square}$

(E) $\pm\sqrt{0.27} = \pm\sqrt{\frac{\square}{100}} = \pm\frac{\sqrt{\square}}{\sqrt{100}} = \pm\frac{\sqrt{\square \cdot 3}}{\square} = \pm\frac{\sqrt{\square} \cdot \sqrt{3}}{\square} = \pm\frac{\square \cdot \sqrt{\square}}{\square}$

Reflect

1. **Discussion** Explain why $\sqrt{6^2}$ and $\sqrt{(-6)^2}$ have the same value.

2. **Discussion** Explain why a must be non-negative when you find $\sqrt{a}$.

3. Does 0 have any square roots? Why or why not?

Explain 1 Solving $ax^2 - c = 0$ by Using Square Roots

Solving a quadratic equation by using square roots may involve either finding square roots of perfect squares or finding square roots of numbers that are not perfect squares. In the latter case, the solution is irrational and can be approximated.

Example 1 **Solve the equation. Give the answer in radical form, and then use a calculator to approximate the solution to two decimal places, if necessary. Use a graphing calculator to graph the related function and compare the roots of the equation to the zeros of the related function.**

(A) $4x^2 - 5 = 2$

Solve the equation for x.

$4x^2 - 5 = 2$	Original equation
$4x^2 - 5 + 5 = 2 + 5$	Add 5 to both sides.
$4x^2 = 7$	Simplify.
$\frac{4x^2}{4} = \frac{7}{4}$	Divide both sides by 4.
$x^2 = 1.75$	Simplify.
$x = \pm\sqrt{1.75}$	Definition of a square root
$x \approx \pm 1.32$	Use a calculator to approximate the square roots.

The approximate solutions of the equation are $x \approx 1.32$ and $x \approx -1.32$.

Use a graphing calculator to graph the related function, $f(x) = 4x^2 - 7$, and find the zeros of the function.

The graph intersects the x-axis at approximately $(1.32, 0)$ and $(-1.32, 0)$. So, the roots of the equation are the zeros of the related function.

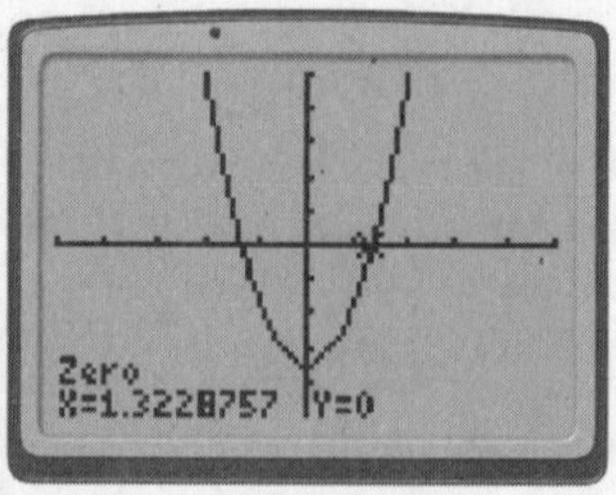

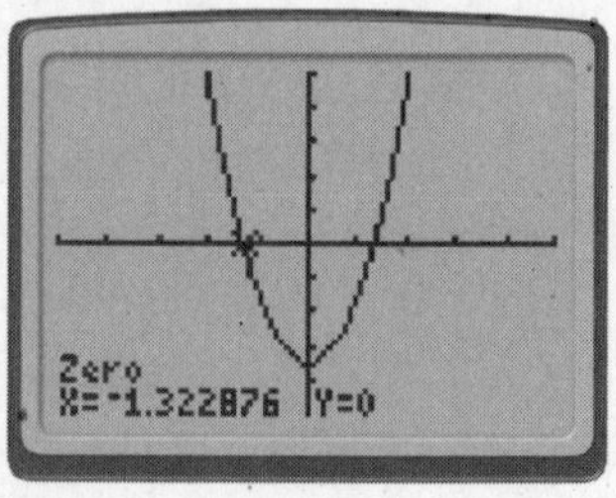

(B) $2x^2 - 8 = 0$

Solve the equation for x.

$2x^2 - 8 = 0$	Original equation
$2x^2 - 8 + \square = 0 + \square$	Add $\square$ to both sides.
$2x^2 = \square$	Simplify.
$\dfrac{2x^2}{\square} = \dfrac{8}{\square}$	Divide both sides by $\square$.
$x^2 = \square$	Simplify.
$x = \pm\sqrt{\square}$	Definition of a square root
$x = \pm \square$	Evaluate the square roots.

The solutions of the equation are $x = \square$ and $x = \square$.

Use a graphing calculator to graph the related function, $f(x) = 2x^2 - 8$, and find the zeros of the function.

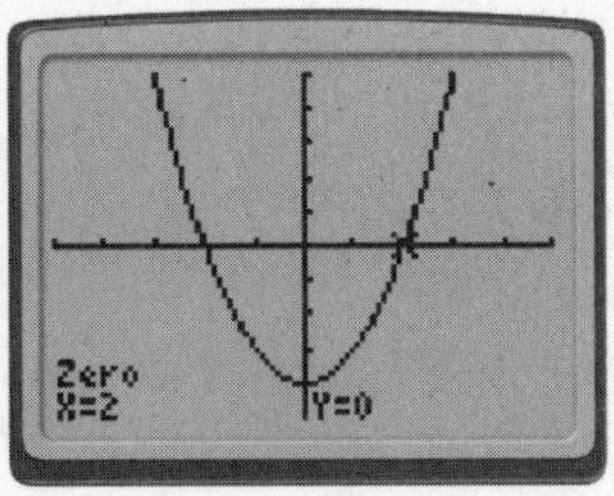

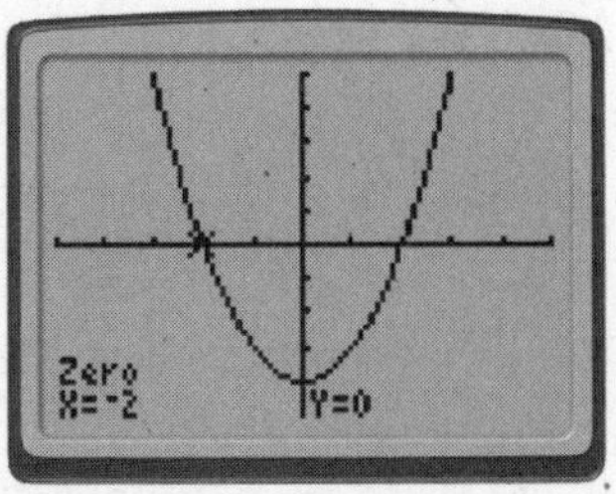

The graph intersects the x-axis at $(\square, \square)$ and $(\square, \square)$. So,

the ________ of the equation are

the __________ of the related function.

Your Turn

Solve the equation. Give the answer in radical form, and then use a calculator to approximate the solution to two decimal places, if necessary. Use a graphing calculator to graph the related function to check your answer.

4. $3x^2 + 6 = 33$

5. $5x^2 - 9 = 2$

Explain 2 Solving $a(x + b)^2 = c$ by Using Square Roots

Solving a quadratic equation may involve isolating the squared part of a quadratic expression on one side of the equation first.

Example 2 **Solve the equation. Give the answer in radical form, and then use a calculator to approximate the solution to two decimal places, if necessary.**

Ⓐ $(x + 5)^2 = 36$

$(x + 5)^2 = 36$	Original equation
$x + 5 = \pm\sqrt{36}$	Take the square root of both sides.
$x + 5 = \pm 6$	Simplify the square root.
$x = \pm 6 - 5$	Subtract 5 from both sides.
$x = -6 - 5$ or $x = 6 - 5$	Solve for both cases.
$x = -11$ $\quad$ $x = 1$	

The solutions are $x = -11$ and $x = 1$.

Ⓑ $3(x - 5)^2 = 18$

$3(x - 5)^2 = 18$	Original equation
$(x - 5)^2 = \square$	Divide both sides by $\square$.
$x - 5 = \pm\sqrt{\square}$	Take the square roots of both sides.
$x = \pm\sqrt{\square} + \square$	Add $\square$ to both sides.
$x = \sqrt{\square} + 5$ or $x = -\sqrt{6} + \square$	Solve for both cases.
$x \approx \square$ or $x \approx \square$	

The approximate solutions are $x \approx \square$ and $x \approx \square$.

Reflect

6. Find the solution(s), if any, of $2(x - 3)^2 = -32$. Explain your reasoning.

Your Turn

Solve the equation. Give the answer in radical form, and then use a calculator to approximate the solution to two decimal places, if necessary.

7. $4(x + 10)^2 = 24$

8. $(x - 9)^2 = 64$

Explain 3 Solving Equation Models by Using Square Roots

Real-world situations can sometimes be analyzed by solving a quadratic equation using square roots.

Example 3 **Solve the problem.**

Ⓐ A contractor is building a fenced-in playground at a daycare. The playground will be rectangular with its width equal to half its length. The total area will be 5000 square feet. Determine how many feet of fencing the contractor will use.

First, find the dimensions.
Let $A = 5000$, $\ell = x$, and $w = \frac{1}{2}x$.

$A = \ell w$

$5000 = x \cdot \frac{1}{2}x$

$5000 = \frac{1}{2}x^2$

$10{,}000 = x^2$

$\pm\sqrt{10{,}000} = x$ Take the square root of both sides.

$\pm 100 = x$ Evaluate the square root.

Since the width of a rectangle cannot be negative, the length of the playground is 100 feet. The width is half the length, or 50 feet.

Find the amount of fencing.

$P = 2\ell + 2w$

$= 2(100) + 2(50)$

$= 200 + 100$ Multiply.

$= 300$ Add.

So, the contractor will use 300 feet of fencing.

(B) A person standing on a second-floor balcony drops keys to a friend standing below the balcony. The keys are dropped from a height of 10 feet. The height in feet of the keys as they fall is given by the function $h(t) = -16t^2 + 10$, where t is the time in seconds since the keys were dropped. The friend catches the keys at a height of 4 feet. Find the elapsed time before the keys are caught.

Let $h(t) = \square$. Substitute the value into the equation and solve for t.

$h(t) = -16t^2 + 10$	Original equation
$\square = -16t^2 + 10$	Substitute.
$4 - \square = -16t^2 + 10 - \square$	Subtract 10 from both sides.
$\square = -16t^2$	Simplify.
$\dfrac{-6}{\square} = \dfrac{-16t^2}{\square}$	Divide both sides by -16.
$\square = t^2$	Simplify.
$\pm\sqrt{\square} = t$	Take the square root of both sides.
$\pm\square \approx t$	Use a calculator to approximate the square roots.

Since time cannot be negative, the elapsed time before the keys are caught is approximately $\square$ second(s).

Your Turn

9. A zookeeper is buying fencing to enclose a pen at the zoo. The pen is an isosceles right triangle. There is already a fence along the hypotenuse, which borders a path. The area of the pen will be 4500 square feet. The zookeeper can buy the fencing in whole feet only. How many feet of fencing should he buy?

Elaborate

10. How many real solutions does $x^2 = -25$ have? Explain.

11. Suppose the function $h(t) = -16t^2 + 20$ models the height in feet of an object after t seconds. If the final height is given as 2 feet, explain why there is only one reasonable solution for the time it takes the object to fall.

12. **Essential Question Check-In** What steps would you take to solve $6x^2 - 54 = 42$?

Evaluate: Homework and Practice

Personal Math Trainer

- Online Homework
- Hints and Help
- Extra Practice

Use the Product Property of Radicals, the Quotient Property of Radicals, or both to simplify each expression.

1. $\pm\sqrt{0.0081}$

2. $\pm\sqrt{\frac{8}{25}}$

3. $\pm\sqrt{96}$

Solve each equation. Give the answer in radical form, and then use a calculator to approximate the solution to two decimal places, if necessary. Use a graphing calculator to graph the related function to check your answer.

4. $5x^2 - 21 = 39$

5. $0.1x^2 - 1.2 = 8.8$

6. $6x^2 - 21 = 33$

7. $6 - \frac{1}{3}x^2 = -20$

8. $5 - 2x^2 = -3$

9. $7x^2 + 10 = 18$

Solve each equation. Give the answer in radical form, and then use a calculator to approximate the solution to two decimal places, if necessary.

10. $5(x - 9)^2 = 15$

11. $(x + 15)^2 = 81$

12. $3(x + 1)^2 = 27$

13. $\frac{2}{3}(x - 40)^2 = 24$

14. $(x - 12)^2 = 54$

15. $(x + 5.4)^2 = 1.75$

16. The area on a wall covered by a rectangular poster is 320 square inches. The length of the poster is 1.25 times longer than the width of the poster. What are the dimensions of the poster?

17. A circle is graphed with its center on the origin. The area of the circle is 144 square units. What are the x-intercepts of the graph? Round to the nearest tenth.

18. The equation $d = 16t^2$ gives the distance d in feet that a golf ball falls in t seconds. How many seconds will it take a golf ball to drop to the ground from a height of 4 feet? 64 feet?

19. Entertainment For a scene in a movie, a sack of money is dropped from the roof of a 600-foot skyscraper. The height of the sack above the ground in feet is given by $h = -16t^2 + 600$, where t is the time in seconds. How long will it take the sack to reach the ground? Round to the nearest tenth of a second.

20. A lot for sale is shaped like a trapezoid. The bases of the trapezoid represent the widths of the front and back yards. The width of the back yard is twice the width of the front yard. The distance from the front yard to the backyard, or the height of the trapezoid, is equal to the width of the back yard. Find the width of the front and back yards, given that the area is 6000 square feet. Round to the nearest foot.

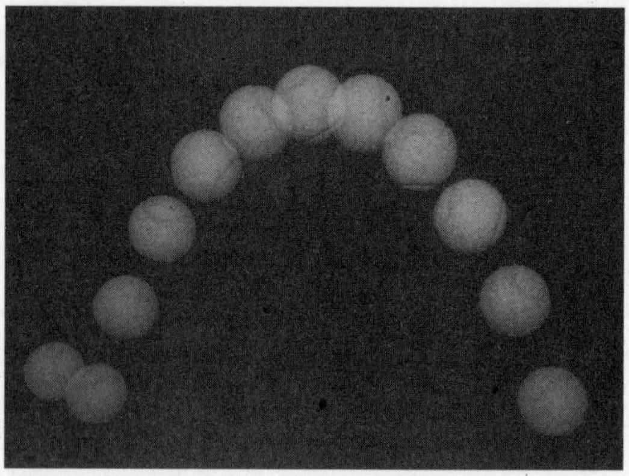

21. To study how high a ball bounces, students drop the ball from various heights. The function $h(t) = -16t^2 + h_0$ gives the height (in feet) of the ball at time t measured in seconds since the ball was dropped from a height of h_0. If the ball is dropped from a height of 8 feet, find the elapsed time until the ball hits the floor. Round to the nearest tenth.

22. Match each equation with its solutions.

a. $2x^2 - 2 = 16$ ________ $= \pm\frac{2\sqrt{33}}{3}$

b. $2(x-2)^2 = 16$ ________ $x = \pm 3$

c. $3x^2 + 4 = 48$ ________ $x = 2 \pm 2\sqrt{2}$

d. $3(x+4)^2 = 48$ ________ $x = -8$ or $x = 0$

H.O.T. Focus on Higher Order Thinking

23. Explain the Error Trent and Lisa solve the same equation, but they disagree on the solution of the equation. Their work is shown. Which solution is correct? Explain.

Trent:	Lisa:
$5x^2 + 1000 = -125$	$5x^2 + 1000 = -125$
$5x^2 = -1125$	$5x^2 = -1125$
$x^2 = -225$	$x^2 = -225$
$x = \pm\sqrt{-225}$	no real solutions
$x = \pm 15$	

24. Multi-Step Construction workers are installing a rectangular, in-ground pool. To start, they dig a rectangular hole in the ground where the pool will be. The area of the ground that they will be digging up is 252 square feet. The length of the pool is twice the width of the pool.

a. What are the dimensions of the pool? Round to the nearest tenth.

b. Once the pool is installed, the workers will build a fence, that encloses a rectangular region, around the perimeter of it. The fence will be 10 feet from the edges of the pool, except at the corners. How many feet of fencing will the workers need?

25. Communicate Mathematical Ideas Explain why the quadratic equation $x^2 + b = 0$ where $b > 0$, has no real solutions, but the quadratic equation $x^2 - b = 0$ where $b > 0$, has two real solutions.

26. Justify Reasoning For the equation $x^2 = a$, describe the values of a that will result in two real solutions, one real solution, and no real solution. Explain your reasoning.

Lesson Performance Task

You have been asked to create a pendulum clock for your classroom. The clock will be placed on one wall of the classroom and go the entire height of the wall. Choose how large you want the face and hands on your clock to be and provide measurements for the body of the clock. The pendulum will start halfway between the center of the clock face and its bottom edge and will initially end 1 foot above the floor. Calculate the period of the pendulum using the formula $L = 9.78t^2$, where L is the length of the pendulum in inches and t is the length of the period in seconds.

Now, adjust the length of your pendulum so the number of periods in 1 minute or 60 seconds is an integer value. How long is your pendulum and how many periods equal one minute?

Name ______________________ Class ______________ Date ________

9.2 Solving Equations by Completing the Square

Resource Locker

Essential Question: How can you use completing the square to solve a quadratic equation?

Explore Modeling Completing the Square

You can use algebra tiles to model a perfect square trinomial.

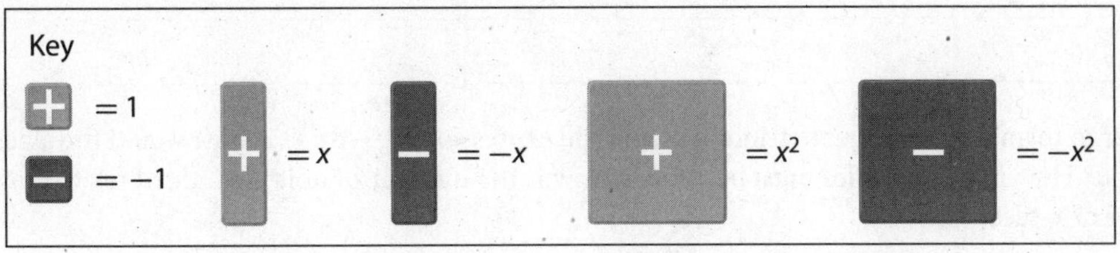

(A) The algebra tiles shown represent the expression $x^2 + 6x$. The expression does not have a constant term, which would be represented with unit tiles. Create a square diagram of algebra tiles by adding the correct number of unit tiles to form a square.

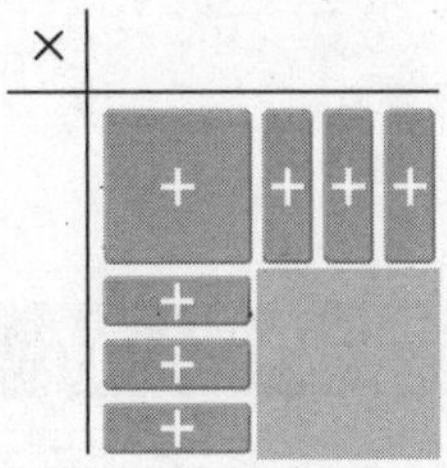

(B) How many unit tiles were added to the expression? ____

(C) Write the trinomial represented by the algebra tiles for the complete square.

$\square x^2 + \square x + \square$

(D) It should be easily recognized that the trinomial $\square x^2 + \square x + \square$ is an example of the special case $(a + b^2) = a^2 + 2ab + b^2$. Recall that trinomials of this form are called perfect-square trinomials. Since the trinomial is a perfect square, it can be factored into two identical binomials.

$\square x^2 + \square x + \square = \left(\square x + \square\right)^2$

(E) Refer to the algebra tiles in the diagram. What expression is represented by the tiles?

$\square x^2 + \square x$

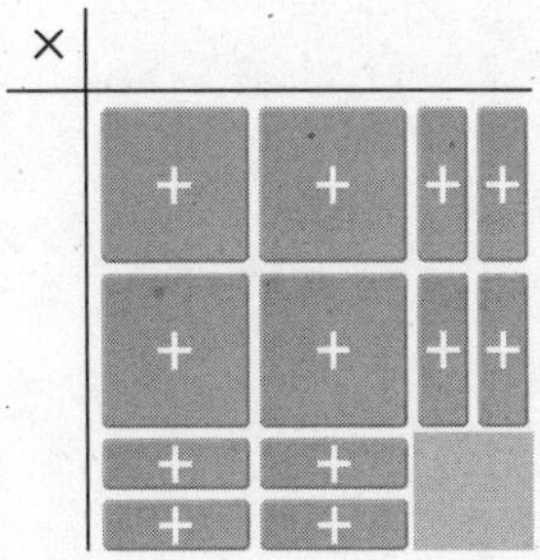

(F) Complete the square in Step E by filling the bottom right corner with unit tiles. How many unit tiles were added to the diagram? ____

(G) Write the trinomial represented by the algebra tiles for the complete square.

$\square x^2 + \square x + \square$

(H) The trinomial is a square of a binomial. Use the algebra tiles to write the trinomial in factored form.

$\square x^2 + \square x + \square = (\square x + \square)^2$

Reflect

1. **Discussion** When using algebra tiles to model the expression $x^2 + 6x + c$, the x-tiles are divided equally, with 3 tiles on the right and bottom sides of the x^2-tile. How does the number 3 relate to the total number of x-tiles? How does the number 3 relate to the total number of unit tiles that were added?

2. In order to form a perfect square trinomial with the expression $x^2 + 8x + c$, how would the algebra tiles be arranged? How many unit tiles must be added? How is the number of unit tiles added related to the total number of x-tiles?

Explain 1 Completing the Square When $a = 1$

Completing the square is a process of rewriting a quadratic expression as a perfect square trinomial so that it can be solved by taking square roots. In the Explore, the method for completing the square when $a = 1$ was modeled with algebra tiles. First, place half of the x-tiles along the right side of the x^2-tile and half underneath the tile. Then add unit tiles to fill in the rectangle started with the x^2 - and x-tiles. The number of unit tiles equals the square of the number of x-tiles on either side of the x^2-tile.

In other words, to complete the square for the expression $x^2 + bx + c$, add $\left(\frac{b}{2}\right)^2$. The perfect-square trinomial will then be $x^2 + bx + \left(\frac{b}{2}\right)^2$ and its factored form will be $\left(x + \frac{b}{2}\right)^2$.

Example 1 **Complete the square to form a perfect-square trinomial.**

(A) $x^2 + 4x$

$x^2 + 4x$

$b = 4$	Identify b.
$\left(\frac{4}{2}\right)^2 = 2^2 = 4$	Find $\left(\frac{b}{2}\right)^2$.
$x^2 + 4x + 4$	Add $\left(\frac{b}{2}\right)^2$ to the expression.

(B) $x^2 - 8x$

$x^2 - 8x$

$b = \square$ Identify b.

$\left(\frac{\square}{2}\right)^2 = \left(\square\right)^2 = \square$ Find $\left(\frac{b}{2}\right)^2$.

$x^2 - 8x + \square$ Add $\left(\frac{b}{2}\right)^2$ to the expression.

Reflect

3. When b is negative, why is the result added to the expression still positive?

____

____

Your Turn

4. Complete the square: $x^2 + 12x$

Explain 2 Solving $x^2 + bx + c = 0$ by Completing the Square

Completing the square can also be used to solve equations in the forms $x^2 + bx + c = 0$ or $x^2 + bx = c$.

Example 2 **Solve each equation by completing the square. Check the answers.**

(A) $x^2 - 4x = 3$

$x^2 - 4x = 3$

$x^2 - 4x + 4 = 3 + 4$ Add $\left(\frac{b}{2}\right)^2 = \left(\frac{-4}{2}\right)^2 = 4$ to both sides.

$(x - 2)^2 = 7$ Factor and simplify.

$x - 2 = \pm\sqrt{7}$ Take the square root of both sides.

$x - 2 = \sqrt{7}$ or $x - 2 = -\sqrt{7}$ Write and solve two equations.

$x = 2 + \sqrt{7}$ $x = 2 - \sqrt{7}$ Add 2 to both sides.

Check the answers.

$(2 + \sqrt{7})^2 - 4(2 + \sqrt{7})$

$= 4 + 4\sqrt{7} + 7 - 8 - 4\sqrt{7}$

$= 4 + 7 - 8 + 4\sqrt{7} - 4\sqrt{7}$

$= 3$

$(2 - \sqrt{7})^2 - 4(2 - \sqrt{7})$

$= 4 - 4\sqrt{7} + 7 - 8 + 4\sqrt{7}$

$= 4 + 7 - 8 - 4\sqrt{7} + 4\sqrt{7}$

$= 3$

$2 + \sqrt{7}$ and $2 - \sqrt{7}$ are both solutions of the equation $x^2 - 4x = 3$.

B $x^2 + 16x = 36$

$$x^2 + 16x = 36$$

$\square x^2 + \square x + \square = \square + \square$ Add $\left(\frac{b}{2}\right)^2 = \square$ to both sides.

$\left(\square x + \square\right)^2 = \square$ Factor and simplify.

$\square x + \square = \pm \square$ Take the square root of both sides.

$\square x + \square = \square$ or $\square x + \square = -\square$

$x = \square$ $\qquad x = \square$

Check the answers.

$$x^2 + 16x = 36$$

$$(-18)^2 + 16 \cdot \square = 36$$

$$\square - \square = 36$$

$$\square = 36$$

$x = -18$ is/is not a solution to the equation $x^2 + 16x = 36$.

$$x^2 + 16x = 36$$

$$2^2 + 16 \cdot \square = 36$$

$$\square + \square = 36$$

$$\square = 36$$

$x = 2$ is/is not a solution to the equation $x^2 + 16x = 36$

Your Turn

Solve each equation by completing the square. Check the answers.

5. $x^2 - 10x = 11$

6. $x^2 + 6x = 2$

Explain 3 Solving $ax^2 + bx + c = 0$ by Completing the Square When a Is a Perfect Square

When a is a perfect square, completing the square is easier than in other cases. Recall that the number of unit tiles needed is equal to the square of b divided by four times a, or $\frac{b^2}{4a}$. This is always the case when a is a perfect square.

Example 3 **Solve each equation by completing the square.**

Ⓐ $4x^2 - 8x = 21$

$4x^2 - 8x = 21$	
$\frac{(-8)^2}{4 \cdot 4} = \frac{64}{16} = 4$	Find $\frac{b^2}{4a}$.
$4x^2 - 8x + 4 = 21 + 4$	Add $\frac{b^2}{4a}$ to both sides.
$(2x - 2)^2 = 25$	Factor and simplify.
$2x - 2 = \pm\sqrt{25}$	Take the square root of the both sides.
$2x - 2 = \pm 5$	Simplify.
$2x - 2 = 5$ or $2x - 2 = -5$	Write and solve 2 equations.
$2x = 7$ or $2x = -3$	Add to both sides.
$x = \frac{7}{2}$ or $x = -\frac{3}{2}$	Divide both sides by 2.

Ⓑ $9x^2 + 6x = 10$

$9x^2 + 6x = 10$	
$\frac{\square^2}{4 \cdot \square} = \frac{\square}{\square} = \square$	Find $\frac{b^2}{4a}$.
$\square x^2 + \square x + \square = 10 + \square$	Add $\frac{b^2}{4a}$ to both sides.
$\left(\square x + \square\right)^2 = \square$	Factor and simplify.
$\square x + \square = \pm\sqrt{\square}$	Take the square root of the both sides.
$\square x + \square = \sqrt{\square}$ or $\square x + \square = -\sqrt{\square}$	Write and solve two equations.
$\square x = -\square + \sqrt{\square}$ $\square x = -\square - \sqrt{\square}$	Subtract $\square$ from both sides.
$x = \frac{-\square + \sqrt{\square}}{\square}$ $x = \frac{-\square - \sqrt{\square}}{\square}$	Divide both sides by $\square$.

Reflect

7. In order for the procedure used in this section to work, why does a have to be a perfect square?

Your Turn

Solve each equation by completing the square.

8. $16x^2 - 16x = 5$

9. $4x^2 + 12x = 5$

Explain 4 Solving $ax^2 + bx + c = 0$ by Completing the Square When a Is Not a Perfect Square

When the leading coefficient a is not a perfect square, the equation can be transformed by multiplying both sides by a value such that a becomes a perfect square.

Example 4 **Solve each equation by completing the square.**

(A) $2x^2 - 6x = 5$

Since the coefficient of x^2 is 2, which is not a perfect square, multiply both sides by a value so the coefficient will have a perfect square. In this case, use 2.

$2x^2 - 6x = 5$	
$2(2x^2 - 6x) = 2(5)$	Multiply both sides by 2.
$4x^2 - 12x = 10$	Simplify.
$\frac{(-12)^2}{4 \cdot 4} = \frac{144}{16} = 9$	Find $\frac{b^2}{4a}$.
$4x^2 - 12x + 9 = 10 + 9$	Add $\frac{b^2}{4a}$ to both sides.
$(2x - 3)^2 = 19$	Factor and simplify.
$2x - 3 = \pm\sqrt{19}$	Take the square root of the both sides.
$2x - 3 = \sqrt{19}$ or $2x - 3 = -\sqrt{19}$	Write and solve 2 equations.
$2x = 3 + \sqrt{19}$ $\quad$ $2x = 3 - \sqrt{19}$	Add to both sides.
$x = \frac{3 + \sqrt{19}}{2}$ $\quad$ $x = \frac{3 - \sqrt{19}}{2}$	Divide both sides by 2.

(B) $3x^2 + 3x = 16$

Since the coefficient of x^2 is ______, which is not a perfect square, multiply both sides by a value so the coefficient will have a perfect square. In this case, use ______.

$3x^2 + 3x = 16$	
$\square(3x^2 + 2x) = \square(16)$	Multiply both sides by $\square$.
$\square x^2 + \square x = \square$	Simplify.
$\dfrac{\square^2}{4 \cdot \square} = \dfrac{\square}{\square} = \square$	Find $\dfrac{b^2}{4a}$.
$\square x^2 + \square x + \square = \square + \square$	Add $\dfrac{b^2}{4a}$ to both sides.
$\left(\square x + \square\right)^2 = \square$	Factor and simplify.
$\square x + \square = \pm\sqrt{\square} = \pm\square$	Take the square root of the both sides.
$\square x + \square = \square$ or $\square x + \square = -\square$	Write and solve two equations.
$\square x = \square$ $\quad$ $\square x = -\square$	Subtract $\square$ from both sides.
$x = \square$ $\quad$ $x = -\square$	Divide both sides by $\square$.

Reflect

10. Consider the equation $2x^2 + 11x = 12$. Why is 2 the best value by which to multiply both sides of the equation before completing the square?

____

____

____

Your Turn

Solve each equation by completing the square.

11. $\frac{1}{2}x^2 + 3x = 14$

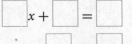

12. $2x^2 - 4x = 16$

Explain 5 Modeling Completing the Square for Quadratic Equations

Completing the square can be useful when solving problems involving quadratic functions, especially if the function cannot be factored. In these cases, complete the square to rewrite the function in vertex form: $f(x) = a(x - h)^2 + k$. Completing the square in this situation is similar to solving equations by completing the square, but instead of adding a term to both sides of the equation, you will both add and subtract it from the function's rule.

Recall that the height of an object moving under the force of gravity, with no other forces acting on it, can be modeled by the quadratic function $h = -16t^2 + vt + s$, where t is the time in seconds, v is the initial vertical velocity, and s is the initial height in feet.

Example 5 **Write a function in standard form for each model. Then, rewrite the equation in vertex form and solve the problem. Graph the function on a graphing calculator and find the x-intercepts and maximum value of the graph.**

Ⓐ **Sports** A baseball is thrown from a height of 5 feet. If the person throws the baseball at a velocity of 30 feet per second, what will be the maximum height of the baseball? How long will it take the baseball to hit the ground?

The function for this situation is $h = -16t^2 + 30t + 5$.

Complete the square to find the vertex of the function's graph.

$$h = -16t^2 + 30t + 5$$

$$h = -1(16t^2 - 30t) + 5 \qquad \text{Factor out } -1.$$

$$h = -1\left(16t^2 - 30t + \frac{225}{16} - \frac{225}{16}\right) + 5 \qquad \text{Complete the square.}$$

$$h = -1\left(\left(4t - \frac{15}{4}\right)^2 - \frac{225}{16}\right) + 5 \qquad \text{Factor the perfect-square trinomial.}$$

$$h = -\left(4t - \frac{15}{4}\right)^2 + \frac{225}{16} + 5 \qquad \text{Distribute the } -1.$$

$$h = -4\left(t - \frac{15}{4}\right)^2 + \frac{305}{16} \qquad \text{Combine the last two terms.}$$

The coordinates of the vertex are $\left(\frac{15}{4}, \frac{305}{16}\right)$, or about (3.75, 19.06). The maximum height will be about 19 feet.

The graph of the function confirms the vertex at about (3.75, 19.06). The t-intercept at about 2.03 indicates that the baseball will hit the ground after about 2 seconds.

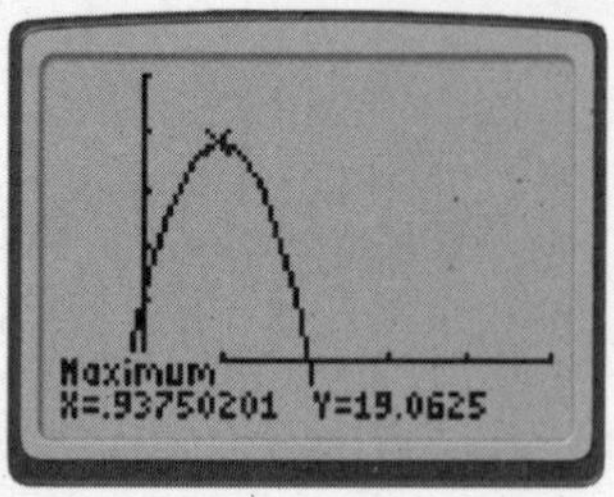

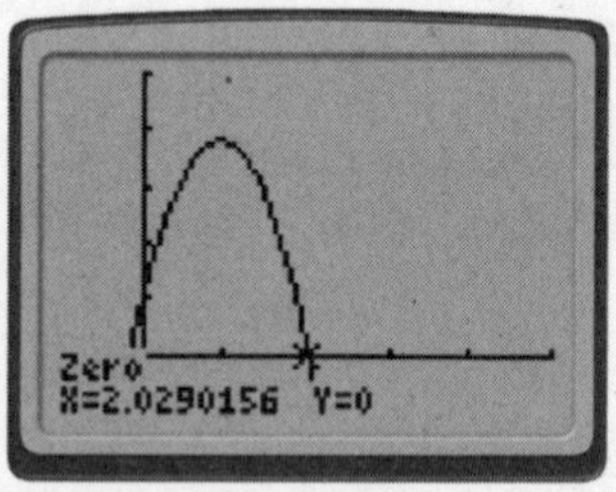

(B) **Sports** A person kicks a soccer ball from the ground with an initial upward velocity of 16 feet per second. What is the maximum height of the soccer ball? When will the soccer ball hit the ground?

An equation for this situation is $h = -16t^2 + \square\, t + \square$.

Complete the square to find the vertex of the function's graph.

$h = -16t^2 + \square\, t + \square$

$h = \square\left(\square t^2 - \square t\right) + \square$ — Factor out $\square$.

$h = \square\left(\square t^2 - \square t + \frac{\square}{\square} - \frac{\square}{\square}\right) + 0$ — Complete the square.

$h = \square\left(\square\left(t - \frac{\square}{\square}\right)^2 - \frac{\square}{\square}\right) + 0$ — Factor the perfect-square trinomial.

$h = \square\left(\square\left(t - \frac{\square}{\square}\right)^2\right) + \frac{\square}{\square} + 0$ — Distribute the -16.

$h = \square\left(\square\left(t - \frac{\square}{\square}\right)^2\right) + \square$ — Combine the last two terms.

The coordinates of the vertex are $\left(\frac{\square}{\square}, \square\right)$.

The soccer ball will be at its highest when it is at its vertex, or at $\square$ feet.

The graph of the function confirms the vertex at (0.5, 4). The x-intercept at 1 indicates that the ball will hit the ground after 1 second.

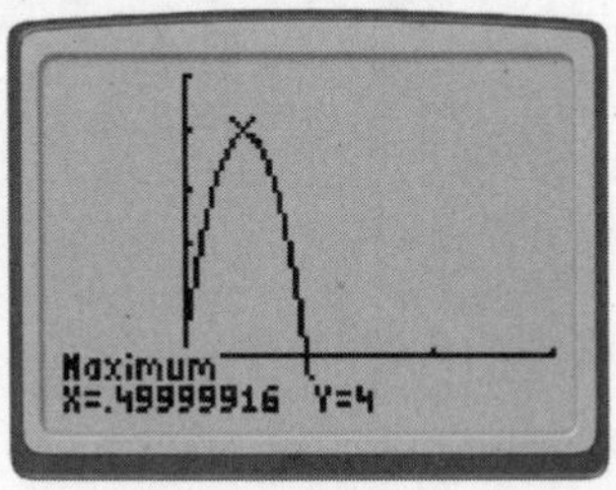

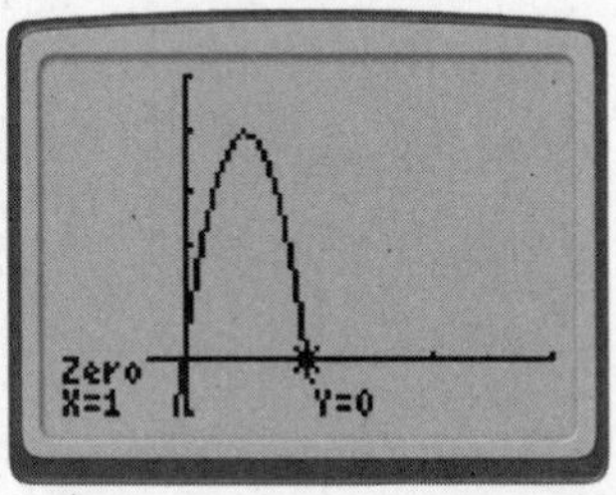

Your Turn

13. Physics A person standing at the edge of a cliff 48 feet tall throws a ball up and just off the cliff with an initial upward velocity of 8 feet per second. What is the maximum height of the ball? When will the ball hit the ground?

Elaborate

14. When $b > 0$, the perfect square-trinomial of the expression $x + bx$ is $x^2 + bx + \left(\frac{b}{2}\right)^2$. What is the perfect-square trinomial when $b < 0$? Does the sign of the constant change? Why or why not?

15. Essential Question Check-In What is the first step in completing the square to solve a quadratic equation of the form $ax^2 + bx = c$?

Evaluate: Homework and Practice

Personal Math Trainer

- Online Homework
- Hints and Help
- Extra Practice

Complete the square to form a perfect-square trinomial.

1. $x^2 + 26x$

2. $x^2 - 18x$

3. $x^2 - 2x$

4. $x^2 - 24x$

Solve each equation by completing the square. Check the answers.

5. $x^2 + 8x = 33$

6. $x^2 - 6x = 8$

7. $x^2 + 12x = 5$

8. $x^2 - 14x = 95$

Solve each equation by completing the square.

9. $9x^2 + 12x = 32$

10. $4x^2 + 20x = 2$

11. $16x^2 - 32x = 65$

12. $9x^2 - 24x = 1$

13. $\frac{1}{2}x^2 + 4x = 10$

14. $3x^2 - 4x = 20$

15. $2x^2 + 14x = 4$

16. $\frac{1}{2}x^2 - 5x = 18$

Projectile Motion **Write an equation for each model, rewrite the equation into vertex form, and solve the problem. Then graph the function on a graphing calculator and state the *x*-intercepts of the graph.**

17. Sports A person kicks a ball from the ground into the air with an initial upward velocity of 8 feet per second. What is the maximum height of the ball? When will the ball hit the ground?

18. Physics A person reaching out to the edge of a building ledge 85 feet off the ground flicks a twig up and off the ledge with an initial upward velocity of 11 feet per second. What is the maximum height of the twig? When will the twig hit the ground?

19. VOLLEYBALL A volleyball player hits a ball from a height of 5 feet with an initial vertical velocity of 16 feet per second. What is the maximum height of the volleyball? Assuming it is not hit by another player, when will the volleyball hit the ground?

20. LACROSSE A lacrosse player throws a ball into the air from a height of 8 feet with an initial vertical velocity of 32 feet per second. What is the maximum height of the ball? When will the ball hit the ground?

21. Identify the value of a in each equation of the form $ax^2 + bx + c = 0$.

a. $11x^2 + 2x = 4$

b. $4x^2 + 5 = 0$

c. $3x^3 = 7$

d. $5x^2 + 11x = 1$

e. $3x^2 = 5$

22. The diagram represents the expression $x^2 + 8x$. Use algebra tiles to model completing the square. Then write the perfect square trinomial expression.

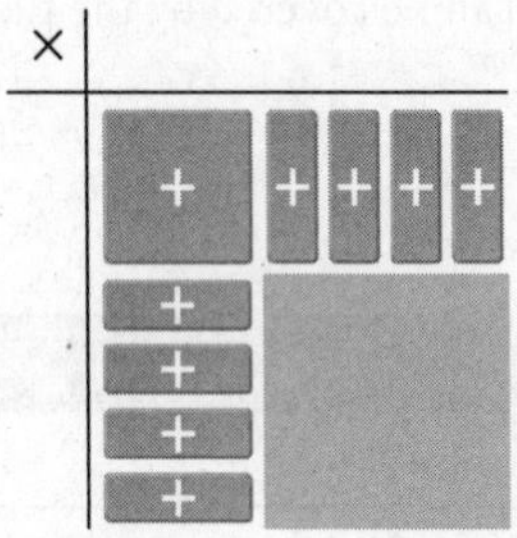

H.O.T. Focus on Higher Order Thinking

23. Explain the Error A student was instructed to solve the equation $x^2 + 4x = 77$ and produced the following work. Explain the student's error. What is the correct solution?

$$x^2 + 4x = 77$$
$$x^2 + 4x + 4 = 77 + 4$$
$$(x + 2)^2 = 81$$
$$x + 2 = 9$$
$$x = 7$$

24. Justify Reasoning Will the equation $x^2 + 6x = -10$ produce an answer that is a real number after the square is completed? Explain.

25. Draw Conclusions When solving a quadratic model, why are some solutions considered extraneous? Is this always the case, or can some quadratic models have two solutions?

Lesson Performance Task

An architect is designing the lobby of a new office building. The company that hired her has reclaimed a large quantity of stone floor tiles from the building previously on the site and wishes to use them to tile the lobby. The lobby needs to be 18 feet longer than it is wide to incorporate an information desk. The table below shows the types of tile available, the general color of the tile, and the area that can be covered by the tile.

Stone	Color	Area in Square Feet
Marble	Cream	175
Marble	Cream with gold flecks	115
Marble	Black	648
Marble	White with black flecks	360
Slate	Gray	280
Slate	Gray with blue gray regions	243
Travertine	Caramel	208
Travertine	Latte	760
Adoquin	Dark gray with black regions	319
Adoquin	Light gray with darker gray regions	403
Limestone	Pewter	448
Limestone	Beige	544

Design the lobby using at least all of one type of tile. You can add additional types of tiles to create patterns in the floor. For this exercise, you can decide on the dimensions of the tiles in order to make any pattern you wish.

Name ______________________ Class ______________ Date ____________

9.3 Using the Quadratic Formula to Solve Equations

Essential Question: What is the quadratic formula, and how can you use it to solve quadratic equations?

Resource Locker

Explore Deriving the Quadratic Formula

You can complete the square on the general form of a quadratic equation to derive a formula that can be used to solve any quadratic equation.

(A) Write the standard form of a quadratic equation.

$ax^2 + bx + c = \square$

(B) Subtract c from both sides.

$ax^2 + bx = \square$

(C) Multiply both sides by $4a$ to make the coefficient of x^2 a perfect square.

$4a^2x^2 + \square = \square$

(D) Add b^2 to both sides of the equation to complete the square.

$4a^2x^2 + 4abx + b^2 = -4ac + \square$

(E) Factor the left side to write the trinomial as the square of a binomial.

$\left(\square\right)^2 = b^2 - 4ac$

(F) Take the square roots of both sides.

$\square = \pm\sqrt{\square}$

(G) Subtract b from both sides.

$2ax = \square \pm \sqrt{\square}$

(H) Divide both sides by $2a$ to solve for x.

$x = \dfrac{\square \pm \sqrt{\square}}{\square}$

(I) The formula you just derived, $x = \frac{-b \pm \sqrt{b^2 - 4ac}}{2a}$, is called the **quadratic formula**. It gives you the values of x that solve any quadratic equation where $a \neq 0$.

Reflect

1. **What If?** If the derivation had begun by dividing each term by a, what would the resulting binomial of x have been after completing the square? Does one derivation method appear to be simpler than the other? Explain.

Explain 1 Using the Discriminant to Determine the Number of Real Solutions

Recall that a quadratic equation, $ax^2 + bx + c$, can have two, one, or no real solutions. By evaluating the part of the quadratic formula under the radical sign, $b^2 - 4ac$, called the **discriminant**, you can determine the number of real solutions.

Example 1 **Determine how many real solutions each quadratic equation has.**

(A) $x^2 - 4x + 3 = 0$

$a = 1, b = -4, c = 3$ — Identify a, b, and c.

$b^2 - 4ac$ — Use the discriminant.

$(-4)^2 - 4(1)(3)$ — Substitute the identified values into the discriminant.

$16 - 12 = 4$ — Simplify.

Since $b^2 - 4ac > 0$, the equation has two real solutions.

(B) $x^2 - 2x + 2 = 0$

$a =$ ☐, $b =$ ☐, $c =$ ☐ — Identify a, b, and c.

$b^2 - 4ac$ — Use the discriminant.

$(☐)^2 - 4(☐)(☐)$ — Substitute the identified values into the discriminant.

☐ $-$ ☐ $=$ ☐ — Simplify.

Since $b^2 - 4ac$ ☐ 0, the equation has ______ real solution(s).

Reflect

2. When the discriminant is positive, the quadratic equation has two real solutions. When the discriminant is negative, there are no real solutions. How many real solutions does a quadratic equation have if its discriminant equals 0? Explain.

Your Turn

Use the discriminant to determine the number of real solutions for each quadratic equation.

3. $x^2 + 4x + 1 = 0$ **4.** $2x^2 - 6x + 15 = 0$ **5.** $x^2 + 6x + 9 = 0$

Explain 2 Solving Equations by Using the Quadratic Formula

To use the quadratic formula to solve a quadratic equation, check that the equation is in standard form. If not, rewrite it in standard form. Then substitute the values of *a*, *b*, and *c* into the formula.

Example 2 **Solve using the quadratic formula.**

(A) $2x^2 + 3x - 5 = 0$

$a = 2, b = 3, c = -5$ Identify *a*, *b*, and *c*.

$x = \frac{-b \pm \sqrt{b^2 - 4ac}}{2a}$ Use the quadratic formula.

$x = \frac{-3 \pm \sqrt{(3)^2 - 4(2)(-5)}}{2(2)}$ Substitute the identified values into the quadratic formula.

$x = \frac{-3 \pm \sqrt{49}}{4}$ Simplify the radicand and the denominator.

$x = \frac{-3 \pm 7}{4}$ Evaluate the square root.

$x = \frac{-3 + 7}{4}$ or $x = \frac{-3 - 7}{4}$ Write as two equations.

$x = 1$ or $x = -\frac{5}{2}$ Simplify both equations.

The solutions are 1 and $-\frac{5}{2}$.

Graph $y = 2x^2 + 3x - 5$ to verify your answers.

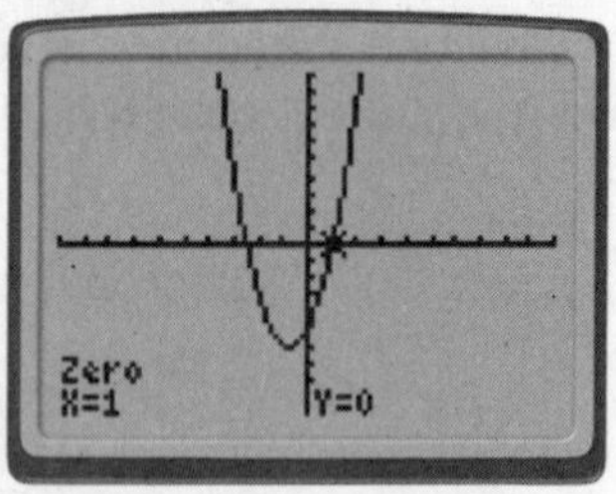

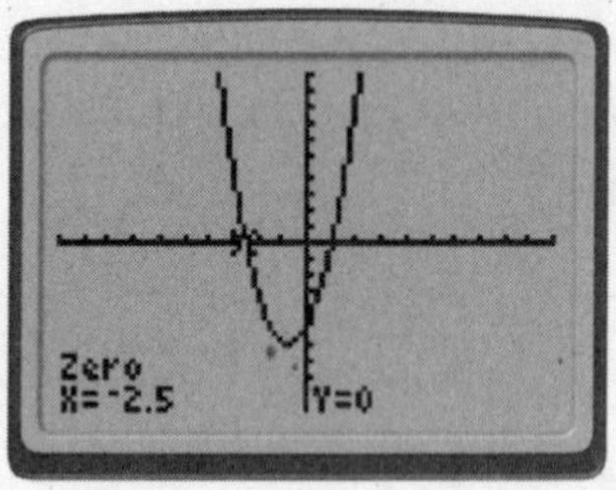

The graph does verify the solutions.

(B) $2x = x^2 - 4$

$x^2 - \square - 4 = 0$ — Write in standard form.

$a = \square$, $b = \square$, $c = \square$ — Identify a, b, and c.

$x = \dfrac{-b \pm \sqrt{b^2 - 4ac}}{2a}$ — Use the quadratic formula.

$x = \dfrac{-(\square) \pm \sqrt{(\square)^2 - 4(\square)(\square)}}{2(\square)}$ — Substitute the identified values into the quadratic formula.

$x = \dfrac{2 \pm \sqrt{\square}}{2}$ — Simplify the radicand and the denominator.

$x = \dfrac{2 \pm \sqrt{\square \cdot 5}}{2} = \dfrac{2 \pm 2\square}{2} = 1 \pm \square$ — Simplify.

$x = \square$ or $x = \square$ — Write as two equations.

$x \approx \square$ or $x \approx \square$ — Use a calculator to find approximate solutions to three decimal places.

The exact solutions are $\square$ and $\square$. The approximate solutions are $\square$ and $\square$.

Graph $y = x^2 - \square - 4$ and find the zeros using the graphing calculator. The calculator will give approximate values.

The graph ________ confirm the solutions.

Reflect

6. Discussion How can you use substitution to check your solutions?

____

Your Turn

Solve using the quadratic formula.

7. $x^2 - 6x - 7 = 0$

8. $2x^2 = 8x - 7$

Explain 3 Using the Discriminant with Real-World Models

Given a real-world situation that can be modeled by a quadratic equation, you can find the number of real solutions to the problem using the discriminant, and then apply the quadratic formula to obtain the solutions. After finding the solutions, check to see if they make sense in the context of the problem.

In projectile motion problems where the projectile height h is modeled by the equation $h = -16t^2 + vt + s$, where t is the time in seconds the object has been in the air, v is the initial vertical velocity in feet per second, and s is the initial height in feet. The -16 coefficient in front of the t^2 term refers to the effect of gravity on the object. This equation can be written using metric units as $h = -4.9t^2 + vt + s$, where the units are converted from feet to meters. Time remains in units of seconds.

Example 3 **For each problem, use the discriminant to determine the number of real solutions for the equation. Then, find the solutions and check to see if they make sense in the context of the problem.**

(A) A diver jumps from a platform 10 meters above the surface of the water. The diver's height is given by the equation $h = -4.9t^2 + 3.5t + 10$, where t is the time in seconds after the diver jumps. For what time t is the diver's height 1 meter?

Substitute $h = 1$ into the height equation. Then, write the resulting quadratic equation in standard form to solve for t.

$1 = -4.9t^2 + 3.5t + 10$ $\quad\quad$ $0 = -4.9t^2 + 3.5t + 9$

First, use the discriminant to find the number of real solutions of the equation.

$b^2 - 4ac$ $\quad\quad$ Use the discriminant.

$(3.5)^2 - 4(-4.9)(9) = 188.65$

Since $b^2 - 4ac > 0$, the equation has two real solutions.

Next, use the quadratic formula to find the real number solutions.

$a = -4.9,\ b = 3.5,\ c = 9$	Identify a, b, and c.
$t = \dfrac{-b \pm \sqrt{b^2 - 4ac}}{2a}$	Use the quadratic formula.
$t = \dfrac{-3.5 \pm \sqrt{188.65}}{2(-4.9)}$	Substitute the identified values into the quadratic formula and the value of the discriminant.
$t \approx \dfrac{-3.5 \pm 13.73}{-9.8}$	Simplify.
$t \approx \dfrac{-3.5 + 13.73}{-9.8}$ or $t \approx \dfrac{-3.5 - 13.73}{-9.8}$	Write as two equations.
$t \approx -1.04$ or $t \approx 1.76$	Solutions

Disregard the negative solution because t represents the seconds after the diver jumps and a negative value has no meaning in this context. So, the diver is at height 1 meter after a time of $t \approx 1.76$ seconds.

B The height in meters of a model rocket on a particular launch can be modeled by the equation $h = -4.9t^2 + 102t + 100$, where t is the time in seconds after its engine burns out 100 meters above the ground. When will the rocket reach a height of 600 meters?

Substitute $h =$ ☐ into the height equation. Then, write the resulting quadratic equation in standard form to solve for t.

$h = -4.9t^2 + 102t + 100$

☐ $= -4.9t^2 + 102t + 100$

$0 = -4.9t^2 + 102t -$ ☐

First, use the discriminant to find the number of real solutions of the equation.

$a = -4.9$, $b =$ ☐, $c =$ ☐	Identify a, b, and c.
$b^2 - 4ac$	Use the discriminant.
$\left(☐\right)^2 - 4(-4.9)\left(☐\right)$	Substitute the identified values into the discriminant.
☐ − ☐ = ☐	Simplify.

Since $b^2 - 4ac$ ☐ 0, the equation has ☐ real solutions.

Next, use the quadratic formula to find the real number solutions.

$t = \frac{-\square \pm \sqrt{\square}}{2(-4.9)}$ Substitute the identified values into the quadratic formula and the value of the discriminant.

$t = \frac{\square \pm \square}{-9.8}$ Simplify.

$t \approx \frac{-102 + \square}{-9.8}$ or $t \approx \frac{-102 - \square}{-9.8}$ Write as two equations.

$t \approx \square$ or $t \approx \square$ Solutions

Disregard the ________ solution because t represents the seconds after the rocket has launched and a ________ value has no meaning in this context. So, the rocket is at height 600 meters after a time of $t \approx \square$ seconds.

Your Turn

For each problem, use the discriminant to determine the number of real solutions for the equation. Then, find the solutions and check to see if they make sense in the context of the problem.

9. A soccer player uses her head to hit a ball up in the air from a height of 2 meters with an initial vertical velocity of 5 meters per second. The height h in meters of the ball is given by $h = -4.9t^2 + 5t + 2$, where t is the time elapsed in seconds. How long will it take the ball to hit the ground if no other players touch it?

10. The quarterback of a football team throws a pass to the team's receiver. The height h in meters of the football can be modeled by $h = -4.9t^2 + 3t + 1.75$, where t is the time elapsed in seconds. The receiver catches the football at a height of 0.25 meters. How long does the ball remain in the air until it is caught by the receiver?

Elaborate

11. How can the discriminant of a quadratic equation be used to determine the number of zeros (x-intercepts) that the graph of the equation will have?

12. What advantage does using the quadratic formula have over other methods of solving quadratic equations?

13. **Essential Question Check-In** How can you derive the quadratic formula?

Evaluate: Homework and Practice

Personal Math Trainer

- Online Homework
- Hints and Help
- Extra Practice

Determine how many real solutions each quadratic equation has.

1. $4x^2 + 4x + 1 = 0$

2. $x^2 - x + 3 = 0$

3. $x^2 - 8x^2 - 9 = 0$

4. $2x^2 - x\sqrt{5} + 2 = 0$

5. $\frac{x^2}{2} - x + \frac{1}{4} = 0$

6. $\frac{x^2}{4} - x\sqrt{7} + 7 = 0$

7. $\frac{x^2}{2} - x\sqrt{2} + 1 = 0$

8. $x^2\sqrt{2} - x + \frac{1}{2} = 0$

Solve using the quadratic formula. Leave answers that are not perfect squares in radical form.

9. $10x + 4 = 6x^2$

10. $x^2 + x - 20 = 0$

11. $4x^2 = 4 - x$

12. $9x^2 + 3x - 2 = 0$

13. $14x + 3 = -8x^2$

14. $x^2 + 3x^2 + 1 = 0$

For each problem, use the discriminant to determine the number of real solutions for the equation. Then, find the solutions and check to see if they make sense in the context of the problem.

15. Sports A soccer player kicks the ball to a height of 1 meter inside the goal. The equation for the height h of the ball at time t is $h = -4.9t^2 - 5t + 2$. Find the time the ball reached the goal.

16. The length and width of a rectangular patio are, $(x + 8)$ feet and $(x + 6)$ feet, respectively. If the area of the patio is 160 square feet, what are the dimensions of the patio?

17. Chemistry A scientist is growing bacteria in a lab for study. One particular type of bacteria grows at a rate of $y = 2t^2 + 3t + 500$. A different bacteria grows at a rate of $y = 3t^2 + t + 300$. In both of these equations, y is the number of bacteria after t minutes. When is there an equal number of both types of bacteria?

Use this information for Exercises 18 and 19. A gymnast, who can stretch her arms up to reach 6 feet, jumps straight up on a trampoline. The height of her feet above the trampoline can be modeled by the equation $h = -16x^2 + 12x$, where x is the time in seconds after her jump.

18. Do the gymnast's hands reach a height of 10 feet above the trampoline? Use the discriminant to explain. (Hint: Since h = height of feet, you must use the difference between the heights of the hands and feet.)

19. Which of the following are possible heights she achieved? Select all that apply.

a. $h = \frac{9}{4}$

b. $h = 4$

c. $h = 3$

d. $h = 0.5$

e. $h = \frac{1}{4}$

20. Explain the Error Dan said that if a quadratic equation does not have any real solutions, then it does not represent a function. Explain Dan's error.

H.O.T. Focus on Higher Order Thinking

21. Communicate Mathematical Ideas Explain why a positive discriminant results in two real solutions.

22. Multi-Step A model rocket is launched from the top of a hill 10 meters above ground level. The rocket's initial speed is 10 meters per second. Its height h can be modeled by the equation $h = -4.9t^2 + 10t + 10$, where t is the time in seconds.

a. When does the rocket achieve a height of 100 meters?

b. How long does it take the rocket to reach ground level?

Lesson Performance Task

A baseball field is next to a building that is 130 feet tall. A series of batters hit pitched balls into the air with the given initial vertical velocities. (Assume each ball is hit from a height of 3 feet.) After the game, a fan reports that several hits resulted in the ball hitting the roof of the building. How can you use the discriminant to determine whether any of the hits described below could be among them? Explain. If any of the balls hit could have hit the roof, identify them. Can you tell if the ball actually did hit the roof?

Player	Initial Vertical Velocity (ft/s)
Janok	99
Jimenez	91
Serrano	88
Sei	89

Name ____________ Class ____________ Date ________

9.4 Choosing a Method for Solving Quadratic Equations

Resource Locker

Essential Question: How can you choose a method for solving a given quadratic equation?

Explore Comparing Solution Methods for Quadratic Equations

$7x^2 - 3x - 5 = 0$

Try to solve the equation by factoring.

(A) Find the factors of 7 and −5 to complete the table:

Factors of 7	Factors of −5	Outer Product + Inner Product
1, 7	1, −5	2
1, 7	5, −1	
1, 7	−1, 5	
1, 7	−5, 1	

(B) None of the sums of the inner and outer products of the factor pairs of 7 and −5 equal −3.

Does this mean the equation cannot be solved? ______.

Now, try to solve the equation by completing the square.

(C) The leading coefficient is not a perfect square. Multiply both sides by a value that makes the coefficient a perfect square.

$\square(7x^2 - 3x - 5) = (0)\square$

$\square x^2 - \square x - \square = \square$

(D) Add or subtract to move the constant term to the other side of the equation.

$\square x^2 - \square x = \square$

(E) Find $\frac{b^2}{4a}$ and reduce to simplest form.

$\frac{b^2}{4a} = \frac{\square^2}{4(\square)} = \frac{\square}{\square} = \frac{\square}{\square}$

Ⓕ Add $\frac{b^2}{4a}$ to both sides of the equation,

$$\square x^2 - \square x + \frac{\square}{\square} = \square + \frac{\square}{\square}$$

$$\square x^2 - \square x + \frac{\square}{\square} = \frac{\square}{\square}$$

Ⓖ Factor the perfect-square trinomial on the left side of the equation.

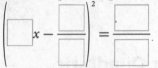

$$\left(\square x - \frac{\square}{\square}\right)^2 = \frac{\square}{\square}$$

Ⓗ Take the square root of both sides.

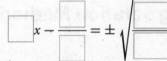

$$\square x - \frac{\square}{\square} = \pm\sqrt{\frac{\square}{\square}}$$

Ⓘ Add the constant to both sides, and then divide by *a*. Find both solutions for *x*.

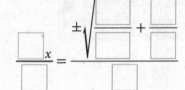

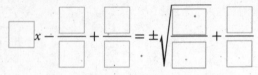

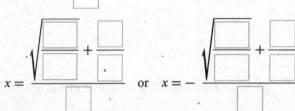

$$\square x - \frac{\square}{\square} + \frac{\square}{\square} = \pm\sqrt{\frac{\square}{\square}} + \frac{\square}{\square}$$

$$\frac{\square x}{\square} = \frac{\pm\sqrt{\frac{\square}{\square}} + \frac{\square}{\square}}{\square}$$

$$x = \frac{\pm\sqrt{\frac{\square}{\square}} + \frac{\square}{\square}}{\square}$$

$$x = \frac{\sqrt{\frac{\square}{\square}} + \frac{\square}{\square}}{\square} \quad \text{or} \quad x = -\frac{\sqrt{\frac{\square}{\square}} + \frac{\square}{\square}}{\square}$$

Ⓙ Solve both equations to three decimal places using your calculator.

$x = \square$ or $x = \square$

Now use the quadratic formula to solve the same equation.

Ⓚ Identify the values of *a*, *b*, and *c*. $a = \square$, $b = \square$, $c = \square$

Ⓛ Substitute values into the quadratic formula.

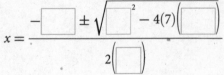

$$x = \frac{-\square \pm \sqrt{\square^2 - 4(7)(\square)}}{2(\square)}$$

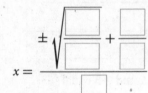

(M) Simplify the discriminant and the denominator.

$$x = \frac{3 \pm \sqrt{\square}}{\square}$$

(N) Use your calculator to finish simplifying the expression for x.

$x = \square$ or $x = \square$

Reflect

1. **Discussion** Another method you learned for solving quadratics is taking square roots. Why would that not work in this case?

____

____

____

Explain 1 Solving Quadratic Equations Using Different Methods

You have seen several ways to solve a quadratic equation, but there are reasons why you might choose one method over another.

Factoring is usually the fastest and easiest method. Try factoring first if it seems likely that the equation is factorable.

Both completing the square and using the quadratic formula are more general. Quadratic equations that are solvable can be solved using either method.

Example 1 **Speculate which method is the most appropriate for each equation and explain your answer. Then solve the equation using factoring (if possible), completing the square, and the quadratic formula.**

(A) $x^2 + 7x + 6 = 0$

Factor the quadratic.

Set up a factor table adding factors of c.

Factors of c	Sum of Factors
1, 6	7
2, 3	5

Substitute in factors. $(x + 1)(x + 6) = 0$

Use the Zero Product Property $x + 1 = 0$ or $x + 6 = 0$

Solve both equations for x. $x = -1$ or $x = -6$

Complete the square.

Move the constant term to the right side. $x^2 + 7x = -6$

Add $\frac{b^2}{4a}$ to both sides. $x^2 + 7x + \frac{49}{4} = -6 + \frac{49}{4}$

Simplify. $x^2 + 7x + \frac{49}{4} = \frac{25}{4}$

Factor the perfect-square trimonial on the left. $\left(x + \frac{7}{2}\right)^2 = \frac{25}{4}$

Take the square root of both sides. $x + \frac{7}{2} = \pm\frac{5}{2}$

Write two equations. $x + \frac{7}{2} = \frac{5}{2}$ or $x + \frac{7}{2} = -\frac{5}{2}$

Solve both equations. $x = -1$ or $x = -6$

Apply the quadratic formula.

Identify the values of a, b, and c. $a = 1, b = 7, c = 6$

Substitute values into the quadratic formula. $x = \frac{-7 \pm \sqrt{7^2 - 4(1)(6)}}{2(1)}$

Simplify the discriminant and denominator. $x = \frac{-7 \pm \sqrt{25}}{2}$

Evaluate the square root and write as two equations. $x = \frac{-7 + 5}{2}$ or $x = \frac{-7 - 5}{2}$

Simplify. $x = -1$ or $x = -6$

Because the list of possible factors that needed to be checked was short, it makes sense to try factoring $x^2 + 7x + 6$ first, even if you don't know if you will be able to factor it. Once factored, the remaining steps are fewer and simpler than either completing the square or using the quadratic formula.

Ⓑ $2x^2 + 8x + 3 = 0$

Factor the quadratic.

Factors of *c*	Factors of *c*	Sum of Inner and Outer Products
1, 2	1, 3	
1, 2	3, 1	

Can the quadratic be factored? ______.

Complete the square.

Move the constant term to the right side. $2x^2 + 8x = -3$

Multiply both sides by $\square$ to make a perfect square. $\square x^2 + 16x = \square$

Add $\frac{b^2}{4a}$ to both sides. $4x^2 + 16x + \square = 10$

Factor the left side. $\left(\square x + \square\right)^2 = 10$

Take the square root of both sides. $2x + 4 = \square$

Write two equations. $2x + 4 = \square$ or $2x + 4 = -\sqrt{10}$

Solve both equations. $x = -2 \square \frac{\sqrt{10}}{2}$ or $x = -2 \square \frac{\sqrt{10}}{2}$

Apply the quadratic formula.

Identify the values of *a*, *b*, and *c*. $a = \square$, $b = \square$, $c = \square$

Substitute values into the quadratic formula. $x = \frac{\square \pm \sqrt{\square^2 - 4(\square)(\square)}}{2(\square)}$

Simplify the discriminant and denominator. $x = \frac{-8 \pm \sqrt{\square}}{4}$

Evaluate the square root and write as two equations. $x = \frac{-8 \pm \square\sqrt{\square}}{4}$

Simplify. $x = \square \pm \frac{\sqrt{10}}{\square}$

Reflect

2. What are the advantages and disadvantages of solving a quadratic equation by taking square roots?

3. What are the advantages and disadvantages of solving a quadratic equation by factoring?

4. What are the advantages and disadvantages of solving a quadratic equation by completing the square?

5. What are the advantages and disadvantages of solving a quadratic equation by using the quadratic formula?

____

____

____

____

____

Your Turn

Solve the quadratic equations by any method you chose. Identify the method and explain why you chose it.

6. $9x^2 - 100 = 0$

7. $x^2 + 4x - 7 = 0$

Explain 2 Choosing Solution Methods for Quadratic Equation Models

Recall that the formula for height, in feet, of a projectile under the influence of gravity is given by $h = -16t^2 + vt + s$, where t is the time in seconds, v is the upward initial velocity (at $t = 0$), and s is the starting height.

Example 2 **Marco is throwing a tennis ball at a kite that is stuck 42 feet up in a tree, trying to knock it loose. He can throw the ball at a velocity of 45 feet per second upward at a height of 4 feet. Will his throw reach the kite? How hard does Marco need to throw the ball to reach the kite?**

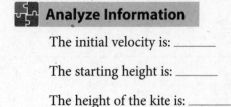

Analyze Information

The initial velocity is: ______

The starting height is: ______

The height of the kite is: ______

Formulate a Plan

Use the projectile motion formula to write an equation for the height of the ball t seconds after Marco throws it.

$h = \square t^2 + \square t + \square$

To determine if the ball can reach the height of the kite, set up the equation to find the time it takes the ball to reach the height of the kite.

$-16t^2 + 45t + 4 = \square$

Convert the equation to standard form.

$-16t^2 + 45t + \square = 0$

This problem will be easiest to solve by ______________________ To check if the ball reaches the kite, begin by calculating the ____________. To determine the velocity that Marco must throw the ball to reach the kite, we should find the velocity where the ____________ is equal to _____, which is the exact moment at which the ball changes direction and falls back to earth.

Solve

Identify values of a, b, and c. $a = \square$, $b = \square$, $c = \square$

Evaluate the discriminant first. $b^2 - 4ac = \square^2 - 4(\square)(\square)$

$= \square$

A negative discriminant means that there are _____ solutions to the equation. Marco's throw will/will not reach as high as the kite.

The velocity with which Marco needs to throw the ball to reach the kite is the coefficient b of the x-term of the quadratic equation.

$b = \square$

Substitute v into the discriminant and solve for a discriminant equal to 0 to find the velocity at which Marco needs to throw the ball.

Identify values of a, b, and c. $a = \square$, $b = \square$, $c = \square$

Evaluate the discriminant first. $\square^2 - 4(\square)(\square) = 0$

Simplify. $v^2 - \square = 0$

This quadratic equation should be solved by ______________ because it has no x-term.

Move the constant term to the right. $v^2 = \square$

Take square roots of both sides. Use your calculator. $v \approx \pm \square$

The negative velocity represents a downward throw and will not result in the ball hitting the kite. The tennis ball must have a velocity of at about ______ feet per second to reach the kite.

Justify and Evaluate

Plot the graph of Marco's throw on your graphing calculator to see that the conclusion you reached (no solution) makes sense because the graphs do not intersect. Sketch the graph.

Then plot the height of the ball when the discriminant is equal to zero. The graphs intersect in one point. Sketch the graph.

Your Turn

8. The wheel of a remote controlled airplane falls off while the airplane is climbing at 40 feet in the air. The wheel starts with an initial upward velocity of 24 feet per second. How long does it take to fall to the ground? Set up the equation to determine the time and pick one method to solve it. Explain why you chose that method.

9. Marco's brother, Jessie, is helping Marco knock a kite from the tree. He can throw the ball 50 feet per second upwards, from a height of 5 feet. Is he throwing the ball hard enough to reach the kite, and if so, how long does it take the ball to reach the kite?

Elaborate

10. Which method do you think is best if you are going to have to use a calculator?

11. Some factorable quadratic expressions are still quite difficult to solve by factoring rather than using another method. What makes an equation difficult to factor?

12. You are taking a test on quadratic equations and you can't decide which method would be the fastest way to solve a particular problem. How could looking at a graph of the equation on a calculator help you decide which method to use?

13. Essential Question Check-In How should you determine a method for solving a quadratic equation?

Evaluate: Homework and Practice

Personal Math Trainer
- Online Homework
- Hints and Help
- Extra Practice

1. Look at this quadratic equation and explain what you think will be the best approach to solving it. Do not solve the equation.

$3.38x^2 + 2.72x - 9.31 = 0$

Solve the quadratic equation by any means. Identify the method and explain why you chose it. Irrational answers may be left in radical form or approximated with a calculator (round to two decimal places).

2. $x^2 - 7x + 12 = 0$

3. $36x^2 - 64 = 0$

4. $4x^2 - 4x - 3 = 2$

5. $8x^2 + 9x + 2 = 1$

6. $5x^2 + 0x - 13 = 0$

7. $7x^2 - 5x - 5 = 0$

8. $3x^2 - 6x = 0$

9. $2x^2 + 4x - 3 = 0$

10. $(x - 5)^2 = 16$

11. $(2x - 1)^2 = x$

12. $2(x + 2)^2 - 5 = 3$

13. $(2x - 3)^2 = 4x$

14. $6x^2 - 5x + 12 = 0$

15. $3x^2 + 6x + 2 = 0$

16. $\frac{1}{2}x^2 + 3x + \frac{5}{2} = 0$

17. $(6x + 7)(x + 1) = 26$

Use the projectile motion formula and solve the quadratic equation by any means. Identify the method and explain why you chose it. Irrational answers and fractions should be converted to decimal form and rounded to two places.

18. Gary drops a pair of gloves off of a balcony that is 64 feet high down to his friend on the ground. How long does it take the pair of gloves to hit the ground?

19. A soccer player jumps up and heads the ball while it is 7 feet above the ground. It bounces up at a velocity of 20 feet per second. How long will it take the ball to hit the ground?

20. A stomp rocket is a toy that is launched into the air from the ground by a sudden burst of pressure exerted by stomping on a pedal. If the rocket is launched at 24 feet per second, how long will it be in the air?

21. A dog leaps off of the patio from 2 feet off of the ground with an upward velocity of 15 feet per second. How long will the dog be in the air?

22. Multipart Classification Indicate whether the following statements about finding solutions to quadratic equations with integer coefficients are true or false.

a. Any quadratic equation with a real solution can be solved by using the quadratic formula. ○ True ○ False

b. Any quadratic equation with a real solution can be solved by completing the square. ○ True ○ False

c. Any quadratic equation with a real solution can be solved by factoring. ○ True ○ False

d. Any quadratic equation with a real solution can be solved by taking the square root of both sides of the equation. ○ True ○ False

e. If the equation can be factored, it has rational solutions. ○ True ○ False

f. If the equation has only one real solution, it cannot be factored. ○ True ○ False

H.O.T. Focus on Higher Order Thinking

23. Justify Reasoning Any quadratic equation with a real solution can be solved with the quadratic formula. Describe the kinds of equations where that would not be the best choice, and explain your reasoning.

24. Critique Reasoning Marisol decides to solve the quadratic equation by factoring $21x^2 + 47x - 24 = 0$. Do you think she chose the best method? How would you solve this equation?

25. Communicate Mathematical Ideas Explain the difference between the statements "The quadratic formula can be used to solve any quadratic equation with a real solution" and "Every quadratic equation has a real solution."

Lesson Performance Task

A landscaper is designing a patio for a customer who has several different ideas about what to make.

Use the given information to set up a quadratic equation modeling the situation and solve it using the quadratic formula. Then determine if another method for solving quadratic equations would have been easier to use and explain why.

a. One of the customer's ideas is to buy bluestone tiles from a home improvement store using several gift cards he has received as presents over the past few years. If the total value of the gift cards is \$6500 and the bluestone costs \$9 per square foot, what are the dimensions of the largest patio that can be made that is 12 feet longer than it is wide?

b. Another of the customer's ideas is simply a quadratic equation scrawled on a napkin.

$x^2 - 54x + 720 = 0$

c. The third idea is also a somewhat random quadratic polynomial.

$x^2 - 40x + 257 = 0$

Name________________________________ Class______________ Date______________

9.5 Solving Nonlinear Systems

Essential Question: How can you solve a system of equations when one equation is linear and the other is quadratic?

Resource Locker

Explore Determining the Possible Number of Solutions of a System of Linear and Quadratic Equations

A system of one linear and one quadratic equation may have zero, one, or two solutions.

(A) The graph of the quadratic function $f(x) = x^2 - 2x - 2$ is shown. On the same coordinate plane, graph the following linear functions:

$g(x) = -x - 2$, $h(x) = 2x - 6$, $j(x) = 0.5x - 5$

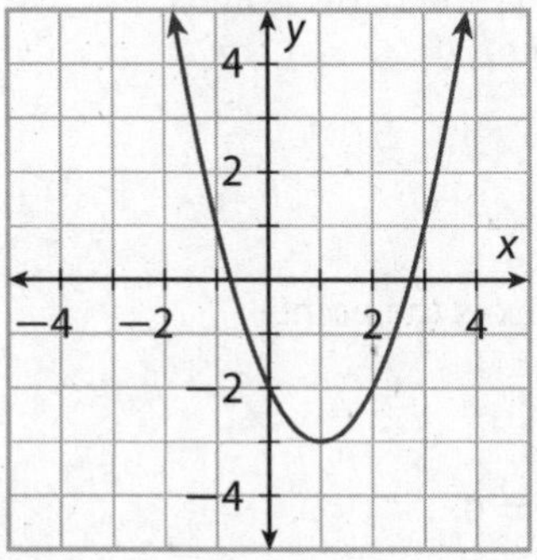

(B) Look at the graph of the system consisting of the quadratic function, $f(x)$, and the linear function, $g(x)$. Based on the intersections of these two graphs, how many solutions exist in a system consisting of these two functions? ________

(C) Look at the graph of the system consisting of the quadratic function, $f(x)$, and the linear function, $h(x)$. Based on the intersections of these two graphs, how many solutions exist in a system consisting of these two functions? ________

(D) Look at the graph of the system consisting of the quadratic function, $f(x)$, and the linear function, $j(x)$. Based on the intersections of these two graphs, how many solutions exist in a system consisting of these two functions? ________

Reflect

1. A system consisting of a quadratic equation and a linear equation can have ______, ______, or ______ solutions.

Explain 1 Solving a System of Linear and Quadratic Equations Graphically

A system of equations consisting of a linear and quadratic equation can be solved graphically by finding the points where the graphs intersect.

Example 1 **Solve the system of equations graphically.**

(A) $\begin{cases} y = (x+1)^2 - 4 \\ y = 2x - 2 \end{cases}$

Graph the quadratic function. The vertex is the point $(-1, -4)$. The x-intercepts are the points where $y = 0$.

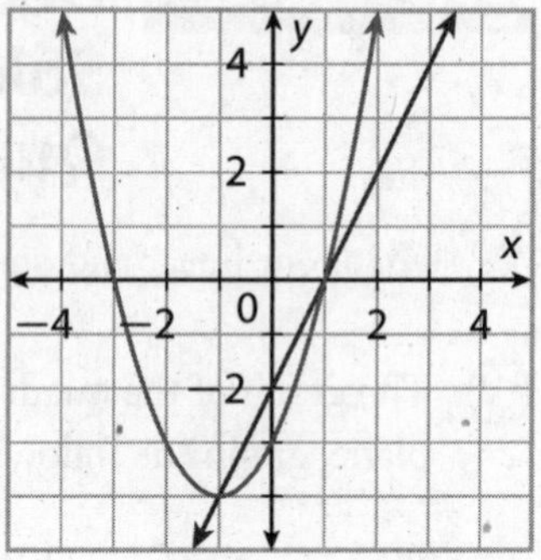

$(x+1)^2 - 4 = 0$

$(x+1)^2 = 4$

$x + 1 = \pm 2$

$x = 1$ or $x = -3$

Graph the linear function on the same coordinate plane.

The solutions of the system are the points where the graphs intersect. The solutions are $(-1, -4)$ and $(1, 0)$.

(B) $\begin{cases} y = 2(x-2)^2 - 2 \\ y = -x - 1 \end{cases}$

Graph the quadratic function. The vertex is the point $(2, \square)$.

The x-intercepts are the points where $y = 0$.

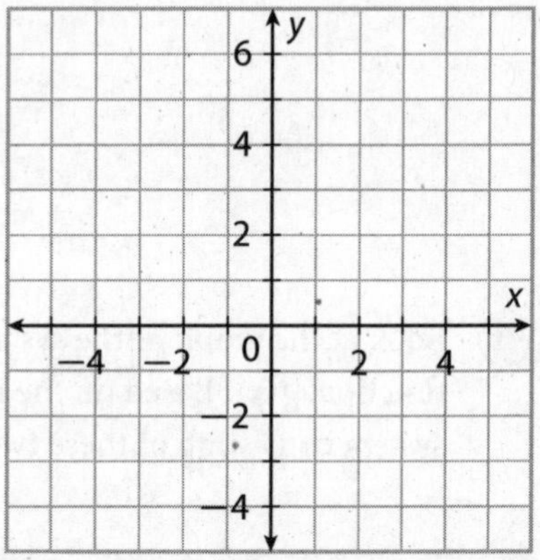

$2(x-2)^2 - 2 = 0$

$2(x-2)^2 = \square$

$(x-2)^2 = \square$

$\square = \pm 1$

$x = \square$ or $x = \square$

Graph the linear function on the same coordinate plane.

There are ______ intersection points. This system has ______ solution(s).

Your Turn **Solve the system of equations graphically.**

2. $\begin{cases} y = -2(x+2)^2 + 8 \\ y = 4x + 16 \end{cases}$

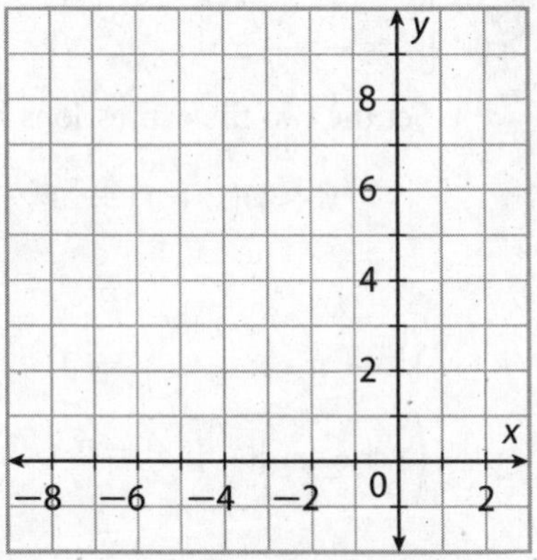

3. $\begin{cases} y = (x+1)^2 - 9 \\ y = 6x - 12 \end{cases}$

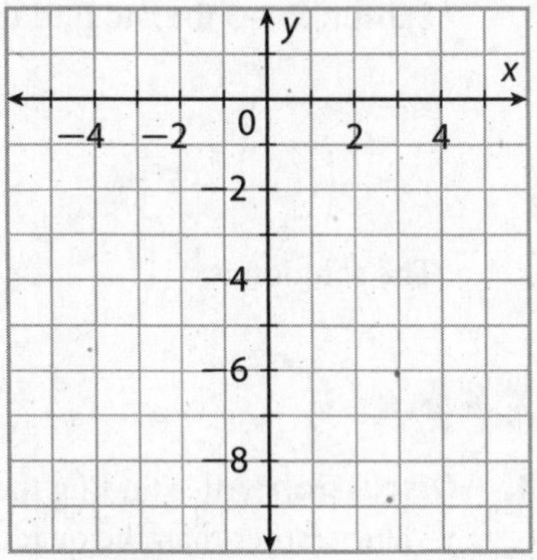

Explain 2 Solving a System of Linear and Quadratic Equations Algebraically

Systems of equations can also be solved algebraically by using the substitution method to eliminate a variable. If the system is one linear and one quadratic equation, the equation resulting after substitution will also be quadratic and can be solved by selecting an appropriate method.

Example 2 **Solve the system of equations algebraically.**

(A) $\begin{cases} y = (x+1)^2 - 4 \\ y = 2x - 2 \end{cases}$

Set the two the expressions for y equal to each other, and solve for x.

$$(x+1)^2 - 4 = 2x - 2$$
$$x^2 + 2x - 3 = 2x - 2$$
$$x^2 - 1 = 0$$
$$x^2 = 1$$
$$x = \pm 1$$

Substitute 1 and −1 for x to find the corresponding y-values.

$y = 2x - 2$ $\qquad$ $y = 2x - 2$

$y = 2(1) - 2 = 0$ $\qquad$ $y = 2(-1) - 2 = -4$

The solutions are $(1, 0)$ and $(-1, -4)$.

Ⓑ $\begin{cases} y = (x+4)(x+1) \\ y = -x - 5 \end{cases}$

Set the two the expressions for y equal to each other, and solve for x.

$$(x+4)(x+1) = \boxed{}$$

$$x^2 + \boxed{}\,x + \boxed{} = -x - 5$$

$$x^2 + \boxed{}\,x + \boxed{} = 0$$

$$\left(x + \boxed{}\right)(x+3) = 0$$

$$x = \boxed{}$$

Substitute -3 for x to find the corresponding y-value.

$$y = -x - 5$$

$$y = -\left(\boxed{}\right) - 5 = \boxed{}$$

The solution is $\boxed{}$.

Reflect

4. Discussion After finding the x-values of the intersection points, why use the linear equation to find the y-values rather than the quadratic? What if the quadratic equation is used instead?

Your Turn **Solve the system of equations algebraically.**

5. $\begin{cases} y = 2x^2 + 9x + 5 \\ y = 3x - 3 \end{cases}$

Explain 3 Solving a Real-World Problem with a System of Linear and Quadratic Equations

Systems of equations can be solved by graphing both equations on a graphing calculator and using the Intersect feature.

Example 3 **Create and solve a system of equations to solve the problem.**

(A) A rock climber is pulling his pack up the side of a cliff that is 175.5 feet tall at a rate of 2 feet per second. The height of the pack in feet after t seconds is given by $h = 2t$. The climber drops a coil of rope from directly above the pack. The height of the coil in feet after t seconds is given by $h = -16t^2 + 175.5$. At what time does the coil of rope hit the pack?

Create the system of equations to solve.

$$\begin{cases} h = -16t^2 + 175.5 \\ h = 2t \end{cases}$$

Graph the functions together and find any points of intersection.

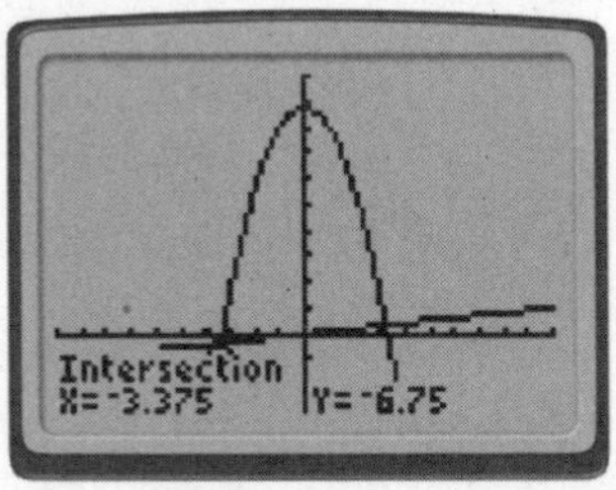

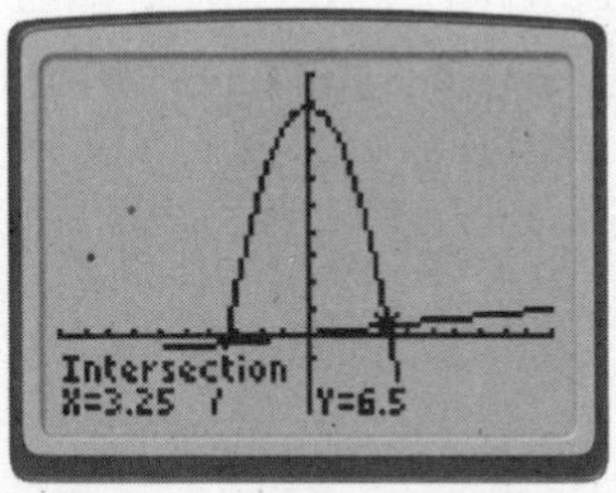

The intersection is at $(-3.375, -6.75)$.

The x-value represents time, so this solution is not reasonable.

The intersection is at $(3.25, 6.5)$.

This solution indicates that the coil hits the pack after 3.25 seconds.

(B) A window washer is ascending the side of a building that is 520 feet tall at a rate of 3 feet per second. The elevation of the window washer after t seconds is given by $h = 3t$. The supplies are lowered to the window washer from the top of the building at the same time that he begins to ascend the building. The height of the supplies in feet after t seconds is given by $h = -2t^2 + 520$. At what time do the supplies reach the window washer?

Create the system of equations to solve.

$$\begin{cases} h = \square\, t^2 + \square \\ h = \square\, t \end{cases}$$

Graph the functions together and find any points of intersection.

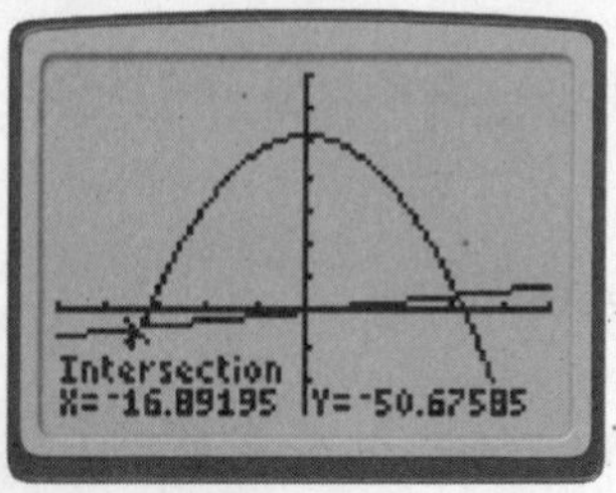

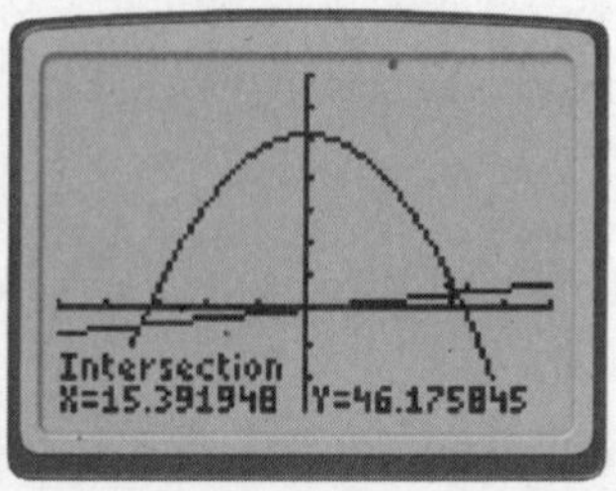

The intersection is at about (☐, ☐).

The x-value represents ______, so this solution is ______________________________

______________________________.

The intersection is at about (☐, ☐).

This solution indicates that ______________

____

______________________________.

Reflect

6. How did you know which intersection to use in the example problems?

____

____

____

Your Turn **Write and solve a system of equations to solve the problem.**

7. A billboard painter is using a pulley system to hoist a can of paint up to a scaffold at a rate of half a meter per second. The height of the can of paint as a function of time is given by $h(t) = 0.5t$. Five seconds after he starts raising the can of paint, his partner accidentally kicks a paint brush off of the scaffolding, which falls to the ground. The height of the falling paint brush can be represented by $h(t) = -4.9\,(t - 5)^2 + 30$. When does the brush pass the paint can?

Elaborate

8. **Discussion** When solving a system of equations consisting of a quadratic equation and a linear equation by graphing, why is it difficult to be sure there is one solution as opposed to 0 or 2?

9. How can you use the discriminant to determine how many solutions a linear-quadratic system has?

10. **Essential Question Check-in** How can the graphs of two functions be used to solve a system of a quadratic and a linear equation?

Evaluate: Homework and Practice

- Online Homework
- Hints and Help
- Extra Practice

1. The graph of the function $f(x) = -\frac{1}{4}(x-3)^2 + 4$ is shown. Graph the functions $g(x) = x + 1$, $h(x) = x + 2$, and $j(x) = x + 3$ with the graph of $f(x)$, and determine how many solutions each system has.

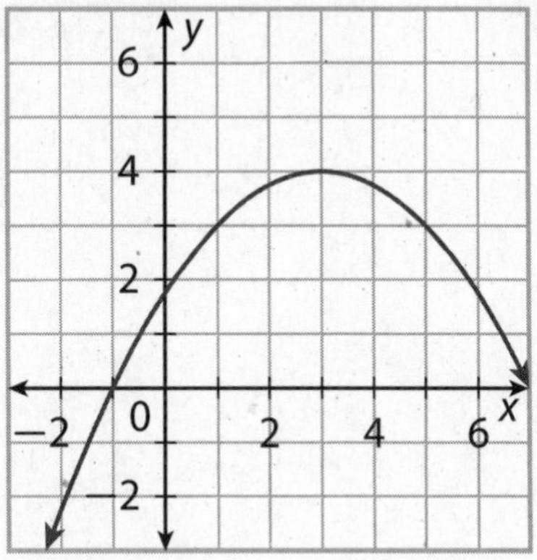

$f(x)$ and $g(x)$: ______

$f(x)$ and $h(x)$: ______

$f(x)$ and $j(x)$: ______

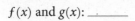

Solve each system of equations graphically.

2. $\begin{cases} y = (x+3)^2 - 4 \\ y = 2x + 2 \end{cases}$

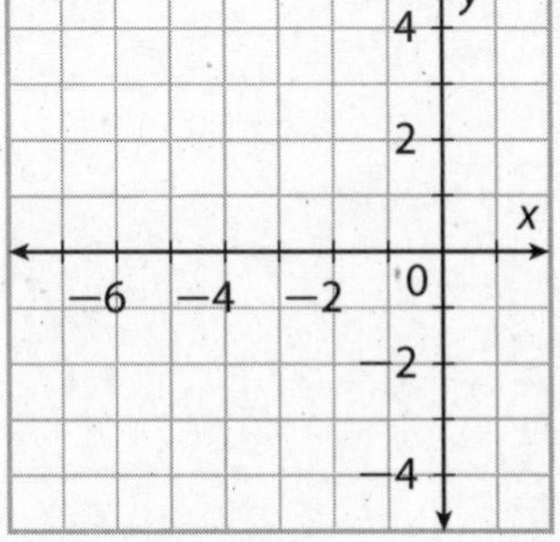

3. $\begin{cases} y = x^2 - 1 \\ y = x - 2 \end{cases}$

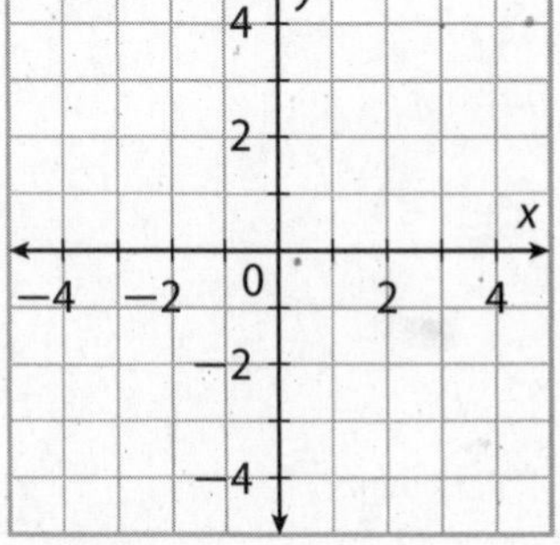

4. $\begin{cases} y = (x-4)^2 - 2 \\ y = -2 \end{cases}$

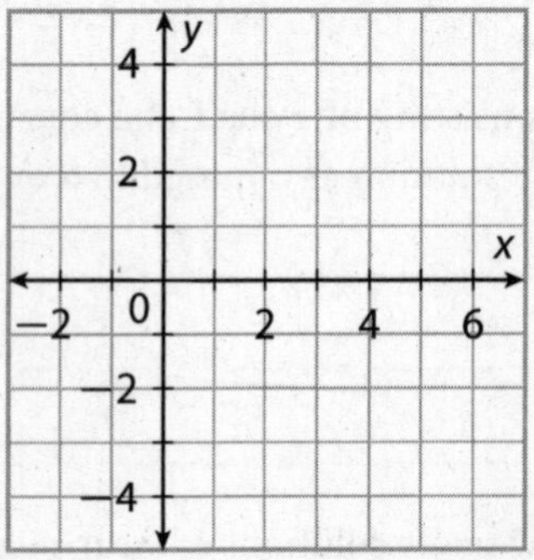

5. $\begin{cases} y = -x^2 + 4 \\ y = -3x + 6 \end{cases}$

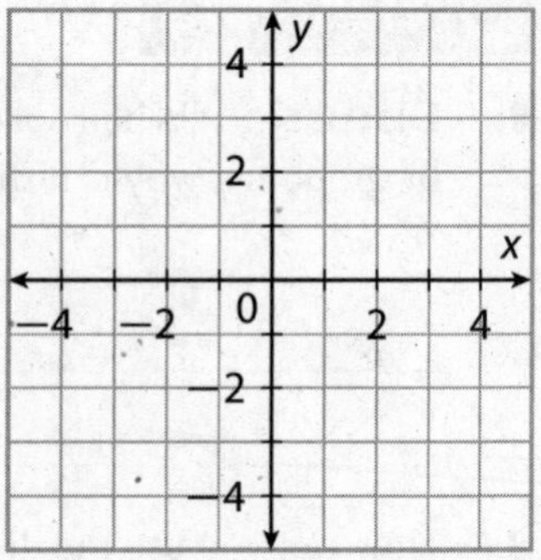

6. $\begin{cases} y = -(x-2)^2 + 9 \\ y = 3x + 3 \end{cases}$

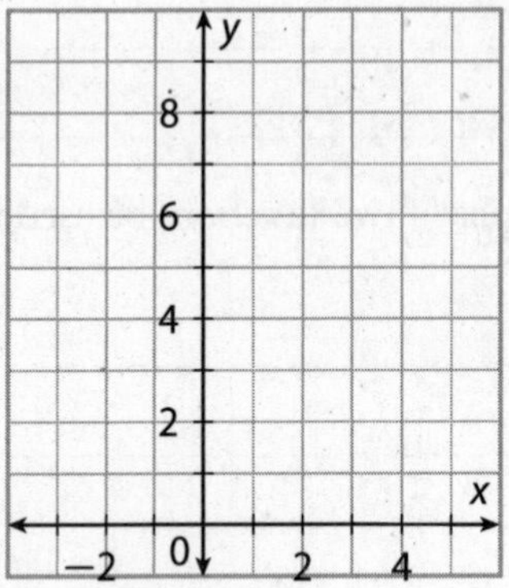

7. $\begin{cases} y = 3(x+1)^2 - 1 \\ y = x - 4 \end{cases}$

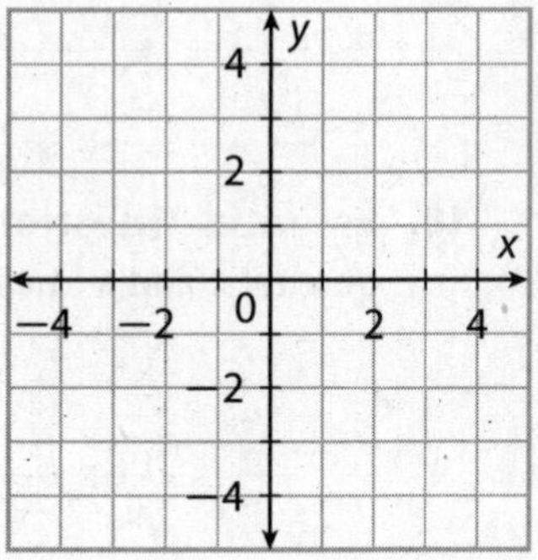

Solve the system of equations algebraically.

8. $\begin{cases} y = x^2 + 1 \\ y = 5 \end{cases}$

9. $\begin{cases} y = x^2 - 3x + 2 \\ y = 4x - 8 \end{cases}$

10. $\begin{cases} y = (x-3)^2 \\ y = 4 \end{cases}$

11. $\begin{cases} y = -x^2 + 4x \\ y = x + 2 \end{cases}$

12. $\begin{cases} y = 2x^2 - 5x + 6 \\ y = 5x - 6 \end{cases}$

13. $\begin{cases} y = x^2 + 7 \\ y = -9x + 29 \end{cases}$

14. $\begin{cases} y = 4x^2 + 45x + 83 \\ y = 5x - 17 \end{cases}$

15. $\begin{cases} y = (x + 2)(x + 4) \\ y = 3x + 2 \end{cases}$

Create and solve a linear quadratic system to solve the problem.

16. The height in feet of a skydiver t seconds after deploying her parachute is given by $h(t) = -300t + 1000$. A ball is thrown up toward the skydiver, and after t seconds, the height of the ball in feet is given by $h(t) = -16t^2 + 100t$. When does the ball reach the skydiver?

17. A wildebeest fails to notice a lion that is charging from behind at 65 feet per second until the lion is 40 feet away. The lion's position as a function of time is given by $p(t) = 65t - 40$. The wildebeest has to begin accelerating from a standstill until it is captured or reaches a top speed fast enough to stay ahead of the lion. The wildebeest's position as a function of time is given by $d(t) = 35t^2$. Does the wildebeest escape?

18. An elevator in a hotel moves at 20 feet per second. Leaving from the ground floor, its height in feet after t seconds is given by the formula $h(t) = 20t$. A bolt comes loose in the elevator shaft above, and its height in feet after falling for t seconds is given by $h(t) = -16t^2 + 200$. At what time and at what height does the bolt hit the elevator?

19. A bungee jumper leaps from a bridge 100 meters over a gorge. Before the 40-meter-long bungee begins to slow him down, his height is characterized by $h(t) = -4.9t^2 + 100$. Two seconds after he jumps, a car on the bridge blows out a tire. The sound of the tire blow-out moves down from the top of the bridge at the speed of sound and has a height given by $h(t) = -340(t - 2) + 100$. How high will the bungee jumper be when he hears the sound of the blowout?

20. Explain the Error A student is asked to solve the system of equations $y = x^2 + 2x - 7$ and $y - 2 = x + 1$. For the first step, the student sets the right hand sides equal to each other to get the equation $x^2 + 2x - 7 = x + 1$. Why does this not give the correct solution?

21. Explain the Error After solving the system of equations in Exercise 18 (the elevator and the bolt), a student concludes that there are two different times that the bolt hits the elevator. What is the error in the student's reasoning?

22. Multi-part Classification

The functions listed are graphed here.

$f_1(x) = 2(x + 3)^2 + 1$ and $f_2(x) = -\frac{3}{4}(x - 2)^2 + 3$

$g_1(x) = x + 3$ and $g_2(x) = 3$ and $g_3(x) = -\frac{1}{2}x + 1$

Use the graph to classify each system as having 0, 1, or 2 solutions.

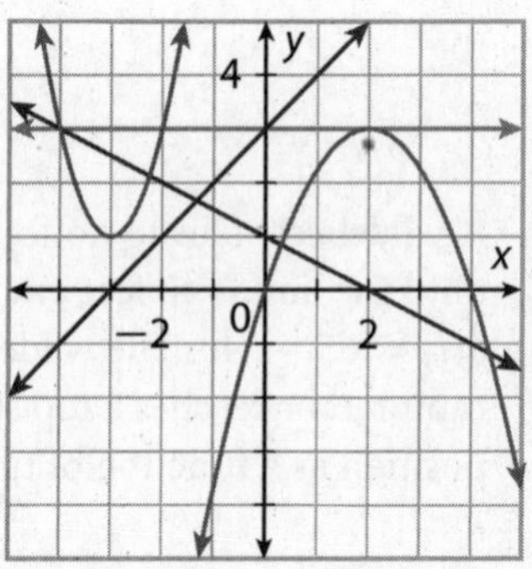

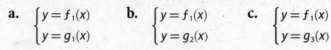

a. $\begin{cases} y = f_1(x) \\ y = g_1(x) \end{cases}$ **b.** $\begin{cases} y = f_1(x) \\ y = g_2(x) \end{cases}$ **c.** $\begin{cases} y = f_1(x) \\ y = g_3(x) \end{cases}$

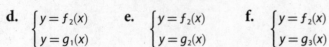

d. $\begin{cases} y = f_2(x) \\ y = g_1(x) \end{cases}$ **e.** $\begin{cases} y = f_2(x) \\ y = g_2(x) \end{cases}$ **f.** $\begin{cases} y = f_2(x) \\ y = g_3(x) \end{cases}$

H.O.T. Focus on Higher Order Thinking

23. Explain the Error After solving the system of equations in Exercise 16 (the skydiver and the ball), a student concludes there are two valid solutions because they both have positive times. The ball must pass by the skydiver twice. What is the error in the student's reasoning?

24. Multi-Part Problem The path of a baseball hit for a home run can be modeled by $y = -\frac{x^2}{484} + x + 3$, where x and y are in feet and home plate is at the origin. The ball lands in the stands, which are modeled by $4y - x = -352$ for $x \geq 400$. Use a graphing calculator to graph the system.

a. What do the variables x and y represent?

b. About how far is the baseball from home plate when it lands?

c. About how high up in the stands does the baseball land?

25. Draw Conclusions A certain system of a linear and a quadratic equation has two solutions, $(2, 7)$ and $(5, 10)$. The quadratic equation is $y = x^2 - 6x + 15$. What is the linear equation? Justify your answer.

26. Justify Reasoning It is possible for a system of two linear equations to have infinitely many solutions. Explain why this is not possible for a system with one linear and one quadratic equation.

Lesson Performance Task

A race car leaves pit row at a speed of 40 feet per second and accelerates at a constant rate of 44 feet per second squared. Its distance from the pit exit is given by the function $d_r(t) = 22t^2 + 40t$. The race car leaves ahead of an approaching pace car traveling at a constant speed of 120 feet per second. In each case, find out if the pace car will catch up to the race car, and if so, how far down the track it will catch up. If there is more than one solution, explain how you know which one to select.

a. The pace car passes by the exit to pit row 1 second after the race car exits.

b. The pace car passes the exit half a second after the race car exits.

STUDY GUIDE REVIEW

Using Square Roots to Solve Quadratic Equations

MODULE 9

Essential Question: How can you use quadratic equations to solve real-world problems?

Key Vocabulary

completing the square *(completar el cuadrado)*

discriminant *(discriminante)*

quadratic formula *(fórmula cuadrática)*

square root *(raíz cuadrada)*

KEY EXAMPLE *(Lesson 9.1)*

Solve $(x-8)^2 = 49$ by taking the square root.

$(x-8)^2 = 49$ — *Equations in the form $a(x+b)^2 = c$ can be solved by taking square roots.*

$x - 8 = \pm 7$ — *Take the square root of both sides.*

$x = \pm 7 + 8$

$x = 7 + 8$ and $x = -7 + 8$ — *Solve both cases.*

$x = 15$ and $x = 1$

KEY EXAMPLE *(Lesson 9.2)*

Solve $9x^2 - 6x = 20$ by completing the square.

$\frac{(-6)^2}{4(9)} = 1$ — *Find $\frac{b^2}{4a}$.*

$9x^2 - 6x + 1 = 20 + 1$ — *Complete the square.*

$(3x-1)^2 = 21$

$x = \frac{\sqrt{21}+1}{3}$ and $x = \frac{-\sqrt{21}+1}{3}$

KEY EXAMPLE *(Lesson 9.3)*

Solve $8x^2 - 8x + 2 = 0$ using the quadratic formula.

$a = 8, b = -8, c = 2$ — *Identify a, b, and c.*

$x = \frac{-b \pm \sqrt{b^2 - 4ac}}{2a}$ — *Use the quadratic formula.*

$x = \frac{8 \pm \sqrt{(-8)^2 - (4)(8)(2)}}{2(8)}$

$x = \frac{8 \pm \sqrt{0}}{16}$ — *Since $b^2 - 4ac = 0$, the equation has one real solution.*

$x = \frac{1}{2}$

EXERCISES

Solve each equation. *(Lessons 9.1, 9.2, 9.3, 9.4)*

1. $x^2 + 12x = -17$

2. $(4x - 11)^2 = 100$

3. $4x^2 + 8x = 10$

4. $3x^2 + 17x + 10 = 0$

5. A diver jumps off a high diving board that is 33 feet above the surface of the pool with an initial upward velocity of 6 feet per second. The height of the diver above the surface of the pool can be represented by the equation $-16t^2 + 6t + 33 = 0$. How long will the diver be in the air, to the nearest hundredth of a second? Identify the method you used to solve the quadratic equation, and explain why you chose it. *(Lesson 9.4)*

MODULE PERFORMANCE TASK

Fireworks Display

You are planning a fireworks show for a local Fourth of July celebration. Fire officials require that all fireworks explode at a height greater than 70 meters so that debris has a chance to cool off as it falls.

The firing platform for the fireworks is 1.9 meters off the ground. You have the option of firing your fireworks at an initial velocity of anywhere between 35 and 42 meters/second. If every firework is timed to explode when it reaches its maximum height, find two different initial velocities that are acceptable to the local fire officials. Then, figure out how long to delay the firing of the slower firework so that it will explode at the same time as the faster firework.

Use your own paper to complete the task. Be sure to write down all your data and assumptions. Then use graphs, tables, or algebra to explain how you reached your conclusion.

Ready to Go On?

9.1–9.5 Using Square Roots to Solve Quadratic Equations

Personal Math Trainer

- Online Homework
- Hints and Help
- Extra Practice

Find the discriminant of each quadratic equation, and determine the number of real solutions of each equation. *(Lesson 9.4)*

1. $3x^2 + 2x + 6 = 0$

2. $4x^2 + 6x = 8$

Solve each equation using the given method. *(Lessons 9.1, 9.2, 9.3, 9.4)*

3. $8x^2 - 72 = 0$; square root

4. $25x^2 + 20x = 6$; completing the square

5. $2x^2 + 14x + 12 = 0$; factoring

6. $3x^2 + 7x + 8 = 0$; quadratic formula

7. Find the solution or solutions of the system of equations $\begin{cases} y = x^2 + 2 \\ y = x + 4 \end{cases}$. *(Lesson 9.5)*

ESSENTIAL QUESTION

8. What are the methods of solving a quadratic equation without factoring? When can you use each method?

MODULE 9
MIXED REVIEW

Assessment Readiness

1. Is the given expression a perfect-square trinomial? Select Yes or No for each expression.

A. $x^2 + 24x + 144$ ○ Yes ○ No

B. $4x^2 + 36x + 9$ ○ Yes ○ No

C. $9x^2 - 6x + 1$ ○ Yes ○ No

2. Consider the following statements. Choose True or False for each.

A. $4x^2 - 64 = 0$ has 2 real solutions. ○ True ○ False

B. $x^2 - 5x - 9 = 0$ has only 1 real solution. ○ True ○ False

C. $3x^2 + 4x + 2 = 0$ has no real solutions. ○ True ○ False

3. Solve $-2x^2 - 9x = -4$. What are the solutions? Explain how you solved the problem.

4. A landscaper is making a garden bed in the shape of a rectangle. The length of the garden bed is 2.5 feet longer than twice the width of the bed. The area of the garden bed is 62.5 square feet. Find the perimeter of the bed. Show your work.

Linear, Exponential, and Quadratic Models

MODULE 10

Essential Question: How can you use linear, exponential, and quadratic models to solve real-world problems?

REAL WORLD VIDEO
The Kemp's Ridley sea turtle is an endangered species of turtle that nests along the Texas coast. Functions can be used to model the survivorship curve of the Kemp's Ridley sea turtle.

MODULE PERFORMANCE TASK PREVIEW

What Model Fits a Survivorship Curve?

Survivorship curves are graphs that show the number or proportion of individuals in a particular population that survive over time. Survivorship curves are used in diverse fields such as actuarial science, demography, biology, and epidemiology. How can you determine what mathematical model best fits a certain type of survivorship curve? Let's find out!

Are YOU Ready?

Complete these exercises to review skills you will need for this module.

Personal Math Trainer
- Online Homework
- Hints and Help
- Extra Practice

Scatter Plots

Example 1 Tell whether the correlation is positive or negative, or if there is no correlation.

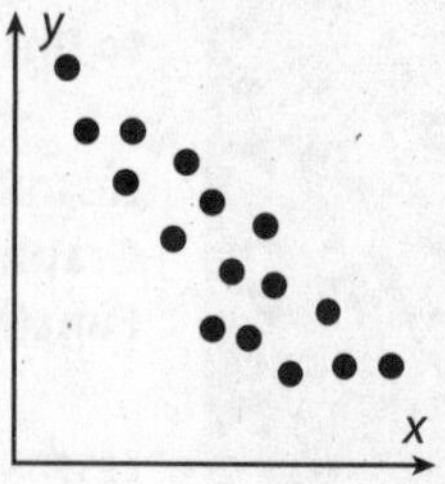

Scatter plots can help you see relationships between two variables.

- In a positive correlation, as the value of one variable increases, the value of the other variable increases.
- In a negative correlation, as the value of one variable decreases, the value of the other variable increases.
- Sometimes there is no correlation, meaning there is no relationship between the variables.

The scatter plot has a negative correlation.

Tell whether the correlation is positive or negative, or if there is no correlation.

1.

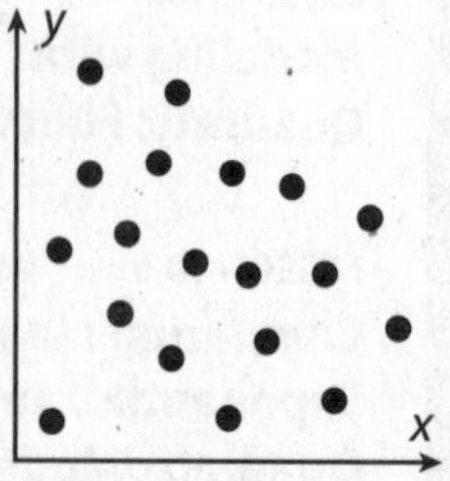

____

2.

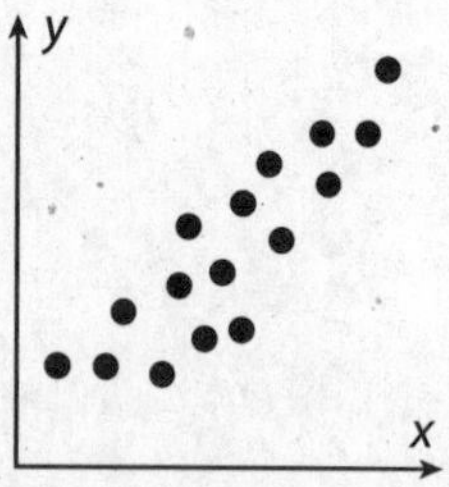

____

Constant Rate of Change

Example 2 Tell if the rate of change is constant.

+1 +1 +1

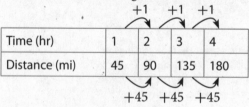

Time (hr)	1	2	3	4
Distance (mi)	45	90	135	180

+45 +45 +45

$$\text{rate of change} = \frac{\text{change in miles}}{\text{change in hours}} = \frac{45}{1}$$

The rate of change is constant.

Tell if the rate of change is constant.

3.

Age (mo)	3	6	9	12
Weight (lb)	12	16	18	20

______

4.

Hours	2	4	6	8
Pay ($)	16	32	48	64

______

Name________________________ Class______________ Date__________

10.1 Fitting a Linear Model to Data

Essential Question: How can you use the linear regression function on a graphing calculator to find the line of best fit for a two-variable data set?

Resource Locker

Explore 1 Plotting and Analyzing Residuals

For any set of data, different lines of fit can be created. Some of these lines will fit the data better than others. One way to determine how well the line fits the data is by using residuals. A **residual** is the signed vertical distance between a data point and a line of fit.

After calculating residuals, a residual plot can be drawn. A **residual plot** is a graph of points whose x-coordinates are the variables of the independent variable and whose y-coordinates are the corresponding residuals.

Looking at the distribution of residuals can help you determine how well a line of fit describes the data. The plots below illustrate how the residuals may be distributed for three different data sets and lines of fit.

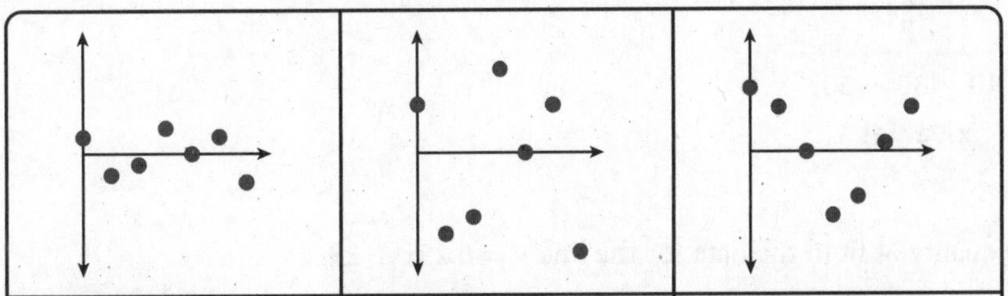

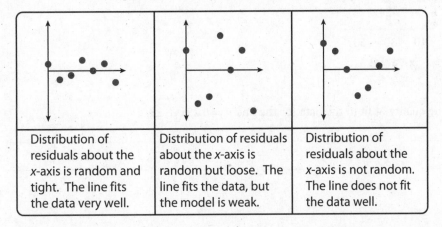

Distribution of residuals about the x-axis is random and tight. The line fits the data very well.	Distribution of residuals about the x-axis is random but loose. The line fits the data, but the model is weak.	Distribution of residuals about the x-axis is not random. The line does not fit the data well.

The table lists the median age of females living in the United States, based on the results of the United States Census over the past few decades. Follow the steps listed to complete the task.

(A) Use the table to create a table of paired values for x and y. Let x represent the time in years after 1970 and y represent the median age of females.

Year	Median Age of Females
1970	29.2
1980	31.3
1990	34.0
2000	36.5
2010	38.2

x					
y					

(B) Use residuals to calculate the quality of fit for the line $y = 0.25x + 29$, where y is median age and x is years since 1970.

x	Actual y	Predicted y based on $y = 0.25x + 29$	Residual *Subtract Predicted from Actual to Find the Residual.*
0	29.2		
10	31.3		
20	34.0		
30	36.5		
40	38.2		

(C) Plot the residuals.

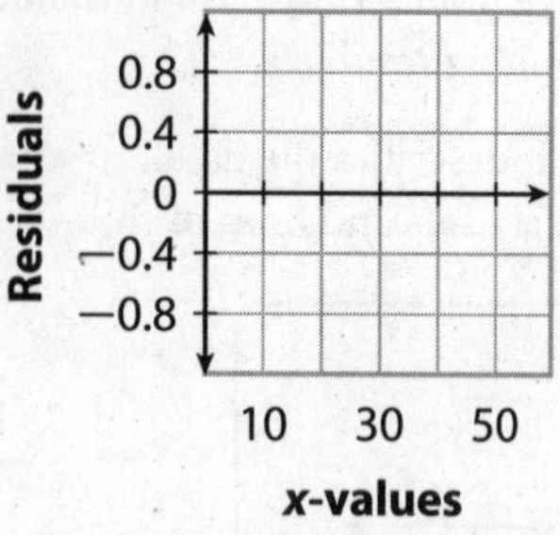

(D) Evaluate the quality of fit to the data for the line $y = 0.25x + 29$.

______

______

Reflect

1. **Discussion** When comparing two lines of fit for a single data set, how does the residual size show which line is the best model?

______

______

2. **Discussion** What would the residual plot look like if a line of fit is not a good model for a data set?

______

______

Explore 2 Analyzing Squared Residuals

When different people fit lines to the same data set, they are likely to choose slightly different lines. Another way to compare the quality of a line of fit is by squaring residuals. In this model, the closer the sum of the squared residuals is to 0, the better the line fits the data.

In the previous section, a line of data was fit for the median age of females over time. After performing this task, two students came up with slightly different results. Student A came up with the equation $y = 0.25x + 29.0$ while Student B came up with the equation $y = 0.25x + 28.8$, where x is the time in years since 1970 and y is the median age of females in both cases.

(A) Complete each table below.

$y = 0.25x + 29.0$				
x	y (Actual)	y (Predicted)	Residual	Square of Residual
0	29.2			
10	31.3			
20	34.0			
30	36.5			
40	38.2			

$y = 0.25x + 28.8$				
x	y (Actual)	y (Predicted)	Residual	Square of Residual
0	29.2			
10	31.3			
20	34.0			
30	36.5			
40	38.2			

(B) Find the sum of squared residuals for each line of fit.

$y = 0.25x + 29.0$: ☐

$y = 0.25x + 28.8$: ☐

(C) Which line has the smaller sum of squared residuals?

____

Reflect

3. How does squaring a residual affect the residual's value?

____

____

4. Are the sums of residuals or the sum of the squares of residuals a better measure of quality of fit?

____

____

Explain 1 Assessing the Fit of Linear Functions from Residuals

The quality of a line of fit can be evaluated by finding the sum of the squared residuals. The closer the sum of the squared residuals is to 0, the better the line fits the data.

Example 1 **The data in the tables are given along with two possible lines of fit. Calculate the residuals for both lines of fit and then find the sum of the squared residuals. Identify the lesser sum and the line with better fit.**

(A)

x	2	4	6	8
y	7	8	4	8

$y = x + 2.2$

$y = x + 2.4$

a. Find the residuals of each line.

x	y (Actual)	y Predicted by $y = x + 2.4$	Residual for $y = x + 2.4$	y Predicted by $y = x + 2.2$	Residual for $y = x + 2.2$
2	7	4.4	2.6	4.2	2.8
4	8	6.4	1.6	6.2	1.8
6	4	8.4	−4.4	8.2	−4.2
8	8	10.4	−2.4	10.2	−2.2

b. Square the residuals and find their sum.

$y = x + 2.4\ (2.6)^2 + (1.6)^2 + (-4.4)^2 + (-2.4)^2 = 6.76 + 2.56 + 19.36 + 5.76 = 34.44$

$y = x + 2.2\ (2.8)^2 + (1.8)^2 + (-4.2)^2 + (-2.2)^2 = 7.84 + 3.24 + 17.64 + 4.84 = 33.56$

The sum of the squared residuals for $y = x + 2.2$ is smaller, so it provides a better fit for the data.

(B)

x	1	2	3	4
y	5	4	6	10

$y = 2x + 3$

$y = 2x + 2.5$

a. Find the residuals of each line.

x	y (Actual)	y Predicted by $y = 2x + 3$	Residual for $y = 2x + 3$	y Predicted by $y = 2x + 2.5$	Residual for $y = 2x + 2.5$
1	5				
2	4				
3	6				
4	10				

b. Square the residuals and find their sum.

$y = 2x + 3: (\square)^2 + (\square)^2 + (\square)^2 + (\square)^2 = \square + \square + \square + \square = \square$

$y = 2x + 2.5: (\square)^2 + (\square)^2 + (\square)^2 + (\square)^2 = \square + \square + \square + \square = \square$

The sum of the squared residuals for $y = \square x + \square$ is smaller, so it provides a better fit for the data.

Reflect

5. How do negative signs on residuals affect the sum of squared residuals?

6. Why do small values for residuals mean that a line of best fit has a tight fit to the data?

Your Turn

7. The data in the table are given along with two possible lines of fit. Calculate the residuals for both lines of fit and then find the sum of the squared residuals. Identify the lesser sum and the line with better fit.

x	1	2	3	4
y	4	7	8	6

$y = x + 4$

$y = x + 4.2$

Explain 2 Performing Linear Regression

The least-squares line for a data set is the line of fit for which the sum of the squared residuals is as small as possible. Therefore the least-squares line is a line of best fit. A **line of best fit** is the line that comes closest to all of the points in the data set, using a given process. **Linear regression** is a method for finding the least-squares line.

Example 2 **Given latitudes and average temperatures in degrees Celsius for several cities, use your calculator to find an equation for the line of best fit. Then interpret the correlation coefficient and use the line of best fit to estimate the average temperature of another city using the given latitude.**

(A)

City	Latitude	Average Temperature (°C)
Barrow, Alaska	71.2°N	−12.7
Yakutsk, Russia	62.1°N	−10.1
London, England	51.3°N	10.4
Chicago, Illinois	41.9°N	10.3
San Francisco, California	37.5°N	13.8
Yuma, Arizona	32.7°N	22.8
Tindouf, Algeria	27.7°N	22.8
Dakar, Senegal	14.0°N	24.5
Mangalore, India	12.5°N	27.1

Estimate the average temperature in Vancouver, Canada at 49.1°N.

Enter the data into data lists on your calculator. Enter the latitudes in column **L1** and the average temperatures in column **L2**.

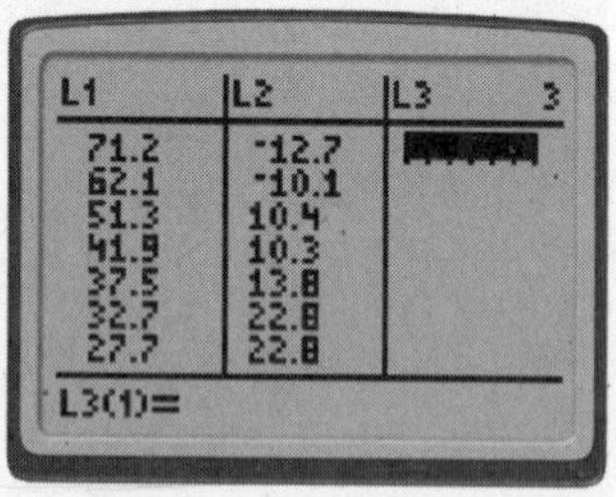

Create a scatter plot of the data.

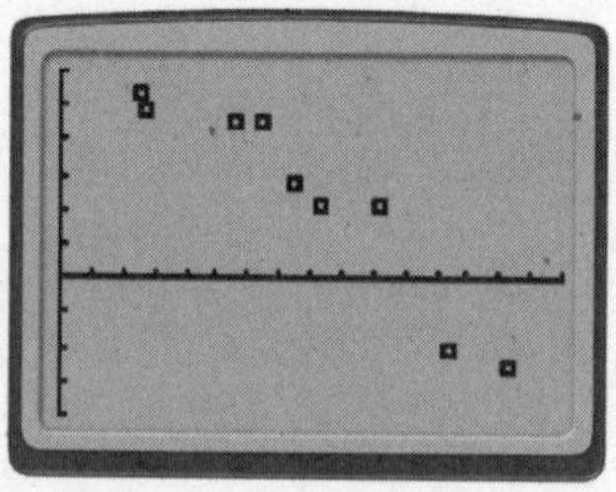

Use the Linear Regression feature to find the equation for the line of best fit using the lists of data you entered. Be sure to have the calculator also display values for the correlation coefficient r and r^2.

The correlation coefficient is about −0.95, which is very strong. This indicates a strong correlation, so we can rely on the line of fit for estimating average temperatures for other locations within the same range of latitudes.

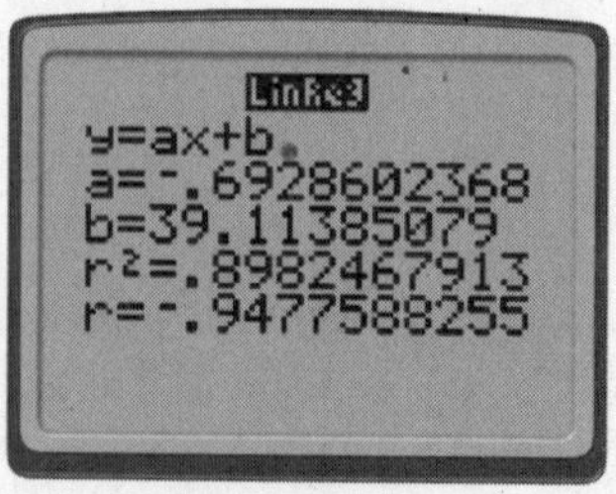

The equation for the line of best fit is $y \approx -0.693x + 39.11$.

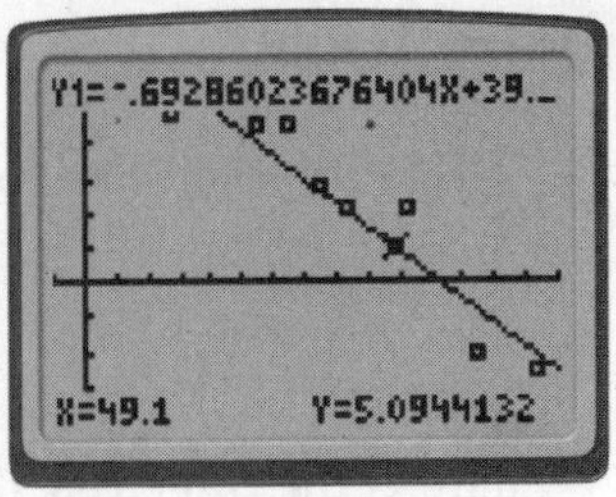

Graph the line of best fit with the data points in the scatter plot.

Use the TRACE function to find the approximate average temperature in degrees Celsius for a latitude of 49.1°N.

The average temperature in Vancouver should be around 5°C.

(B)

City	Latitude	Average Temperature (°F)
Fairbanks, Alaska	64.5°N	30
Moscow, Russia	55.5°N	39
Ghent, Belgium	51.0°N	46
Kiev, Ukraine	50.3°N	49
Prague, Czech Republic	50.0°N	50
Winnipeg, Manitobia	49.5°N	52
Luxembourg	49.4°N	53
Vienna, Austria	48.1°N	56
Bern, Switzerland	46.6°N	59

Estimate the average temperature in degrees Fahrenheit in Bath, England, at 51.4°N.

Enter the data into data lists on your calculator.

Use the Linear Regression feature to find the equation for the line of best fit using the lists of data you entered. Be sure to have the calculator also display values for the correlation coefficient r and r^2.

The correlation coefficient is about ________, which indicates a ____________ correlation. The correlation coefficient indicates that the line of best fit [is/ is not] reliable for estimating temperatures of other locations within the same range of latitudes.

The equation for the line of best fit is $y \approx -$ [ ] $x +$ [ ].

Use the equation to estimate the average temperature in Bath, England at 51.4°N.

$y \approx -$ [ ] $x +$ [ ]

The average temperature in degrees Fahrenheit in Bath, England, should be around [ ] °F.

Graph the line of best fit with the data points in the scatter plot. Then use the TRACE function to find the approximate average temperature in degrees Fahrenheit for a latitude of 51.4°N.

Reflect

8. Interpret the slope of the line of best fit in terms of the context for Example 2A.

9. Interpret the y-intercept of the line of best fit in terms of the context for Example 2A.

Your Turn

10. Use the given data and your calculator to find an equation for the line of best fit. Then interpret the correlation coefficient and use the line of best fit to estimate the average temperature of another city using the given latitude.

City	Latitude	Average Temperature (°F)
Anchorage, United States	61.1°N	18
Dublin, Ireland	53.2°N	29
Zurich, Switzerland	47.2°N	34
Florence, Italy	43.5°N	37
Trenton, New Jersey	40.1°N	
Algiers, Algeria	36.5°N	46
El Paso, Texas	31.5°N	49
Dubai, UAE	25.2°N	56
Manila, Philippines	14.4°N	61

Elaborate

11. What type of line does linear regression analysis make?

12. Why are squared residuals better than residuals?

13. Essential Question Check-In What four keys are needed on a graphing calculator to perform a linear regression?

Evaluate: Homework and Practice

Personal Math Trainer

- Online Homework
- Hints and Help
- Extra Practice

The data in the tables below are shown along with two possible lines of fit. Calculate the residuals for both lines of fit and then find the sum of the squared residuals. Identify the lesser sum and the line with better fit.

1.

x	2	4	6	8
y	1	3	5	7

$y = x + 5$

$y = x + 4.9$

2.

x	1	2	3	4
y	1	7	3	5

$y = 2x + 1$

$y = 2x + 1.1$

3.

x	2	4	6	8
y	2	8	4	6

$y = 3x + 4$

$y = 3x + 4.1$

4.

x	1	2	3	4
y	2	1	4	3

$y = x + 1$

$y = x + 0.9$

5.

x	2	4	6	8
y	1	5	4	3

$y = 3x + 1.2$

$y = 3x + 1$

6.

x	1	2	3	4
y	4	1	3	2

$y = x + 5$

$y = x + 5.3$

7.

x	2	4	6	8
y	3	6	4	5

$y = 2x + 1$

$y = 2x + 1.4$

8.

x	1	2	3	4
y	5	3	6	4

$y = x + 2$

$y = x + 2.2$

9.

x	2	4	6	8
y	1	5	7	3

$y = x + 3$

$y = x + 2.6$

10.

x	1	2	3	4
y	2	5	4	3

$y = x + 1.5$

$y = x + 1.7$

11.

x	1	2	3	4
y	2	9	7	12

$y = 2x + 3.1$

$y = 2x + 3.5$

12.

x	1	3	5	7
y	2	6	8	13

$y = 1.6x + 4$

$y = 1.8x + 4$

13.

x	1	2	3	4
y	7	5	11	8

$y = x + 5$

$y = 1.3x + 5$

14.

x	1	2	3	4
y	4	11	5	15

$y = 2x + 3$

$y = 2.4x + 3$

Use the given data and your calculator to find an equation for the line of best fit. Then interpret the correlation coefficient and use the line of best fit to estimate the average temperature of another city using the given latitude.

15.

City	Latitude	Average Temperature (°F)
Calgary, Alberta	51.0°N	24
Munich, Germany	48.1°N	26
Marseille, France	43.2°N	29
St. Louis, Missouri	38.4°N	34
Seoul, South Korea	37.3°N	36
Tokyo, Japan	35.4°N	38
New Delhi, India	28.4°N	43
Honululu, Hawaii	21.2°N	52
Bangkok, Thailand	14.2°N	58
Panama City, Panama	8.6°N	

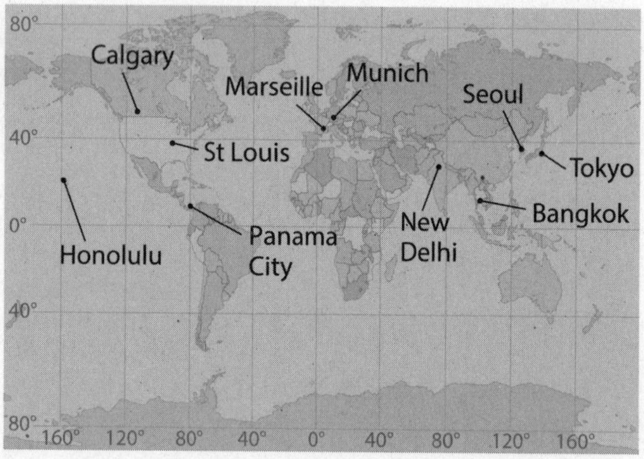

16.

City	Latitude	Average Temperature (°F)
Oslo, Norway	59.6°N	21
Warsaw, Poland	52.1°N	28
Milan, Italy	45.2°N	34
Vatican City, Vatican City	41.5°N	41
Beijing, China	39.5°N	42
Tel Aviv, Israel	32.0°N	48
Kuwait City, Kuwait	29.2°N	☐
Key West, Florida	24.3°N	55
Bogota, Columbia	4.4°N	64
Mogadishu, Somalia	2.0°N	66

17.

City	Latitude	Average Temperature (°F)
Tornio, Finland	65.5°N	28
Riga, Latvia	56.6°N	36
Minsk, Belarus	53.5°N	39
Quebec City, Quebec	46.5°N	45
Turin, Italy	45.0°N	47
Pittsburgh, Pennsylvania	40.3°N	49
Lisbon, Portugal	38.4°N	52
Jerusalem, Israel	31.5°N	☐
New Orleans, Louisiana	29.6°N	60
Port-au-Prince, Haiti	18.3°N	69

18.

City	Latitude (°N)	Average Temperature (°F)
Juneau, Alaska	58.2	15
Amsterdam, Netherlands	52.2	24
Salzburg, Austria	47.5	36
Belgrade, Serbia	44.5	38
Philadelphia, Pennsylvania	39.6	41
Tehran, Iran	35.4	44
Nassau, Bahamas	25.0	52
Mecca, Saudi Arabia	21.3	56
Dakar, Senegal	14.4	
Georgetown, Guyana	6.5	65

Demographics **Each table lists the median age of people living in the United States, based on the results of the United States Census over the past few decades. Use residuals to calculate the quality of fit for the line $y = 0.5x + 20$, where y is median age and x is years since 1970.**

19.

Year	Median age of men
1970	25.3
1980	26.8
1990	29.1
2000	31.4
2010	35.6

20.

Year	Median Age of Texans
1970	27.1
1980	29.3
1990	31.1
2000	33.8
2010	37.6

21. State the residuals based on the actual y and predicted y values.

a. Actual: 23, Predicted: 21

b. Actual: 25.6, Predicted: 23.3

c. Actual: 24.8, Predicted: 27.4

d. Actual: 34.9, Predicted: 31.3

H.O.T. Focus on Higher Order Thinking

22. Critical Thinking The residual plot of an equation has x-values that are close to the x-axis from $x = 0$ to $x = 10$, but has values that are far from the axis from $x = 10$ to $x = 30$. Is this a strong or weak relationship?

23. Communicate Mathematical Ideas In a squared residual plot, the residuals form a horizontal line at $y = 6$. What does this mean?

24. Interpret the Answer Explain one situation other than those in this section where squared residuals are useful.

Lesson Performance Task

The table shows the latitudes and average temperatures for the 10 largest cities in the Southern Hemisphere.

City	Latitude (°S)	Average Temperature (°F)
Sao Paulo, Brazil	23.9	69
Buenos Aires, Argentina	34.8	64
Rio de Janeiro, Brazil	22.8	76
Jakarta, Indonesia	6.3	81
Lodja, DRC	3.5	73
Lima, Peru	12.0	68
Santiago de Chile, Chile	33.2	58
Sydney, Australia	33.4	64
Melbourne, Australia	37.7	58
Johannesburg, South Africa	26.1	61

a. Use a graphing calculator to find a line of best fit for this data set. What is the equation for the best-fit line? Interpret the meaning of the slope of this line.

b. The city of Piggs Peak, Swaziland, is at latitude 26.0 °S. Use the equation of your best-fit line to predict the average temperature in Piggs Peak. The actual average temperature for Piggs Peak is 65.3 °F. How might you account for the difference in predicted and actual values?

c. Assume that you graphed the latitude and average temperature for 10 cities in the Northern Hemisphere. Predict how the line of best fit for that data set might compare with the best-fit line for the Southern Hemisphere cities.

Name________________________ Class________________ Date__________

10.2 Graphing Exponential Functions

Essential Question: How do you graph an exponential function of the form $f(x) = ab^x$?

Resource Locker

Explore Exploring Graphs of Exponential Functions

Exponential functions follow the general shape $y = ab^x$.

(A) Graph the exponential functions on a graphing calculator, and match the graph to the correct function rule.

1. $y = 3(2)^x$

2. $y = 0.5(2)^x$

3. $y = 3(0.5)^x$

4. $y = -3(2)^x$

a.

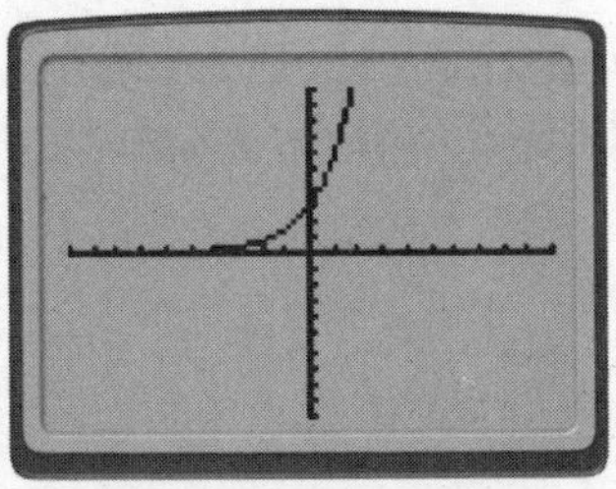

b.

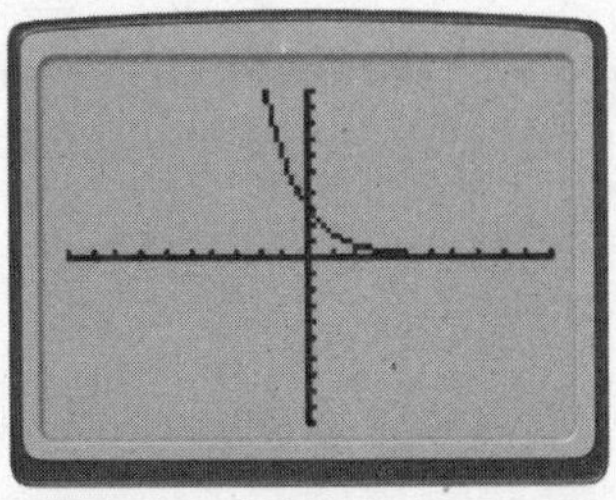

c.

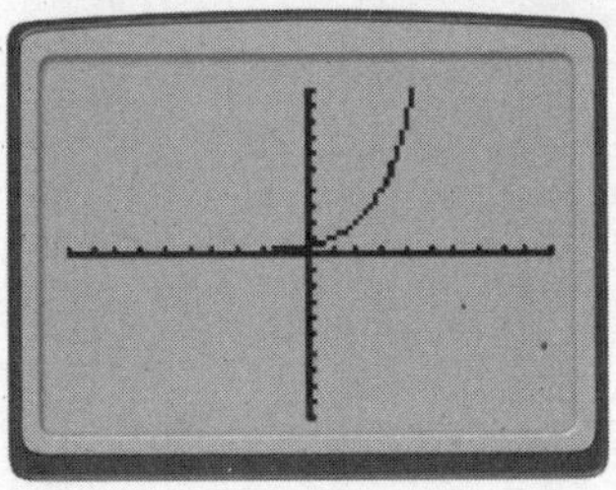

d.

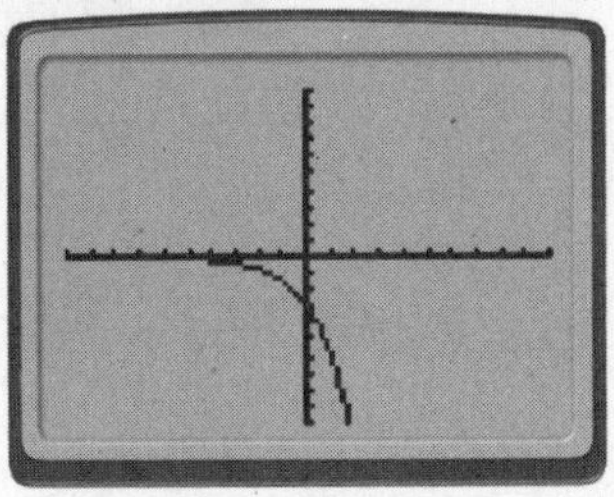

(B) In all the functions 1–4 above, the base $b > 0$.

Use the graphs to make a conjecture: State the domain and range of $y = ab^x$ if $a > 0$.

____

____

(C) In all the functions 1–4 above, the base $b > 0$.

Use the graphs to make a conjecture: State the domain and range of $y = ab^x$ if $a < 0$.

____

____

(D) What is the y-intercept of $f(x) = 0.5(2)^x$?

____

(E) Note the similarities between the y-intercept and a. What is their relationship?

Reflect

1. **Discussion** What is the domain for any exponential function $y = ab^x$?

2. **Discussion** Describe the values of b for all functions $y = ab^x$.

Explain 1 Graphing Increasing Positive Exponential Functions

The symbol ∞ represents *infinity*. We can describe the *end behavior* of a function by describing what happens to the function values as x approaches positive infinity ($x \to \infty$) and as x approaches negative infinity ($x \to -\infty$).

Example 1 **Graph each exponential function. After graphing, identify a and b, the y-intercept, and the end behavior of the graph.**

(A) $f(x) = 2^x$

Choose several values of x and generate ordered pairs.

x	$f(x) = 2^x$
−1	0.5
0	1
1	2
2	4

Graph the ordered pairs and connect them with a smooth curve.

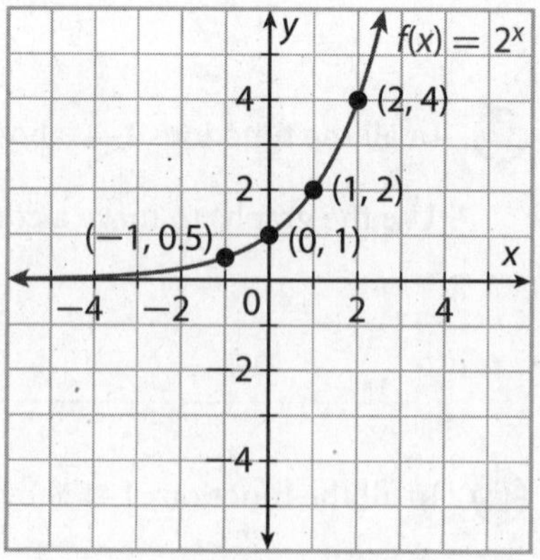

$a = 1$

$b = 2$

y-intercept: $(0, 1)$

End Behavior: As x-values approach positive infinity ($x \to \infty$), y-values approach positive infinity ($y \to \infty$).
As x-values approach negative infinity ($x \to -\infty$), y-values approach zero ($y \to 0$).

Using symbols only, we say: As $x \to \infty$, $y \to \infty$, and as $x \to -\infty$, $y \to 0$.

Ⓑ $f(x) = 3(4)^x$

Choose several values of x and generate ordered pairs.

x	$f(x) = 3(4)^x$
−1	
0	
1	
2	

Graph the ordered pairs and connect them with a smooth curve.

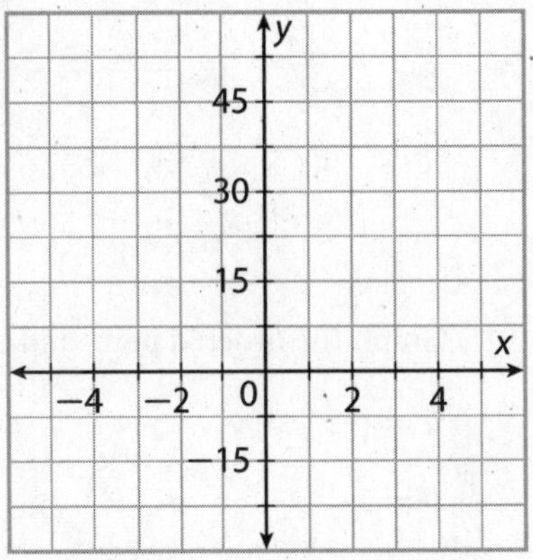

$a =$ ☐

$b =$ ☐

y-intercept: (☐, ☐)

End Behavior: As $x \to \infty$, $y \to$ ☐ and as $x \to -\infty$, $y \to$ ☐.

Reflect

3. If $a > 0$ and $b > 1$, what is the end behavior of the graph?

4. Describe the y-intercept of the exponential function $f(x) = ab^x$ in terms of a and b.

Your Turn

5. Graph the exponential function $f(x) = 2(2)^x$

After graphing, identify a and b, the y-intercept, and the end behavior of the graph.

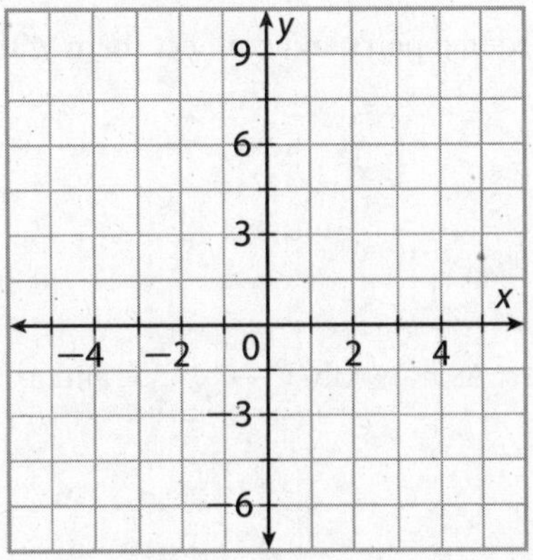

Explain 2 Graphing Decreasing Negative Exponential Functions

Example 2 **Graph each exponential function. After graphing, identify *a* and *b*, the *y*-intercept, and the end behavior of the graph.**

(A) $f(x) = -2(3)^x$

Choose several values of x and generate ordered pairs.

x	$f(x) = -2(3)^x$
−1	−0.7
0	−2
1	−6
2	−18

Graph the ordered pairs and connect them with a smooth curve.

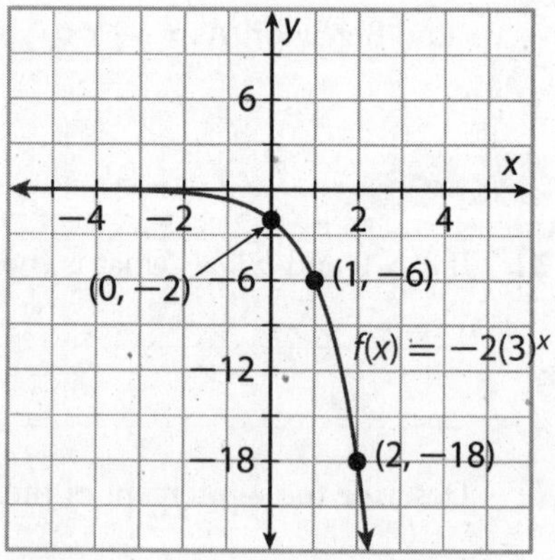

$a = -2$

$b = 3$

y-intercept: $(0, -2)$

End Behavior: As $x \to \infty$, $y \to -\infty$ and as $x \to -\infty$, $y \to 0$.

(B) $f(x) = -3(4)^x$

Choose several values of x and generate ordered pairs.

x	$f(x) = -3(4)^x$
−1	
0	
1	
2	

Graph the ordered pairs and connect them with a smooth curve.

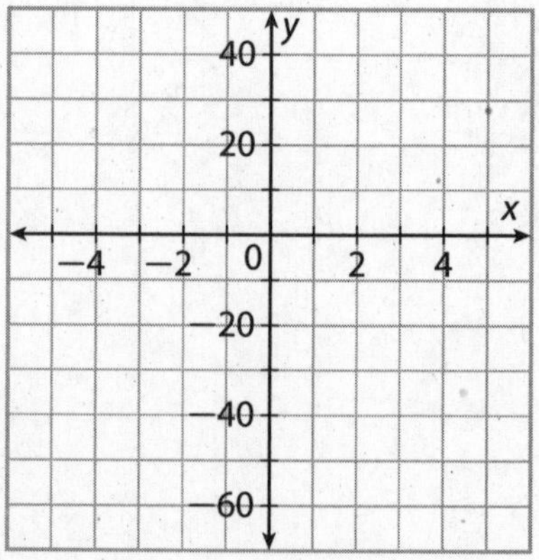

$a =$ ☐

$b =$ ☐

y-intercept: (☐, ☐)

End Behavior: As $x \to \infty$, $y \to$ ☐ and as $x \to -\infty$, $y \to$ ☐.

Reflect

6. If $a < 0$ and $b > 1$, what is the end behavior of the graph?

Your Turn

7. Graph the exponential function. $f(x) = -3(3)^x$

After graphing, identify a and b, the y-intercept, and the end behavior of the graph.

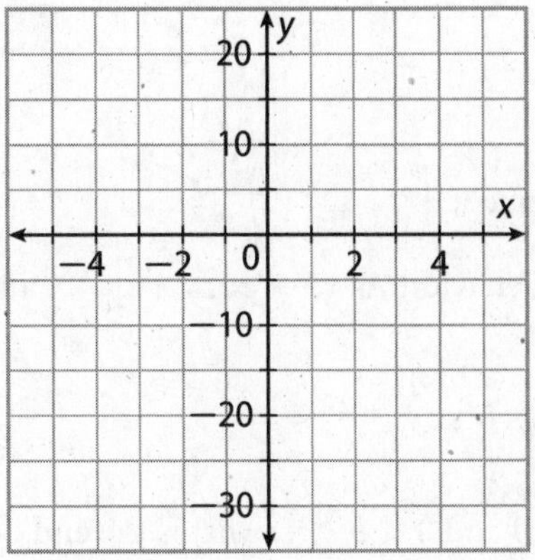

Explain 3 Graphing Decreasing Positive Exponential Functions

Example 3 **Graph each exponential function. After graphing, identify *a* and *b*, the *y*-intercept, and the end behavior of the graph. Use inequalities to discuss the behavior of the graph.**

(A) $f(x) = (0.5)^x$

Choose several values of x and generate ordered pairs.

x	$f(x) = (0.5)^x$
−1	2
0	1
1	0.5
2	0.25

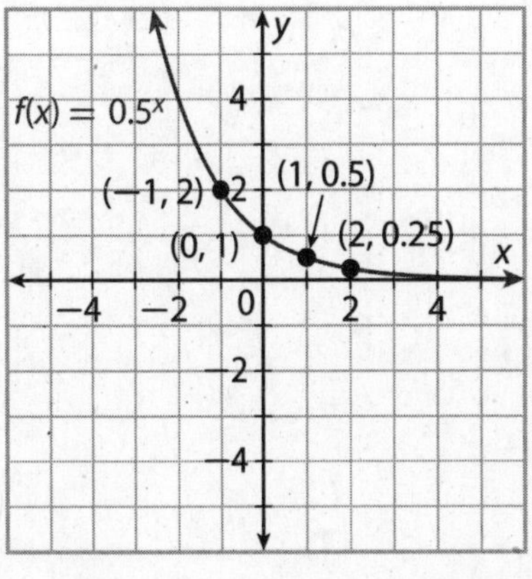

Graph the ordered pairs and connect them with a smooth curve.

$a = 1$

$b = 0.5$

y-intercept: $(0, 1)$

End Behavior: As $x \to \infty$, $y \to 0$ and as $x \to -\infty$, $y \to \infty$.

(B) $f(x) = 2(0.4)^x$

Choose several values of x and generate ordered pairs.

x	$f(x) = 2(0.4)^x$
−1	
0	
1	
2	

Graph the ordered pairs and connect them with a smooth curve.

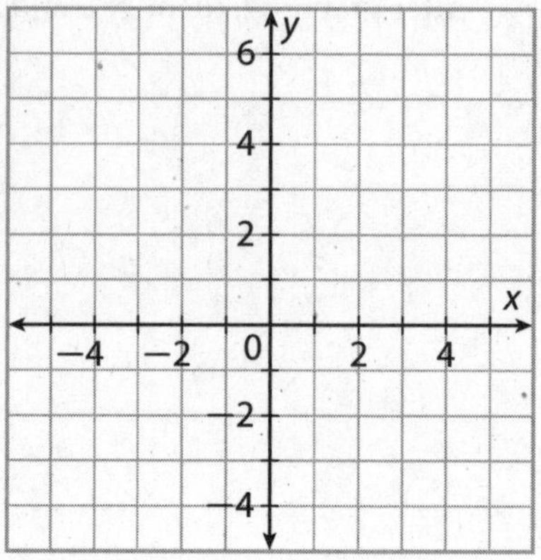

$a =$ ☐

$b =$ ☐

y-intercept: (☐, ☐)

End Behavior: As $x \to \infty$, $y \to$ ☐ and as $x \to -\infty$, $y \to$ ☐.

Reflect

8. If $a > 0$ and $0 < b < 1$, what is the end behavior of the graph?

____

____

Your Turn

9. Graph the exponential function. After graphing, identify a and b, the y-intercept, and the end behavior of the graph.

$f(x) = 3(0.5)^x$

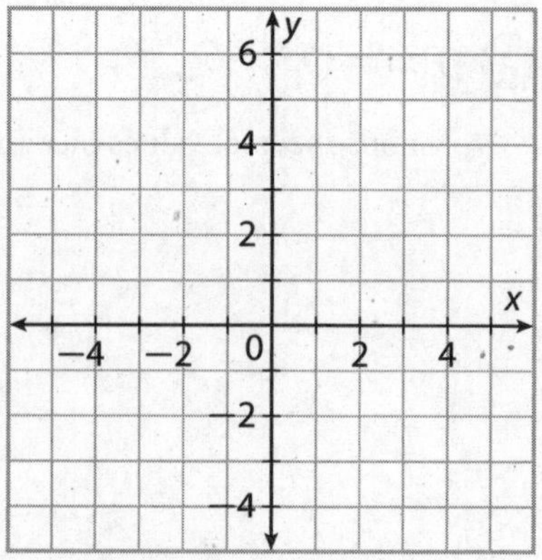

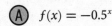

Explain 4 Graphing Increasing Negative Exponential Functions

Example 4 **Graph each exponential function. After graphing, identify a and b, the y-intercept, and the end behavior of the graph.**

(A) $f(x) = -0.5^x$

Choose several values of x and generate ordered pairs.

x	$f(x) = -0.5^x$
−1	−2
0	−1
1	−0.5
2	−0.25

Graph the ordered pairs and connect them with a smooth curve.

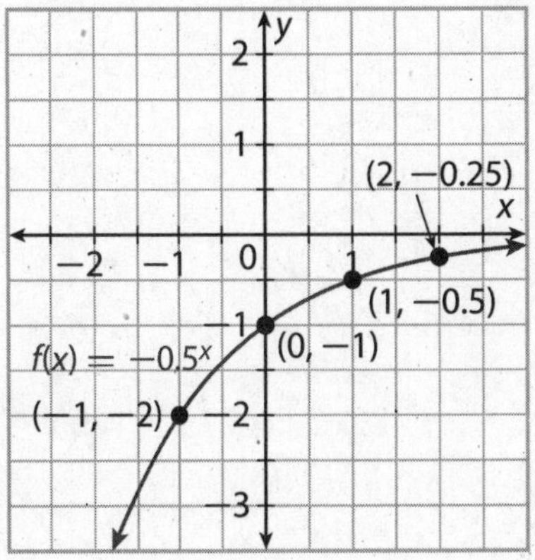

$a = -1$

$b = 0.5$

y-intercept: $(0, -1)$

End Behavior: As $x \to \infty$, $y \to 0$ and as $x \to -\infty$, $y \to -\infty$.

(B) $f(x) = -3(0.4)^x$

Choose several values of x and generate ordered pairs.

x	$f(x) = -3(0.4)^x$
−1	
0	
1	
2	

Graph the ordered pairs and connect them with a smooth curve.

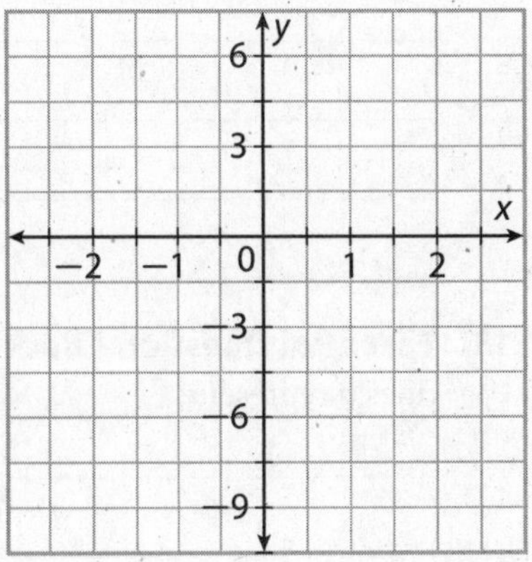

$a =$ ☐

$b =$ ☐

y-intercept: (☐, ☐)

End Behavior: As $x \to \infty$, $y \to$ ☐ and as $x \to -\infty$, $y \to$ ☐.

Reflect

10. If $a < 0$ and $0 < b < 1$, what is the end behavior of the graph?

____

____

Your Turn

11. Graph the exponential function. After graphing, identify a and b, the y-intercept, and the end behavior of the graph.
$f(x) = -2(0.5)^x$

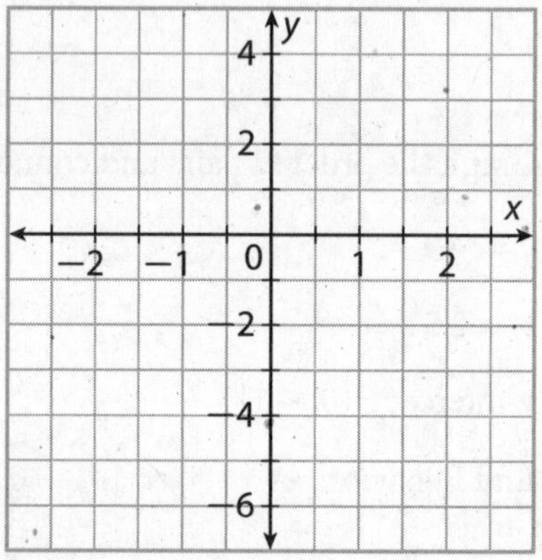

Elaborate

12. Why is $f(x) = 3(-0.5)^x$ not an exponential function?

____

____

____

____

____

____

13. Essential Question Check-In When an exponential function of the form $f(x) = ab^x$ is graphed, what does a represent?

____

____

✩ Evaluate: Homework and Practice

Personal Math Trainer

- Online Homework
- Hints and Help
- Extra Practice

State *a*, *b*, and the *y*-intercept then graph the function on a graphing calculator.

1. $f(x) = 2(3)^x$

2. $f(x) = -6(2)^x$

3. $f(x) = -5(0.5)^x$

4. $f(x) = 3(0.8)^x$

5. $f(x) = 6(3)^x$

6. $f(x) = -4(0.2)^x$

7. $f(x) = 7(0.9)^x$

8. $f(x) = -3(2)^x$

State *a*, *b*, and the *y*-intercept then graph the function and describe the end behavior of the graphs.

9. $f(x) = 3(3)^x$

10. $f(x) = 5(0.6)^x$

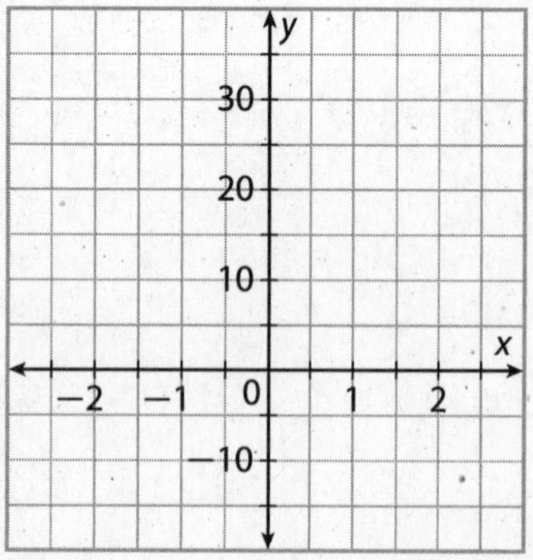

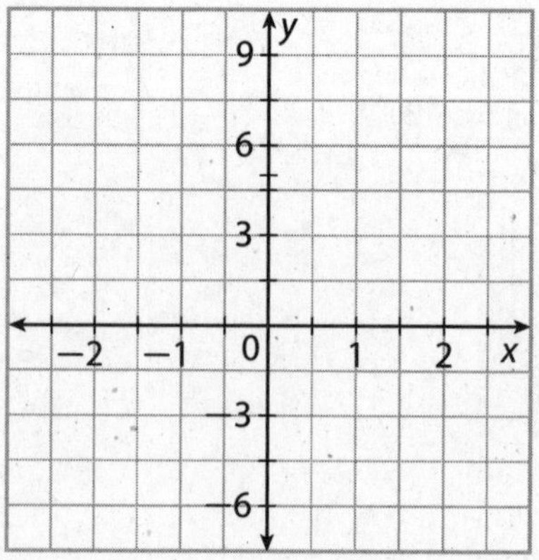

11. $f(x) = -6(0.7)^x$

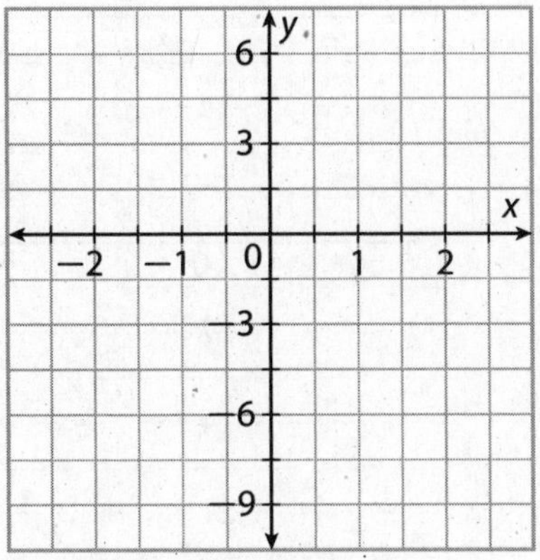

12. $f(x) = -4(3)^x$

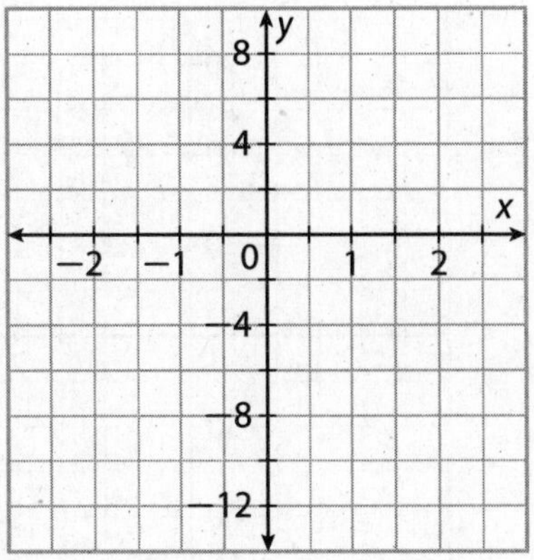

13. $f(x) = 5(2)^x$

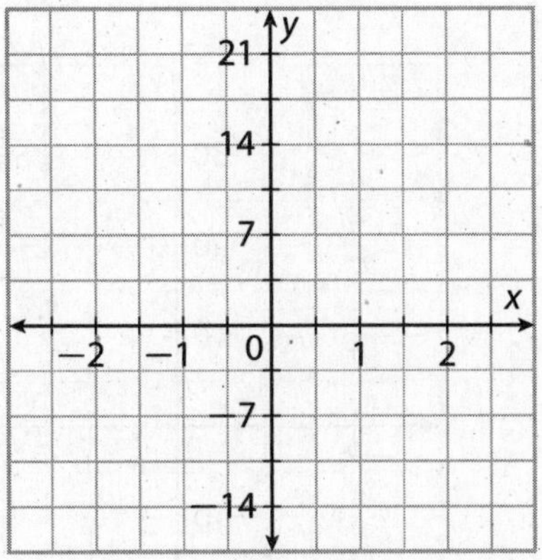

14. $f(x) = -2(0.8)^x$

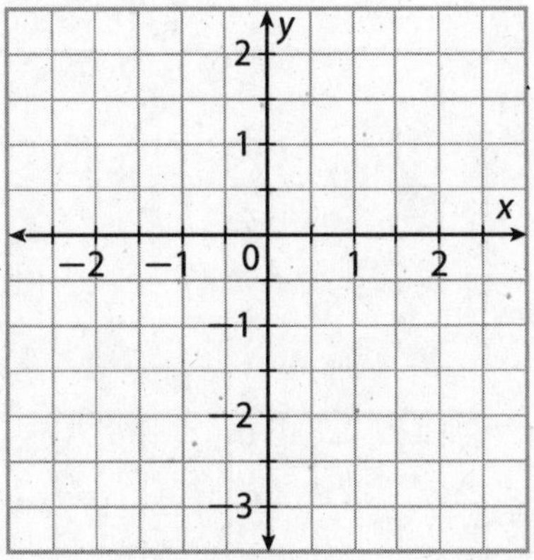

15. $f(x) = 9(3)^x$

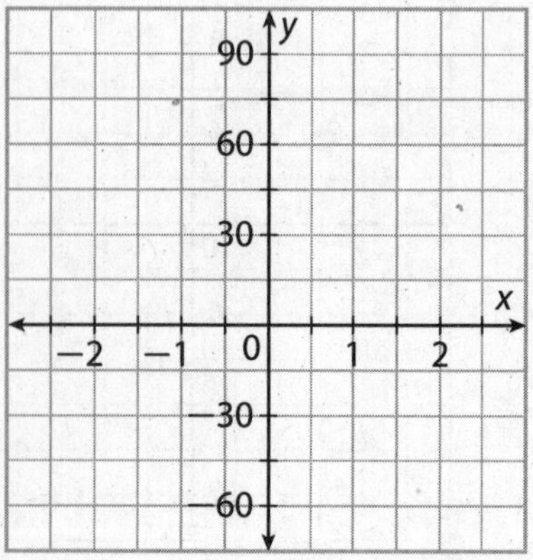

16. $f(x) = -5(2)^x$

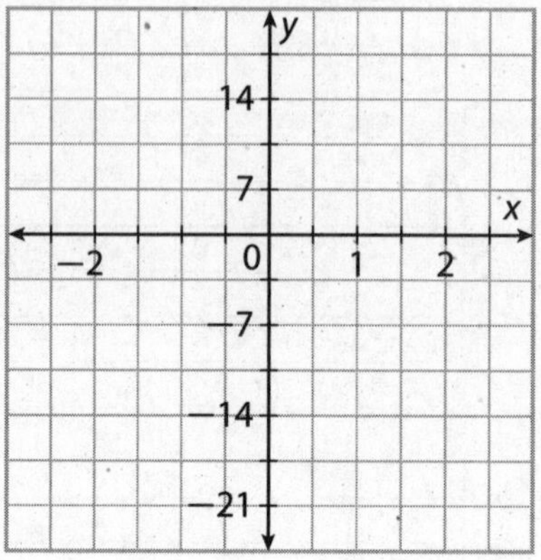

17. $f(x) = 7(0.4)^x$

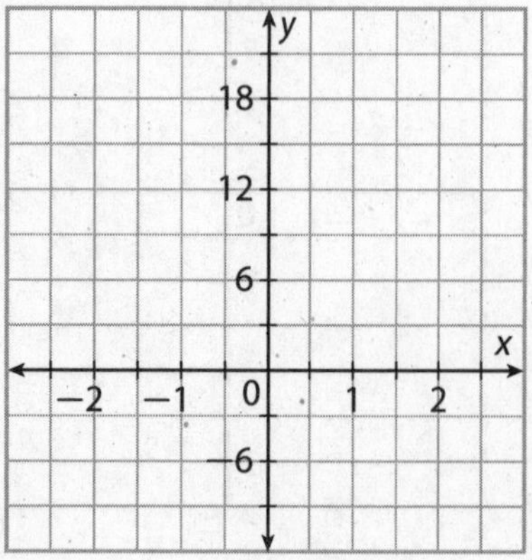

18. $f(x) = 6(2)^x$

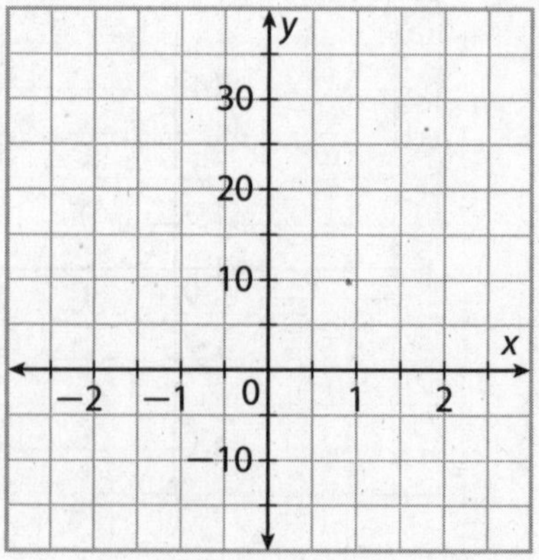

19. Identify the domain and range of each function. Make sure to provide these answers using inequalities.

a. $f(x) = 3(2)^x$

b. $f(x) = 7(0.4)^x$

c. $f(x) = -2(0.6)^x$

d. $f(x) = -3(4)^x$

e. $f(x) = 2(22)^x$

20. Statistics In 2000, the population of Massachusetts was 6.3 million people and was growing at a rate of about 0.32% per year. At this growth rate, the function $f(x) = 6.3(1.0032)^x$ gives the population, in millions x years after 2000. Using this model, find the year when the population reaches 7 million people.

21. Physics A ball is rolling down a slope and continuously picks up speed. Suppose the function $f(x) = 1.2(1.11)^x$ describes the speed of the ball in inches per minute. How fast will the ball be rolling in 20 minutes? Round the answer to the nearest whole number.

H.O.T. Focus on Higher Order Thinking

22. Draw Conclusions Assume that the domain of the function $f(x) = 3(2)^x$ is the set of all real numbers. What is the range of the function?

23. What If? If $b = 1$ in an exponential function, what will the graph of the function look like?

24. Critical Thinking Using the graph of an exponential function, how can b be found?

25. Critical Thinking Use the table to write the equation for the exponential function.

x	$f(x)$
-1	$\frac{4}{5}$
0	4
1	20
2	100

Lesson Performance Task

A pumpkin is being grown for a contest at the state fair. Its growth can be modeled by the equation $P = 25(1.56)^n$, where P is the weight of the pumpkin in pounds and n is the number of weeks the pumpkin has been growing. By what percentage does the pumpkin grow every week? After how many weeks will the pumpkin be 80 pounds?

After the pumpkin grows to 80 pounds, it grows more slowly. From then on, its growth can be modeled by $P = 25(1.23)^n$, where n is the number of weeks since the pumpkin reached 80 pounds. Estimate when the pumpkin will reach 150 pounds.

Name ____________________ Class ____________ Date ________

10.3 Modeling Exponential Growth and Decay

Resource Locker

Essential Question: How can you use exponential functions to model the increase or decrease of a quantity over time?

Explore 1 Describing End Behavior of a Growth Function

When you graph a function $f(x)$ in a coordinate plane, the x-axis represents the independent variable and the y-axis represents the dependent variable. Therefore, the graph of $f(x)$ is the same as the graph of the equation $y = f(x)$. You will use this form when you use a calculator to graph functions.

Ⓐ Use a graphing calculator to graph the exponential growth function $f(x) = 200(1.10)^x$, using Y_1 for $f(x)$. Use a viewing window from -20 to 20 for x, with a scale of 2, and from -100 to 1000 for y, with a scale of 50. Sketch the curve on the axes provided.

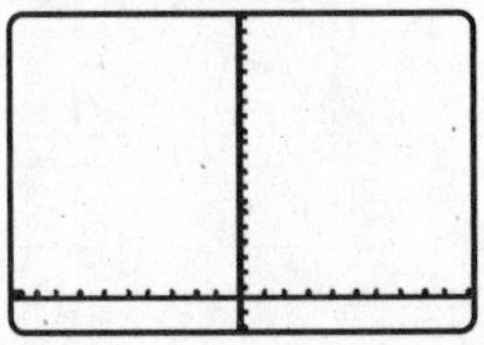

Ⓑ To describe the end behavior of the function, you describe the function values as x increases or decreases without bound. Using the TRACE feature, move the cursor to the right along the curve. Describe the end behavior as x increases without bound.

____

Ⓒ Using the TRACE feature, move the cursor to the left along the curve. Describe the end behavior as x decreases without bound.

____

Reflect

1. Describe the domain and range of the function using inequalities.

____

2. Identify the y-intercept of the graph of the function.

____

3. An asymptote of a graph is a line the graph approaches more and more closely. Identify an asymptote of this graph.

____

4. **Discussion** Why is the value of the function always greater than 0?

____

____

Explore 2 Describing End Behavior of a Decay Function

Use the form from the first Explore exercise to graph another function on your calculator.

(A) Use a graphing calculator to graph the exponential decay function $f(x) = 500(0.8)^x$, using Y_1 for $f(x)$. Use a viewing window from -10 to 10 for x, with a scale of 1, and from -500 to 5000 for y, with a scale of 500. Sketch the curve on the axes provided.

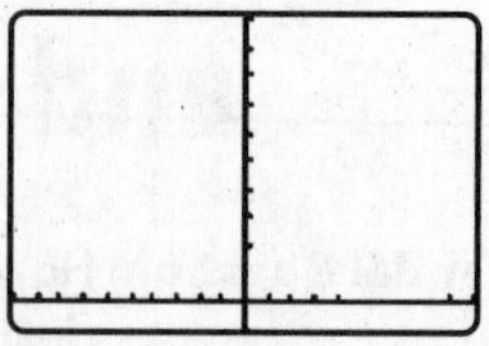

(B) Using the TRACE feature, move the cursor to the right along the curve. Describe the end behavior as x increases without bound.

____

____

(C) Using the TRACE feature, move the cursor to the left along the curve. Describe the end behavior as x decreases without bound.

____

____

Reflect

5. Discussion Describe the domain and range of the function using inequalities.

____

____

6. Identify the y-intercept of the graph of the function.

____

____

7. Identify an asymptote of this graph. Why is this line an asymptote?

____

____

Explain 1 Modeling Exponential Growth

Recall that a function of the form $y = ab^x$ represents exponential growth when $a > 0$ and $b > 1$. If b is replaced by $1 + r$ and x is replaced by t, then the function is the **exponential growth model** $y = a(1 + r)^t$, where a is the initial amount, the base $(1 + r)$ is the growth factor, r is the growth rate, and t is the time interval. The value of the model increases with time.

Example 1 **Write an exponential growth function for each situation. Graph each function and state its domain, range and an asymptote. What does the y-intercept represent in the context of the problem?**

(A) A painting is sold for \$1800, and its value increases by 11% each year after it is sold. Find the value of the painting in 30 years.

Write the exponential growth function for this situation.

$$y = a(1 + r)^t$$
$$= 1800(1 + 0.11)^t$$
$$= 1800(1.11)^t$$

Find the value in 30 years.

$$y = 1800(1.11)^t$$
$$= 1800(1.11)^{30}$$
$$\approx 41{,}206.13$$

After 30 years, the painting will be worth approximately \$41,206.

Create a table of values to graph the function.

t	y	(t, y)
0	1800	(0, 1800)
8	4148	(8, 4148)
16	9560	(16, 9560)
24	22,030	(24, 22,030)
32	50,770	(32, 50,770)

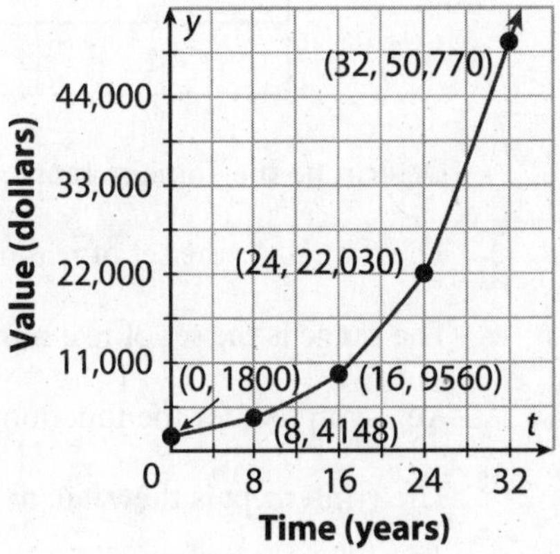

Determine the domain, range and an asymptote of the function.

The domain is the set of real numbers t such that $t \geq 0$.

The range is the set of real numbers y such that $y \geq 1800$.

An asymptote for the function is $y = 0$.

The y-intercept is the value of y when $t = 0$, which is the value of the painting when it was sold.

Ⓑ **A baseball trading card is sold for \$2, and its value increases by 8% each year after it is sold. Find the value of the baseball trading card in 10 years.**

Write the exponential growth function for this situation.

$y = a(1 + r)^t$

$= \square\left(1 + \square\right)^t$

$= \square\left(\square\right)^t$

Find the value in 10 years.

$y = a(1 + r)^t$

$= \square\left(\square\right)^t$

$= \square\left(\square\right)^{\square}$

$\approx \square$

After 10 years, the baseball trading card will be worth approximately \$________.

Create a table of values to graph the function.

t	y	(t, y)
0		
3		
6		
9		
12		

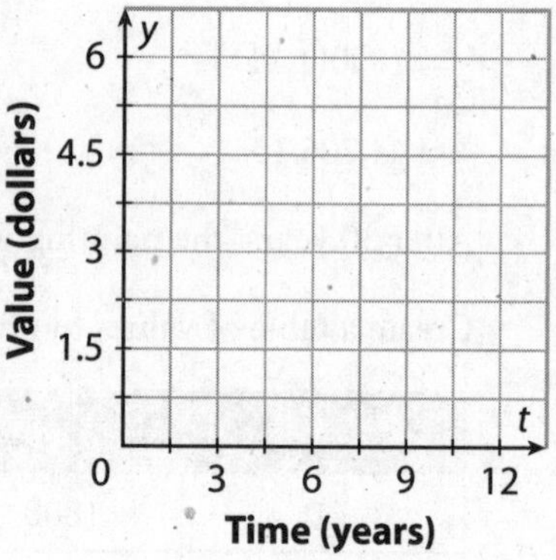

Determine the domain, range, and an asymptote of the function.

The domain is the set of real numbers t such that $t \geq \square$.

The range is the set of real numbers y such that $y \geq \square$.

An asymptote for the function is ________.

The y-intercept is the value of y when $t = 0$, which is the ________.

Reflect

8. Find a recursive rule that models the exponential growth of $y = 1800(1.11)^t$.

____

9. Find a recursive rule that models the exponential growth of $y = 2(1.08)^t$.

____

Your Turn

10. Write and graph an exponential growth function, and state the domain and range. Tell what the y-intercept represents. Sara sold a coin for \$3, and its value increases by 2% each year after it is sold. Find the value of the coin in 8 years.

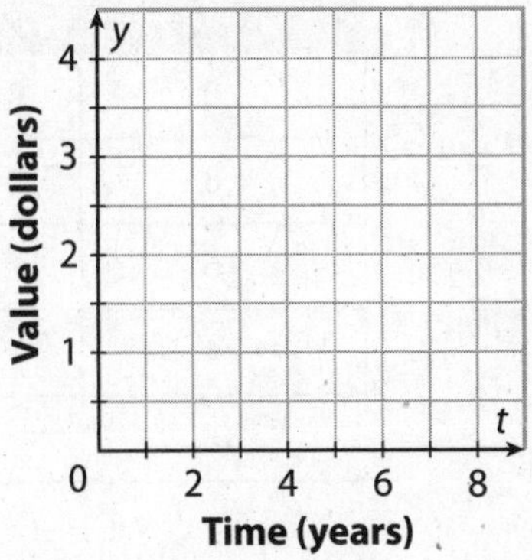

Explain 2 Modeling Exponential Decay

Recall that a function of the form $y = ab^x$ represents exponential decay when $a > 0$ and $0 < b < 1$. If b is replaced by $1 - r$ and x is replaced by t, then the function is the **exponential decay model** $y = a(1 - r)^t$, where a is the initial amount, the base $(1 - r)$ is the decay factor, r is the decay rate, and t is the time interval.

Example 2 **Write an exponential decay function for each situation. Graph each function and state its domain and range. What does the *y*-intercept represent in the context of the problem?**

(A) The population of a town is decreasing at a rate of 3% per year. In 2005, there were 1600 people. Find the population in 2013.

Write the exponential decay function for this situation.

$$y = a(1 - r)^t$$
$$= 1600(1 - 0.03)^t$$
$$= 1600(0.97)^t$$

Find the value in 8 years.

$$y = 1600(0.97)^t$$
$$= 1600(0.97)^8$$
$$\approx 1254$$

After 8 years, the town's population will be about 1254 people.

Create a table of values to graph the function.

t	y	(t, y)
0	1600	(0, 1600)
8	1254	(8, 1254)
16	983	(16, 983)
24	770	(24, 770)
32	604	(32, 604)

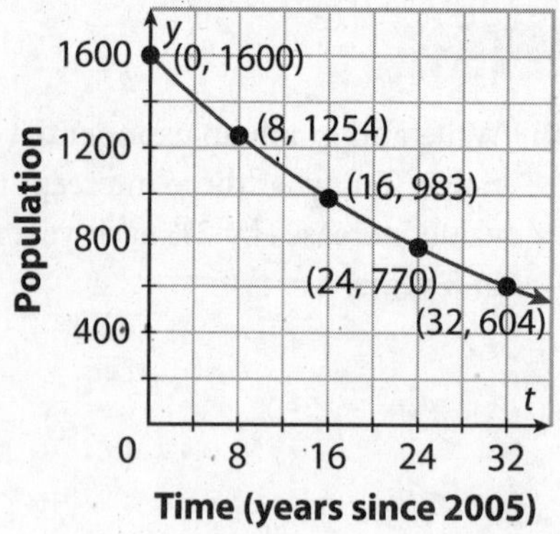

Determine the domain and range of the function.

The domain is the set of real numbers t such that $t \geq 0$. The range is the set of real numbers y such that $0 \leq y \leq 1600$.

The y-intercept is the value of y when $t = 0$, the number of people before it started to lose population.

B The value of a car is depreciating at a rate of 5% per year. In 2010, the car was worth \$32,000. Find the value of the car in 2013.

Write the exponential decay function for this situation.

$y = a(1 - r)^t$

$= \square\left(1 - \square\right)^t$

$= \square\left(\square\right)^t$

Find the value in 3 years.

$y = a(1 - r)^t$

$= \square\left(\square\right)^t$

$= \square\left(\square\right)^{\square} \approx \square$

After 3 years, the car's value will be \$$\square$.

Create a table of values to graph the function.

t	y	(t, y)
0		
1		
2		
3		

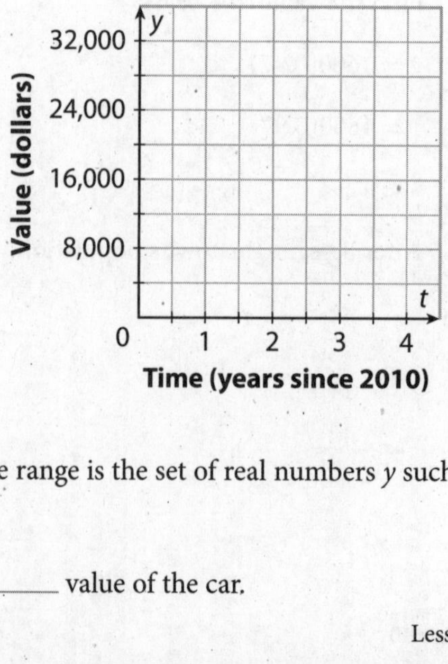

Determine the domain and range of the function.

The domain is the set of real numbers t such that $t \geq \square$. The range is the set of real numbers y such that $\square \leq y \leq \square$.

The y-intercept, 32,000, is the value of y when $t = 0$, the ________ value of the car.

Reflect

11. Find a recursive rule that models the exponential decay of $y = 1600(0.97)^t$.

12. Find a recursive rule that models the exponential decay of $y = 32{,}000(0.95)^t$.

Your Turn

13. The value of a boat is depreciating at a rate of 9% per year. In 2006, the boat was worth \$17,800. Find the worth of the boat in 2013. Write an exponential decay function for this situation. Graph the function and state its domain and range. What does the y-intercept represent in the context of the problem?

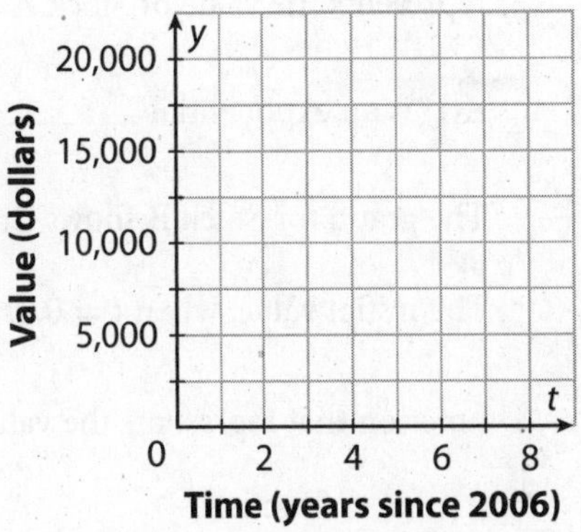

Explain 3 Comparing Exponential Growth and Decay

Graphs can be used to describe and compare exponential growth and exponential decay models over time.

Example 3 **Use the graphs provided to write the equations of the functions. Then describe and compare the behaviors of both functions.**

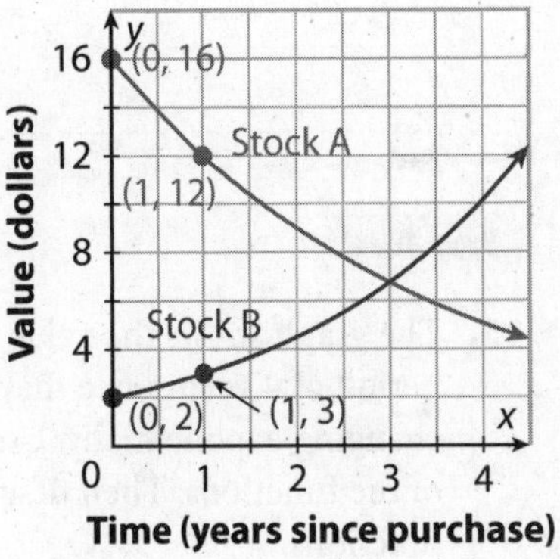

(A) The graph shows the value of two different shares of stock over the period of 4 years since they were purchased. The values have been changing exponentially.

The graph for Stock A shows that the value of the stock is decreasing as time increases.

The initial value, when $t = 0$, is 16. The value when $t = 1$ is 12. Since $12 \div 16 = 0.75$, the function that represents the value of Stock A after t years is $A(t) = 16(0.75)^t$. $A(t)$ is an exponential decay function.

The graph for Stock B shows that the value of the stock is increasing as time increases.

The initial value, when $t = 0$, is 2. The value when $t = 1$ is 3. Since $3 \div 2 = 1.5$, the function that represents the value of Stock B after t years is $B(t) = 2(1.5)^t$. $B(t)$ is an exponential growth function.

The value of Stock A is going down over time. The value of Stock B is going up over time. The initial value of Stock A is greater than the initial value of Stock B. However, after about 3 years, the value of Stock B becomes greater than the value of Stock A.

Ⓑ The graph shows the value of two different shares of stocks over the period of 4 years since they were purchased. The values have been changing exponentially.

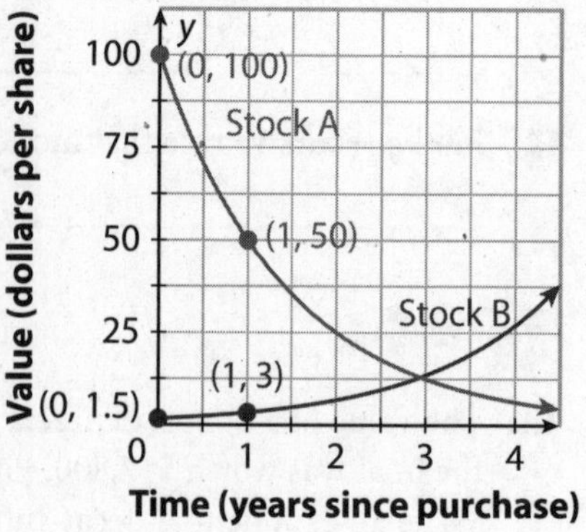

The graph for Stock A shows that the value of the stock is ________ as time increases.

The initial value, when $t = 0$, is ☐. The value when $t = 1$ is ☐. Since ☐ ÷ ☐ = ☐, the function that represents the value of Stock A after t years is $A(t) = \square\left(\square\right)^t$. $A(t)$ is an exponential ________ function.

The graph for Stock B shows that the value of the stock is ________ as time increases.

The initial value, when $t = 0$, is ☐. The value when $t = 1$ is ☐. Since ☐ ÷ ☐ = ☐, the function that represents the value of Stock B after t years is $B(t) = \square\left(\square\right)^t$. $B(t)$ is an exponential ________ function.

The value of Stock A is going ________ over time. The value of Stock B is going ________ over time.

The initial value of Stock A is ________ than the initial value of Stock B. However, after about ☐ years, the value of Stock B becomes ________ than the value of Stock A.

Reflect

14. Discussion In the function $B(t) = 1.5(2)^t$, is it likely that the value of B can be accurately predicted in 50 years?

____

____

Your Turn

15. The graph shows the value of two different shares of stocks over the period of 4 years since they were purchased. The values have been changing exponentially. Use the graphs provided to write the equations of the functions. Then describe and compare the behaviors of both functions.

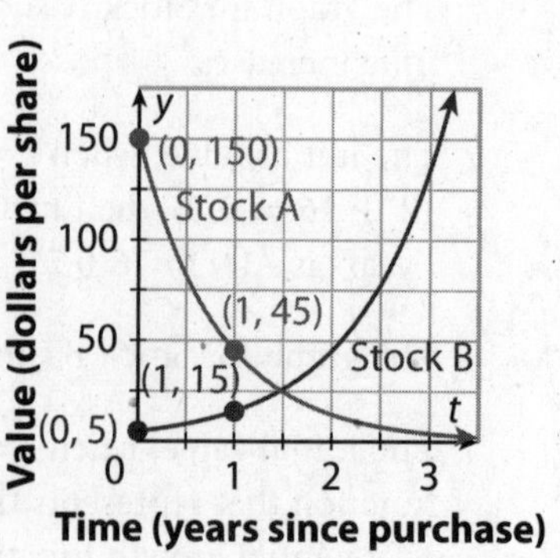

Elaborate

16. If $b > 1$ in a function of the form $y = ab^x$, is the function an example of exponential growth or an example of exponential decay?

17. What is an asymptote of the function $y = 35(1.1)^x$?

18. **Essential Question Check-In** What equation should be used when modeling an exponential function that models a decrease in a quantity over time?

Evaluate: Homework and Practice

Personal Math Trainer

- Online Homework
- Hints and Help
- Extra Practice

Graph the function on a graphing calculator, and state its domain, range, end behavior, and an asymptote.

1. $f(x) = 300(1.16)^x$

2. $f(x) = 800(0.85)^x$

3. $f(x) = 65(1.64)^x$

4. $f(x) = 57(0.77)^x$

Write an exponential function to model each situation. Then find the value of the function after the given amount of time.

5. Annual sales for a company are \$155,000 and increases at a rate of 8% per year for 9 years.

6. The value of a textbook is \$69 and decreases at a rate of 15% per year for 11 years.

7. A new savings account is opened with $300 and gains 3.1% yearly for 5 years.

8. The value of a car is $7800 and decreases at a rate of 8% yearly for 6 years.

9. The starting salary at a construction company is fixed at $55,000 and increases at a rate of 1.8% yearly for 4 years.

10. The value of a piece of fine jewelry is $280 and decreases at a rate of 3% yearly for 7 years.

11. The population of a town is 24,000 and is increasing at a rate of 6% per year for 3 years.

12. The value of a new stadium is $3.4 million and decreases at a rate of 2.39% yearly for 10 years.

Write an exponential function for each situation. Graph each function and state its domain and range. Determine what the *y*-intercept represents in the context of the problem.

13. The value of a boat is depreciating at a rate of 7% per year. In 2004, the boat was worth $192,000. Find the value of the boat in 2013.

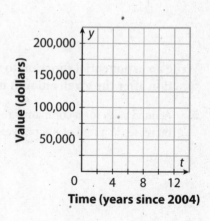

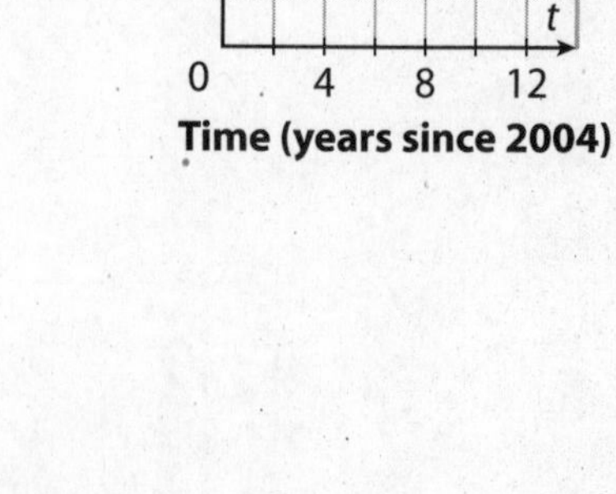

14. The value of a collectible baseball card is increasing at a rate of 0.5% per year. In 2000, the card was worth \$1350. Find the value of the card in 2013.

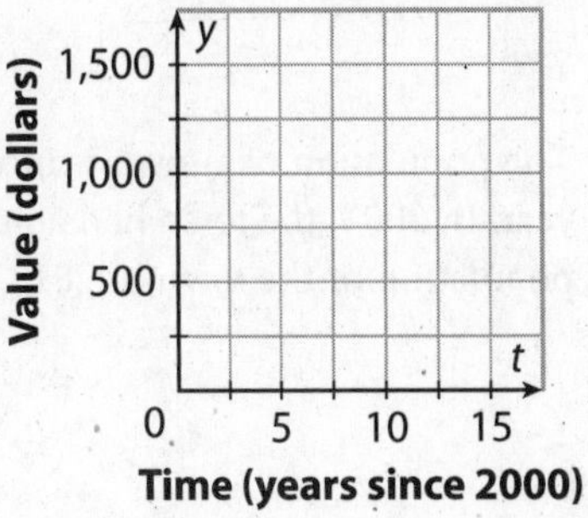

15. The value of an airplane is depreciating at a rate of 7% per year. In 2004, the airplane was worth \$51.5 million. Find the value of the airplane in 2013.

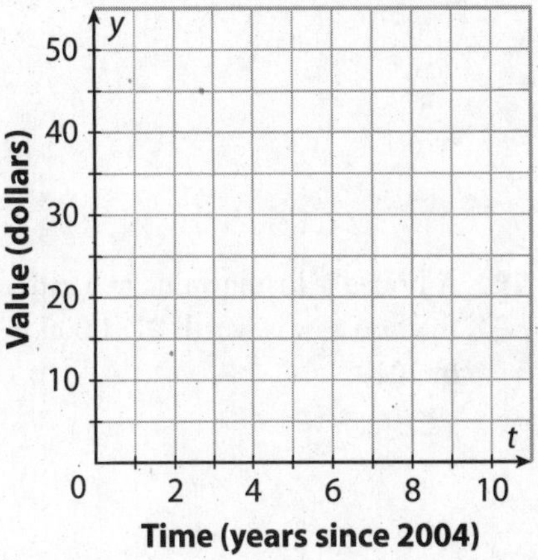

16. The value of a movie poster is increasing at a rate of 3.5% per year. In 1990, the poster was worth \$20.25. Find the value of the poster in 2013.

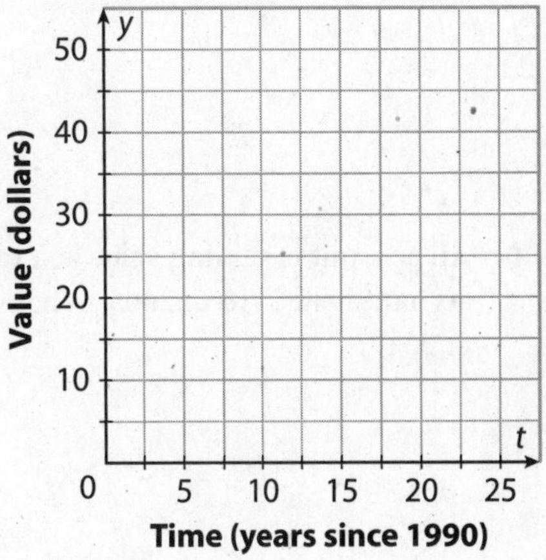

17. The value of a couch is decreasing at a rate of 6.2% per year. In 2007, the couch was worth $1232. Find the value of the couch in 2014.

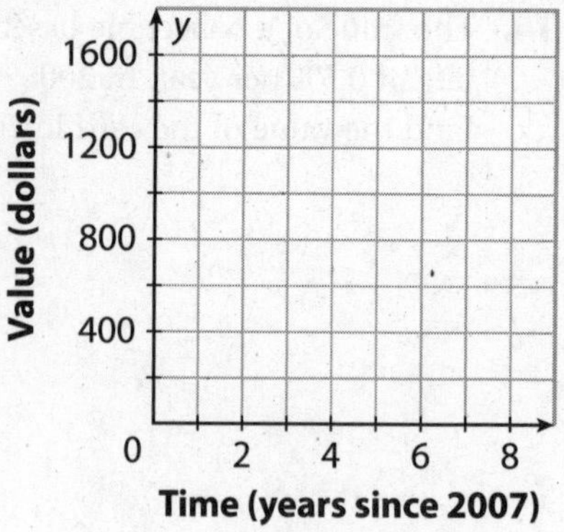

18. The population of a town is increasing at a rate of 2.2% per year. In 2001, the town had a population of 34,567. Find the population of the town in 2018.

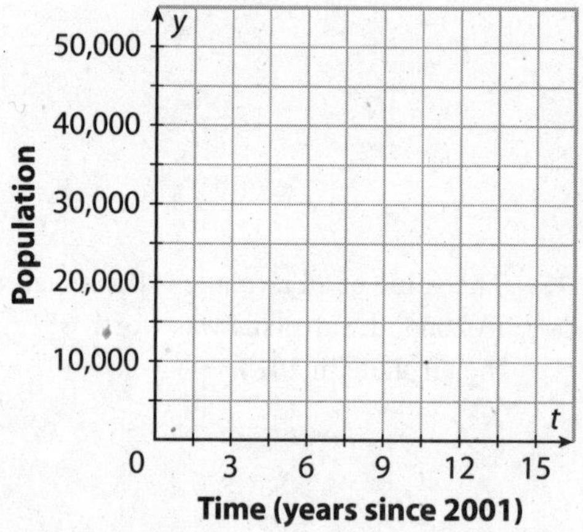

19. A house is losing value at a rate of 5.4% per year. In 2009, the house was worth $131,000. Find the value of the house in 2019.

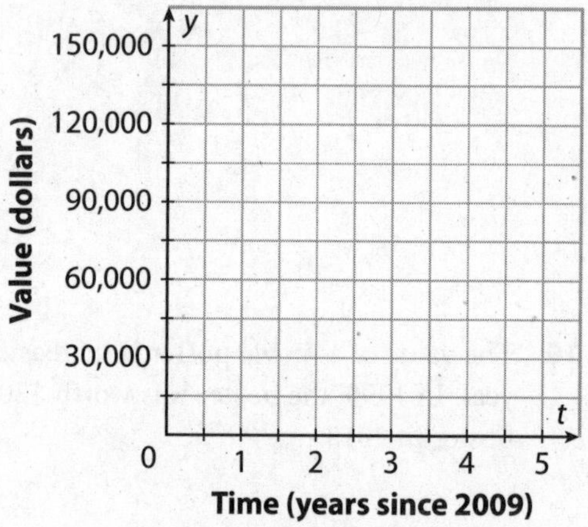

20. An account is gaining value at a rate of 4.94% per year. The account held $113 in 2005. What will the bank account hold in 2017?

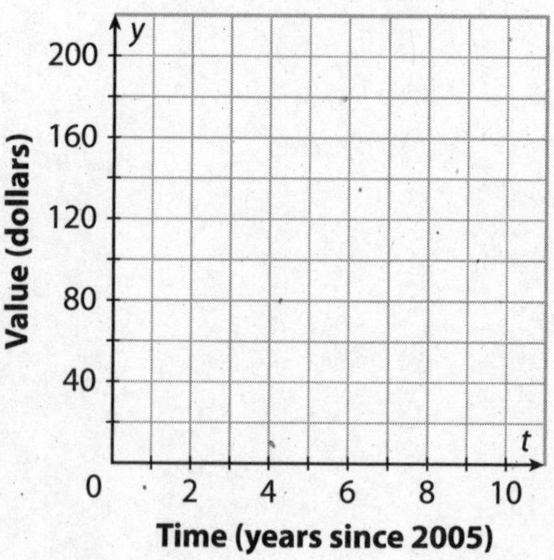

Describe and compare each pair of functions.

21. $A(t) = 13(0.6)^t$ and $B(t) = 4(3.2)^t$

22. $A(t) = 9(0.4)^t$ and $B(t) = 0.6(1.4)^t$

23. $A(t) = 547(0.32)^t$ and $B(t) = 324(3)^t$

24. $A(t) = 2(0.6)^t$ and $B(t) = 0.2(1.4)^t$

25. Identify the y-intercept of each of the exponential functions.

a. $3123(432{,}543)^x$

b. $76(89{,}047{,}832)^x$

c. $45(54)^x$

H.O.T. Focus on Higher Order Thinking

26. Explain the Error A student was asked to find the value of a \$2500 item after 4 years. The item was depreciating at a rate of 20% per year. What is wrong with the student's work?

$2500(0.2)^4$

\$4

27. Make a Conjecture The value of a certain car can be modeled by the function $y = 18000(0.76)^t$, where t is time in years. Will the value of the function ever be 0?

28. Communicate Mathematical Ideas Explain how a graph of an exponential function may resemble the graph of a linear function.

Lesson Performance Task

Archeologists have several methods of determining the age of recovered artifacts. One method is radioactive dating.

All matter is made of atoms. Atoms, in turn, are made of protons, neutrons, and electrons. An "element" is defined as an atom with a given number of protons. Carbon, for example, has exactly 6 protons. Carbon atoms can, however, have different numbers of neutrons. These are known as "isotopes" of carbon. Carbon-12 has 6 neutrons, carbon-13 has 7 neutrons, and carbon-14 has 8 neutrons. All carbon-based life forms contain these different isotopes of carbon.

Carbon-12 and carbon-13 account for over 99% of all the carbon in living things. Carbon-14, however, accounts for approximately 1 part per trillion or 0.0000000001% of the total carbon in living things. More importantly, carbon-14 is unstable and has a half-life of approximately 5700 years. This means that, within the span of 5700 years, one-half of any amount of carbon will "decay" into another atom. In other words, if you had 10 g of carbon-14 today, only 5 g would remain after 5700 years.

But, as long as an organism is living, it keeps taking in and releasing carbon-14, so the level of it in the organism, as small as it is, remains constant. Once an organism dies, however, it no longer ingests carbon-14, so the level of carbon-14 in it drops due to radioactive decay. Because we know how much carbon-14 an organism had when it was alive, as well as how long it takes for that amount to become half of what it was, you can determine the age of the organism by comparing these two values.

Use the information presented to create a function that will model the amount of carbon-14 in a sample as a function of its age. Create the model $C(n)$ where C is the amount of carbon-14 in parts per quadrillion (1 part per trillion is 1000 parts per quadrillion) and n is the age of the sample in half-lives. Graph the model.

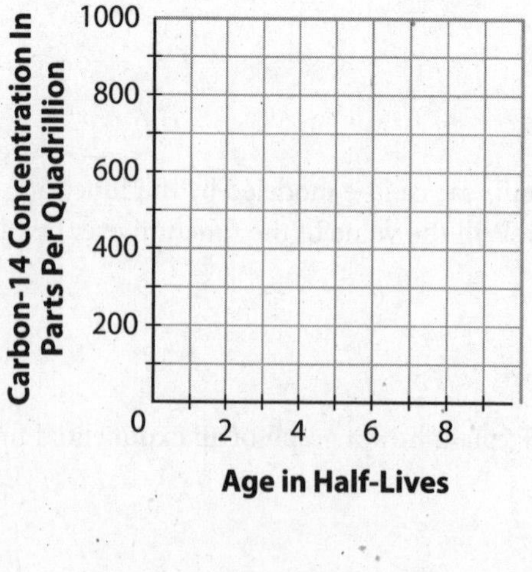

Name______________________ Class______________ Date__________

10.4 Modeling with Quadratic Functions

Essential Question: How can you use tables to recognize quadratic functions and use technology to create them?

Resource Locker

Explore Using Second Differences to Identify Quadratic Functions

A linear function is a straight line, a quadratic function is a parabola, and an exponential function is a curve that approaches a horizontal asymptote in one direction and curves upward to infinity in the other direction.

You can determine if the function is linear or exponential when the values of x and y are presented in a table. For a constant change in x-values, if the difference between the associated y-values is constant, then the function is linear. If the ratio of the associated y-values is constant, then the function is exponential.

What if neither the ratio of successive terms nor the first differences are roughly constant? There is a clue in the method for recognizing a linear function. Find the second difference. The second difference is the value obtained by subtracting consecutive first differences. If this number is non-zero, then the function will be quadratic. Examine the graph of the given quadratic function; then construct a table with values for x, y, and the first and second differences.

Ⓐ Graph the function $f(x) = x^2$ on the given axes.

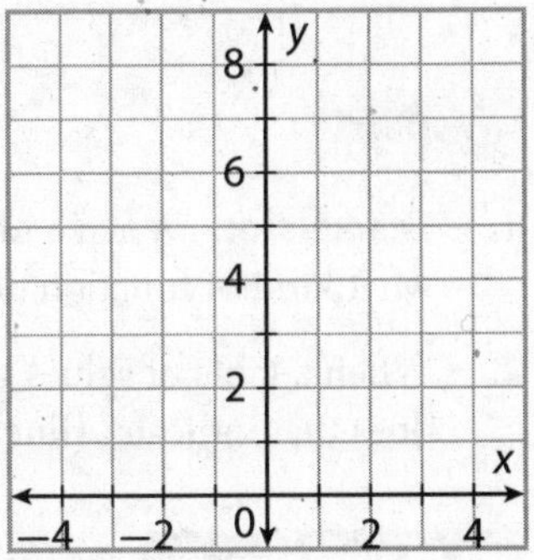

Use the table to complete Steps B, D, and F.

x	$y = f(x)$	First Difference	Second Difference
1	1	______	______
2	$2^2 =$ ____	$4 - 1 =$ ____	______
3	$3^2 =$ ____	$9 - 4 =$ ____	$5 - 3 =$ ____
4	$4^2 =$ ____	____ $-$ ____ $=$ ____	$7 - 5 =$ ____
5	$5^2 =$ ____	____ $-$ ____ $=$ ____	____ $-$ ____ $= 2$

Ⓑ Complete the $y = f(x)$ column of the table with indicated values of $f(x) = x^2$.

Ⓒ Is there a constant difference between x-values? yes/no

Ⓓ Recall that the differences between y-values are called the *first differences*. Complete the First Difference column of the table with the indicated first differences.

Ⓔ Are the first differences constant (the same)? yes/no

Ⓕ The differences between the first differences are called the **second differences**. Complete the Second Difference column of the table with the indicated second differences.

Ⓖ Are the second differences constant (the same)? yes/no

Ⓗ Complete the table for another quadratic function: $f(x) = -3x^2$.

x	$y = f(x)$	First Difference	Second Difference
1	$-3 \cdot 1 =$ ______	______	______
2	$-3 \cdot 2^2 =$ ______	$-12 - (-3) =$ ______	______
3	$-3 \cdot 3^2 =$ ______	______ − ______ = ______	$-15 - (-9) =$ ______
4	$-3 \cdot 4^2 =$ ______	______ − ______ = ______	______ $- (-15) =$ ______
5	$-3 \cdot 5^2 =$ ______	______ − ______ = ______	______ − ______ = ______

Ⓘ Is there a constant difference between x-values? yes/no

Are the first differences constant (the same)? yes/no

Are the second differences constant (the same)? yes/no

Reflect

1. **Discussion** When a table of values with constant x-values leads to constant y-values (*first* differences), what kind of function does that indicate? (linear/quadratic)

2. When a table of values with constant x-values leads to constant *second* differences, what kind of function does that indicate? (linear/quadratic)

Explain 1 Verify Quadratic Relationships Using Quadratic Regression

The second differences for $f(x) = x^2$, the parent quadratic function, are constant for values of y when the corresponding differences between x-values are constant. Now, do the reverse. For a given set of data, verify that the second differences are constant and then use a graphing calculator to find a quadratic model for the data. Enter the independent variable into List 1 and the dependent variable into List 2, and perform a **quadratic regression** on the data. When your calculator performs a quadratic regression, it uses a specific statistical method to fit a quadratic model to the data.

As with linear regression, the data will not be perfect. When finding a model, if the first differences are close but not exactly equal, a linear model will still be a good fit. Likewise, if the second differences aren't exactly the same, a quadratic model will be a good fit if the second differences are close to being the same.

Example 1 **Find a quadratic model for the given situation. Begin by creating a scatter plot of the given data on your graphing calculator, and then find the second differences to verify the data is quadratic. Finally, use a graphing calculator to perform a quadratic regression on the data and graph the regression equation on the scatter plot.**

Ⓐ A student is measuring the kinetic energy of a pickup truck as it is travels at various speeds. The speed is given in meters per second, and the kinetic energy is given in kilojoules. Use the given data to find a quadratic model for the data.

Speed x	Kinetic Energy $y = K(x)$	First Difference	Second Difference
20	410	______	______
25	640	230	______
30	922	282	52
35	1256	334	52
40	1640	384	50
45	2076	436	52
50	2563	487	51

Enter the data into a graphing calculator, placing the x-values into List 1 and the y-values into List 2.

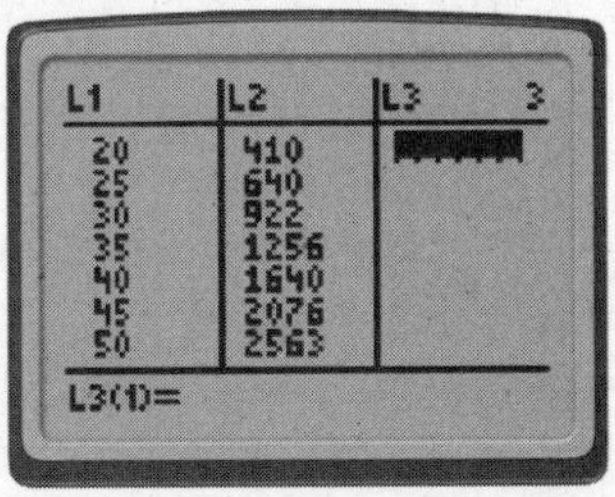

Next view a scatter plot of the data points. The calculator window shown is $15 < x < 55$ with an x-scale of 5 and $0 < y < 3000$ with a y-scale of 500.

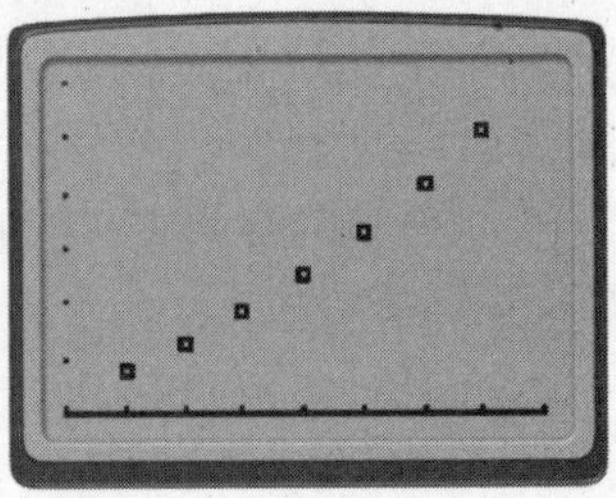

Next find the first and second differences and fill in the table.

The first difference of the first and second y-value is found by evaluating the expression below.

$K(25) - K(20)$

$640 - 410$

230

Find the next first difference in the same manner.

$K(30) - K(25)$

$922 - 640$

282

Find the rest of the first differences and fill in the table.

The first of the second differences is the difference between the values in the third and fourth rows of the first difference column.

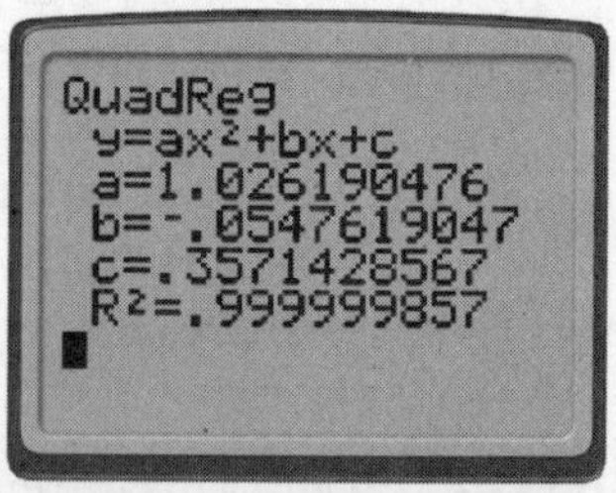

$282 - 230 = 52$

Find the rest of the second differences and fill in the rest of the table.

Notice that the second differences are very close to being constant.

Use a graphing calculator to find the equation for the quadratic regression. $y \approx 1.026x^2 - 0.0548x + 0.3571$

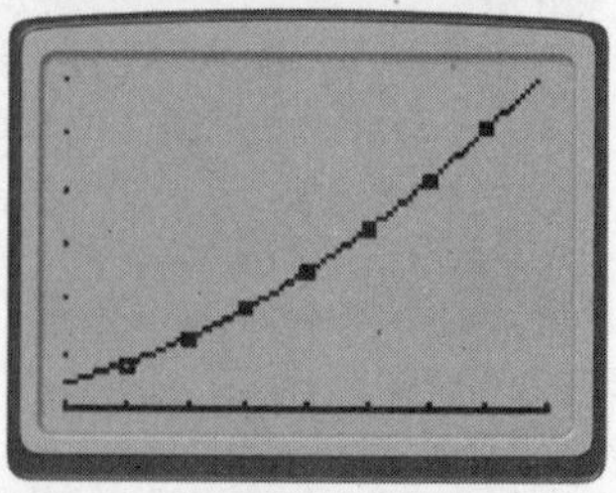

Note that the correlation coefficient is very close to 1, so the model is a good fit.

Plot the regression equation over the scatter plot.

(B) The table shows the speed of a car in meters per second as it accelerates from a stop at a constant rate, measured every 2 seconds.

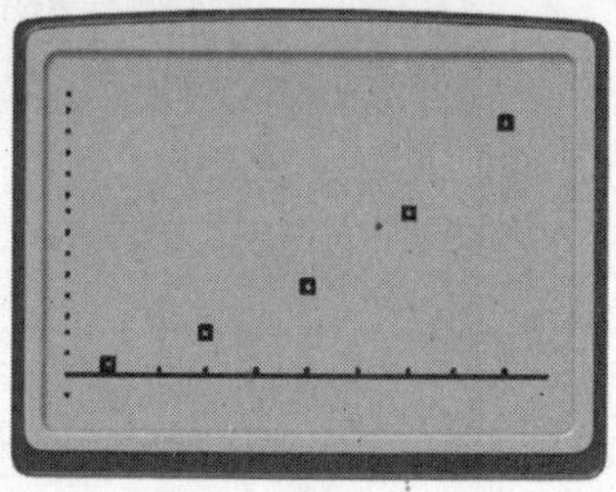

Time	2	4	6	8	10
Speed	5.1	20.4	45.8	81.2	126.1

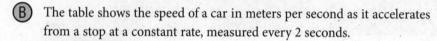

Create a scatter plot of the data using a graphing calculator.

Find the first and second differences and fill out the table.

Time x	Speed y	First Difference	Second Difference
2	5.1	______	______
4	20.4	☐	______
6	45.8	☐	☐
8	81.2	☐	☐
10	126.1	☐	☐

Find the regression equation using a graphing calculator. Report the results to 4 significant digits.

____

Based on the correlation coefficient, the model ____ a good fit.

Plot the regression equation over the scatter plot.

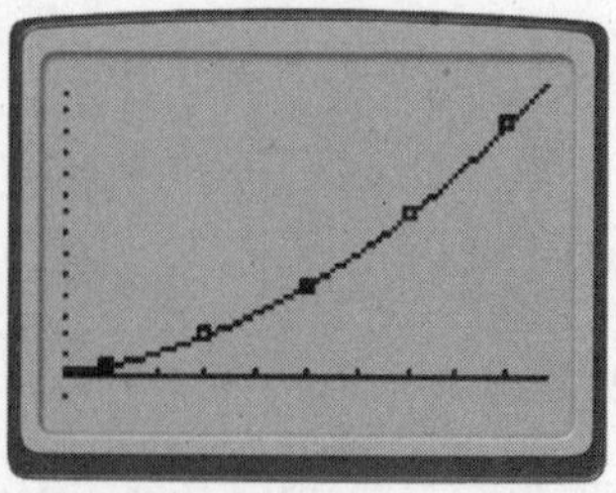

Reflect

3. **Discussion** Give examples of reasons why the second differences in real-world data won't necessarily be equal.

Your Turn

Find a quadratic model for the given situation. Begin by creating a scatter plot of the given data on your graphing calculator, and then find the second differences to verify the data is quadratic. Finally, use a graphing calculator to perform a quadratic regression on the data and graph the regression equation on the scatter plot.

4. The table shows the height of a soccer ball in feet for every half-second after a goalie dropkicks it.

Time	0.5	1.0	1.5	2.0	2.5	3.0	3.5
Height	54	104	142	173	195	208	216

5. A company that makes flying discs to use as promotional materials will produce a flying disc of any size. The table shows the cost of 100 flying discs based on the desired size.

Size	4	4.5	5	5.5	6	6.5	7
Cost	34.99	44.99	54.99	66.99	79.99	92.99	107.99

Explain 2 Using Quadratic Regression to Solve a Real-World Problem

After performing quadratic regression on a given data set, the regression equation can be used to answer questions about the scenario represented by the data.

Example 2 **Use a graphing calculator to perform quadratic regression on the data given. Then solve the problem and identify and interpret the domain and range of the function.**

(A) The height of a model rocket in feet *t* seconds after it is launched vertically is shown in the following table. Determine the maximum height the rocket attains.

Time	1	2	3	4	5	6	7	8
Height	342	667	902	1163	1335	1459	1584	1864

Enter the data into List 1 and List 2 of a graphing calculator and perform the quadratic regression.

Then plot the regression function over a scatter plot of the data.

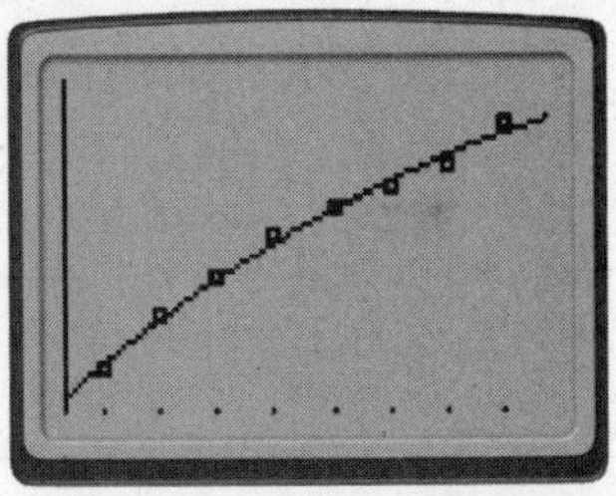

Increase the values of Xmax and Ymax until you can see the maximum value of the function. Then use the maximum function on your graphing calculator to find the maximum height of the rocket.

The model rocket attains a maximum height of approximately 2150 feet 13.5 seconds after launch.

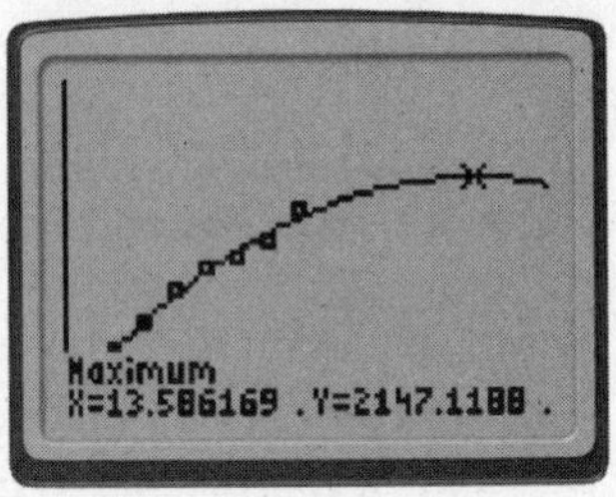

The domain of the function will be $0 \leq t \leq +\infty$. Because the independent variable is time, it doesn't make sense to consider negative time.

The range of the function is $0 \leq y \leq 2150$ because the height of the rocket should never be negative and it will not go higher than its maximum height.

(B) When a rock is thrown into a pond, it makes a series of circular waves. The area enclosed by the first wave is recorded every second and is shown in the table below. If the rock lands 15 meters from shore, when will the first wave reach the shoreline?

Time	1	2	3	4	5	6
Area	9.0	35.8	79.8	145.2	225.1	319.1

Enter the values into List 1 and List 2 of a graphing calculator and use ____________ or ____________ to find the model.

$y \approx$ [ ] $x^2 +$ [ ] $x +$ [ ] $\quad R^2 \approx$ [ ]

$y \approx$ [ ]

Based on the value of R^2, this function ________ a close fit for the data.

The area enclosed by the wave is a circle, so the wave will reach the shore when the ________ of the wave is ________ meters.

The area of a circle is given by $A = \pi r^2$.

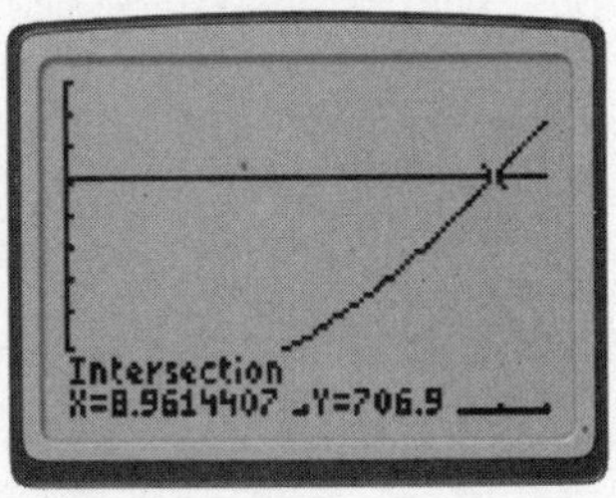

$A = \pi r^2$

$= \pi$ [ ]^2 $=$ [ ] $\pi \cong$ [ ]

Plot the regression equation as Y_2 and let $Y_2 =$ [ ].

Find the ____________ of the two lines.

The model intersects the line $y = 706.9$ at $x =$ ☐. The first wave will reach the shoreline in ________.

The function only makes sense while the wave is still ________. Once it reaches ________, the wave will no longer increase in size in the same way. Therefore, the domain of the function is ________ and the range is ________.

Your Turn

Use a graphing calculator to perform quadratic regression on the data given. Then solve the problem and identify and interpret the domain and range of the function.

6. A company needs boxes to package the goods it produces. One product has a standard shape and thickness but comes in a variety of sizes. The sizes are given as integers. The costs of the various sizes in cents are shown in the table. When the packaging cost reaches $2.00, the company will need to add a surcharge. What is the first size that will have the surcharge added?

Size	1	2	3	4	5	6	7
Cost	7.1	13.8	20.1	29.3	50.1	62.3	86.9

7. A company sells simple circular wall clocks in a variety of sizes. The production cost of each clock is dependent on the diameter of the clock in inches. The costs of making several sizes of clocks in dollars are given in the table. How big would a clock be that costs $4.00 to make? (Round to the nearest eighth.)

Size	8	$8\frac{1}{2}$	9	$9\frac{3}{8}$	$9\frac{1}{2}$	10	12
Cost	1.07	1.16	1.30	1.32	1.36	1.53	2.23

Elaborate

8. Are there any limitations to identifying data that can be modeled by a quadratic function using the method of second differences?

____

____

9. A function modeling a situation can be represented as both a function and a graph. Identify some situations where one representation is more helpful than the other.

____

____

____

____

10. Essential Question Check-In When using technology to create a regression model, name two methods for judging the fit of the regression equation.

____

____

____

Evaluate: Homework and Practice

Personal Math Trainer
- Online Homework
- Hints and Help
- Extra Practice

Determine if the function represented in the table is quadratic by finding the second differences.

1.

x	$f(x)$	First Difference	Second Difference
1	2	________	________
2	4		________
3	8		
4	16		
5	32		
6	64		

The function ________ quadratic.

2.

x	$f(x)$	First Difference	Second Difference
1	3	________	________
2	12		________
3	27		
4	48		
5	75		
6	108		

The function ________ quadratic.

3.

x	$f(x)$	First Difference	Second Difference
1	9	________	________
2	13		________
3	17		
4	21		
5	25		
6	29		

The function ________ quadratic.

4.

x	$f(x)$	First Difference	Second Difference
1	2	________	________
2	18		________
3	48		
4	92		
5	150		
6	222		

The function ________ quadratic.

Find the second differences of the given data to verify that the relationship will be quadratic. Then use a graphing calculator to find the quadratic regression equation and R^2 with a precision of 4 digits.

5.

x	1	7	13	19	25	31	37	43	49	55	61	67
y	93	107	125	148	174	203	237	274	316	361	410	462

6.

x	8	11.4	14.8	18.2	21.6	25	28.4	31.8	35.2	38.6	42	45.4
y	24	60	106	161	227	302	387	483	588	703	827	962

7.

x	3.6	17.9	32.2	46.5	60.8	75.1	89.4	103.7	118	132.3	146.6	160.9
y	1946	1684	1442	1219	1012	821	648	494	357	237	133	44

8.

x	9	9.2	9.4	9.6	9.8	10	10.2	10.4	10.6	10.8	11	11.2
y	44	465	844	1180	1475	1728	1941	2117	2255	2355	2409	2416

9.

x	17	20.1	23.2	26.4	29.5	32.7	35.8	38.9	42.1	45.2	48.4	51.5
y	1000	995	974	936	882	814	729	627	510	376	225	58

Find a quadratic model for the given situation. Begin by creating a scatter plot of the given data on your graphing calculator, and then find the second differences to verify the data is quadratic. Finally, use a graphing calculator to perform a quadratic regression on the data.

10. The table shows the height of an arrow in feet x seconds after being released toward a target down range by an archery student.

Time	0.25	0.5	0.75	1.0	1.25	1.5	1.75
Height	12.0	23.7	32.5	39.3	44.6	47.5	47.8

11. The table shows the cost of cleaning a lap pool based on the number of lanes it has.

Number of Lanes	6	8	10	12	14	16
Cleaning Cost	30	95	263	518	875	1299

Use a graphing calculator to find a quadratic model for the given data.

12.

x	2.9	3.9	4.7	5.6	6.9	7.7	8.5
y	8	14	23	29	40	53	70

13.

x	4.7	6.7	8.5	10.1	12.8	14.3	15.9
y	32	17	−27	−94	−193	−321	−499

14.

x	−2.7	−1.9	−0.9	0	0.9	1.9	2.7
y	−13	−8	−6	−4	−5	−8	−13

Use a graphing calculator to perform quadratic regression on the given data. Then solve the problem and identify and interpret the domain and range of the function.

15. The revenue of a company based on the price of its product is in the table below. How much should the company sell the product for to maximize revenue?

Price	1	2	2.75	4	4.5	6	8	8.4	9
Revenue	90	228	303	384	406	396	282	229	135

16. A scuba diver brought an air-filled balloon 150 feet underwater to the bottom of a lake. The diver conducts an experiment to measure the surface area of the balloon while ascending back to the surface. The results of the measurements are shown in the table. How far will the balloon have risen when it has doubled in surface area?

Distance from Bottom	0	20	40	60	80	100	120
Surface Area	28.6	32.2	35.4	39.5	45.0	52.8	65.4

17. The height of a ski jumper with respect to the low point of the ramp in meters is measured every 0.3 seconds. The results are given in the table. If the skier lands at a point 30 meters below the reference point, how long was the skier in the air?

Time	0.3	0.6	0.9	1.2	1.5	1.8	2.1	2.4
Height	11.2	14.06	16.32	18.47	19.48	20.52	21.01	21.01

H.O.T. Focus on Higher Order Thinking

Use the table for Exercises 18 and 19.

x	1	1.25	1.5	1.75	2	3	4	5	6	7	8	9
y	2	2.378	2.828	3.364	4	8	16	32	64	128	256	512

18. What If? If you perform a quadratic regression on the data, will the value of R^2 be close to 1? Justify your answer.

19. Communicate Mathematical Ideas Perform a quadratic regression on the data; then perform a quadratic regression using only the first four data points. Explain the difference in R^2 values between the two models.

20. Multi-Part A trebuchet is a catapult that was used in the Middle Ages to hurl projectiles during a siege. It is now used in various regions of the United States to throw pumpkins. Teams build trebuchets to compete to see who can throw a pumpkin the farthest. On the practice field, one team has measured the height of its pumpkin after it is launched at 1-second intervals. The results are displayed in the table below.

Time	1	2	3	4	5	6	7	8
Height	152	265	377	441	470	450	396	342

a. Find a quadratic function that models the data.

b. Determine the flight time of the pumpkin.

c. If the pumpkin travels horizontally at a speed of 120 feet per second, how far does it travel before it hits the ground?

d. At the official competition, the trebuchet is situated on a slight rise 10 feet above the targeting area. How far will the pumpkin travel in the competition, assuming the height relative to the base of the trebuchet is modeled by the same function and it moves with the same horizontal speed?

Lesson Performance Task

A student stands at the top of a lighthouse that is 200 feet tall. The base of the lighthouse is an additional 300 feet above the ocean below, and the student has a clear shot to the water below to examine the claims made by Galileo. But, this being the 21st century, the student also has a sophisticated laser tracker that continually tracks the exact height of the dropped object from the ground as well as the length of time elapsed from the drop. At the end of the trial, the student gets sample data in the form of a table.

Time	Height above Ground
0	200
0.5	196
1	184
1.5	164
2	136
2.5	100
3	56
3.5	4
4	−56
4.5	−124
5	−200

Examine the data and determine the relationship between time and height. Then find the function that models the data. (Hint: Negative values represent when the object passes the base of the lighthouse.)

Name ______________________ Class ______________ Date ________

10.5 Comparing Linear, Exponential, and Quadratic Models

Resource Locker

Essential Question: How can you determine whether a given data set is best modeled by a linear, quadratic, or exponential function?

Explore — Exploring End Behavior of Linear, Quadratic, and Exponential Functions

Recall that you learned to characterize the end behavior of a function by recognizing what the behavior of the function is as x approaches positive or negative infinity. Look at the three graphs to see what the function does as x approaches infinity or negative infinity.

Linear	Quadratic	Exponential
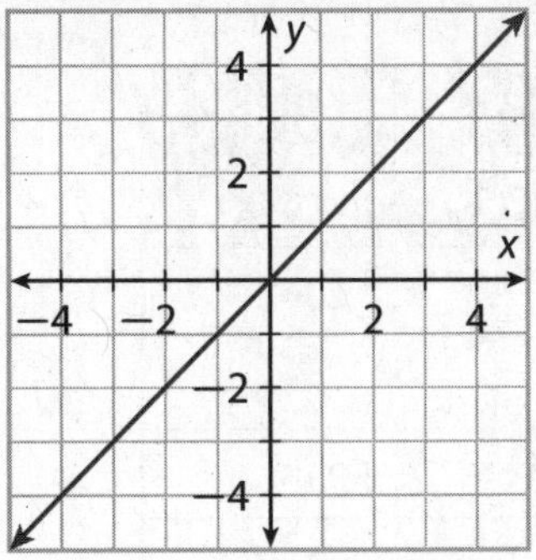	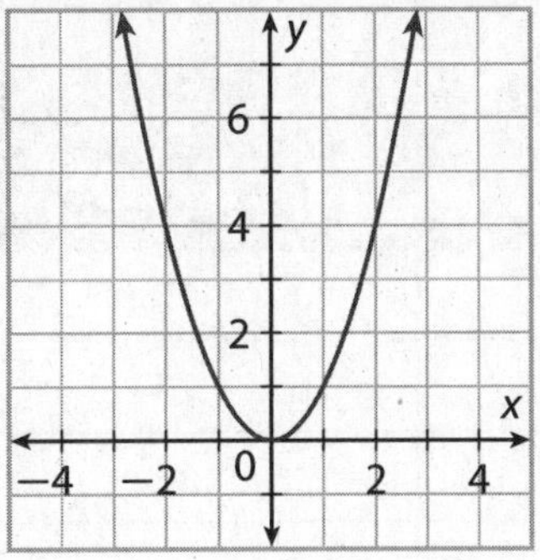	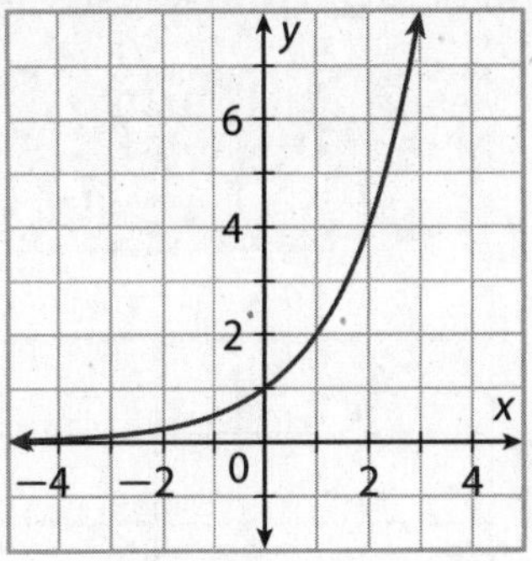

(A) For the linear function, $f(x)$, as x approaches infinity, $f(x)$ ______________, and as x approaches negative infinity, $f(x)$ ______________.

(B) For the quadratic function, $g(x)$, as x approaches infinity, $g(x)$ ______________, and as x approaches negative infinity, $g(x)$ ______________.

(C) For the exponential function, $h(x)$, as x approaches infinity, $h(x)$ ______________, and as x approaches negative infinity, $h(x)$ ______________.

Examine the end behavior and the rate of the change of the three function types by filling in the values of the table.

(D) Fill in the missing values of the table.

	Linear	Quadratic	Exponential
x	$L(x) = 5x - 2$	$Q(x) = 5x^2 - 2$	$E(x) = 5^x - 2$
1	3	3	3
2	8	18	
3	13	43	123
4		78	623
5	23		3123
6	28	178	15,623
7	33	243	
8	38	318	390,623

(E) Use first differences to find the growth rate over each interval and determine which function ultimately grows fastest.

	Linear	Quadratic	Exponential
x	$L(x+1) - L(x)$	$Q(x+1) - Q(x)$	$E(x+1) - E(x)$
1	5	15	20
2	5	25	
3		35	500
4	5		2500
5	5	55	

(F) The fastest growing function of the three is the ___________.

Reflect

1. What is the end behavior of $y = 7x + 12$?

____

____

2. What is the end behavior of $y = 5x^2 + x + 2$?

____

____

3. What is the end behavior of $y = 3^x - 5$?

____

____

4. Make a Conjecture Does an increasing exponential function always grow faster than an increasing quadratic function? Will the growth rate of an increasing exponential function eventually exceed that of an increasing quadratic function?

Explain 1 Justifying a Quadratic Model as More Appropriate Than a Linear Model

The first step in modeling data is selecting an appropriate functional form. If you are trying to decide between a quadratic and a linear model, for example, you may compare interval rates of change or the end behavior. First and second differences are useful for identifying linear and quadratic functions if the data points have equally spaced x-values.

Example 1 **Examine the data sets provided and determine whether a quadratic or linear model is more appropriate by examining the graph, the end behavior, and the first and second differences.**

(A)

x	$f(x)$
0	3
1	1.5
2	1
3	1.5
4	3
5	5.5
6	9

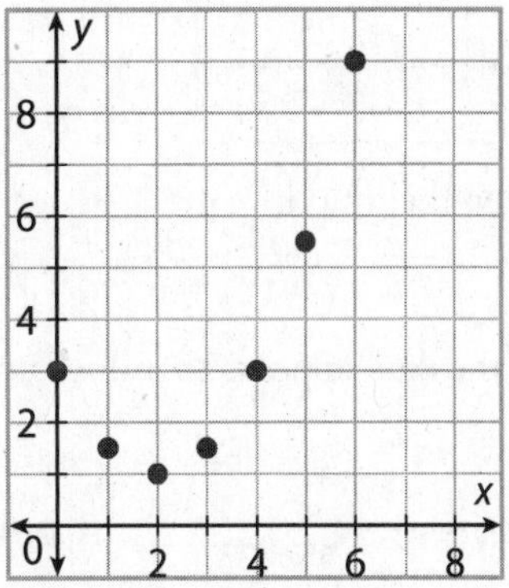

Shape:

The graph of the data appears to follow a curved path that starts downward and turns back upward.

End Behavior:

The path appears to increase without end as x approaches infinity and to increase without end as x approaches negative infinity.

Based on the apparent curvature and end behavior, the function is quadratic.

Interval Behavior:

x	$f(x)$	First Difference	Second Difference
0	3	______	______
1	1.5	−1.5	______
2	1	−0.5	1
3	1.5	0.5	1
4	3	1.5	1
5	5.5	2.5	1
6	9	3.5	1

The first differences increase as x increases, while the second differences are constant, which is characteristic of a quadratic function.

(B)

x	$f(x)$
0	8
1	6.75
2	5
3	2.75
4	0
5	−3.25
6	−7

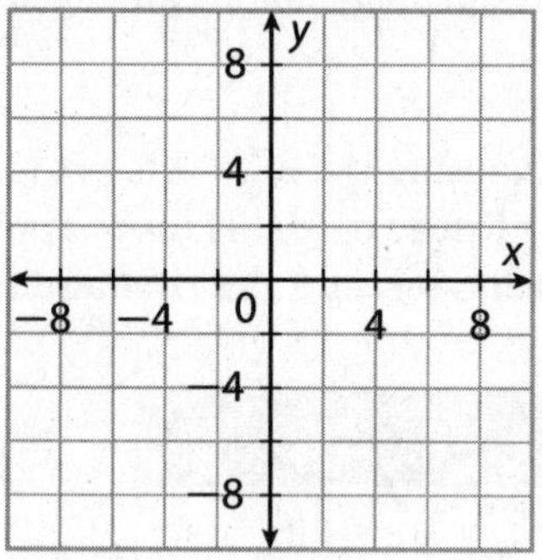

Plot the data on the graph.

Shape:

The graph of the data appears to follow a curved | straight, downward | upward path.

End Behavior:

The path appears to ______ as x increases and to ______ as x decreases.

The curvature is more consistent with a quadratic than a line, but the apparent end behavior is not. Fill in the first and second differences to discuss internal behavior.

Interval Behavior:

x	$f(x)$	First Differences	Second Differences
0	8	______	______
1	6.75	−1.25	______
2	5		
3	2.75		
4	0		
5	−3.25		
6	−7		

The absolute values of the first differences ______ as x increases, while the second differences are constant, which is characteristic of a quadratic function.

Reflect

5. Was the end behavior helpful in determining that the function in Example 1B was a quadratic? Explain.

6. **Discussion** Can you always tell that a function is quadratic by looking at a graph of it?

Your Turn

7.

x	$f(x)$
0	−4
1	−3.8
2	−3.2
3	−2.2
4	−0.8
5	1
6	3.2

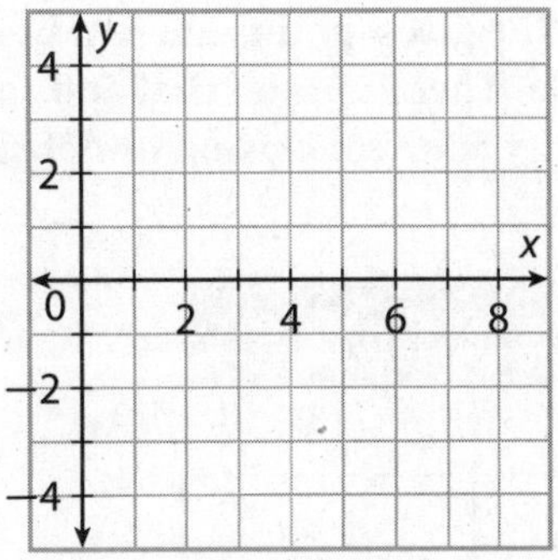

Examine the data set and determine whether a quadratic or linear model is more appropriate by examining the graph, the end behavior, and the first and second differences.

x	$f(x)$	First Difference	Second Difference
0	−4	______	______
1	−3.8		______
2	−3.2		
3	−2.2		
4	−0.8		
5	1		
6	3.2		

Explain 2 Justifying a Quadratic Model as More Appropriate Than an Exponential Model

Previously, you learned to model data with an exponential function. How do you choose between a quadratic and an exponential function to model a given set of data? Graph the given data points and compare the trend of the data with the general shape and end behavior of the parent quadratic and exponential functions. Use the results to decide if the function appears to be quadratic or exponential. Then examine the first and second differences and the ratios of the function using the function values corresponding to x-values separated by a constant amount.

Properties of $f(x) = x^2$ and $g(x) = b^x$		
	$f(x) = x^2$	$g(x) = b^x$ with $b > 1$
End behavior as:		
x approaches infinity	$f(x)$ approaches infinity	$g(x)$ approaches infinity
x approaches negative infinity	$f(x)$ approaches infinity	$g(x)$ approaches zero

Example 2 **Determine if the function represented in the given table is quadratic or exponential. Plot the given points and analyze the graph. Draw a conclusion if possible. Then find the first and second differences and ratios and either verify your conclusion or determine the family of the function.**

(A)

x	$f(x)$
−3	3
−2	1.5
−1	1
0	1.5
1	3
2	5.5
3	9

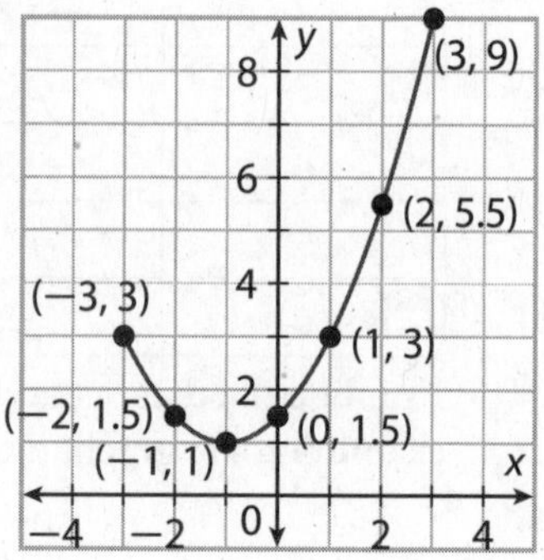

Graph $f(x)$ on the axes provided by plotting the given points and connecting them with a smooth curve.

The data appears to be parabolic.

Also, as x approaches infinity, $f(x)$ appears to increase without end, and as x approaches negative infinity, $f(x)$ appears to increase without end.

It appears that $f(x)$ is a quadratic function.

Now find the first and second differences and the ratio of the values of $f(x)$.

x	$f(x)$	First Difference	Second Difference	Ratio
−3	3	______	______	______
−2	1.5	−1.5	______	0.5
−1	1	−0.5	1	0.67
0	1.5	0.5	1	1.5
1	3	1.5	1	2
2	5.5	2.5	1	1.83
3	9	3.5	1	1.64

The second differences are constant so the function is quadratic as predicted.

(B)

x	$f(x)$	First Difference	Second Difference	Ratio
−2	4	______	______	______
0	3.5		______	
2	2			
4	−0.5			
6	−4			
8	−8.5			

Graph $f(x)$ on the axes provided by plotting the given points and connecting them with a smooth curve.

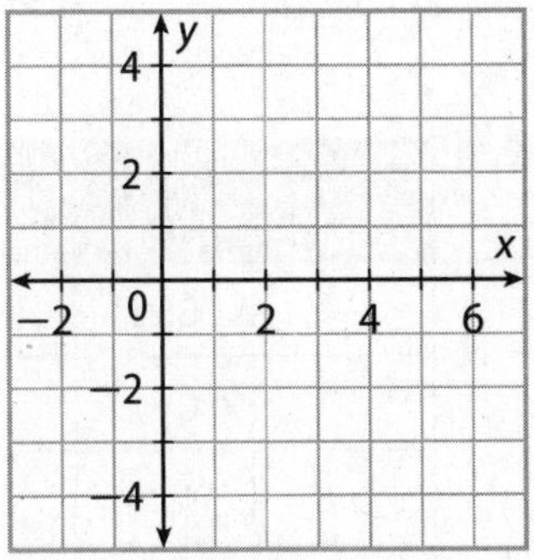

The data appears to be ______________________.

As x approaches infinity, $f(x)$ ______________________.

As x approaches negative infinity, $f(x)$ ______________________.

It appears that $f(x)$ ______________________.

Now find the first and second differences and the ratio of the values of $f(x)$.

The ______________ are constant so the function is ______________.

Your Turn

Determine if the function represented in the given table is quadratic or exponential. Plot the given points and analyze the graph. Draw a conclusion if possible. Then find the first and second differences and ratios and either verify your conclusion or determine the family of the function.

8.

x	$f(x)$	First Difference	Second Difference	Ratio
−3	−5	______	______	______
−2	−3.11		______	
−1	−1.44			
0	0			
1	1.22			
2	2.22			
3	3			
4	3.56			
5	3.89			
6	4			

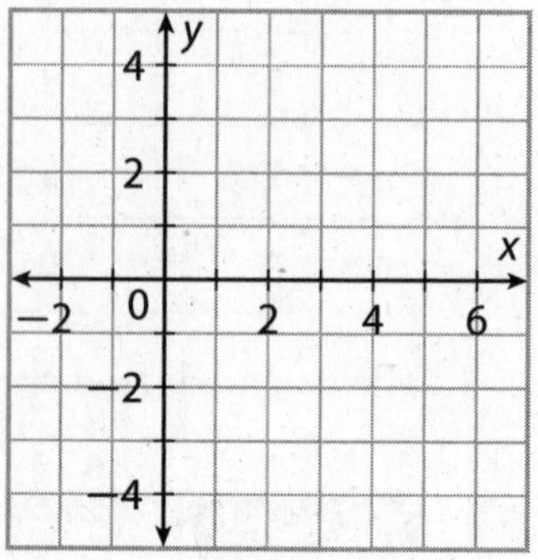

9.

x	$f(x)$	First Difference	Second Difference	Ratio
−2	8.25	______	______	______
0	6		______	
2	4.25			
4	3			
6	2.25			
8	2			

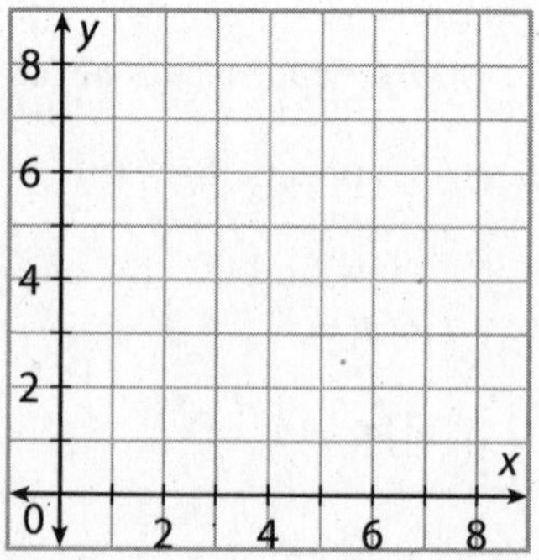

Explain 3 Selecting an Appropriate Model Given Linear, Exponential, or Quadratic Data

It is important to be able to choose among a variety of models when solving real-world problems.

Example 3 **Decide which type of function is best represented by each of the following data sets. Then perform the following steps:**

1. Graph the data on a scatterplot and draw a fit curve.
2. Identify which function the data appear to represent.
3. Predict the function's end behavior as x approaches infinity.
4. Use a function table to calculate the first differences, second differences, and ratios.
5. Perform the appropriate regression on a graphing calculator. Plot the regression line and data together to evaluate the fit of regression.
6. Answer any additional questions.

(A) **Demographics** The data table describes the average lifespan in the United States over time.

Year	Average Lifespan (years)
1900	47.3
1910	50.0
1920	54.1
1930	59.7
1940	62.9
1950	68.2
1960	69.7
1970	70.8
1980	73.1
1990	75.4

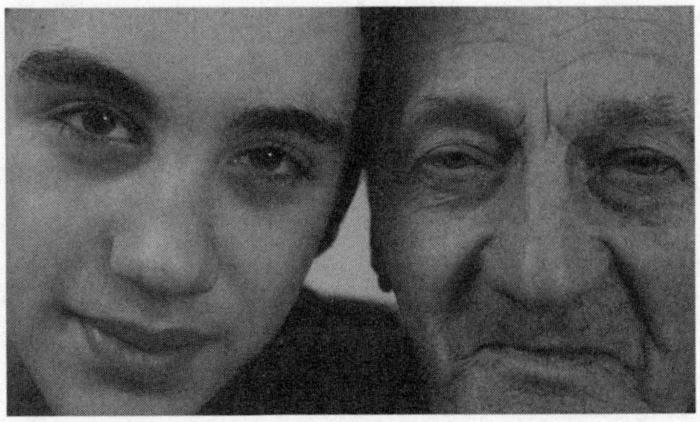

What will be the estimated average lifespan in 2000?

Graph the scatterplot and an approximate line of fit to determine the best function to use for this data set.

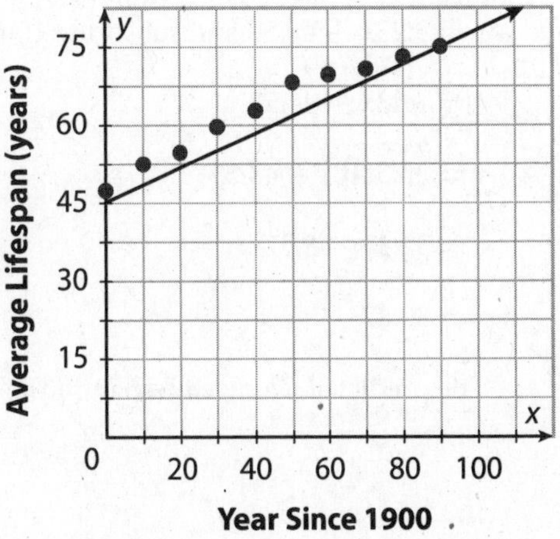

The data set appears to best fit a linear function.

The end behavior of the data is that as x approaches infinity, $f(x)$ approaches infinity.

Complete the function table for first differences, second differences, and ratios.

Year	Average Lifespan (years)	First Difference	Second Difference	Ratio
1900	47.3	______	______	______
1910	50.0	2.7	______	$\frac{50.0}{47.3} = 1.06$
1920	54.1	4.1	1.4	$\frac{54.1}{50.0} = 1.08$
1930	59.7	5.6	1.5	$\frac{59.7}{54.1} = 1.10$
1940	62.9	3.2	−2.4	$\frac{62.9}{59.7} = 1.05$
1950	68.2	5.3	2.1	$\frac{68.2}{62.9} = 1.08$
1960	69.7	1.5	−3.8	$\frac{69.7}{68.2} = 1.02$
1970	70.8	1.1	−0.4	$\frac{70.8}{69.7} = 1.02$
1980	73.1	2.3	1.2	$\frac{73.1}{70.8} = 1.03$
1990	75.4	2.3	0	$\frac{75.4}{73.1} = 1.03$

Since the ratios are dropping, it is possible that the data set can be modeled by an exponential regression. Since the average of the second differences is around 0, however, it is most likely that the data set should be modeled by a linear regression.

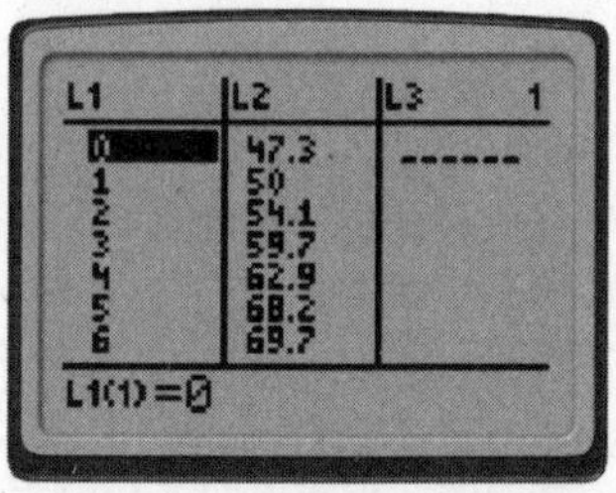

Perform the linear regression by first creating a data table by using the STAT function on a calculator. Use the numbers 0 through 9 to represent the years, starting with 0 for 1900.

Go to STAT, move over to CALC, type 4, and press ENTER to perform the regression.

Press ZOOM and 9 to fit the data. Plot the line from the regression to test its fit.

The linear regression is a good fit for the data set.

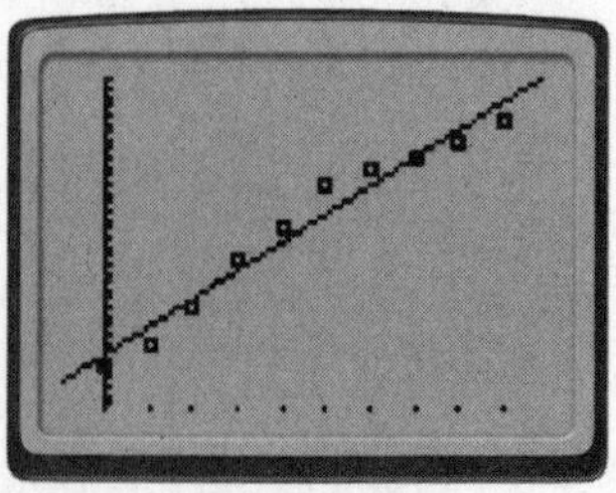

To find the estimated average lifespan in 2000, use the equation $y = 3.23x + 48.57$ and substitute 10 for x.

$y = 3.23x + 48.57$

$y = 3.23(10) + 48.57$

$= 32.3 + 48.57$

$= 80.87$

The predicted average lifespan in the year 2000 is 80.87 years.

(B) **Biology** The data table lists the whooping crane population over time.

Whooping Crane	
Year	**Population**
1940	22
1950	34
1960	33
1970	56
1980	76
1990	146
2000	177
2010	281

How many whooping cranes will exist in 2020?

Graph the scatterplot and an approximate line of fit to determine the best function to use for this data set.

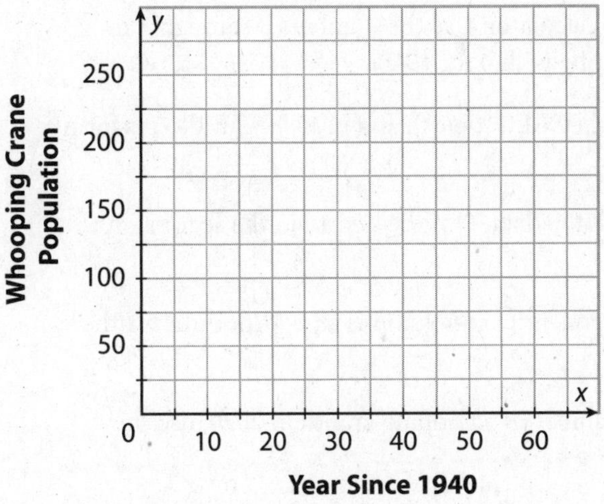

The data set appears to best fit an linear/quadratic/exponential function.

The end behavior of this data is that as x approaches infinity, $f(x)$, approaches infinity.

Complete the function table for first differences, second differences, and ratios.

Year	Population	First Difference	Second Difference	Ratio
1940	22	______	______	______
1950	34	12	______	$\frac{34}{22} = 1.55$
1960	33	−1	−13	
1970	56			
1980	76			
1990	146			
2000	177			
2010	281			

Since the ratios are changing/not changing and the second difference does/does not have an average that is close to 0, linear/quadratic/exponential regression should be used.

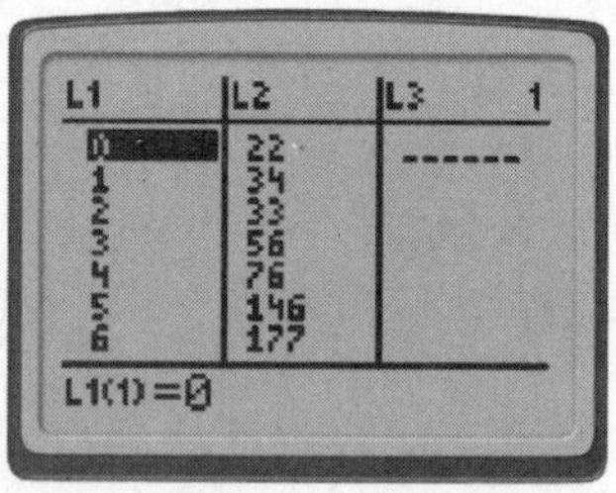

Perform the exponential regression by first creating a data table by using the STAT function on a calculator. Use the numbers 0 through 7 to represent the years, starting with 0 for 1940.

Go to STAT, move over to CALC, type 0, and press ENTER to perform the regression.

Press ZOOM and 9 to fit the data. Plot the line from the regression to test its fit.

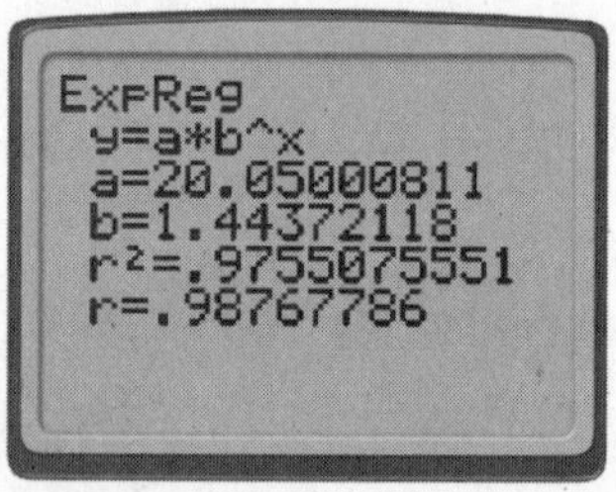

The linear/quadratic/exponential regression is a good/poor fit for the data set.

To find the estimated number of whooping cranes in 2020, use the

equation $y =$ [ ] and substitute ______ for x.

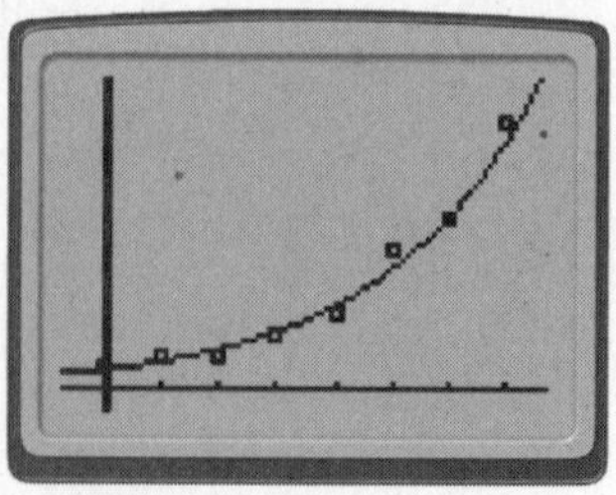

$y =$ [ ]

$y =$ [ ]

$=$ [ ]

$=$ [ ]

Since it is unrealistic to round up in this situation, the number of whooping cranes in 2020 will be ______.

Your Turn

Decide which type of function is best represented by each of the following data sets. Then perform the following steps:

1. Graph the data on a scatterplot and draw a fit curve.
2. Identify which function the data appear to represent.
3. Predict the function's end behavior as x approaches infinity.
4. Use a function table to calculate the first differences, second differences, and ratios.
5. Perform the appropriate regression on a graphing calculator. Plot the regression line and data together to evaluate the fit of regression.
6. Answer any additional questions.

10. Population The data table describes the percentage of people living in central cities in the United States over time. What percentage of people were living in central cities in the United States in 2000?

Year	% of People
1910	21.2
1920	24.2
1930	30.8
1940	32.5
1950	32.8
1960	32.3
1970	31.4
1980	30.0

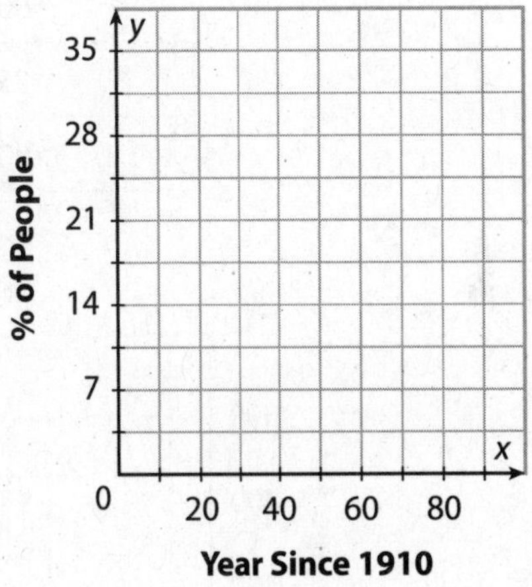

11. Automobiles The data table describes the car weight versus horsepower for automobiles produced in 2012. If a car weighed 6500 pounds in 2012, how much horsepower should the car have?

Car Weight (pounds)	Horsepower in 2012
2000	70
2500	105
3000	145
3500	179
4000	259
4500	338
5000	400
5500	557
6000	556

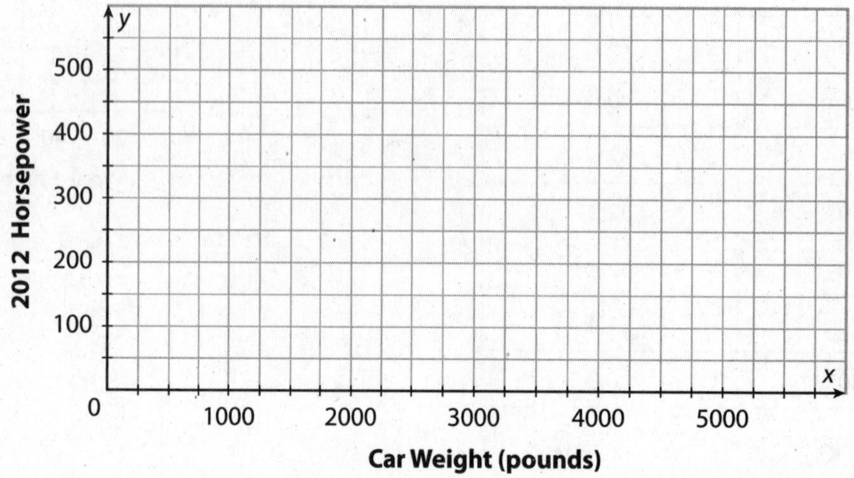

Elaborate

12. In general, what are three possible end behaviors of exponential, linear, and quadratic graphs as x increases without bound? When do these end behaviors occur?

13. What do function tables tell you that graphs don't? How can this information be used to help you select a model?

14. When does a graph help determine an appropriate model better than examining first and second differences and ratios?

15. Can two different models be created that represent the same set of data?

16. **Essential Question Check-In** How can a graph be used to determine whether a given data set is best modeled by a linear, quadratic, or exponential function?

Evaluate: Homework and Practice

Personal Math Trainer
- Online Homework
- Hints and Help
- Extra Practice

1. For the two function $f(x) = 2x + 1$ and $g(x) = 2^x + 1$ which function has the greatest average rate of change over the interval from 0 to 1? What about the interval from 2 to 3?

2. Plot the data and describe the observed shape and end behavior. Does it appear linear or quadratic? Calculate first and second differences and identify the type of function.

x	$f(x)$	First Difference	Second Difference
0	−0.79		
1	2.81		
2	4.41		
3	4.01		
4	1.61		
5	−2.79		

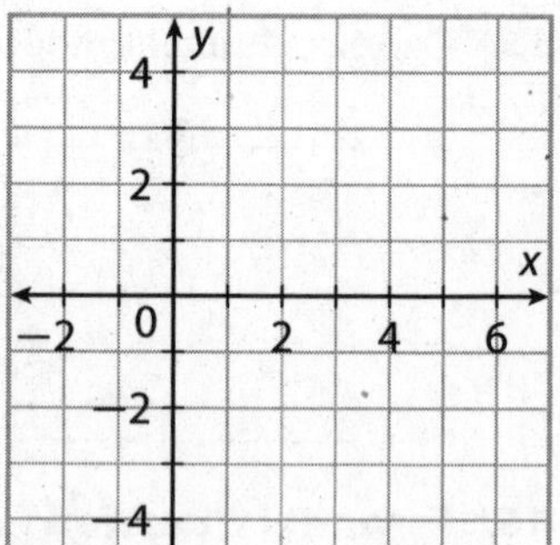

3. Plot the data that fits on the grid and describe the observed shape and end behavior. Does it appear to be linear or quadratic? Calculate first and second differences and identify the type of function.

x	$f(x)$	First Difference	Second Difference
−2	−4	______	______
−1	−3.3		______
0	−1.2		
1	2.3		
2	7.2		
3	13.5		

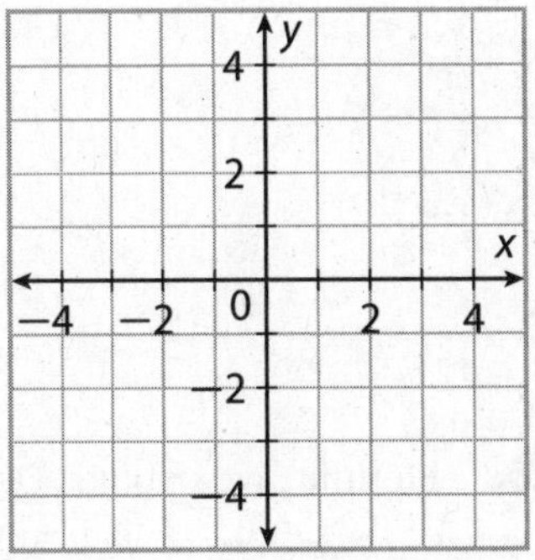

4. Plot the data on the grid and describe the observed shape and end behavior. Does it appear linear or quadratic? Calculate first and second differences and identify the type of function.

x	$f(x)$	First Difference	Second Difference
0	7.6	______	______
1	6.25		______
2	4.6		
3	2.65		
4	0.4		

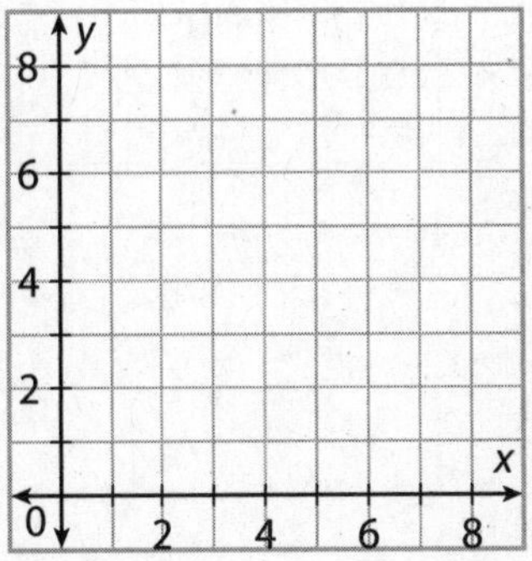

5. Plot the data and describe the observed the shape and end behavior. Does it appear linear or quadratic Calculate first and second differences and identify the type of function?

x	f(x)	First Difference	Second Difference
1	−7.2	______	______
2	−3.8		______
3	0		
4	4.2		
5	8.8		

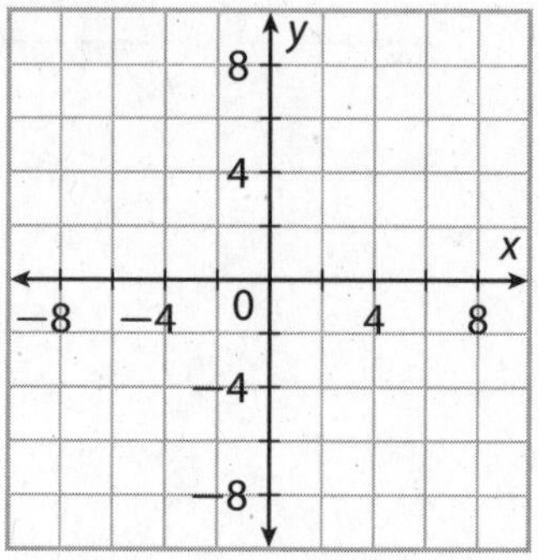

6. Plot the given points. Describe the general shape and end behavior of the graph. Draw a conclusion about the function, if possible. Then complete the table and use the differences to to verify your conclusions.

x	f(x)	First Difference	Second Difference	Ratio
−2	−5.75	______	______	______
0	1		______	
2	6.25			
4	10			
6	12.25			
8	13			
10	12.25			
12	10			
14	6.25			

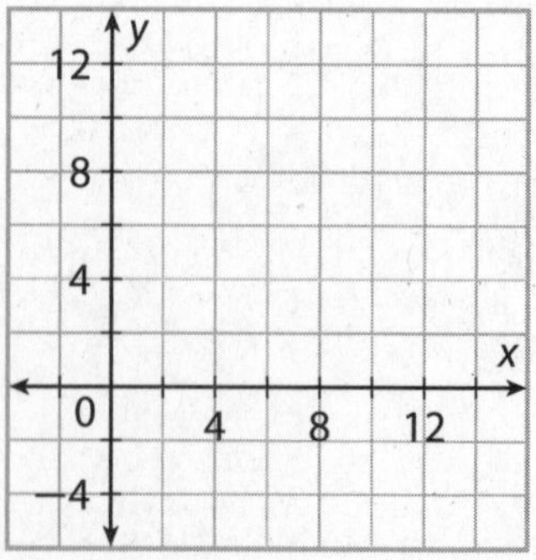

7. Plot the given points. Describe the general shape and end behavior of the graph. Draw a conclusion about the function, if possible. Then complete the table and use the differences to to verify your conclusions.

x	$f(x)$	First Difference	Second Difference	Ratio
−2	9	______	______	______
0	5.5		______	
2	3			
4	1.5			
6	1			

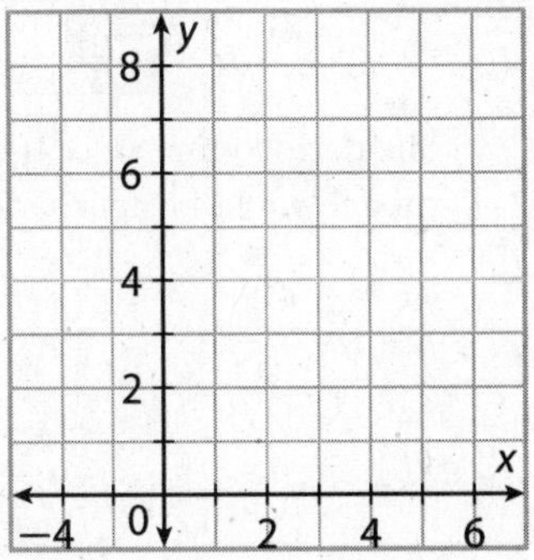

8. Plot the given points. Describe the general shape and end behavior of the graph. Draw a conclusion about the function, if possible. Then complete the table and use the differences to to verify your conclusions.

x	$f(x)$	First Difference	Second Difference	Ratio
−5	−3	______	______	______
−2	−2		______	
1	1			
4	6			
7	13			

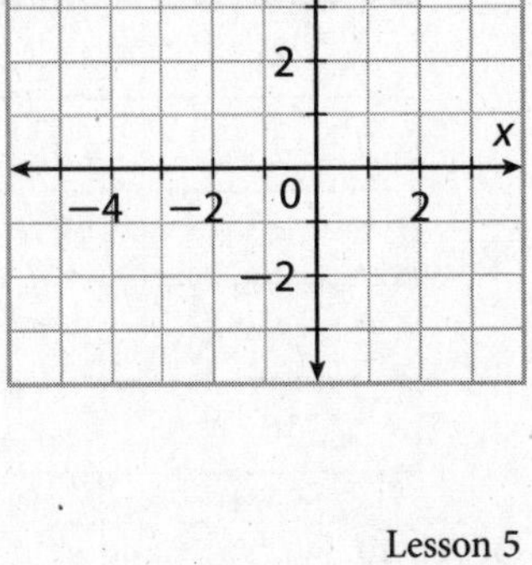

H.O.T. Focus on Higher Order Thinking

9. Critical Thinking A set of data was modeled by using the quadratic, linear, and exponential forms of regression. Nearly identical statistically significant r^2-values were produced in all three situations. Which type of regression model should be used? Explain.

10. Explain the Error To determine if the data represents a linear model, Louise looked at the difference in y-values: 110, 110, 110, 110.

x	7	9	12	14	18
y	150	260	370	480	590

She decided that since the differences between the y-values are all the same, a linear model would be appropriate. Explain her mistake.

11. Critical Thinking Suppose that the following r-values were produced from an unknown set of data.

r-values		
Linear	**Quadratic**	**Exponential**
0.15	0.11	0.13

What type of regression model should be chosen for this data set? Explain.

Lesson Performance Task

The table shows general guidelines for the weight of a Great Dane at various ages. Create a function modeling the ideal weight for a Great Dane at any age. Justify your choice of models. How well do you think your model will do when the puppy is one or two years old?

Age (months)	Weight (kg)
2	12
4	23
6	33
8	40
10	45

STUDY GUIDE REVIEW

Linear, Exponential, and Quadratic Models

MODULE 10

Essential Question: How can you use linear, exponential, and quadratic models to solve real-world problems?

Key Vocabulary
correlation *(correlación)*
exponential function *(función exponencial)*
exponential regression *(regresión exponencial)*
line of best fit *(línea de mejor ajuste)*
linear regression *(regresión lineal)*
quadratic regression *(regresión cuadrática)*

KEY EXAMPLE (Lesson 10.3)

A comic book is sold for \$3, and its value increases by 6% each year after it is sold. Write an exponential growth function to find the value of the comic book in 25 years.

Write the exponential growth function for this situation.

$y = a(1 + r)^t$

$= 3(1 + 0.06)^t$

$= 3(1.06)^t$

Find the value in 25 years.

$y = 3(1.06)^t$

$= 3(1.06)^{25}$

≈ 12.88

After 25 years, the comic book will be worth approximately \$12.88.

KEY EXAMPLE (Lesson 10.4)

Find the second differences of the given data to verify that the relationship will be quadratic. Use a graphing calculator to find the quadratic regression equation for the data and R^2 to 4 significant digits.

The table below shows the cost of shipping a box that has a volume of x cubic feet.

Volume	Cost (\$)	First Difference	Second Difference
1	\$6.15		
2	\$8.00	$8 - 6.15 = 1.85$	
3	\$13.90	$13.9 - 8 = 5.9$	$5.9 - 1.85 = 4.05$
4	\$23.75	$23.75 - 13.9 = 9.85$	$9.85 - 5.9 = 3.95$
5	\$38.25	$38.25 - 23.75 = 14.5$	$14.5 - 9.85 = 4.65$

$a \approx 2.09$

$b \approx -4.54$

$c \approx 8.65$

$R^2 \approx 0.9999$

The second differences are close to being constant. Plug the volumes, as the x-values, and the costs, as the y-values, into the graphing calculator and run a quadratic regression.

The quadratic regression equation is $y \approx 2.09x^2 - 4.54x + 8.65$.

EXERCISES

State whether each situation is best represented by an exponential or linear function. Then write an exponential or linear function for the model and state whether the model is increasing or decreasing. *(Lessons 10.1, 10.3)*

1. A customer borrows $950 at 6% interest compounded annually.

2. The population of a town is 8548 people and decreases by 90 people each year.

3. The table below shows the height of a baseball in inches x seconds after it was thrown. Fill in the table with the first differences and second differences. Then, use a graphing calculator to find the quadratic regression equation for the data. *(Lesson 10.4)*

Time	Height	First Difference	Second Difference
0	60		
0.25	59		
0.5	57		
0.75	52		
1	44		
1.25	35		

MODULE PERFORMANCE TASK

What Model Fits a Survivorship Curve?

A survivorship curve shows the number of surviving members of a population over time from a given set of births. The graph shows the three types of survivorship curves that commonly occur. Which types of functions would appear to best model each type of curve?

The data table presents the results of a survivorship study for a population of 1000 goats. What type of survivorship curve most closely matches the goat data? Can you find a good mathematical model for these data, using either a linear, quadratic, or exponential function, or a combination?

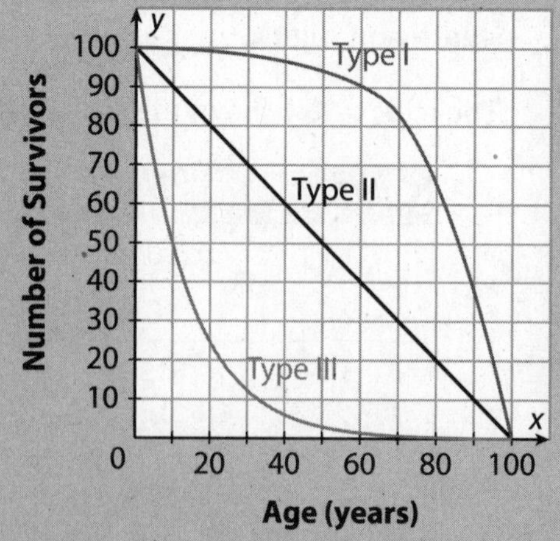

Age (years)	1	2	3	4	5	6	7	8	9	10
Number of Deaths During Year	12	13	9	11	12	11	9	11	11	11
Age (years)	**11**	**12**	**13**	**14**	**15**	**16**	**17**	**18**	**19**	**20**
Number of Deaths During Year	28	14	46	62	52	92	101	133	159	203

Ready to Go On?

10.1–10.5 Linear, Exponential, and Quadratic Models

Personal Math Trainer
- Online Homework
- Hints and Help
- Extra Practice

1. The table shows numbers of books read by students in an English class over a summer and the students' grades for the following semester.

Books	0	0	0	0	1	1	1	2	2	3	5	8	10	14	20
Grade	64	68	69	72	71	74	76	75	79	85	86	91	94	99	98

Find an equation for the line of best fit. Calculate and interpret the correlation coefficient. Then use your equation to predict the grade of a student who read 7 books. *(Lesson 10.1)*

2. The height of a plant, in inches, x weeks after it was planted is given in the table below. Use a graphing calculator to write a quadratic regression equation for the data set given. About how many weeks did it take the plant to reach a height of 40 inches? *(Lesson 10.4)*

Weeks	5	10	15	20	25
Height	15	31	55	87	127

3. Graph the data represented in the given table. Determine if the function represented in the given table is best represented by a linear, exponential, or quadratic function. Explain your answer. *(Lesson 10.5)*

x	−3	−2	−1	0	1	2	3
$f(x)$	5.5	3.5	1.5	1	0.6	0.3	0.1

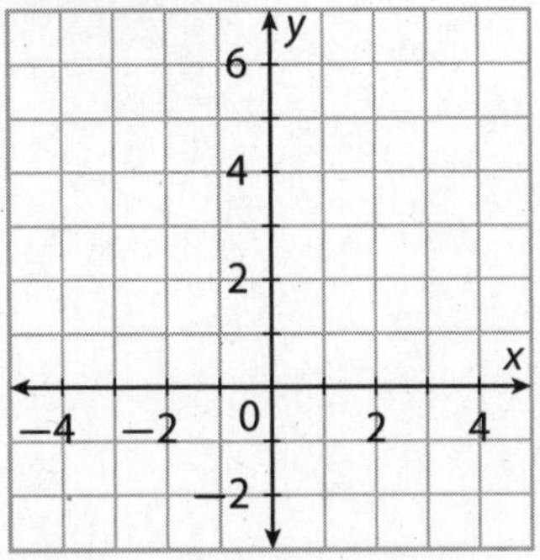

ESSENTIAL QUESTION

4. How can you determine if a function is linear, quadratic, or exponential?

MODULE 10
MIXED REVIEW

Assessment Readiness

1. Consider each data set and if it is best represented by a linear, exponential, or quadratic model. Choose True or False for each statement.

   A. $\{(-5, 2), (-3, 6), (-1, 10), (1, 14), (3, 18)\}$ is best represented by a linear model. ○ True ○ False

   B. $\{(-2, 12), (-1, 6), (0, 3), (1, 1.5), (2, 0.75)\}$ is best represented by a quadratic model. ○ True ○ False

   C. $\{(-5, 4), (-4, 1), (-3, 0), (-2, 1), (-1, 4)\}$ is best represented by an exponential model. ○ True ○ False

2. Does the given equation have 2 real solutions? Select Yes or No for each equation.

   A. $6x^2 + 15 = 0$ ○ Yes ○ No

   B. $8x^2 - 50 = 0$ ○ Yes ○ No

   C. $3x^2 + 4x - 10 = 0$ ○ Yes ○ No

3. Consider data represented by the following points: $\{(-2, 0.25), (-1, 1.5), (0, 4), (1, 15), (2, 60)\}$. Determine if the data are best represented by a linear, exponential, or quadratic function. Explain your answer.

4. The equation $2x^2 + 8x + c = 0$ has one real solution. What is the value of c? Explain how you found the value of c.

Assessment Readiness

Personal Math Trainer

- Online Homework
- Hints and Help
- Extra Practice

1. A quadratic equation has the solutions –3 and 6. Can the quadratic equation be the given equation?

A. $(2x + 6)(x - 6) = 0$ ○ Yes ○ No

B. $(6x - 1)(x + 3) = 0$ ○ Yes ○ No

C. $-3x(x - 6) = 0$ ○ Yes ○ No

2. Factor and solve each equation. Does the equation have a solution of $x = -5$?

A. $3x^2 + 14x - 5 = 0$ ○ Yes ○ No

B. $x^2 + 3x - 40 = 0$ ○ Yes ○ No

C. $x^2 - 3x - 40 = 0$ ○ Yes ○ No

3. Consider the equation $4x^2 - 20 = 0$. Is the given statement True or False?

A. The equation has 2 solutions. ○ True ○ False

B. A solution of the equation is $-\sqrt{20}$. ○ True ○ False

C. A solution of the equation is $\sqrt{5}$. ○ True ○ False

4. Solve $\left(2x + \frac{2}{3}\right)(x + 5) = 0$. Is the given value a solution of the equation?

A. $x = -\frac{1}{3}$ ○ Yes ○ No

B. $x = -5$ ○ Yes ○ No

C. $x = \frac{2}{3}$ ○ Yes ○ No

5. The equation $ax^2 + 12x + c = 0$ has one solution. Can a and c equal each of the following values?

A. $a = 4, c = 9$ ○ Yes ○ No

B. $a = 9, c = 16$ ○ Yes ○ No

C. $a = 36, c = 1$ ○ Yes ○ No

6. The table given has been filled out for the function $g(x)$. The values of $g(x)$ are not shown. Is $g(x)$ a linear or quadratic function? Justify your answer.

x	−2		0		2		4		6
$g(x)$									
First difference		−4		−4		−4		−4	
Second difference			0		0		0		

7. The area of a square table top can be represented by $\left(9x^2 - 30x + 25\right)$ ft². The perimeter of the table top is 34 feet. What is the value of x? Explain how you solved this problem.

8. Solve $4x^2 + 8x = -3$. Which of the following solution methods did you use: factoring, completing the square, or the quadratic formula? Why? Show your work.

Performance Tasks

★ **9.** Abigail has a rectangular quilt with dimensions 36 inches by 48 inches. She decides to sew a border on the quilt, so that the total area of the quilt is 1900 square inches. What will be the width of the border?

★★10. The table shows the average weight of a particular variety of sheep at various ages.

A. None of the three models—linear, quadratic, or exponential—fits the data exactly. Which of these is the best model for the data? Explain your choice.

B. What would you predict for the weight of a sheep that is 1 year old?

C. Do you think you could use your model to find the weight of a sheep at any age? Why or why not?

Sheep	
Age (mo)	Weight (lb)
2	36
4	69
6	99
8	120
10	135

★★★11. Examine the two models that represent annual tuition for two colleges.

A. Describe each model as linear, quadratic, or exponential.

B. Write a function rule for each model.

C. Both models have the same values for 2004. What does this mean?

D. Why do both models have the same value for year 1?

Years After 2004	Tuition at College 1 ($)	Tuition at College 2 ($)
0	2000.00	2000.00
1	2200.00	2200.00
2	2400.00	2420.00
3	2600.00	2662.00
4	2800.00	2928.20

MATH IN CAREERS

Competitive Diver Franco and Grace are competitive divers. Grace dives from a 20-meter cliff into the water, with an initial upward speed of 3.2 m/s. Franco dives from a springboard that is 10 meters above the water surface with an initial upward speed of 4.2 m/s.

The height in meters of an object projected into the air with an initial vertical velocity of v meters per second and initial height of h_0 can be modeled by $h(t) = -4.9t^2 + vt + h_0$.

a. Write a function $h_{\text{Grace}}(t)$ that models the height of Grace's dive.

b. Write a function $h_{\text{Franco}}(t)$ that models the height of Franco's dive.

c. Use a graphing calculator to graph both functions on the same screen. Label each function.

d. What are the domain and range of each function in terms of the situation? Explain. Round values to the nearest tenth.

e. Compare the maximum heights and the time that elapses before each diver hits the water.

UNIT 5

Extending Quadratic Equations

MATH IN CAREERS

Ichthyologist An ichthyologist is a biologist who specializes in the study of fish. Ichthyologists work in a variety of disciplines relating to fish and their environment, including ecology, taxonomy, behavior, and conservation. Ichthyologists might perform tasks such as monitoring water quality, designing and conducting experiments, evaluating data using statistics, and publishing results in scientific journals. Ichthyologists utilize mathematical models and collect and analyze experimental and observational data to help them understand fish and their environment.

If you are interested in a career as an ichthyologist, you should study these mathematical subjects:

- Geometry
- Algebra
- Statistics
- Calculus

Research other careers that require using mathematical models to understand an organism and its environment. Check out the career activity at the end of the unit to find out how **ichthyologists** use math.

Vocabulary

Review Words

- ✔ axis of symmetry *(eje de simetría)*
- ✔ discriminant *(discriminante)*
- ✔ elimination *(eliminación)*
- ✔ parabola *(parábola)*
- ✔ quadratic formula *(fórmula cuadrática)*
- ✔ substitution *(sustitución)*
- ✔ vertex *(vértice)*

Preview Words

- complex number *(número complejo)*
- directrix *(directriz)*
- focus *(foco)*
- imaginary number *(número imaginario)*
- inverse function *(función inversa)*
- inverse relation *(relación inversa)*
- matrix *(matriz)*
- radical function *(función radical)*

Visualize Vocabulary

Use the ✔ words to complete the graphic. Place one word in each of the four sections of the frame.

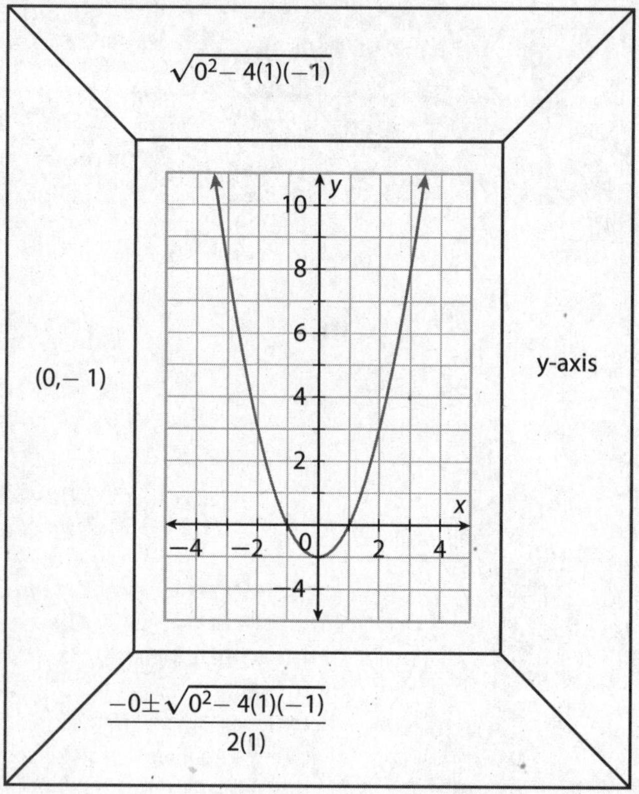

Understand Vocabulary

To become familiar with some of the vocabulary terms in the module, consider the following. You may refer to the module, the glossary, or a dictionary.

1. Every point on a parabola is equidistant from a fixed line, called the ____________________, and a fixed point, called the ____________________.

2. A ____________________ is any number that can be written as $a + bi$, where a and b are real numbers and $i = \sqrt{-1}$.

3. A ____________________ is a rectangular array of numbers.

Active Reading

Four-Corner Fold Before beginning each lesson, create a four-corner fold to help you organize the characteristics of key concepts. As you study each lesson, define new terms, including an example and a graph or diagram where applicable.

MODULE 11

Quadratic Equations and Complex Numbers

Essential Question: How can you use quadratic equations and complex numbers to solve real-world problems?

REAL WORLD VIDEO
Safe drivers are aware of stopping distances and carefully judge how fast they can travel based on road conditions. Stopping distance is one of many everyday functions that can be modeled with quadratic equations.

MODULE PERFORMANCE TASK PREVIEW

Can You Stop in Time?

When a driver applies the brakes, the car continues to travel for a certain distance until coming to a stop. The stopping distance for a vehicle depends on many factors, including the initial speed of the car and road conditions. How far will a car travel after the brakes are applied? Let's hit the road and find out!

Are YOU Ready?

Complete these exercises to review skills you will need for this module.

Personal Math Trainer

- Online Homework
- Hints and Help
- Extra Practice

One-Step Inequalities

Example 1

Solve $-2x \leq 9$ for x.

$x \geq -4.5$

Divide both sides by −2. Because you are dividing by a negative number, flip the inequality symbol.

Solve each inequality.

1. $n - 12 > 9$ ________

2. $-3p < -27$ ________

3. $\frac{k}{4} \geq -1$ ________

Exponents

Example 2

Simplify $\frac{3a^5b^2}{9a^2b}$.

$$\frac{3a^5b^2}{9a^2b} = \frac{3^1a^5b^2}{3^2a^2b^1} = \frac{a^{5-2}b^{2-1}}{3^{2-1}} = \frac{a^3b}{3}$$

Subtract exponents when dividing.

Simplify each expression.

4. $\frac{16p^2}{2p^4}$ ________

5. $5vw^5 \cdot 2v^4$ ________

6. $\frac{3x^7y}{6x^4y^2}$ ________

Solving Quadratic Equations by Factoring

Example 3

Factor to solve $x^2 + 2x - 15 = 0$ for x.

Pairs of factors of −15 are:

1 and −15

3 and −5

5 and −3

15 and −1

The pair with the sum of the middle term, 2, is 5 and −3.

$(x + 5)(x - 3) = 0$

Either $x + 5 = 0$ or $x - 3 = 0$, so x-values are −5 and 3.

Factor to solve each equation.

7. $x^2 - 7x + 6 = 0$ ________

8. $x^2 - 18x + 81 = 0$ ________

9. $x^2 - 16 = 0$ ________

Name__________ Class__________ Date__________

11.1 Solving Quadratic Equations by Taking Square Roots

Essential Question: What is an imaginary number, and how is it useful in solving quadratic equations?

Resource Locker

Explore Investigating Ways of Solving Simple Quadratic Equations

There are many ways to solve a quadratic equation. Here, you will use three methods to solve the equation $x^2 = 16$: by graphing, by factoring, and by taking square roots.

(A) Solve $x^2 = 16$ by graphing.

First treat each side of the equation as a function, and graph the two functions, which in this case are $f(x) = x^2$ and $g(x) = 16$, on the same coordinate plane.

Then identify the x-coordinates of the points where the two graphs intersect.

$x = \square$ or $x = \square$

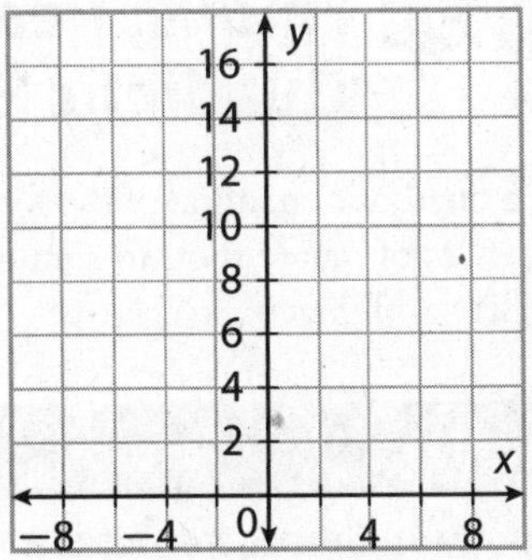

(B) Solve $x^2 = 16$ by factoring.

This method involves rewriting the equation so that 0 is on one side in order to use the *zero-product property*, which says that the product of two numbers is 0 if and only if at least one of the numbers is 0.

Write the equation.	$x^2 = 16$
Subtract 16 from both sides.	$x^2 - \square = 0$
Factor the difference of two squares.	$(x + \square)(x - 4) = 0$
Apply the zero-product property.	$x + \square = 0$ or $x - 4 = 0$
Solve for x.	$x = \square$ or $x = 4$

(C) Solve $x^2 = 16$ by taking square roots.

A real number x is a *square root* of a nonnegative real number a provided $x^2 = a$. A square root is written using the radical symbol $\sqrt{}$. Every positive real number a has both a positive square root, written $\sqrt{a}$, and a negative square root, written $-\sqrt{a}$. For instance, the square roots of 9 are $\pm\sqrt{9}$ (read "plus or minus the square root of 9"), or ± 3. The number 0 has only itself as its square root: $\pm\sqrt{0} = 0$.

Write the equation.	$x^2 = 16$
Use the definition of square root.	$x = \pm\sqrt{16}$
Simplify the square roots.	$x = \square$

Reflect

1. Which of the three methods would you use to solve $x^2 = 5$? Explain, and then use the method to find the solutions.

2. Can the equation $x^2 = -9$ be solved by any of the three methods? Explain.

Explain 1 Finding Real Solutions of Simple Quadratic Equations

When solving a quadratic equation of the form $ax^2 + c = 0$ by taking square roots, you may need to use the following properties of square roots to simplify the solutions. (In a later lesson, these properties are stated in a more general form and then proved.)

Property Name	Words	Symbols	Numbers
Product property of square roots	The square root of a product equals the product of the square roots of the factors.	$\sqrt{ab} = \sqrt{a} \cdot \sqrt{b}$ where $a \geq 0$ and $b \geq 0$	$\sqrt{12} = \sqrt{4 \cdot 3}$ $= \sqrt{4} \cdot \sqrt{3}$ $= 2\sqrt{3}$
Quotient property of square roots	The square root of a fraction equals the quotient of the square roots of the numerator and the denominator.	$\sqrt{\frac{a}{b}} = \frac{\sqrt{a}}{\sqrt{b}}$ where $a \geq 0$ and $b > 0$	$\sqrt{\frac{5}{9}} = \frac{\sqrt{5}}{\sqrt{9}}$ $= \frac{\sqrt{5}}{3}$

Using the quotient property of square roots may require an additional step of *rationalizing the denominator* if the denominator is not a rational number. For instance, the quotient property allows you to write $\sqrt{\frac{2}{7}}$ as $\frac{\sqrt{2}}{\sqrt{7}}$, but $\sqrt{7}$ is not a rational number. To rationalize the denominator, multiply $\frac{\sqrt{2}}{\sqrt{7}}$ by $\frac{\sqrt{7}}{\sqrt{7}}$ (a form of 1) and get this result: $\frac{\sqrt{2}}{\sqrt{7}} \cdot \frac{\sqrt{7}}{\sqrt{7}} = \frac{\sqrt{14}}{\sqrt{49}} = \frac{\sqrt{14}}{7}$.

Example 1 **Solve the quadratic equation by taking square roots.**

(A) $2x^2 - 16 = 0$

Add 16 to both sides.	$2x^2 = 16$
Divide both sides by 2.	$x^2 = 8$
Use the definition of square root.	$x = \pm\sqrt{8}$
Use the product property.	$x = \pm\sqrt{4} \cdot \sqrt{2}$
Simplify.	$x = \pm 2\sqrt{2}$

(B) $-5x^2 + 9 = 0$

Subtract 9 from both sides.	$-5x^2 = \square$
Divide both sides by $\square$.	$x^2 = \square$
Use the definition of square root.	$x = \pm\sqrt{\square}$
Use the quotient property.	$x = \pm \square$
Simplify the numerator.	$x = \pm \square$
Rationalize the denominator.	$x = \pm \square$

Your Turn

Solve the quadratic equation by taking square roots.

3. $x^2 - 24 = 0$

4. $-4x^2 + 13 = 0$

Explain 2 Solving a Real-World Problem Using a Simple Quadratic Equation

Two commonly used quadratic models for falling objects near Earth's surface are the following:

- Distance fallen (in feet) at time t (in seconds): $d(t) = 16t^2$
- Height (in feet) at time t (in seconds): $h(t) = h_0 - 16t^2$ where h_0 is the object's initial height (in feet)

For both models, time is measured from the instant that the object begins to fall. A negative value of t would represent a time before the object began falling, so negative values of t are excluded from the domains of these functions. This means that for any equation of the form $d(t) = c$ or $h(t) = c$ where c is a constant, a negative solution should be rejected.

Example 2 **Write and solve an equation to answer the question. Give the exact answer and, if it's irrational, a decimal approximation (to the nearest tenth of a second).**

(A) If you drop a water balloon, how long does it take to fall 4 feet?

Using the model $d(t) = 16t^2$, solve the equation $d(t) = 4$.

Write the equation. $16t^2 = 4$

Divide both sides by 16. $t^2 = \frac{1}{4}$

Use the definition of square root. $t = \pm\sqrt{\frac{1}{4}}$

Use the quotient property. $t = \pm\frac{1}{2}$

Reject the negative value of t. The water balloon falls 4 feet in $\frac{1}{2}$ second.

(B) The rooftop of a 5-story building is 50 feet above the ground. How long does it take the water balloon dropped from the rooftop to pass by a third-story window at 24 feet?

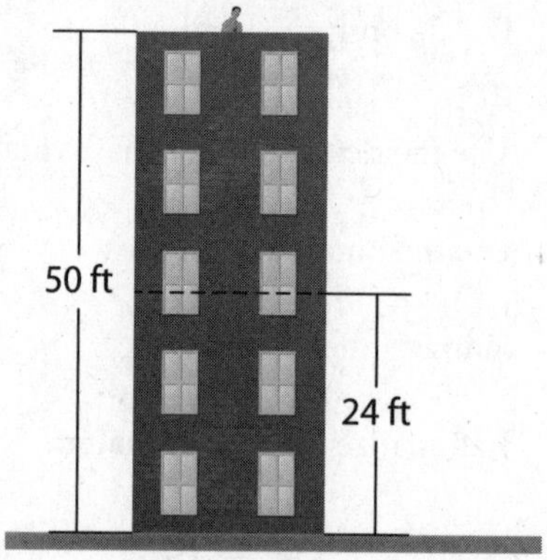

Using the model $h(t) = h_0 - 16t^2$, solve the equation $h(t) = 24$. (When you reach the step at which you divide both sides by -16, leave 16 in the denominator rather than simplifying the fraction because you'll get a rational denominator when you later use the quotient property.)

Write the equation. $\square - 16t^2 = \square$

Subtract 50 from both sides. $-16t^2 = \square$

Divide both sides by -16. $t^2 = \square$

Use the definition of square root. $t = \pm\sqrt{\square}$

Use the quotient property to simplify. $t = \pm\square$

Reject the negative value of t. The water balloon passes by the third-story window in $\square \approx \square$ seconds.

Reflect

5. **Discussion** Explain how the model $h(t) = h_0 - 16t^2$ is built from the model $d(t) = 16t^2$.

Your Turn

Write and solve an equation to answer the question. Give the exact answer and, if it's irrational, a decimal approximation (to the nearest tenth of a second).

6. How long does it take the water balloon described in Part B to hit the ground?

7. On the moon, the distance d (in feet) that an object falls in time t (in seconds) is modeled by the function $d(t) = \frac{8}{3}t^2$. Suppose an astronaut on the moon drops a tool. How long does it take the tool to fall 4 feet?

Explain 3 Defining Imaginary Numbers

You know that the quadratic equation $x^2 = 1$ has two real solutions, the equation $x^2 = 0$ has one real solution, and the equation $x^2 = -1$ has no real solutions. By creating a new type of number called *imaginary numbers*, mathematicians allowed for solutions of equations like $x^2 = -1$.

Imaginary numbers are the square roots of negative numbers. These numbers can all be written in the form bi where b is a nonzero real number and i, called the **imaginary unit**, represents $\sqrt{-1}$. Some examples of imaginary numbers are the following:

- $2i$
- $-5i$
- $-\frac{i}{3}$ or $-\frac{1}{3}i$
- $i\sqrt{2}$ (Write the i in front of the radical symbol for clarity.)
- $\frac{i\sqrt{3}}{2}$ or $\frac{\sqrt{3}}{2}i$

Given that $i = \sqrt{-1}$, you can conclude that $i^2 = -1$. This means that the square of any imaginary number is a negative real number. When squaring an imaginary number, use the power of a product property of exponents: $(ab)^m = a^m \cdot b^m$.

Example 3 **Find the square of the imaginary number.**

(A) $5i$

$$(5i)^2 = 5^2 \cdot i^2$$
$$= 25(-1)$$
$$= -25$$

(B) $-i\sqrt{2}$

$$(-i\sqrt{2})^2 = \left(\boxed{}\right)^2 \cdot i^2$$
$$= \boxed{}(-1)$$
$$= \boxed{}$$

Reflect

8. By definition, i is a square root of -1. Does -1 have another square root? Explain.

Your Turn

Find the square of the imaginary number.

9. $-2i$

10. $\frac{\sqrt{3}}{3}i$

Explain 4 Finding Imaginary Solutions of Simple Quadratic Equations

Using imaginary numbers and the property below you can solve simple quadratic equations that do not have real solutions.

Square Root of a Negative Number Property
For a positive real number r, $\sqrt{-r} = i\sqrt{r}$. For example, $\sqrt{-6} = i\sqrt{6}$.

Note that this property effectively extends the Product Property of Square Roots to cases where one of the radicands is negative. The property cannot be extended to cases where both radicands are negative because then $i^2 = \sqrt{-1} \cdot \sqrt{-1} = \sqrt{(-1)(-1)} = \sqrt{1} = 1$, which contradicts the fact that $i^2 = -1$.

Example 4 **Solve the quadratic equation by taking square roots. Allow for imaginary solutions.**

(A) $x^2 + 12 = 0$

Write the equation. $x^2 + 12 = 0$

Subtract 12 from both sides. $x^2 = -12$

Use the definition of square root. $x = \pm\sqrt{-12}$

Use the fact that for $r > 0$, $\sqrt{-r} = i\sqrt{r}$. $x = \pm i\sqrt{12}$

Use the product property of square roots. $x = \pm i\sqrt{(4)(3)} = \pm 2i\sqrt{3}$

B $4x^2 + 11 = 6$

Write the equation.	$4x^2 + 11 = 6$
Subtract 11 from both sides.	$\square x^2 = \square$
Divide both sides by $\square$.	$x^2 = \square$
Use the definition of square root.	$x = \pm\sqrt{\square}$
Use the fact that for $r > 0$, $\sqrt{-r} = i\sqrt{r}$.	$x = \pm i\sqrt{\square}$
Use the quotient property of square roots.	$x = \pm \square$

Your Turn

Solve the quadratic equation by taking square roots. Allow for imaginary solutions.

11. $\frac{1}{4}x^2 + 9 = 0$

12. $-5x^2 + 3 = 10$

Elaborate

13. The quadratic equations $4x^2 + 32 = 0$ and $4x^2 - 32 = 0$ differ only by the sign of the constant term. Without actually solving the equations, what can you say about the relationship between their solutions?

14. What kind of a number is the square of an imaginary number?

15. Why do you reject negative values of t when solving equations based on the models for a falling object near Earth's surface, $d(t) = 16t^2$ for distance fallen and $h(t) = h_0 - 16t^2$ for height during a fall?

16. **Essential Question Check-In** Describe how to find the square roots of a negative number.

Evaluate: Homework and Practice

Personal Math Trainer

- Online Homework
- Hints and Help
- Extra Practice

1. Solve the equation $x^2 - 2 = 7$ using the indicated method.

 a. Solve by graphing.

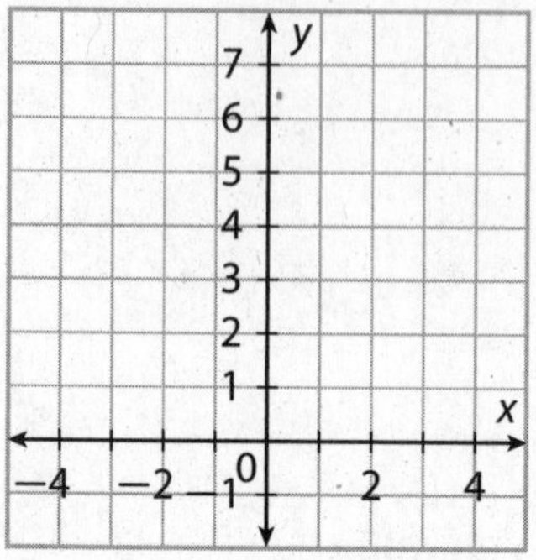

 b. Solve by factoring.

 c. Solve by taking square roots.

2. Solve the equation $2x^2 + 3 = 5$ using the indicated method.

 a. Solve by graphing.

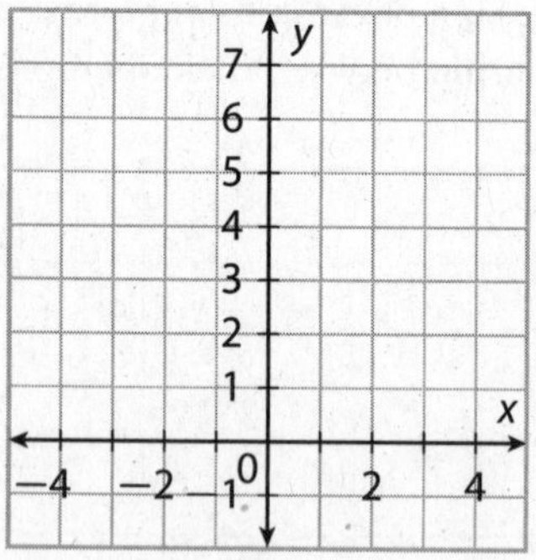

 b. Solve by factoring.

 c. Solve by taking square roots.

Solve the quadratic equation by taking square roots.

3. $4x^2 = 24$

4. $-\frac{x^2}{5} + 15 = 0$

5. $2(5 - 5x^2) = 5$

6. $3x^2 - 8 = 12$

Write and solve an equation to answer the question. Give the exact answer and, if it's irrational, a decimal approximation (to the nearest tenth of a second).

7. A squirrel in a tree drops an acorn. How long does it take the acorn to fall 20 feet?

8. A person washing the windows of an office building drops a squeegee from a height of 60 feet. How long does it take the squeegee to pass by another window washer working at a height of 20 feet?

Geometry Determine the lengths of the sides of the rectangle using the given area. Give answers both exactly and approximately (to the nearest tenth).

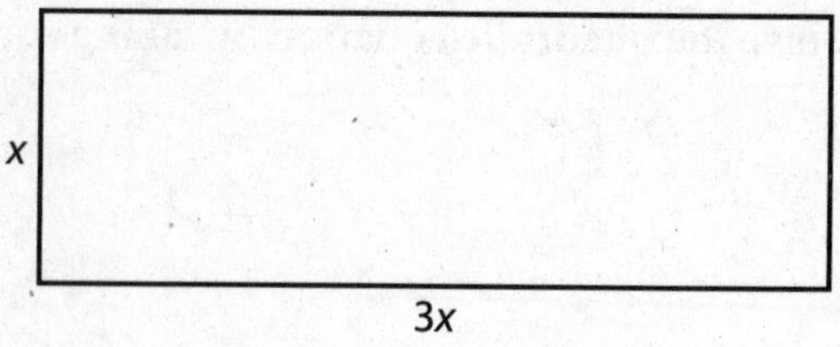

9. The area of the rectangle is 45 cm^2.

10. The area of the rectangle is 54 cm^2.

Find the square of the imaginary number.

11. $3i$

12. $i\sqrt{5}$

13. $-i\frac{\sqrt{2}}{2}$

Determine whether the quadratic equation has real solutions or imaginary solutions by solving the equation.

14. $15x^2 - 10 = 0$

15. $\frac{1}{2}x^2 + 12 = 4$

16. $5(2x^2 - 3) = 4(x^2 - 10)$

Solve the quadratic equation by taking square roots. Allow for imaginary solutions.

17. $x^2 = -81$

18. $x^2 + 64 = 0$

19. $5x^2 - 4 = -8$

20. $7x^2 + 10 = 0$

Geometry Determine the length of the sides of each square using the given information. Give answers both exactly and approximately (to the nearest tenth).

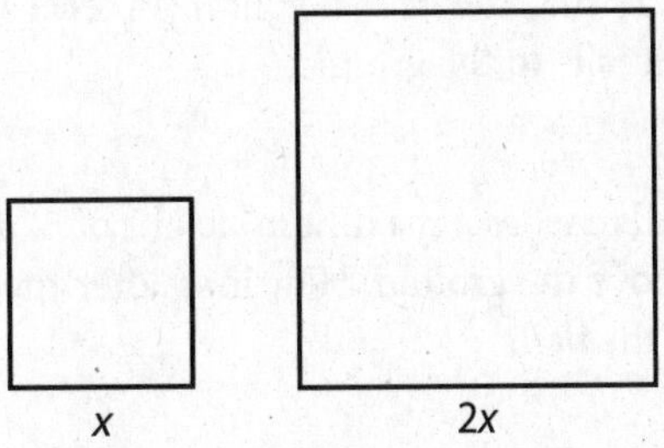

21. The area of the larger square is 42 cm^2 more than the area of the smaller square.

22. If the area of the larger square is decreased by 28 cm^2, the result is half of the area of the smaller square.

23. Determine whether each of the following numbers is real or imaginary.

a. i ☐ Real ☐ Imaginary

b. A square root of 5 ☐ Real ☐ Imaginary

c. $(2i)^2$ ☐ Real ☐ Imaginary

d. $(-5)^2$ ☐ Real ☐ Imaginary

e. $\sqrt{-3}$ ☐ Real ☐ Imaginary

f. $-\sqrt{10}$ ☐ Real ☐ Imaginary

H.O.T. Focus on Higher Order Thinking

24. Critical Thinking When a batter hits a baseball, you can model the ball's height using a quadratic function that accounts for the ball's initial vertical velocity. However, once the ball reaches its maximum height, its vertical velocity is momentarily 0 feet per second, and you can use the model $h(t) = h_0 - 16t^2$ to find the ball's height h (in feet) at time t (in seconds) as it falls to the ground.

a. Suppose a fly ball reaches a maximum height of 67 feet and an outfielder catches the ball 3 feet above the ground. How long after the ball begins to descend does the outfielder catch the ball?

b. Can you determine (without writing or solving any equations) the total time the ball was in the air? Explain your reasoning and state any assumptions you make.

25. Represent Real-World Situations The aspect ratio of an image on a screen is the ratio of image width to image height. An HDTV screen shows images with an aspect ratio of 16:9. If the area of an HDTV screen is 864 in^2, what are the dimensions of the screen?

26. Explain the Error Russell wants to calculate the amount of time it takes for a load of dirt to fall from a crane's clamshell bucket at a height of 16 feet to the bottom of a hole that is 32 feet deep. He sets up the following equation and tries to solve it.

$$16 - 16t^2 = 32$$
$$-16t^2 = 16$$
$$t^2 = -1$$
$$t = \pm\sqrt{-1}$$
$$t = \pm i$$

Does Russell's answer make sense? If not, find and correct Russell's error.

Lesson Performance Task

A suspension bridge uses two thick cables, one on each side of the road, to hold up the road. The cables are suspended between two towers and have a parabolic shape. Smaller vertical cables connect the parabolic cables to the road. The table gives the lengths of the first few vertical cables starting with the shortest one.

Displacement from the Shortest Vertical Cable (m)	Height of Vertical Cable (m)
0	3
1	3.05
2	3.2
3	3.45

Find a quadratic function that describes the height (in meters) of a parabolic cable above the road as a function of the horizontal displacement (in meters) from the cable's lowest point. Use the function to predict the distance between the towers if the parabolic cable reaches a maximum height of 48 m above the road at each tower.

Name ______________________ Class ______________ Date ________

11.2 Complex Numbers

Essential Question: What is a complex number, and how can you add, subtract, and multiply complex numbers?

Resource Locker

Explore Exploring Operations Involving Complex Numbers

In this lesson, you'll learn to perform operations with *complex numbers*, which have a form similar to linear binomials such as $3 + 4x$ and $2 - x$.

(A) Add the binomials $3 + 4x$ and $2 - x$.

Group like terms. $(3 + 4x) + (2 - x) = (3 + \square) + (4x + \square)$

Combine like terms. $= (\square + \square)$

(B) Subtract $2 - x$ from $3 + 4x$.

Rewrite as addition. $(3 + 4x) - (2 - x) = (3 + 4x) + (-2 + \square)$

Group like terms. $= (3 + \square) + (4x + \square)$

Combine like terms. $= (\square + \square)$

(C) Multiply the binomials $3 + 4x$ and $2 - x$.

Use FOIL. $(3 + 4x)(2 - x) = 6 + (-3x) + \square + \square$

Combine like terms. $= 6 + \square + \square$

Reflect

1. In Step A, you found that $(3 + 4x) + (2 - x) = 5 + 3x$. Suppose $x = i$ (the imaginary unit).

What equation do you get? ______________________

2. In Step B, you found that $(3 + 4x) + (2 - x) = 1 + 5x$. Suppose $x = i$ (the imaginary unit).

What equation do you get? ______________________

3. In Step C, you found that $(3 + 4x)(2 - x) = 6 + 5x - 4x^2$. Suppose $x = i$ (the imaginary unit). What equation do you get? How can you further simplify the right side of this equation?

____

____

Explain 1 Defining Complex Numbers

A **complex number** is any number that can be written in the form $a + bi$, where a and b are real numbers and $i = \sqrt{-1}$. For a complex number $a + bi$ a is called the *real part* of the number, and b is called the *imaginary part.* (Note that "imaginary part" refers to the real multiplier of i; it does not refer to the imaginary number bi.) The Venn diagram shows some examples of complex numbers.

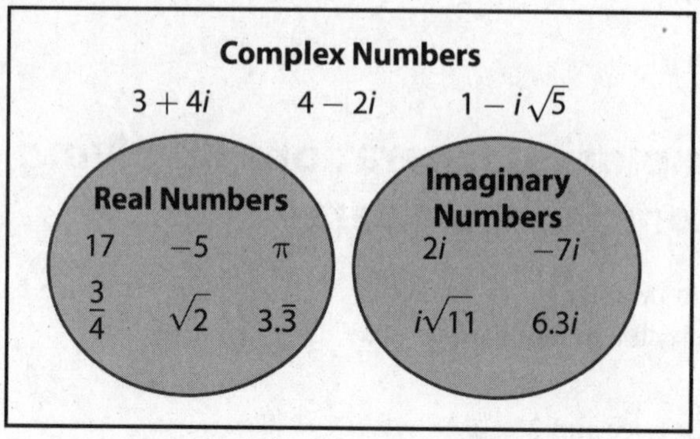

Notice that the set of real numbers is a subset of the set of complex numbers. That's because a real number a can be written in the form $a + 0i$ (whose imaginary part is 0). Likewise, the set of imaginary numbers is also a subset of the set of complex numbers, because an imaginary number bi (where $b \neq 0$) can be written in the form $0 + bi$ (whose real part is 0).

Example 1 **Identify the real and imaginary parts of the given number. Then tell which of the following sets the number belongs to: real numbers, imaginary numbers, and complex numbers.**

(A) $9 + 5i$

The real part of $9 + 5i$ is 9, and the imaginary part is 5. Because both the real and imaginary parts of $9 + 5i$ are nonzero; the number belongs only to the set of complex numbers.

(B) $-7i$

The real part of $-7i$ is ____, and the imaginary part is ____. Because the real/imaginary part is 0, the number belongs to these sets: ________________________________.

Your Turn

Identify the real and imaginary parts of the given number. Then tell which of the following sets the number belongs to: real numbers, imaginary numbers, and complex numbers.

4. 11

5. $-1+i$

Explain 2 Adding and Subtracting Complex Numbers

To add or subtract complex numbers, add or subtract the real parts and the imaginary parts separately.

Example 2 **Add or subtract the complex numbers.**

(A) $(-7+2i)+(5-11i)$

Group like terms. $(-7+2i)+(5-11i)=(-7+5)+(2i+(-11i))$

Combine like terms. $=-2+(-9i)$

Write addition as subtraction. $=-2-9i$

(B) $(18+27i)-(2+3i)$

Group like terms. $(18+27i)-(2+3i)=\left(18-\boxed{}\right)+\left(\boxed{}-3i\right)$

Combine like terms. $=\boxed{}+\boxed{}\,i$

Reflect

6. Is the sum $(a+bi)+(a-bi)$ where a and b are real numbers, a real number or an imaginary number? Explain.

Your Turn

Add or subtract the complex numbers.

7. $(17-6i)-(9+10i)$

8. $(16+17i)+(-8-12i)$

Explain 3 Multiplying Complex Numbers

To multiply two complex numbers, use the distributive property to multiply each part of one number by each part of the other. Use the fact that $i^2 = -1$ to simplify the result.

Example 3 **Multiply the complex numbers.**

(A) $(4 + 9i)(6 - 2i)$

Use the distributive property. $(4 + 9i)(6 - 2i) = 24 - 8i + 54i - 18i^2$

Substitute -1 for i^2. $= 24 - 8i + 54i - 18(-1)$

Combine like terms. $= 42 + 46i$

(B) $(-3 + 12i)(7 + 4i)$

Use the distributive property. $(-3 + 12i)(7 + 4i) = \square - 12i + \square + 48i^2$

Substitute -1 for i^2. $= \square - 12i + \square + 48(-1)$

Combine like terms. $= \square + \square i$

Reflect

9. Is the product of $(a + bi)(a - bi)$, where a and b are real numbers, a real number or an imaginary number? Explain.

Your Turn

Multiply the complex numbers.

10. $(6 - 5i)(3 - 10i)$

11. $(8 + 15i)(11 + i)$

Explain 4 Solving a Real-World Problem Using Complex Numbers

Electrical engineers use complex numbers when analyzing electric circuits. An electric circuit can contain three types of components: resistors, inductors, and capacitors. As shown in the table, each type of component has a different symbol in a circuit diagram, and each is represented by a different type of complex number based on the phase angle of the current passing through it.

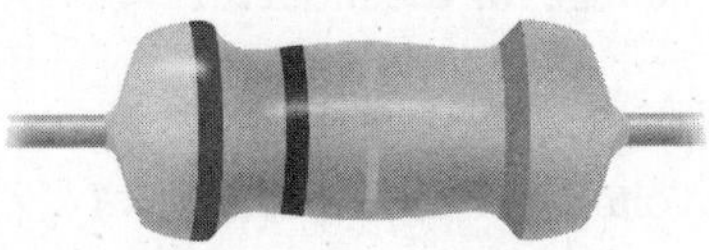

Circuit Component	Symbol in Circuit Diagram	Phase Angle	Representation as a Complex Number
Resistor		0°	A real number a
Inductor		90°	An imaginary number bi where $b > 0$
Capacitor	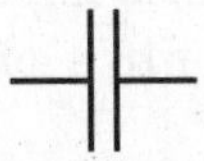	−90°	An imaginary number bi where $b < 0$

A diagram of an alternating current (AC) electric circuit is shown along with the *impedance* (measured in ohms, Ω) of each component in the circuit. An AC power source, which is shown on the left in the diagram and labeled 120 V (for volts), causes electrons to flow through the circuit. Impedance is a measure of each component's opposition to the electron flow.

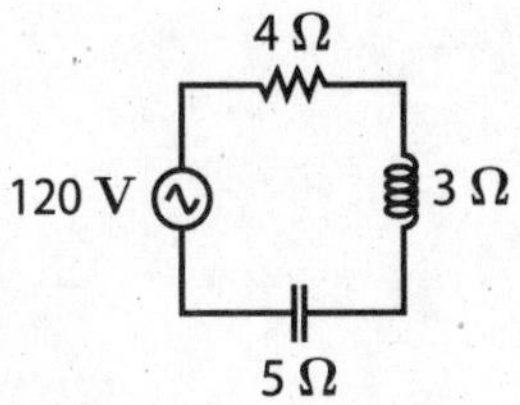

Example 4 **Use the diagram of the electric circuit to answer the following questions.**

(A) The total impedance in the circuit is the sum of the impedances for the individual components. What is the total impedance for the given circuit?

Write the impedance for each component as a complex number.

- Impedance for the resistor: 4
- Impedance for the inductor: $3i$
- Impedance for the capacitor: $-5i$

Then find the sum of the impedances.

Total impedance $= 4 + 3i + (-5i) = 4 - 2i$

(B) Ohm's law for AC electric circuits says that the voltage V (measured in volts) is the product of the current I (measured in amps) and the impedance Z (measured in ohms): $V = I \cdot Z$. For the given circuit, the current I is $24 + 12i$ amps. What is the voltage V for each component in the circuit?

Use Ohm's law, $V = I \cdot Z$, to find the voltage for each component. Remember that Z is the impedance from Part A.

Voltage for the resistor $= I \cdot Z = (24 + 12i)\left(\boxed{}\right) = 96 + \boxed{}\,i$

Voltage for the inductor $= I \cdot Z = (24 + 12i)\left(\boxed{}\right) = -36 + \boxed{}\,i$

Voltage for the capacitor $= I \cdot Z = (24 + 12i)\left(\boxed{}\right) = \boxed{} - 120i$

Reflect

12. Find the sum of the voltages for the three components in Part B. What do you notice?

Your Turn

13. Suppose the circuit analyzed in Example 4 has a second resistor with an impedance of 2 Ω added to it. Find the total impedance. Given that the circuit now has a current of $18 + 6i$ amps, also find the voltage for each component in the circuit.

Elaborate

14. What kind of number is the sum, difference, or product of two complex numbers?

15. When is the sum of two complex numbers a real number? When is the sum of two complex numbers an imaginary number?

16. Discussion What are the similarities and differences between multiplying two complex numbers and multiplying two binomial linear expressions in the same variable?

17. Essential Question Check-In How do you add and subtract complex numbers?

Evaluate: Homework and Practice

Personal Math Trainer

- Online Homework
- Hints and Help
- Extra Practice

1. Find the sum of the binomials $3 + 2x$ and $4 - 5x$. Explain how you can use the result to find the sum of the complex numbers $3 + 2i$ and $4 - 5i$.

2. Find the product of the binomials $1 - 3x$ and $2 + x$. Explain how you can use the result to find the product of the complex numbers $1 - 3i$ and $2 + i$.

Identify the real and imaginary parts of the given number. Then tell which of the following sets the number belongs to: real numbers, imaginary numbers, and complex numbers.

3. $5 + i$

4. $7 - 6i$

5. 25

6. $i\sqrt{21}$

Add.

7. $(3 + 4i) + (7 + 11i)$

8. $(2 + 3i) + (6 - 5i)$

9. $(-1 - i) + (-10 + 3i)$

10. $(-9 - 7i) + (6 + 5i)$

Subtract.

11. $(2 + 3i) - (7 + 6i)$

12. $(4 + 5i) - (14 - i)$

13. $(-8 - 3i) - (-9 - 5i)$

14. $(5 + 2i) - (5 - 2i)$

Multiply.

15. $(2 + 3i)(3 + 5i)$

16. $(7 + i)(6 - 9i)$

17. $(-4 + 11i)(-5 - 8i)$

18. $(4 - i)(4 + i)$

Use the diagram of the electric circuit and the given current to find the total impedance for the circuit and the voltage for each component.

19.

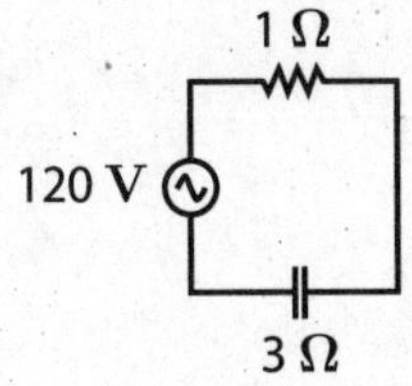

The circuit has a current of $12 + 36i$ amps.

20.

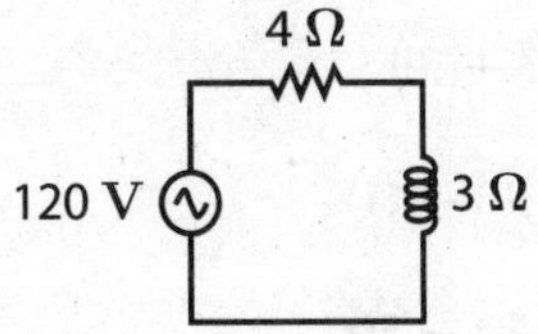

The circuit has a current of $19.2 - 14.4i$ amps.

21.

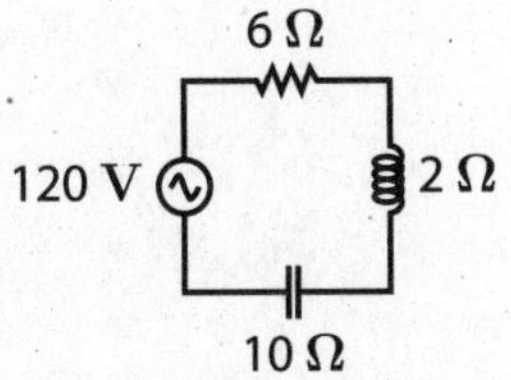

The circuit has a current of $7.2 + 9.6i$ amps.

22.

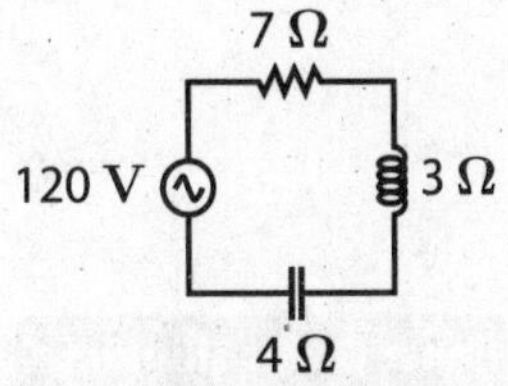

The circuit has a current of $16.8 + 2.4i$ amps.

23. Match each product on the right with the corresponding expression on the left.

A. $(3 - 5i)(3 + 5i)$ ______________ $-16 + 30i$

B. $(3 + 5i)(3 + 5i)$ ______________ -34

C. $(-3 - 5i)(3 + 5i)$ ______________ 34

D. $(3 - 5i)(-3 - 5i)$ ______________ $16 - 30i$

H.O.T. Focus on Higher Order Thinking

24. Explain the Error While attempting to multiply the expression $(2 - 3i)(3 + 2i)$, a student made a mistake. Explain and correct the error.

$$(2 - 3i)(3 + 2i) = 6 - 9i + 4i - 6i^2$$
$$= 6 - 9(-1) + 4(-1) - 6(1)$$
$$= 6 + 9 - 4 - 6$$
$$= 5$$

25. Critical Thinking Show that $\sqrt{3} + i\sqrt{3}$ and $-\sqrt{3} - i\sqrt{3}$ are the square roots of $6i$.

26. Justify Reasoning What type of number is the product of two complex numbers that differ only in the sign of their imaginary parts? Prove your conjecture.

Lesson Performance Task

Just as real numbers can be graphed on a real number line, complex numbers can be graphed on a complex *plane*, which has a horizontal real axis and a vertical imaginary axis. When a set that involves complex numbers is graphed on a complex plane, the result can be an elaborate self-similar figure called a *fractal*. Such a set is called a Julia set.

Consider Julia sets having the quadratic recursive rule $f(n+1) = \left(f(n)\right)^2 + c$ for some complex number $f(0)$ and some complex constant c. For a given value of c, a complex number $f(0)$ either belongs or doesn't belong to the "filled-in" Julia set corresponding to c depending on what happens with the sequence of numbers generated by the recursive rule.

a. Letting $c = i$, generate the first few numbers in the sequence defined by $f(0) = 1$ and $f(n+1) = \left(f(n)\right)^2 + i$. Record your results in the table.

n	$f(n)$	$f(n+1) = \left(f(n)\right)^2 + i$
0	$f(0) = 1$	$f(1) = \left(f(0)\right)^2 + i = (1)^2 + i = 1 + i$
1	$f(1) = 1 + i$	$f(2) = \left(f(1)\right)^2 + i = (1+i)^2 + i = \square$
2	$f(2) = \square$	$f(3) = \left(f(2)\right)^2 + i = \left(\square\right)^2 + i = \square$
3	$f(3) = \square$	$f(4) = \left(f(3)\right)^2 + i = \left(\square\right)^2 + i = \square$

b. The *magnitude* of a complex number $a + bi$ is the real number $\sqrt{a^2 + b^2}$. In the complex plane, the magnitude of a complex number is the number's distance from the origin. If the magnitudes of the numbers in the sequence generated by a Julia set's recursive rule, where $f(0)$ is the starting value, remain bounded, then $f(0)$ belongs to the "filled-in" Julia set. If the magnitudes increase without bound, then $f(0)$ doesn't belong to the "filled-in" Julia set. Based on your completed table for $f(0) = 1$, would you say that the number belongs to the "filled-in" Julia set corresponding to $c = i$? Explain.

c. Would you say that $f(0) = i$ belongs to the "filled-in" Julia set corresponding to $c = i$? Explain.

Name______________________ Class______________ Date__________

11.3 Finding Complex Solutions of Quadratic Equations

Resource Locker

Essential Question: How can you find the complex solutions of any quadratic equation?

Explore Investigating Real Solutions of Quadratic Equations

(A) Complete the table.

$ax^2 + bx + c = 0$	$ax^2 + bx = -c$	$f(x) = ax^2 + bx$	$g(x) = -c$
$2x^2 + 4x + 1 = 0$			
$2x^2 + 4x + 2 = 0$			
$2x^2 + 4x + 3 = 0$			

(B) The graph of $f(x) = 2x^2 + 4x$ is shown. Graph each $g(x)$. Complete the table.

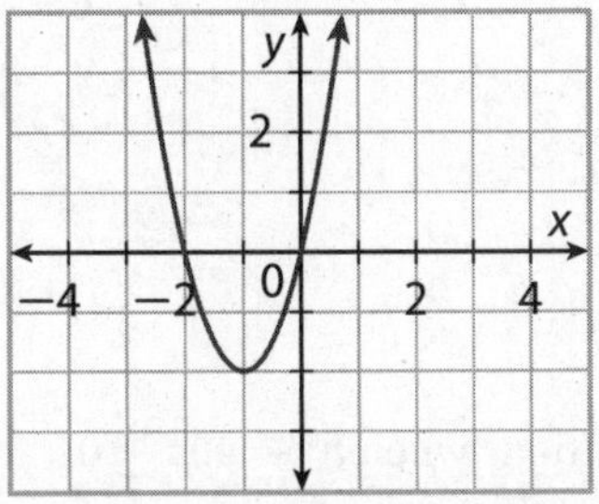

Equation	Number of Real Solutions
$2x^2 + 4x + 1 = 0$	
$2x^2 + 4x + 2 = 0$	
$2x^2 + 4x + 3 = 0$	

(C) Repeat Steps A and B when $f(x) = -2x^2 + 4x$.

$ax^2 + bx + c = 0$	$ax^2 + bx = -c$	$f(x) = ax^2 + bx$	$g(x) = -c$
$-2x^2 + 4x - 1 = 0$			
$-2x^2 + 4x - 2 = 0$			
$-2x^2 + 4x - 3 = 0$			

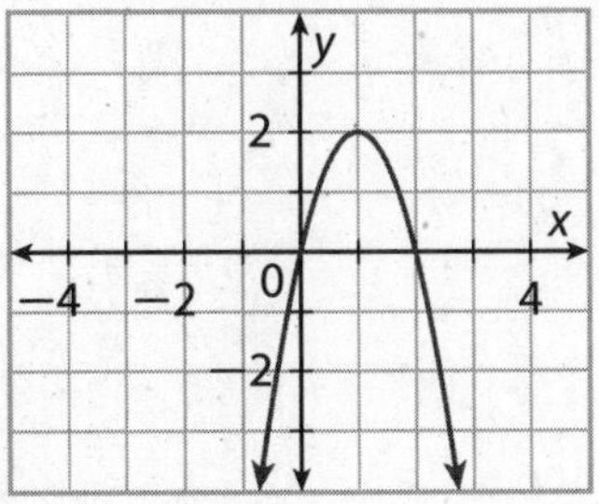

Equation	Number of Real Solutions
$-2x^2 + 4x - 1 = 0$	
$-2x^2 + 4x - 2 = 0$	
$-2x^2 + 4x - 3 = 0$	

Reflect

1. Look back at Steps A and B. Notice that the minimum value of $f(x)$ in Steps A and B is -2. Complete the table by identifying how many real solutions the equation $f(x) = g(x)$ has for the given values of $g(x)$.

Value of $g(x)$	Number of Real Solutions of $f(x) = g(x)$
$g(x) = -2$	
$g(x) > -2$	
$g(x) < -2$	

2. Look back at Step C. Notice that the maximum value of $f(x)$ in Step C is 2. Complete the table by identifying how many real solutions the equation $f(x) = g(x)$ has for the given values of $g(x)$.

Value of $g(x)$	Number of Real Solutions of $f(x) = g(x)$
$g(x) = 2$	
$g(x) > 2$	
$g(x) < 2$	

3. You can generalize Reflect 1: For $f(x) = ax^2 + bx$ where $a > 0$, $f(x) = g(x)$ where $g(x) = -c$ has real solutions when $g(x)$ is greater than or equal to the minimum value of $f(x)$. The minimum value of $f(x)$ is

$$f\left(-\frac{b}{2a}\right) = a\left(-\frac{b}{2a}\right)^2 + b\left(-\frac{b}{2a}\right) = a\left(\frac{b^2}{4a^2}\right) - \frac{b^2}{2a} = \frac{b^2}{4a} - \frac{b^2}{2a} = \frac{b^2}{4a} - \frac{2b^2}{4a} = -\frac{b^2}{4a}.$$

So, $f(x) = g(x)$ has real solutions when $g(x) \geq -\frac{b^2}{4a}$.

Substitute $-c$ for $g(x)$. $-c \geq -\frac{b^2}{4a}$

Add $\frac{b^2}{4a}$ to both sides. $\frac{b^2}{4a} - c \geq 0$

Multiply both sides by $4a$, which is positive. $b^2 - 4ac \geq 0$

In other words, the equation $ax^2 + bx + c = 0$ where $a > 0$ has real solutions when $b^2 - 4ac \geq 0$.

Generalize the results of Reflect 2 in a similar way. What do you notice?

Explain 1 Finding Complex Solutions by Completing the Square

Recall that completing the square for the expression $x^2 + bx$ requires adding $\left(\frac{b}{2}\right)^2$ to it, resulting in the perfect square trinomial $x^2 + bx + \left(\frac{b}{2}\right)^2$, which you can factor as $\left(x + \frac{b}{2}\right)^2$. Don't forget that when $x^2 + bx$ appears on one side of an equation, adding $\left(\frac{b}{2}\right)^2$ to it requires adding $\left(\frac{b}{2}\right)^2$ to the other side as well.

Example 1 **Solve the equation by completing the square. State whether the solutions are real or non-real.**

Ⓐ $3x^2 + 9x - 6 = 0$

1. Write the equation in the form $x^2 + bx = c$.

$$3x^2 + 9x - 6 = 0$$
$$3x^2 + 9x = 6$$
$$x^2 + 3x = 2$$

2. Identify b and $\left(\frac{b}{2}\right)^2$.

$$b = 3$$
$$\left(\frac{b}{2}\right)^2 = \left(\frac{3}{2}\right)^2 = \frac{9}{4}$$

3. Add $\left(\frac{b}{2}\right)^2$ to both sides of the equation.

$$x^2 + 3x + \frac{9}{4} = 2 + \frac{9}{4}$$

4. Solve for x.

$$\left(x + \frac{3}{2}\right)^2 = 2 + \frac{9}{4}$$
$$\left(x + \frac{3}{2}\right)^2 = \frac{17}{4}$$
$$x + \frac{3}{2} = \pm\sqrt{\frac{17}{4}}$$
$$x + \frac{3}{2} = \pm\frac{\sqrt{17}}{2}$$
$$x = -\frac{3}{2} \pm \frac{\sqrt{17}}{2}$$
$$x = \frac{-3 \pm \sqrt{17}}{2}$$

There are two real solutions: $\frac{-3 + \sqrt{17}}{2}$ and $\frac{-3 - \sqrt{17}}{2}$.

Ⓑ $x^2 - 2x + 7 = 0$

1. Write the equation in the form $x^2 + bx = c$.

2. Identify b and $\left(\frac{b}{2}\right)^2$.

$$b = \square$$
$$\left(\frac{b}{2}\right)^2 = \left(\frac{\square}{2}\right)^2 = \square$$

3. Add $\left(\frac{b}{2}\right)^2$ to both sides.

$$x^2 - 2x + \square = -7 + \square$$

4. Solve for x.

$$x^2 + 2x \square = -7 + \square$$
$$\left(x - \square\right)^2 = \square$$
$$x - \square = \pm\sqrt{\square}$$
$$x = 1 \pm \sqrt{\square}$$

There are two real/non-real solutions: ________ and ________.

Reflect

4. How many complex solutions do the equations in Parts A and B have? Explain.

Your Turn

Solve the equation by completing the square. State whether the solutions are real or non-real.

5. $x^2 + 8x + 17 = 0$

6. $x^2 + 10x - 7 = 0$

Explain 2 Identifying Whether Solutions Are Real or Non-real

By completing the square for the general quadratic equation $ax^2 + bx + c = 0$, you can obtain the *quadratic formula*, $x = \frac{-b \pm \sqrt{b^2 - 4ac}}{2a}$, which gives the solutions of the general quadratic equation. In the quadratic formula, the expression under the radical sign, $b^2 - 4ac$, is called the *discriminant*, and its value determines whether the solutions of the quadratic equation are real or non-real.

Value of Discriminant	Number and Type of Solutions
$b^2 - 4ac > 0$	Two real solutions.
$b^2 - 4ac = 0$	One real solution
$b^2 - 4ac < 0$	Two non-real solutions

Example 2 **Answer the question by writing an equation and determining whether the solutions of the equation are real or non-real.**

(A) A ball is thrown in the air with an initial vertical velocity of 14 m/s from an initial height of 2 m. The ball's height h (in meters) at time t (in seconds) can be modeled by the quadratic function $h(t) = -4.9t^2 + 14t + 2$. Does the ball reach a height of 12 m?

Set $h(t)$ equal to 12. $-4.9t^2 + 14t + 2 = 12$

Subtract 12 from both sides. $-4.9t^2 + 14t + 10 = 0$

Find the value of the discriminant. $14^2 - 4(-4.9)(-10) = 196 - 196 = 0$

Because the discriminant is zero, the equation has one real solution, so the ball does reach a height of 12 m.

(B) A person wants to create a vegetable garden and keep the rabbits out by enclosing it with 100 feet of fencing. The area of the garden is given by the function $A(w) = w(50 - w)$ where w is the width (in feet) of the garden. Can the garden have an area of 700 ft^2?

Set $A(w)$ equal to 700. $w(50 - w) = \square$

Multiply on the left side. $50w - w^2 = \square$

Subtract 700 from both sides. $-w^2 + 50w - \square = 0$

Find the value of the discriminant.

Because the discriminant is [positive/zero/negative], the equation has [two real/one real/two non-real] solutions, so the garden [can/cannot] have an area of 700 ft^2.

Your Turn

Answer the question by writing an equation and determining if the solutions are real or non-real.

7. A hobbyist is making a toy sailboat. For the triangular sail, she wants the height h (in inches) to be twice the length of the base b (in inches). Can the area of the sail be 10 in^2?

Explain 3 Finding Complex Solutions Using the Quadratic Formula

When using the quadratic formula to solve a quadratic equation, be sure the equation is in the form $ax^2 + bx + c = 0$.

Example 3 **Solve the equation using the quadratic formula. Check a solution by substitution.**

(A) $-5x^2 - 2x - 8 = 0$

Write the quadratic formula. $x = \dfrac{-b \pm \sqrt{b^2 - 4ac}}{2a}$

Substitute values. $= \dfrac{-(-2) \pm \sqrt{(-2)^2 - 4(-5)(-8)}}{2(-5)}$

Simplify. $= \dfrac{2 \pm \sqrt{-156}}{-10} = \dfrac{1 \pm i\sqrt{39}}{-5}$

So, the two solutions are $-\frac{1}{5} - \frac{i\sqrt{39}}{5}$ and $-\frac{1}{5} + \frac{i\sqrt{39}}{5}$.

Check by substituting one of the values.

Substitute. $-5\left(-\frac{1}{5} - \frac{i\sqrt{39}}{5}\right)^2 - 2\left(-\frac{1}{5} - \frac{i\sqrt{39}}{5}\right) - 8 \stackrel{?}{=} 0$

Square. $-5\left(\frac{1}{25} + \frac{2i\sqrt{39}}{25} - \frac{39}{25}\right) - 2\left(-\frac{1}{5} - \frac{i\sqrt{39}}{5}\right) - 8 \stackrel{?}{=} 0$

Distribute. $-\frac{1}{5} - \frac{2i\sqrt{39}}{5} + \frac{39}{5} + \frac{2}{5} + \frac{2i\sqrt{39}}{5} - 8 \stackrel{?}{=} 0$

Simplify. $\frac{40}{5} - 8 \stackrel{?}{=} 0$

$0 = 0$

(B) $7x^2 + 2x + 3 = -1$

Write the equation with 0 on one side. $7x^2 + 2x + \square = 0$

Write the quadratic formula. $x = \frac{-b \pm \sqrt{b^2 - 4ac}}{2a}$

Substitute values. $= \frac{-\square \pm \sqrt{\left(\square\right)^2 - 4\left(\square\right)\left(\square\right)}}{2\left(\square\right)}$

Simplify. $= \frac{-\square \pm \sqrt{-\square}}{14}$

$= \frac{-\square \pm \square i\sqrt{\square}}{14} = \frac{-\square \pm \square i\sqrt{\square}}{7}$

So, the two solutions are ________________ and ________________.

Check by substituting one of the values.

Substitute.

Square.

Distribute.

Simplify.

Your Turn

Solve the equation using the quadratic formula. Check a solution by substitution.

8. $6x^2 - 5x - 4 = 0$

9. $x^2 + 8x + 12 = 2x$

Elaborate

10. Discussion Suppose that the quadratic equation $ax^2 + bx + c = 0$ has $p + qi$ where $q \neq 0$ as one of its solutions. What must the other solution be? How do you know?

11. Discussion You know that the graph of the quadratic function $f(x) = ax^2 + bx + c$ has the vertical line $x = -\frac{b}{2a}$ as its axis of symmetry. If the graph of $f(x)$ crosses the x-axis, where do the x-intercepts occur relative to the axis of symmetry? Explain.

12. Essential Question Check-In Why is using the quadratic formula to solve a quadratic equation easier than completing the square?

Evaluate: Homework and Practice

Personal Math Trainer

- Online Homework
- Hints and Help
- Extra Practice

1. The graph of $f(x) = x^2 + 6x$ is shown. Use the graph to determine how many real solutions the following equations have: $x^2 + 6x + 6 = 0$, $x^2 + 6x + 9 = 0$, and $x^2 + 6x + 12 = 0$. Explain.

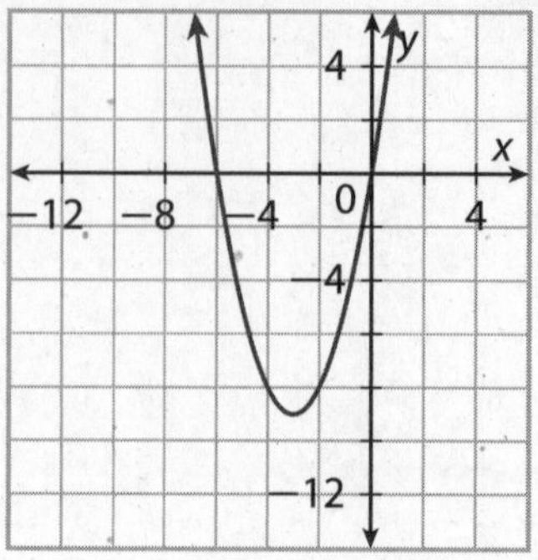

2. The graph of $f(x) = -\frac{1}{2}x^2 + 3x$ is shown. Use the graph to determine how many real solutions the following equations have: $-\frac{1}{2}x^2 + 3x - 3 = 0$, $-\frac{1}{2}x^2 + 3x - \frac{9}{2} = 0$, and $-\frac{1}{2}x^2 + 3x - 6 = 0$. Explain.

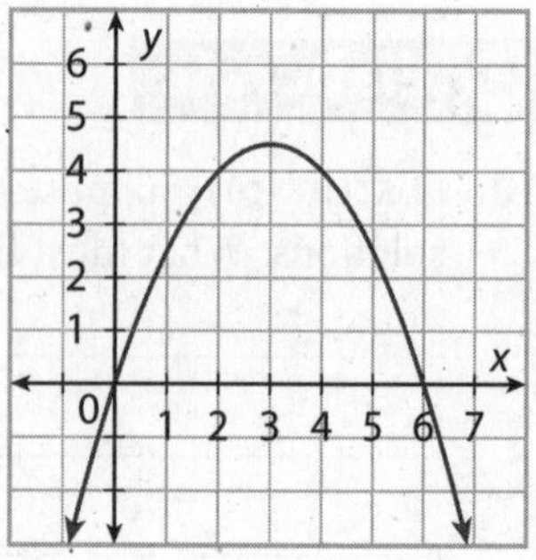

Solve the equation by completing the square. State whether the solutions are real or non-real.

3. $x^2 + 4x + 1 = 0$

4. $x^2 + 2x + 8 = 0$

5. $x^2 - 5x = -20$

6. $5x^2 - 6x = 8$

7. $7x^2 + 13x = 5$

8. $-x^2 - 6x - 11 = 0$

Without solving the equation, state the number of solutions and whether they are real or non-real.

9. $-16x^2 + 4x + 13 = 0$

10. $7x^2 - 11x + 10 = 0$

11. $-x^2 - \frac{2}{5}x = 1$

12. $4x^2 + 9 = 12x$

Answer the question by writing an equation and determining whether the solutions of the equation are real or non-real.

13. A gardener has 140 feet of fencing to put around a rectangular vegetable garden. The function $A(w) = 70w - w^2$ gives the garden's area A (in square feet) for any width w (in feet). Does the gardener have enough fencing for the area of the garden to be 1300 ft^2?

14. A golf ball is hit with an initial vertical velocity of 64 ft/s. The function $h(t) = -16t^2 + 64t$ models the height h (in feet) of the golf ball at time t (in seconds). Does the golf ball reach a height of 60 ft?

15. As a decoration for a school dance, the student council creates a parabolic arch with balloons attached to it for students to walk through as they enter the dance. The shape of the arch is modeled by the equation $y = x(5 - x)$, where x and y are measured in feet and where the origin is at one end of the arch. Can a student who is 6 feet 6 inches tall walk through the arch without ducking?

16. A small theater company currently has 200 subscribers who each pay \$120 for a season ticket. The revenue from season-ticket subscriptions is \$24,000. Market research indicates that for each \$10 increase in the cost of a season ticket, the theater company will lose 10 subscribers. A model for the projected revenue R (in dollars) from season-ticket subscriptions is $R(p) = (120 + 10p)(200 - 10p)$, where p is the number of \$10 price increases. According to this model, is it possible for the theater company to generate \$25,600 in revenue by increasing the price of a season ticket?

Solve the equation using the quadratic formula. Check a solution by substitution.

17. $x^2 - 8x + 27 = 0$

18. $x^2 - 30x + 50 = 0$

19. $x + 3 = x^2$

20. $2x^2 + 7 = 4x$

21. Place an X in the appropriate column of the table to classify each equation by the number and type of its solutions.

Equation	Two Real Solutions	One Real Solution	Two Non-Real Solutions
$x^2 - 3x + 1 = 0$			
$x^2 - 2x + 1 = 0$			
$x^2 - x + 1 = 0$			
$x^2 + 1 = 0$			
$x^2 + x + 1 = 0$			
$x^2 + 2x + 1 = 0$			
$x^2 + 3x + 1 = 0$			

H.O.T. Focus on Higher Order Thinking

22. Explain the Error A student used the method of completing the square to solve the equation $-x^2 + 2x - 3 = 0$. Describe and correct the error.

$$-x^2 + 2x - 3 = 0$$
$$-x^2 + 2x = 3$$
$$-x^2 + 2x + 1 = 3 + 1$$
$$(x + 1)^2 = 4$$
$$x + 1 = \pm\sqrt{4}$$
$$x + 1 = \pm 2$$
$$x = -1 \pm 2$$

So, the two solutions are $-1 + 2 = 1$ and $-1 - 2 = -3$.

23. Make a Conjecture Describe the values of c for which the equation $x^2 + 8x + c = 0$ has two real solutions, one real solution, and two non-real solutions.

24. Analyze Relationships When you rewrite $y = ax^2 + bx + c$ in vertex form by completing the square, you obtain these coordinates for the vertex: $\left(-\frac{b}{2a}, c - \frac{b^2}{4a}\right)$. Suppose the vertex of the graph of $y = ax^2 + bx + c$ is located on the x-axis. Explain how the coordinates of the vertex and the quadratic formula are in agreement in this situation.

Lesson Performance Task

Matt and his friends are enjoying an afternoon at a baseball game. A batter hits a towering home run, and Matt shouts, "Wow, that must have been 110 feet high!" The ball was 4 feet off the ground when the batter hit it, and the ball came off the bat traveling vertically at 80 feet per second.

a. Model the ball's height h (in feet) at time t (in seconds) using the projectile motion model $h(t) = -16t^2 + v_0 t + h_0$ where v_0 is the projectile's initial vertical velocity (in feet per second) and h_0 is the projectile's initial height (in feet). Use the model to write an equation based on Matt's claim, and then determine whether Matt's claim is correct.

b. Did the ball reach a height of 100 feet? Explain.

c. Let h_{max} be the ball's maximum height. By setting the projectile motion model equal to h_{max}, show how you can find h_{max} using the discriminant of the quadratic formula.

d. Find the time at which the ball reached its maximum height.

STUDY GUIDE REVIEW

Quadratic Equations and Complex Numbers

MODULE 11

Essential Question: How can you use quadratic equations and complex numbers to solve real-world problems?

Key Vocabulary

complex number *(número complejo)*

imaginary number *(número imaginario)*

imaginary unit *(unidad imaginaria)*

pure imaginary number *(número imaginario puro)*

KEY EXAMPLE (Lessons 11.1, 11.2)

Take square roots to solve the quadratic equations.

$3x^2 - 27 = 9$

$3x^2 = 36$ Add 27 to both sides.

$x^2 = 12$ Divide both sides by 3.

$x = \pm\sqrt{12}$ Square root

$x = \pm\sqrt{4} \cdot \sqrt{3}$ Product Property

$x = \pm 2\sqrt{3}$ Simplify.

$x^2 + 20 = 0$

$x^2 = -20$ Subtract 20 on both sides.

$x = \pm\sqrt{-20}$ Square root

$x = \pm\sqrt{(-1)(5)(4)}$ Product Property

$x = \pm 2i\sqrt{5}$ Simplify.

KEY EXAMPLE (Lesson 11.3)

Solve $2x^2 + 4x - 8 = 0$ by completing the square.

$2x^2 + 4x = 8$ Write the equation in the form $x^2 + bx = c$.

$x^2 + 2x = 4$ Divide both sides by 2.

$x^2 + 2x + 1 = 4 + 1$ Add $\left(\frac{b}{2}\right)^2$ to both sides of the equation.

$(x + 1)^2 = 5$ Solve for *x*.

$x + 1 = \pm\sqrt{5}$

$x = -1 \pm \sqrt{5}$

EXERCISES

Solve using the method stated. *(Lessons 11.1, 11.3)*

1. $x^2 - 16 = 0$ (square root)

2. $2x^2 - 10 = 0$ (square root)

3. $3x^2 - 6x - 12 = 0$ (completing the square)

4. $x^2 + 6x + 10 = 0$ (completing the square)

5. $x^2 - 4x + 4 = 0$ (factoring)

6. $x^2 - x - 30 = 0$ (factoring)

7. Explain when a quadratic equation can be solved using factoring. *(Lessons 11.1, 11.3)*

8. Can any quadratic equation be solved by completing the square Explain. *(Lessons 11.1, 11.3)*

MODULE PERFORMANCE TASK

Can You Stop in Time?

A driver sees a tree fall across the road 125 feet in front of the car. The driver is barely able to stop the car before hitting the tree. Below what speed in miles per hour must the car have been traveling when the driver saw the tree fall?

The equation for braking distance is $d = \frac{v^2}{2\mu g}$, where d is braking distance, v is speed of the car, μ is the coefficient of friction between the tires and the road, and g is the acceleration due to gravity, 32.2 ft/s^2.

Start by listing on your own paper the information you will need and the steps you will take to solve the problem. Then complete the task, using numbers, words, or algebra to explain how you reached your conclusion.

Ready to Go On?

11.1–11.3 Quadratic Equations and Complex Numbers

Personal Math Trainer

- Online Homework
- Hints and Help
- Extra Practice

Solve the equations by taking square roots, completing the square, factoring, or using the quadratic formula. *(Lessons 11.1, 11.2, 11.3)*

1. $2x^2 - 16 = 0$

2. $2x^2 - 6x - 20 = 0$

3. $2x^2 + 2x - 2 = 0$

4. $x^2 + x = 30$

5. $x^2 - 5x = 24$

6. $-4x^2 + 8 = 24$

7. $x^2 + 30 = 24$

8. $x^2 + 4x + 3 = 0$

ESSENTIAL QUESTION

9. Write a real world situation that could be modeled by the equation $7m \cdot 5m = 875$. *(Lesson 11.1)*

MODULE 11
MIXED REVIEW

Assessment Readiness

1. Which of the following equations, when graphed, has two x-intercepts?

A. $x^2 + 16 = 0$ ○ Yes ○ No

B. $2x^2 - 20 = 10$ ○ Yes ○ No

C. $-3x^2 - 6 = 0$ ○ Yes ○ No

2. Consider the equation $4x^2 + 4x - 16 = 0$. Choose True or False for each statement.

A. To solve this equation using complete the square, $\left(\frac{b}{2}\right)^2 = \left(\frac{4}{2}\right)^2 = 4$. ○ True ○ False

B. If solving this equation using factoring, then $(x + 4)(x - 4) = 0$ ○ True ○ False

C. After completing the square, $x = -\frac{1}{2} \pm \frac{\sqrt{17}}{2}$. ○ True ○ False

3. Consider the equation $ax^2 + bx = 25$. For what values of a and b would you solve this equation by taking a square root? For what values of a would the square root result in an imaginary number? Explain your answers.

4. Consider the equation $f(x) = ax^2 + bx + c$. For what values of a would the quadratic function open upward? For what values of a would the quadratic function open downward? What would happen to the function if the value of a were 0? Explain.

Quadratic Relations and Systems of Equations

MODULE 12

Essential Question: How can you use systems of equations to solve real-world problems?

LESSON 12.1
Circles

LESSON 12.2
Parabolas

LESSON 12.3
Solving Linear-Quadratic Systems

REAL WORLD VIDEO
Video game designers need a solid understanding of algebra, including systems of quadratic equations, in order to program realistic interactions within the game environment.

MODULE PERFORMANCE TASK PREVIEW

How Can You Hit a Moving Target with a Laser Beam?

Video games can be a lot of fun. They can also help players to develop and hone skills such as following instructions, using logic in problem solving, hand-eye coordination, and fine motor and spatial abilities. Video game designers often use mathematics to program realistic interactions in the video world. How can math be used to aim a laser beam to hit a virtual clay disk flying through the air? Set your sights on the target and let's get started!

Are YOU Ready?

Complete these exercises to review skills you will need for this module.

Personal Math Trainer
- Online Homework
- Hints and Help
- Extra Practice

Graphing Linear Nonproportional Relationships

Example 1 Graph $y = -2x - 3$.

x	0	−2	−3
y	−3	1	3

Make a table of values. Plot the points and draw a line through them.

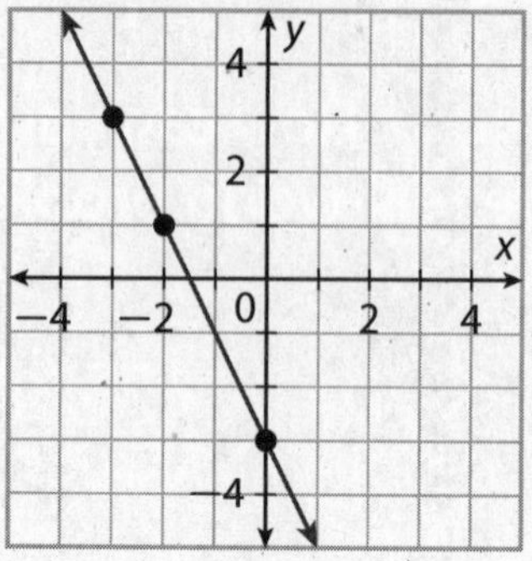

Graph each equation.

1. $y = -x + 5$

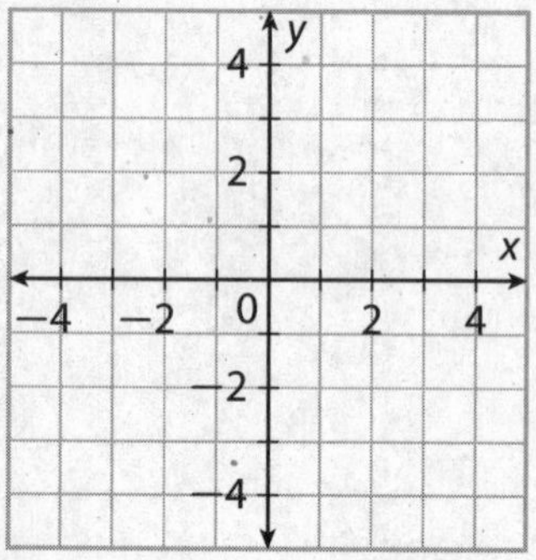

2. $y = 3x - 2$

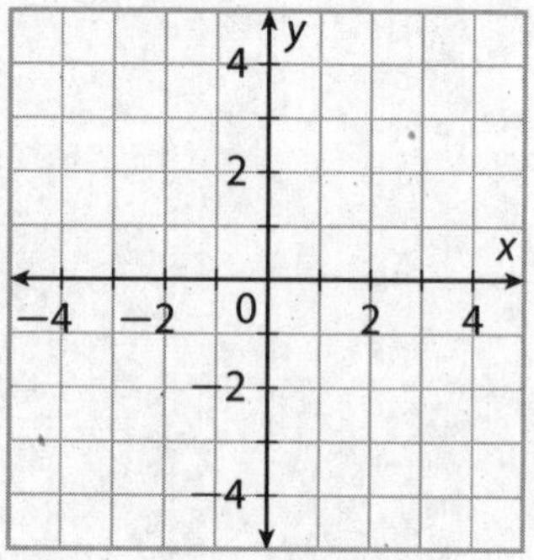

Multi-Step Equations

Example 2 Solve $4(x - 2) = 12$ for x.

$4x - 8 = 12$ Distribute.

$4x = 20$ Add 8 to both sides.

$x = 5$ Divide by 4.

Solve each equation.

3. $5 - 3x = 7(x - 1)$ ________ **4.** $3x + 2(x - 1) = 28$ ________ **5.** $2(6 - 5x) = 5x + 9$ ________

Solving Systems of Two Linear Equations

Example 3 Solve the system $\begin{cases} y = 2x + 8 \\ 3x + 2y = 2 \end{cases}$

$3x + 2(2x + 8) = 2$ Substitute.

$x = -2$ Solve for x.

$y = 2(-2) + 8 = 4$ Solve for y.

The solution is $(-2, 4)$.

Solve each system.

6. $\begin{cases} y = 10 - 3x \\ 5x - y = 6 \end{cases}$ ________ **7.** $\begin{cases} 2x - 3y = 4 \\ -x + 2y = 3 \end{cases}$ ________ **8.** $\begin{cases} 5x - 2y = 4 \\ 3x + 2y = -12 \end{cases}$ ________

Name________________________ Class______________ Date__________

12.1 Circles

Essential Question: What is the standard form for the equation of a circle, and what does the standard form tell you about the circle?

Resource Locker

Explore Deriving the Standard-Form Equation of a Circle

Recall that a circle is the set of points in a plane that are a fixed distance, called the radius, from a given point, called the center.

Ⓐ The coordinate plane shows a circle with center $C(h, k)$ and radius r. $P(x, y)$ is an arbitrary point on the circle but is not directly above or below or to the left or right of C. $A(x, k)$ is a point with the same x-coordinate as P and the same y-coordinate as C. Explain why $\triangle CAP$ is a right triangle.

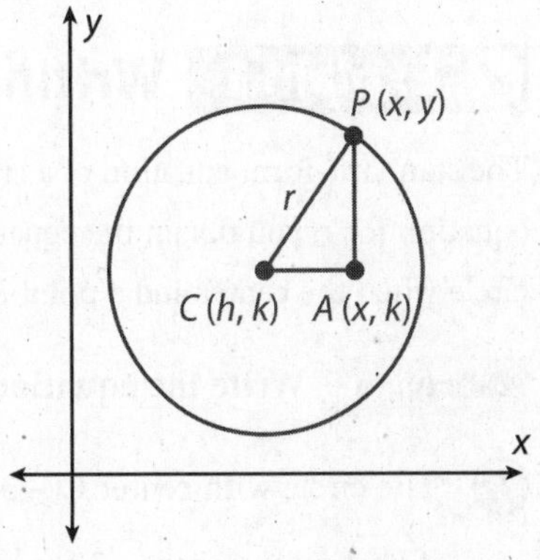

____

____

____

____

____

____

Ⓑ Identify the lengths of the sides of $\triangle CAP$. Remember that point P is arbitrary, so you cannot rely upon the diagram to know whether the x-coordinate of P is greater than or less than h or whether the y-coordinate of P is greater than or less than k, so you must use absolute value for the lengths of the legs of $\triangle CAP$. Also, remember that the length of the hypotenuse of $\triangle CAP$ is just the radius of the circle.

The length of segment AC is $|\square|$.

The length of segment AP is $|\square|$.

The length of segment CP is ______.

Ⓒ Apply the Pythagorean Theorem to $\triangle CAP$ to obtain an equation of the circle.

$$(x - \square)^2 + (y - \square)^2 = \square^2$$

Reflect

1. **Discussion** Why isn't absolute value used in the equation of the circle?

2. **Discussion** Why does the equation of the circle also apply to the cases in which P has the same x-coordinate as C or the same y-coordinate as C so that $\triangle CAP$ doesn't exist?

Explain 1 Writing the Equation of a Circle

The standard-form equation of a circle with center $C(h, k)$ and radius r is $(x - h)^2 + (y - k)^2 = r^2$. If you solve this equation for r, you obtain the equation $r = \sqrt{(x - h)^2 + (y - k)^2}$, which gives you a means for finding the radius of a circle when the center and a point $P(x, y)$ on the circle are known.

Example 1 **Write the equation of the circle.**

(A) The circle with center $C(-3, 2)$ and radius $r = 4$

Substitute -3 for h, 2 for k, and 4 for r into the general equation and simplify.

$$(x - (-3))^2 + (y - 2)^2 = 4^2$$

$$(x + 3)^2 + (y - 2)^2 = 16$$

(B) The circle with center $C(-4, -3)$ and containing the point $P(2, 5)$

Step 1 Find the radius.

$$r = CP$$

$$= \sqrt{(\square - (-4))^2 + (\square - (-3))^2}$$

$$= \sqrt{(\square)^2 + (\square)^2}$$

$$= \sqrt{\square + \square}$$

$$= \sqrt{\square} = \square$$

Step 2 Write the equation of the circle.

$$(x - (-4))^2 + (y - (-3))^2 = \square^2$$

$$(x + 4)^2 + (y + 3)^2 = \square$$

Your Turn

Write the equation of the circle.

3. The circle with center $C(1, -4)$ and radius $r = 2$

4. The circle with center $C(-2, 5)$ and containing the point $P(-2, -1)$

Explain 2 Rewriting an Equation of a Circle to Graph the Circle

Expanding the standard-form equation $(x - h)^2 + (y - k)^2 = r^2$ results in a general second-degree equation in two variables having the form $x^2 + y^2 + cx + dy + e = 0$. In order to graph such an equation or an even more general equation of the form $ax^2 + ay^2 + cx + dy + e = 0$. you must complete the square on both x and y to put the equation in standard form and identify the circle's center and radius.

Example 2 **Graph the circle after writing the equation in standard form.**

(A) $x^2 + y^2 - 10x + 6y + 30 = 0$

Write the equation. $x^2 + y^2 - 10x + 6y + 30 = 0$

Prepare to complete the square on x and y. $\left(x^2 - 10x + \blacksquare\right) + \left(y^2 + 6y + \blacksquare\right) = -30 + \blacksquare + \blacksquare$

Complete both squares. $\left(x^2 - 10x + 25\right) + \left(y^2 + 6y + 9\right) = -30 + 25 + 9$

Factor and simplify. $(x - 5)^2 + (y + 3)^2 = 4$

The center of the circle is $C(5, -3)$, and the radius is $r = \sqrt{4} = 2$.

Graph the circle.

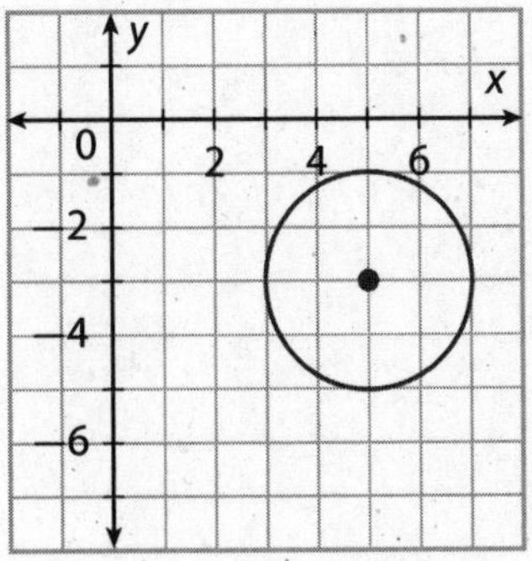

B $4x^2 + 4y^2 + 8x - 16y + 11 = 0$

Write the equation.	$4x^2 + 4y^2 + 8x - 16y + 11 = 0$
Factor 4 from the x terms and the y terms.	$4(x^2 + 2x) + 4(y^2 - 4y) + 11 = 0$
Prepare to complete the square on x and y.	$4(x^2 + 2x + \blacksquare) + 4(y^2 - 4y + \blacksquare) = -11 + 4(\blacksquare) + 4(\blacksquare)$
Complete both squares.	$4(x^2 + 2x + \square) + 4(y^2 - 4y + \square) = -11 + 4(\square) + 4(\square)$
Factor and simplify.	$4(x + \square)^2 + 4(y - \square)^2 = \square$
Divide both sides by 4.	$(x + \square)^2 + (y - \square)^2 = \square$

The center is $C(\square, \square)$, and the radius is $r = \sqrt{\square} = \square$.

Graph the circle.

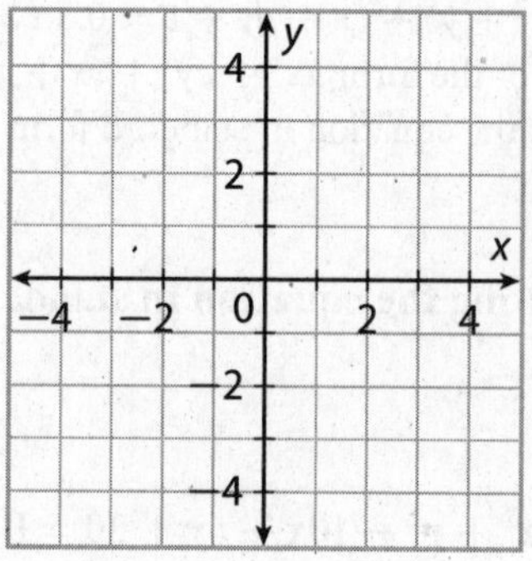

Your Turn

Graph the circle after writing the equation in standard form.

5. $x^2 + y^2 + 4x + 6y + 4 = 0$

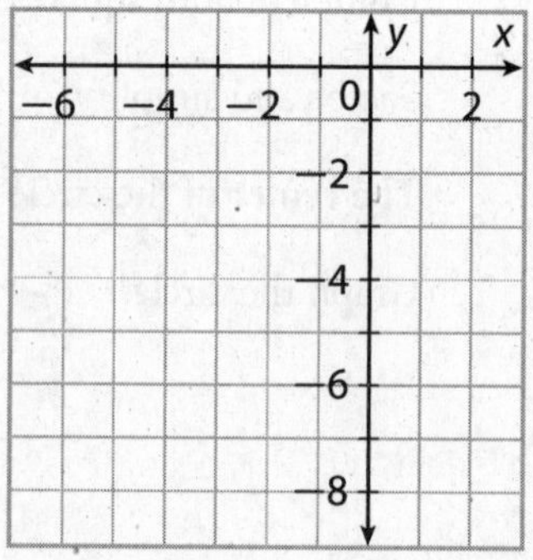

6. $9x^2 + 9y^2 - 54x - 72y + 209 = 0$

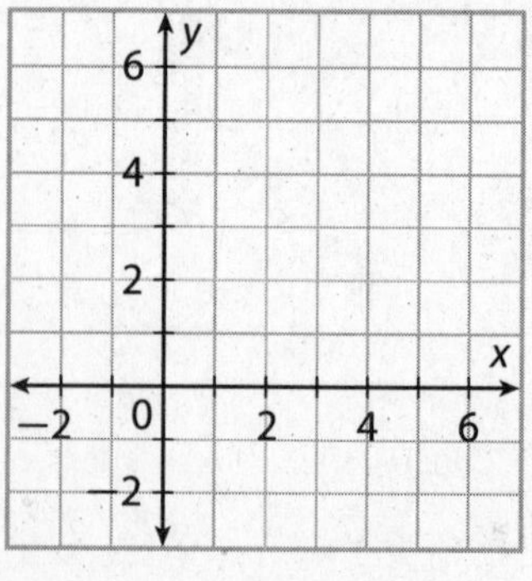

Explain 3 Solving a Real-World Problem Involving a Circle

A circle in a coordinate plane divides the plane into two regions: points inside the circle and points outside the circle. Points inside the circle satisfy the inequality $(x-h)^2+(y-k)^2<r^2$, while points outside the circle satisfy the inequality $(x-h)^2+(y-k)^2>r^2$.

Example 3 **Write an inequality representing the given situation, and draw a circle to solve the problem.**

(A) The table lists the locations of the homes of five friends along with the locations of their favorite pizza restaurant and the school they attend. The friends are deciding where to have a pizza party based on the fact that the restaurant offers free delivery to locations within a 3-mile radius of the restaurant. At which homes should the friends hold their pizza party to get free delivery?

Place	Location
Alonzo's home	$A(3, 2)$
Barbara's home	$B(2, 4)$
Constance's home	$C(-2, 3)$
Dion's home	$D(0, -1)$
Eli's home	$E(1, -4)$
Pizza restaurant	$(-1, 1)$
School	$(1, -2)$

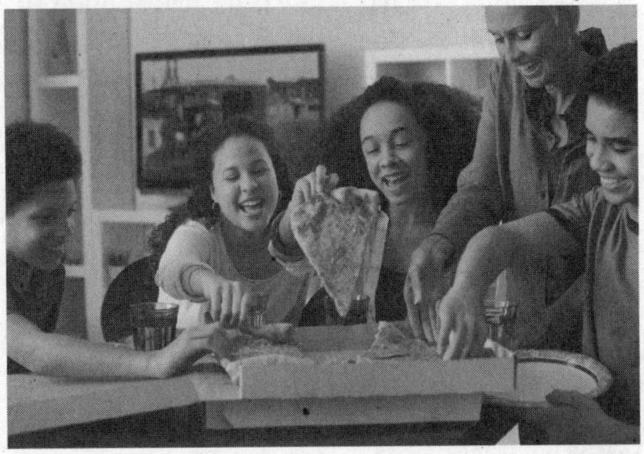

Write the equation of the circle with center $(-1, 1)$ and radius 3.

$(x-(-1))^2+(y-1)^2=3^2$, or $(x+1)^2+(y-1)^2=9$

The inequality $(x+1)^2+(y-1)^2<9$ represents the situation. Plot the points from the table and graph the circle.

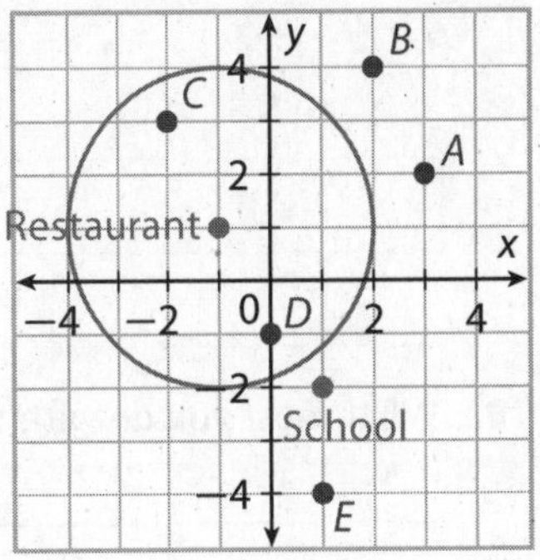

The points inside the circle satisfy the inequality. So, the friends should hold their pizza party at either Constance's home or Dion's home to get free delivery.

(B) In order for a student to ride the bus to school, the student must live more than 2 miles from the school. Which of the five friends are eligible to ride the bus?

Write the equation of the circle with center $(\square, \square)$ and radius ____.

$(x-\square)^2+(y-(\square))^2=\square^2$

$(x-\square)^2+(y+\square)^2=\square$

The inequality $(x-\square)^2+(y+\square)^2>\square$ represents the situation.

Use the coordinate grid in Part A to graph the circle.

The points ________ the circle satisfy the inequality. So, ________________ are eligible to ride the bus.

Reflect

7. For Part B, how do you know that point E isn't outside the circle?

Your Turn

Write an inequality representing the given situation, and draw a circle to solve the problem.

8. Sasha delivers newspapers to subscribers that live within a 4-block radius of her house. Sasha's house is located at point $(0, -1)$. Points A, B, C, D, and E represent the houses of some of the subscribers to the newspaper. To which houses does Sasha deliver newspapers?

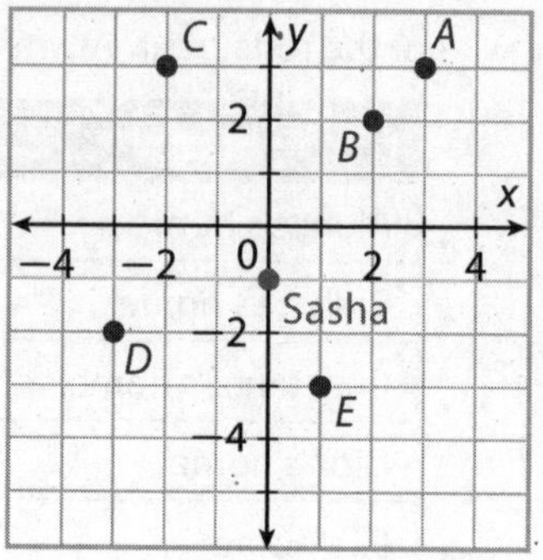

Elaborate

9. Describe the process for deriving the equation of a circle given the coordinates of its center and its radius.

10. What must you do with the equation $ax^2 + ay^2 + cx + dy + e = 0$ in order to graph it?

11. What do the inequalities $(x - h)^2 + (y - k)^2 < r^2$ and $(x - h)^2 + (y - k)^2 > r^2$ represent?

12. Essential Question Check-In What information must you know or determine in order to write an equation of a circle in standard form?

Evaluate: Homework and Practice

Personal Math Trainer

- Online Homework
- Hints and Help
- Extra Practice

Write the equation of the circle.

1. The circle with $C(4, -11)$ and radius $r = 16$

2. The circle with $C(-7, -1)$ and radius $r = 13$

3. The circle with center $C(-8, 2)$ and containing the point $P(-1, 6)$

4. The circle with center $C(5, 9)$ and containing the point $P(4, 8)$

In Exercises 5–12, graph the circle after writing the equation in standard form.

5. $x^2 + y^2 - 2x - 8y + 13 = 0$

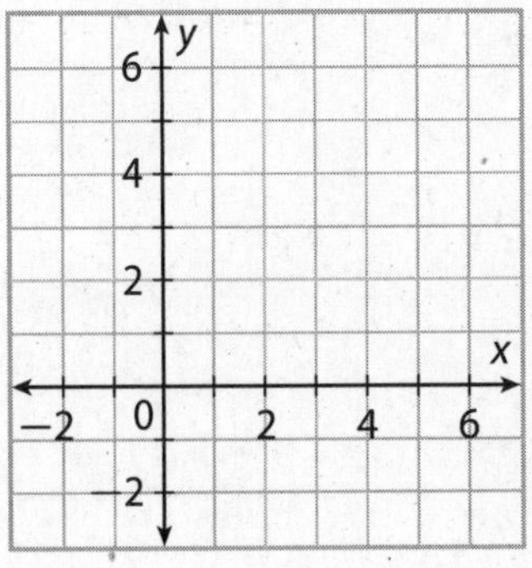

Graph the circle after writing the equation in standard form.

6. $x^2 + y^2 + 6x - 10y + 25 = 0$

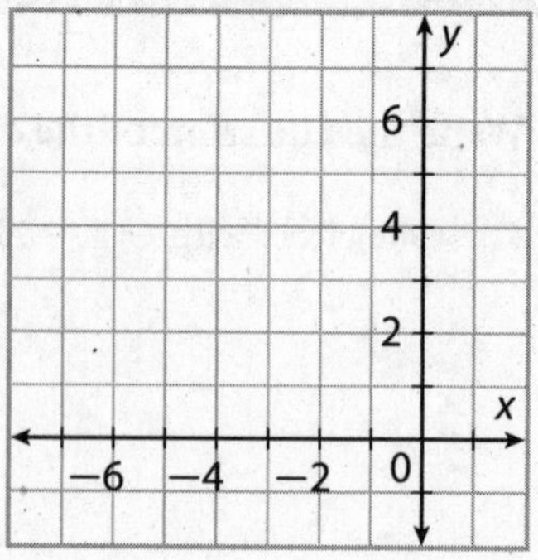

7. $x^2 + y^2 + 4x + 12y + 39 = 0$

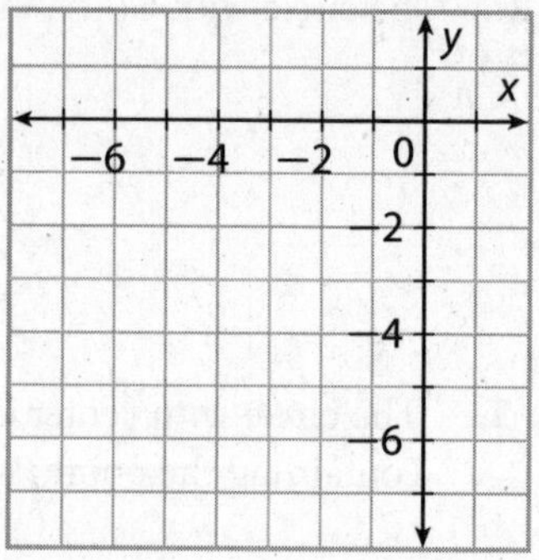

8. $x^2 + y^2 - 8x + 4y + 16 = 0$

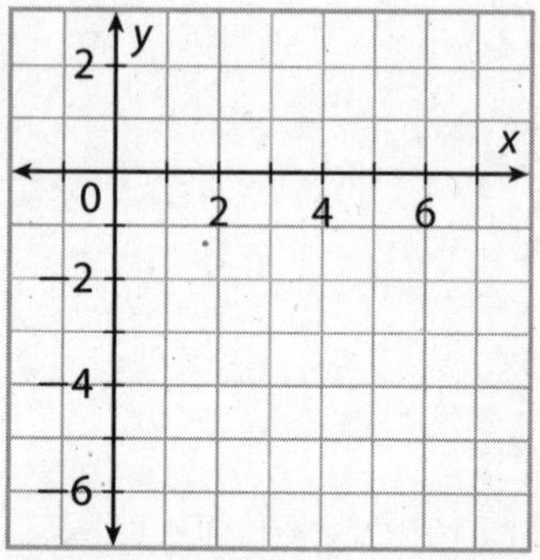

9. $8x^2 + 8y^2 - 16x - 32y - 88 = 0$

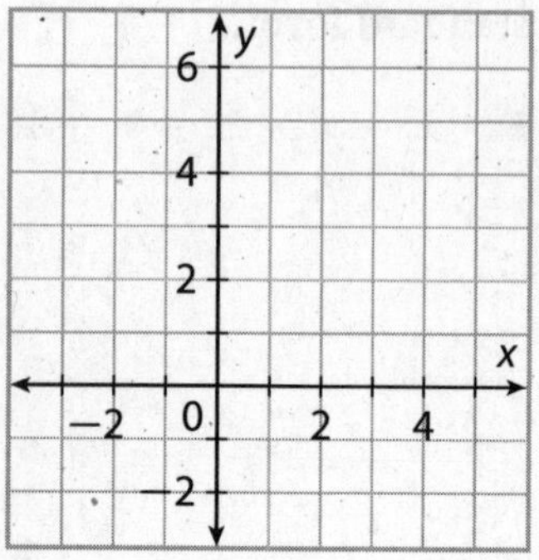

10. $2x^2 + 2y^2 + 20x + 12y + 50 = 0$

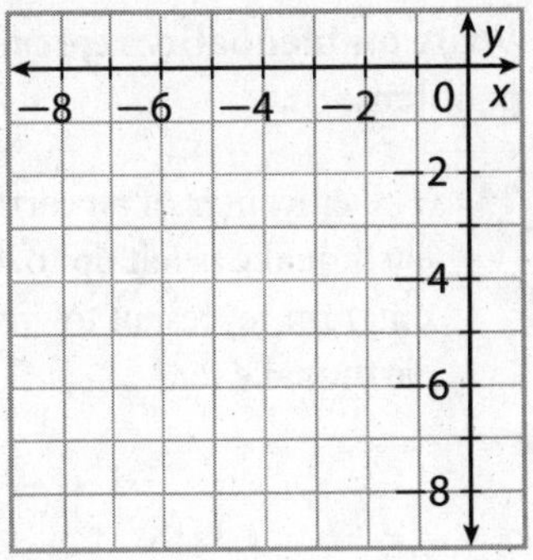

11. $12x^2 + 12y^2 - 96x - 24y + 201 = 0$

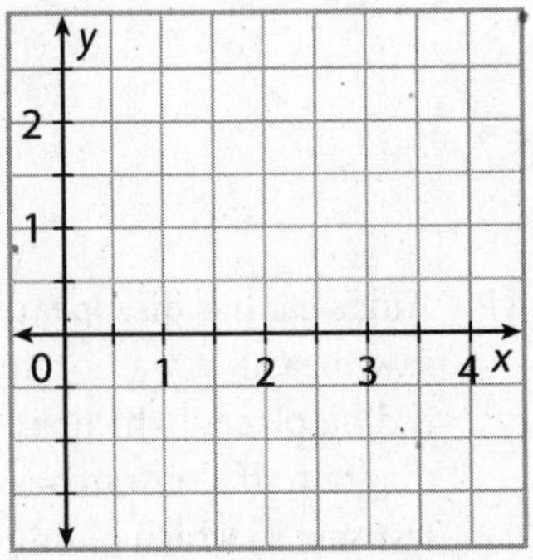

12. $16x^2 + 16y^2 + 64x - 96y + 199 = 0$

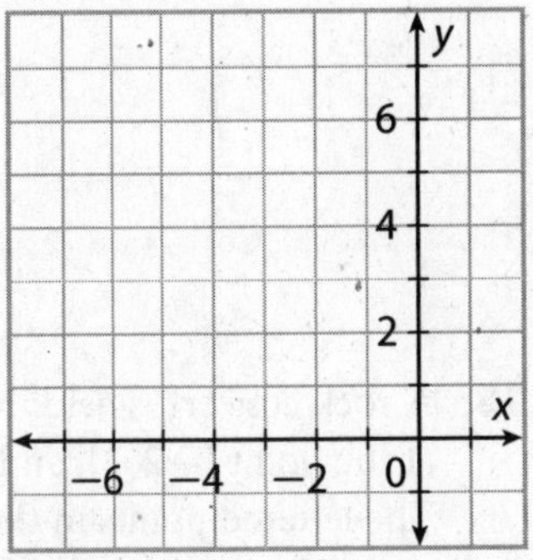

In Exercises 13–20, write an inequality representing the problem, and draw a circle to solve the problem.

13. A router for a wireless network on a floor of an office building has a range of 35 feet. The router is located at the point (30, 30). The lettered points in the coordinate diagram represent computers in the office. Which computers will be able to connect to the network through the router?

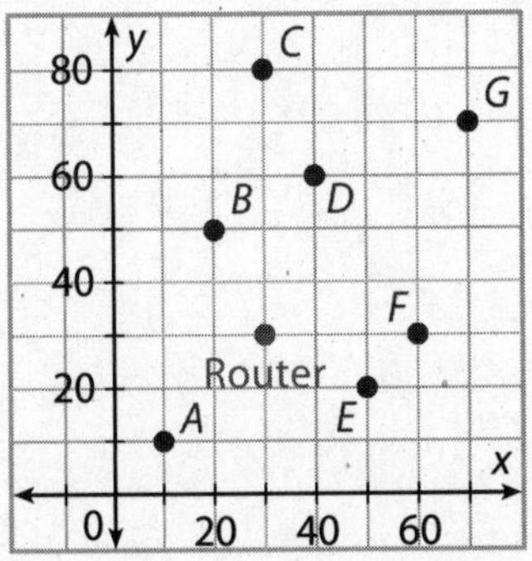

Write an inequality representing the problem, and draw a circle to solve the problem.

14. The epicenter of an earthquake is located at the point $(20, -30)$. The earthquake is felt up to 40 miles away. The labeled points in the coordinate diagram represent towns near the epicenter. In which towns is the earthquake felt?

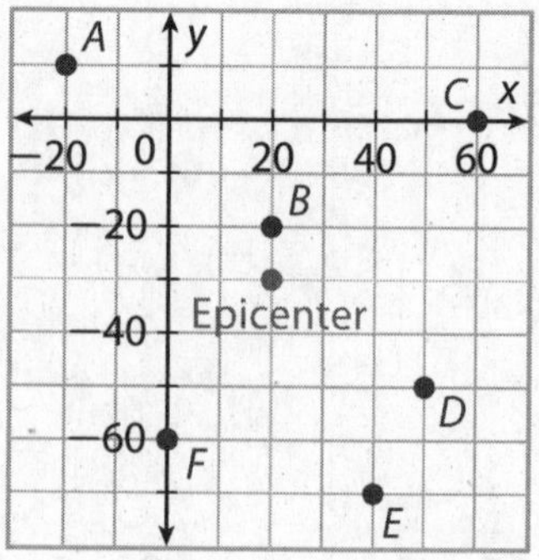

15. Aida's cat has disappeared somewhere in her apartment. The last time she saw the cat, it was located at the point $(30, 40)$. Aida knows all of the cat's hiding places, which are indicated by the lettered points in the coordinate diagram. If she searches for the cat no farther than 25 feet from where she last saw it, which hiding places will she check?

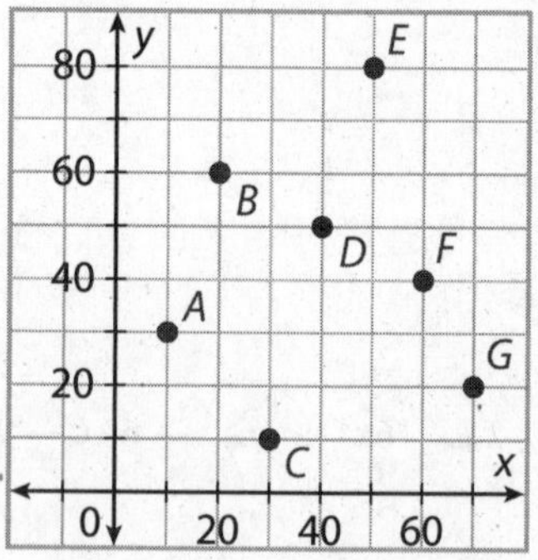

16. A rock concert is held in a large state park. The concert stage is located at the point $(-2, 2)$, and the music can be heard as far as 4 miles away. The lettered points in the coordinate diagram represent campsites within the park. At which campsites can the music be heard?

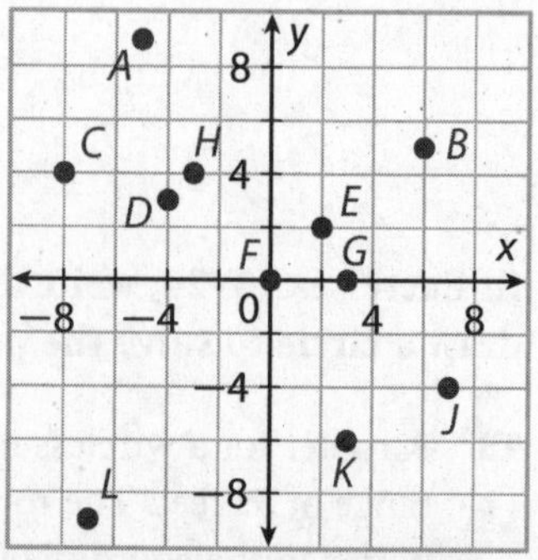

17. Business When Claire started her in-home computer service and support business, she decided not to accept clients located more than 10 miles from her home. Claire's home is located at the point (5, 0), and the lettered points in the coordinate diagram represent the homes of her prospective clients. Which prospective clients will Claire not accept?

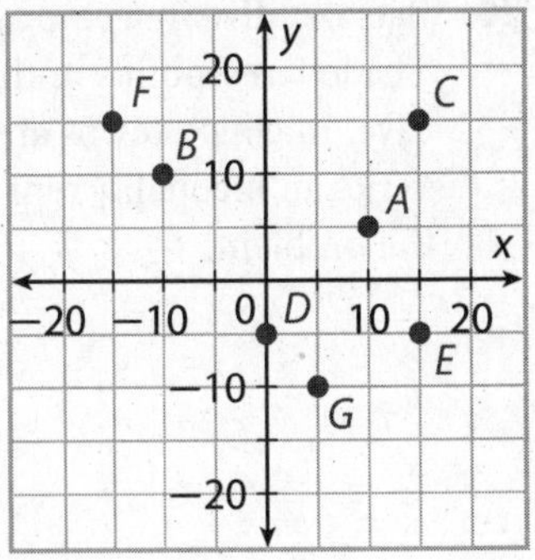

18. Aviation An airport's radar system detects airplanes that are in flight as far as 60 miles from the airport. The airport is located at $(-20, 40)$. The lettered points in the coordinate diagram represent the locations of airplanes currently in flight. Which airplanes does the airport's radar system detect?

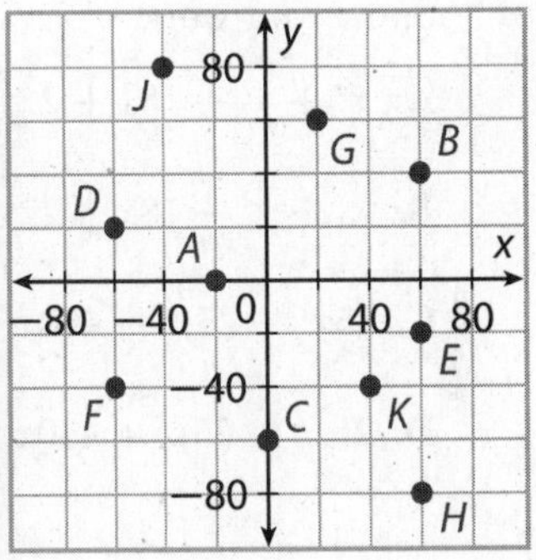

19. Due to a radiation leak at a nuclear power plant, the towns up to a distance of 30 miles from the plant are to be evacuated. The nuclear power plant is located at the point $(-10, -10)$. The lettered points in the coordinate diagram represent the towns in the area. Which towns are in the evacuation zone?

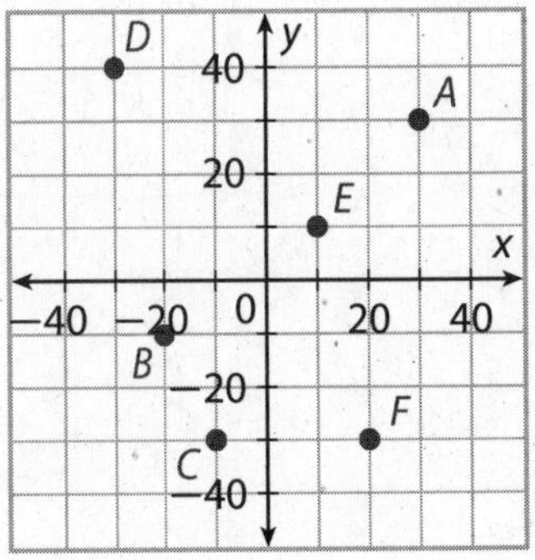

20. Bats that live in a cave at point $(-10, 0)$ have a feeding range of 40 miles. The lettered points in the coordinate diagram represent towns near the cave. In which towns are bats from the cave not likely to be observed? Write an inequality representing the problem, and draw a circle to solve the problem.

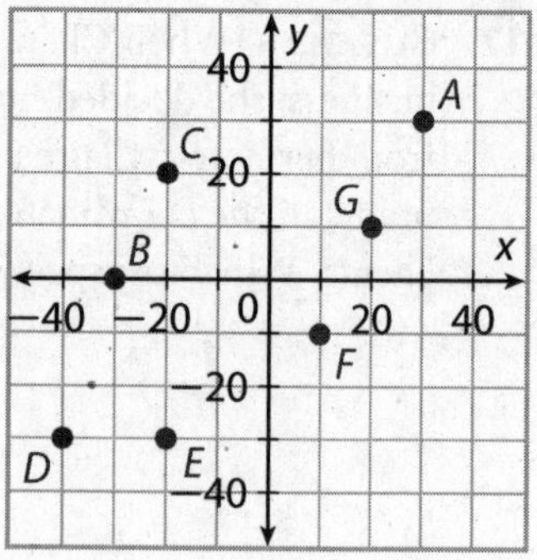

21. Match the equations to the center and radius of the circle each represents. Show your work.

A. $x^2 + y^2 + 18x + 22y - 23 = 0$ ______ $C(9, -11); r = 13$

B. $x^2 + y^2 - 18x + 22y + 33 = 0$ ______ $C(9, 11); r = 15$

C. $25x^2 + 25y^2 - 450x - 550y - 575 = 0$ ______ $C(-9, -11); r = 15$

D. $25x^2 + 25y^2 + 450x - 550y + 825 = 0$ ______ $C(-9, 11); r = 13$

H.O.T. Focus on Higher Order Thinking

22. Multi-Step A garden sprinkler waters the plants in a garden within a 12-foot spray radius. The sprinkler is located at the point (5, −10). The lettered points in the coordinate diagram represent the plants. Use the diagram for parts a–c.

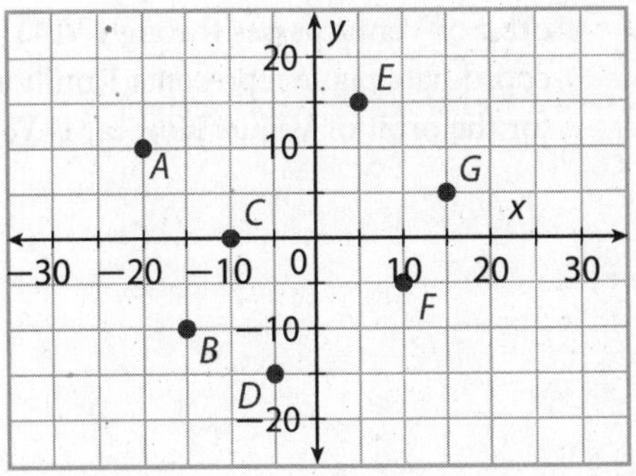

a. Write an inequality that represents the region that does not get water from the sprinkler. Then draw a circle and use it to identify the plants that do not get water from the sprinkler.

b. Suppose a second sprinkler with the same spray radius is placed at the point (10, 10). Write a system of inequalities that represents the region that does not get water from either sprinkler. Then draw a second circle and use it to identify the plants that do not get water from either sprinkler.

c. Where would you place a third sprinkler with the same spray radius so all the plants get water from a sprinkler? Write a system of inequalities that represents the region that does not get water from any of the sprinklers. Then draw a third circle to show that every plant receives water from a sprinkler.

23. Represent Real-World Situations The orbit of the planet Venus is nearly circular. An astronomer develops a model for the orbit in which the Sun has coordinates $S(0, 0)$, the circular orbit of Venus passes through $V(41, 53)$, and each unit of the coordinate plane represents 1 million miles. Write an equation for the orbit of Venus. How far is Venus from the sun?

24. Draw Conclusions The *unit circle* is defined as the circle with radius 1 centered at the origin. A *Pythagorean triple* is an ordered triple of three positive integers, (a, b, c), that satisfy the relationship $a^2 + b^2 = c^2$. An example of a Pythagorean triple is (3, 4, 5). In parts a–d, you will draw conclusions about Pythagorean triples.

a. Write the equation of the unit circle.

b. Use the Pythagorean triple $(3, 4, 5)$ and the symmetry of a circle to identify the coordinates of two points on the part of the unit circle that lies in Quadrant I. Explain your reasoning.

c. Use your answer from part b and the symmetry of a circle to identify the coordinates of six other points on the unit circle. This time, the points should be in Quadrants II, III, and IV.

d. Find a different Pythagorean triple and use it to identify the coordinates of eight points on the unit circle.

25. Make a Conjecture In a two-dimensional plane, coordinates are given by ordered pairs of the form (x, y). You can generalize coordinates to three-dimensional space by using ordered triples of the form (x, y, z) where the coordinate z is used to indicate displacement above or below the xy-plane. Generalize the standard-form equation of a circle to find the general equation of a sphere. Explain your reasoning.

Lesson Performance Task

A highway that runs straight east and west passes 6 miles south of a radio tower. The broadcast range of the station is 10 miles.

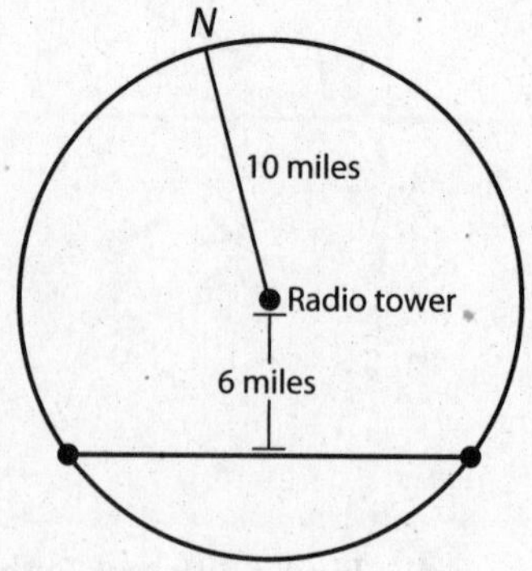

a. Determine the distance along the highway that a car will be within range of the radio station's signal.

b. Given that the car is traveling at a constant speed of 60 miles per hour, determine the amount of time the car is within range of the signal.

Name ____________ Class ____________ Date ____________

12.2 Parabolas

Essential Question: How is the distance formula connected with deriving equations for both vertical and horizontal parabolas?

Resource Locker

Explore Deriving the Standard-Form Equation of a Parabola

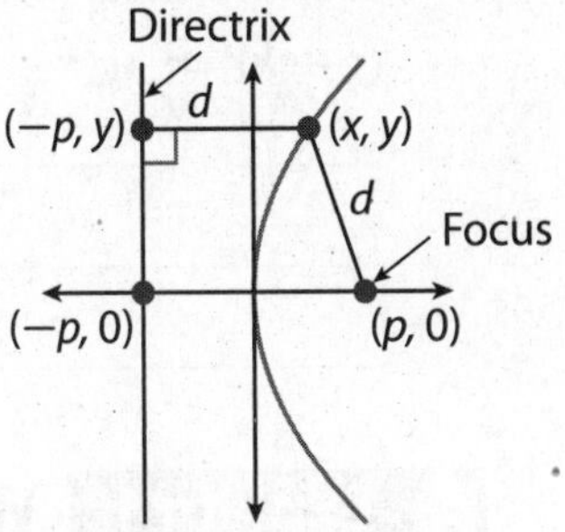

A **parabola** is defined as a set of points equidistant from a line (called the **directrix**) and a point (called the **focus**). The focus will always lie on the axis of symmetry, and the directrix will always be perpendicular to the axis of symmetry. This definition can be used to derive the equation for a horizontal parabola opening to the right with its vertex at the origin using the distance formula. (The derivations of parabolas opening in other directions will be covered later.)

(A) The coordinates for the focus are given by $\square$.

(B) Write down the expression for the distance from a point (x, y) to the coordinates of the focus:

$$d = \sqrt{(\square - \square)^2 + (\square - \square)^2}$$

(C) The distance from a point to a line is measured by drawing a perpendicular line segment from the point to the line. Find the point where a horizontal line from (x, y) intersects the directrix (defined by the line $x = -p$ for a parabola with its vertex on the origin).

$\square$

(D) Write down the expression for the distance from a point, (x, y) to the point from Step C:

$$d = \sqrt{(\square - \square)^2 + (\square - \square)^2}$$

(E) Setting the two distances the same and simplifying gives.

$$\sqrt{(x - p)^2 + y^2} = \sqrt{(x + p)^2}$$

To continue solving the problem, square both sides of the equation and expand the squared binomials.

$$\square x^2 + \square xp + \square p^2 + y^2 = \square x^2 + \square xp + \square p^2$$

(F) Collect terms.

$$\square x^2 + \square px + \square p^2 + y^2 = 0$$

(G) Finally, simplify and arrange the equation into the **standard form for a horizontal parabola** (with vertex at (0, 0)):

$$y^2 = \square$$

Reflect

1. Why was the directrix placed on the line $x = -p$?

2. **Discussion** How can the result be generalized to arrive at the standard form for a horizontal parabola with a vertex at (h, k):
$(y - k)^2 = 4p(x - h)$?

Explain 1 Writing the Equation of a Parabola with Vertex at (0, 0)

The equation for a horizontal parabola with vertex at $(0, 0)$ is written in the standard form as $y^2 = 4px$. It has a vertical directrix along the line $x = -p$, a horizontal axis of symmetry along the line $y = 0$, and a focus at the point $(p, 0)$. The parabola opens toward the focus, whether it is on the right or left of the origin $(p > 0 \text{ or } p < 0)$. Vertical parabolas are similar, but with horizontal directrices and vertical axes of symmetry:

Parabolas with Vertices at the Origin		
	Vertical	**Horizontal**
Equation in standard form	$x^2 = 4py$	$y^2 = 4px$
$p > 0$	Opens upward	Opens rightward
$p < 0$	Opens downward	Opens leftward
Focus	$(0, p)$	$(p, 0)$
Directrix	$y = -p$	$x = -p$
Axis of Symmetry	$x = 0$	$y = 0$

Example 1 **Find the equation of the parabola from the description of the focus and directrix. Then make a sketch showing the parabola, the focus, and the directrix.**

Ⓐ Focus $(-8, 0)$, directrix $x = 8$

A vertical directrix means a horizontal parabola.

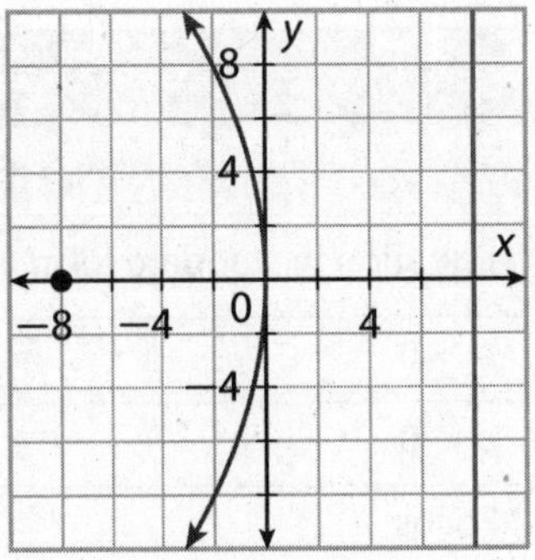

Confirm that the vertex is at $(0, 0)$:

a. The y-coordinate of the vertex is the same as the focus: 0.

b. The x-coordinate is halfway between the focus (-8) and the directrix $(+8)$: 0.

c. The vertex is at $(0, 0)$.

Use the equation for a horizontal parabola, $y^2 = 4px$, and replace p with the x coordinate of the focus: $y^2 = 4(-8)x$

Simplify: $y^2 = -32x$

Plot the focus and directrix and sketch the parabola.

Ⓑ Focus $(0, -2)$, directrix $y = 2$

A [vertical/horizontal] directrix means a [vertical/horizontal] parabola.

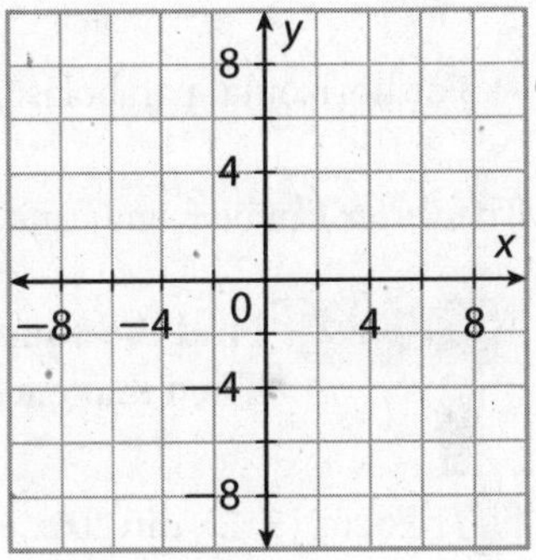

Confirm that the vertex is at $(0, 0)$:

a. The x-coordinate of the vertex is the same as the focus: 0.

b. The y-coordinate is halfway between the focus, ☐ and the directrix, ☐ : 0

c. The vertex is at $(0, 0)$.

Use the equation for a vertical parabola, ☐, and replace p with the y-coordinate of the focus: $x^2 = 4 \cdot$ ☐ $\cdot\, y$

Simplify: $x^2 =$ ☐

Plot the focus, the directrix, and the parabola.

Your Turn

Find the equation of the parabola from the description of the focus and directrix. Then make a sketch showing the parabola, the focus, and the directrix.

3. Focus $(2, 0)$, directrix $x = -2$

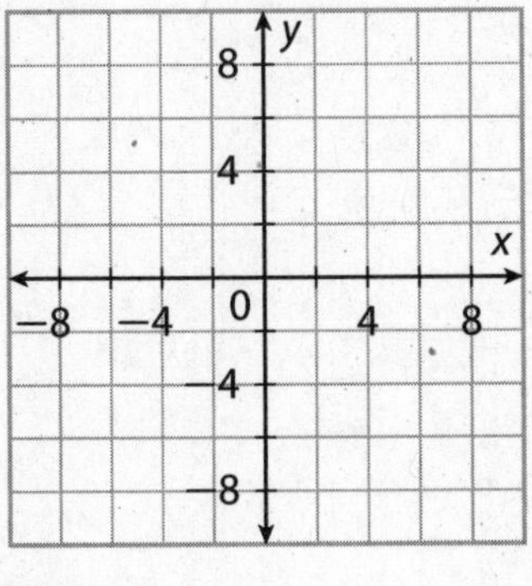

4. Focus $\left(0, -\frac{1}{2}\right)$, directrix $y = \frac{1}{2}$

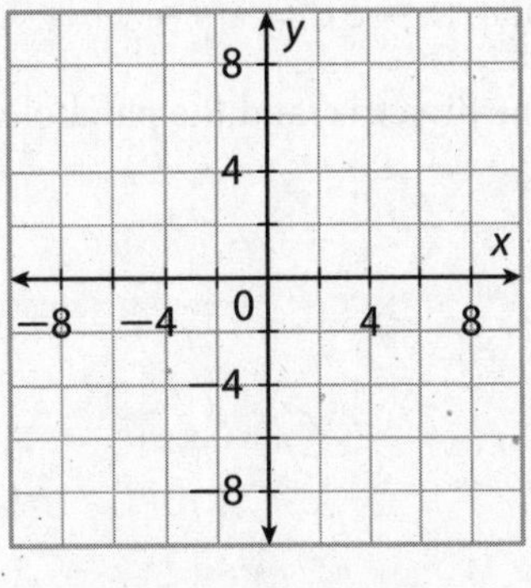

Explain 2 Writing the Equation of a Parabola with Vertex at (h, k)

The standard equation for a parabola with a vertex (h, k) can be found by translating from $(0, 0)$ to (h, k): substitute $(x - h)$ for x and $(y - k)$ for y. This also translates the focus and directrix each by the same amount.

Parabolas with Vertex (h, k)		
	Vertical	**Horizontal**
Equation in standard form	$(x-h)^2 = 4p(y-k)$	$(y-k)^2 = 4p(x-h)$
$p > 0$	Opens upward	Opens rightward
$p < 0$	Opens downward	Opens leftward
Focus	$(h, k+p)$	$(h+p, k)$
Directrix	$y = k - p$	$x = h - p$
Axis of Symmetry	$x = h$	$y = k$

p is found halfway from the directrix to the focus:

- For vertical parabolas: $p = \dfrac{(y \text{ value of focus}) - (y \text{ value of directrix})}{2}$
- For horizontal parabolas: $p = \dfrac{(x \text{ value of focus}) - (x \text{ value of directrix})}{2}$

The vertex can be found from the focus by relating the coordinates of the focus to h, k, and p.

Example 2 **Find the equation of the parabola from the description of the focus and directrix. Then make a sketch showing the parabola, the focus, and the directrix.**

(A) Focus $(3, 2)$, directrix $y = 0$

A horizontal directrix means a vertical parabola.

$p = \dfrac{(y \text{ value of focus}) - (y \text{ value of directrix})}{2} = \dfrac{2 - 0}{2} = 1$

$h =$ the x-coordinate of the focus $= 3$

Solve for k: The y-value of the focus is $k + p$, so

$k + p = 2$

$k + 1 = 2$

$k = 1$

Write the equation: $(x - 3)^2 = 4(y - 1)$

Plot the focus, the directrix, and the parabola.

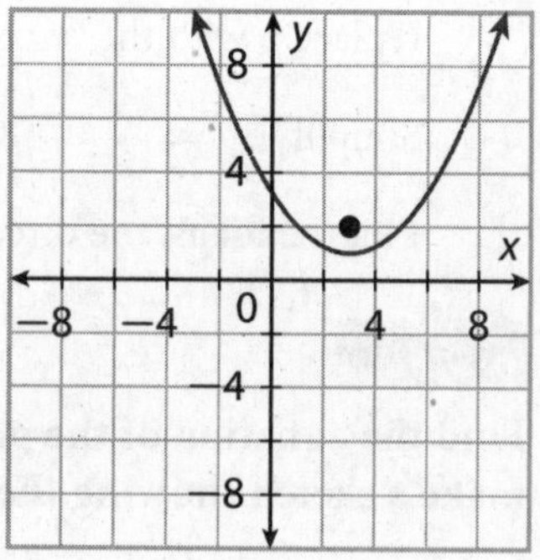

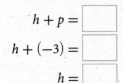

(B) Focus $(-1, -1)$, directrix $x = 5$

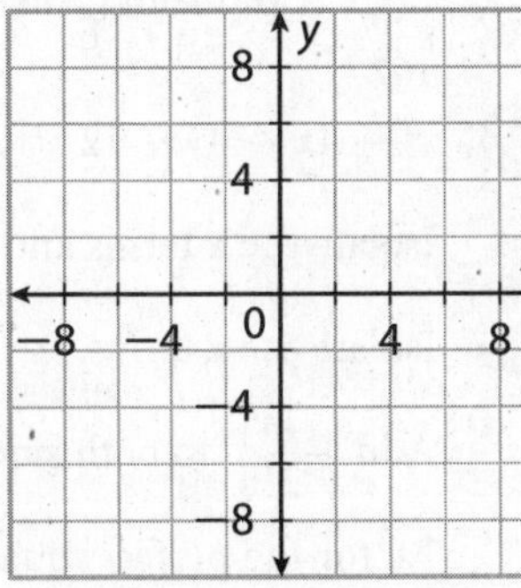

A vertical directrix means a ____________ parabola.

$p = \frac{(x \text{ value of focus}) - (x \text{ value of directrix})}{2} = \frac{\square - \square}{2} = \square$

$k =$ the y-coordinate of the focus $= \square$

Solve for h: The x-value of the focus is $h + p$, so

$h + p = \square$

$h + (-3) = \square$

$h = \square$

Write the equation: $(y + 1)^2 = \square(x - \square)$

Your Turn

Find the equation of the parabola from the description of the focus and directrix. Then make a sketch showing the parabola, the focus, and the directrix.

5. Focus $(5, -1)$, directrix $x = -3$

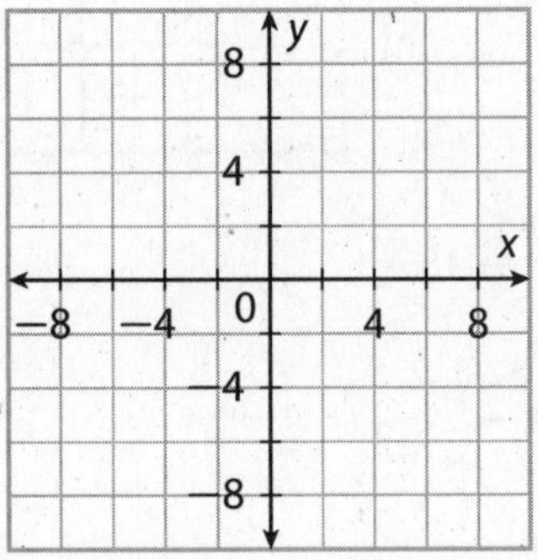

6. Focus $(-2, 0)$, directrix $y = 4$

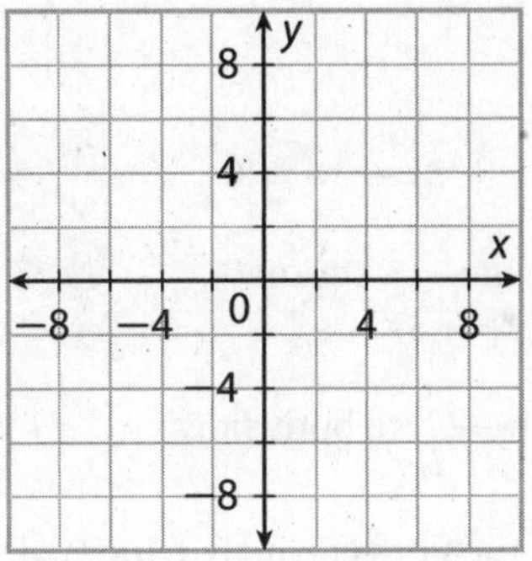

Explain 3 Rewriting the Equation of a Parabola to Graph the Parabola

A **second-degree equation in two variables** is an equation constructed by adding terms in two variables with powers no higher than 2. The general form looks like this:

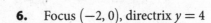

$ax^2 + by^2 + cx + dy + e = 0$

Expanding the standard form of a parabola and grouping like terms results in a second-degree equation with either $a = 0$ or $b = 0$, depending on whether the parabola is vertical or horizontal. To graph an equation in this form requires the opposite conversion, accomplished by completing the square of the squared variable.

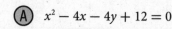

Example 3 **Convert the equation to the standard form of a parabola and graph the parabola, the focus, and the directrix.**

(A) $x^2 - 4x - 4y + 12 = 0$

Isolate the x terms and complete the square on x.

Isolate the x terms. $x^2 - 4x = 4y - 12$

Add $\left(\frac{-4}{2}\right)^2$ to both sides. $x^2 - 4x + 4 = 4y - 8$

Factor the perfect square trinomial on the left side. $(x - 2)^2 = 4y - 8$

Factor out 4 from the right side. $(x - 2)^2 = 4(y - 2)$

This is the standard form for a vertical parabola. Now find p, h, and k from the standard form $(x - h)^2 = 4p(y - k)$ in order to graph the parabola, focus, and directrix.

$4p = 4$, so $p = 1$ Vertex $= (h, k) = (2, 2)$

$h = 2$, $k = 2$ Focus $= (h, k + p) = (2, 2 + 1) = (2, 3)$

Directrix: $y = k - p = 2 - 1$, or $y = 1$

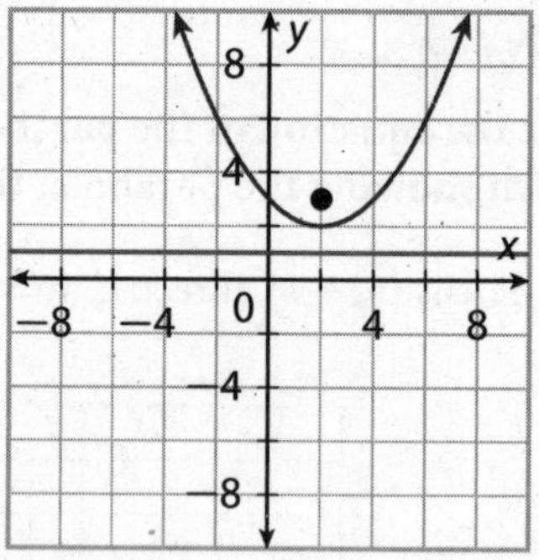

(B) $y^2 + 2x + 8y + 18 = 0$

Isolate the ☐ terms. $y^2 + 8y = -2x - 18$

Add $\left(\frac{\square}{2}\right)^2$ to both sides. $y^2 + 8y + \square = -2x - \square$

Factor the perfect square trinomial. $(y + \square)^2 = -2x - \square$

Factor out ☐ on the right. $(y + \square)^2 = \square(x + \square)$

Identify the features of the graph using the standard form of a horizontal parabola, $(y - k)^2 = 4p(x - h)$:

$4p = \square$, so $p = \square$

$h = \square$, $k = \square$

Vertex $= (h, k) = (\square, \square)$

Focus $= (h + p, k) = (\square, \square)$

Directrix: $x = h - p$, or $x = \square$

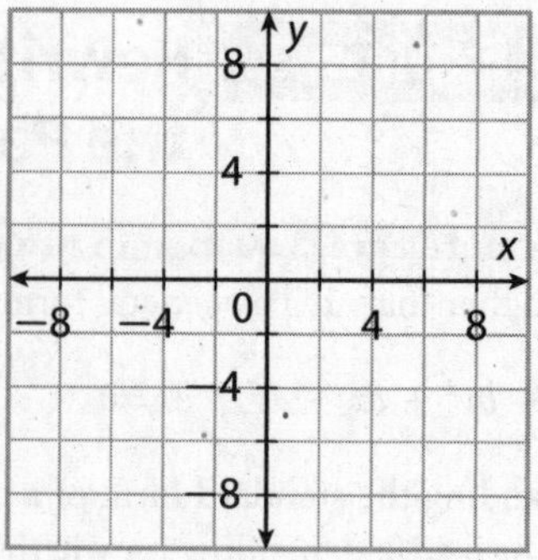

Your Turn

Convert the equation to the standard form of a parabola and graph the parabola, the focus, and the directrix.

7. $y^2 - 12x - 4y + 64 = 0$

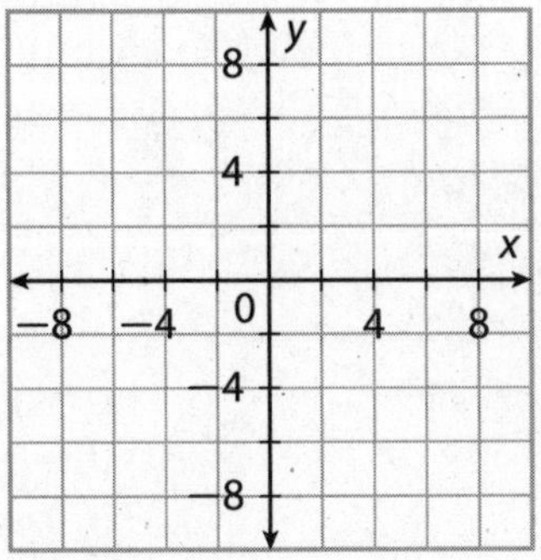

8. $x^2 + 8x - 16y - 48 = 0$

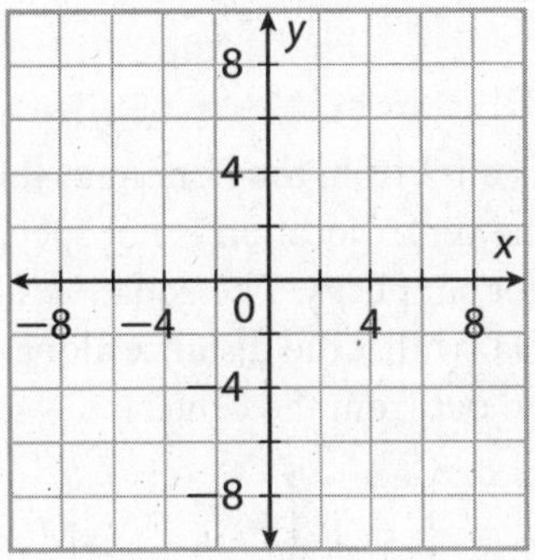

Explain 4 Solving a Real-World Problem

Parabolic shapes occur in a variety of applications in science and engineering that take advantage of the concentrating property of reflections from the parabolic surface at the focus.

Example 4

(A) Parabolic microphones are so-named because they use a parabolic dish to bounce sound waves toward a microphone placed at the focus of the parabola in order to increase sensitivity. The dish shown has a cross section dictated by the equation $x = 32y^2$ where x and y are in inches. How far from the center of the dish should the microphone be placed?

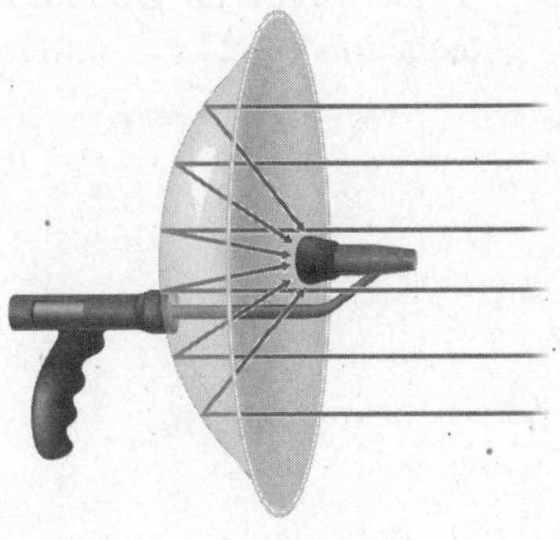

The cross section matches the standard form of a horizontal parabola with $h = 0$, $k = 0$, $p = 8$.

Therefore the vertex, which is the center of the dish, is at $(0, 0)$ and the focus is at $(8, 0)$, 8 inches away.

Ⓑ A reflective telescope uses a parabolic mirror to focus light rays before creating an image with the eyepiece. If the focal length (the distance from the bottom of the mirror's bowl to the focus) is 140 mm and the mirror has a 70 mm diameter (width), what is the depth of the bowl of the mirror?

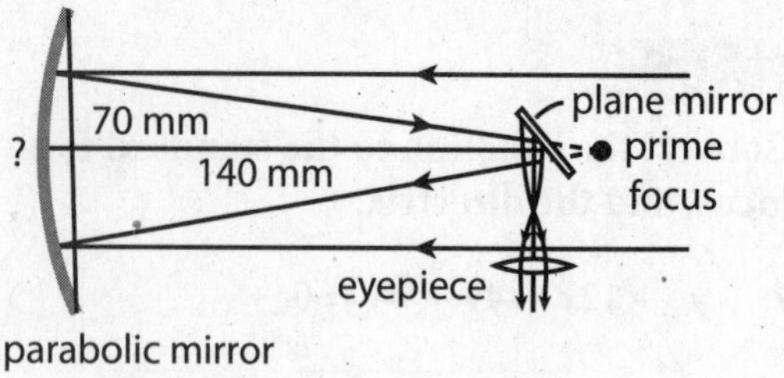

The distance from the bottom of the mirror's bowl to the focus is p. The vertex location is not specified (or needed), so use $(0, 0)$ for simplicity. The equation for the mirror is a horizontal parabola (with x the distance along the telescope and y the position out from the center).

$$\left(y - \square\right)^2 = 4p\left(x - \square\right)$$

$$y^2 = \square\, x$$

Since the diameter of the bowl of the mirror is 70 mm, the points at the rim of the mirror have y-values of 35 mm and -35 mm. The x-value of either point will be the same as the x-value of the point directly above the bottom of the bowl, which equals the depth of the bowl. Since the points on the rim lie on the parabola, use the equation of the parabola to solve for the x-value of either edge of the mirror.

$$\square^2 = \square\, x$$

$$x \approx \square \text{ mm}$$

The bowl is approximately 2.19 mm deep.

Your Turn

9. A football team needs one more field goal to win the game. The goalpost that the ball must clear is 10 feet (~3.3 yd) off the ground. The path of the football after it is kicked for a 35-yard field goal is given by the equation $y - 11 = -0.0125\,(x - 20)^2$, in yards. Does the team win?

Elaborate

10. Examine the graphs in this lesson and determine a relationship between the separation of the focus and the vertex, and the shape of the parabola. Demonstrate this by finding the relationship between p for a vertical parabola with vertex of $(0, 0)$ and a, the coefficient of the quadratic parent function $y = ax^2$.

11. Essential Question Check-In How can you use the distance formula to derive an equation relating x and y from the definition of a parabola based on focus and directrix?

Evaluate: Homework and Practice

Personal Math Trainer

- Online Homework
- Hints and Help
- Extra Practice

Find the equation of the parabola with vertex at $(0, 0)$ from the description of the focus and directrix and plot the parabola, the focus, and the directrix.

1. Focus at $(3, 0)$, directrix: $x = -3$

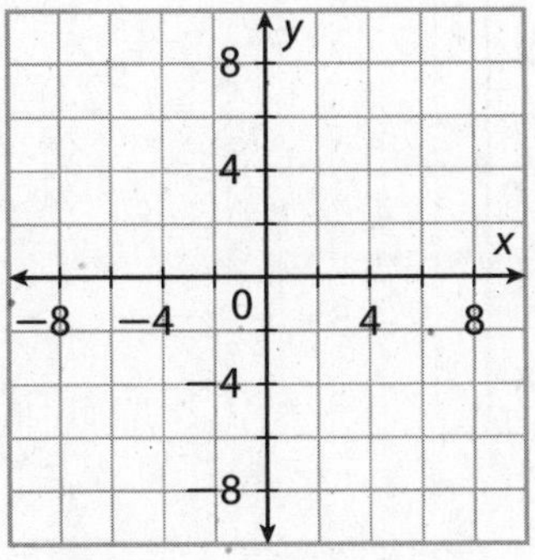

2. Focus at $(0, -5)$, directrix: $y = 5$

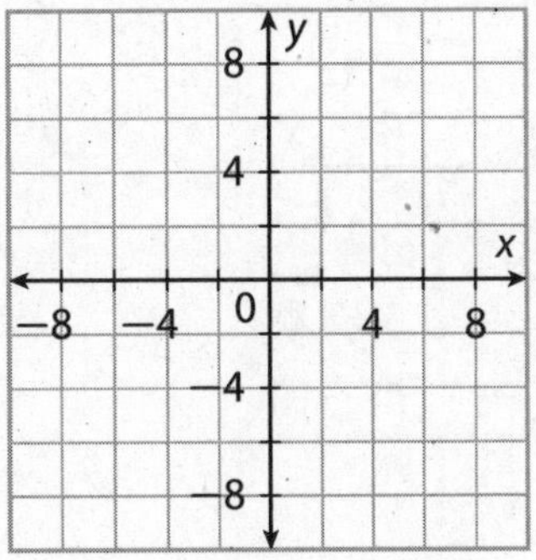

3. Focus at $(-1, 0)$, directrix: $x = 1$

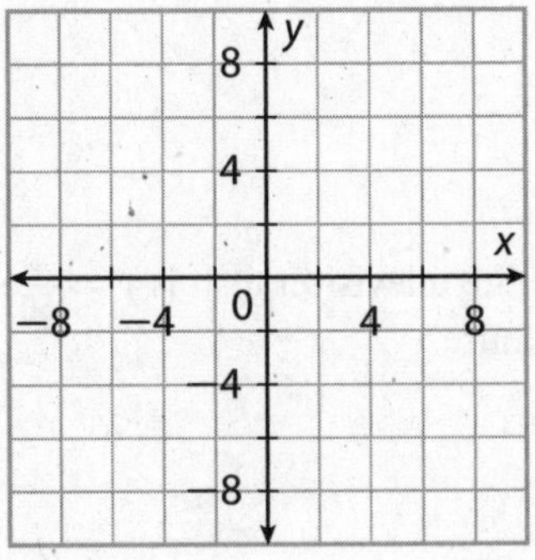

4. Focus at $(0, 2)$, directrix: $y = -2$

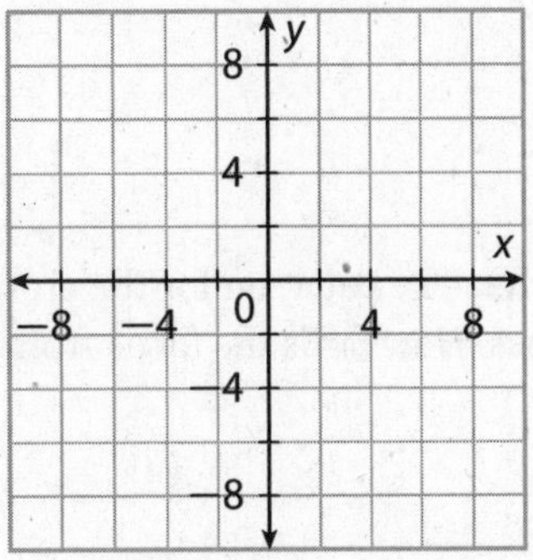

Find the equation of the parabola with the given information.

5. Vertex: $(-3, 6)$; Directrix: $x = -1.75$

6. Vertex: $(6, 20)$; Focus: $(6, 11)$

Find the equation of the parabola with vertex at (h, k) from the description of the focus and directrix and plot the parabola, the focus, and the directrix.

7. Focus at $(5, 3)$, directrix: $y = 7$

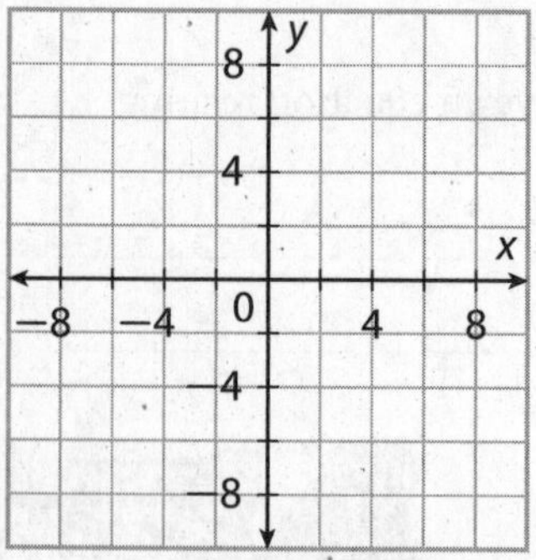

8. Focus at $(-3, 3)$, directrix: $x = 3$

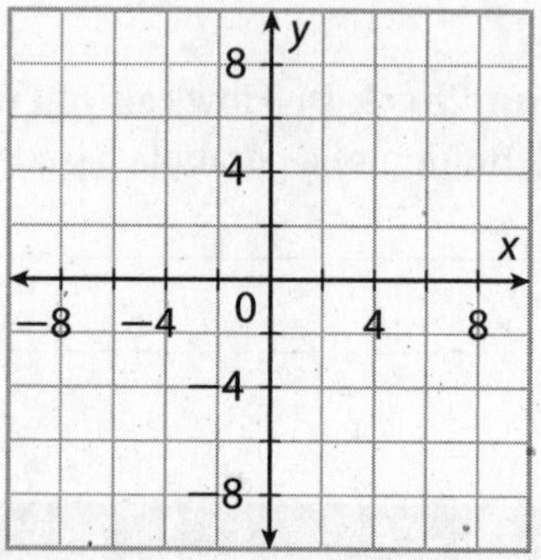

Convert the equation to the standard form of a parabola and graph the parabola, the focus, and the directrix.

9. $y^2 - 20x - 6y - 51 = 0$

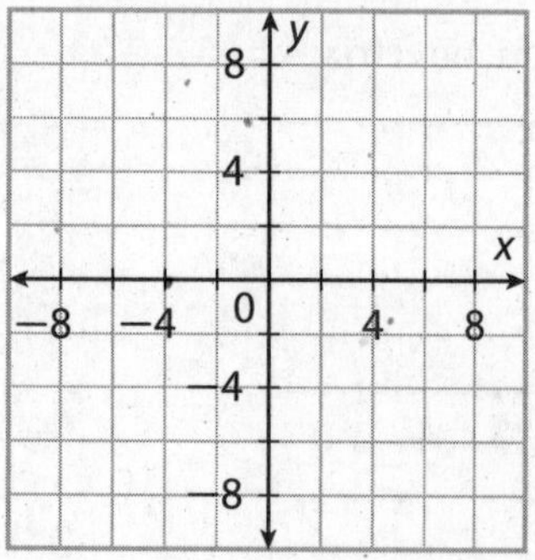

10. $x^2 - 14x - 12y + 73 = 0$

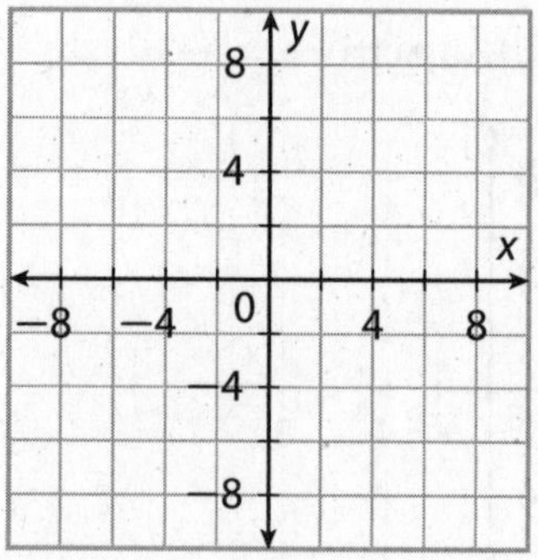

11. Communications The equation for the cross section of a parabolic satellite television dish is $y = \frac{1}{50}x^2$, measured in inches. How far is the focus from the vertex of the cross section?

12. **Engineering** The equation for the cross section of a spotlight is $y + 5 = \frac{1}{12}x^2$, measured in inches. The bulb is located at the focus. How far is the bulb from the vertex of the cross section?

13. When a ball is thrown into the air, the path that the ball travels is modeled by the parabola $y - 7 = -0.0175(x - 20)^2$, measured in feet. What is the maximum height the ball reaches? How far does the ball travel before it hits the ground?

14. A cable for a suspension bridge is modeled by $y - 55 = 0.0025x^2$, where x is the horizontal distance, in feet, from the support tower and y is the height, in feet, above the bridge. How far is the lowest point of the cable above the bridge?

15. Match each equation to its graph.

____ $y + 1 = \frac{1}{16}(x - 2)^2$ ____ $y - 1 = \frac{1}{16}(x + 2)^2$ ____ $x + 1 = -\frac{1}{16}(y - 2)^2$

A.
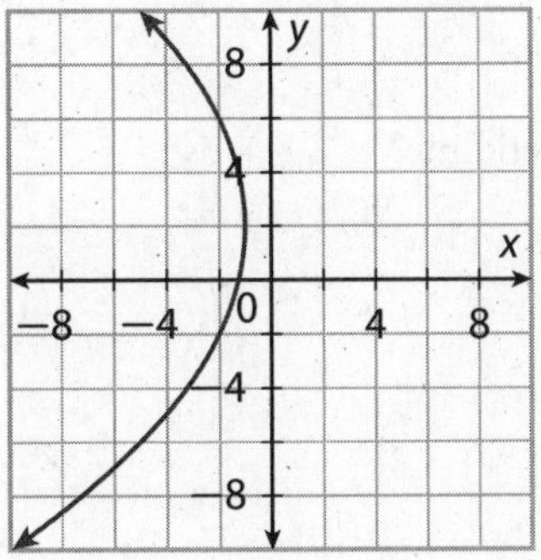

B.
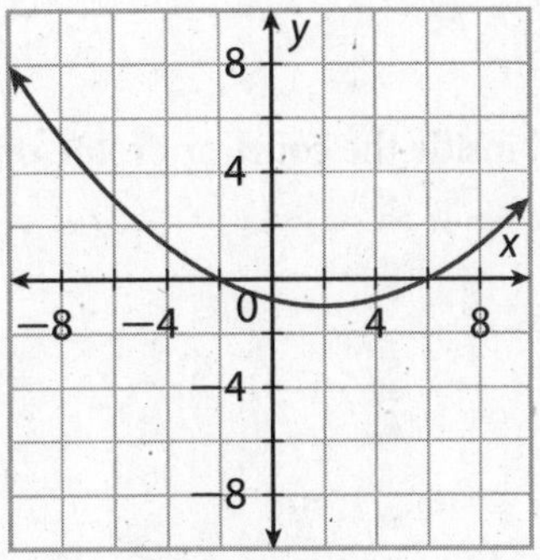

C.
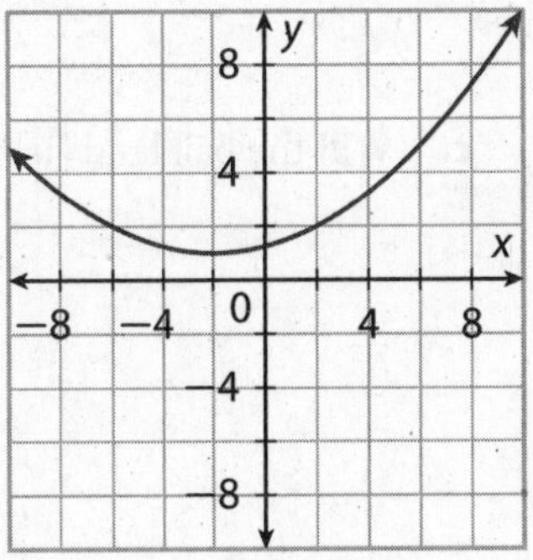

Derive the equation of the parabolas with the given information.

16. An upward-opening parabola with a focus at $(0, p)$ and a directrix $y = -p$.

17. A leftward-opening parabola with a focus at $(-p, 0)$ and directrix at $x = p$.

H.O.T. Focus on Higher Order Thinking

18. Multi-Step A tennis player hits a tennis ball just as it hits one end line of the court. The path of the ball is modeled by the equation $y - 4 = -\frac{4}{1521}(x - 39)^2$ where $x = 0$ is at the end line. The tennis net is 3 feet high, and the total length of the court is 78 feet.

a. How far is the net located from the player?

b. Explain why the ball will go over the net.

c. Will the ball land "in," that is, inside the court or on the opposite endline?

19. Critical Thinking The latus rectum of a parabola is the line segment perpendicular to the axis of symmetry through the focus, with endpoints on the parabola. Find the length of the latus rectum of a parabola. Justify your answer. *Hint*: Set the coordinate system such that the vertex is at the origin and the parabola opens rightward with the focus at $(p, 0)$.

20. Explain the Error Lois is finding the focus and directrix of the parabola $y - 8 = -\frac{1}{2}(x + 2)^2$. Her work is shown. Explain what Lois did wrong, and then find the correct answer.

$h = -2, k = 8$

$4p = -\frac{1}{2}$, so $p = -\frac{1}{8}$, or $p = -0.125$

Focus $= (h, k + p) = (-2, 7.875)$

Directrix: $y = k - p$, or $y = 8.125$

Lesson Performance Task

Parabolic microphones are used for field audio during sports events. The microphones are manufactured such that the equation of their cross section is $x = \frac{1}{34}y^2$, in inches. The feedhorn part of the microphone is located at the focus.

a. How far is the feedhorn from the edge of the parabolic surface of the microphone?

b. What is the diameter of the microphone? Explain your reasoning.

c. If the diameter is increased by 5 inches, what is the new equation of the cross section of the microphone?

Name________________________ Class______________ Date__________

12.3 Solving Linear-Quadratic Systems

Resource Locker

Essential Question: How can you solve a system composed of a linear equation in two variables and a quadratic equation in two variables?

Explore Investigating Intersections of Lines and Graphs of Quadratic Equations

There are many real-world situations that can be modeled by linear or quadratic functions. What happens when the two situations overlap? Examine graphs of linear functions and quadratic functions and determine the ways they can intersect.

(A) Examine the two graphs below to consider the ways a line could intersect the parabola.

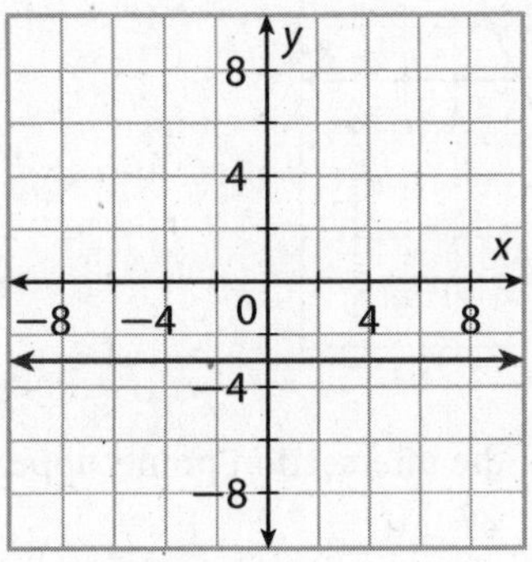
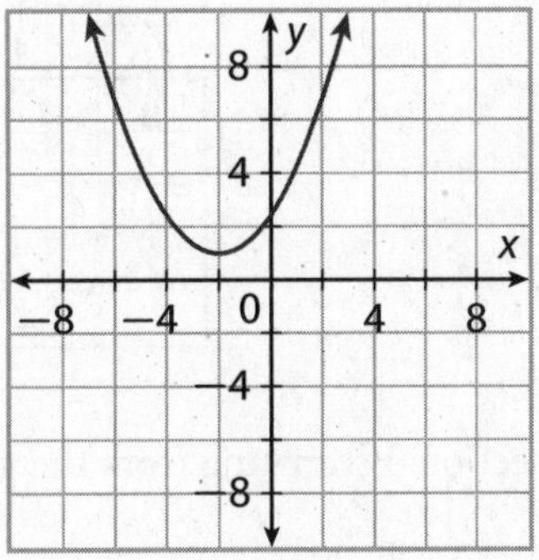

(B) Sketch three graphs of a line and a parabola: one showing intersection in one point, one showing intersection in two points, and one not showing intersection.

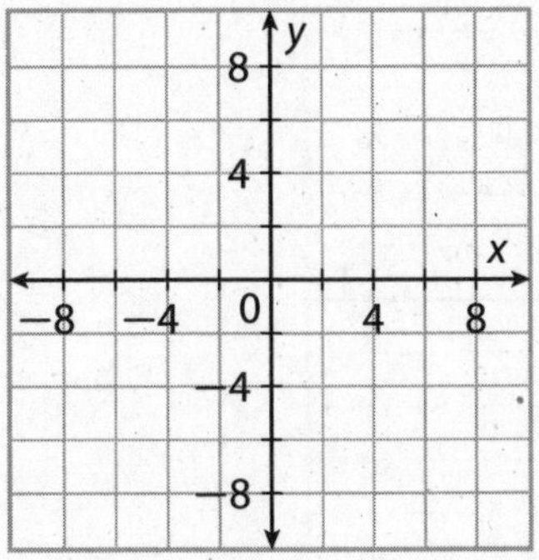
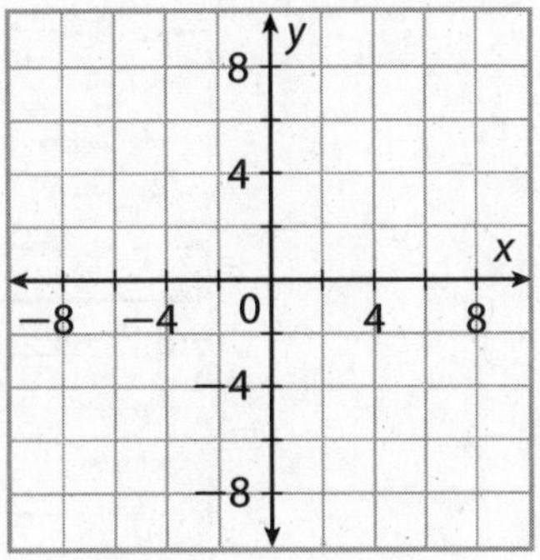
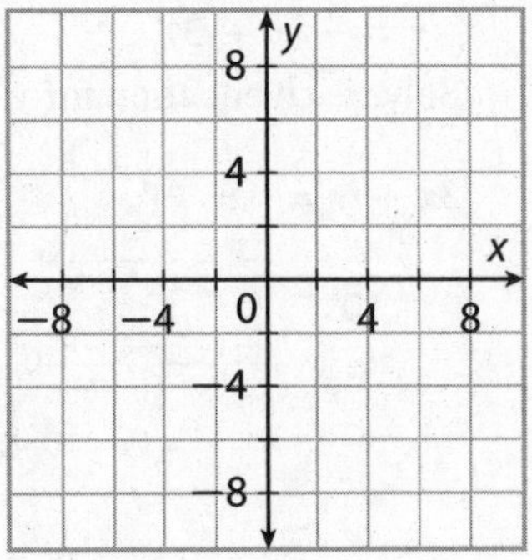

(C) So a constant linear function and a quadratic function can intersect at ________ points.

Reflect

1. If a line intersects a circle at one point, what is the relationship between the line and the radius of the circle at that point?

____

2. **Discussion** Does a line have to be horizontal to intersect a parabola at exactly one point?

____

Explain 1 Solving Linear-Quadratic Systems Graphically

Graph each equation by hand and find the set of points where the two graphs intersect.

Example 1 **Solve the given linear-quadratic system graphically.**

Ⓐ $\begin{cases} 2x - y = 3 \\ y + 6 = 2(x + 1)^2 \end{cases}$

Plot the line and the parabola.

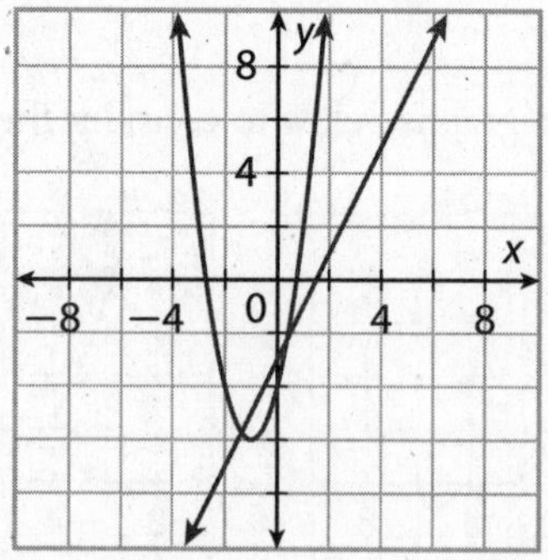

Solve each equation for y.

$2x - y = 3$
$y = 2x - 3$

$y + 6 = 2(x + 1)^2$
$y = 2(x + 1)^2 - 6$

Find the approximate points of intersection: Estimating from the graph, the intersection points appear to be near (−1.5, −5.5) and (0.5, −2.5).

The exact solutions (which can be found algebraically) are $\left(\frac{-1 - \sqrt{3}}{2}, -\sqrt{3} - 4\right)$ and $\left(\frac{-1 + \sqrt{3}}{2}, \sqrt{3} - 4\right)$, or about (−1.37, −5.73) and (0.37, −2.27).

Ⓑ $\begin{cases} 3x + y = 4.5 \\ y = \frac{1}{2}(x - 3)^2 \end{cases}$

Plot the line and the parabola on the axes provided.

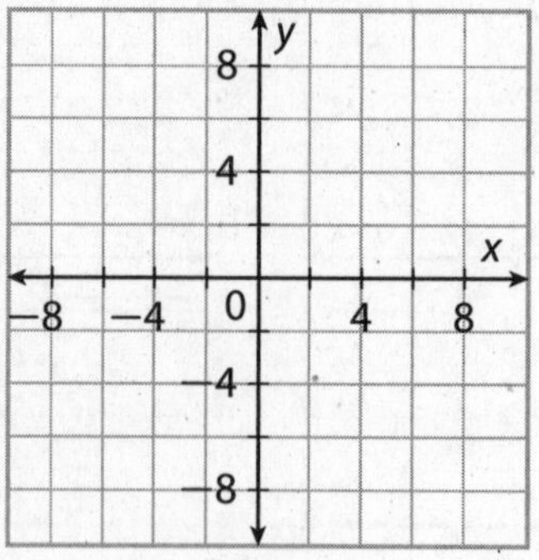

Solve each equation for y.

$3x + y = 4.5$

$y =$ ☐

$y =$ ☐

Find the approximate point(s) of intersection: ______ .

Note that checking these coordinates in the original system shows that this is an exact solution.

Your Turn

Solve the given linear-quadratic system graphically.

3. $\begin{cases} y + 3x = 0 \\ y - 6 = -3x^2 \end{cases}$

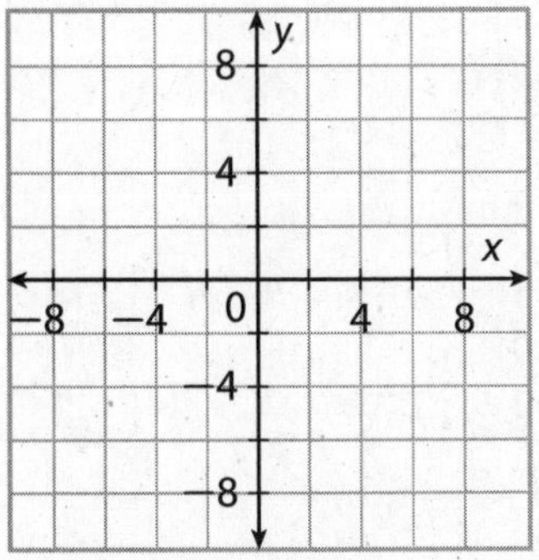

4. $\begin{cases} y + 1 = \frac{1}{2}(x - 3)^2 \\ x - y = 6 \end{cases}$

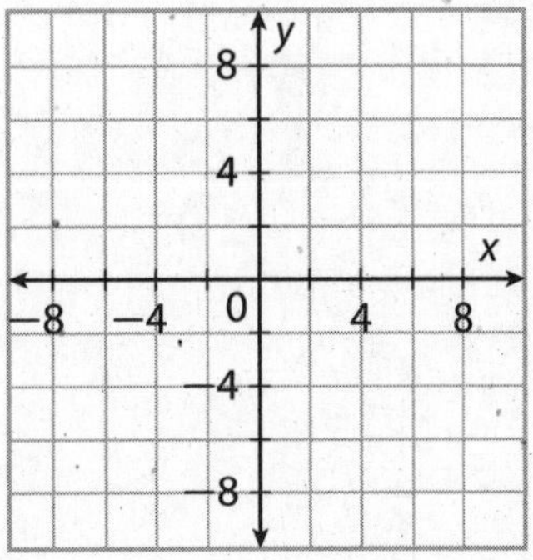

Explain 2 Solving Linear-Quadratic Systems Algebraically

Use algebra to find the solution. Use substitution or elimination.

Example 2 **Solve the given linear-quadratic system algebraically.**

Ⓐ $\begin{cases} 3x - y = 7 \\ y + 4 = 2(x + 5)^2 \end{cases}$

Solve this system using elimination. First line up the terms.

$$7 + y = 3x$$
$$4 + y = 2(x + 5)^2$$

Subtract the second equation from the first to eliminate the y variable.

$$7 + y = 3x$$
$$-\left(4 + y = 2(x + 5^2)\right)$$
$$3 = 3x - 2(x + 5)^2$$

Solve the resulting equation for x using the quadratic formula.

$$3 = 3x - 2(x + 5)^2$$
$$3 = 3x - 2(x^2 + 10x + 25)$$
$$3 = 3x - 2x^2 - 20x - 50$$
$$0 = -2x^2 - 17x - 53$$
$$2x^2 + 17x + 53 = 0$$
$$x = \frac{-17 \pm \sqrt{17^2 - 4 \cdot 2 \cdot 53}}{2 \cdot 2}$$
$$= \frac{-17 \pm \sqrt{289 - 424}}{4}$$
$$= \frac{-17 \pm \sqrt{-135}}{4}$$

There is no real number equivalent to $\sqrt{-135}$, so the system has no solution.

(B) $\begin{cases} y = \frac{1}{4}(x-3)^2 \\ 3x - 2y = 13 \end{cases}$

Solve the system by substitution. The first equation is already solved for y. Substitute the expression $\frac{1}{4}(x-3)^2$ for y in the second equation.

$$3x - 2\left(\frac{1}{4}(x-3)^2\right) = 13$$

Now, solve for x.

$$13 = 3x - 2\left(\frac{1}{4}(x-3)^2\right)$$

$$13 = 3x - \boxed{}\,(x-3)^2$$

$$13 = 3x - \frac{1}{2}\left(\boxed{}\right)$$

$$13 = 3x - \frac{1}{2}x^2 + 3x - \frac{9}{2}$$

$$13 = -\frac{1}{2}x^2 + \boxed{} - \frac{9}{2}$$

$$0 = -\frac{1}{2}x^2 + 6x - \frac{35}{2}$$

$$0 = x^2 \boxed{}$$

$$0 = \left(x \boxed{}\right)\left(x \boxed{}\right)$$

$$x = \left(\boxed{}\right) \text{ or } x = \left(\boxed{}\right)$$

So the line and the parabola intersect at two points. Use the x-coordinates of the intersections to find the points.

Solve $3x - 2y = 13$ for y.

$$3x - 2y = 13$$

$$-2y = 13 - 3x$$

Find y when $x = 5$ and when $x = 7$.

$$y = \boxed{}$$

$$y = -\frac{13 - 3 \cdot 5}{2} \qquad y = -\frac{13 - 3 \cdot 7}{2}$$

$$= -\frac{13 - 15}{2} \qquad = -\frac{13 - 21}{2}$$

$$= -\frac{-2}{2} \qquad = -\frac{-8}{2}$$

$$= 1 \qquad = 4$$

So the solutions to the system are ________________.

Reflect

5. How can you check algebraic solutions for reasonableness?

____

____

Your Turn

Solve the given linear-quadratic system algebraically.

6. $\begin{cases} x - 6 = -\frac{1}{6}y^2 \\ 2x + y = 6 \end{cases}$

7. $\begin{cases} x - y = 7 \\ x^2 - y = 7 \end{cases}$

Explain 3 Solving Real-World Problems

You can use the techniques from the previous examples to solve real-world problems.

Example 3 **Solve each problem.**

(A) A tour boat travels around an island in a pattern that can be modeled by the equation $36x^2 + 25y^2 = 900$. A fishing boat approaches the island on a path that can be modeled by the equation $3x - 2y = -8$. Is there a danger of collision? If so, where?

Write the system of equations.

$$\begin{cases} 36x^2 + 25y^2 = 900 \\ 3x - 2y = -8 \end{cases}$$

Solve the second equation for x.

$$3x - 2y = -8$$

$$3x = 2y - 8$$

$$x = \frac{2y - 8}{3}$$

Substitute for x in the first equation.

$$36x^2 + 25y^2 = 900$$

$$36\left(\frac{2y-8}{3}\right)^2 + 25y^2 = 900$$

$$36\left(\frac{4y^2 - 32y + 64}{9}\right) + 25y^2 = 900$$

$$4\left(4y^2 - 32y + 64\right) + 25y^2 = 900$$

$$16y^2 - 128y + 256 + 25y^2 = 900$$

$$41y^2 - 128y - 644 = 0$$

Solve using the quadratic equation.

$$y = \frac{128 \pm \sqrt{128^2 - 4(41)(-644)}}{2(41)}$$

$$= \frac{128 \pm \sqrt{122{,}000}}{82}$$

$$\approx -2.70 \text{ or } 5.82$$

Collisions can occur when $y \approx -2.70$ or $y \approx 5.82$.

To find the x-values, substitute the y-values into $x = \frac{2y-8}{3}$.

$$x = \frac{2(-2.70) - 8}{3} \qquad x = \frac{2(5.82) - 8}{3}$$

$$= \frac{-5.40 - 8}{3} \qquad = \frac{11.64 - 8}{3}$$

$$= \frac{-13.40}{3} \qquad = \frac{3.64}{3}$$

$$\approx -4.47 \qquad \approx 1.21$$

So the boats could collide at approximately $(-4.47, -2.70)$ or $(1.21, 5.82)$.

(B) The range of the signal from a radio station is bounded by a circle described by the equation $x^2 + y^2 = 2025$. A stretch of highway near the station is modeled by the equation $y - 15 = \frac{1}{20}x$. At which points, if any, does a car on the highway enter and exit the broadcast range of the station?

Write the system of equations.

$$\begin{cases} x^2 + y^2 = 2025 \\ y - 15 = \frac{1}{20}x \end{cases}$$

Solve the second equation for y.

$$y - 15 = \frac{1}{20}x$$

$$y = \boxed{}$$

Substitute for x in the first equation.

$$x^2 + y^2 = 2025$$

$$x^2 + \left(\boxed{}\right)^2 = 2025$$

$$x^2 + \boxed{} = 2025$$

$$\boxed{}x^2 + \frac{3}{2}x + 225 = 2025$$

$$\frac{401}{400}x^2 + \frac{3}{2}x - \boxed{} = 0$$

$$401x^2 + 600x - 720000 = 0$$

Solve using the quadratic formula.

$$y = \frac{-600 \pm \sqrt{600^2 - 4(401)(-720000)}}{2(401)}$$

$$= \frac{600 \pm \sqrt{1,155,240,000}}{802}$$

$\approx \boxed{}$ or $\boxed{}$ (rounded to the nearest hundredth)

To find the y-values, substitute the x-values into $y = \frac{1}{20}x + 15$.

The car will be within the radio station's broadcast area between ______________________.

Your Turn

8. An asteroid is traveling toward Earth on a path that can be modeled by the equation $y = \frac{1}{28}x - 7$. It approaches a satellite in orbit on a path that can be modeled by the equation $\frac{x^2}{49} + \frac{y^2}{51} = 1$. What are the approximate coordinates of the points where the satellite and asteroid might collide?

9. The owners of a circus are planning a new act. They want to have a trapeze artist catch another acrobat in mid-air as the second performer comes into the main tent on a zip-line. If the path of the trapeze can be modeled by the parabola $y = \frac{1}{4}x^2 + 16$ and the path of the zip-line can be modeled by $y = 2x + 12$, at what point can the trapeze artist grab the second acrobat?

Elaborate

10. A parabola opens to the left. Identify an infinite set of parallel lines that will intersect the parabola only once.

____

11. If a parabola can intersect a line from the set of lines $\left\{x = a \middle| a \in R\right\}$ in 0, 1, or 2 points, what do you know about the parabola?

____

12. Essential Question Check-In How can you solve a system composed of a linear equation in two variables and a quadratic equation in two variables?

____

____

Evaluate: Homework and Practice

1. How many points of intersection are on the graph?

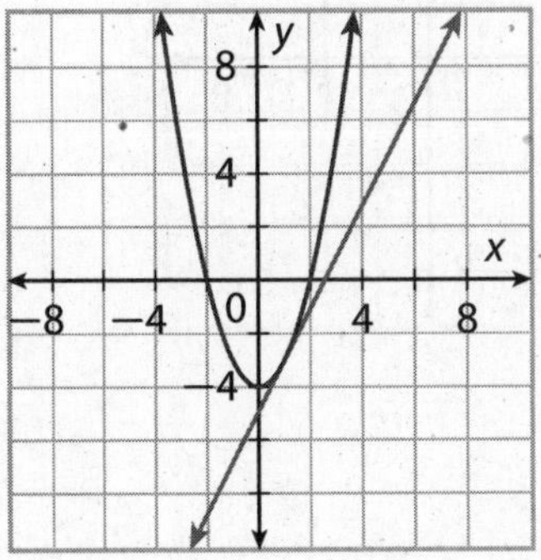

2. How many points of intersection are there on the graph of $\begin{cases} y = x^2 + 3x - 2 \\ y - x = 4 \end{cases}$?

Solve each given linear-quadratic system graphically. If necessary, round to the nearest integer.

3. $\begin{cases} y = -(x - 2)^2 + 4 \\ y = -5 \end{cases}$

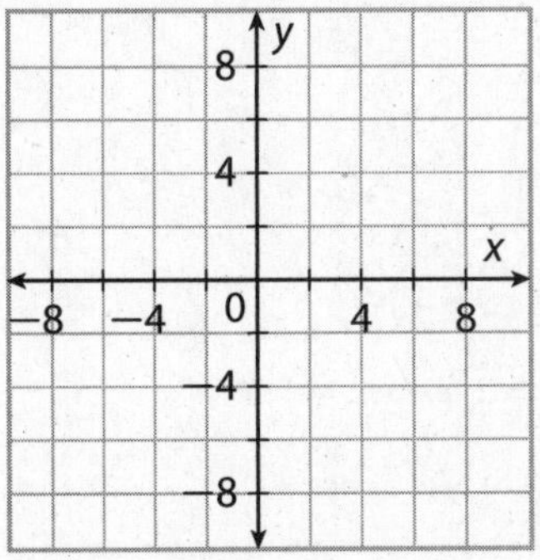

4. $\begin{cases} y - 3 = (x - 1)^2 \\ 2x + y = 5 \end{cases}$

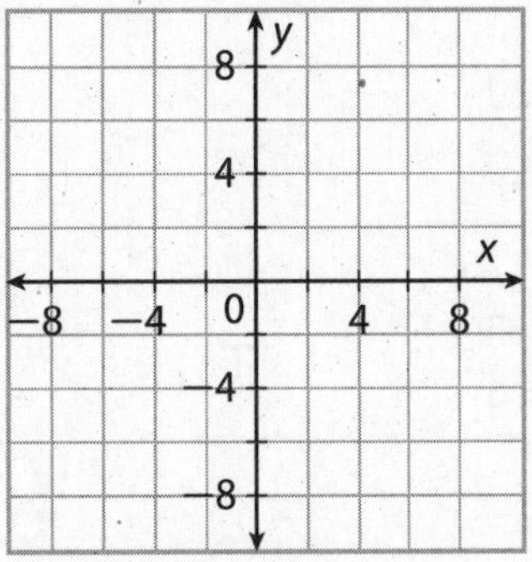

5. $\begin{cases} x = y^2 - 5 \\ -x + 2y = 12 \end{cases}$

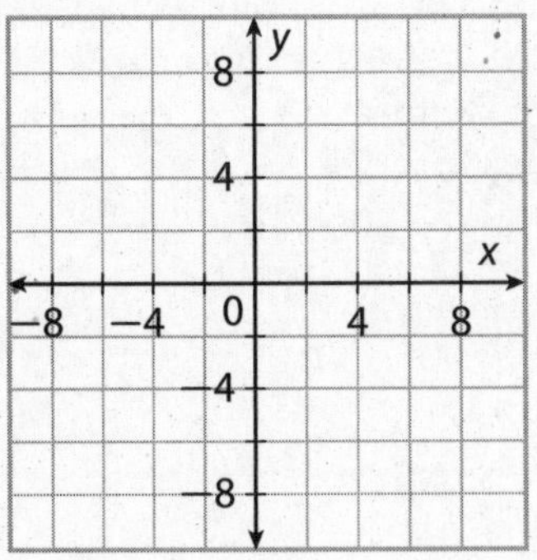

6. $\begin{cases} x - 4 = (y + 1)^2 \\ 3x - y = 17 \end{cases}$

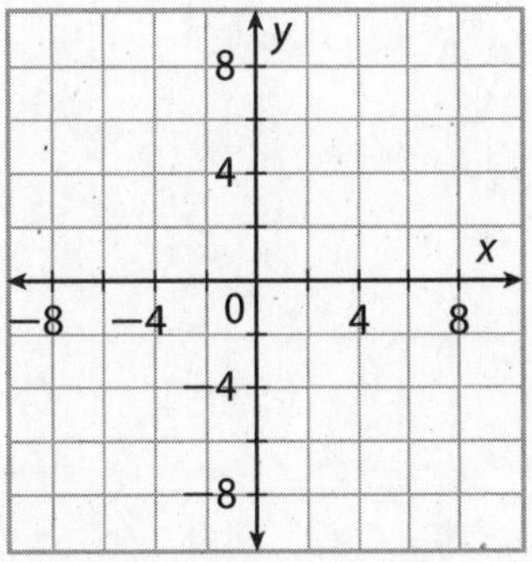

7. $\begin{cases} (y-4)^2 + x^2 = -12x - 20 \\ x = y \end{cases}$

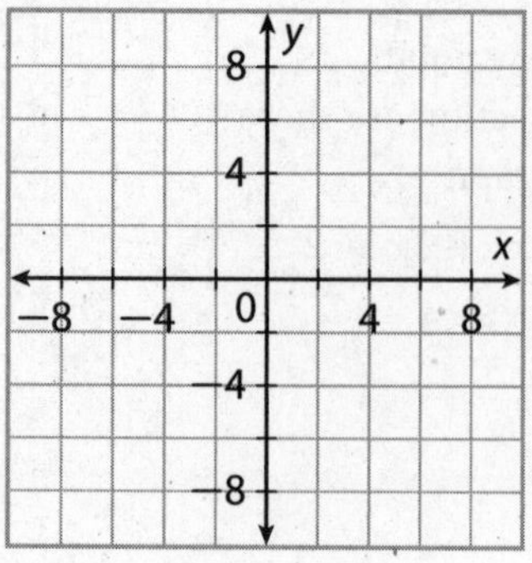

8. $\begin{cases} 5 - y = x^2 + x \\ y + 1 = \frac{3}{4}x \end{cases}$

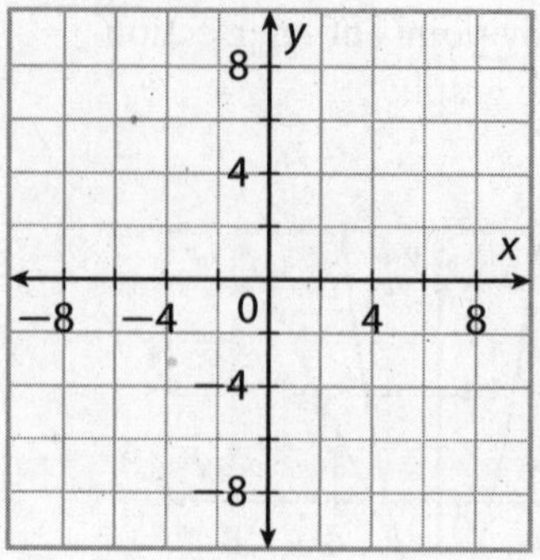

Solve each linear-quadratic system algebraically.

9. $\begin{cases} 6x + y = -16 \\ y + 7 = x^2 \end{cases}$

10. $\begin{cases} y - 5 = (x-2)^2 \\ x + 2y = 6 \end{cases}$

11. $\begin{cases} y^2 - 26 = -x^2 \\ x - y = 6 \end{cases}$

12. $\begin{cases} y - 3 = x^2 - 2x \\ 2x + y = 1 \end{cases}$

13. $\begin{cases} y = x^2 + 1 \\ y - 1 = x \end{cases}$

14. $\begin{cases} y = x^2 + 2x + 7 \\ y - 7 = x \end{cases}$

15. Jason is driving his car on a highway at a constant rate of 60 miles per hour when he passes his friend Alan whose car is parked on the side of the road. Alan has been waiting for Jason to pass so that he can follow him to a nearby campground. To catch up to Jason's passing car, Alan accelerates at a constant rate. The distance d, in miles, that Alan's car travels as a function of time t, in hours, since Jason's car has passed is given by $d = 3600t^2$. Find how long it takes Alan's car to catch up with Jason's car.

16. The flight of a cannonball toward a hill is described by the parabola $y = 2 + 0.12x - 0.002x^2$.

The hill slopes upward along a path given by $y = 0.15x$.

Where on the hill does the cannonball land?

17. Amy throws a quarter from the top of a building at the same time that a balloon is released from the ground. The equation describing the height y above ground of the quarter in feet is $y = 64 - 2x^2$, where x is the time in seconds. The equation describing the elevation of the balloon in feet is $y = 6x + 8$, where x is the time in seconds. After how many seconds will the balloon and quarter pass each other? Check your solution for reasonableness.

18. The range of an ambulance service is a circular region bounded by the equation $x^2 + y^2 = 400$. A straight road within the service area is represented by $y = 3x + 20$. Find the length of the road, in miles, that lies within the range of the ambulance service (round your answer to the nearest hundredth).

Recall that the distance formula is $d = \sqrt{(x_2 - x_1)^2 + (y_2 - y_1)^2}$.

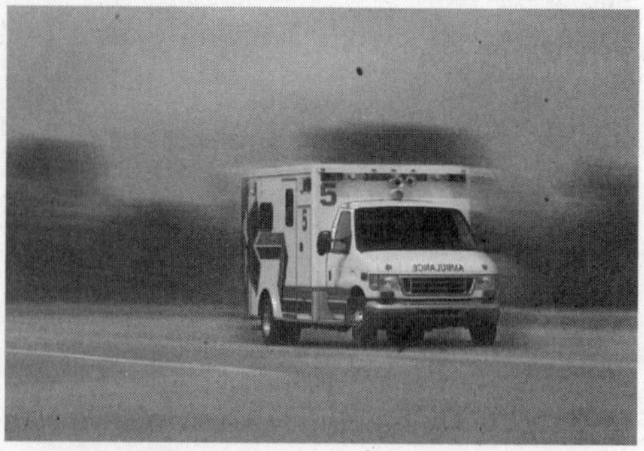

19. Match the equations with their solutions.

______ $\begin{cases} y = x - 2 \\ -x^2 + y = 4x - 2 \end{cases}$ **A.** (4, 3) (−4, −3)

______ $\begin{cases} y = (x - 2)^2 \\ y = -5x - 8 \end{cases}$ **B.** (0, −2) (5, 3)

______ $\begin{cases} 4y = 3x \\ x^2 + y^2 = 25 \end{cases}$ **C.** (2, 0)

______ $\begin{cases} y = (x - 2)^2 \\ y = 0 \end{cases}$ **D.** No solution

20. A student solved the system $\begin{cases} y - 7 = x^2 - 5x \\ y - 2x = 1 \end{cases}$ graphically and determined the only solution to be (1, 3). Was this a reasonable answer? How do you know?

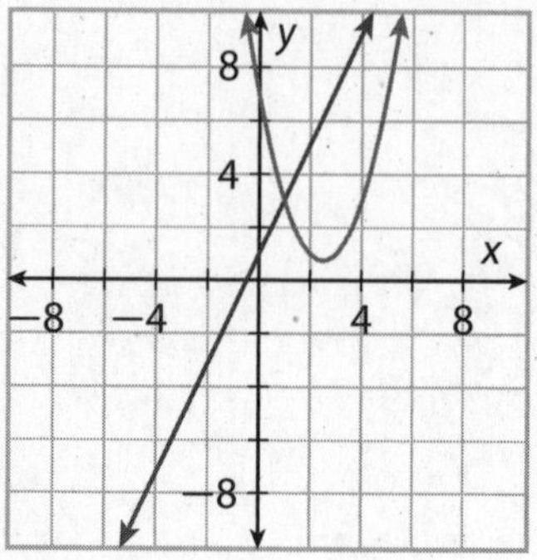

H.O.T. Focus on Higher Order Thinking

21. Explain the Error A student was asked to come up with a system of equations, one linear and one quadratic, that has two solutions. The student gave $\begin{cases} y^2 = -(x+1)^2 + 9 \\ y = x^2 - 4x + 3 \end{cases}$ as the answer. What did the student do wrong?

22. Analyze Relationships The graph shows a quadratic function and a linear function $y = d$. If the linear function were changed to $y = d + 3$, how many solutions would the new system have? If the linear function were changed to $y = d - 5$, how many solutions would the new system have? Give reasons for your answers.

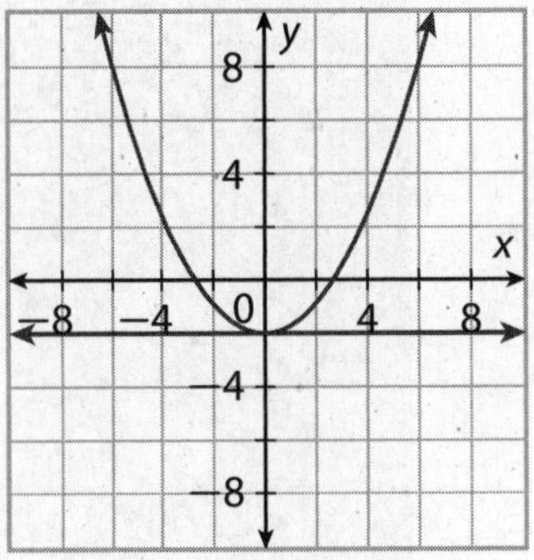

23. Make a Conjecture Given $y = 100x^2$ and $y = 0.0001x^2$, what can you say about any line that goes through the vertex of each but is not horizontal or vertical?

24. Communicate Mathematical Ideas Explain why a system of a linear equation and a quadratic equation cannot have an infinite number of solutions.

Lesson Performance Task

Suppose an aerial freestyle skier goes off a ramp with her path represented by the equation $y = -0.024(x - 25)^2 + 40$ where $x = 0$ represents the end of the ramp. If the surface of the mountain is represented by the linear equation $y = -0.5x + 25$, find the horizontal distance in feet the skier lands from the end of the ramp.

Quadratic Relations and Systems of Equations

Essential Question: How can you use systems of equations to solve real-world problems?

Key Vocabulary

directrix *(directriz)*
focus of a parabola *(foco de una parábola)*
linear equation in three variables *(ecuación lineal en tres variables)*
matrix *(matriz)*
ordered triple *(tripleta ordenada)*

KEY EXAMPLE (Lesson 12.1)

Write the equation of a circle that has a center at (–3, 5) and a radius of 9.

$(x-h)^2 + (y-k)^2 = r^2$	The standard form of the equation of a circle
$h = -3$	x-coordinate of center
$k = 5$	y-coordinate of center
$r = 9$	radius
$(x-(-3))^2 + (y-5)^2 = 9^2$	Substitute.
$(x+3)^2 + (y-5)^2 = 81$	Simplify.

KEY EXAMPLE (Lesson 12.3)

Solve the system using elimination.

$$\begin{cases} -5x + y = 10 \\ y + 2 = 3(x+4)^2 \end{cases}$$

First, line up the terms.

$$y - 10 = 5x$$
$$y + 2 = 3(x+4)^2$$

Subtract the second equation from the first.

$$\begin{array}{r} \cancel{y} - 10 = 5x \\ -\cancel{y} + (-2) = -3(x+4)^2 \\ \hline -12 = 5x - 3(x+4)^2 \end{array}$$

Solve the resulting equation for x.

$$-12 = 5x - 3(x+4)^2$$
$$-12 = 5x - 3x^2 - 24x - 48$$
$$0 = -3x^2 - 19x - 36$$
$$x = \frac{19 \pm \sqrt{(-19)^2 - 4(-3)(-36)}}{2(-3)}$$
$$x = \frac{19 \pm i\sqrt{71}}{-6}$$

There is no real number equivalent, so the system has no solution.

EXERCISES

Find the equation of the circle with the given characteristics. *(Lessons 12.1)*

1. Center: (3, 4)

Radius: 6

2. Center: (–7.5, 15)

Radius: 1.5

Find the center and radius of the given circle. *(Lessons 12.1)*

3. $(x-5)^2+(y-8)^2=144$

4. $x^2+(y+6)^2=50$

Find the solution to the system of equations using graphing or elimination. *(Lessons 12.2, 12.3)*

5. $\begin{cases} 4x+3y=1 \\ y=x^2-x-1 \end{cases}$

6. $\begin{cases} x-3y=2 \\ y=x^2+2x-34 \end{cases}$

MODULE PERFORMANCE TASK

How Can You Hit a Moving Target with a Laser Beam?

A video game designer is creating a game similar to skeet shooting, where a player will use a laser beam to hit a virtual clay disk launched into the air. The disk is launched from the ground and, if nothing blows it up, it reaches a maximum height of 30 meters and returns to the ground 60 meters away. The laser is fired from a height of 5 meters above the ground. Where should the designer point the laser to hit the disk at its maximum height?

Use your own paper to complete the task. Be sure to write down all your data and assumptions. Then use graphs, numbers, words, or algebra to explain how you reached your conclusion.

Ready to Go On?

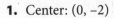

12.1–12.3 Quadratic Relations and Systems of Equations

Personal Math Trainer

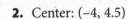

- Online Homework
- Hints and Help
- Extra Practice

Find the equation of the circle with the given characteristics. *(Lesson 12.1)*

1. Center: (0, –2)

Radius: 1

2. Center: (–4, 4.5)

Radius: 16

Find the center and radius of the given circle. *(Lesson 12.1)*

3. $x^2 + y^2 = 25$

4. $(x - 18)^2 + (y + 18)^2 = 70$

Solve the system of equations using any method. *(Lesson 12.3)*

5. $\begin{cases} y + 12 = 4x \\ y - 20 = x^2 - 8x \end{cases}$

6. $\begin{cases} y = x + 2 \\ 2y - 12 = 2x^2 - 8x \end{cases}$

ESSENTIAL QUESTION

7. Describe a real-world situation that might involve solving a linear equation and a quadratic equation. *(Lesson 12.3)*

MODULE 12
MIXED REVIEW

Assessment Readiness

1. Look at each focus and directrix. Is the resulting parabola horizontal? Select Yes or No for A–C.

A. Focus $(-5, 0)$, Directrix $x = 5$ ○ Yes ○ No

B. Focus $(4, 0)$, Directrix $x = -4$ ○ Yes ○ No

C. Focus $(0, -3)$, Directrix $y = 3$ ○ Yes ○ No

2. Consider the system of equations $\begin{cases} y = x^2 + 6x + 10 \\ y + 6 = 2x \end{cases}$. Choose Yes or No for each statement.

A. Another way to write this system is ○ Yes ○ No

$$\begin{cases} y = x^2 + 6x + 10 \\ y = 2x - 6 \end{cases}$$

B. The only way to solve this system is by graphing. ○ Yes ○ No

C. There is only one solution to the system, $(-4, 2)$. ○ Yes ○ No

3. Is it possible for a system made up of one linear equation and one quadratic equation to have infinitely many solutions? Why or why not?

4. Robin solved a quadratic equation using the process shown. Describe and correct her mistake.

$$0 = \frac{x^2}{4} - 2x + 7$$

$$x = \frac{-(-2) \pm \sqrt{(-2)^2 - 4\left(\frac{1}{4}\right)(7)}}{2(1/4)}$$

$$= \frac{2 \pm \sqrt{-4 - 7}}{\frac{1}{2}}$$

$$= 4 \pm 2\sqrt{-11}$$

$$= 4 \pm 2i\sqrt{11}$$

Functions and Inverses

MODULE 13

Essential Question: How can you use functions and inverses to solve real-world problems?

REAL WORLD VIDEO
Balls of different diameters and volumes can present a variety of packaging challenges for sports equipment manufacturers. Check out how inverse functions can help lead to efficient solutions.

MODULE PERFORMANCE TASK PREVIEW

The Smallest Cube

If you know the dimensions of a box that is shaped like a rectangular prism, you can easily find the volume of the box using the formula $v = l \times w \times h$. But what if you know the volume and want to know the dimensions? That's the problem package designers face when they know the size of a new product and must find the dimensions of the package it will be sold in. You'll do just that after you learn to "unpack" functions in this module—that is, find their inverses.

Are YOU Ready?

Complete these exercises to review skills you will need for this module.

Personal Math Trainer

- Online Homework
- Hints and Help
- Extra Practice

Squares and Square Roots

Example 1 Evaluate $\sqrt{225}$.

Since $15^2 = 15 \cdot 15 = 225$, the square root of 225 is 15.

Evaluate.

1. $\sqrt{144}$ ________

2. $\sqrt{256}$ ________

3. $\sqrt{\frac{4}{9}}$ ________

Cubes and Cube Roots

Example 2 Evaluate $\sqrt[3]{-27}$.

Since $(-3)^3 = (-3) \cdot (-3) \cdot (-3) = -27$, the cube root of -27 is -3.

Evaluate.

4. $\sqrt[3]{1000}$ ________

5. $\sqrt[3]{-125}$ ________

6. $\sqrt[3]{-64}$ ________

Linear Functions

Example 3 Write $8x - 2y = 20$ in slope-intercept form.

$-2y = -8x + 20$ Isolate the y-term.

$y = 4x - 10$ Divide both by -2.

Write each equation in slope-intercept form.

7. $2x + 3y = 24$ ________

8. $3(2y - x) = -15$ ________

9. $3x + 0.4y = -1$ ________

Name________________________ Class________________ Date__________

13.1 Graphing Polynomial Functions

Essential Question: How does the value of *n* affect the behavior of the function $f(x) = x^n$?

Resource Locker

Explore Exploring Graphs of Cubic and Quartic Functions

The **end behavior** of a function is a description of the values of the function as x approaches positive infinity ($x \to +\infty$) or negative infinity ($x \to -\infty$). The degree and leading coefficient of a polynomial function determine its end behavior.

(A) Use your graphing calculator to plot each of the cubic functions in the table, and complete the table to describe each function's general shape and end behavior.

Function	Number of Direction Changes	End Behavior as $x \to +\infty$	End Behavior as $x \to -\infty$
$f(x) = x^3 - 5x$		$f(x) \to$ ☐	$f(x) \to$ ☐
$f(x) = -2x^3$		$f(x) \to$ ☐	$f(x) \to$ ☐
$f(x) = \frac{3}{2}x^3 + x + 1$		$f(x) \to$ ☐	$f(x) \to$ ☐

(B) All three of these functions are cubic, which means that they have degree ________. Their shapes vary, but one feature they all share is that the end behavior is the same/opposite on the two ends.

(C) The graphs show quartic functions. Fill in the blanks to describe each function's general shape and end behavior.

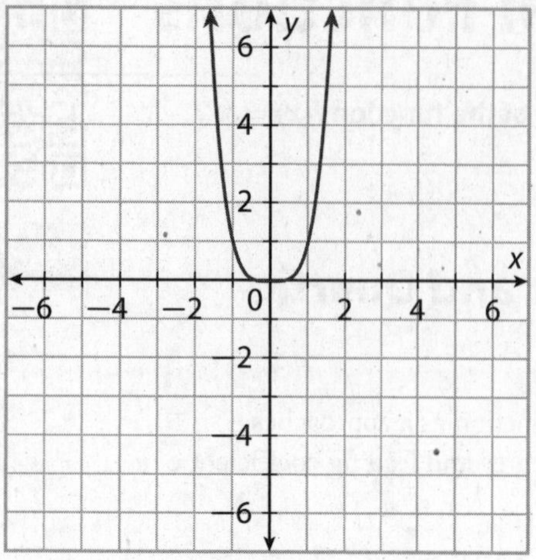

$f(x) = x^4$

____ direction change(s)

As $x \to +\infty$, $f(x) \to$ ☐.

As $x \to -\infty$, $f(x) \to$ ☐.

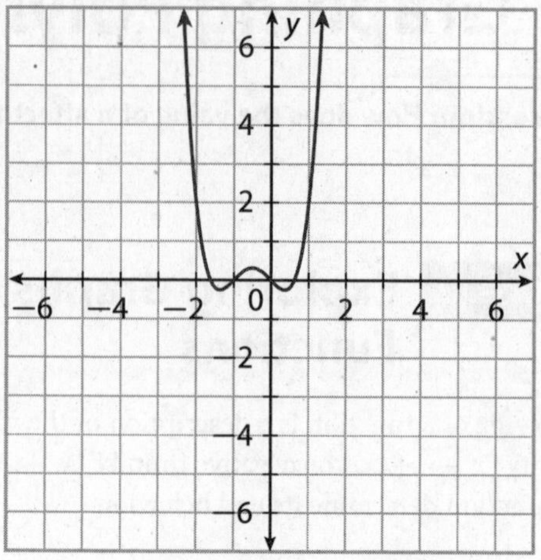

$f(x) = x^4 + 2x^3 - x$

____ direction change(s)

As $x \to +\infty$, $f(x) \to$ ☐.

As $x \to -\infty$, $f(x) \to$ ☐.

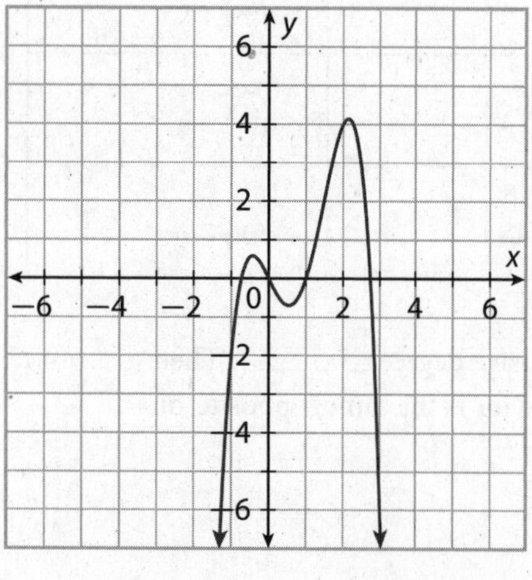

$f(x) = -x^4 + 3x^3 - 2x$

____ direction change(s)

As $x \to +\infty$, $f(x) \to$ ☐.

As $x \to -\infty$, $f(x) \to$ ☐.

(D) All three of these functions are quartic, which means that they have degree ________. Their shapes vary, but one feature they all share is that the end behavior is the same/opposite on the two ends.

Each of the graphs of the functions in Steps A and C change directions at least once. These direction changes are called **turning points**.

Reflect

1. **Discussion** How many turning points did the cubic functions have? the quartic functions? Do you notice a pattern?

____

____

____

Explain 1 Even and Odd Degree Polynomial Functions

The degree of a polynomial affects the shape of its graph. The table shows representative graphs for polynomial functions with degrees from 1 through 5. A polynomial of degree n can have up to $n - 1$ turning points.

Notice that for functions with odd degrees (1, 3, 5, ...), the end behaviors of graphs are opposite, and for functions with even degrees (2, 4, 6, ...), the end behaviors of graphs are the same.

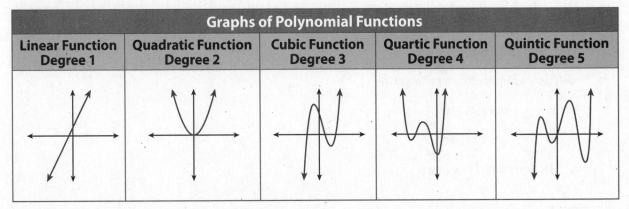

Graphs of Polynomial Functions

Linear Function Degree 1	Quadratic Function Degree 2	Cubic Function Degree 3	Quartic Function Degree 4	Quintic Function Degree 5
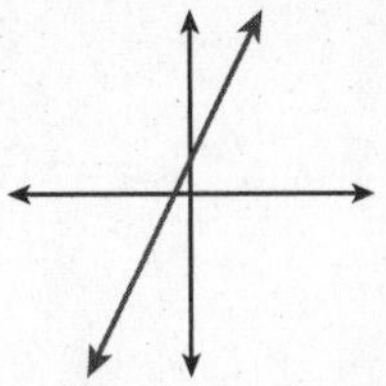	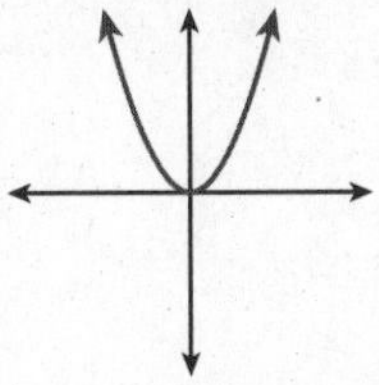	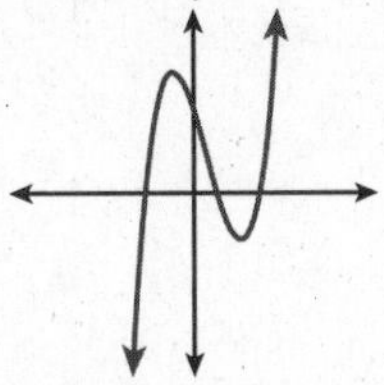	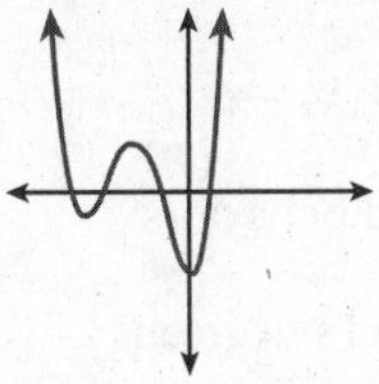	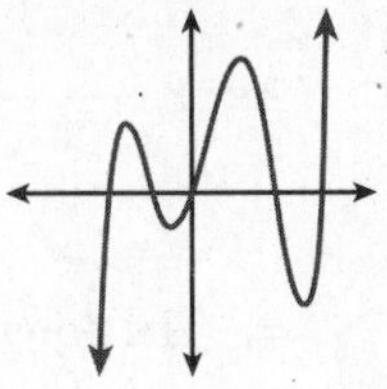

The sign of the leading coefficient determines the end behavior. The table summarizes the end behavior rules for polynomials.

$f(x)$ is a polynomial with...	Odd Degree	Even Degree
Leading coefficient $a > 0$	As $x \to +\infty$, $f(x) \to +\infty$ 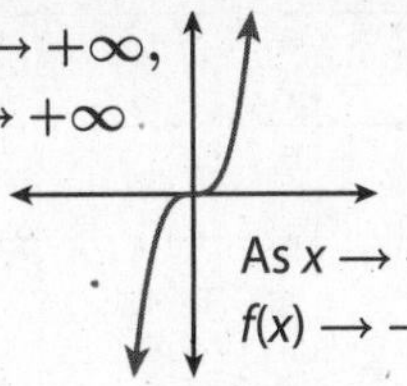 As $x \to -\infty$, $f(x) \to -\infty$	As $x \to -\infty$, $f(x) \to +\infty$ 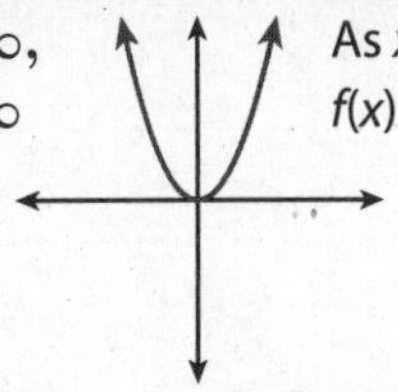 As $x \to +\infty$, $f(x) \to +\infty$
Leading coefficient $a < 0$	As $x \to -\infty$, $f(x) \to +\infty$ 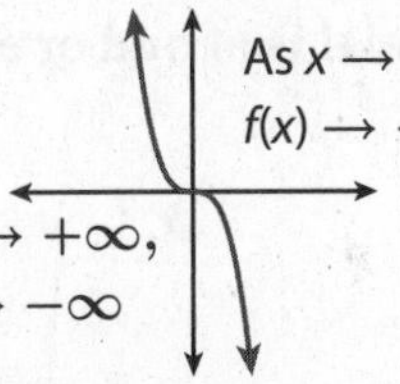 As $x \to +\infty$, $f(x) \to -\infty$	As $x \to -\infty$, $f(x) \to -\infty$ 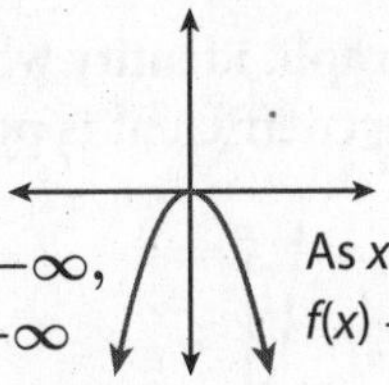 As $x \to +\infty$, $f(x) \to -\infty$

Example 1 **For each graph, identify whether the polynomial $f(x)$ is of odd or even degree, and whether the leading coefficient is positive or negative.**

(A)

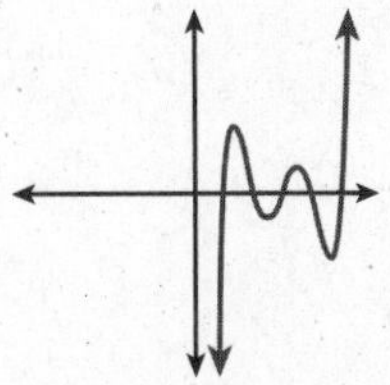

End behavior:

As $x \to +\infty$, $f(x) \to +\infty$.

The leading coefficient is positive.

As $x \to -\infty$, $f(x) \to -\infty$

$\Rightarrow$ Opposite end behaviors

$\Rightarrow$ The polynomial's degree is odd.

(B)

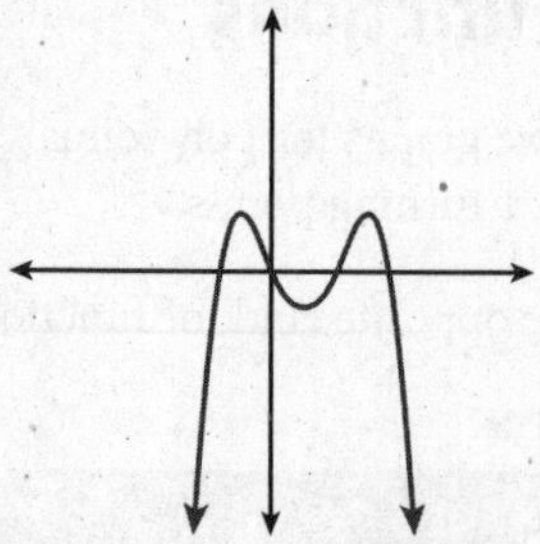

As $x \rightarrow +\infty$, $f(x) \rightarrow$ ______.

$\Rightarrow$ The leading coefficient is negative.

As of $x \rightarrow -\infty$, $f(x) \rightarrow$ ______.

$\Rightarrow$ ______ end behaviors

$\Rightarrow$ The polynomial's degree is ______.

Reflect

2. Discussion Explain why the leading coefficient is the only polynomial coefficient that determines end-behavior.

____

____

____

Your Turn

For each graph, identify whether the polynomial is of odd or even degree, and whether the leading coefficient is positive or negative.

3.

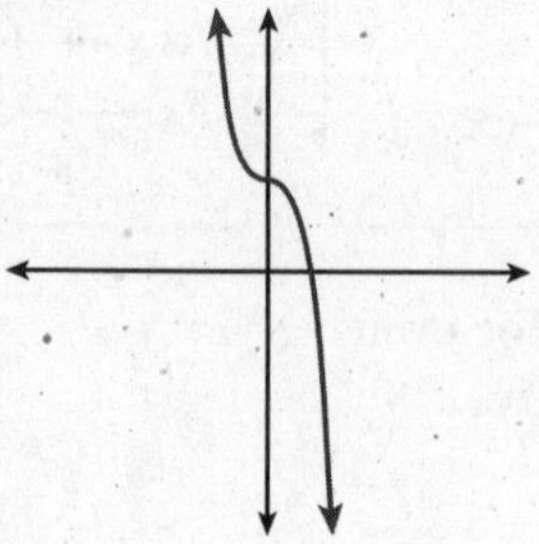

4.

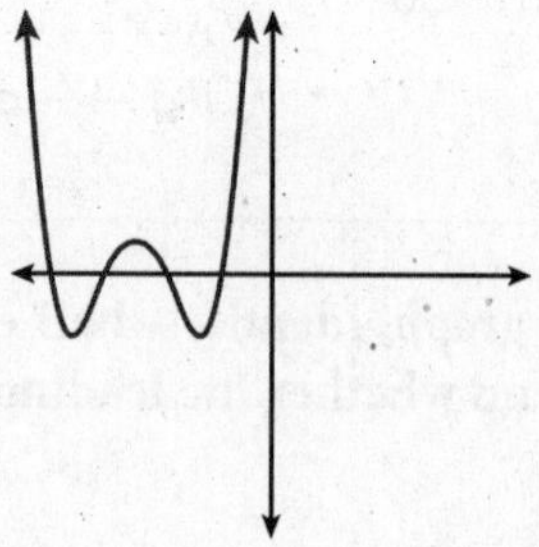

Explain 2 Classifying Even and Odd Functions

A function is an **even function** if $f(-x) = f(x)$ for all values of x. This means that if the point (x, y) is on the graph, then the point $(-x, y)$ is also on the graph.

A function is an **odd function** if $f(-x) = -f(x)$ for all values of x. This means that if the point (x, y) is on the graph, then the point $(-x, -y)$ is also on the graph.

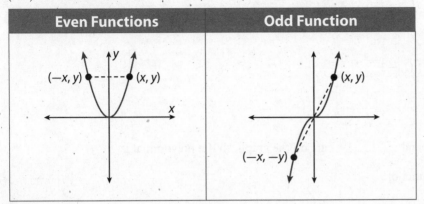

Even Functions	Odd Function
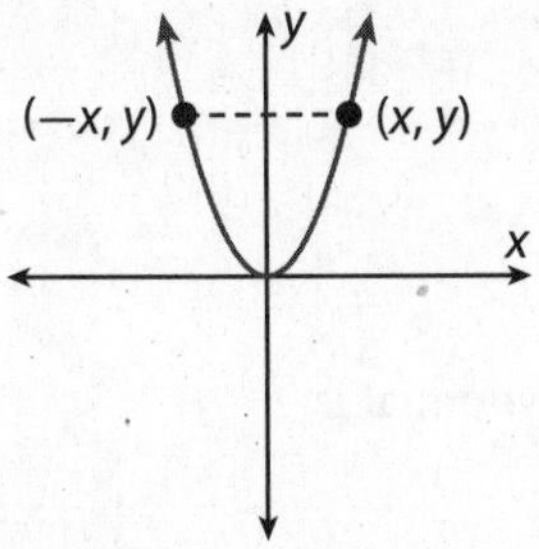	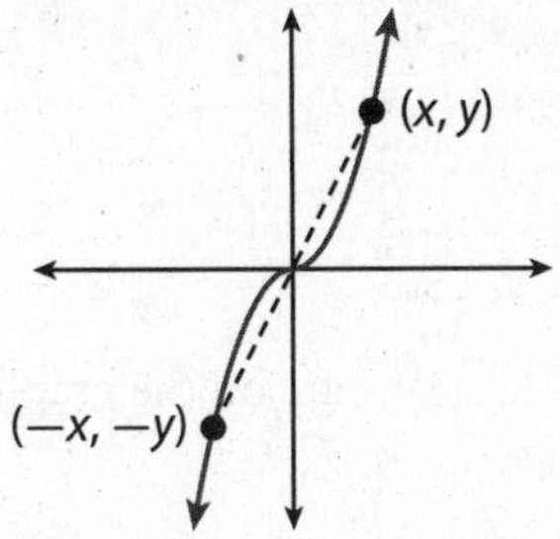

Example 2 **Classify each graphed polynomial as an odd or even function, and identify whether the leading coefficient is positive or negative.**

(A)

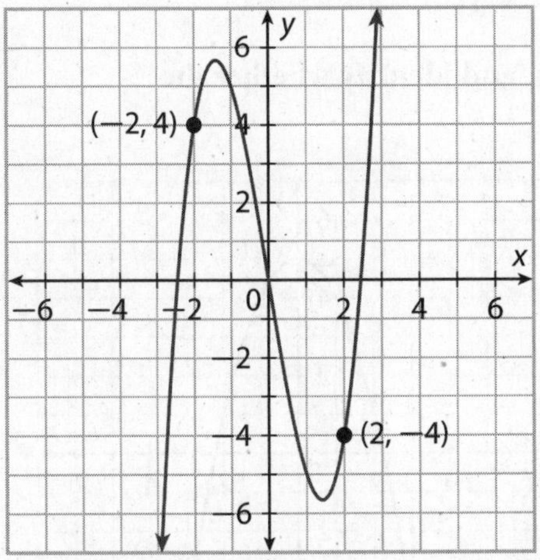

The points $(-2, 4)$ and $(2, -4)$ are on the graph, so the polynomial is an odd function.

End Behavior:

As $x \to +\infty$, $f(x) \to +\infty$, so the leading coefficient is positive.

B

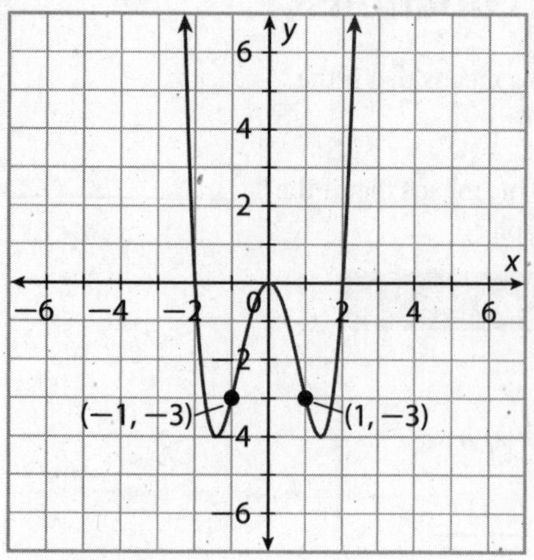

The points ________ and ________ are on the graph, so the polynomial is

a(n) ____________ function.

End Behavior:

As $x \to +\infty$, $f(x) \to$ ☐, so the leading coefficient is ________.

Your Turn

Classify each graphed polynomial as an odd or even function, and identify whether the leading coefficient is positive or negative.

5.

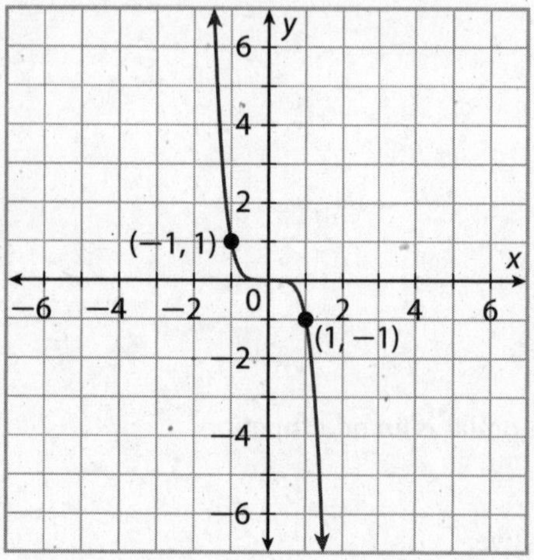

6.

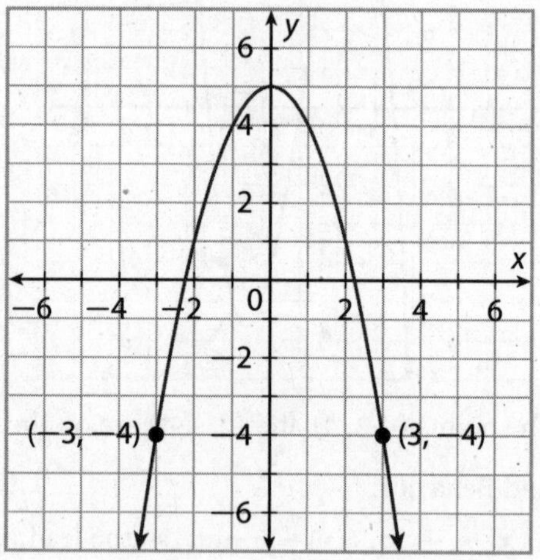

Elaborate

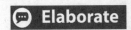

7. How can you tell based on the end behavior that an odd degree polynomial must have an even number of turning points, and an even degree polynomial must have an odd number?

8. If $f(x)$ is a polynomial and $f(-x) = -f(x)$, how do you know that the polynomial has an odd degree?

9. **Essential Question Check-In** How does the degree of a polynomial affect its end behavior?

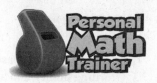

Evaluate: Homework and Practice

Personal Math Trainer
- Online Homework
- Hints and Help
- Extra Practice

1. Use a graphing calculator to plot the function $f(x) = x^3 + 2x^2 - 3x - 4$ and determine how many turning points there are and what the end behavior is.

For each graph, identify whether the polynomial $f(x)$ is of odd or even degree, and whether the leading coefficient is positive or negative.

2.
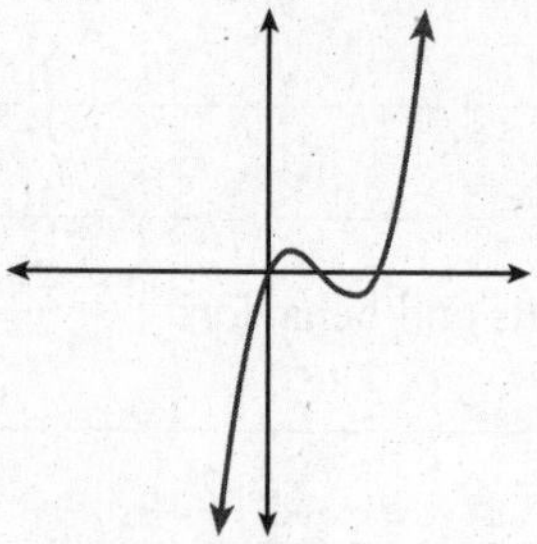

3.
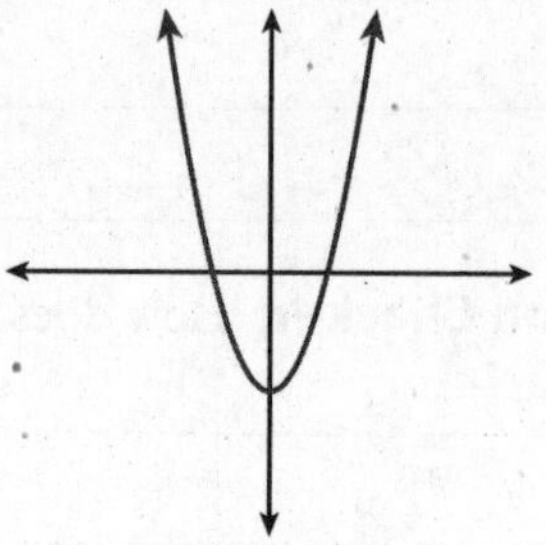

4.
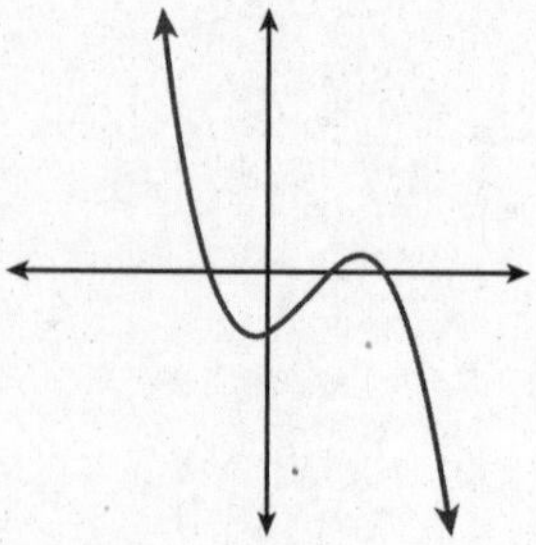

5.
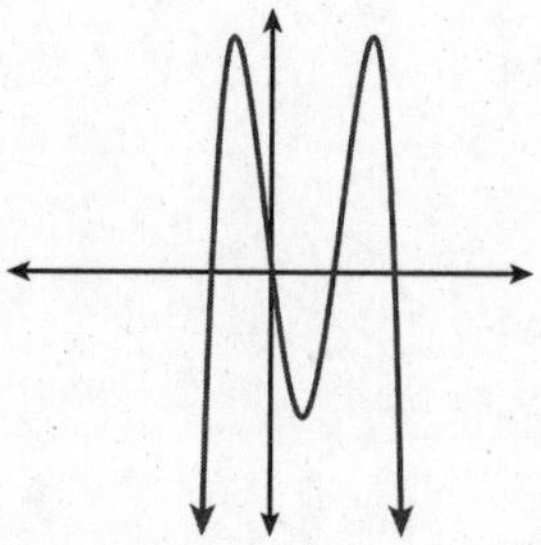

6.
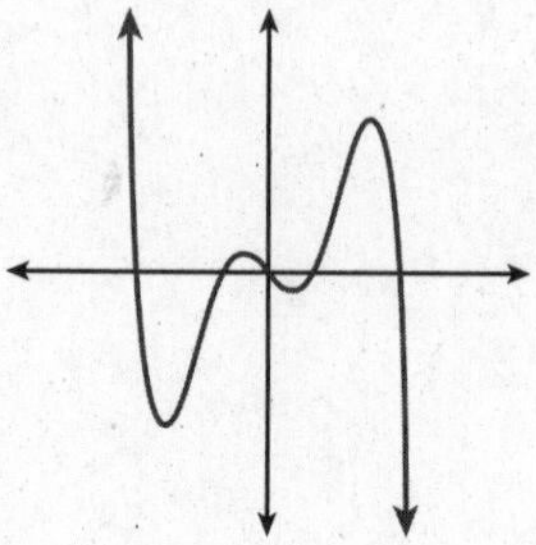

7.
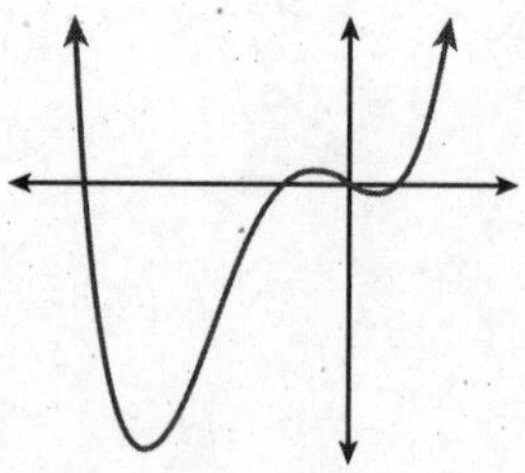

8.
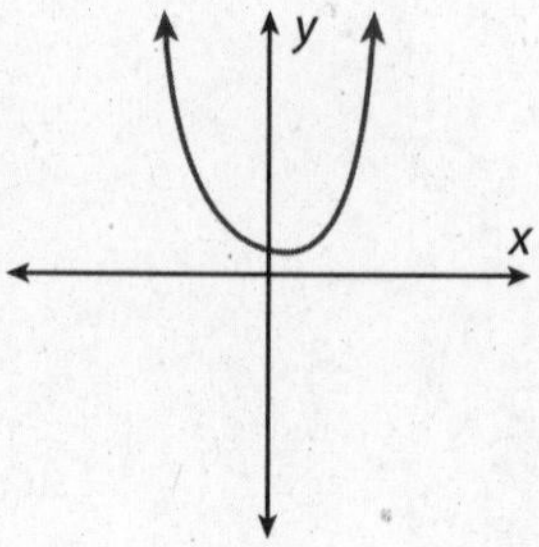

9.
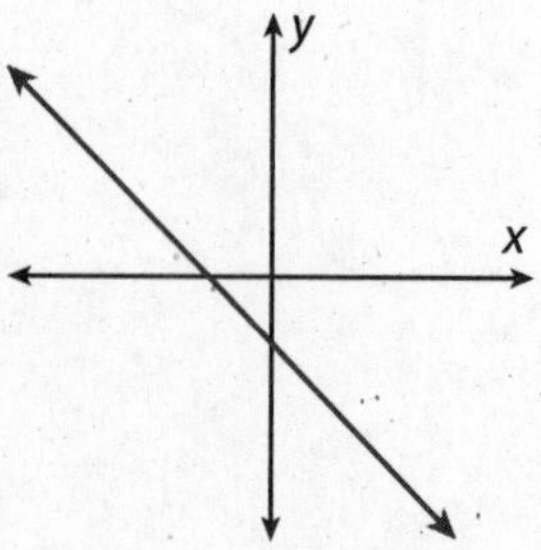

10.

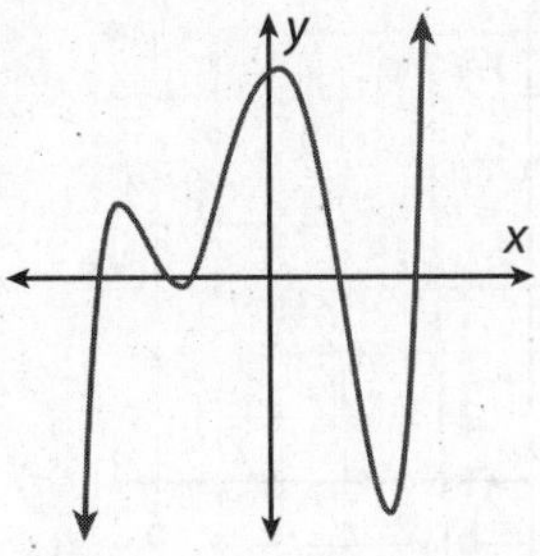

11.

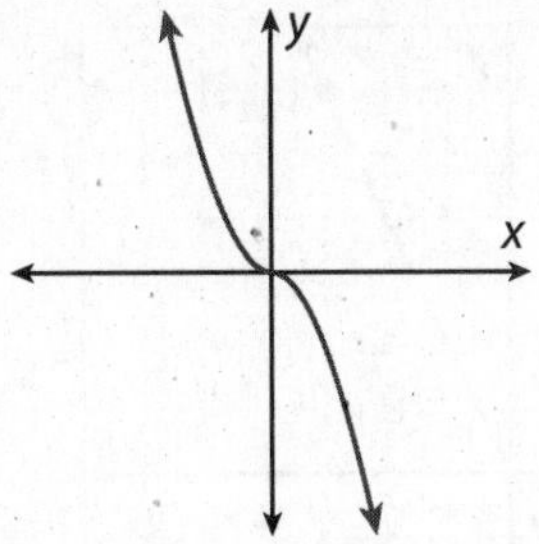

Label each function as an odd or even function, and identify the sign of the leading coefficient.

12.

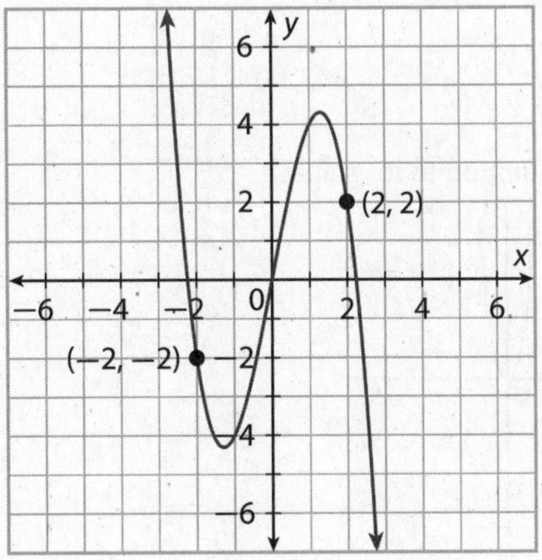

13.

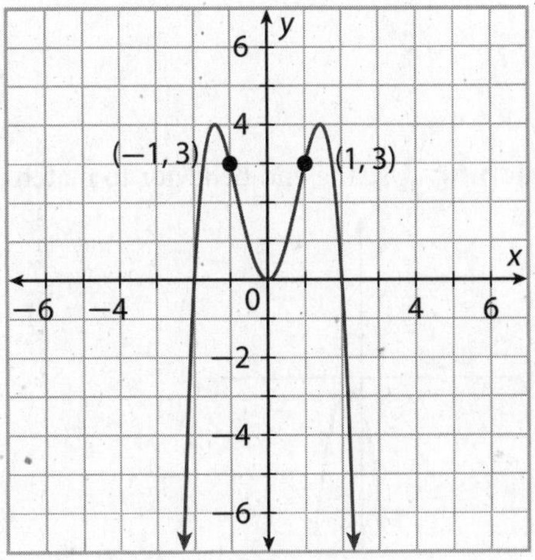

14.

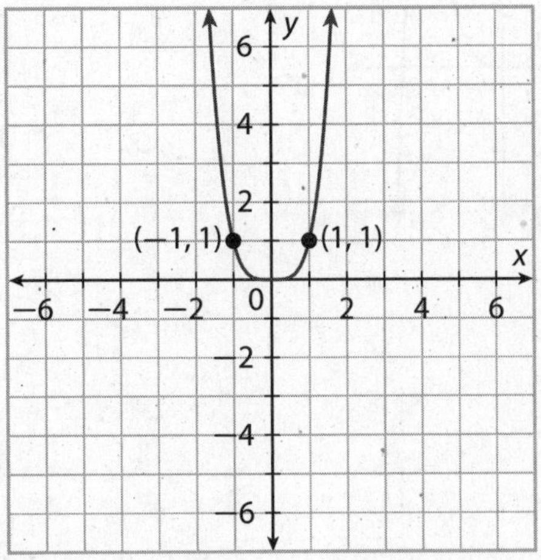

15.

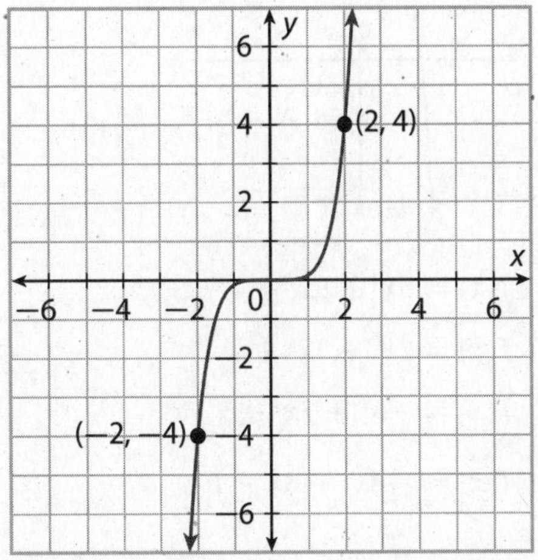

16.

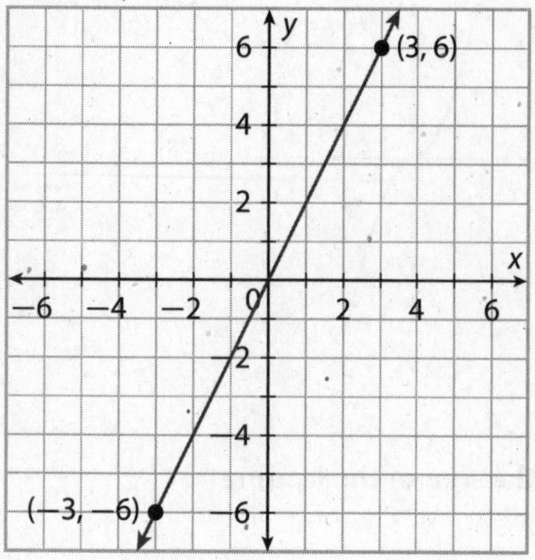

17.

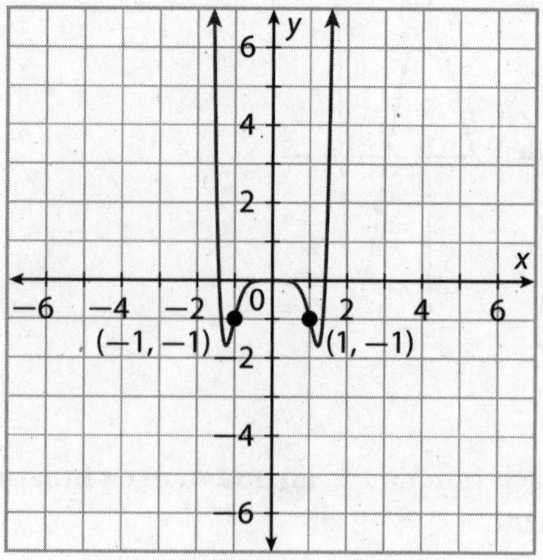

18. Matching Use the end behavior to match each polynomial function to its graph.

a.

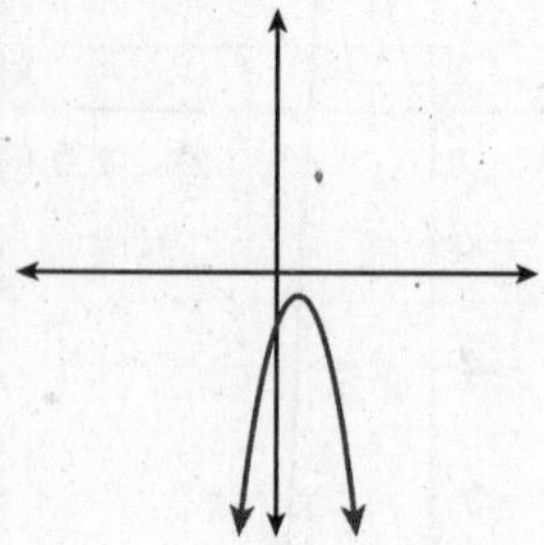

b.

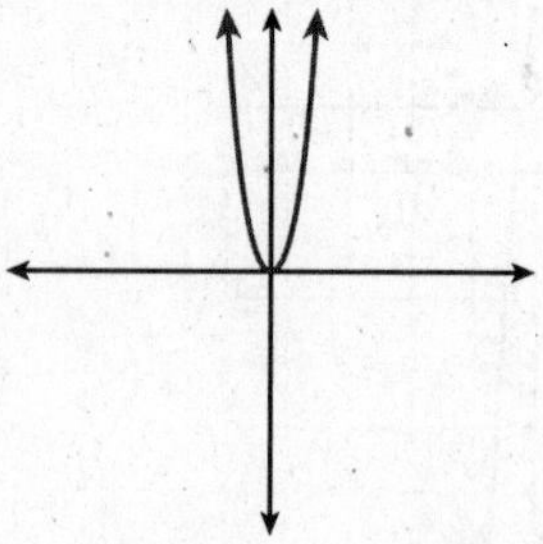

c.

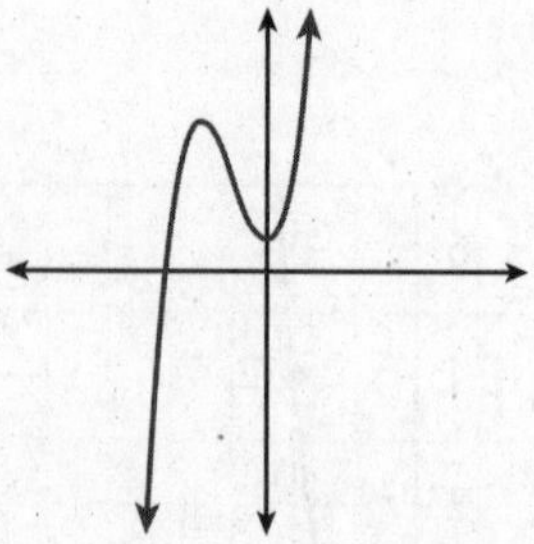

d.

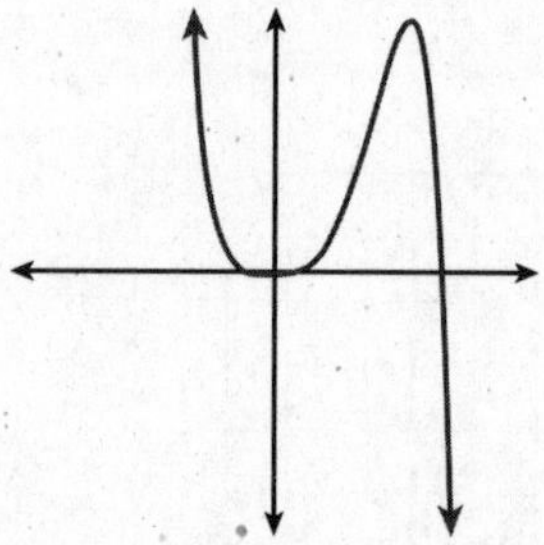

1. $f(x) = 5x^3 + 9x^2 + 1$

2. $f(x) = 2x^6 + 3x^4 + 5x^2$

3. $f(x) = -x^5 + 3x^4 + x$

4. $f(x) = -4x^2 + 3x - 1$

H.O.T. Focus on Higher Order Thinking

19. **Communicate Mathematical Ideas** Predict the end behavior of the polynomial function $f(x) = -x^9$.

20. **Communicate Mathematical Ideas** Is the function $f(x) = x^3$ an odd or even function? Show your reasoning.

21. **Explain the Error** Carlos and Rhonda are disagreeing over the answer to a math problem. Rhonda claims that the polynomial function $f(x) = \frac{1}{3}x^3 + 6x^2 + 21x + 16$ should approach negative infinity as x approaches negative infinity, because the leading term has a positive coefficient and is of odd degree.

Carlos entered the function on his graphing calculator and produced the following graph, which appears to show the function approaching positive infinity as x approaches negative infinity.

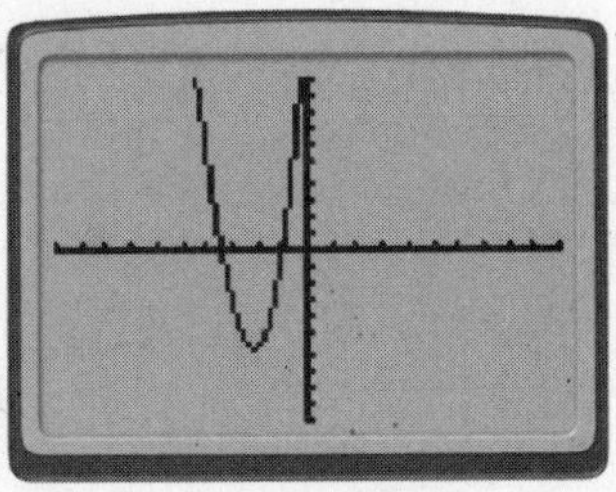

Who is right? Can you figure out what the mistake is?

Lesson Performance Task

A company that specializes in gift baskets is making a pyramid-shaped package with a rectangular base. The base must have a perimeter of 54 centimeters, and the height of the package must be equal to the length of its base.

a. Write a polynomial function, $V(x)$, for the volume of the package, where x is the length of the base. What are the constraints on x for this situation?

b. Use a graphing calculator to find the maximum volume of the package. What value of x corresponds to the maximum volume?

c. What dimensions result in a package with the maximum volume?

Name________ Class________ Date________

13.2 Understanding Inverse Functions

Resource Locker

Essential Question: How can you recognize inverses of functions from their graphs and how can you find inverses of functions?

Explore Exploring Inverses of Functions

You can use a graphing calculator to explore inverse functions and their relationships to the linear function $f(x) = x$.

(A) Using a standard viewing window, graph the function $y = 2^x$ and the linear function $y = x$ on a graphing calculator. Describe the end behavior of $y = 2^x$ as $x \to +\infty$.

(B) Use the DrawInv feature on the calculator to draw the graph of the inverse of $y = 2^x$ along with $y = 2^x$ and $y = x$. How are the graphs of $y = 2^x$ and its inverse related? Is the inverse of $y = 2^x$ a function? Explain your answer.

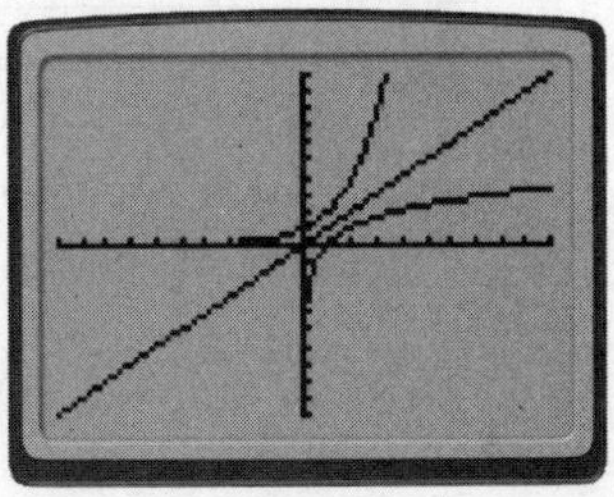

(C) Now graph the function $y = x^2$ and the linear function $y = x$ on a graphing calculator. Use the DrawInv feature to draw the graph of the inverse $y = x^2$ along with $y = x^2$ and $y = x$. How are the graphs of $y = x^2$ and its inverse related? Is the inverse of $y = x^2$ a function? Explain your answer.

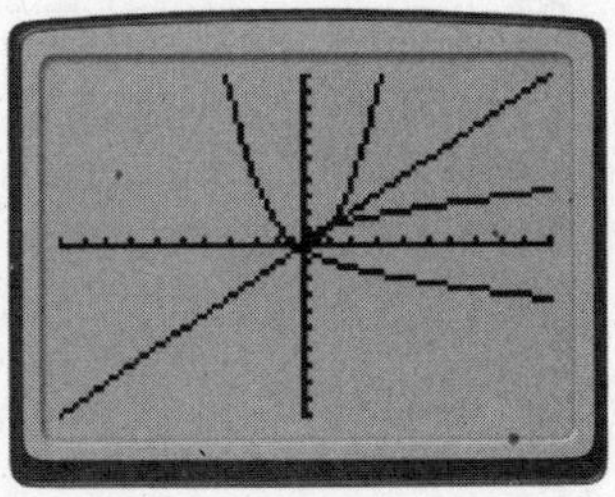

Reflect

1. **Make a Conjecture** Functions and their inverses appear to be reflections across which line?

2. Do you think all inverses of functions are functions? Why or why not?

Explain 1 Graphing Inverse Relations

You have seen the word *inverse* used in various ways.

The additive inverse of 3 is −3.

The multiplicative inverse of 5 is $\frac{1}{5}$.

You can also find and apply inverses to relations, which are sets of ordered pairs, and functions. To graph the **inverse relation**, you can reflect each point across the line $y = x$. This is equivalent to switching the x- and y-values in each ordered pair of the relation.

Example 1 **Graph the relation and connect the points. Then graph the inverse. Identify the domain and range of each relation.**

(A)

x	0	1	2	4	8
y	2	4	5	6	7

Graph each ordered pair and connect the points.

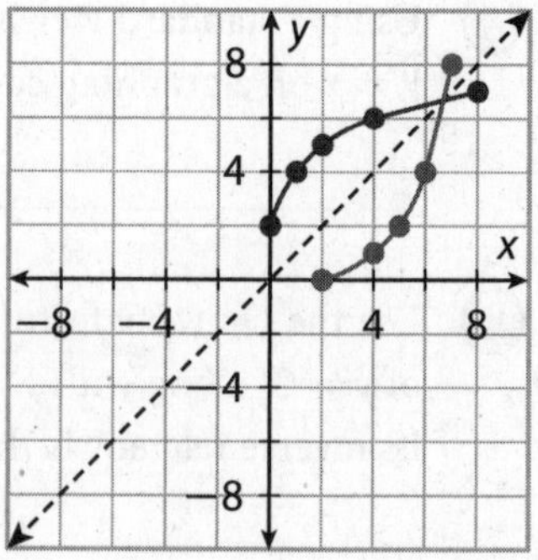

Switch the x- and y-values in each ordered pair.

x	2	4	5	6	7
y	0	1	2	4	8

Reflect each point across $y = x$, and connect the new points. Make sure the points match those in the table.

Original relation: Domain: $0 \le x \le 8$ Range: $2 \le y \le 7$

Inverse relation: Domain: $2 \le x \le 7$ Range: $0 \le y \le 8$

(B)

x	1	3	4	5	6
y	0	1	2	3	5

Graph each ordered pair and connect the points.

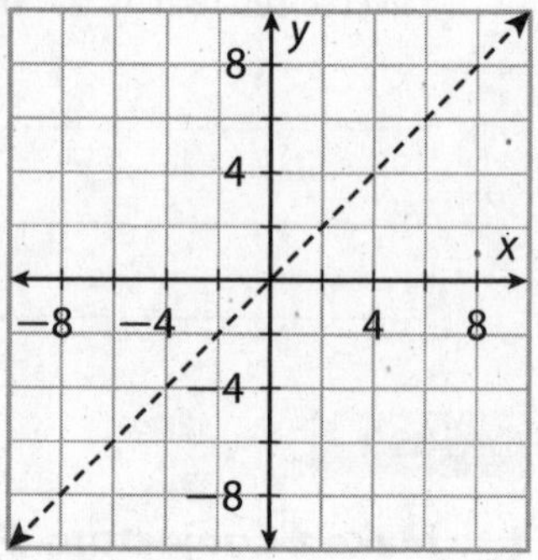

Switch the x- and y-values in each ordered pair.

x	0				
y	1				

Reflect each point across $y = x$, and connect the new points. Make sure the points match those in the table.

Original relation: Domain: ☐ $\le x \le$ ☐ Range: ☐ $\le y \le$ ☐

Inverse relation: Domain: ☐ $\le x \le$ ☐ Range: ☐ $\le y \le$ ☐

Reflect

3. **Discussion** How are the domain and range of a relation related to the domain and range of its inverse?

Your Turn

Graph the relation and connect the points. Then graph the inverse. Identify the domain and range of each relation.

4.

x	1	2	3	5	7
y	2	4	6	8	9

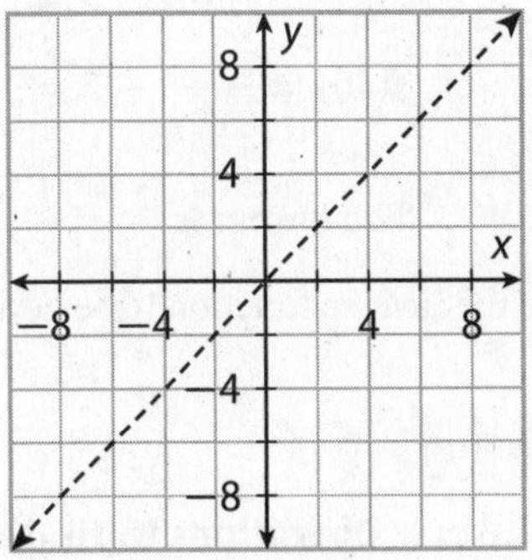

Explain 2 Writing Inverse Functions by Using Inverse Operations

When the relation is also a function, you can write the inverse of the function $f(x)$ as $f^{-1}(x)$. This notation does *not* indicate a reciprocal.

Functions that undo each other are called **inverse functions**.

You can find the inverse function by writing the original function with x and y switched and solving for y.

Example 2 **Use inverse operations to find each inverse. Then check your solution.**

(A) $f(x) = 2x$

$y = 2x$	Write y for $f(x)$.
$x = 2y$	Switch x and y.
$y = \frac{x}{2}$	Solve for y.

The inverse is $f^{-1}(x) = \frac{x}{2}$.

Check:

1. Use the input $x = 7$ in $f(x)$.

$f(x) = 2x$

$f(7) = 2(7) = 14$

The output is 14.

2. Verify that the output, 14, gives the input, 7.

$f^{-1}(x) = \frac{x}{2}$

$f^{-1}(14) = \frac{14}{2} = 7$

Since the inverse function *does* undo the original function, $f^{-1}(x) = \frac{x}{2}$ is correct.

(B) $f(x) = \frac{x}{4} - 5$

$y = \frac{x}{4} - 5$ Write y for $\square$.

$\square = \frac{\square}{4} - 5$ Switch $\square$ and y.

$y = \square\left(x + \square\right)$ Solve for $\square$.

Check:

1. Use the input $x = 40$ in $f(x)$.

$f(40) = \frac{\square}{4} - 5 = \square - 5 = \square$

The output is $\square$.

2. Verify that the output, $\square$, gives the input, $\square$.

$f^{-1}\left(\square\right) = 4\left(\square + 5\right) = 4\left(\square\right) = \square$

Since the inverse function (does/does not) undo the original function, it (is/is not) correct.

Your Turn

Use inverse operations to find the inverse. Then check your solution.

5. $f(x) = 5x - 7$

Explain 3 Graphing Inverse Functions

A function and its inverse are reflections across the line $y = x$.

Example 3 **Write the inverse of each function. Then graph the function together with its inverse.**

(A) $f(x) = 3x + 6$

$y = 3x + 6$ Write y for $f(x)$.

$x = 3y + 6$ Switch x and y.

$y = \frac{x - 6}{3}$ Solve for y.

$y = \frac{1}{3}x - 2$ Simplify.

The inverse is $f^{-1}(x) = \frac{1}{3}x - 2$.

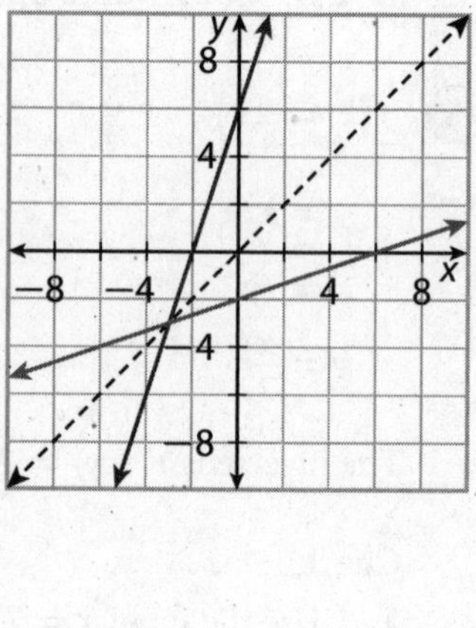

(B) $f(x) = \frac{2}{3}x + 2$

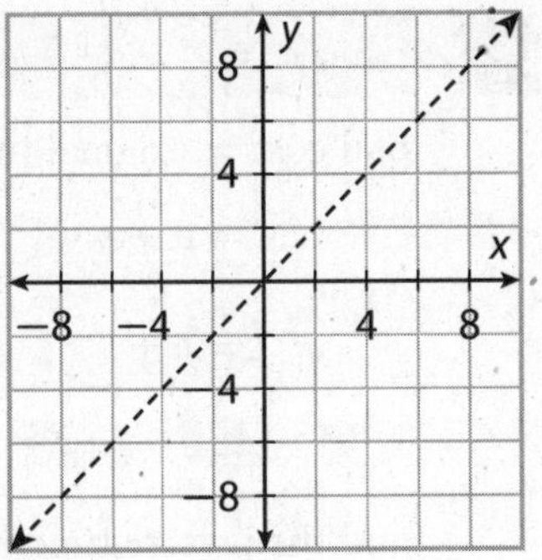

$\square = \frac{2}{3}x + 2$ Write y for $f(x)$.

$\square = \frac{2}{3}\square + 2$ Switch x and y.

$\square = \frac{\square}{\square}\left(x - \square\right)$ Solve for $\square$.

$y = \frac{\square}{\square}x - \square$ Simplify.

The inverse is $f^{-1}(x) = \frac{\square}{\square}x - \square$.

Your Turn

Write the inverse of each function. Then graph the function together with its inverse.

6. $f(x) = 2x - 4$

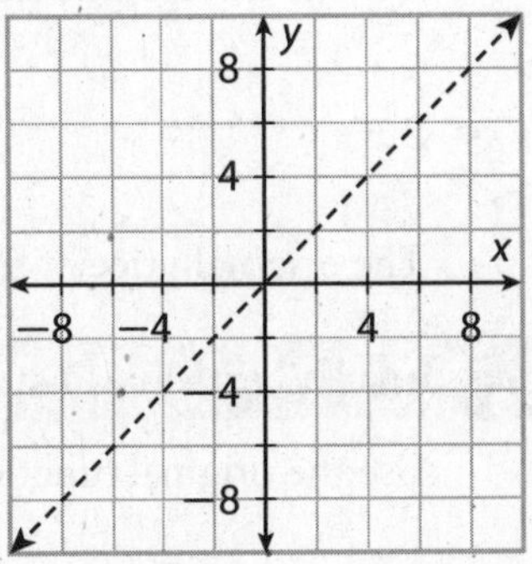

Explain 4 Using Inverse Functions to Solve Real-World Problems

Any time you need to work backward from a result to the original input, you can apply inverse functions.

Example 4 **Solve each problem by finding and evaluating the inverse function.**

Represent Real-World Problems Lloyd is trying to find the original price of a camera he bought as a gift, but he does not have the store receipt. From the bank transaction, he knows that including a \$3 gift-wrap charge and 8% tax, the total was \$103.14. What was the original price of the camera? Justify your answer.

Analyze Information

Identify the important information.

- Lloyd paid a total of \$ $\square$ for the camera.
- The total includes a gift-wrapping charge of \$ $\square$ and a sales tax of $\square$ % of the original price.

Formulate a Plan

Build a function for the total cost t of the camera. Then determine the inverse of the function, and use it to find the original price p.

Solve

total cost = original price + tax + gift-wrapping charge

$t = p + p \cdot \square \% + \square$

$t = p + \square p + \square$

$t = \square p + \square$

Find the inverse function.

$t = \square p + \square$

$t - \square = \square p$

$\frac{t - \square}{\square} = p$

Use the inverse function to find the original price p for a total price of \$$\square$.

$p = \frac{\square - \square}{\square} \approx \square$

The original price of the camera was \$$\square$.

Justify and Evaluate

Use the original function to check your answer.

$t = \square p + \square$

$t = \square \cdot \left(\square \right) + \square \approx \square$

Since the inverse function (does/does not) undo the original function, it (is/is not) correct.

Reflect

7. What are the domain and range of the function for the total cost and its inverse in Example 4?

Your Turn

8. To make tea, use $\frac{1}{6}$ teaspoon of tea per ounce of water plus a teaspoon for the pot. Use the inverse to find the number of ounces of water needed if 7 teaspoons of tea are used. Check your answer.

Elaborate

9. Explain the result of interchanging x and y to find the inverse function of $f(x) = x$. How could you have predicted this from the graph of $f(x)$?

10. Give an example of a function whose inverse is a function. Give an example of a function whose inverse is not a function.

11. Describe what happens when you take the inverse of the inverse of a function. Is the result necessarily a function? Explain.

12. **Essential Question Check-In** Inverses are reflections of functions across which line?

Evaluate: Homework and Practice

Personal Math Trainer

- Online Homework
- Hints and Help
- Extra Practice

Graph the relation and connect the points. Then graph the inverse. Identify the domain and range of each relation.

1.

x	1	2	3	4
y	1	2	4	8

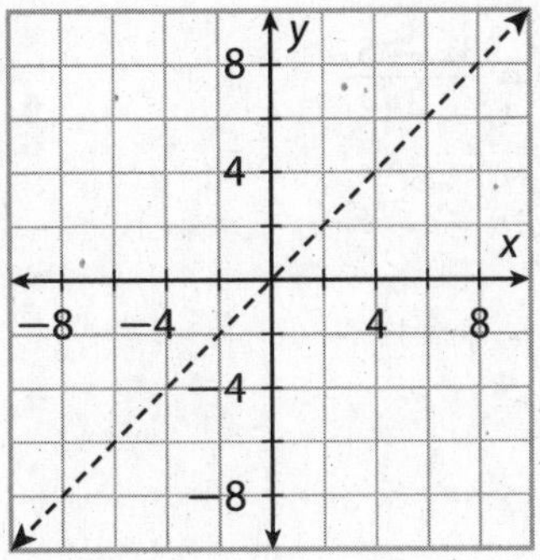

2.

x	3	4	1	−1
y	−1	−2	−4	−4

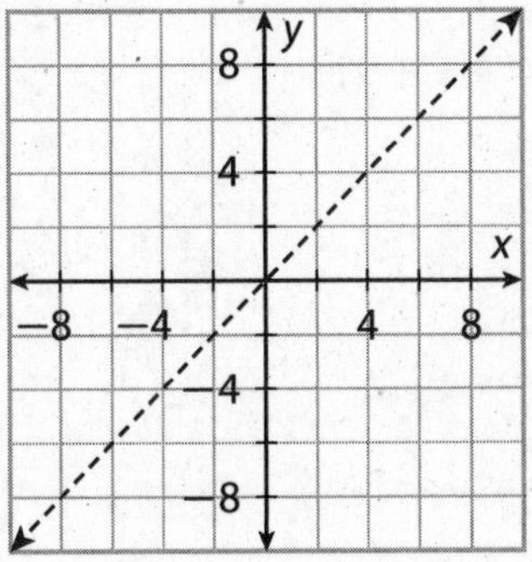

3.

x	1	3	5	7
y	0	3	6	9

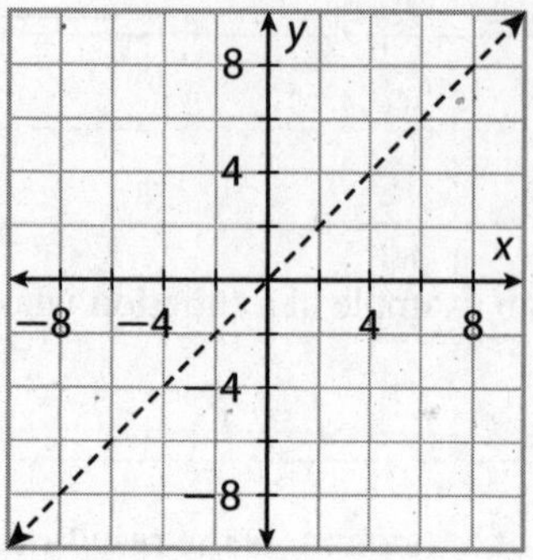

4.

x	−2	0	3	7
y	0	−1	−4	−9

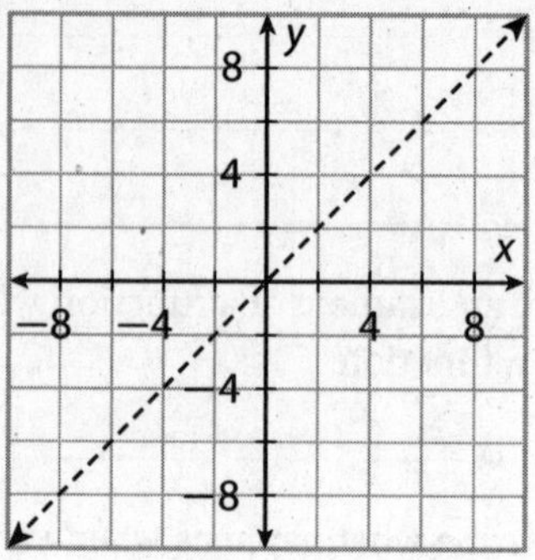

Use inverse operations to find each inverse. Then check your solution.

5. $f(x) = 5x - 1$

6. $f(x)= \frac{x}{2} + 3$

7. $f(x)= 3 - \frac{1}{2}x$

8. $f(x)= \frac{1}{2}(3 - 3x)$

9. $f(x)= 4(x + 1)$

10. $f(x)= \frac{3x - 5}{2}$

Write the inverse of each function. Then graph the function together with its inverse.

11. $f(x) = 5 - 2x$

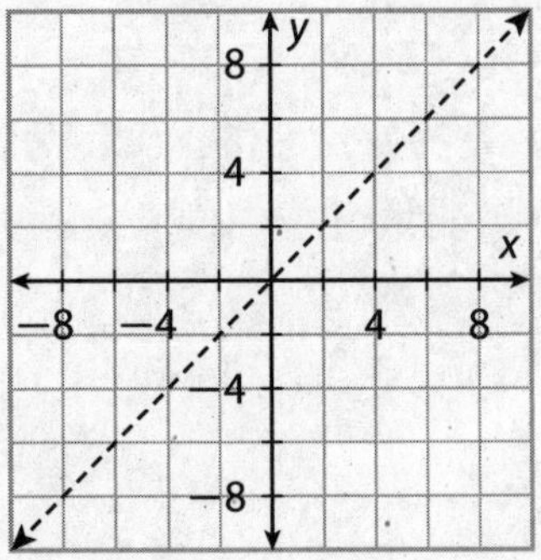

12. $f(x) = \frac{x}{4} + 2$

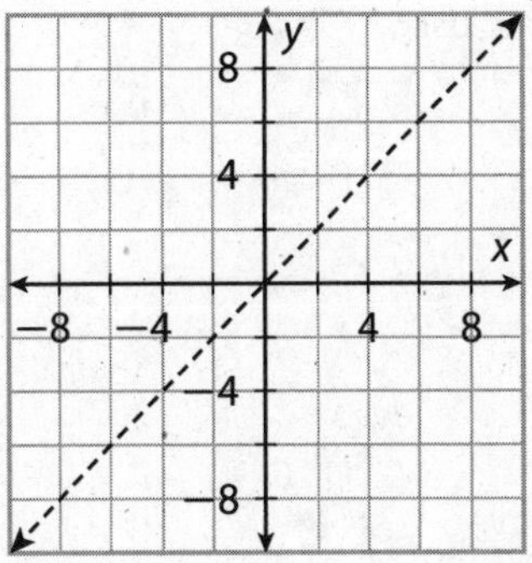

13. $f(x) = 10 + 0.6x$

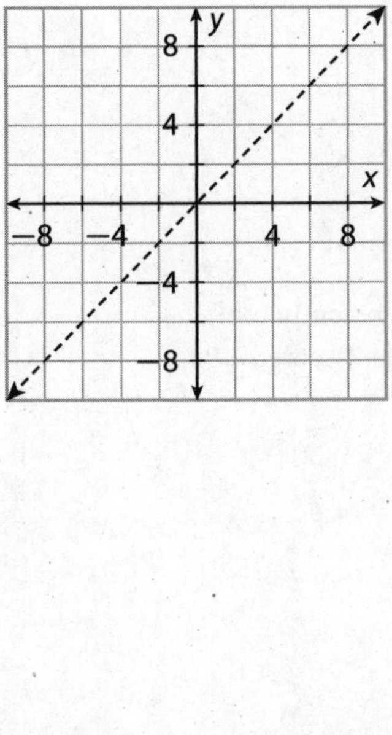

14. $f(x) = 2 + 3x$

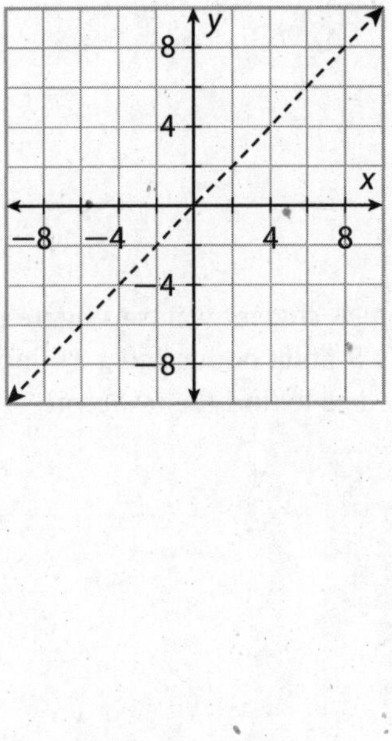

Solve each problem using an inverse function.

15. Meteorology The formula $C = \frac{5}{9}(F - 32)$ gives degrees Celsius as a function of degrees Fahrenheit. Find the inverse of this function to convert degrees Celsius to degrees Fahrenheit, and use it to find 16 °C in degrees Fahrenheit.

16. To make coffee using a home drip coffee maker, use $\frac{1}{4}$ tablespoon of coffee grounds per ounce of water plus 2 tablespoons for the coffee pot. Use the inverse to find the number of ounces of water needed if 11 tablespoons of coffee grounds are used.

17. Shopping A shopping attendant needs to price a large jigsaw puzzle returned by a customer. The customer paid a total of $33.14, including a convenience charge of $1.50 and 11% sales tax on the subtotal. Use the inverse to find the original price of the puzzle.

18. Education A student wants to figure out her raw score on a test she recently took. Including a 5-point bonus and a 2% increase after the bonus, the student scored a 94. Use the inverse to find the raw score.

19. Currency At one point, the currency exchange rate between the U.S. dollar and the British pound sterling was 0.600 pound per dollar after a 3-dollar exchange fee. Use the inverse to determine how many U.S. dollars 100 British pounds would be worth.

20. Travel A taxi driver charges \$2 for service plus 65¢ per mile. Use the inverse to determine the number of miles driven if the total charge is \$11.75.

21. Identify whether you need to use an additive inverse, multiplicative inverse, or both to find the inverse of the given function. Select the correct answer for each lettered part.

A. $f(x) = 3x$	○ Additive Inverse	○ Multiplicative Inverse	○ Both
B. $f(x) = 3x + 4$	○ Additive Inverse	○ Multiplicative Inverse	○ Both
C. $f(x) = \frac{x}{6}$	○ Additive Inverse	○ Multiplicative Inverse	○ Both
D. $f(x) = 5x + 6$	○ Additive Inverse	○ Multiplicative Inverse	○ Both
E. $f(x) = \frac{x+6}{x+2}$	○ Additive Inverse	○ Multiplicative Inverse	○ Both

22. Use a graphing calculator to graph the function $y = 3^x$ on a standard viewing window along with its inverse and the line $y = x$. Is the function's inverse a function? Explain your answer.

H.O.T. Focus on Higher Order Thinking

23. Critical Thinking Find the inverse of $f(x) = \frac{x-3}{x+4}$. Then use a sample input and output to check your answer.

24. Explain the Error A student produced the following result when attempting to find the inverse of $f(x) = \frac{x}{6} + 5$. Explain the student's error and state the correct answer.

$$y = \frac{x}{6} + 5$$

$$x = \frac{y}{6} + 5$$

$$x - 5 = \frac{y}{6}$$

$$6x - 5 = y$$

Lesson Performance Task

The population p in thousands for the state of Oregon can be modeled by the linear function $p = 39.016t + 1039.614$, where t is the time in years since 1940.

A. Find an equation for the inverse function, rounding the constants and coefficients to three decimal places. What is the meaning of the slope and y-intercept of the inverse function?

B. Use the inverse function to estimate when the population of Oregon was 3,000,000.

C. The population of Oregon was estimated as 3,930,065 in 2013. Use the model to predict when the population of Oregon will be 4,800,000. What would have to be assumed for your answer to be valid?

Name________________________ Class________________ Date__________

13.3 Graphing Square Root Functions

Essential Question: How can you use transformations of the parent square root function to graph functions of the form $f(x) = a\sqrt{x - h} + k$?

Resource Locker

Explore 1 Exploring the Inverse of $y = x^2$

Use the steps that follow to explore the inverse of $y = x^2$.

(A) Use a graphing calculator to graph $y = x^2$ and $y = x$. Describe the graph.

____

____

____

(B) Use the DrawInv feature to graph the inverse of $y = x^2$ along with $y = x^2$ and $y = x$. Describe the new graph.

____

____

(C) State whether the inverse is a function. Explain your reasoning.

____

____

(D) Use inverse operations to write the inverse of $y = x^2$.

Switch x and y in the equation: $x = y^2$

Take the square root of both sides of the equation. $\_\_\_\_\_\_ = y$

Reflect

1. **Discussion** Explain why the inverse of $y = x^2$ is not a function.

____

____

Explore 2 Graphing the Parent Square Root Function

The graph shows $y = \pm\sqrt{x}$, $y = x^2$, and $y = x$. You have discovered that $y = \pm\sqrt{x}$ is not a function. You will find out how to alter $y = \pm\sqrt{x}$ so that it becomes a function.

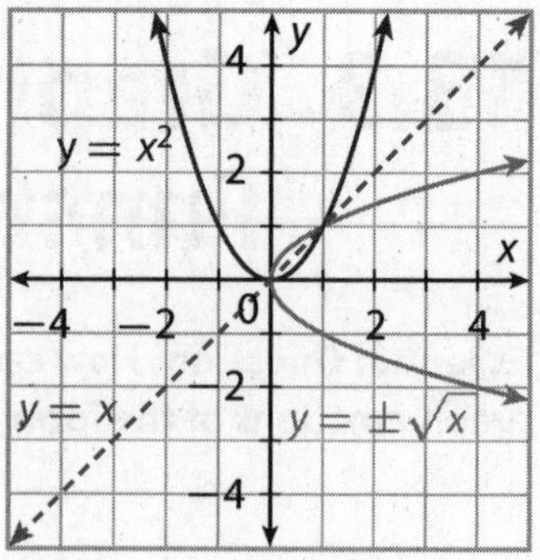

(A) For $y = \pm\sqrt{x}$ can x be negative? Explain your reasoning.

____

____

(B) If the domain of $y = x^2$ was restricted to $x \leq 0$, would the inverse be a function? Explain your reasoning.

____

____

(C) If the domain of $y = x^2$ was restricted to $x \geq 0$, would the inverse be a function? Explain your reasoning.

____

____

(D) Typically the domain of $y = x^2$ is restricted to $x \geq 0$ before findng its inverse to create the parent square root function. What is the equation of the parent square root function?

____

(E) A **radical function** is a function whose rule is a radical expression. A **square root function** is a radical function involving $\sqrt{x}$.

Graph the parent square root function $y = \sqrt{x}$ by first making a table of values.

x	$y = \sqrt{x}$	(x, y)
0	$\sqrt{0}$	(0, 0)
1	______	(1, __)
4	______	(4, __)
9	______	(9, __)

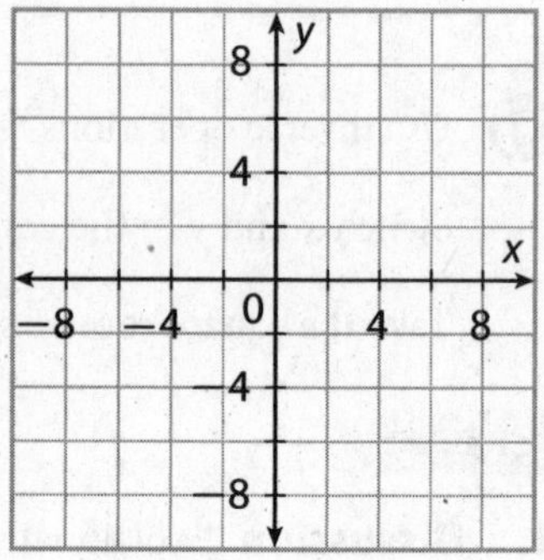

(F) Plot the points on the graph and draw a smooth curve through them.

Reflect

2. What are the domain and range of the parent square root function?

____

____

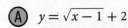

Explain 1 Graphing Translations of the Parent Square Root Function

You discovered in Explore 2 that the parent square root function is $y = \sqrt{x}$. The equation $y = \sqrt{x - h} + k$ is the parent square root function with horizontal and vertical translations, where h and k are constants. The constant h will cause a horizontal shift and k will cause a vertical shift.

Example 1 **Graph each function by using a table and plotting the points. State the direction of the shift from the parent square root function, and by how many units. Then state the domain and range. Confirm your graph by graphing with a graphing calculator.**

Ⓐ $y = \sqrt{x - 1} + 2$

x	$y = \sqrt{x - 1} + 2$	(x, y)
1	$\sqrt{1 - 1} + 2$	(1, 2)
2	$\sqrt{2 - 1} + 2$	(2, 3)
5	$\sqrt{5 - 1} + 2$	(5, 4)
10	$\sqrt{10 - 1} + 2$	(10, 5)

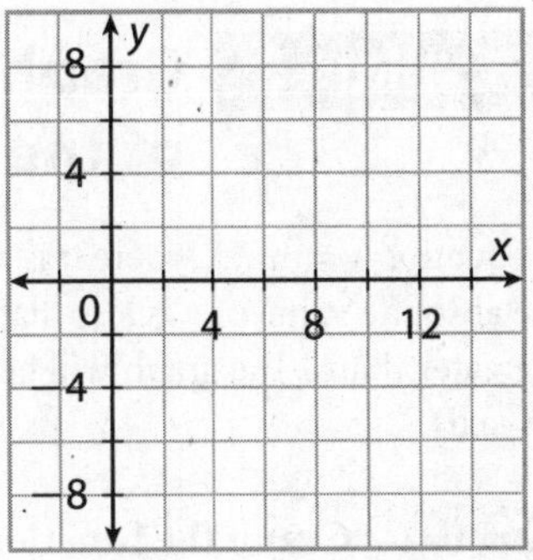

The graph is translated 2 units up and 1 unit right.

Domain: $x \geq 1$ Range: $y \geq 2$

Ⓑ $y = \sqrt{x + 3} - 2$

x	$y = \sqrt{x + 3} - 2$	(x, y)
−3	$\sqrt{-3 + 3} - 2$	(−3, −2)
−2		
1		
6		
13		

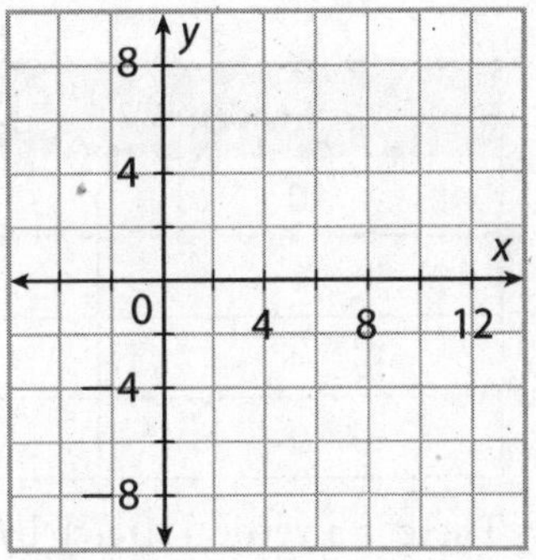

The graph is translated ____ unit(s) (up/down) and

____ unit(s) to the(left/right).

Domain: ____________ Range: ____________

Your Turn

3. $y = \sqrt{x + 1}$

x	$y = \sqrt{x + 1}$	(x, y)
−1		
0		
3		
8		

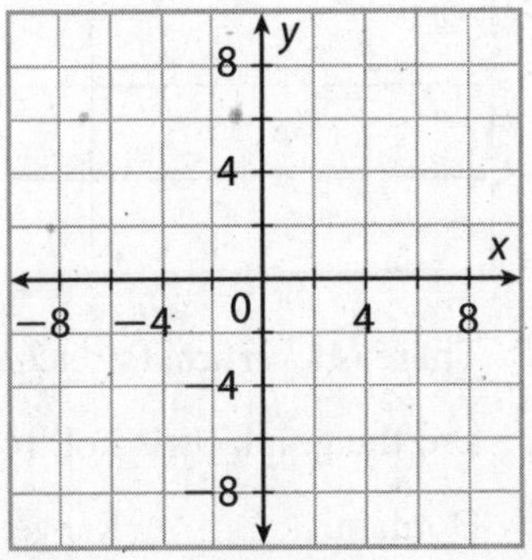

4. $y = \sqrt{x} - 4$

x	$y = \sqrt{x} - 4$	(x, y)
0		
1		
4		
9		

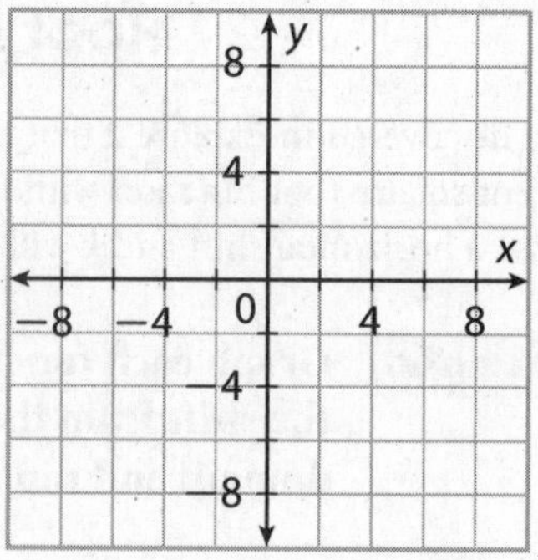

Explain 2 Graphing Stretches/Compressions and Reflections of the Parent Square Root Function

The equation $y = a\sqrt{x}$, where a is a constant, is the parent square root function with a vertical stretch or compression. If the absolute value of a is less than 1 the graph will be compressed by a factor of $|a|$, and if the absolute value of a is greater than 1 the graph will be stretched by a factor of $|a|$. If a is negative, the graph will be reflected across the x-axis.

Example 2 **Graph the functions by using a table and plotting the points. State the stretch/compression factor and whether the graph of the parent function was reflected or not. Then state the domain and range. Confirm your graph by graphing with a graphing calculator.**

Ⓐ $y = -2\sqrt{x}$

x	$y = -2\sqrt{x}$	(x, y)
0	$-2\sqrt{0}$	(0, 0)
1	$-2\sqrt{1}$	(1, −2)
4	$-2\sqrt{4}$	(4, −4)
9	$-2\sqrt{9}$	(9, −6)

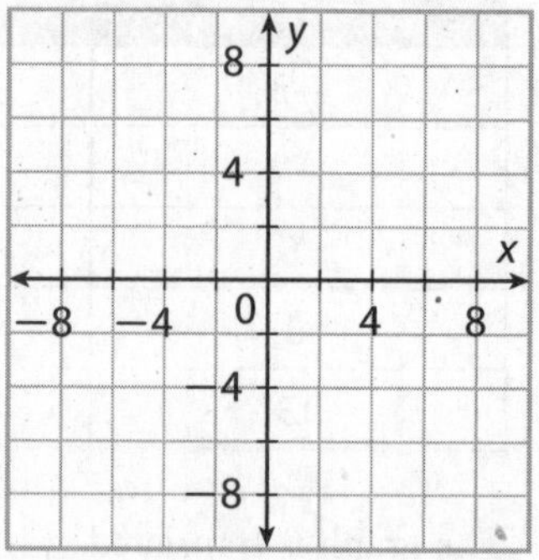

There is a vertical stretch by a factor of 2, and the graph is reflected across the x-axis.

Domain: $x \geq 0$ Range: $y \leq 0$

Ⓑ $y = \frac{1}{2}\sqrt{x}$

x	$y = \frac{1}{2}\sqrt{x}$	(x, y)
0	$\frac{1}{2}\sqrt{0}$	(0, 0)
1		
4		
9		

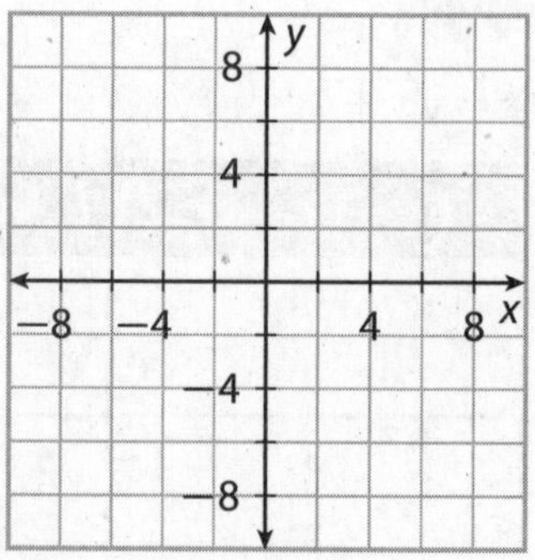

There is a vertical (stretch/compression) by a factor of ______,

and the graph (is/is not) reflected across the x–axis.

Domain: __________ Range: __________

Your Turn

Graph the functions by using a table and plotting the points. State the stretch/compression factor and whether the graph of the parent function was reflected or not. Then state the domain and range. Confirm your graph by graphing with a graphing calculator.

5. $y = 3\sqrt{x}$

x	$y = 3\sqrt{x}$	(x, y)
0	$3\sqrt{0}$	(0, 0)
1		
4		
9		

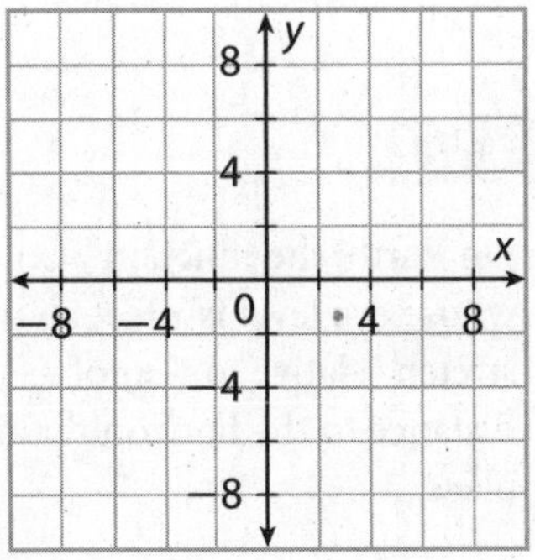

6. $y = -\frac{1}{4}\sqrt{x}$

x	$y = -\frac{1}{4}\sqrt{x}$	(x, y)
0	$-\frac{1}{4}\sqrt{0}$	(0, 0)
1		
4		
9		

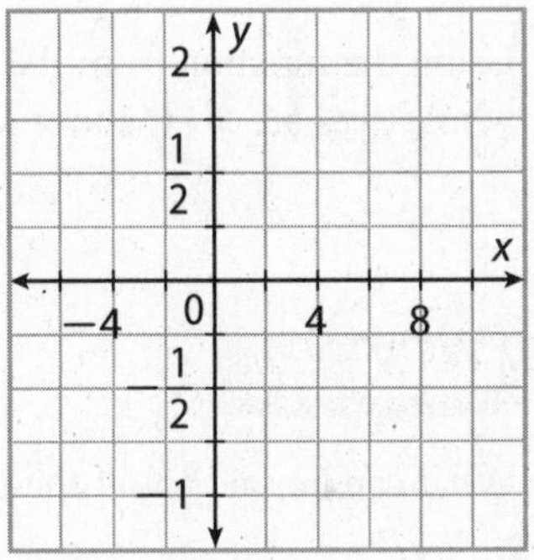

Explain 3 Modeling Real-World Situations with Square Root Functions

You can use transformations of square root functions to model real-world situations.

Example 3 **Construct a square root function to solve each problem.**

(A) On Earth, the function $f(x) = \frac{6}{5}\sqrt{x}$ approximates the distance in miles to the horizon observed by a person whose eye level is x feet above the ground. Use the function to estimate the distance to the horizon for someone whose eyes are 6.5 ft above Earth's surface, rounding to one decimal place.

$f(x) = \frac{6}{5}\sqrt{x}$

$f(6.5) = \frac{6}{5}\sqrt{6.5}$ Substitute 6.5 for x.

$f(6.5) \approx 3.1$ miles Simplify.

(B) Using the function from Example 3A, estimate the distance to the horizon for someone whose eyes are 5.8 ft above Earth's surface, rounding to one decimal place.

$f(x) = \frac{6}{5}\sqrt{x}$

$f(\_\_\_) = \frac{6}{5}\sqrt{\_\_\_}$ Substitute ______ for x.

$f(\_\_\_) \approx$ ______ miles Simplify.

Your Turn

7. On Earth, the function $f(x) = \frac{6}{5}\sqrt{x}$ approximates the distance in miles to the horizon observed by a person whose eye level is x feet above the ground. The graph of the corresponding function for Mars has a vertical stretch relative to $f(x)$ of $\frac{\sqrt{5}}{3}$. Write the corresponding function $g(x)$ for Mars and use it to estimate the distance to the horizon for an astronaut whose eyes are 6.2 ft above Mars's surface, rounding to one decimal place.

8. Using the function from the previous question, estimate the distance to the horizon for an astronaut whose eyes are 5.5 ft above Mars's surface, rounding to one decimal place.

Elaborate

9. What can be said about the inverse of $y = x^2$ when the domain isn't restricted?

10. Are there any square root functions that do not have a restricted domain? Explain.

11. Essential Question Check-In What is the domain and range of the function $f(x) = \sqrt{x - h} + k$?

Evaluate: Homework and Practice

Personal Math Trainer
- Online Homework
- Hints and Help
- Extra Practice

1. What is the inverse of $y = x^2$? Select the correct answer.

A. $y = \sqrt{x}$ B. $y = \pm\sqrt{x}$ C. $y = -\sqrt{x}$ D. $y = x$

2. What is the parent square root function? What is its domain and range?

For Exercises 3–14, graph each function, describe any transformation from the parent function, and state the domain and range.

3. $y = \sqrt{x+1} - 4$

x	$y = \sqrt{x+1} - 4$	(x, y)
−1	$\sqrt{-1+1} - 4$	$(-1, -4)$
0		
3		
8		

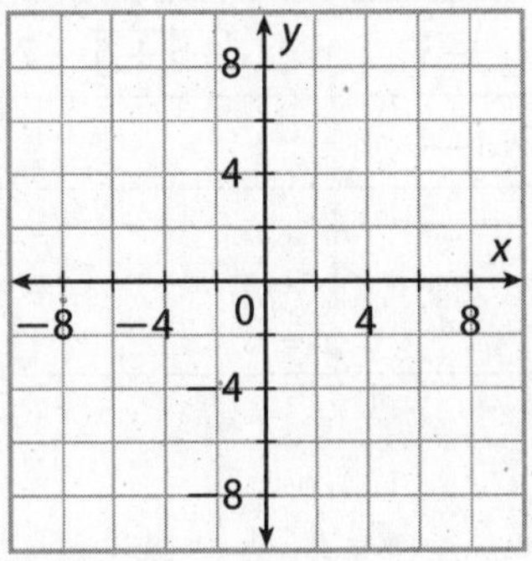

4. $y = \sqrt{x} + 6$

x	$y = \sqrt{x} + 6$	(x, y)
0	$\sqrt{0} + 6$	$(0, 6)$
1		
4		
9		

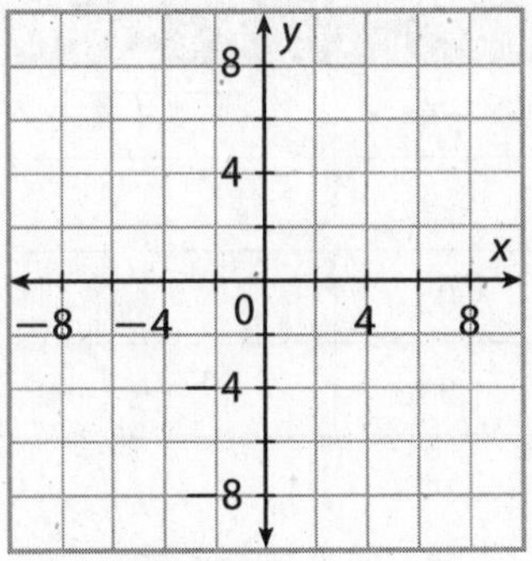

5. $y = \sqrt{x+8}$

x	$y = \sqrt{x+8}$	(x, y)
−8	$\sqrt{-8+8}$	$(-8, 0)$
−7		
−4		
1		
8		

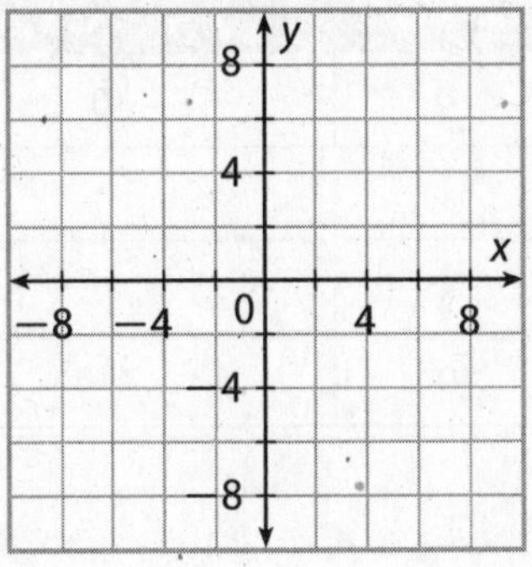

6. $y = \sqrt{x - 4} + 3$

x	$y = \sqrt{x - 4} + 3$	(x, y)
4	$\sqrt{4 - 4} + 3$	$(4, 3)$
5		
8		

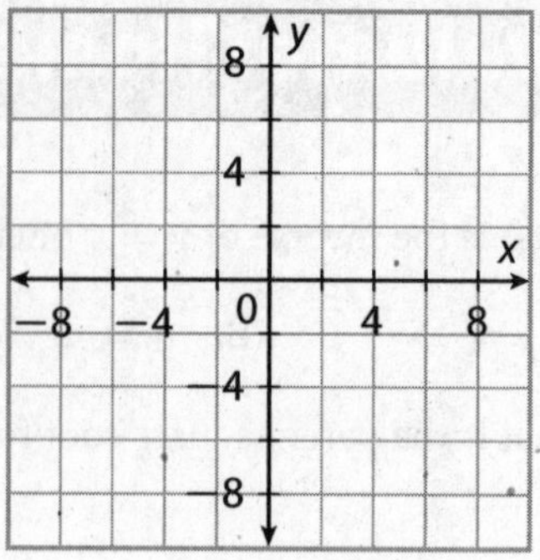

7. $y = \sqrt{x + 5} - 7$

x	$y = \sqrt{x + 5} - 7$	(x, y)
−5	$\sqrt{-5 + 5} - 7$	$(-5, -7)$
−4		
−1		
4		

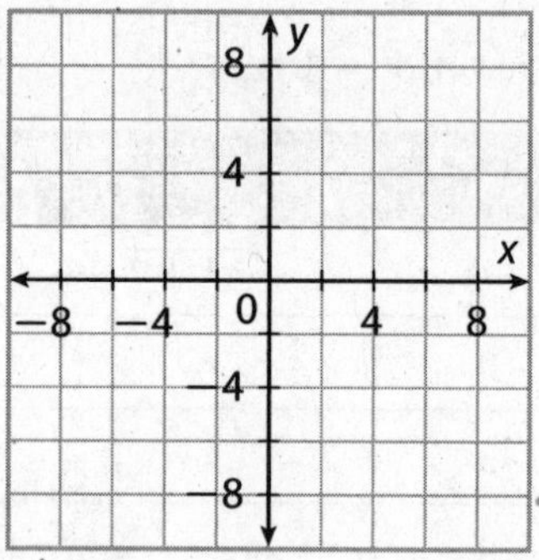

8. $y = \sqrt{x + 4} + 7$

x	$y = \sqrt{x + 4} + 7$	(x, y)
−4	$\sqrt{-4 + 4} + 7$	$(-4, 7)$
−3		
0		
5		

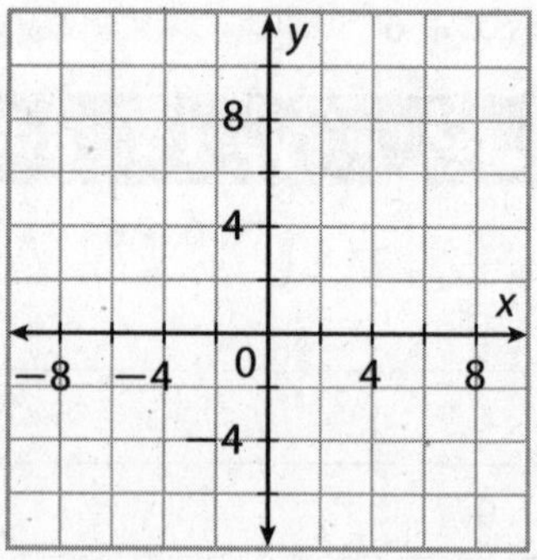

9. $y = -\sqrt{x}$

x	$y = -\sqrt{x}$	(x, y)
0	$-\sqrt{0}$	$(0, 0)$
1		
4		
9		

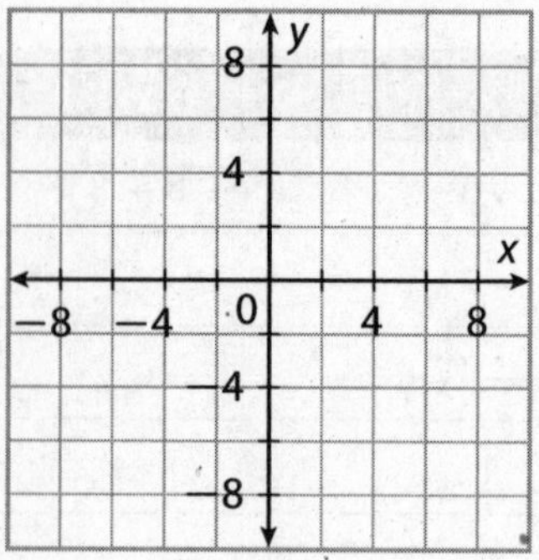

10. $y = \frac{1}{10}\sqrt{x}$

x	$y = \frac{1}{10}\sqrt{x}$	(x, y)
0	$\frac{1}{10}\sqrt{0}$	$(0, 0)$
1		
4		
9		

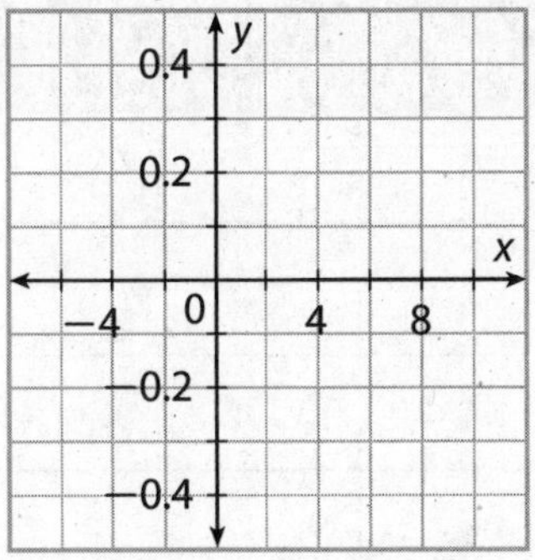

11. $y = -5\sqrt{x}$

x	$y = -5\sqrt{x}$	(x, y)
0	$-5\sqrt{0}$	$(0, 0)$
1		
4		
9		

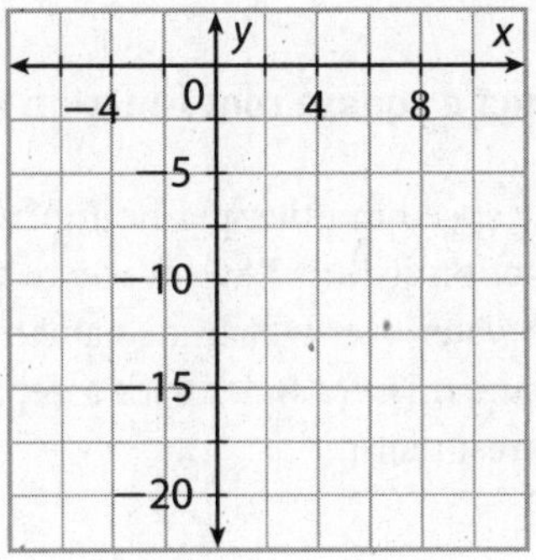

12. $y = \frac{1}{3}\sqrt{x}$

x	$y = \frac{1}{3}\sqrt{x}$	(x, y)
0	$\frac{1}{3}\sqrt{0}$	$(0, 0)$
1		
4		
9		

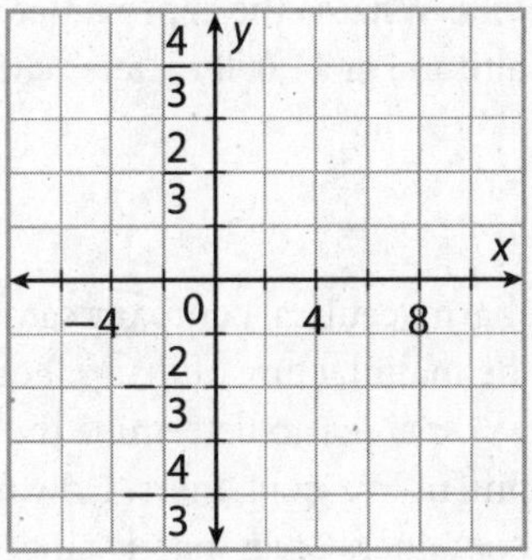

13. $y = 6\sqrt{x}$

x	$y = 6\sqrt{x}$	(x, y)
0	$6\sqrt{0}$	$(0, 0)$
1		
4		
9		
16		

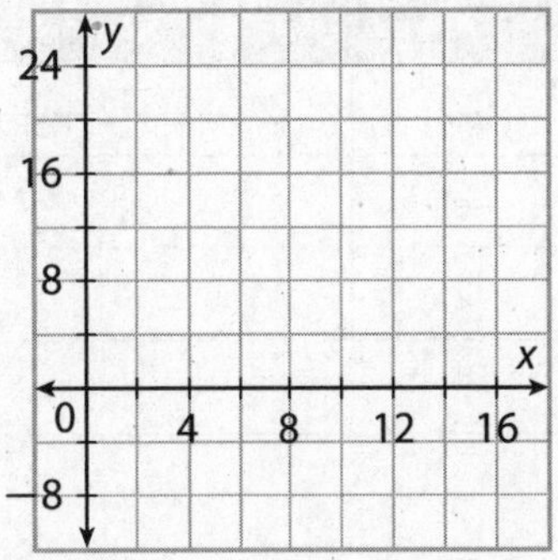

14. $y = -\frac{1}{2}\sqrt{x}$

x	$y = -\frac{1}{2}\sqrt{x}$	(x, y)
0	$-\frac{1}{2}\sqrt{0}$	$(0, 0)$
1		
4		
9		

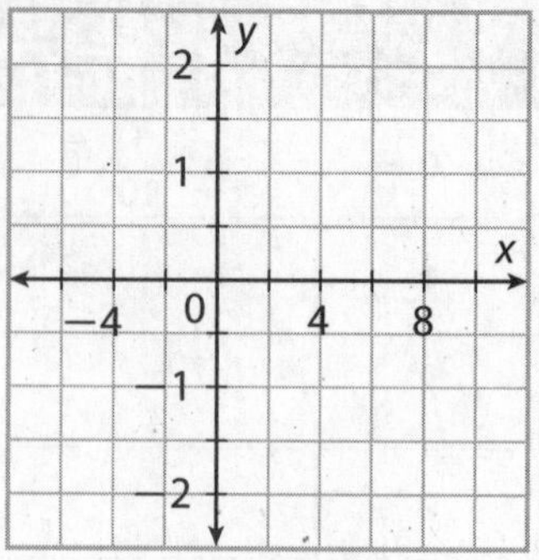

Construct a square root function to solve the problem.

15. The speed in miles per hour of a tsunami can be modeled by the function $s(d) = 3.86\sqrt{d}$, where d is the average depth in feet of the water over which the tsunami travels. Predict the speed of a tsunami over water with a depth of 1500 feet, rounding to the nearest tenth.

16. Pilots use the function $D(A) = 3.56\sqrt{A}$ to approximate the distance D in kilometers to the horizon from an altitude A in meters. What is the approximate distance to the horizon observed by a pilot flying at an altitude of 11,000 meters? (Round to the nearest tenth of a kilometer.)

17. A pharmaceutical company samples the raw materials it receives before they are used in the manufacture of drugs. For inactive ingredients, the company uses the function $s(x) = \sqrt{x} + 1$ to determine the number of samples s that should be taken from a shipment of x containers. How many samples should be taken from a shipment of 45 containers of an inactive ingredient? (Round to the nearest whole number.)

18. Graph the equation $y = 2\sqrt{x + 2} + 2$. Then state the domain and range.

x	$y = 2\sqrt{x + 2} + 2$	(x, y)
−2	$2\sqrt{-2 + 2} + 2$	$(-2, 2)$
−1		
2		
7		

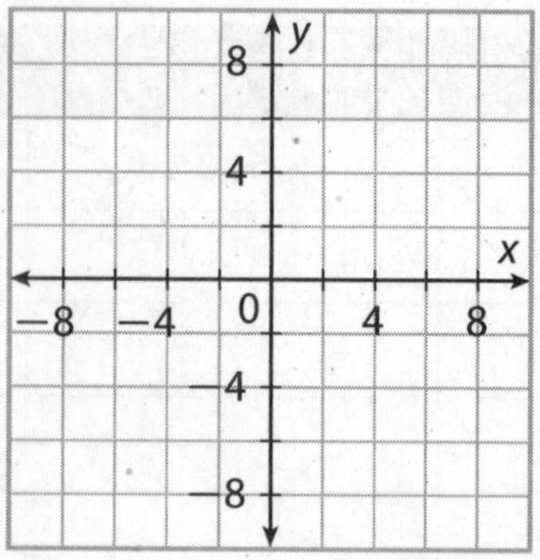

Write an equation for each graph. Explain your reasoning.

19.

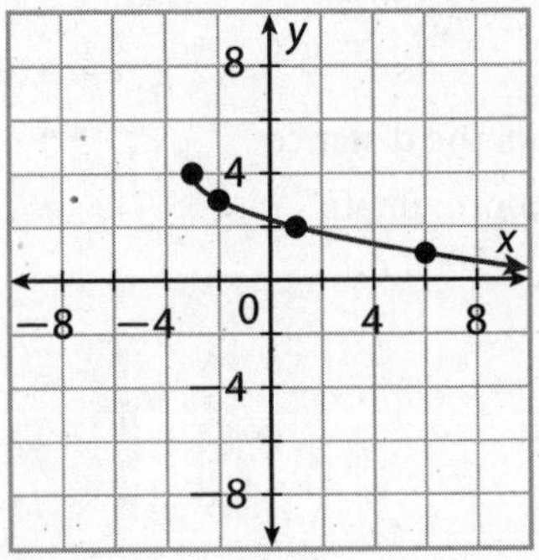

20.

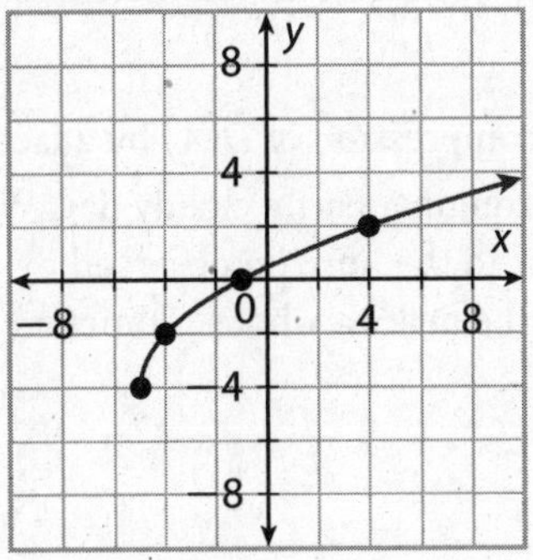

H.O.T. Focus on Higher Order Thinking

21. Explain the Error A student said the domain and range for the equation $y = \frac{1}{2}\sqrt{x + 10} - 7$ was $x \leq -10$ and $y \geq 7$. Is the student correct? If not, give the mistake and the correct answer.

22. Multi-Step The time t in seconds required for an object to fall from a certain height can be modeled by the function $t(h) = \frac{1}{4}\sqrt{h}$, where h is the initial height of the object in feet. How much longer will it take for a piece of an iceberg to fall into the ocean from a height of 240 ft than from a height of 100 ft? (Round to the nearest hundredth of a second.)

23. Analyze Relationships Describe how a horizontal translation and a vertical translation of the function $f(x) = \sqrt{x}$ each affect the function's domain and range.

24. Represent Real-World Problems Pilots use the function $D(A) = 3.56\sqrt{A}$ to approximate the distance D in kilometers to the horizon from an altitude A in meters on a clear day.

a. A vertical compression of $D(A)$ by a factor of $\frac{1}{4}$ can be used to model the distance to the horizon on a partly cloudy day. Write the new function and approximate the distance to the horizon observed by a pilot flying at an altitude of 5000 m. (Round to the nearest whole kilometer.)

b. How will the distance to the horizon on a partly cloudy day change if the pilot descends by 1500 m?

Lesson Performance Task

On a clear day, the ability to see a faraway unobstructed object on flat land is limited by the curvature of Earth. For an object with a height H in meters being observed by a person at height h in meters above the ground, the approximate distance d, in kilometers, at which the object falls below the horizon is given by the function $d(H) = 3.57\sqrt{H} + 3.57\sqrt{h}$.

A. What is the effect of the observer's height h on the graph of $d(H)$?

B. An observational tower has two levels, one at 100 meters and the second at 200 meters, so more visitors are able to visit the tower and the visitors have two different perspectives. Several tall buildings are in different directions and are all unobstructed from the observational tower. Plot two functions for the distance required to see a building over the horizon versus the height of the building, one for each level on the observational tower.

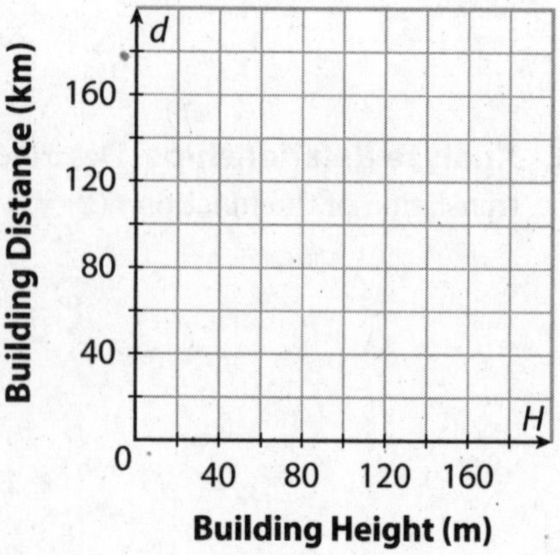

C. Building A is 40 meters tall and 60 kilometers away, building B is 80 meters tall and 62 kilometers away, building C is 110 meters tall and is 68 kilometers away, and building D is 150 meters tall and is 80 kilometers away. Which buildings can be seen from both levels on a clear day? Which buildings can be seen from the top level on a clear day? Explain.

Name________________________ Class________________ Date________________

13.4 Graphing Cube Root Functions

Essential Question: How can you use transformations of the parent cube root function to graph functions of the form $f(x) = a\sqrt[3]{x - h} + k$?

Resource Locker

Explore 1 Exploring the Inverse of $y = x^3$

The inverse of a function can be found both algebraically and graphically. Explore the graph of the inverse of $y = x^3$ first and then find the functional form.

(A) Use your graphing calculator to plot the functions $y = x^3$ and $y = x$, with the standard window settings. The graph of ______ produces a diagonal line across the screen.

(B) Use the DrawInv feature to draw the graph of the inverse of $y = x^3$ along with $y = x^2$ and $y = x$.

The newly drawn inverse should look like a __________ of the parent function across the line, $y = x$.

(C) The inverse graph drawn by the calculator passes the ________ line test, indicating that it is a function.

(D) Cube roots are the inverse operation of cubing. Use inverse operations to write the inverse of $y = x^3$.

Switch x and y in the equation. $x = y^3$

Take the cube roots of both sides of the equation. ______ $= y$

Reflect

1. **Discussion** When you take the cube root of a number or variable, do you have to consider both positive and negative cases? Explain why or why not.

____

____

____

Explore 2 Graphing the Parent Cube Root Function

The graph shows and $y = x^3$ and $y = \sqrt[3]{x}$.

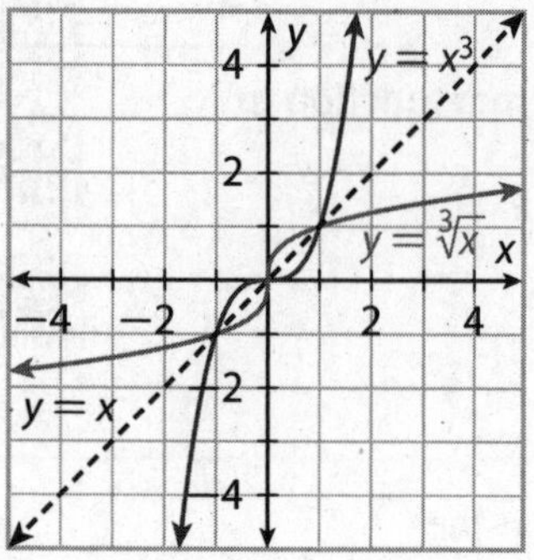

Ⓐ What is the range of $y = x^3$?

☐ $< y <$ ☐

Ⓑ What values of y cannot result from evaluating the cubic function, $y = x^3$? ______

Ⓒ If any value of y can result from evaluating the cubic function, $y = x^3$, then ______ value of x can be used to evaluate the function, $y = \sqrt[3]{x}$.

Ⓓ The domain of $y = \sqrt[3]{x}$ is ☐ $< x <$ ☐.

Ⓔ Is there any need to restrict the domain of $y = \sqrt[3]{x}$? ______

Ⓕ A **cube root function** is a function whose rule is a cube root completing. $y = \sqrt[3]{x}$ is the, and plotting the points parent cube root function. Plot the function for yourself by completing the table of values, and plotting the points.

x	$y = \sqrt[3]{x}$
−8	−2
−1	
0	
1	
8	

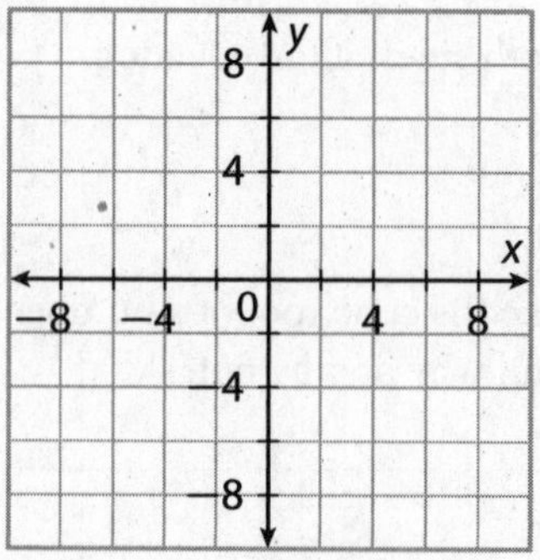

Reflect

2. Why is it that x can be a negative number in the cube root function, but not the square root function?

Explain 1 Graphing Translations of the Parent Cube Root Function

Functions of the form $y = \sqrt[3]{x - h} + k$ are translations of the cube root parent function $y = \sqrt[3]{x}$. For example, the graph of $y = \sqrt[3]{x - h} + k$ looks like the graph of $y = \sqrt[3]{x}$ shifted to the right by h units and up by k units. Positive values of h would result in a shift to the left, and negative values of k would result in a downward shift.

Example 1 **Use a table of values to add the graph of the transformed function to the parent function provided. Describe how the parent function was shifted. State the domain and range. Check your graphs on a graphing calculator.**

(A) $y = \sqrt[3]{x - 3} - 4$

x	y
−5	−6
2	−5
3	−4
4	−3
11	−2

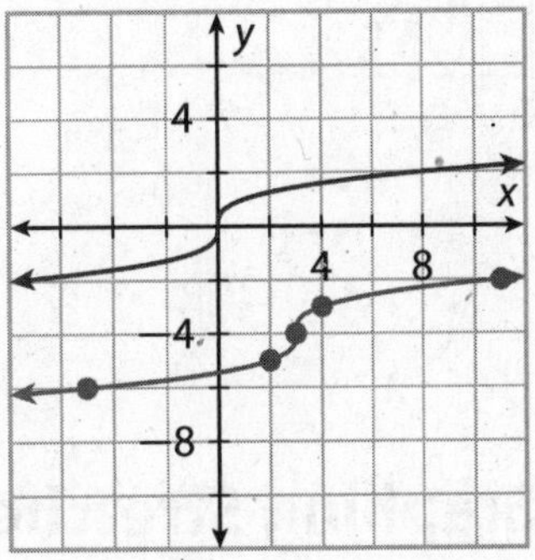

The transformed function was shifted right by 3 units and down by 4 units.

Domain: $-\infty < x < \infty$

Range: $-\infty < y < \infty$

(B) $y = \sqrt[3]{x + 2} + 8$

x	y
−10	
−3	
−2	
−1	
6	

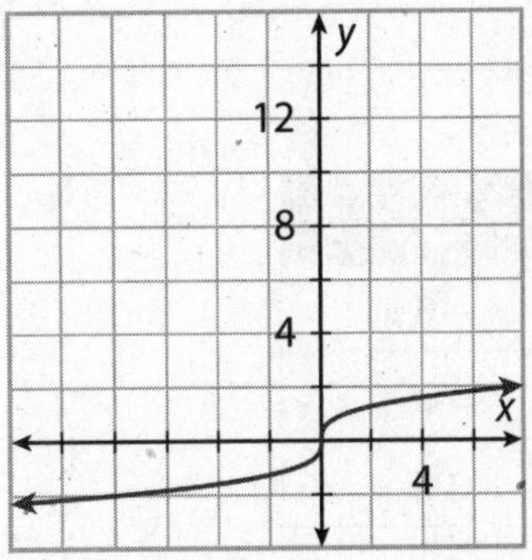

The transformed function was shifted ______ by 2 units and ______ by 8 units.

Domain: ☐ $< x <$ ☐

Range: ☐ $< y <$ ☐

YourTurn

Graph the function and compare it to the parent cube root function. State the shift in direction and by how many units. Then state the domain and range.

3. $y = \sqrt[3]{x+3} - 6$

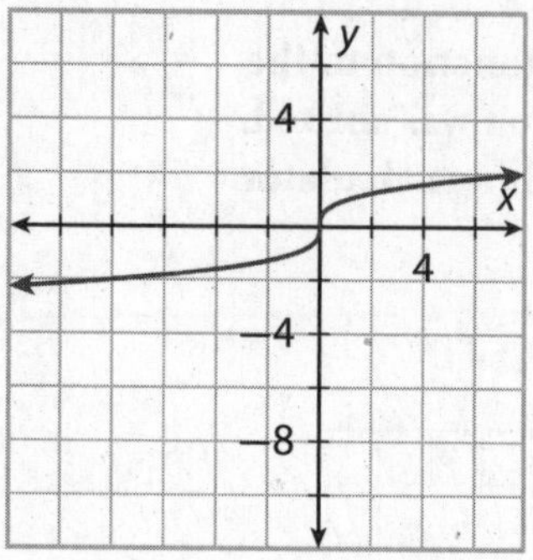

Explain 2 Graphing Stretches/Compressions and Reflections of the Parent Cube Root Function

Functions of the form $y = a\sqrt[3]{x}$ with $a \neq 0$ are vertical stretches and compressions of the cube root parent function. The graph of $y = a\sqrt[3]{x}$ looks like the graph of $y = \sqrt[3]{x}$ but will be stretched vertically by a factor of $|a|$ if $|a| > 1$ or compressed vertically by a factor of $\left|\frac{1}{a}\right|$ if $|a| < 1$. If $a < 0$, the graph will also be reflected across the x-axis.

Example 2 **Use a table of values to add the graph of the transformed function to the parent function provided. Describe how the parent function was stretched, compressed, and/or reflected. State the domain and range. Check your graphs on a graphing calculator.**

Ⓐ $y = \frac{1}{2}\sqrt[3]{x}$

x	y
−1	−0.5
0	0
1	0.5

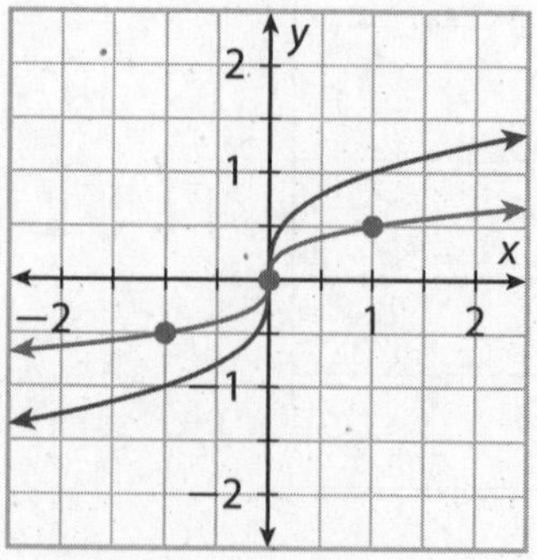

The transformed plot was compressed by a factor of $\frac{1}{2}$ and is not reflected across the x-axis.

Domain: $-\infty < x < \infty$

Range: $-\infty < y < \infty$

Ⓑ $y = -4\sqrt[3]{x}$

x	y
−8	
−1	
0	
1	
8	

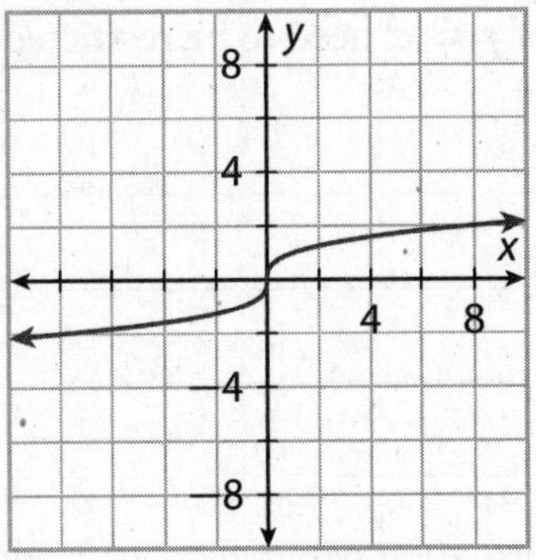

The transformed plot was stretched by a factor of ____ and __________ across the x-axis.

Domain: ☐ $< x <$ ☐

Range: ☐ $< y <$ ☐

YourTurn

Graph the function and compare it to the parent cube root function. State the stretch/compression factor and whether it was reflected or not. Then state the domain and range.

4. $y = 2\sqrt[3]{x}$

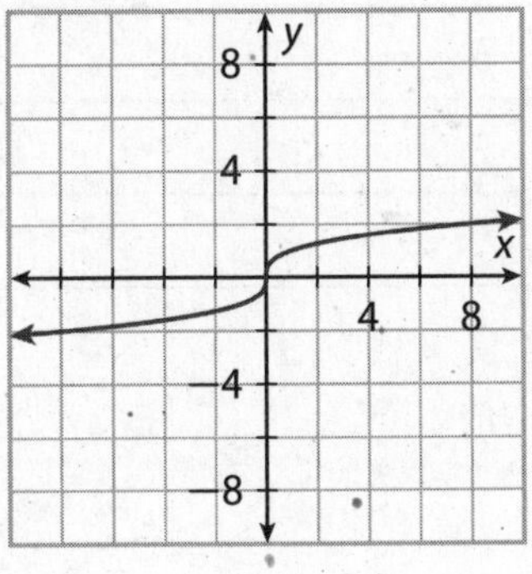

Elaborate

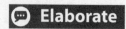

5. Does the domain of $y = x^3$ need to be restricted in order for its inverse to be a function? Explain why or why not.

6. How do the transformation parameters, a, h, and k affect the domain and range of $y = a\sqrt[3]{x - h} + k$?

7. **Essential Question Check-In** Describe how the parameters a, h, and k affect the graph of $y = a\sqrt[3]{x - h} + k$ as they are changed.

Evaluate: Homework and Practice

Personal Math Trainer

- Online Homework
- Hints and Help
- Extra Practice

1. Use inverse operations to find the inverse of $y = 8x^3$.

2. Graph $y = \sqrt[3]{x}$ together with $y = \sqrt{x}$ shown from 0 to 10. What for what positive values of x is the cube root of x greater than the square root of x? What for what positive values of x is the square root of x greater than the cube root of x?

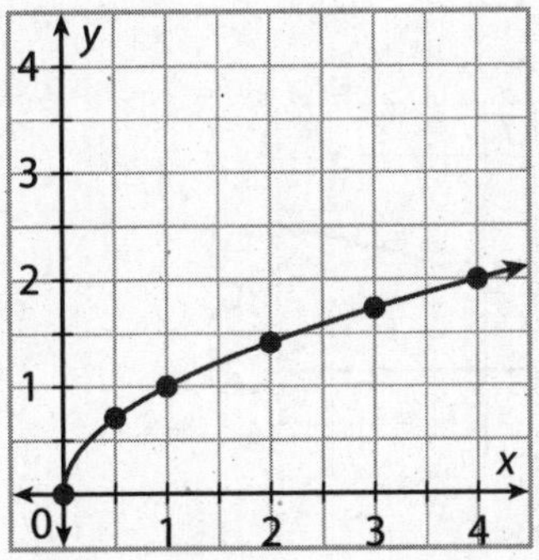

Graph each function by making a table of values.

3. $y = \sqrt[3]{x - 4}$

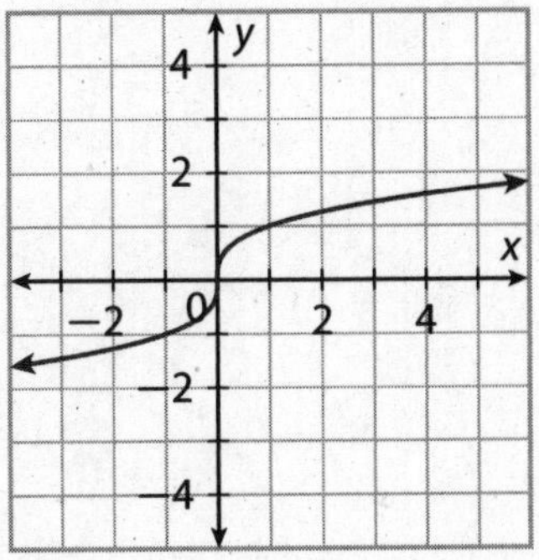

4. $y = \sqrt[3]{x} - 5$

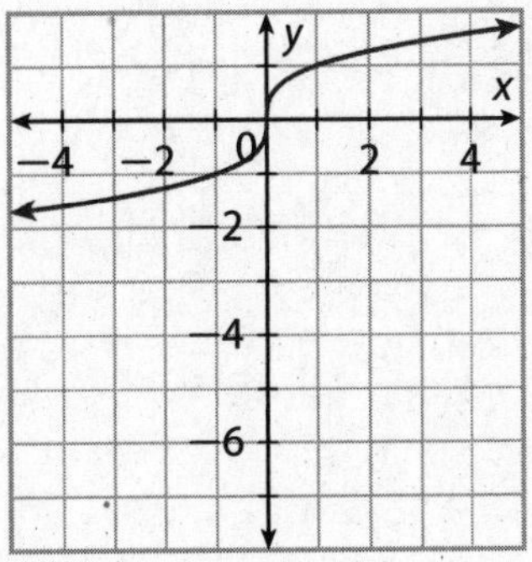

5. $y = \sqrt[3]{x - 2} - 2$

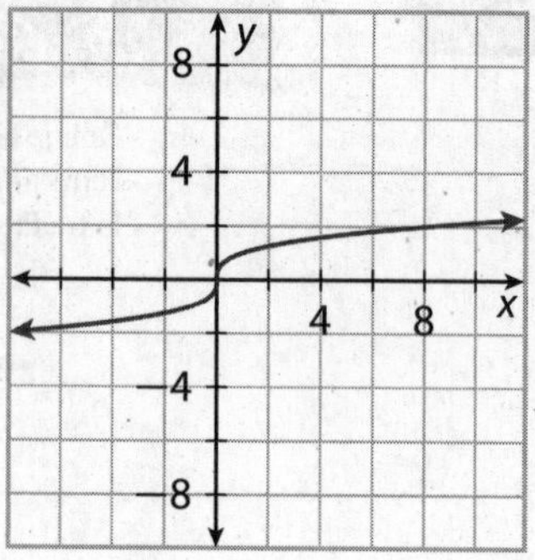

6. $y = \sqrt[3]{x + 3} + 7$

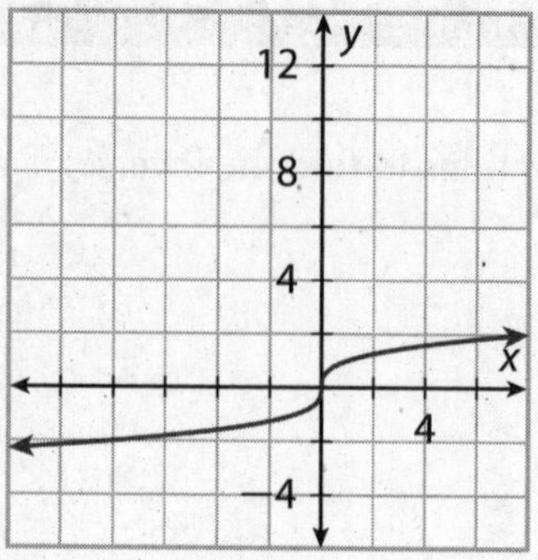

7. $y = -2\sqrt[3]{x}$

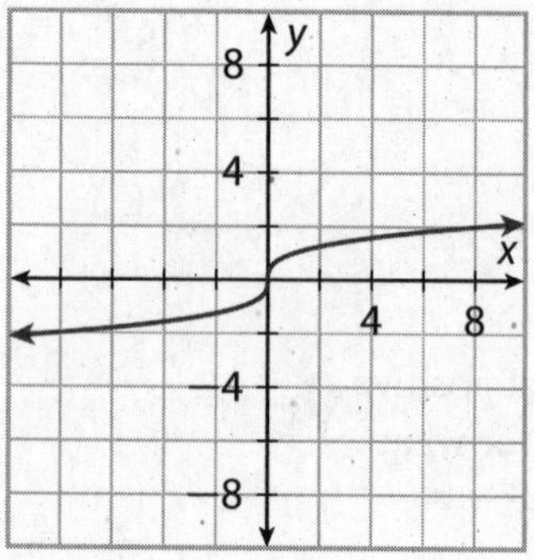

8. $y = \frac{1}{4}\sqrt[3]{x}$

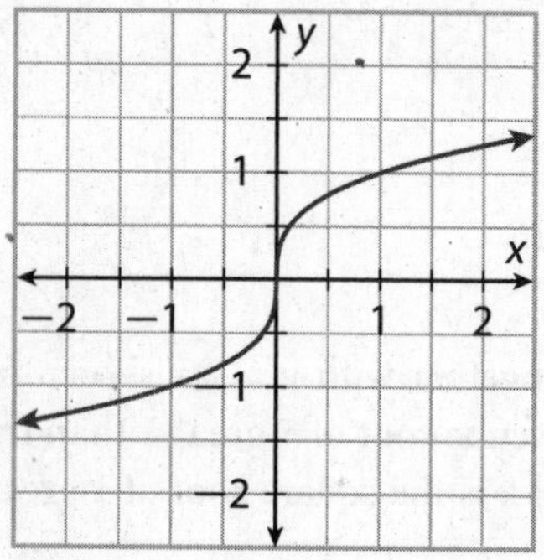

9. $y = 5\sqrt[3]{x}$

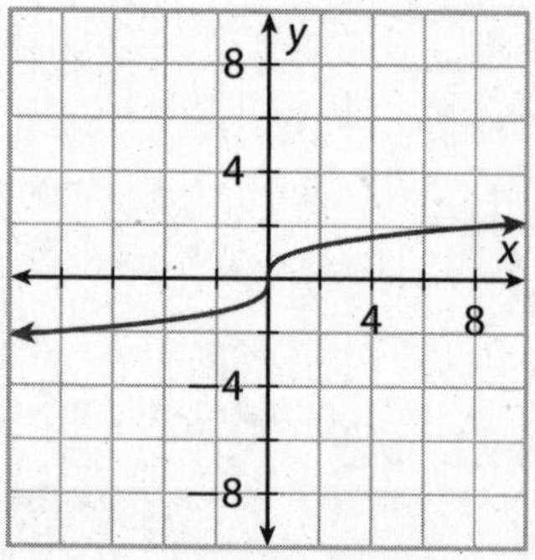

10. $y = -\frac{1}{2}\sqrt[3]{x}$

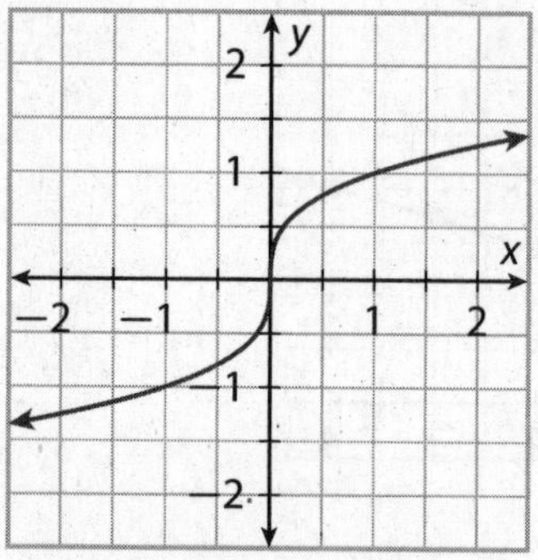

Describe the transformation or transformations of each function from the parent cube root function, $y = \sqrt[3]{x}$.

11. $y = \sqrt[3]{x - 1} + 5$

12. $y = \sqrt[3]{x + 5} + 5$

13. $y = \sqrt[3]{x - 3} - 3$

14. $y = \sqrt[3]{x + 7} - 2\frac{1}{2}$

15. $y = 3\sqrt[3]{x}$

16. $y = -\frac{3}{2}\sqrt[3]{x}$

17. $y = -\frac{1}{5}\sqrt[3]{x}$

18. $y = \frac{1}{10}\sqrt[3]{x}$

19. A cylindrical water holding tank with a height equal to its diameter has a height of $h = \sqrt[3]{\frac{4}{\pi}}\sqrt[3]{V}$, where V is the volume of the tank. Graph the height function on the grid provided.

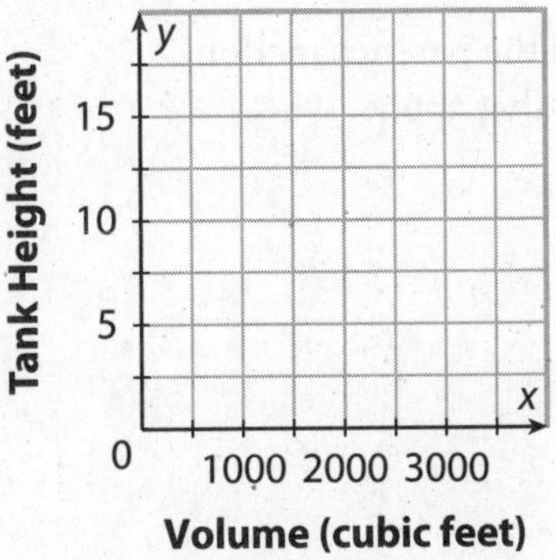

20. Geometry The Louvre Palace in Paris has a large glass pyramid in the main court. For a square pyramid with height equal to length, the height is related to the volume by $h = \sqrt[3]{3}\sqrt[3]{V}$. Graph the height of a pyramid as a function of volume on the grid provided.

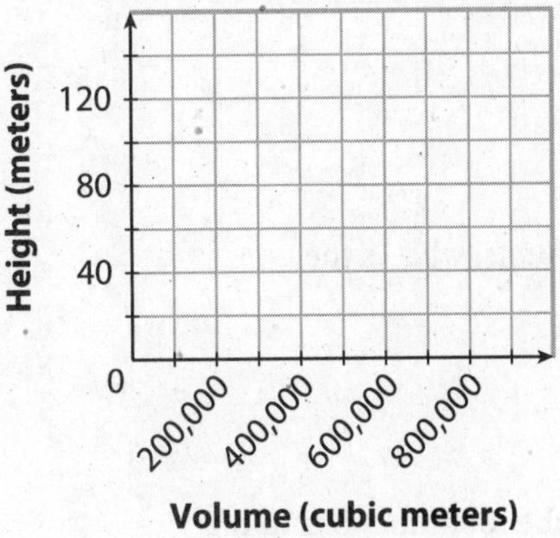

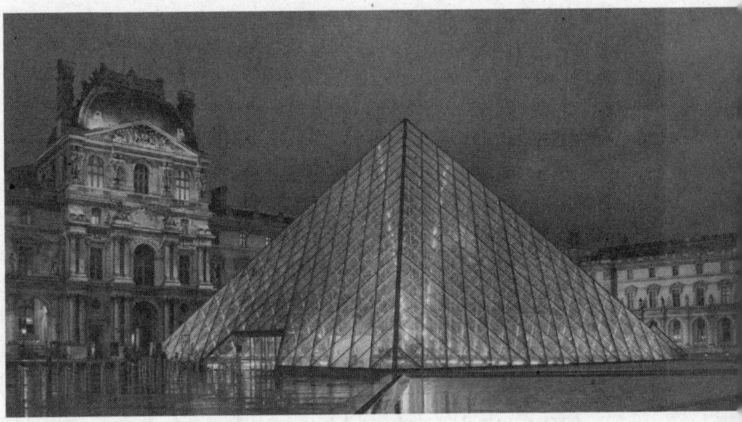

21. Geometry The diameter of a ball as a function of its volume is given by $d = 2\sqrt[3]{\frac{3}{4\pi}}\sqrt[3]{V} \approx 1.24\sqrt[3]{V}$. Describe the transformations of a graph of the radius of a sphere compared to parent cube root function, $d = \sqrt[3]{V}$, and graph the function on the grid provided.

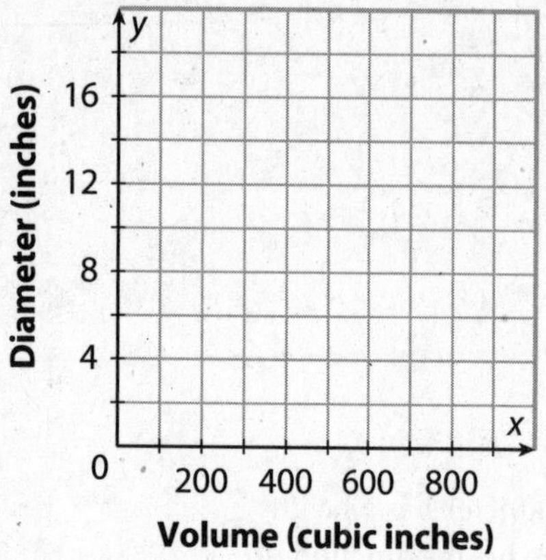

22. The function, $y = \frac{1}{3}\sqrt[3]{x+2} - 5$, has been transformed from the parent function, $y = \sqrt[3]{x}$, by which of the following transformations? Select all that apply.

A. vertical stretch by $\frac{1}{3}$

B. vertical compression by $\frac{1}{3}$

C. reflection across the y-axis

D. reflection across the x-axis

E. shifted up by 5

F. shifted down by 5

G. shifted right by 2

H. shifted left by 2

H.O.T. Focus on Higher Order Thinking

23. Critical Thinking If the graph of $y = \frac{1}{2}\sqrt[3]{x}$ is shifted left 2 units, what is the equation of the translated graph?

24. Communicate Mathematical Ideas Mitchio says that cube root functions of the form $y = a\sqrt[3]{x}$ should be considered to have a limited domain, because a cannot equal 0. Explain why you do or do not agree with Mitchio.

25. Multi-step The length of a cube as a function of total volume is given by $\ell = \sqrt[3]{V_t}$.

a. Write the function for the length of a cubic box needed to hold a cube-shaped glass vase that has a volume of 125 cubic inches and the packing material that surrounds the vase V_p.

b. What are the domain and range of this function?

c. Graph the function on the grid.

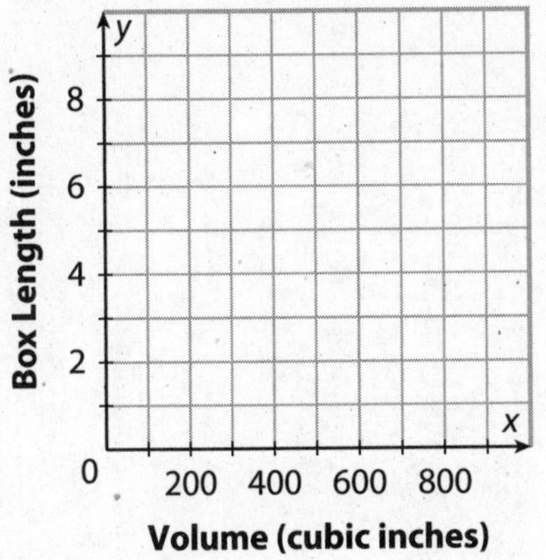

Lesson Performance Task

A manufacturer wants to make a ball bearing that is made of a mixture of zinc, iron, and copper and has come down to two alloys. Alloy A has a density of $7.5 \frac{g}{cm^3}$ and alloy B has a density of $8.5 \frac{g}{cm^3}$.

A. Use the formula for the volume of a sphere, $V = \frac{4}{3}\pi r^3$ and the formula for density, $D = \frac{m}{V}$, to write an equation for m as a function of r for each alloy.

B. Find the inverse of each function. Write the function in terms of $r = a\sqrt{m}$, where a is rounded to three decimal places.

C. How does the graph of each inverse function compare to the parent cube root function? For a given mass, which alloy would have a greater radius?

D. The manufacturer wants the ball bearings to have a mass of 12 grams and to have a radius as close to 0.7 cm as possible. Which alloy would be closer to the manufacturer's desired specifications? Explain.

Functions and Inverses

Essential Question: How can you use functions and inverses to solve real-world problems?

Key Vocabulary
cube root function
(función de raíz cubo)
inverse function
(inverso de una function)
radical function
(radical de una function)
square root function
(función de raíz cuadrada)

KEY EXAMPLE *(Lessons 13.1, 13.2, 13.3)*

Graph $f(x) = x^2 + 1$ and its inverse.

$$y = x^2 + 1$$
$$x = y^2 + 1$$
$$x - 1 = y^2$$
$$\pm\sqrt{x-1} = y$$

To find the inverse of $f(x)$, or $f^{-1}(x)$, switch x and y, and solve for y.

For the inverse to be a function, restrict it to nonnegative numbers, $f^{-1}(x) = \sqrt{x-1}$.

Fill in a table of values for $f(x)$ and $f^{-1}(x)$.

x	$f(x)$	$f^{-1}(x)$
-2	$(-2)^2 + 1 = 5$	not a real number
-1	$(-1)^2 + 1 = 2$	not a real number
0	$(0)^2 + 1 = 1$	not a real number
1	$(1)^2 + 1 = 2$	$\sqrt{1-1} = 0$
2	$(2)^2 + 1 = 5$	$\sqrt{2-1} = 1$
3	$(3)^2 + 1 = 10$	$\sqrt{3-1} \approx 1.41$
4	$(4)^2 + 1 = 17$	$\sqrt{4-1} \approx 1.73$

Graph the ordered pairs.

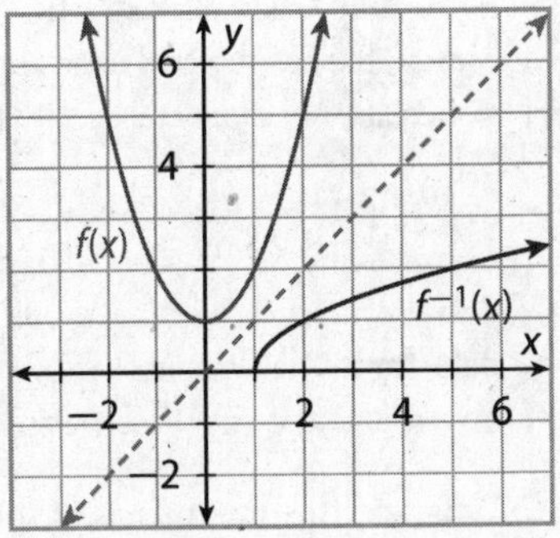

$f^{-1}(x)$ is a reflection of $f(x)$ over $y = x$ for nonnegative values of x.

The domain of $f(x)$ is all real numbers, and the range of $f(x)$ is $y \geq 1$.

The domain of $f^{-1}(x)$ is $x \geq 1$, and the range of $f^{-1}(x)$ is $y \geq 0$.

EXERCISES

1. Graph $f(x) = \frac{1}{2}(x + 2)^3$. ***(Lesson 13.1)***

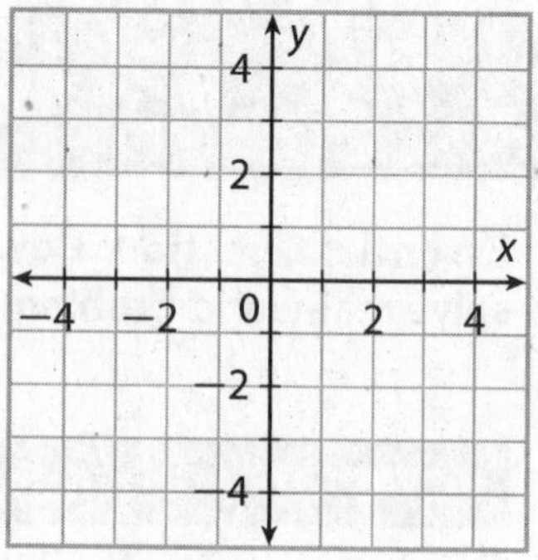

Write the inverse of each function. ***(Lesson 13.2)***

2. $g(x) = 4x^2 + 7$

3. $t(x) = (x + 15)^3 - 4$

4. Graph $h(x) = \sqrt[3]{x} - 2$. Find the domain and range of $h(x)$. ***(Lesson 13.4)***

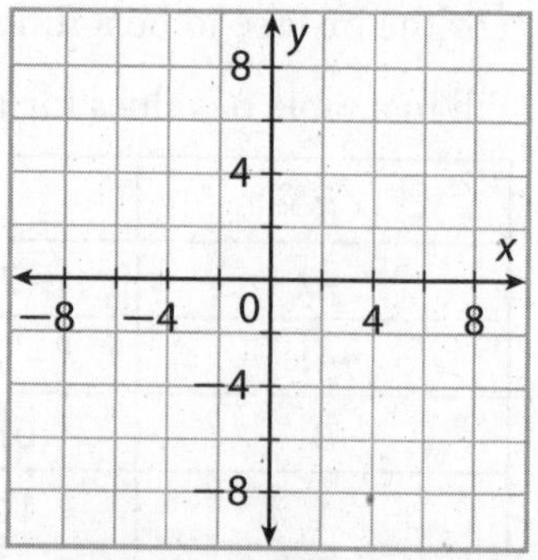

MODULE PERFORMANCE TASK

The Smallest Cube

Foolish Sports makes sporting equipment for people who play unusual sports like lawnmower racing, pie eating, and cheese rolling. For some reason, companies that make footballs, roller skates, and hockey sticks make a lot more money.

So, Foolish is going into the ordinary-sports business. Its first project is to make and sell baseballs, basketballs, and golf balls. The company's package designer found the typical volumes of the three products and now must determine the dimensions of the boxes they will be sold in. Each box must be cubical and must be the smallest box that can contain the ball.

Basketball	448 cu in.
Baseball	14.1 cu in.
Golf ball	2.48 cu in

What are the dimensions of the three boxes? Explain how you found the dimensions.

Start by listing in the space below the information you will need to solve the problem. Then use your own paper to work on the task. Use numbers, words, or algebra to explain how you reached your conclusion.

Ready to Go On?

13.1–13.4 Functions and Inverses

Personal Math Trainer

- Online Homework
- Hints and Help
- Extra Practice

Graph each function. *(Lesson 13.1)*

1. Graph $g(x) = \frac{1}{4}(x + 1)^3 - 4$.

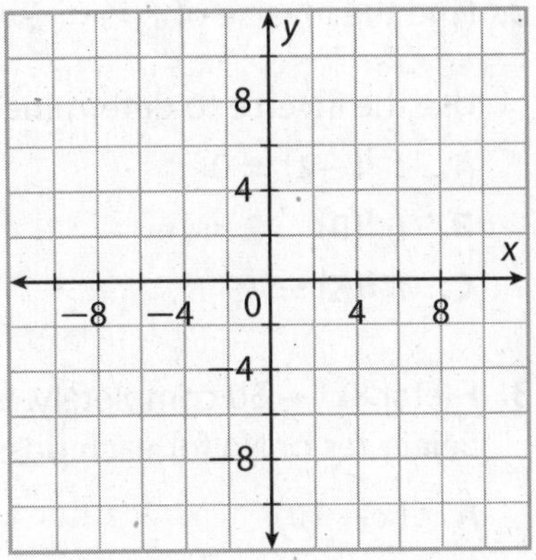

2. Find and graph the inverse of $f(x) = 2x^2 - 4$. *(Lessons 13.2, 13.3)*

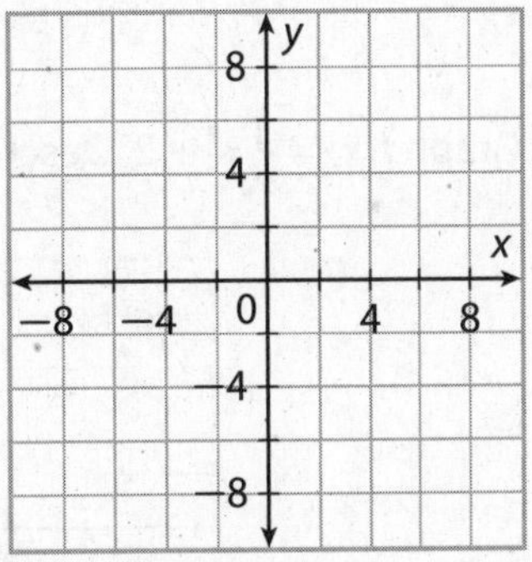

3. Graph $h(x) = 2\sqrt[3]{x + 6} + 4$. *(Lesson 13.4)*

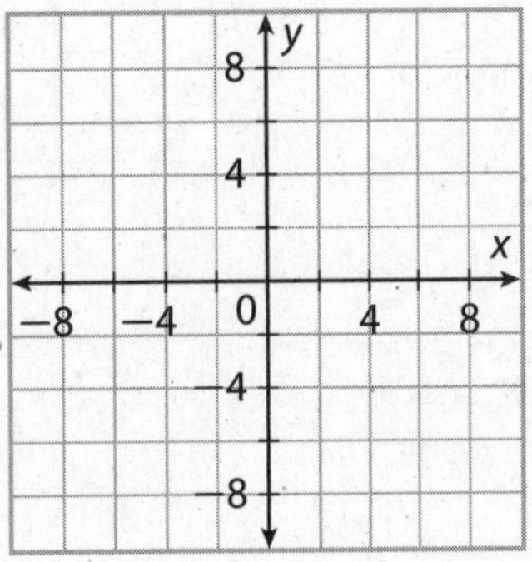

ESSENTIAL QUESTION

4. How could you sketch the inverse of an exponential function?

MODULE 13
MIXED REVIEW

Assessment Readiness

1. Find the solutions of $-2x(x+1)(3x+5)=0$. Is the given value of x a solution? Select Yes or No for each possible solution.

A. $x=-\frac{5}{3}$ ○ Yes ○ No

B. $x=0$ ○ Yes ○ No

C. $x=1$ ○ Yes ○ No

2. Find the inverse of $f(x)=\frac{1}{3}x-2$.

Use the inverse to determine if each of the following equations is True or False.

A. $f^{-1}(-2)=0$ ○ True ○ False

B. $f^{-1}(0)=2$ ○ True ○ False

C. $f^{-1}(3)=15$ ○ True ○ False

3. Factor $8x^2-50$ completely. Is the following expression a factor of this expression? Select Yes or No for each possible factor.

A. $(x-10)$ ○ Yes ○ No

B. $(2x+5)$ ○ Yes ○ No

C. 2 ○ Yes ○ No

4. Graph $f(x)=\frac{1}{2}x^3+2$. Describe the end behavior of the graph.

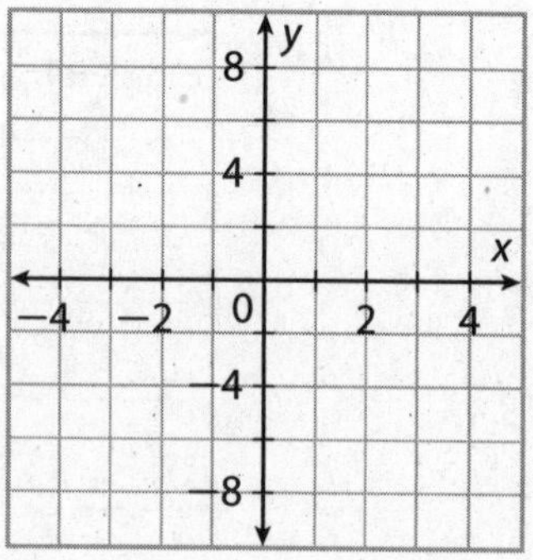

Assessment Readiness

Personal Math Trainer
- Online Homework
- Hints and Help
- Extra Practice

1. Consider the system $\begin{cases} y \leq \frac{1}{2}x + 3 \\ y \geq 2x \end{cases}$. Is each of the following a solution of the system?

Select Yes or No for each possible solution.

A. $(-2, -5)$ ○ Yes ○ No

B. $(2, 4)$ ○ Yes ○ No

C. $(3, -1)$ ○ Yes ○ No

2. Factor and solve each of the following equations. Is –4 a solution of the equation?

Select Yes or No for each equation.

A. $x^2 + 4x + 16 = 0$ ○ Yes ○ No

B. $2x^2 - 8x + 32 = 0$ ○ Yes ○ No

C. $5x^2 - 80 = 0$ ○ Yes ○ No

3. Find the inverse of $f(x) = x^2 - 2$. Determine if the given statement is True of False.

A. $f^{-1}(x)$ is a square root function. ○ True ○ False

B. The domain of is $f^{-1}(x)$ is $x \geq -2$. ○ True ○ False

C. The range of $f^{-1}(x)$ is all real numbers. ○ True ○ False

4. Look at each focus and directrix. Is the resulting parabola vertical? Select Yes or No for A–C.

A. Focus $(6, -3)$, Directrix $x = 2$ ○ Yes ○ No

B. Focus $(-4, -2)$, Directrix $y = -3$ ○ Yes ○ No

C. Focus $(0, 1)$, Directrix $y = 2$ ○ Yes ○ No

5. The graph of $f(x) = \frac{1}{3}x + 1$ is shown. Find and graph the inverse of $f(x)$.

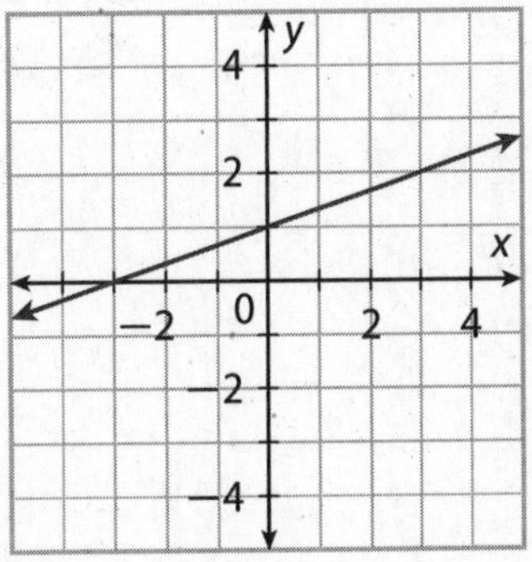

6. Consider the equation $-4x^2 + x = 3$. What method should be used to most easily solve the equation if you have a choice between taking the square root, completing the square, using the quadratic formula, or factoring? Explain your reasoning, and then solve the equation.

7. Graph $f(x) = (x + 2)^3$. Use the graph to solve $-8 = (x + 2)^3$.

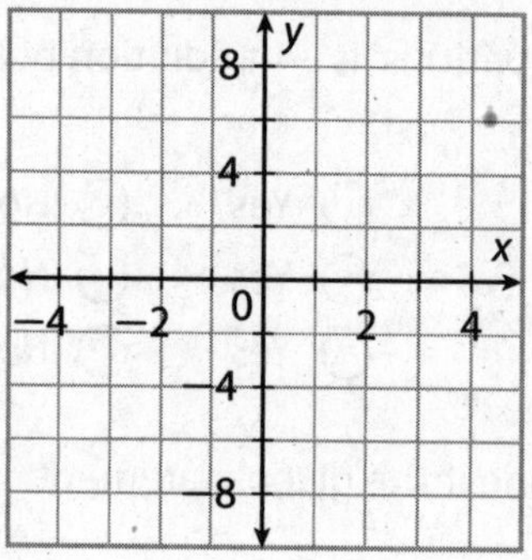

Performance Tasks

★ 8. The relationship between the radius r, in centimeters, of a solid gold sphere and its mass m, in grams, is given by $r = 0.23\sqrt[3]{m}$. Graph this relationship for the interval $0 \leq m \leq 10$.

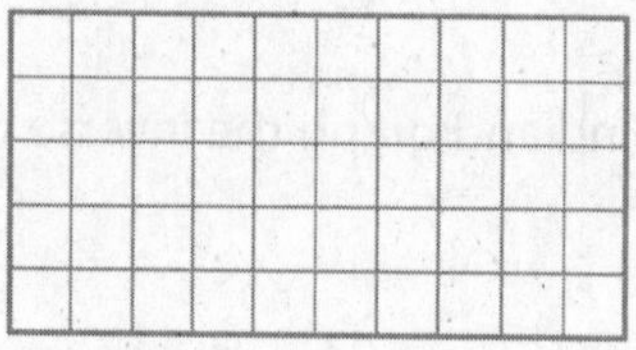

★★ **9.** The spittlebug is the world's highest-jumping animal relative to its body length of about 6 millimeters. The height h of a spittlebug's jump in millimeters can be modeled by the function $h(t) = -4000t^2 + 3000t$, where t is the time in seconds.

A. What is the maximum height that the spittlebug will reach? Explain how you found your answer.

B. What is the ratio of a spittlebug's maximum jumping height to its body length? In the best human jumpers, this ratio is about 1.38 to 1. Compare the ratio for spittlebugs with the ratio for the best human jumpers.

★★★**10.** The distance, d, in meters, an object falls after time t, in seconds, is given by $d = 4.9t^2$.

A. Find the inverse of this function.

B. How much time does it take for a stone dropped from the edge of a cliff to hit the ground 80 meters below? Round your answer to the nearest tenth of a second.

C. The relationship between the temperature in degrees Fahrenheit and Kelvin is given by $F = \frac{9}{5}(K - 273) + 32$. Find the inverse of this function

D. If the speed of sound in air is given by $s = 20.1\sqrt{K}$, where s is in meters per second, how long after dropping the stone can the sound of the stone striking the ground be heard at the edge of the cliff, if the temperature is 77°F? Explain how you got your answer.

MATH IN CAREERS

Ichthyologist A pike is a type of freshwater fish. A ichthyologist uses the function $W(L) = \frac{L^3}{3500}$ to find the approximate weight W in pounds of a pike with length L inches.

a. Write the inverse function $L(W)$.

b. Graph the inverse function.

c. What is the significance in the context of the problem of the point at approximately (6, 28) on the graph of $L(W)$?

d. What are the reasonable domain and range of the function $L(W)$?

Glossary/Glosario

A

ENGLISH	SPANISH	EXAMPLES
absolute value The absolute value of x is the distance from zero to x on a number line, denoted $\lvert x \rvert$. $\lvert x \rvert = \begin{cases} x & \text{if } x \geq 0 \\ -x & \text{if } x < 0 \end{cases}$	**valor absoluto** El valor absoluto de x es la distancia de cero a x en una recta numérica, y se expresa $\lvert x \rvert$. $\lvert x \rvert = \begin{cases} x & \text{si } x \geq 0. \\ -x & \text{si } x < 0 \end{cases}$	$\lvert 3 \rvert = 3$ $\lvert -3 \rvert = 3$
absolute-value equation An equation that contains absolute-value expressions.	**ecuación de valor absoluto** Ecuación que contiene expresiones de valor absoluto.	$\lvert x+4 \rvert = 7$
absolute-value function A function whose rule contains absolute-value expressions.	**función de valor absoluto** Función cuya regla contiene expresiones de valor absoluto.	$y = \lvert x+4 \rvert$
absolute-value inequality An inequality that contains absolute-value expressions.	**desigualdad de valor absoluto** Desigualdad que contiene expresiones de valor absoluto.	$\lvert x+4 \rvert > 7$
acute angle An angle that measures greater than 0° and less than 90°.	**ángulo agudo** Ángulo que mide más de 0° y menos de 90°.	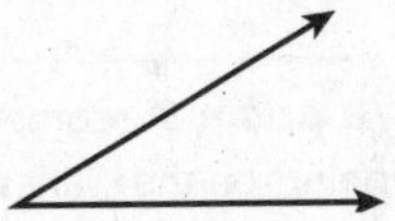
acute triangle A triangle with three acute angles.	**triángulo acutángulo** Triángulo con tres ángulos agudos.	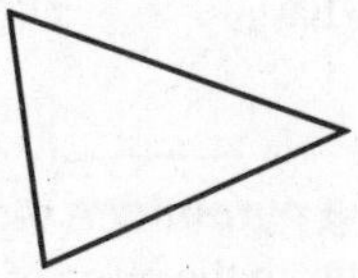
adjacent angles Two angles in the same plane with a common vertex and a common side, but no common interior points.	**ángulos adyacentes** Dos ángulos en el mismo plano que tienen un vértice y un lado común pero no comparten puntos internos.	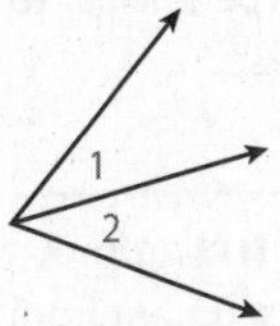 $\angle 1$ and $\angle 2$ are adjacent angles.
adjacent arcs Two arcs of the same circle that intersect at exactly one point.	**arcos adyacentes** Dos arcos del mismo círculo que se cruzan en un punto exacto.	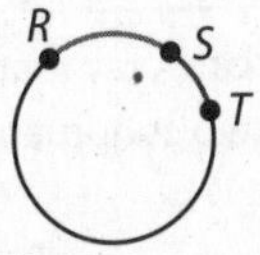 $\overset{\frown}{RS}$ and $\overset{\frown}{ST}$ are adjacent arcs.

ENGLISH	SPANISH	EXAMPLES
alternate exterior angles For two lines intersected by a transversal, a pair of angles that lie on opposite sides of the transversal and outside the other two lines.	**ángulos alternos externos** Dadas dos líneas cortadas por una transversal, par de ángulos no adyacentes ubicados en los lados opuestos de la transversal y fuera de las otras dos líneas.	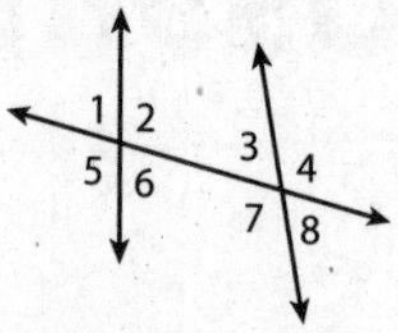 ∠4 and ∠5 are alternate exterior angles.
alternate interior angles For two lines intersected by a transversal, a pair of nonadjacent angles that lie on opposite sides of the transversal and between the other two lines.	**ángulos alternos internos** Dadas dos líneas cortadas por una transversal, par de ángulos no adyacentes ubicados en los lados opuestos de la transversal y entre las otras dos líneas.	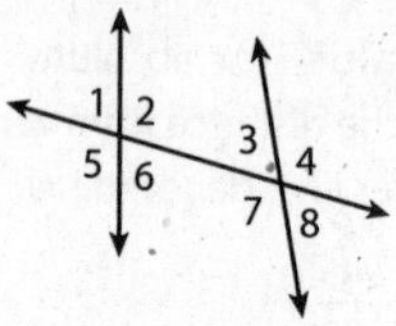 ∠3 and ∠6 are alternate interior angles.
altitude of a cone A segment from the vertex to the plane of the base that is perpendicular to the plane of the base.	**altura de un cono** Segmento que se extiende desde el vértice hasta el plano de la base y es perpendicular al plano de la base.	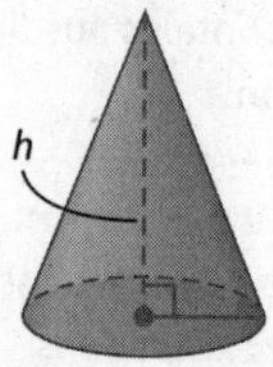
altitude of a cylinder A segment with its endpoints on the planes of the bases that is perpendicular to the planes of the bases.	**altura de un cilindro** Segmento con sus extremos en los planos de las bases que es perpendicular a los planos de las bases.	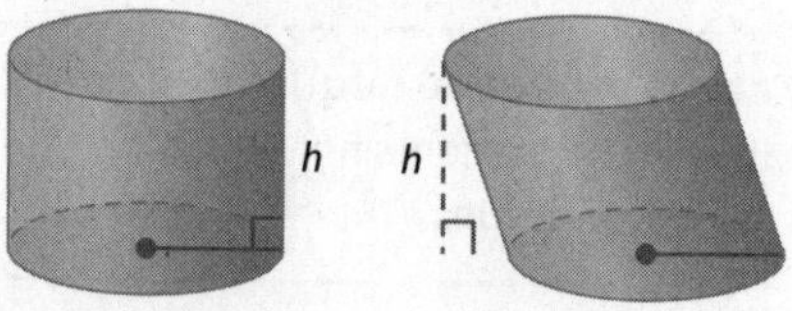
altitude of a prism A segment with its endpoints on the planes of the bases that is perpendicular to the planes of the bases.	**altura de un prisma** Segmento con sus extremos en los planos de las bases que es perpendicular a los planos de las bases.	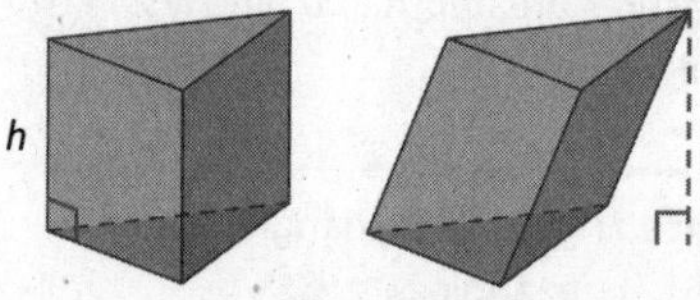
altitude of a pyramid A segment from the vertex to the plane of the base that is perpendicular to the plane of the base.	**altura de una pirámide** Segmento que se extiende desde el vértice hasta el plano de la base y es perpendicular al plano de la base.	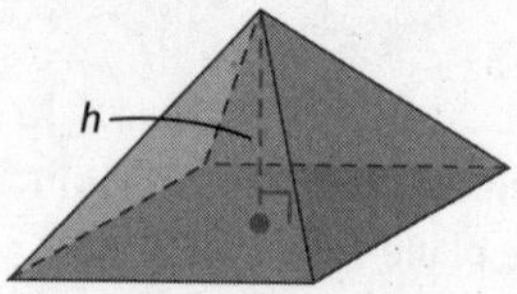
altitude of a triangle A perpendicular segment from a vertex to the line containing the opposite side.	**altura de un triángulo** Segmento perpendicular que se extiende desde un vértice hasta la línea que forma el lado opuesto.	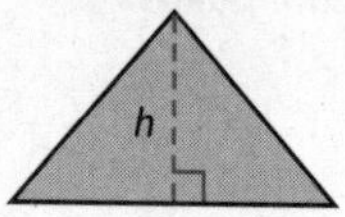
angle bisector A ray that divides an angle into two congruent angles.	**bisectriz de un ángulo** Rayo que divide un ángulo en dos ángulos congruentes.	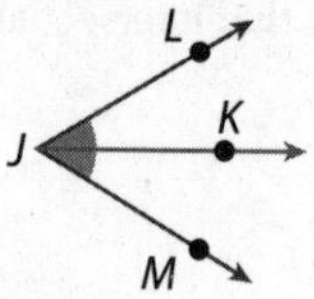 $\overrightarrow{JK}$ is an angle bisector of ∠LJM.

ENGLISH	SPANISH	EXAMPLES
angle of rotation An angle formed by a rotating ray, called the terminal side, and a stationary reference ray, called the initial side.	**ángulo de rotación** Ángulo formado por un rayo rotativo, denominado lado terminal, y un rayo de referencia estático, denominado lado inicial.	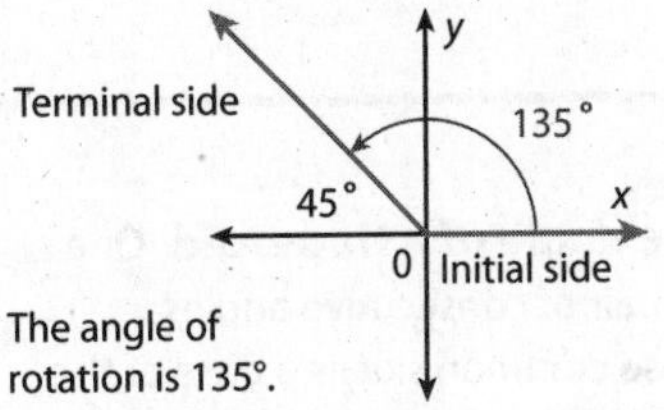
angle of rotational symmetry The smallest angle through which a figure with rotational symmetry can be rotated to coincide with itself.	**ángulo de simetría de rotación** El ángulo más pequeño alrededor del cual se puede rotar una figura con simetría de rotación para que coincida consigo misma.	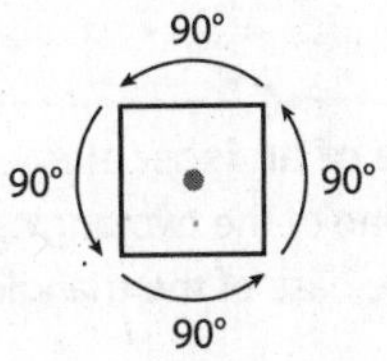
arc An unbroken part of a circle consisting of two points on the circle, called the endpoints, and all the points on the circle between them.	**arco** Parte continua de una circunferencia formada por dos puntos de la circunferencia denominados extremos y todos los puntos de la circunferencia comprendidos entre éstos.	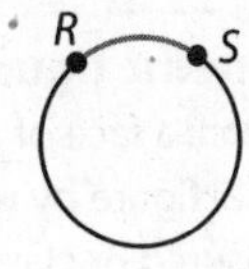
arc length The distance along an arc measured in linear units.	**longitud de arco** Distancia a lo largo de un arco medida en unidades lineales.	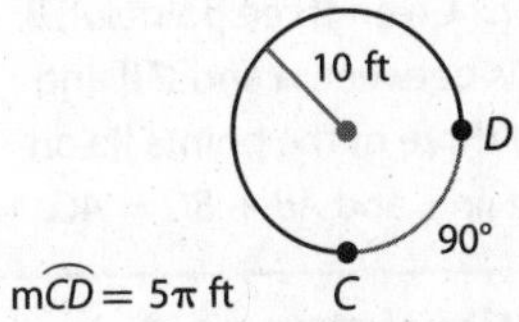
arc marks Marks used on a figure to indicate congruent angles.	**marcas de arco** Marcas utilizadas en una figura para indicar ángulos congruentes.	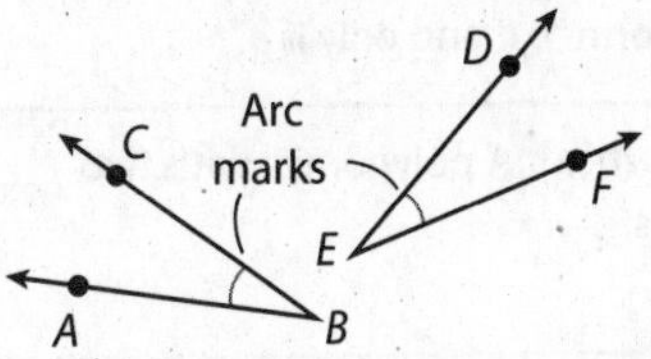
auxiliary line A line drawn in a figure to aid in a proof.	**línea auxiliar** Línea dibujada en una figura como ayuda en una demostración.	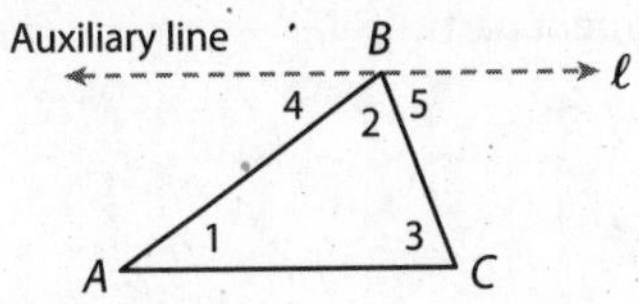
axiom *See* postulate.	**axioma** *Ver* postulado.	
axis of symmetry A line that divides a plane figure or a graph into two congruent reflected halves.	**eje de simetría** Línea que divide una figura plana o una gráfica en dos mitades reflejadas congruentes.	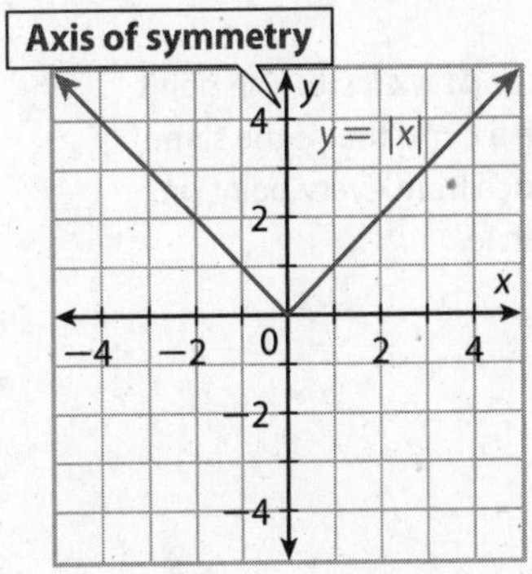

Glossary/Glosario

ENGLISH	SPANISH	EXAMPLES

B

base angle of a trapezoid One of a pair of consecutive angles whose common side is a base of the trapezoid.

ángulo base de un trapecio Uno de los dos ángulos consecutivos cuyo lado en común es la base del trapecio.

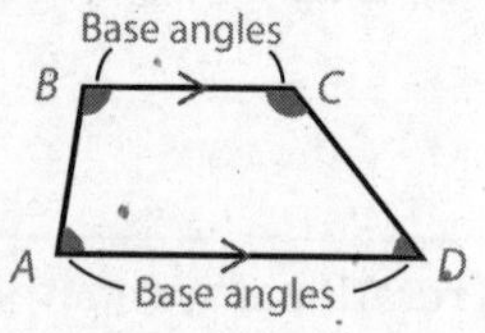

---

base angle of an isosceles triangle One of the two angles that have the base of the triangle as a side.

ángulo base de un triángulo isósceles Uno de los dos ángulos que tienen como lado la base del triángulo.

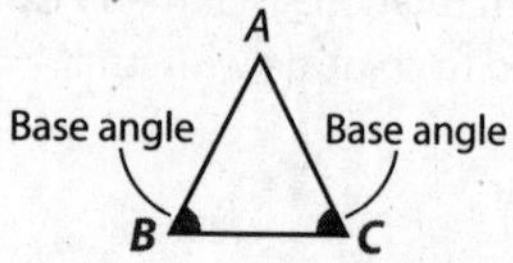

---

base of a geometric figure A side of a polygon; a face of a three-dimensional figure by which the figure is measured or classified.

base de una figura geométrica Lado de un polígono; cara de una figura tridimensional por la cual se mide o clasifica la figura.

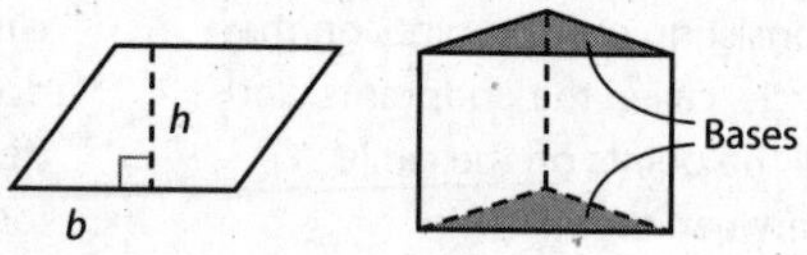

---

between Given three points A, B, and C, B is between A and C if and only if all three of the points lie on the same line, and $AB + BC = AC$.

entre Dados tres puntos A, B y C, B está entre A y C si y sólo si los tres puntos se encuentran en la misma línea y $AB + BC = AC$.

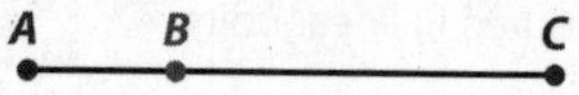

---

biconditional statement A statement that can be written in the form "*p* if and only if *q*."

enunciado bicondicional Enunciado que puede expresarse en la forma "*p* si y sólo si *q*".

A figure is a triangle if and only if it is a three-sided polygon.

---

binomial A polynomial with two terms.

binomio Polinomio con dos términos.

$x + y$

$2a^2 + 3$

$4m^3n^2 + 6mn^4$

---

bisect To divide into two congruent parts.

trazar una bisectriz Dividir en dos partes congruentes.

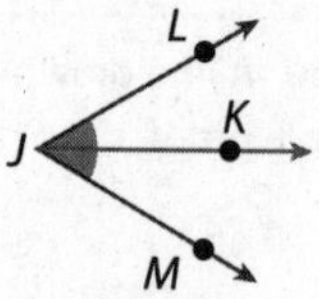

$\overrightarrow{JK}$ bisects $\angle LJM$.

C

center of a circle The point inside a circle that is the same distance from every point on the circle.

centro de un círculo Punto dentro de un círculo que se encuentra a la misma distancia de todos los puntos del círculo.

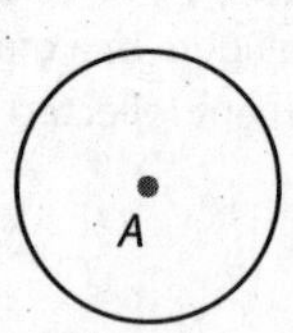

ENGLISH	SPANISH	EXAMPLES

center of a sphere The point inside a sphere that is the same distance from every point on the sphere.

centro de una esfera Punto dentro de una esfera que está a la misma distancia de cualquier punto de la esfera.

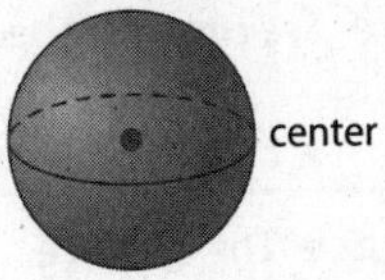

---

center of dilation The intersection of the lines that connect each point of the image with the corresponding point of the preimage.

centro de dilatación Intersección de las líneas que conectan cada punto de la imagen con el punto correspondiente de la imagen original.

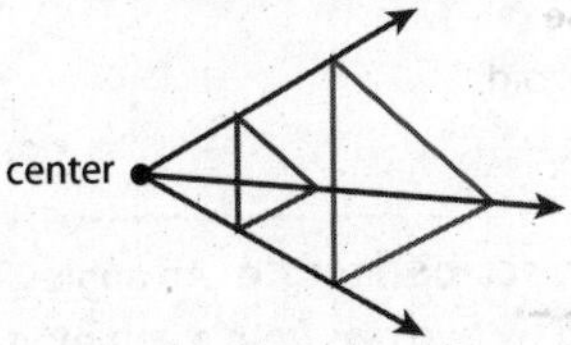

---

center of rotation The point around which a figure is rotated.

centro de rotación Punto alrededor del cual rota una figura.

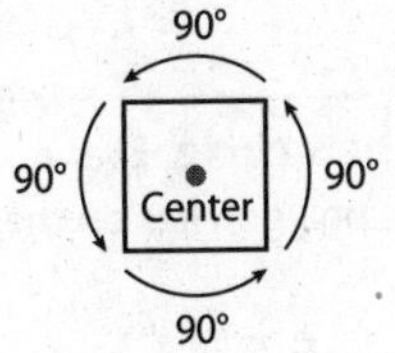

---

central angle of a circle An angle with measure less than or equal to 180° whose vertex is the center of a circle.

ángulo central de un círculo Ángulo con medida inferior o igual a 180° cuyo vértice es el centro de un círculo.

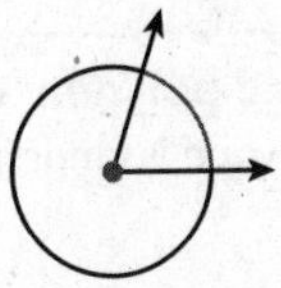

---

centroid of a triangle The point of concurrency of the three medians of a triangle. Also known as the *center of gravity*.

centroide de un triángulo Punto donde se encuentran las tres medianas de un triángulo. También conocido como *centro de gravedad*.

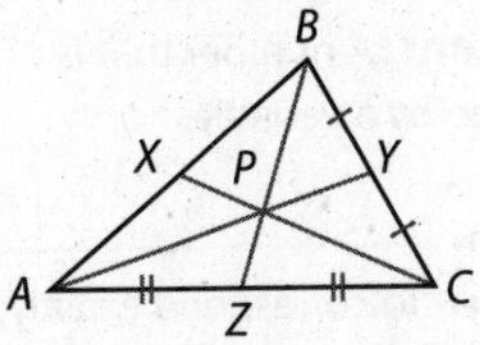

The centroid is *P*.

---

chord A segment whose endpoints lie on a circle.

cuerda Segmento cuyos extremos se encuentran en un círculo.

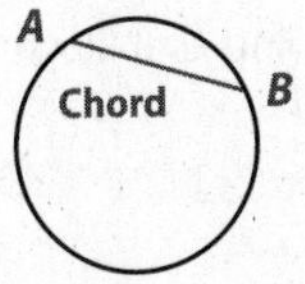

---

circle The set of points in a plane that are a fixed distance from a given point called the center of the circle.

círculo Conjunto de puntos en un plano que se encuentran a una distancia fija de un punto determinado denominado centro del círculo.

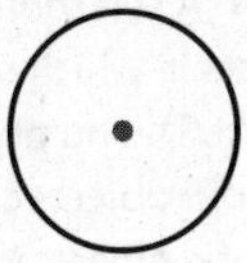

---

circumcenter of a triangle The point of concurrency of the three perpendicular bisectors of a triangle.

circuncentro de un triángulo Punto donde se cortan las tres mediatrices de un triángulo.

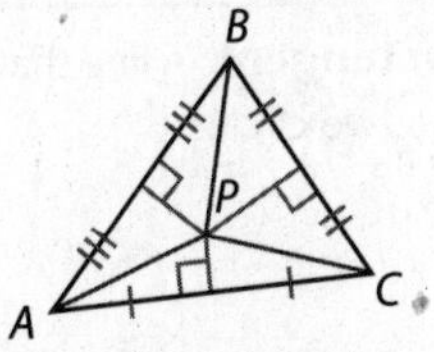

The circumcenter is *P*.

ENGLISH	SPANISH	EXAMPLES
circumcircle *See* circumscribed circle.	**circuncírculo** *Véase* círculo circunscrito.	
circumference The distance around the circle.	**circunferencia** Distancia alrededor del círculo.	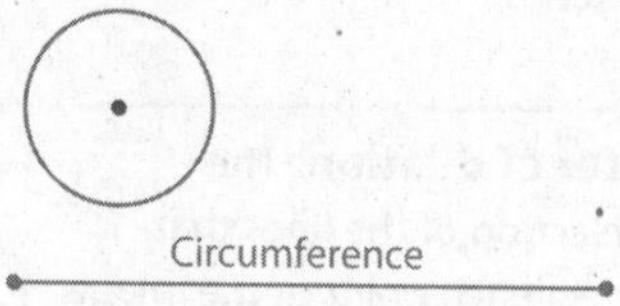 Circumference
circumscribed angle An angle formed by two rays from a common endpoint that are tangent to a circle	**ángulo circunscrito** Ángulo formado por dos semirrectas tangentes a un círculo que parten desde un extremo común.	
circumscribed circle Every vertex of the polygon lies on the circle.	**círculo circunscrito** Todos los vértices del polígono se encuentran sobre el círculo.	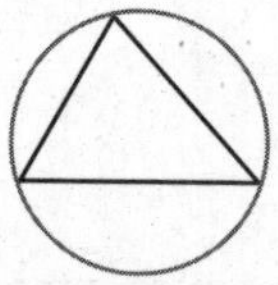
circumscribed polygon Each side of the polygon is tangent to the circle.	**polígono circunscrito** Todos los lados del polígono son tangentes al círculo.	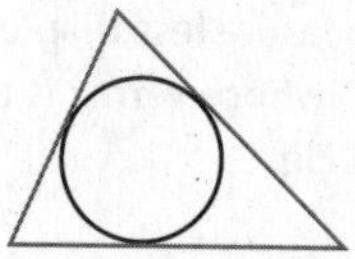
coefficient A number that is multiplied by a variable.	**coeficiente** Número que se multiplica por una variable.	In the expression $2x + 3y$, 2 is the coefficient of x and 3 is the coefficient of y.
coincide To correspond exactly; to be identical.	**coincidir** Corresponder exactamente, ser idéntico.	
collinear Points that lie on the same line.	**colineal** Puntos que se encuentran sobre la misma línea.	 *K*, *L*, and *M* are collinear points.
combination A selection of a group of objects in which order is *not* important. The number of combinations of *r* objects chosen from a group of *n* objects is denoted $_nC_r$.	**combinación** Selección de un grupo de objetos en la cual el orden *no* es importante. El número de combinaciones de *r* objetos elegidos de un grupo de *n* objetos se expresa así: $_nC_r$.	For 4 objects *A*, *B*, *C*, and *D*, there are $_4C_2 = 6$ different combinations of 2 objects: *AB*, *AC*, *AD*, *BC*, *BD*, *CD*.
common tangent A line that is tangent to two circles.	**tangente común** Línea que es tangente a dos círculos.	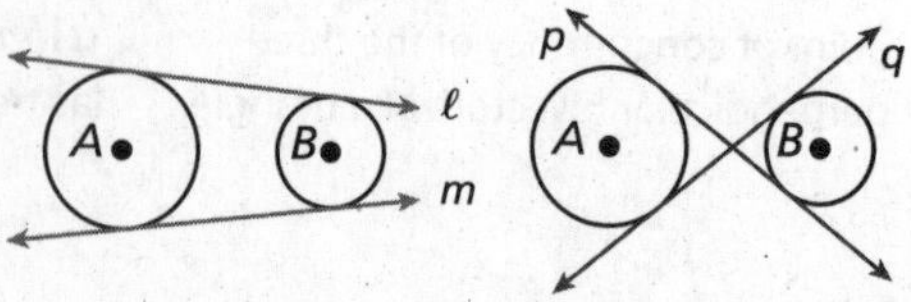

ENGLISH	SPANISH	EXAMPLES
complement of an angle The sum of the measures of an angle and its complement is 90°.	**complemento de un ángulo** La suma de las medidas de un ángulo y su complemento es 90°.	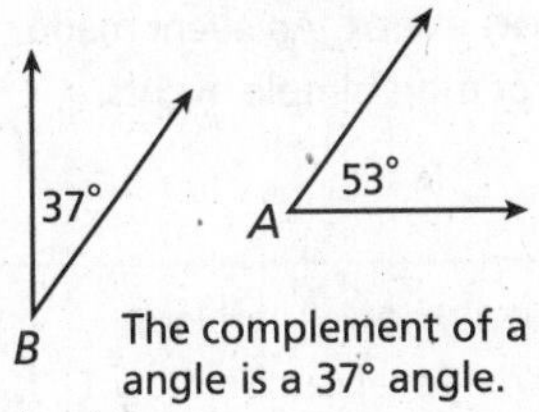 The complement of a 53° angle is a 37° angle.
complement of an event All outcomes in the sample space that are not in an event E, denoted $\overline{E}$.	**complemento de un suceso** Todos los resultados en el espacio muestral que no están en el suceso E y se expresan $\overline{E}$.	In the experiment of rolling a number cube, the complement of rolling a 3 is rolling a 1, 2, 4, 5, or 6.
complementary angles Two angles whose measures have a sum of 90°.	**ángulos complementarios** Dos ángulos cuyas medidas suman 90°.	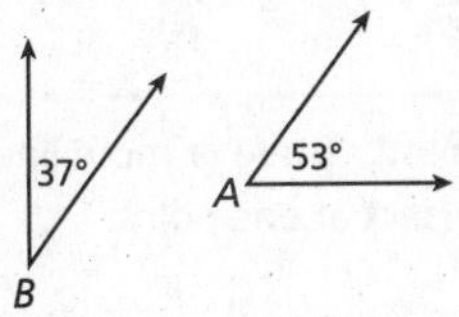
completing the square A process used to form a perfect-square trinomial. To complete the square of $x^2 + bx$, add $\left(\frac{b}{2}\right)^2$.	**completar el cuadrado** Proceso utilizado para formar un trinomio cuadrado perfecto. Para completar el cuadrado de $x^2 + bx$, hay que sumar $\left(\frac{b}{2}\right)^2$.	$x^2 + 6x + \blacksquare$ Add $\left(\frac{6}{2}\right)^2 = 9$. $x^2 + 6x + 9$
complex number Any number that can be written as $a + bi$, where a and b are real numbers and $i = \sqrt{-1}$.	**número complejo** Todo número que se puede expresar como $a + bi$, donde a y b son números reales e $i = \sqrt{-1}$.	$4 + 2i$ $5 + 0i = 5$ $0 - 7i = -7i$
component form The form of a vector that lists the vertical and horizontal change from the initial point to the terminal point.	**forma de componente** Forma de un vector que muestra el cambio horizontal y vertical desde el punto inicial hasta el punto terminal.	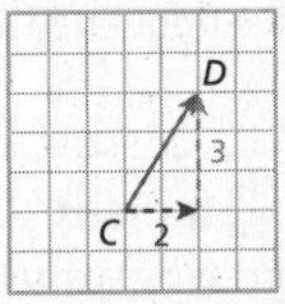 The component form of $\overline{CD}$ is $\langle 2, 3 \rangle$.
composite figure A plane figure made up of triangles, rectangles, trapezoids, circles, and other simple shapes, or a three-dimensional figure made up of prisms, cones, pyramids, cylinders, and other simple three-dimensional figures.	**figura compuesta** Figura plana compuesta por triángulos, rectángulos, trapecios, círculos y otras figuras simples, o figura tridimensional compuesta por prismas, conos, pirámides, cilindros y otras figuras tridimensionales simples.	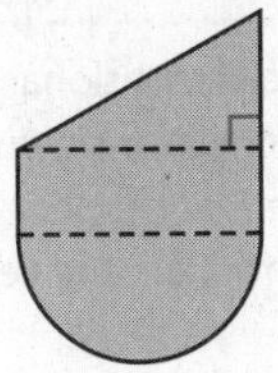
composition of transformations One transformation followed by another transformation.	**composición de transformaciones** Una transformación seguida de otra transformación.	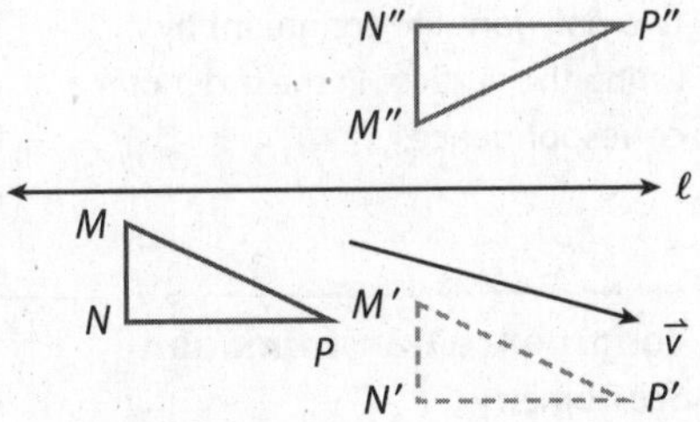

ENGLISH	SPANISH	EXAMPLES
compound event An event made up of two or more simple events.	**suceso compuesto** Suceso formado por dos o más sucesos simples.	In the experiment of tossing a coin and rolling a number cube, the event of the coin landing heads and the number cube landing on 3.
concave polygon A polygon in which a diagonal can be drawn such that part of the diagonal contains points in the exterior of the polygon.	**polígono cóncavo** Polígono en el cual se puede trazar una diagonal tal que parte de la diagonal contiene puntos ubicados fuera del polígono.	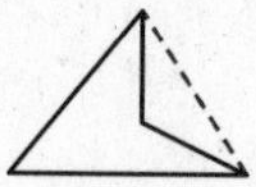 Concave quadrilateral
conclusion The part of a conditional statement following the word *then*.	**conclusión** Parte de un enunciado condicional que sigue a la palabra *entonces*.	If $x + 1 = 5$, then $\underbrace{x = 4}_{\text{Conclusion}}$.
concurrent Three or more lines that intersect at one point.	**concurrente** Tres o más líneas que se cortan en un punto.	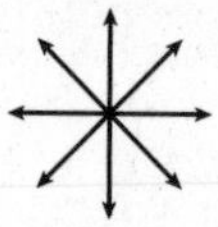
conditional probability The probability of event *B*, given that event *A* has already occurred or is certain to occur, denoted $P(B \mid A)$; used to find probability of dependent events.	**probabilidad condicional** Probabilidad del suceso *B*, dado que el suceso *A* ya ha ocurrido o es seguro que ocurrirá, expresada como $P(B \mid A)$; se utiliza para calcular la probabilidad de sucesos dependientes.	
conditional relative frequency The ratio of a joint relative frequency to a related marginal relative frequency in a two-way table.	**frecuencia relativa condicional** Razón de una frecuencia relativa conjunta a una frecuencia relativa marginal en una tabla de doble entrada.	
conditional statement A statement that can be written in the form "if *p*, then *q*," where *p* is the hypothesis and *q* is the conclusion.	**enunciado condicional** Enunciado que se puede expresar como "si *p*, entonces *q*", donde *p* es la hipótesis y *q* es la conclusión.	If $\underbrace{x + 1 = 5}_{\text{Hypothesis}}$, then $\underbrace{x = 4}_{\text{Conclusion}}$.
cone A three-dimensional figure with a circular base and a curved lateral surface that connects the base to a point called the vertex.	**cono** Figura tridimensional con una base circular y una superficie lateral curva que conecta la base con un punto denominado vértice.	
congruence statement A statement that indicates that two polygons are congruent by listing the vertices in the order of correspondence.	**enunciado de congruencia** Enunciado que indica que dos polígonos son congruentes enumerando los vértices en orden de correspondencia.	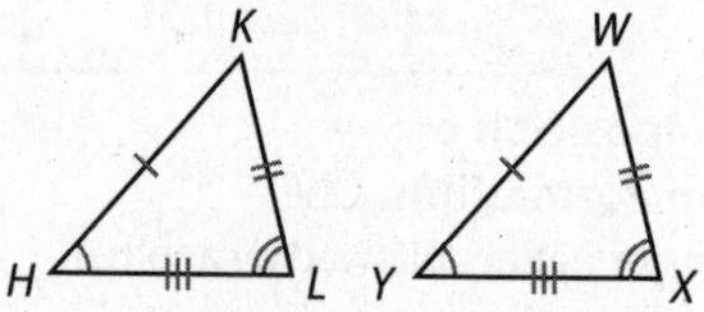 $\triangle HKL \cong \triangle YWX$
congruence transformation *See* isometry.	**transformación de congruencia** *Ver* isometría.	

ENGLISH	SPANISH	EXAMPLES
congruent Having the same size and shape, denoted by ≅.	**congruente** Que tiene el mismo tamaño y la misma forma, expresado por ≅.	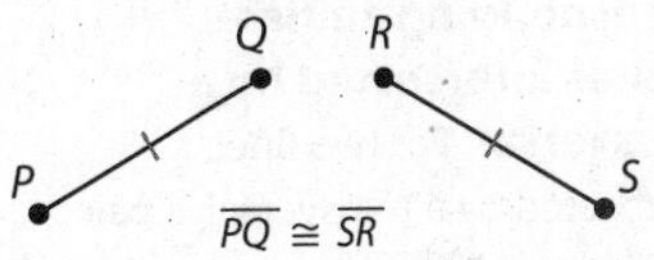 $\overline{PQ} \cong \overline{SR}$
congruent polygons Two polygons whose corresponding sides and angles are congruent.	**polígonos congruentes** Dos polígonos cuyos lados y ángulos correspondientes son congruentes.	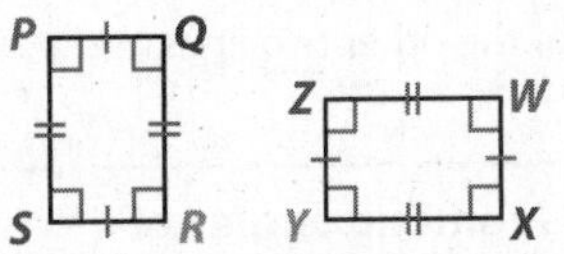
conjecture A statement that is believed to be true.	**conjetura** Enunciado que se supone verdadero.	A sequence begins with the terms 2, 4, 6, 8, 10. A reasonable conjecture is that the next term in the sequence is 12.
consecutive interior angles *See* same-side interior angles.	**ángulos internos consecutivos** *Ver* ángulos internos del mismo lado.	
contrapositive The statement formed by both exchanging and negating the hypothesis and conclusion of a conditional statement.	**contrarrecíproco** Enunciado que se forma al intercambiar y negar la hipótesis y la conclusión de un enunciado condicional.	Statement: If $n + 1 = 3$, then $n = 2$. Contrapositive: If $n \neq 2$, then $n + 1 \neq 3$.
converse The statement formed by exchanging the hypothesis and conclusion of a conditional statement.	**recíproco** Enunciado que se forma intercambiando la hipótesis y la conclusión de un enunciado condicional.	Statement: If $n + 1 = 3$, then $n = 2$. Converse: If $n = 2$, then $n + 1 = 3$.
convex polygon A polygon in which no diagonal contains points in the exterior of the polygon.	**polígono convexo** Polígono en el cual ninguna diagonal contiene puntos fuera del polígono.	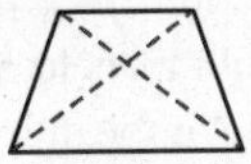 Convex quadrilateral
coordinate A number used to identify the location of a point. On a number line, one coordinate is used. On a coordinate plane, two coordinates are used, called the *x*-coordinate and the *y*-coordinate. In space, three coordinates are used, called the *x*-coordinate, the *y*-coordinate, and the *z*-coordinate.	**coordenada** Número utilizado para identificar la ubicación de un punto. En una recta numérica se utiliza una coordenada. En un plano cartesiano se utilizan dos coordenadas, denominadas coordenada *x* y coordenada *y*. En el espacio se utilizan tres coordenadas, denominadas coordenada *x*, coordenada *y* y coordenada *z*.	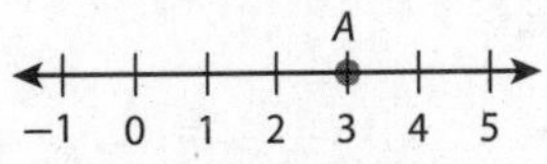 The coordinate of point *A* is 3. 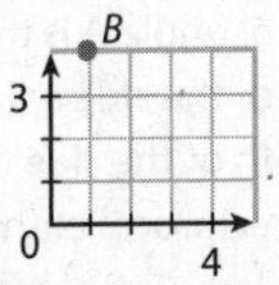 The coordinates of point *B* are (1, 4).
coplanar Points that lie in the same plane.	**coplanar** Puntos que se encuentran en el mismo plano.	
corollary A theorem whose proof follows directly from another theorem.	**corolario** Teorema cuya demostración proviene directamente de otro teorema.	

Glossary/Glosario

ENGLISH	SPANISH	EXAMPLES

corresponding angles of lines intersected by a transversal For two lines intersected by a transversal, a pair of angles that lie on the same side of the transversal and on the same sides of the other two lines.

ángulos correspondientes de líneas cortadas por una transversal Dadas dos líneas cortadas por una transversal, el par de ángulos ubicados en el mismo lado de la transversal y en los mismos lados de las otras dos líneas.

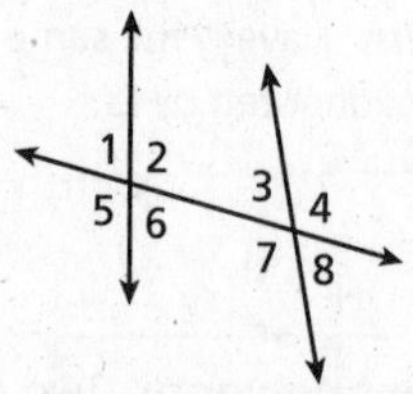

$\angle 1$ and $\angle 3$ are corresponding.

---

corresponding angles of polygons Angles in the same position in two different polygons that have the same number of angles.

ángulos correspondientes de los polígonos Ángulos que tienen la misma posición en dos polígonos diferentes que tienen el mismo número de ángulos.

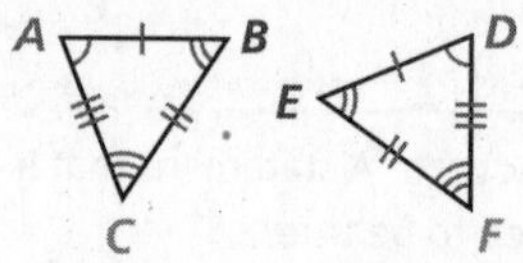

$\angle A$ and $\angle D$ are corresponding angles.

---

corresponding sides of polygons Sides in the same position in two different polygons that have the same number of sides.

lados correspondientes de los polígonos Lados que tienen la misma posición en dos polígonos diferentes que tienen el mismo número de lados.

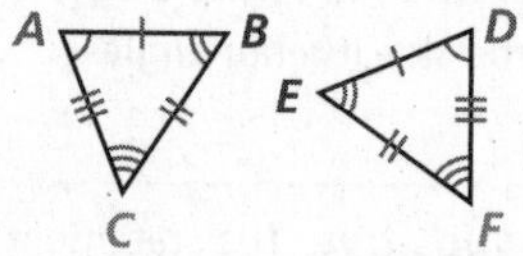

$\overline{AB}$ and $\overline{DE}$ are corresponding sides.

---

cosecant In a right triangle, the cosecant of angle *A* is the ratio of the length of the hypotenuse to the length of the side opposite *A*. It is the reciprocal of the sine function.

cosecante En un triángulo rectángulo, la cosecante del ángulo *A* es la razón entre la longitud de la hipotenusa y la longitud del cateto opuesto a *A*. Es la inversa de la función seno.

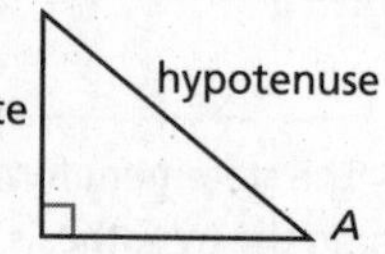

$$\csc A = \frac{\text{hypotenuse}}{\text{opposite}} = \frac{1}{\sin A}$$

---

cosine In a right triangle, the cosine of angle *A* is the ratio of the length of the leg adjacent to angle *A* to the length of the hypotenuse. It is the reciprocal of the secant function.

coseno En un triángulo rectángulo, el coseno del ángulo *A* es la razón entre la longitud del cateto adyacente al ángulo *A* y la longitud de la hipotenusa. Es la inversa de la función secante.

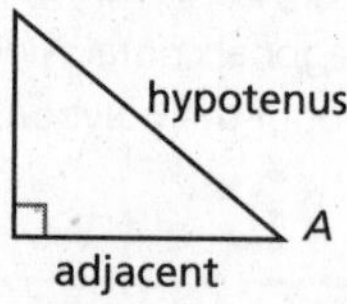

$$\cos A = \frac{\text{adjacent}}{\text{hypotenuse}} = \frac{1}{\sec A}$$

---

cotangent In a right triangle, the cotangent of angle A is the ratio of the length of the side adjacent to *A* to the length of the side opposite *A*. It is the reciprocal of the tangent function.

cotangente En un triángulo rectángulo, la cotangente del ángulo *A* es la razón entre la longitud del cateto adyacente a *A* y la longitud del cateto opuesto a *A*. Es la inversa de la función tangente.

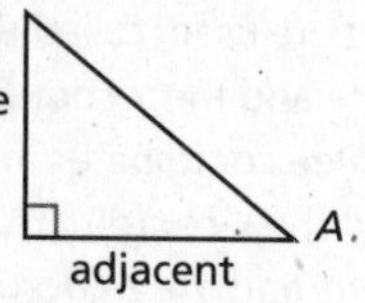

$$\cot A = \frac{\text{adjacent}}{\text{opposite}} = \frac{1}{\tan A}$$

---

counterexample An example that proves that a conjecture or statement is false.

contraejemplo Ejemplo que demuestra que una conjetura o enunciado es falso.

ENGLISH	SPANISH	EXAMPLES
CPCTC An abbreviation for "Corresponding Parts of Congruent Triangles are Congruent," which can be used as a justification in a proof after two triangles are proven congruent.	**PCTCC** Abreviatura que significa "Las partes correspondientes de los triángulos congruentes son congruentes", que se puede utilizar para justificar una demostración después de demostrar que dos triángulos son congruentes (CPCTC, por sus siglas en inglés).	
cross section The intersection of a three-dimensional figure and a plane.	**sección transversal** Intersección de una figura tridimensional y un plano.	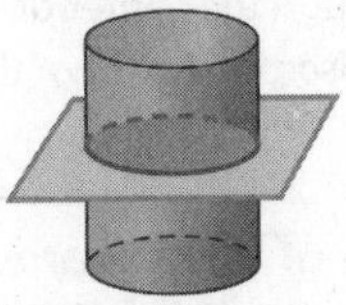
cube A prism with six square faces.	**cubo** Prisma con seis caras cuadradas.	
cylinder A three-dimensional figure with two parallel congruent circular bases and a curved lateral surface that connects the bases.	**cilindro** Figura tridimensional con dos bases circulares congruentes y paralelas y una superficie lateral curva que conecta las bases.	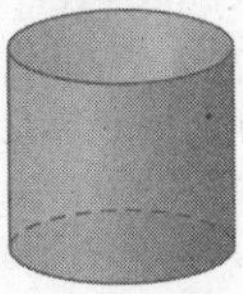

D

ENGLISH	SPANISH	EXAMPLES
decagon A ten-sided polygon.	**decágono** Polígono de diez lados.	
deductive reasoning The process of using logic to draw conclusions.	**razonamiento deductivo** Proceso en el que se utiliza la lógica para sacar conclusiones.	
definition A statement that describes a mathematical object and can be written as a true biconditional statement.	**definición** Enunciado que describe un objeto matemático y se puede expresar como un enunciado bicondicional verdadero.	
degree A unit of angle measure; one degree is $\frac{1}{360}$ of a circle.	**grado** Unidad de medida de los ángulos; un grado es $\frac{1}{360}$ de un círculo.	
degree of a polynomial The degree of the term of the polynomial with the greatest degree.	**grado de un polinomio** Grado del término del polinomio con el grado máximo.	$3x^2y^2 + 4xy^5 - 12x^3y^2$ (Degree 4, Degree 6, Degree 5)
dependent events Events for which the occurrence or nonoccurrence of one event affects the probability of the other event.	**sucesos dependientes** Dos sucesos son dependientes si el hecho de que uno de ellos se cumpla o no afecta la probabilidad del otro.	From a bag containing 3 red marbles and 2 blue marbles, drawing a red marble, and then drawing a blue marble without replacing the first marble.

ENGLISH | **SPANISH** | **EXAMPLES**

diagonal of a polygon A segment connecting two nonconsecutive vertices of a polygon.

diagonal de un polígono Segmento que conecta dos vértices no consecutivos de un polígono.

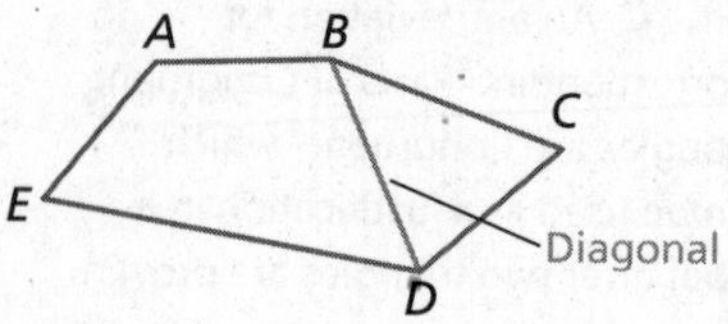

---

diameter A segment that has endpoints on the circle and that passes through the center of the circle; also the length of that segment.

diámetro Segmento que atraviesa el centro de un círculo y cuyos extremos están sobre la circunferencia; longitud de dicho segmento.

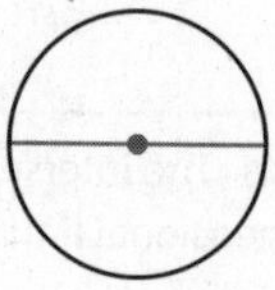

---

difference of two squares A polynomial of the form $a^2 - b^2$, which may be written as the product $(a + b)(a - b)$.

diferencia de dos cuadrados Polinomio del tipo $a^2 - b^2$, que se puede expresar como el producto $(a + b)(a - b)$.

$x^2 - 4 = (x + 2)(x - 2)$

---

dilation A transformation in which the lines connecting every point P with its preimage P' all intersect at a point C known as the center of dilation, and $\frac{CP'}{CP}$ is the same for every point P; a transformation that changes the size of a figure but not its shape.

dilatación Transformación en la cual las líneas que conectan cada punto P con su imagen original P' se cruzan en un punto C conocido como centro de dilatación, y $\frac{CP'}{CP}$ es igual para cada punto P; transformación que cambia el tamaño de una figura pero no su forma.

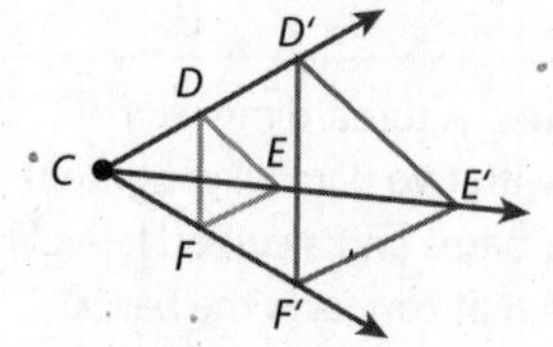

---

directed line segment A segment between two points A and B with a specified direction, from A to B or from B to A.

segmento de una línea con dirección Un segmento entro dos puntos con una dirección especificada.

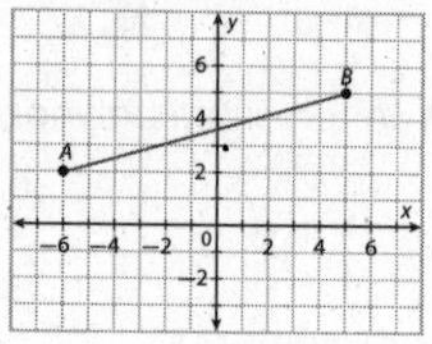

---

directrix A fixed line used to define a *parabola*. Every point on the parabola is equidistant from the directrix and a fixed point called the *focus*.

directriz Línea fija utilizada para definir una *parábola*. Cada punto de la parábola es equidistante de la directriz y de un punto fijo denominado *foco*.

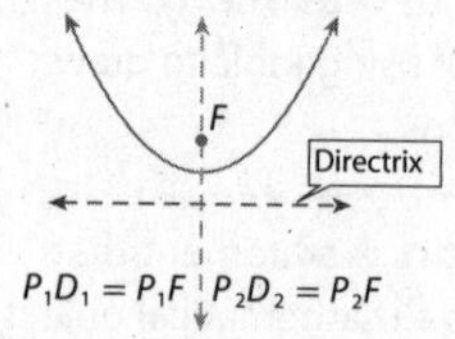

---

direction of a vector The orientation of a vector, which is determined by the angle the vector makes with a horizontal line.

dirección de un vector Orientación de un vector, determinada por el ángulo que forma el vector con una línea horizontal.

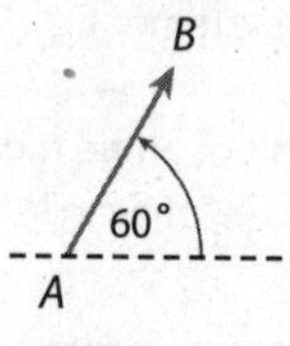

---

discrete function A function whose graph is made up of unconnected points.

función discreta Función cuya gráfica compuesta de puntos no conectados.

---

discriminant The discriminant of the quadratic equation $ax^2 + bx + c = 0$ is $b^2 - 4ac$.

discriminante El discriminante de la ecuación cuadrática $ax^2 + bx + c = 0$ es $b^2 - 4ac$.

The discriminant of $2x^2 - 5x - 3 = 0$ is $(-5)^2 - 4(2)(-3)$ or 49.

ENGLISH	SPANISH	EXAMPLES
distance between two points The absolute value of the difference of the coordinates of the points.	**distancia entre dos puntos** Valor absoluto de la diferencia entre las coordenadas de los puntos.	 $AB = \|a - b\| = \|b - a\|$
distance from a point to a line The length of the perpendicular segment from the point to the line.	**distancia desde un punto hasta una línea** Longitud del segmento perpendicular desde el punto hasta la línea.	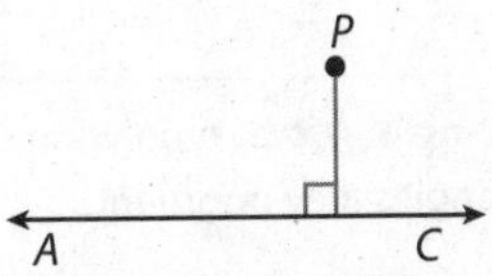 The distance from P to $\overleftrightarrow{AC}$ is 5 units.
dodecagon A 12-sided polygon.	**dodecágono** Polígono de 12 lados.	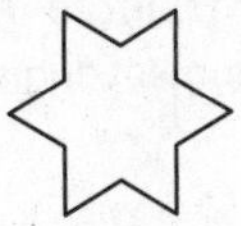
domain The set of all possible input values of a relation or function.	**dominio** Conjunto de todos los posibles valores de entrada de una función o relación.	The domain of the function $f(x) = \sqrt{x}$ is $\{x \mid x \geq 0\}$.

E

ENGLISH	SPANISH	EXAMPLES
element of a set An item in a set.	**elemento de un conjunto** Componente de un conjunto.	4 is an element of the set of even numbers. $4 \in \{\text{even numbers}\}$
empty set A set with no elements.	**conjunto vacío** Conjunto sin elementos.	The solution set of $\|x\| < 0$ is the empty set, $\{\ \}$, or $\varnothing$.
end behavior The trends in the y-values of a function as the x-values approach positive and negative infinity.	**comportamiento extremo** Tendencia de los valores de y de una función a medida que los valores de x se aproximan al infinito positivo y negativo.	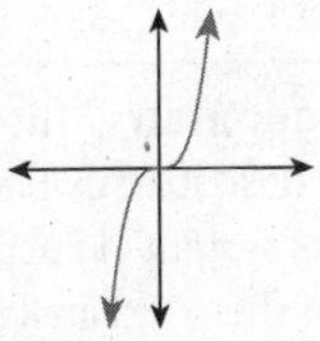 End behavior: $f(x) \to \infty$ as $x \to \infty$ $f(x) \to -\infty$ as $x \to -\infty$
endpoint A point at an end of a segment or the starting point of a ray.	**extremo** Punto en el final de un segmento o punto de inicio de un rayo.	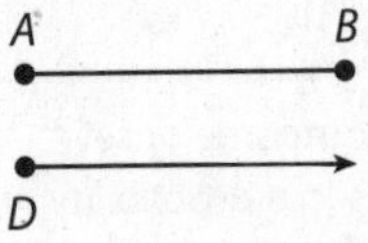
enlargement A dilation with a scale factor greater than 1. In an enlargement, the image is larger than the preimage.	**agrandamiento** Dilatación con un factor de escala mayor que 1. En un agrandamiento, la imagen es más grande que la imagen original.	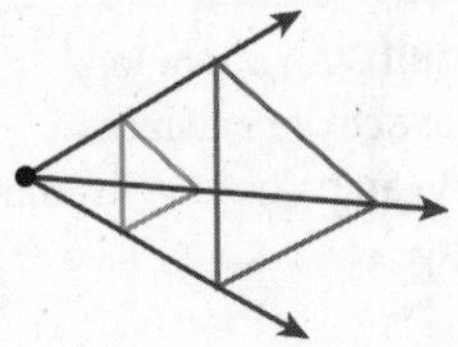

ENGLISH	SPANISH	EXAMPLES
equally likely outcomes Outcomes are equally likely if they have the same probability of occurring. If an experiment has *n* equally likely outcomes, then the probability of each outcome is $\frac{1}{n}$.	**resultados igualmente probables** Los resultados son igualmente probables si tienen la misma probabilidad de ocurrir. Si un experimento tiene *n* resultados igualmente probables, entonces la probabilidad de cada resultado es $\frac{1}{n}$.	If a coin is tossed, and heads and tails are equally likely, then $P(\text{heads}) = P(\text{tails}) = \frac{1}{2}$.
equiangular polygon A polygon in which all angles are congruent.	**polígono equiangular** Polígono cuyos ángulos son todos congruentes.	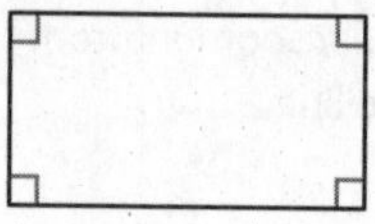
equiangular triangle A triangle with three congruent angles.	**triángulo equiangular** Triángulo con tres ángulos congruentes.	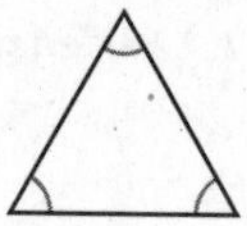
equidistant The same distance from two or more objects.	**equidistante** Igual distancia de dos o más objetos.	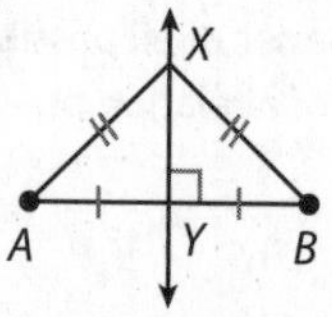 *X* is equidistant from *A* and *B*.
equilateral polygon A polygon in which all sides are congruent.	**polígono equilátero** Polígono cuyos lados son todos congruentes.	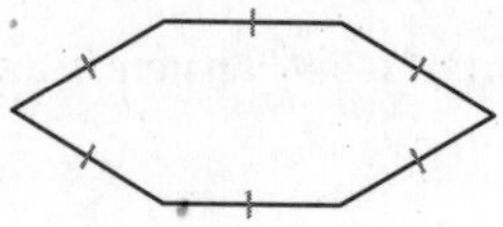
equilateral triangle A triangle with three congruent sides.	**triángulo equilátero** Triángulo con tres lados congruentes.	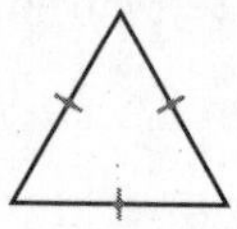
Euclidean geometry The system of geometry described by Euclid. In particular, the system of Euclidean geometry satisfies the Parallel Postulate, which states that there is exactly one line through a given point parallel to a given line.	**geometría euclidiana** Sistema geométrico desarrollado por Euclides. Específicamente, el sistema de la geometría euclidiana cumple con el postulado de las paralelas, que establece que por un punto dado se puede trazar una única línea paralela a una línea dada.	
event An outcome or set of outcomes in a probability experiment.	**suceso** Resultado o conjunto de resultados en un experimento de probabilidad.	In the experiment of rolling a number cube, the event "an odd number" consists of the outcomes 1, 3, 5.
experiment An operation, process, or activity in which outcomes can be used to estimate probability.	**experimento** Una operación, proceso o actividad en la que se usan los resultados para estimar una probabilidad.	Tossing a coin 10 times and noting the number of heads.

ENGLISH	SPANISH	EXAMPLES
experimental probability The ratio of the number of times an event occurs to the number of trials, or times, that an activity is performed.	**probabilidad experimental** Razón entre la cantidad de veces que ocurre un suceso y la cantidad de pruebas, o veces, que se realiza una actividad.	Kendra made 6 of 10 free throws. The experimental probability that she will make her next free throw is $P(\text{free throw}) = \frac{\text{number made}}{\text{number attempted}} = \frac{6}{10}$.
exterior of a circle The set of all points outside a circle.	**exterior de un círculo** Conjunto de todos los puntos que se encuentran fuera de un círculo.	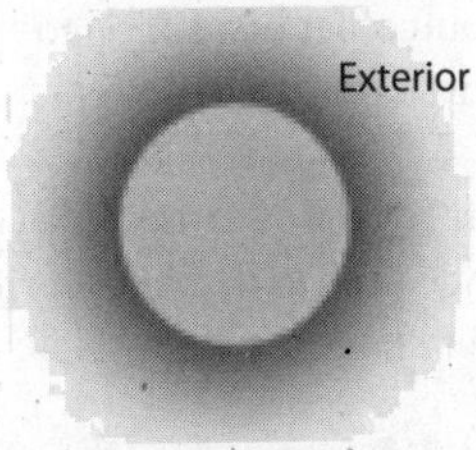
exterior of an angle The set of all points outside an angle.	**exterior de un ángulo** Conjunto de todos los puntos que se encuentran fuera de un ángulo.	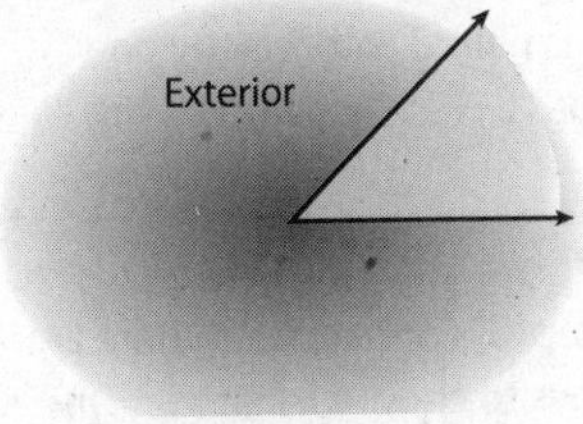
exterior of a polygon The set of all points outside a polygon.	**exterior de un polígono** Conjunto de todos los puntos que se encuentran fuera de un polígono.	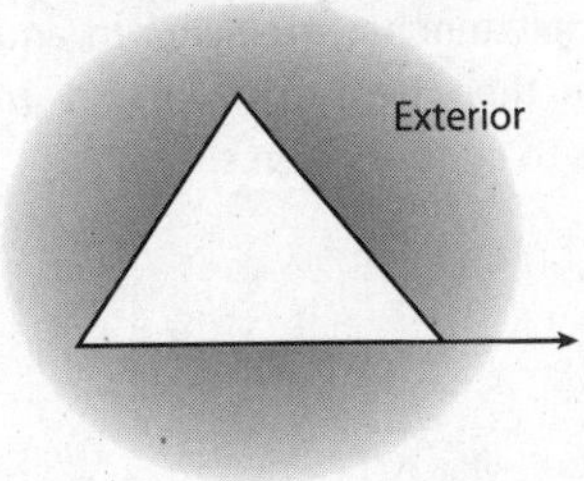
exterior angle of a polygon An angle formed by one side of a polygon and the extension of an adjacent side.	**ángulo externo de un polígono** Ángulo formado por un lado de un polígono y la prolongación del lado adyacente.	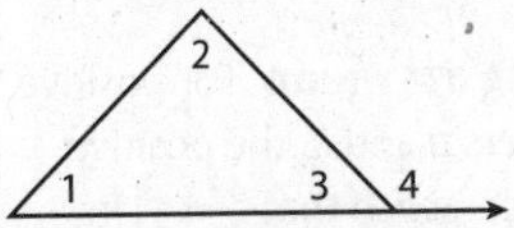 $\angle 4$ is an exterior angle.
external secant segment A segment of a secant that lies in the exterior of the circle with one endpoint on the circle.	**segmento secante externo** Segmento de una secante que se encuentra en el exterior del círculo y tiene un extremo sobre el círculo.	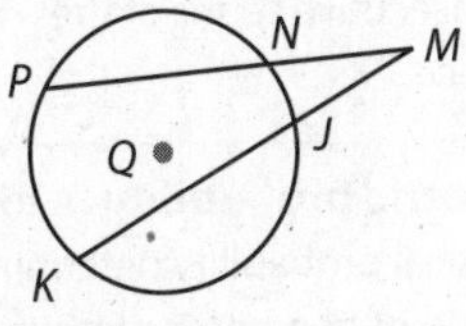 $\overline{NM}$ is an external secant segment.

F

factorial If n is a positive integer, then n factorial, written $n!$, is $n \cdot (n-1) \cdot (n-2) \cdot \ldots \cdot 2 \cdot 1$. The factorial of 0 is defined to be 1.	**factorial** Si n es un entero positivo, entonces el factorial de n, expresado como $n!$, es $n \cdot (n-1) \cdot (n-2) \cdot \ldots \cdot 2 \cdot 1$. Por definición, el factorial de 0 será 1.	$7! = 7 \cdot 6 \cdot 5 \cdot 4 \cdot 3 \cdot 2 \cdot 1 = 5040$ $0! = 1$

Glossary/Glosario

ENGLISH	SPANISH	EXAMPLES
fair When all outcomes of an experiment are equally likely.	**justo** Cuando todos los resultados de un experimento son igualmente probables.	When tossing a fair coin, heads and tails are equally likely. Each has a probability of $\frac{1}{2}$.
favorable outcome The occurrence of one of several possible outcomes of a specified event or probability experiment.	**resultado favorable** Cuando se produce uno de varios resultados posibles de un suceso específico o experimento de probabilidad.	In the experiment of rolling an odd number on a number cube, the favorable outcomes are 1, 3, and 5.
focus (pl. foci) of a parabola A fixed point F used with a *directrix* to define a *parabola*.	**foco de una parábola** Punto fijo F utilizado con una *directriz* para definir una *parábola*.	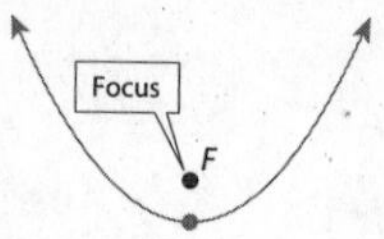
function A relation in which every input is paired with exactly one output.	**función** Una relación en la que cada entrada corresponde exactamente a una salida.	Function: $\{(0, 5), (1, 3), (2, 1), (3, 3)\}$ Not a Function: $\{(0, 1), (0, 3), (2, 1), (2, 3)\}$
Fundamental Counting Principle For n items, if there are m_1 ways to choose a first item, m_2 ways to choose a second item after the first item has been chosen, and so on, then there are $m_1 \cdot m_2 \cdot ... \cdot m_n$ ways to choose n items.	**Principio fundamental deconteo** Dados n elementos, si existen m_1 formas de elegir un primer elemento, m_2 formas de elegir un segundo elemento después de haber elegido el primero, y así sucesivamente, entonces existen $m_1 \cdot m_2 \cdot ... \cdot m_n$ formas de elegir n elementos.	If there are 4 colors of shirts, 3 colors of pants, and 2 colors of shoes, then there are $4 \cdot 3 \cdot 2 = 24$ possible outfits.

G

ENGLISH	SPANISH	EXAMPLES
geometric mean For positive numbers a and b, the positive number x such that $\frac{a}{x} = \frac{x}{b}$. In a geometric sequence, a term that comes between two given nonconsecutive terms of the sequence.	**media geométrica** Dados los números positivos a y b, el número positivo x tal que $\frac{a}{x} = \frac{x}{b}$. En una sucesión geométrica, un término que está entre dos términos no consecutivos dados de la sucesión.	$\frac{a}{x} = \frac{x}{b}$ $x^2 = ab$ $x = \sqrt{ab}$
geometric probability A form of theoretical probability determined by a ratio of geometric measures such as lengths, areas, or volumes.	**probabilidad geométrica** Una forma de la probabilidad teórica determinada por una razón de medidas geométricas, como longitud, área o volumen.	 The probability of the pointer landing on 80° is $\frac{2}{9}$.
great circle A circle on a sphere that divides the sphere into two hemispheres.	**círculo máximo** En una esfera, círculo que divide la esfera en dos hemisferios.	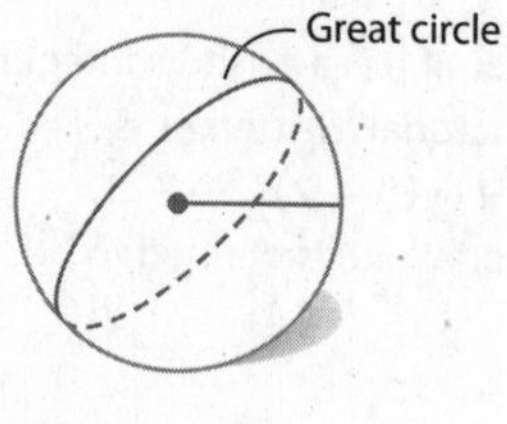

ENGLISH	SPANISH	EXAMPLES

H

height of a figure The length of an altitude of the figure.	**altura de una figura** Longitud de la altura de la figura.	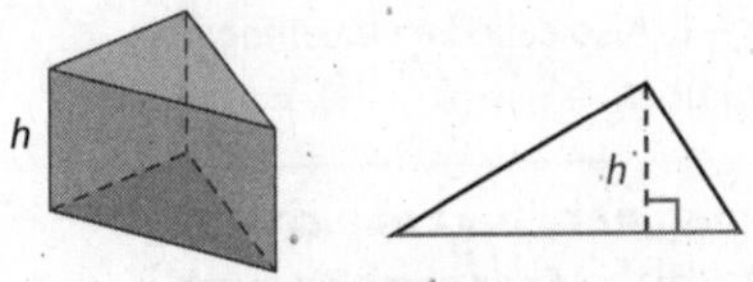
hemisphere Half of a sphere.	**hemisferio** Mitad de una esfera.	
heptagon A seven-sided polygon.	**heptágono** Polígono de siete lados.	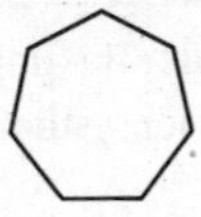
hexagon A six-sided polygon.	**hexágono** Polígono de seis lados.	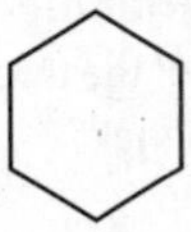
hypotenuse The side opposite the right angle in a right triangle.	**hipotenusa** Lado opuesto al ángulo recto de un triángulo rectángulo.	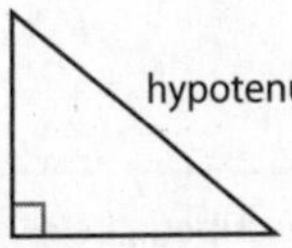
hypothesis The part of a conditional statement following the word *if*.	**hipótesis** La parte de un enunciado condicional que sigue a la palabra *si*.	If $x + 1 = 5$, then $x = 4$. Hypothesis

I

identity An equation that is true for all values of the variables.	**identidad** Ecuación verdadera para todos los valores de las variables.	$3 = 3$ $2(x - 1) = 2x - 2$
image A shape that results from a transformation of a figure known as the preimage.	**imagen** Forma resultante de la transformación de una figura conocida como imagen original.	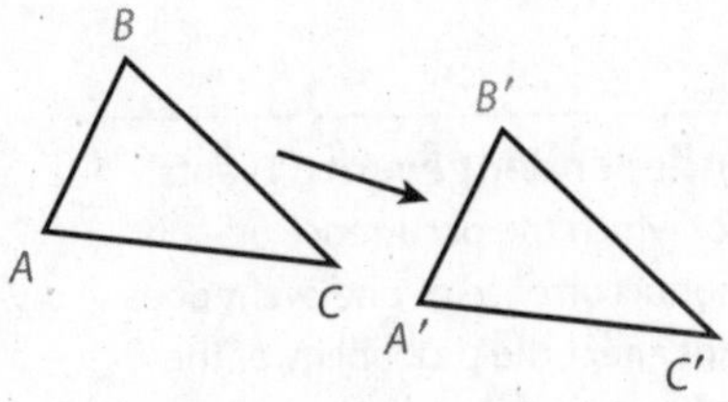

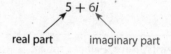

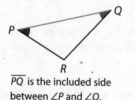

ENGLISH	SPANISH	EXAMPLES
imaginary number The square root of a negative number, written in the form *bi*, where *b* is a real number and *i* is the imaginary unit, $\sqrt{-1}$. Also called a *pure imaginary number.*	**número imaginario** Raíz cuadrada de un número negativo, expresado como *bi*, donde *b* es un número real e *i* es la unidad imaginaria, $\sqrt{-1}$. También se denomina *número imaginario puro.*	$\sqrt{-16} = \sqrt{16} \cdot \sqrt{-1} = 4i$
imaginary part of a complex number For a complex number of the form $a + bi$, the real number *b* is called the imaginary part, represented graphically as *b* units on the imaginary axis of a complex plane.	**parte imaginaria de un número complejo** Dado un número complejo del tipo $a + bi$, el número real *b* se denomina parte imaginaria y se representa gráficamente como *b* unidades en el eje imaginario de un plano complejo.	$5 + 6i$ (real part: 5; imaginary part: 6i)
imaginary unit The unit in the imaginary number system, $\sqrt{-1}$.	**unidad imaginaria** Unidad del sistema de números imaginarios, $\sqrt{-1}$.	$\sqrt{-1} = i$
incenter of a triangle The point of concurrency of the three angle bisectors of a triangle.	**incentro de un triángulo** Punto donde se encuentran las tres bisectrices de los ángulos de un triángulo.	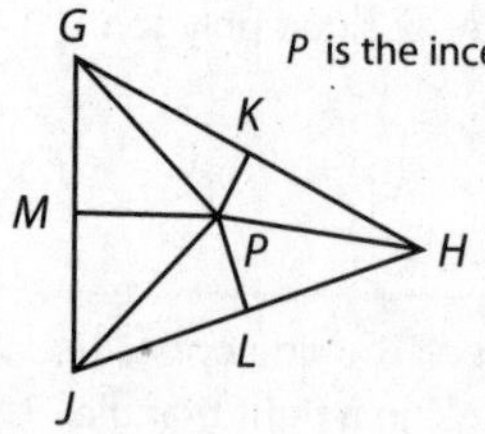 *P* is the incenter.
incircle *See* inscribed circle.	**incírculo** *Véase* círculo inscrito.	
included angle The angle formed by two adjacent sides of a polygon.	**ángulo incluido** Ángulo formado por dos lados adyacentes de un polígono.	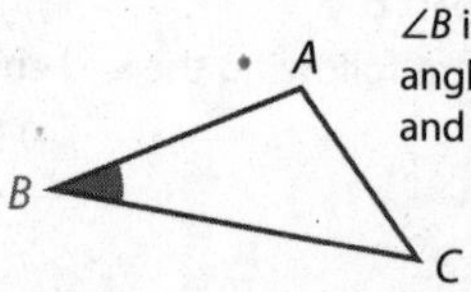 $\angle B$ is the included angle between $\overline{AB}$ and $\overline{BC}$.
included side The common side of two consecutive angles of a polygon.	**lado incluido** Lado común de dos ángulos consecutivos de un polígono.	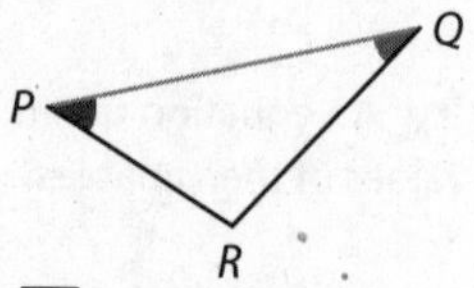 $\overline{PQ}$ is the included side between $\angle P$ and $\angle Q$.
independent events Events for which the occurrence or nonoccurrence of one event does not affect the probability of the other event.	**sucesos independientes** Dos sucesos son independientes si el hecho de que se produzca o no uno de ellos no afecta la probabilidad del otro suceso.	From a bag containing 3 red marbles and 2 blue marbles, drawing a red marble, replacing it, and then drawing a blue marble.
index In the radical $\sqrt[n]{x}$, which represents the *n*th root of *x*, *n* is the index. In the radical $\sqrt{x}$, the index is understood to be 2.	**índice** En el radical $\sqrt[n]{x}$, que representa la enésima raíz de *x*, *n* es el índice. En el radical $\sqrt{x}$, se da por sentado que el índice es 2.	The radical $\sqrt[3]{8}$ has an index of 3.

ENGLISH	SPANISH	EXAMPLES
indirect measurement A method of measurement that uses formulas, similar figures, and/or proportions.	**medición indirecta** Método para medir objetos mediante fórmulas, figuras semejantes y/o proporciones.	
indirect proof A proof in which the statement to be proved is assumed to be false and a contradiction is shown.	**demostración indirecta** Prueba en la que se supone que el enunciado a demostrar es falso y se muestra una contradicción.	
indirect reasoning *See* indirect proof.	**razonamiento indirecto** *Ver* demostración indirecta.	
inductive reasoning The process of reasoning that a rule or statement is true because specific cases are true.	**razonamiento inductivo** Proceso de razonamiento por el que se determina que una regla o enunciado son verdaderos porque ciertos casos específicos son verdaderos.	
inequality A statement that compares two expressions by using one of the following signs: $<$, $>$, $\leq$, $\geq$, or $\neq$.	**desigualdad** Enunciado que compara dos expresiones utilizando uno de los siguientes signos: $<$, $>$, $\leq$, $\geq$, o $\neq$.	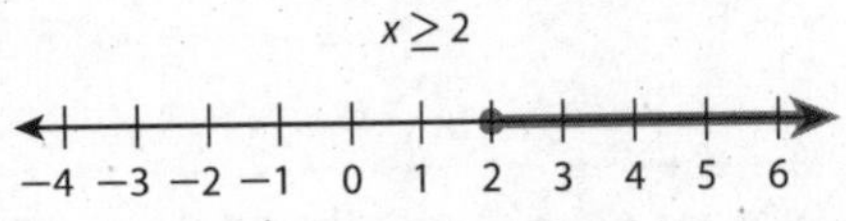
initial point of a vector The starting point of a vector.	**punto inicial de un vector** Punto donde comienza un vector.	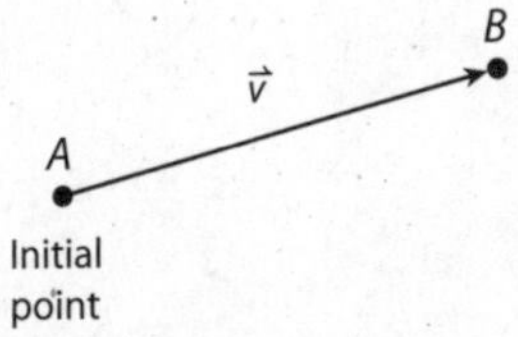
initial side The ray that lies on the positive *x*-axis when an angle is drawn in standard position.	**lado inicial** Rayo que se encuentra sobre el eje *x* positivo cuando se traza un ángulo en posición estándar.	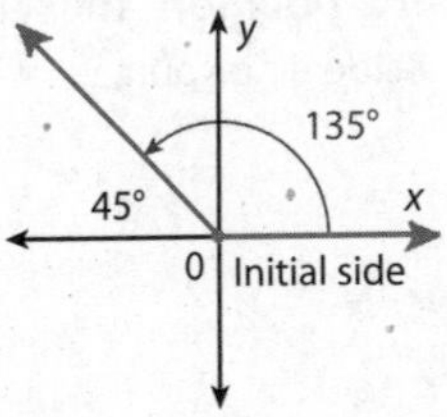
inscribed angle An angle whose vertex is on a circle and whose sides contain chords of the circle.	**ángulo inscrito** Ángulo cuyo vértice se encuentra sobre un círculo y cuyos lados contienen cuerdas del círculo.	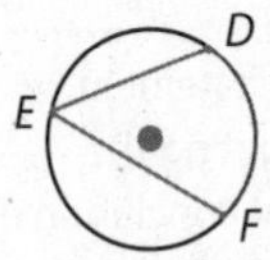
inscribed circle A circle in which each side of the polygon is tangent to the circle.	**círculo inscrito** Círculo en el que cada lado del polígono es tangente al círculo.	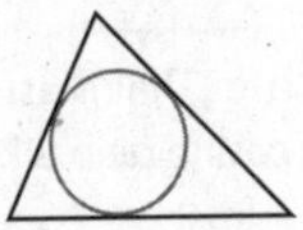
inscribed polygon A polygon in which every vertex of the polygon lies on the circle.	**polígono inscrito** Polígono cuyos vértices se encuentran sobre el círculo.	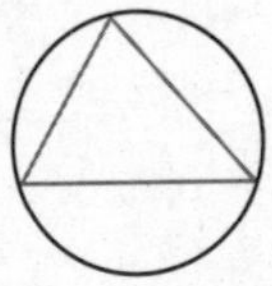

Glossary/Glosario

ENGLISH	SPANISH	EXAMPLES

Glossary/Glosario

intercepted arc An arc that consists of endpoints that lie on the sides of an inscribed angle and all the points of the circle between the endpoints.

arco abarcado Arco cuyos extremos se encuentran en los lados de un ángulo inscrito y consta de todos los puntos del círculo ubicados entre dichos extremos.

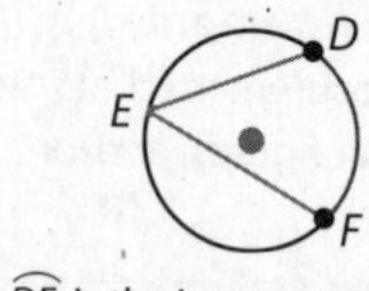

$\widehat{DF}$ is the intercepted arc.

---

interior angle An angle formed by two sides of a polygon with a common vertex.

ángulo interno Ángulo formado por dos lados de un polígono con un vértice común.

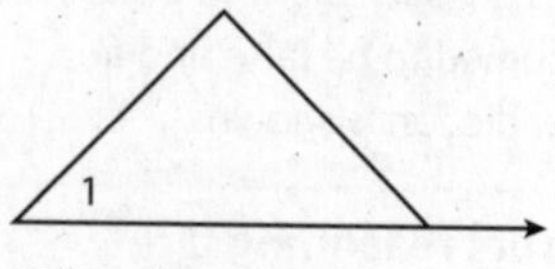

$\angle 1$ is an interior angle.

---

interior of a circle The set of all points inside a circle.

interior de un círculo Conjunto de todos los puntos que se encuentran dentro de un círculo.

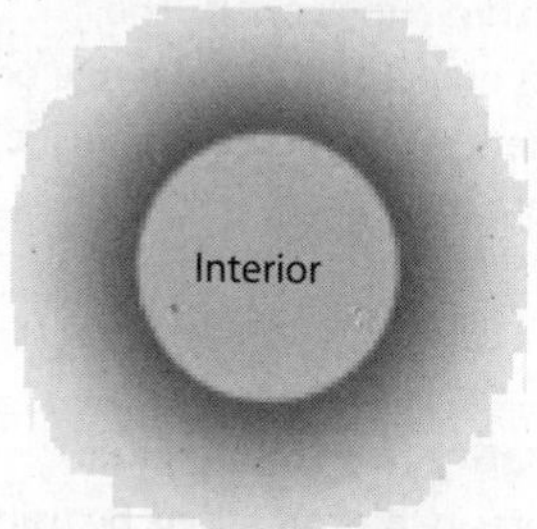

---

interior of an angle The set of all points between the sides of an angle.

interior de un ángulo Conjunto de todos los puntos entre los lados de un ángulo.

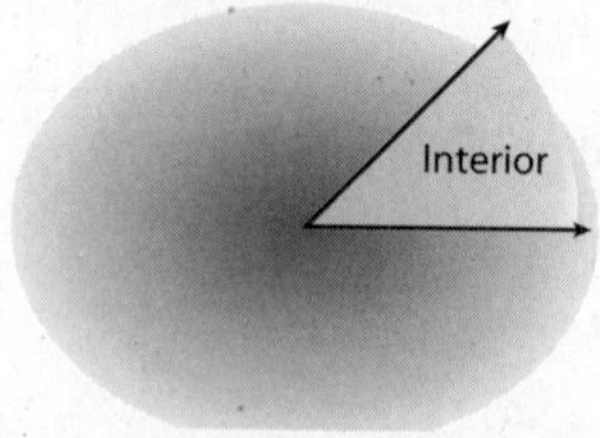

---

interior of a polygon The set of all points inside a polygon.

interior de un polígono Conjunto de todos los puntos que se encuentran dentro de un polígono.

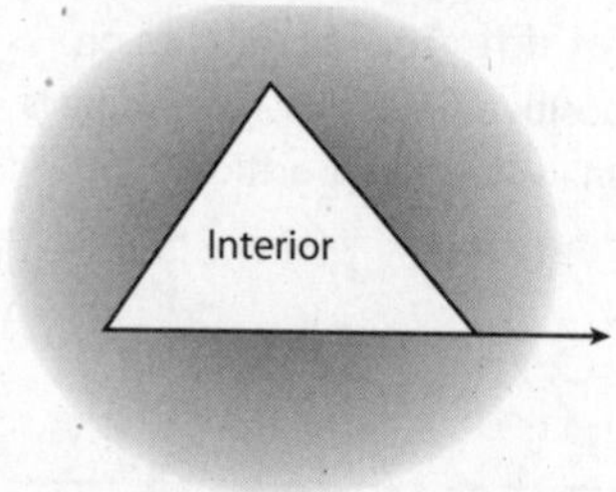

---

inverse The statement formed by negating the hypothesis and conclusion of a conditional statement.

inverso Enunciado formado al negar la hipótesis y la conclusión de un enunciado condicional.

Statement: If $n + 1 = 3$, then $n = 2$.

Inverse: If $n + 1 \neq 3$, then $n \neq 2$.

---

inverse cosine The measure of an angle whose cosine ratio is known.

coseno inverso Medida de un ángulo cuya razón coseno es conocida.

If $\cos A = x$, then $\cos^{-1} x = m\angle A$.

ENGLISH	SPANISH	EXAMPLES

inverse function The function that results from exchanging the input and output values of a one-to-one function. The inverse of $f(x)$ is denoted $f^{-1}(x)$.

función inversa Función que resulta de intercambiar los valores de entrada y salida de una función uno a uno. La función inversa de $f(x)$ se indica $f^{-1}(x)$.

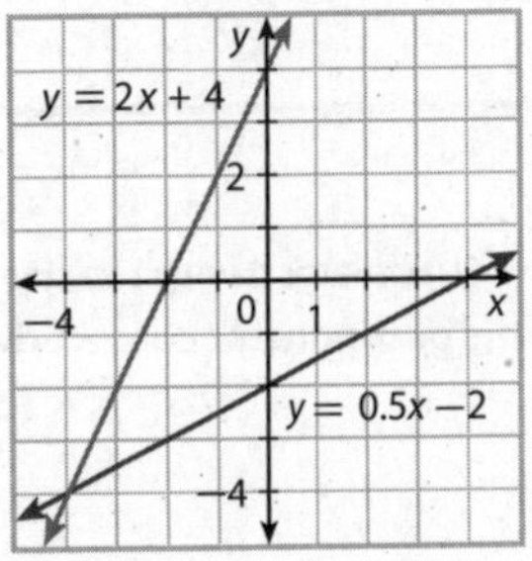

The function $y = \frac{1}{2}x - 2$ is the inverse of the function $y = 2x + 4$.

inverse sine The measure of an angle whose sine ratio is known.

seno inverso Medida de un ángulo cuya razón seno es conocida.

If $\sin A = x$, then $\sin^{-1} x = m\angle A$.

inverse tangent The measure of an angle whose tangent ratio is known.

tangente inversa Medida de un ángulo cuya razón tangente es conocida.

If $\tan A = x$, then $\tan^{-1} x = m\angle A$.

irregular polygon A polygon that is not regular.

polígono irregular Polígono que no es regular.

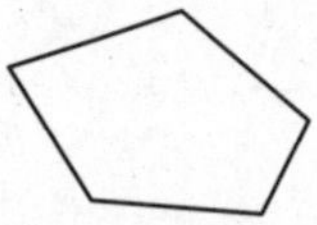

isometry A transformation that does not change the size or shape of a figure.

isometría Transformación que no cambia el tamaño ni la forma de una figura.

Reflections, translations, and rotations are all examples of isometries.

isosceles trapezoid A trapezoid in which the legs are congruent but not parallel.

trapecio isósceles Trapecio cuyos lados no paralelos son congruentes.

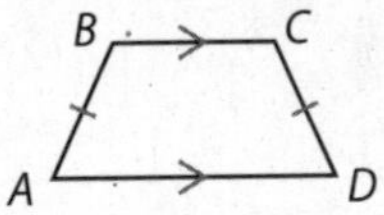

isosceles triangle A triangle with at least two congruent sides.

triángulo isósceles Triángulo que tiene al menos dos lados congruentes.

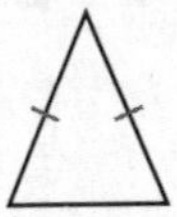

iteration The repetitive application of the same rule.

iteración Aplicación repetitiva de la misma regla.v

J

joint relative frequency The ratio of the frequency in a particular category divided by the total number of data values.

frecuencia relativa conjunta La razón de la frecuencia en una determinada categoría dividida entre el número total de valores.

ENGLISH | **SPANISH** | **EXAMPLES**

K

kite A quadrilateral with exactly two pairs of congruent consecutive sides.

cometa o papalote Cuadrilátero con exactamente dos pares de lados congruentes consecutivos.

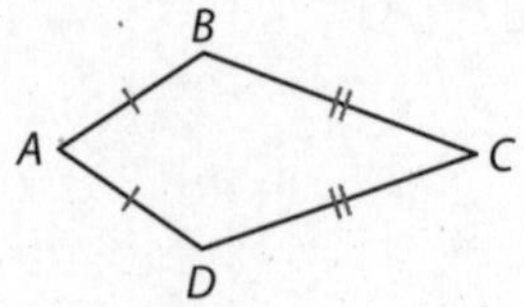

Kite *ABCD*

L

lateral area The sum of the areas of the lateral faces of a prism or pyramid, or the area of the lateral surface of a cylinder or cone.

área lateral Suma de las áreas de las caras laterales de un prisma o pirámide, o área de la superficie lateral de un cilindro o cono.

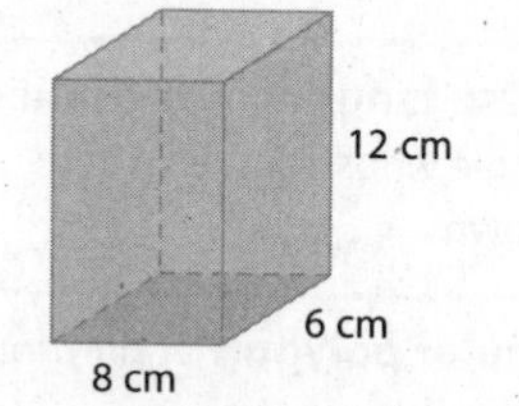

Lateral area $= 4(6)(12) = 288 \text{ cm}^2$

lateral edge An edge of a prism or pyramid that is not an edge of a base.

arista lateral Arista de un prisma o pirámide que no es la arista de una base.

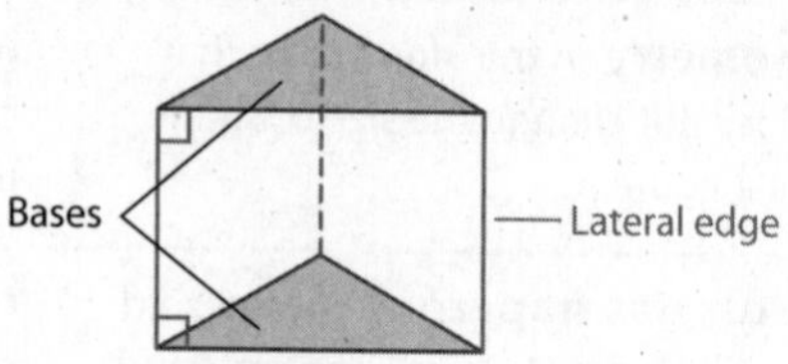

Right prism

lateral face A face of a prism or a pyramid that is not a base.

cara lateral Cara de un prisma o pirámide que no es la base.

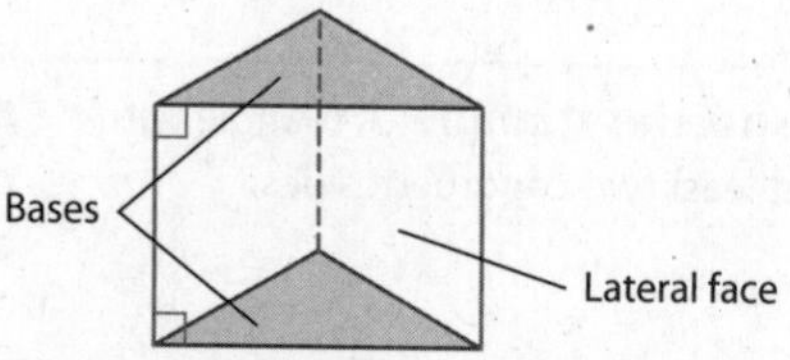

Right prism

lateral surface The curved surface of a cylinder or cone.

superficie lateral Superficie curva de un cilindro o cono.

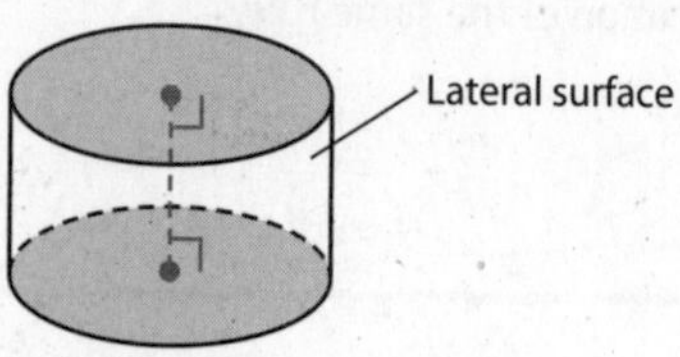

Right cylinder

leading coefficient The coefficient of the first term of a polynomial in standard form.

coeficiente principal Coeficiente del primer término de un polinomio en forma estándar.

$3x^2 + 7x - 2$
Leading coefficient: 3

leg of a right triangle One of the two sides of the right triangle that form the right angle.

cateto de un triángulo rectángulo Uno de los dos lados de un triángulo rectángulo que forman el ángulo recto.

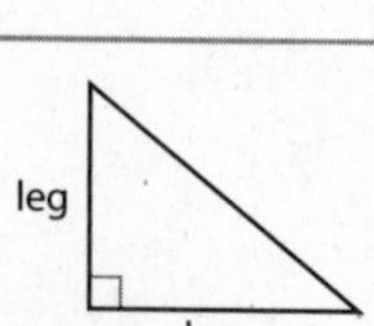

ENGLISH	SPANISH	EXAMPLES
leg of an isosceles triangle One of the two congruent sides of the isosceles triangle.	**cateto de un triángulo isósceles** Uno de los dos lados congruentes del triángulo isósceles.	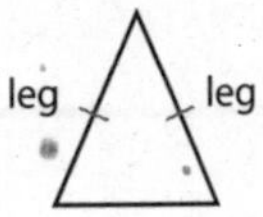
legs of a trapezoid The sides of the trapezoid that are not the bases.	**catetos de un trapecio** Los lados del trapecio que no son las bases.	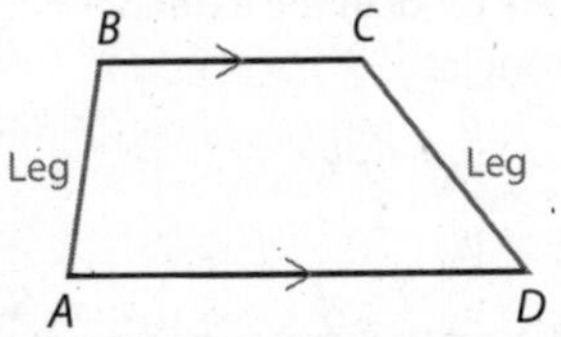
length The distance between the two endpoints of a segment.	**longitud** Distancia entre los dos extremos de un segmento.	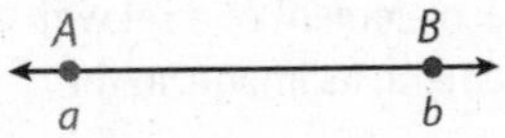 $AB = \|a - b\| = \|b - a\|$
line An undefined term in geometry, a line is a straight path that has no thickness and extends forever.	**línea** Término indefinido en geometría; una línea es un trazo recto que no tiene grosor y se extiende infinitamente.	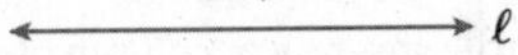
line of symmetry A line that divides a plane figure into two congruent reflected halves.	**eje de simetría** Línea que divide una figura plana en dos mitades reflejas congruentes.	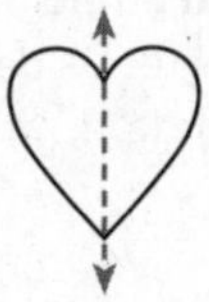
line segment *See* segment of a line.	**segmento** *Véase* segmento de recta.	
line symmetry A figure that can be reflected across a line so that the image coincides with the preimage.	**simetría axial** Figura que puede reflejarse sobre una línea de forma tal que la imagen coincida con la imagen original.	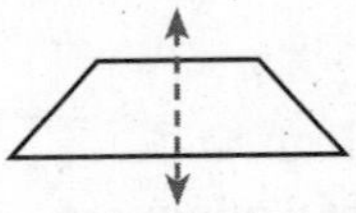
linear equation in three variables An equation with three distinct variables, each of which is either first degree or has a coefficient of zero.	**ecuación lineal en tres variables** Ecuación con tres variables diferentes, sean de primer grado o tengan un coeficiente de cero.	$5 = 3x + 2y + 6z$
linear pair A pair of adjacent angles whose noncommon sides are opposite rays.	**par lineal** Par de ángulos adyacentes cuyos lados no comunes son rayos opuestos.	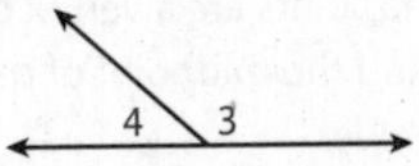 ∠3 and ∠4 form a linear pair.

ENGLISH	SPANISH	EXAMPLES

M

major arc An arc of a circle whose points are on or in the exterior of a central angle.

arco mayor Arco de un círculo cuyos puntos están sobre un ángulo central o en su exterior.

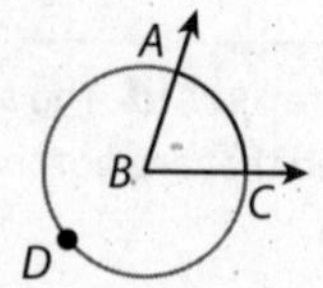

$\overset{\frown}{ADC}$ is a major arc of the circle.

mapping An operation that matches each element of a set with another element, its image, in the same set.

correspondencia Operación que establece una correlación entre cada elemento de un conjunto con otro elemento, su imagen, en el mismo conjunto.

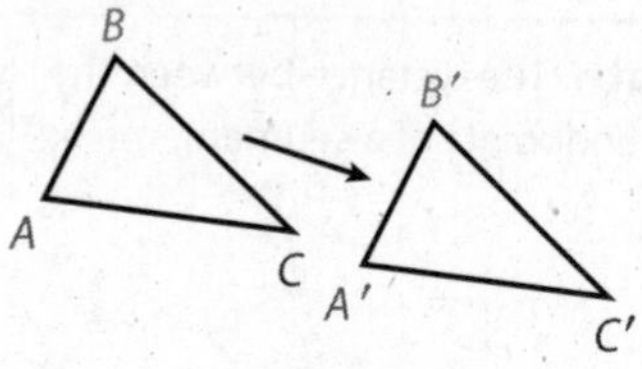

marginal relative frequency The sum of the joint relative frequencies in a row or column of a two-way table.

frecuencia relativa marginal La suma de las frecuencias relativas conjuntas en una fila o columna de una tabla de doble entrada.

measure of an angle Angles are measured in degrees. A degree is $\frac{1}{360}$ of a complete circle.

medida de un ángulo Los ángulos se miden en grados. Un grado es $\frac{1}{360}$ de un círculo completo.

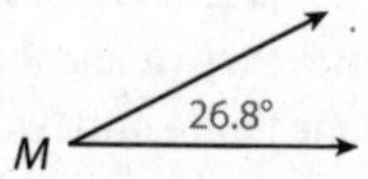

$m\angle M = 26.8°$

measure of a major arc The difference of 360° and the measure of the associated minor arc.

medida de un arco mayor Diferencia entre 360° y la medida del arco menor asociado.

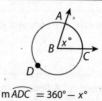

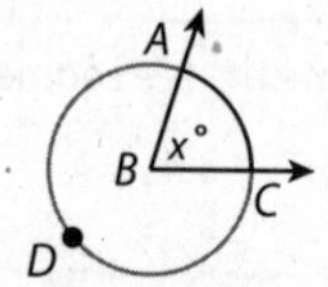

$m\overset{\frown}{ADC} = 360° - x°$

measure of a minor arc The measure of its central angle.

medida de un arco menor Medida de su ángulo central.

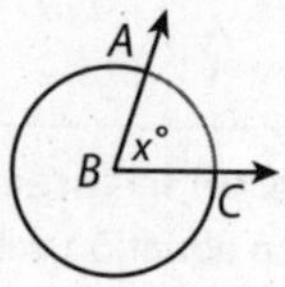

$m\overset{\frown}{AC} = x°$

median of a triangle A segment whose endpoints are a vertex of the triangle and the midpoint of the opposite side.

mediana de un triángulo Segmento cuyos extremos son un vértice del triángulo y el punto medio del lado opuesto.

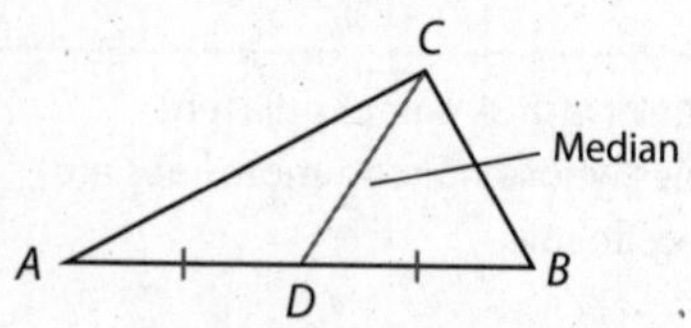

midpoint The point that divides a segment into two congruent segments.

punto medio Punto que divide un segmento en dos segmentos congruentes.

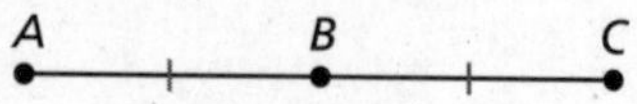

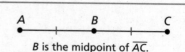

B is the midpoint of $\overline{AC}$.

Glossary/Glosario

ENGLISH	SPANISH	EXAMPLES

midsegment of a trapezoid The segment whose endpoints are the midpoints of the legs of the trapezoid.

segmento medio de un trapecio Segmento cuyos extremos son los puntos medios de los catetos del trapecio.

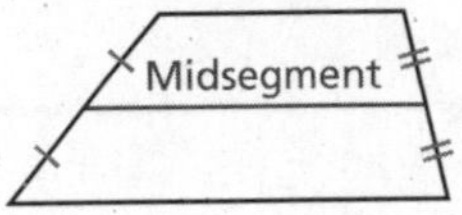

midsegment triangle The triangle formed by the three midsegments of a triangle.

triángulo de segmentos medios Triángulo formado por los tres segmentos medios de un triángulo.

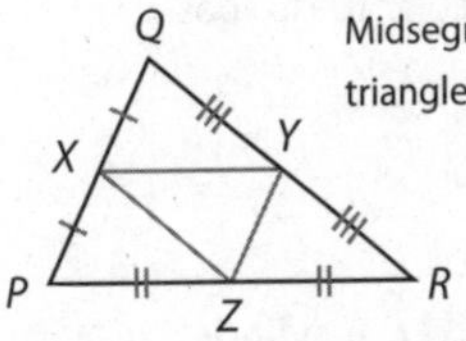

Midsegment triangle: $\triangle XYZ$

minor arc An arc of a circle whose points are on or in the interior of a central angle.

arco menor Arco de un círculo cuyos puntos están sobre un ángulo central o en su interior.

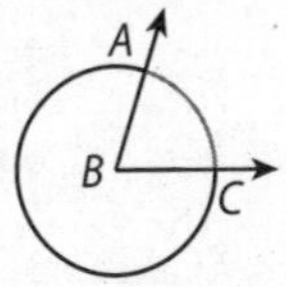

$\overset{\frown}{AC}$ is a minor arc of the circle.

monomial A number or a product of numbers and variables with whole-number exponents, or a polynomial with one term.

monomio Número o producto de números y variables con exponentes de números cabales, o polinomio con un término.

$3x^2y^4$

mutually exclusive events Two events are mutually exclusive if they cannot both occur in the same trial of an experiment.

sucesos mutuamente excluyentes Dos sucesos son mutuamente excluyentes si ambos no pueden ocurrir en la misma prueba de un experimento.

In the experiment of rolling a number cube, rolling a 3 and rolling an even number are mutually exclusive events.

N

***n*-gon** An *n*-sided polygon.

***n*-ágono** Polígono de *n* lados.

nonagon A nine-sided polygon.

nonágono Polígono de nueve lados.

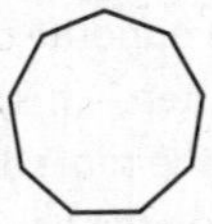

noncollinear Points that do not lie on the same line.

no colineal Puntos que no se encuentran sobre la misma línea.

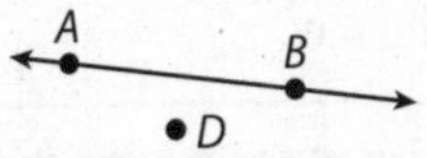

Points *A*, *B*, and *D* are not collinear.

noncoplanar Points that do not lie on the same plane.

no coplanar Puntos que no se encuentran en el mismo plano.

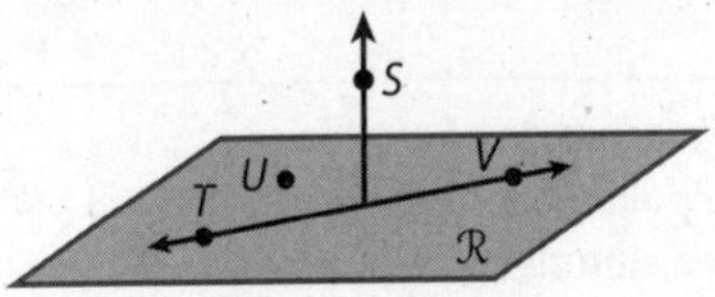

T, *U*, *V*, and *S* are not coplanar.

ENGLISH	SPANISH	EXAMPLES

O

oblique cone A cone whose axis is not perpendicular to the base.

cono oblicuo Cono cuyo eje no es perpendicular a la base.

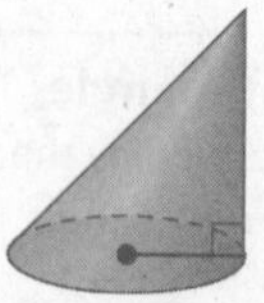

oblique cylinder A cylinder whose axis is not perpendicular to the bases.

cilindro oblicuo Cilindro cuyo eje no es perpendicular a las bases.

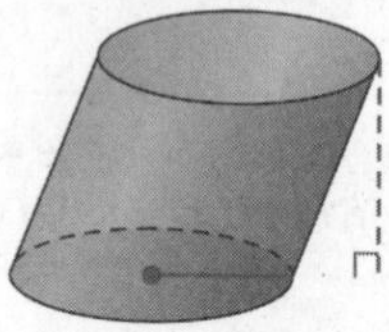

oblique prism A prism that has at least one nonrectangular lateral face.

prisma oblicuo Prisma que tiene por lo menos una cara lateral no rectangular.

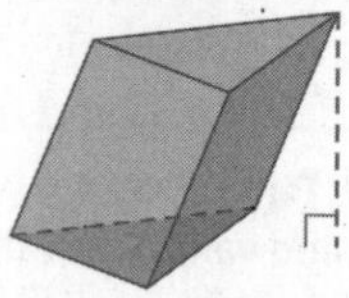

obtuse angle An angle that measures greater than 90° and less than 180°.

ángulo obtuso Ángulo que mide más de 90° y menos de 180°.

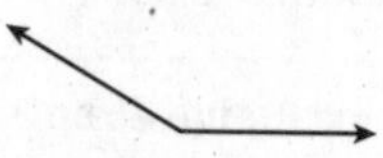

obtuse triangle A triangle with one obtuse angle.

triángulo obtusángulo Triángulo con un ángulo obtuso.

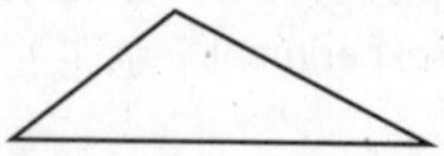

octagon An eight-sided polygon.

octágono Polígono de ocho lados.

opposite The opposite of a number a, denoted $-a$, is the number that is the same distance from zero as a, on the opposite side of the number line. The sum of opposites is 0.

opuesto El opuesto de un número a, expresado $-a$, es el número que se encuentra a la misma distancia de cero que a, del lado opuesto de la recta numérica. La suma de los opuestos es 0.

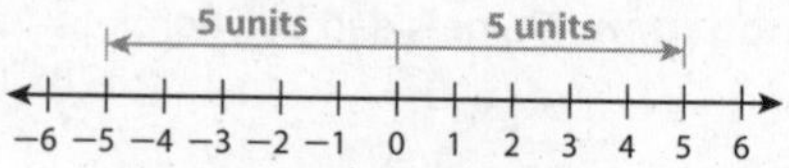

5 and −5 are opposites.

opposite rays Two rays that have a common endpoint and form a line.

rayos opuestos Dos rayos que tienen un extremo común y forman una línea.

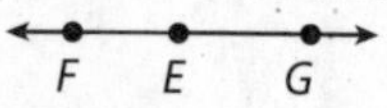

$\overrightarrow{EF}$ and $\overrightarrow{EG}$ are opposite rays.

orthocenter of a triangle The point of concurrency of the three altitudes of a triangle.

ortocentro de un triángulo Punto de intersección de las tres alturas de un triángulo.

P is the orthocenter.

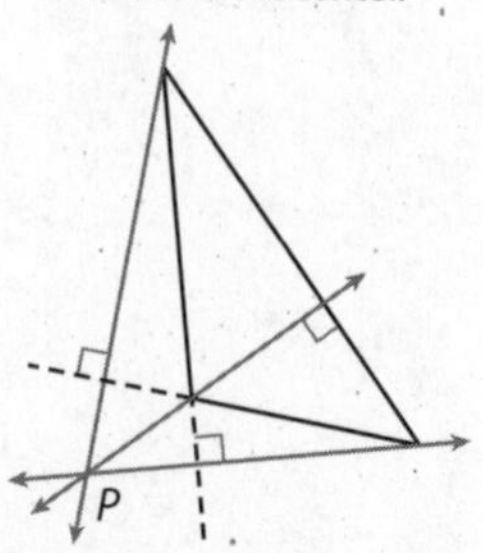

Glossary/Glosario

ENGLISH	SPANISH	EXAMPLES
outcome A possible result of a probability experiment.	**resultado** Resultado posible de un experimento de probabilidad.	In the experiment of rolling a number cube, the possible outcomes are 1, 2, 3, 4, 5, and 6.
overlapping events Events that have one or more outcomes in common. Also called inclusive events.	**sucesos superpuestos** Sucesos que tienen uno o más resultados en común. También se denominan sucesos inclusivos.	Rolling an even number and rolling a prime number on a number cube are overlapping events because they both contain the outcome rolling a 2.

P

ENGLISH	SPANISH	EXAMPLES
parabola The shape of the graph of a quadratic function. Also, the set of points equidistant from a point F, called the focus, and a line d, called the *directrix*.	**parábola** Forma de la gráfica de una función cuadrática. También, conjunto de puntos equidistantes de un punto F, denominado *foco*, y una línea d, denominada *directriz*.	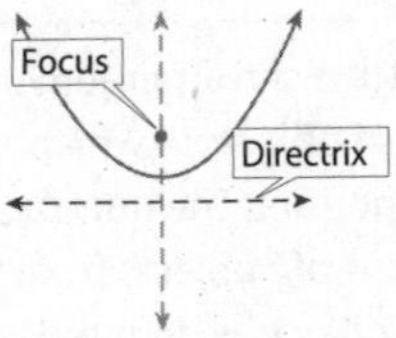
parameter One of the constants in a function or equation that may be changed. Also the third variable in a set of parametric equations.	**parámetro** Una de las constantes en una función o ecuación que se puede cambiar. También es la tercera variable en un conjunto de ecuaciones paramétricas.	$y = (x - h)^2 + k$ parameters
parallel lines Lines in the same plane that do not intersect.	**líneas paralelas** Líneas rectas en el mismo plano que no se cruzan.	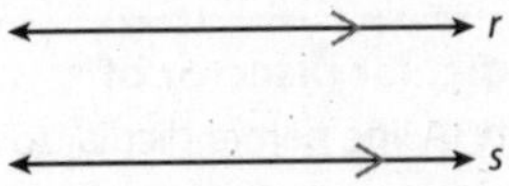 $r \parallel s$
parallel planes Planes that do not intersect.	**planos paralelos** Planos que no se cruzan.	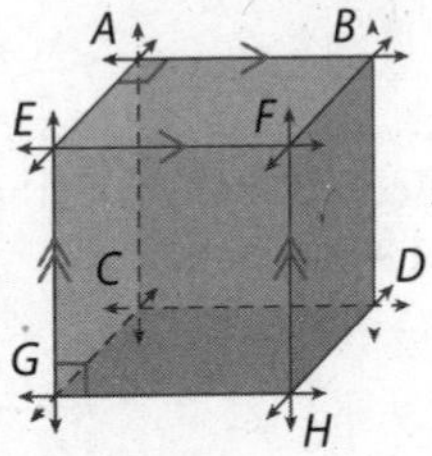 Plane *AEF* and plane *CGH* are parallel planes.
parallelogram A quadrilateral with two pairs of parallel sides.	**paralelogramo** Cuadrilátero con dos pares de lados paralelos.	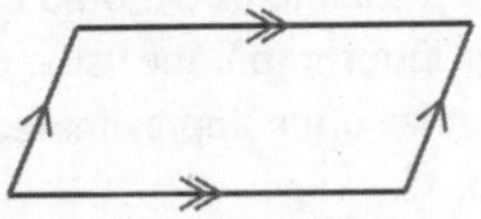
pentagon A five-sided polygon.	**diagrama** Polígono de cinco lados.	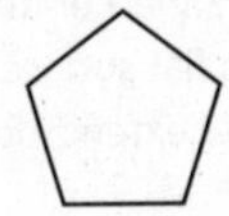

Glossary/Glosario

ENGLISH	SPANISH	EXAMPLES

perfect-square trinomial A trinomial whose factored form is the square of a binomial. A perfect-square trinomial has the form $a^2 - 2ab + b^2 = (a - b)^2$ or $a^2 + 2ab + b^2 = (a + b)^2$.

trinomio cuadrado perfecto Trinomio cuya forma factorizada es el cuadrado de un binomio. Un trinomio cuadrado perfecto tiene la forma $a^2 - 2ab + b^2 = (a - b)^2$ o $a^2 + 2ab + b^2 = (a + b)^2$.

$x^2 + 6x + 9$ is a perfect-square trinomial, because $x^2 + 6x + 9 = (x + 3)^2$.

---

perimeter The sum of the side lengths of a closed plane figure.

perímetro Suma de las longitudes de los lados de una figura plana cerrada.

Perimeter $= 18 + 6 + 18 + 6 = 48$ ft

---

permutation An arrangement of a group of objects in which order is important. The number of permutations of r objects from a group of n objects is denoted ${}_nP_r$.

permutación Arreglo de un grupo de objetos en el cual el orden es importante. El número de permutaciones de r objetos de un grupo de n objetos se expresa ${}_nP_r$.

For 4 objects A, B, C, and D, there are ${}_4P_2 = 12$ different permutations of 2 objects: AB, AC, AD, BC, BD, CD, BA, CA, DA, CB, DB, and DC.

---

perpendicular Intersecting to form 90° angles, denoted by $\perp$.

perpendicular Que se cruza para formar ángulos de 90°, expresado por $\perp$.

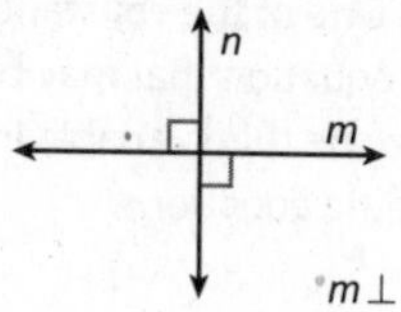

$m \perp n$

---

perpendicular bisector of a segment A line perpendicular to a segment at the segment's midpoint.

mediatriz de un segmento Línea perpendicular a un segmento en el punto medio del segmento.

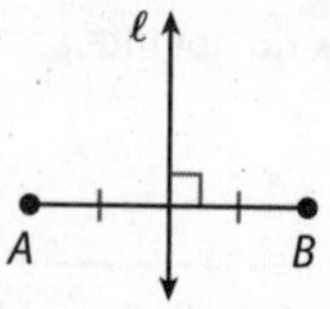

ℓ is the perpendicular bisector of $\overline{AB}$.

---

perpendicular lines Lines that intersect at 90° angles.

líneas perpendiculares Líneas que se cruzan en ángulos de 90°.

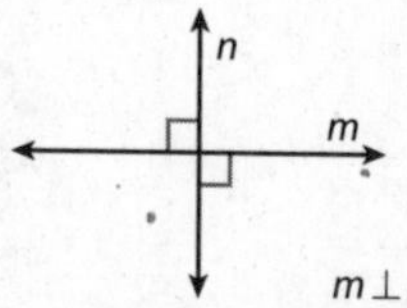

$m \perp n$

---

pi The ratio of the circumference of a circle to its diameter, denoted by the Greek letter π (pi). The value of π is irrational, often approximated by 3.14 or $\frac{22}{7}$.

pi Razón entre la circunferencia de un círculo y su diámetro, expresado por la letra griega π (pi). El valor de π es irracional y por lo general se aproxima a 3.14 ó $\frac{22}{7}$.

If a circle has a diameter of 5 inches and a circumference of C inches, then $\frac{C}{5} = \pi$, or $C = 5\pi$ inches, or about 15.7 inches.

---

plane An undefined term in geometry, it is a flat surface that has no thickness and extends forever.

plano Término indefinido en geometría; un plano es una superficie plana que no tiene grosor y se extiende infinitamente.

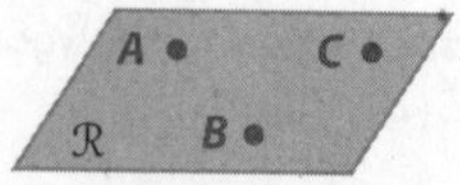

plane R or plane ABC

ENGLISH	SPANISH	EXAMPLES
plane symmetry A three-dimensional figure that can be divided into two congruent reflected halves by a plane has plane symmetry.	**simetría de plano** Una figura tridimensional que se puede dividir en dos mitades congruentes reflejadas por un plano tiene simetría de plano.	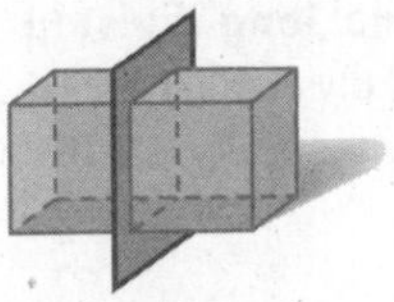 Plane symmetry
Platonic solid One of the five regular polyhedra: a tetrahedron, a cube, an octahedron, a dodecahedron, or an icosahedron.	**sólido platónico** Uno de los cinco poliedros regulares: tetraedro, cubo, octaedro, dodecaedro o icosaedro.	
point An undefined term in geometry, it names a location and has no size.	**punto** Término indefinido de la geometría que denomina una ubicación y no tiene tamaño.	*P* • point *P*
point of concurrency A point where three or more lines coincide.	**punto de concurrencia** Punto donde se cruzan tres o más líneas.	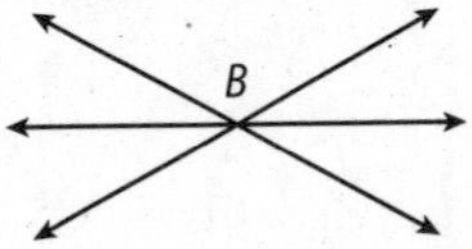
point of tangency The point of intersection of a circle or sphere with a tangent line or plane.	**punto de tangencia** Punto de intersección de un círculo o esfera con una línea o plano tangente.	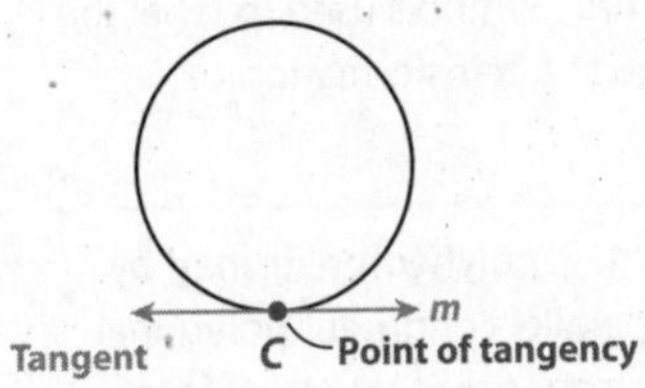
point-slope form $y - y_1 = m(x - x_1)$, where m is the slope and (x_1, y_1) is a point on the line.	**forma de punto y pendiente** $(y - y_1) = m(x - x_1)$, donde m es la pendiente y (x_1, y_1)es un punto en la línea.	
polygon A closed plane figure formed by three or more segments such that each segment intersects exactly two other segments only at their endpoints and no two segments with a common endpoint are collinear.	**polígono** Figura plana cerrada formada por tres o más segmentos tal que cada segmento se cruza únicamente con otros dos segmentos sólo en sus extremos y ningún segmento con un extremo común a otro es colineal con éste.	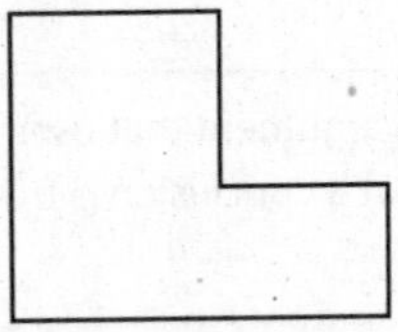
polyhedron A closed three-dimensional figure formed by four or more polygons that intersect only at their edges.	**poliedro** Figura tridimensional cerrada formada por cuatro o más polígonos que se cruzan sólo en sus aristas.	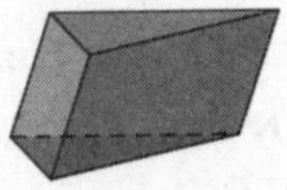
polynomial A monomial or a sum or difference of monomials.	**polinomio** Monomio o suma o diferencia de monomios.	$2x^2 + 3xy - 7y^2$

ENGLISH	SPANISH	EXAMPLES
polynomial long division A method of dividing one polynomial by another.	**división larga polinomial** Método por el que se divide un polinomio entre otro.	$x+2\overline{)\,x^2+3x+5}$ with quotient $x+1$; $-(x^2+2x)$; $x+5$; $-(x+2)$; 3 $\frac{x^2+3x+5}{x+2}=x+1+\frac{3}{x+2}$
postulate A statement that is accepted as true without proof. Also called an *axiom*.	**postulado** Enunciado que se acepta como verdadero sin demostración. También denominado *axioma*.	
preimage The original figure in a transformation.	**imagen original** Figura original en una transformación.	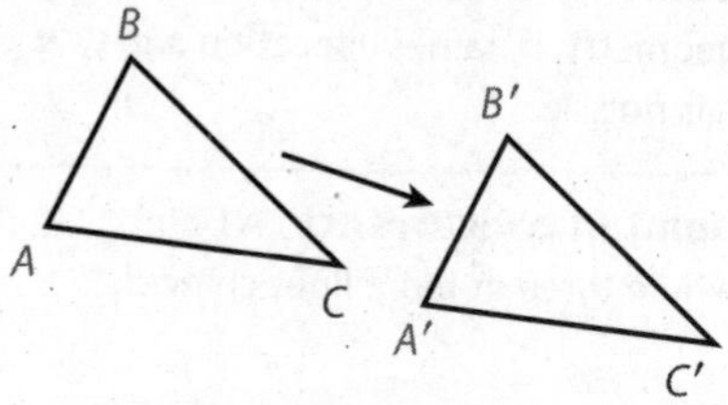
primes Symbols used to label the image in a transformation.	**apóstrofos** Símbolos utilizados para identificar la imagen en una transformación.	$A'B'C'$
prism A polyhedron formed by two parallel congruent polygonal bases connected by lateral faces that are parallelograms.	**prisma** Poliedro formado por dos bases poligonales congruentes y paralelas conectadas por caras laterales que son paralelogramos.	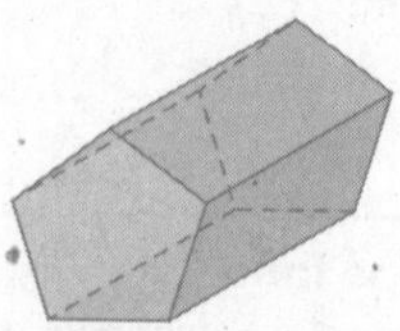
probability A number from 0 to 1 (or 0% to 100%) that is the measure of how likely an event is to occur.	**probabilidad** Número entre 0 y 1 (o entre 0% y 100%) que describe cuán probable es que ocurra un suceso.	A bag contains 3 red marbles and 4 blue marbles. The probability of randomly choosing a red marble is $\frac{3}{7}$.
proof An argument that uses logic to show that a conclusion is true.	**demostración** Argumento que se vale de la lógica para probar que una conclusión es verdadera.	
proof by contradiction *See* indirect proof.	**demostración por contradicción** *Ver* demostración indirecta.	
pure imaginary number *See* imaginary number.	**número imaginario puro** Ver número imaginario.	$3i$
pyramid A polyhedron formed by a polygonal base and triangular lateral faces that meet at a common vertex.	**pirámide** Poliedro formado por una base poligonal y caras laterales triangulares que se encuentran en un vértice común.	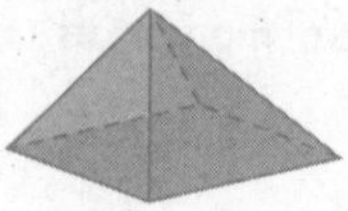

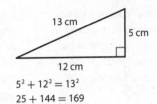

ENGLISH	SPANISH	EXAMPLES
Pythagorean Theorem If a right triangle has legs of lengths a and b and a hypotenuse of length c, then $a^2 + b^2 = c^2$.	**Teorema de Pitágoras** Dado un triángulo rectángulo con catetos de longitudes a y b y una hipotenusa de longitud c, entonces $a^2 + b^2 = c^2$.	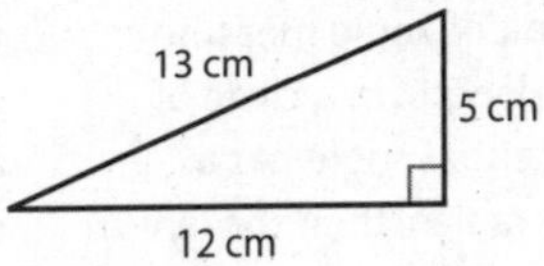 $5^2 + 12^2 = 13^2$ $25 + 144 = 169$
Pythagorean triple A set of three nonzero whole numbers a, b, and c such that $a^2 + b^2 = c^2$.	**Tripleta de Pitágoras** Conjunto de tres números cabales distintos de cero a, b y c tal que $a^2 + b^2 = c^2$.	$\{3, 4, 5\}$ $3^2 + 4^2 = 5^2$

Q

ENGLISH	SPANISH	EXAMPLES
quadratic equation An equation that can be written in the form $ax^2 + bx + c = 0$, where a, b, and c are real numbers and $a \neq 0$.	**ecuación cuadrática** Ecuación que se puede expresar como $ax^2 + bx + c = 0$, donde a, b y c son números reales y $a \neq 0$.	$x^2 + 3x - 4 = 0$ $x^2 - 9 = 0$
Quadratic Formula The formula $x = \frac{-b \pm \sqrt{b^2 - 4ac}}{2a}$, which gives solutions, or roots, of equations in the form $ax^2 + bx + c = 0$, where $a \neq 0$.	**fórmula cuadrática** La fórmula $x = \frac{-b \pm \sqrt{b^2 - 4ac}}{2a}$, que da soluciones, o raíces, para las ecuaciones del tipo $ax^2 + bx + c = 0$, donde $a \neq 0$.	The solutions of $2x^2 - 5x - 3 = 0$ are given by $x = \frac{-(-5) \pm \sqrt{(-5)^2 - 4(2)(-3)}}{2(2)}$ $= \frac{5 \pm \sqrt{25 + 24}}{4} = \frac{5 \pm 7}{4}$ $x = 3$ or $x = -\frac{1}{2}$
quadratic function A function that can be written in the form $f(x) = ax^2 + bx + c$, where a, b, and c are real numbers and $a \neq 0$.	**función cuadrática** Función que se puede expresar como $f(x) = ax^2 + bx + c$, donde a, b y c son números reales y $a \neq 0$.	$f(x) = x^2 - 6x + 8$
quadratic polynomial A polynomial of degree 2.	**polinomio cuadrático** Polinomio de grado 2.	$x^2 - 6x + 8$
quadratic regression A statistical method used to fit a quadratic model to a given data set.	**regresión cuadrática** Método estadístico utilizado para ajustar un modelo cuadrático a un conjunto de datos determinado.	
quadrilateral A four-sided polygon.	**cuadrilátero** Polígono de cuatro lados.	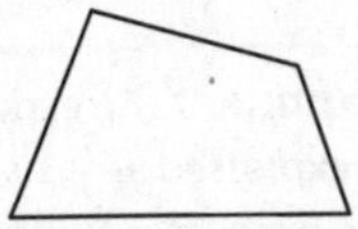

R

ENGLISH	SPANISH	EXAMPLES
radial symmetry *See* rotational symmetry.	**simetría radial** *Ver* simetría de rotación.	

ENGLISH	SPANISH	EXAMPLES
radian A unit of angle measure based on arc length. In a circle of radius r, if a central angle has a measure of 1 radian, then the length of the intercepted arc is r units. 2π radians $= 360°$ 1 radian $\approx 57°$	**radián** Unidad de medida de un ángulo basada en la longitud del arco. En un círculo de radio r, si un ángulo central mide 1 radián, entonces la longitud del arco abarcado es r unidades. 2π radians $= 360°$ 1 radian $\approx 57°$	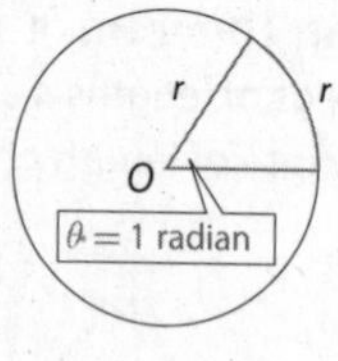
radical equation An equation that contains a variable within a radical.	**ecuación radical** Ecuación que contiene una variable dentro de un radical.	$\sqrt{x+3}+4=7$
radical expression An expression that contains a radical sign.	**expresión radical** Expresión que contiene un signo de radical.	$\sqrt{x+3}+4$
radius of a circle A segment whose endpoints are the center of a circle and a point on the circle; the distance from the center of a circle to any point on the circle.	**radio de un círculo** Segmento cuyos extremos son el centro y un punto de la circunferencia; distancia desde el centro de un círculo hasta cualquier punto de la circunferencia.	
radius of a sphere A segment whose endpoints are the center of a sphere and any point on the sphere; the distance from the center of a sphere to any point on the sphere.	**radio de una esfera** Segmento cuyos extremos son el centro de una esfera y cualquier punto sobre la esfera; distancia desde el centro de una esfera hasta cualquier punto sobre la esfera.	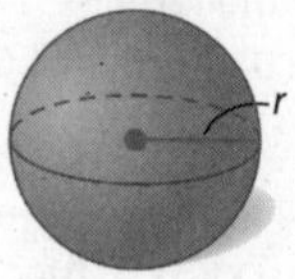
range of a data set The difference of the greatest and least values in the data set.	**rango de un conjunto de datos** La diferencia del mayor y menor valor en un conjunto de datos.	The data set $\{3, 3, 5, 7, 8, 10, 11, 11, 12\}$ has a range of $12 - 3 = 9$.
range of a function or relation The set of output values of a function or relation.	**rango de una función o relación** Conjunto de los valores desalida de una función o relación.	The range of $y = x^2$ is $\{y \mid y \geq 0\}$.
rational equation An equation that contains one or more rational expressions.	**ecuación racional** Ecuación que contiene una o más expresiones racionales.	$\frac{x+2}{x^2+3x-1}=6$
rational exponent An exponent that can be expressed as $\frac{m}{n}$ such that if m and n are integers, then $b^{\frac{m}{n}} = \sqrt[n]{b^m} = \left(\sqrt[n]{b}\right)^m$.	**exponente racional** Exponente que se puede expresar como $\frac{m}{n}$ tal que si m y n son números enteros, entonces $b^{\frac{m}{n}} = \sqrt[n]{b^m} = \left(\sqrt[n]{b}\right)^m$.	$64^{\frac{1}{6}} = \sqrt[6]{64}$
rational expression An algebraic expression whose numerator and denominator are polynomials and whose denominator has a degree ≥ 1.	**expresión racional** Expresión algebraica cuyo numerador y denominador son polinomios y cuyo denominador tiene un grado ≥ 1.	$\frac{x+2}{x^2+3x-1}$

ENGLISH	SPANISH	EXAMPLES
rational function A function whose rule can be written as a rational expression.	**función racional** Función cuya regla se puede expresar como una expresión racional.	$f(x) = \frac{x+2}{x^2+3x-1}$
rational number A number that can be written in the form $\frac{a}{b}$, where a and b are integers and $b \neq 0$.	**número racional** Número que se puede expresar como $\frac{a}{b}$, donde a y b son números enteros y $b \neq 0$.	$3, 1.75, 0.\overline{3}, -\frac{2}{3}, 0$
rationalizing the denominator A method of rewriting a fraction by multiplying by another fraction that is equivalent to 1 in order to remove radical terms from the denominator.	**racionalizar el denominador** Método que consiste en escribir nuevamente una fracción multiplicándola por otra fracción equivalente a 1 a fin de eliminar los términos radicales del denominador.	$\frac{1}{\sqrt{2}} \cdot \frac{\sqrt{2}}{\sqrt{2}} = \frac{\sqrt{2}}{2}$
ray A part of a line that starts at an endpoint and extends forever in one direction.	**rayo** Parte de una línea que comienza en un extremo y se extiende infinitamente en una dirección.	
rectangle A quadrilateral with four right angles.	**rectángulo** Cuadrilátero con cuatro ángulos rectos.	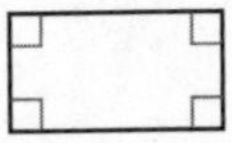
reduction A dilation with a scale factor greater than 0 but less than 1. In a reduction, the image is smaller than the preimage.	**reducción** Dilatación con un factor de escala mayor que 0 pero menor que 1. En una reducción, la imagen es más pequeña que la imagen original.	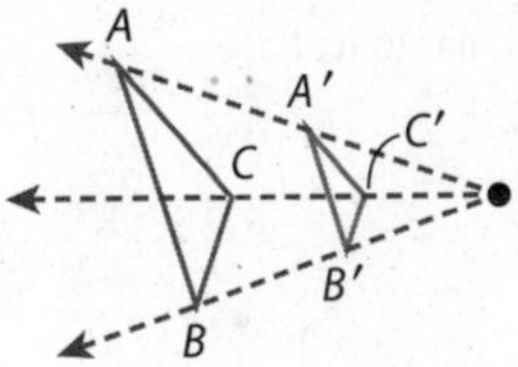
reflection A transformation across a line, called the line of reflection, such that the line of reflection is the perpendicular bisector of each segment joining each point and its image.	**reflexión** Transformación sobre una línea, denominada la línea de reflexión. La línea de reflexión es la mediatriz de cada segmento que une un punto con su imagen.	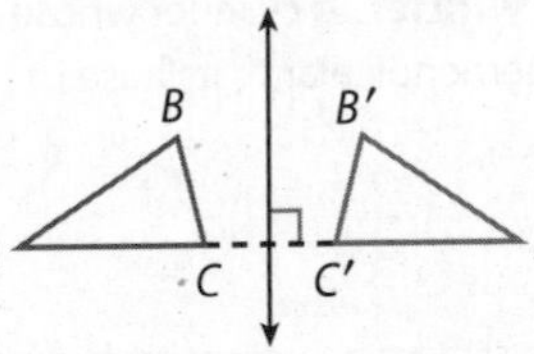
reflection symmetry *See* line symmetry.	**simetría de reflexión** *Ver* simetría axial.	
regular polygon A polygon that is both equilateral and equiangular.	**polígono regular** Polígono equilátero de ángulos iguales.	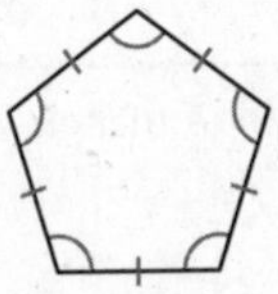
regular polyhedron A polyhedron in which all faces are congruent regular polygons and the same number of faces meet at each vertex. *See also* Platonic solid.	**poliedro regular** Poliedro cuyas caras son todas polígonos regulares congruentes y en el que el mismo número de caras se encuentran en cada vértice. *Ver también* sólido platónico.	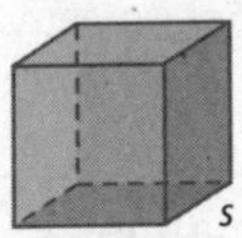

ENGLISH | **SPANISH** | **EXAMPLES**

regular pyramid A pyramid whose base is a regular polygon and whose lateral faces are congruent isosceles triangles.

pirámide regular Pirámide cuya base es un polígono regular y cuyas caras laterales son triángulos isósceles congruentes.

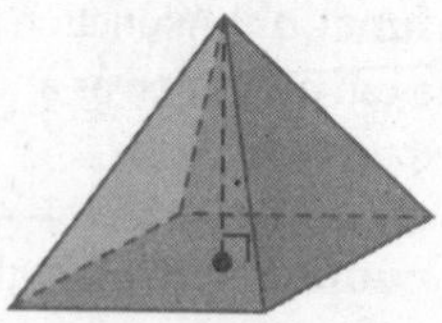

---

remote interior angle An interior angle of a polygon that is not adjacent to the exterior angle.

ángulo interno remoto Ángulo interno de un polígono que no es adyacente al ángulo externo.

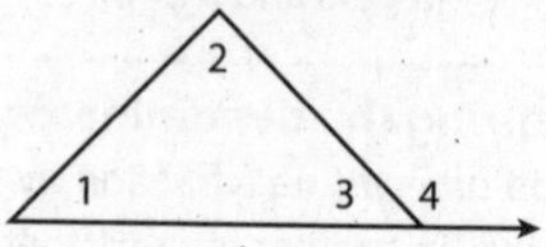

The remote interior angles of ∠4 are ∠1 and ∠2.

---

rhombus A quadrilateral with four congruent sides.

rombo Cuadrilátero con cuatro lados congruentes.

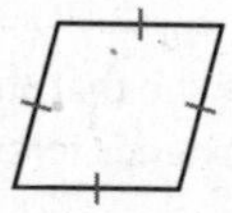

---

right angle An angle that measures 90°.

ángulo recto Ángulo que mide 90°.

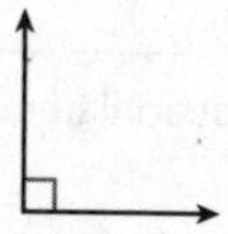

---

right cone A cone whose axis is perpendicular to its base.

cono recto Cono cuyo eje es perpendicular a su base.

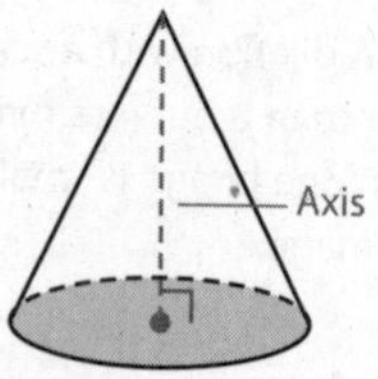

---

right cylinder A cylinder whose axis is perpendicular to its bases.

cilindro recto Cilindro cuyo eje es perpendicular a sus bases.

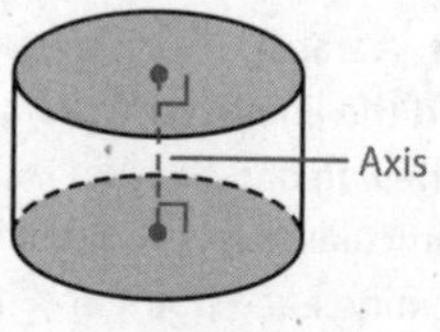

---

right prism A prism whose lateral faces are all rectangles.

prisma recto Prisma cuyas caras laterales son todas rectángulos.

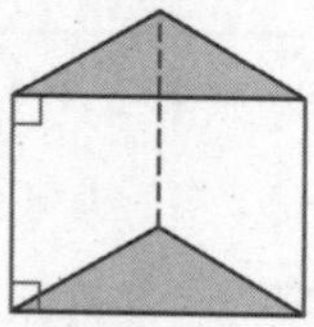

---

right triangle A triangle with one right angle.

triángulo rectángulo Triángulo con un ángulo recto.

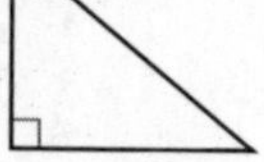

---

rigid motion *See* isometry.

movimiento rígido *Ver* isometría.

---

rigid transformation A transformation that does not change the size or shape of a figure.

transformación rígida Transformación que no cambia el tamaño o la forma de una figura.

ENGLISH | **SPANISH** | **EXAMPLES**

rise The difference in the *y*-values of two points on a line.

distancia vertical Diferencia entre los valores de *y* de dos puntos de una línea.

For the points $(3, -1)$ and $(6, 5)$, the rise is $5 - (-1) = 6$.

---

rotation A transformation about a point *P*, also known as the center of rotation, such that each point and its image are the same distance from *P*. All of the angles with vertex *P* formed by a point and its image are congruent.

rotación Transformación sobre un punto *P*, también conocido como el centro de rotación, tal que cada punto y su imagen estén a la misma distancia de *P*. Todos los ángulos con vértice *P* formados por un punto y su imagen son congruentes.

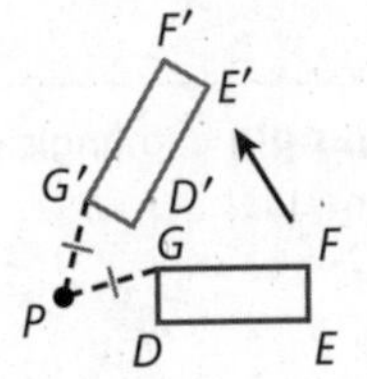

---

run The difference in the *x*-values of two points on a line.

distancia horizontal Diferencia entre los valores de *x* de dos puntos de una línea.

For the points $(3, -1)$ and $(6, 5)$, the run is $6 - 3 = 3$.

S

same-side interior angles For two lines intersected by a transversal, a pair of angles that lie on the same side of the transversal and between the two lines.

ángulos internos del mismo lado Dadas dos líneas cortadas por una transversal, el par de ángulos ubicados en el mismo lado de la transversal y entre las dos líneas.

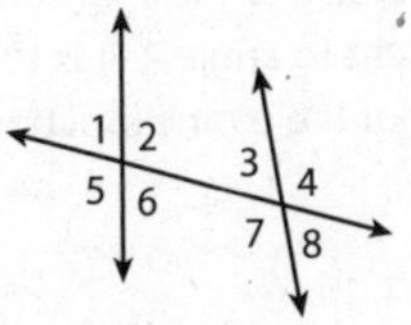

$\angle 2$ and $\angle 3$ are same-side interior angles.

---

sample space The set of all possible outcomes of a probability experiment.

espacio muestral Conjunto de todos los resultados posibles de un experimento de probabilidad.

In the experiment of rolling a number cube, the sample space is $\{1, 2, 3, 4, 5, 6\}$.

---

scale The ratio between two corresponding measurements.

escala Razón entre dos medidas correspondientes.

1 cm : 5 mi

---

scale drawing A drawing that uses a scale to represent an object as smaller or larger than the actual object.

dibujo a escala Dibujo que utiliza una escala para representar un objeto como más pequeño o más grande que el objeto original.

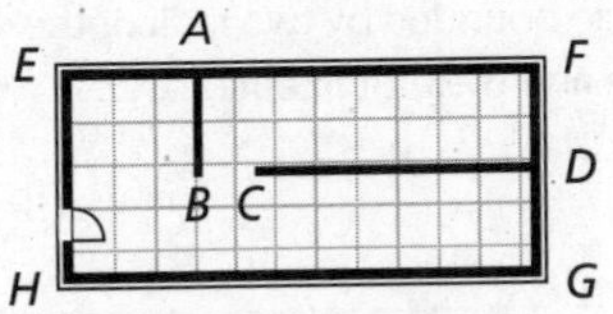

A blueprint is an example of a scale drawing.

---

scale factor The multiplier used on each dimension to change one figure into a similar figure.

factor de escala El multiplicador utilizado en cada dimensión para transformar una figura en una figura semejante.

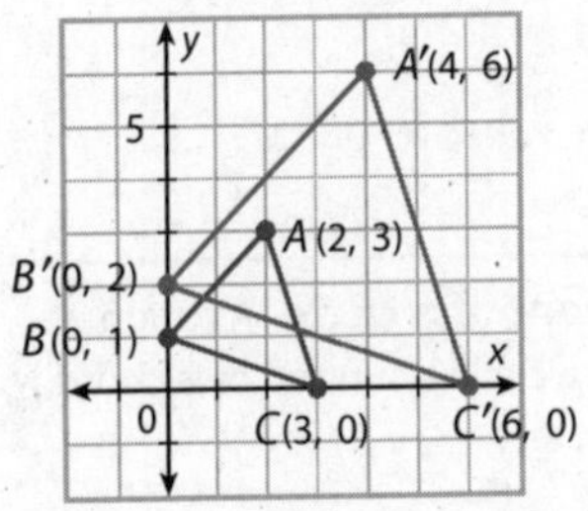

Scale factor: 2

ENGLISH	SPANISH	EXAMPLES
scale model A three-dimensional model that uses a scale to represent an object as smaller or larger than the actual object.	**modelo a escala** Modelo tridimensional que utiliza una escala para representar un objeto como más pequeño o más grande que el objeto real.	
scalene triangle A triangle with no congruent sides.	**triángulo escaleno** Triángulo sin lados congruentes.	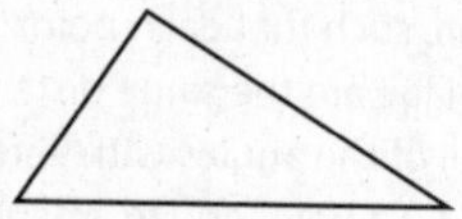
secant of a circle A line that intersects a circle at two points.	**secante de un círculo** Línea que corta un círculo en dos puntos.	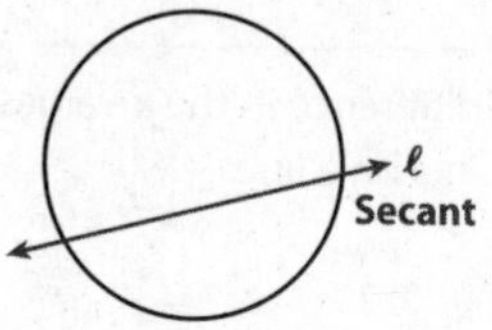
secant of an angle In a right triangle, the ratio of the length of the hypotenuse to the length of the side adjacent to angle *A*. It is the reciprocal of the cosine function.	**secante de un ángulo** En un triángulo rectángulo, la razón entre la longitud de la hipotenusa y la longitud del cateto adyacente al ángulo *A*. Es la inversa de la función coseno.	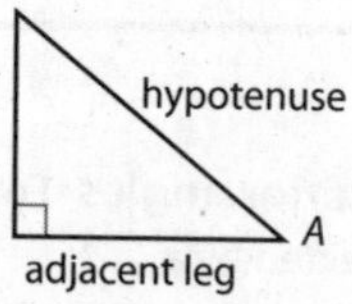 $\sec A = \frac{\text{hypotenuse}}{\text{adjacent}} = \frac{1}{\cos A}$
secant segment A segment of a secant with at least one endpoint on the circle.	**segmento secante** Segmento de una secante que tiene al menos un extremo sobre el círculo.	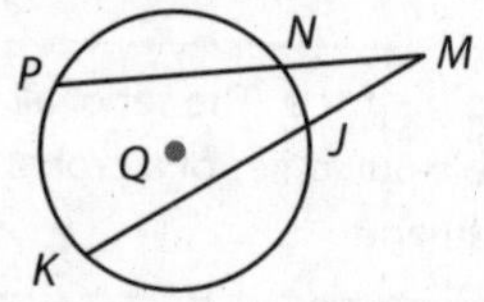 $\overline{NM}$ is an external secant segment. $\overline{JK}$ is an internal secant segment.
sector of a circle A region inside a circle bounded by two radii of the circle and their intercepted arc.	**sector de un círculo** Región dentro de un círculo delimitado por dos radios del círculo y por su arco abarcado.	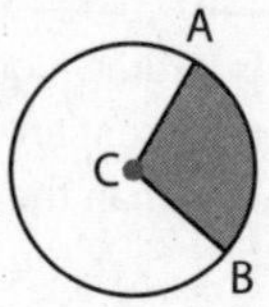
segment bisector A line, ray, or segment that divides a segment into two congruent segments.	**bisectriz de un segmento** Línea, rayo o segmento que divide un segmento en dos segmentos congruentes.	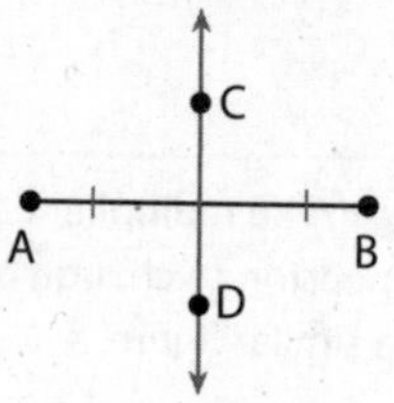
segment of a circle A region inside a circle bounded by a chord and an arc.	**segmento de un círculo** Región dentro de un círculo delimitada por una cuerda y un arco.	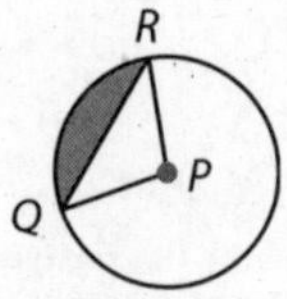

ENGLISH	SPANISH	EXAMPLES
segment of a line A part of a line consisting of two endpoints and all points between them.	**segmento de una línea** Parte de una línea que consiste en dos extremos y todos los puntos entre éstos.	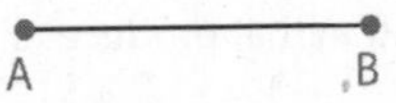
semicircle An arc of a circle whose endpoints lie on a diameter.	**semicírculo** Arco de un círculo cuyos extremos se encuentran sobre un diámetro.	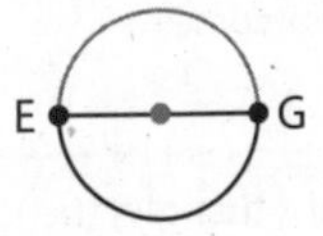
set A collection of items called elements.	**conjunto** Grupo de componentes denominados elementos.	$\{1, 2, 3\}$
side of a polygon One of the segments that form a polygon.	**lado de un polígono** Uno de los segmentos que forman un polígono.	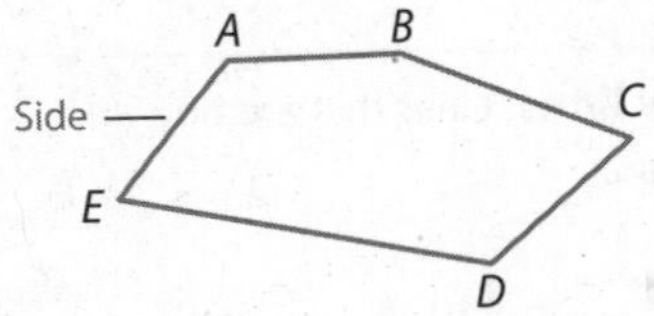
side of an angle One of the two rays that form an angle.	**lado de un ángulo** Uno de los dos rayos que forman un ángulo.	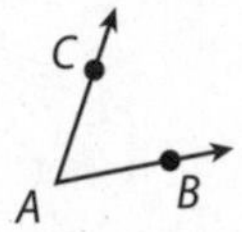 $\overrightarrow{AC}$ and $\overrightarrow{AB}$ are sides of $\angle CAB$.
similar Two figures are similar if they have the same shape but not necessarily the same size.	**semejantes** Dos figuras con la misma forma pero no necesariamente del mismo tamaño.	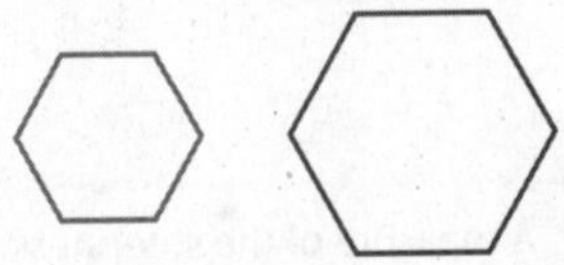
similar polygons Two polygons whose corresponding angles are congruent and whose corresponding side lengths are proportional.	**polígonos semejantes** Dos polígonos cuyos ángulos correspondientes son congruentes y cuyos lados correspondientes tienen longitudes proporcionales.	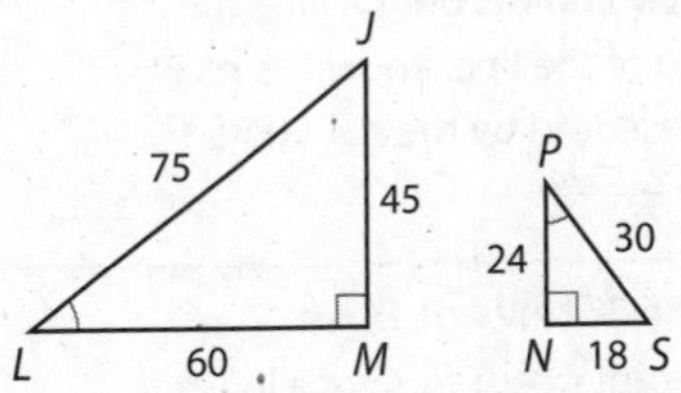
similarity ratio The ratio of two corresponding linear measurements in a pair of similar figures.	**razón de semejanza** Razón de dos medidas lineales correspondientes en un par de figuras semejantes.	Similarity ratio: $\frac{3.5}{2.1} = \frac{5}{3}$
similarity statement A statement that indicates that two polygons are similar by listing the vertices in the order of correspondence.	**enunciado de semejanza** Enunciado que indica que dos polígonos son semejantes enumerando los vértices en orden de correspondencia.	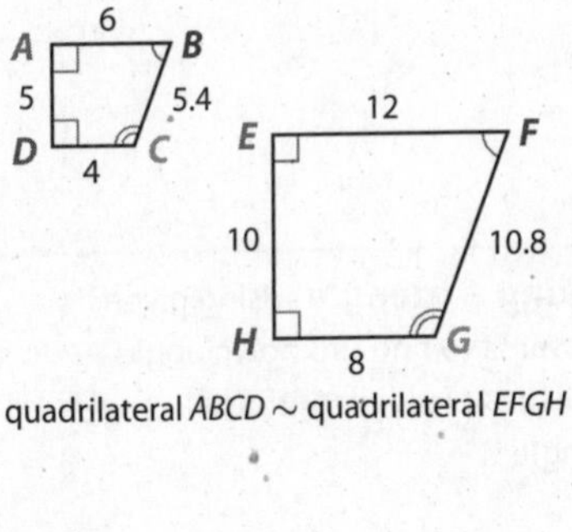 quadrilateral $ABCD \sim$ quadrilateral $EFGH$

Glossary/Glosario

ENGLISH	SPANISH	EXAMPLES
similarity transformation A transformation that produces similar figures.	**transformación de semejanza** Una transformación que resulta en figuras semejantes.	Dilations are similarity transformations.
simple event An event consisting of only one outcome.	**suceso simple** Suceso que contiene sólo un resultado.	In the experiment of rolling a number cube, the event consisting of the outcome 3 is a simple event.
sine In a right triangle, the ratio of the length of the leg opposite $\angle A$ to the length of the hypotenuse.	**seno** En un triángulo rectángulo, razón entre la longitud del cateto opuesto a $\angle A$ y la longitud de la hipotenusa.	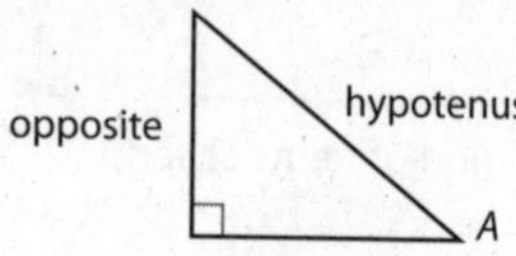 $\sin A = \frac{\text{opposite}}{\text{hypotenuse}}$
skew lines Lines that are not coplanar.	**líneas oblicuas** Líneas que no son coplanares.	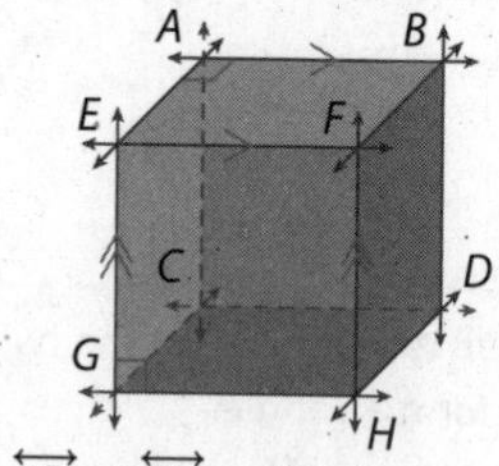 $\overleftrightarrow{AE}$ and $\overleftrightarrow{CD}$ are skew lines.
slide *See* translation.	**deslizamiento** *Ver* traslación.	
slope A measure of the steepness of a line. If (x_1, y_1) and (x_2, y_2) are any two points on the line, the slope of the line, known as m, is represented by the equation $m = \frac{y_2 - y_1}{x_2 - x_1}$.	**pendiente** Medida de la inclinación de una línea. Dados dos puntos (x_1, y_1) y (x_2, y_2) en una línea, la pendiente de la línea, denominada m, se representa con la ecuación $m = \frac{y_2 - y_1}{x_2 - x_1}$.	
slope-intercept form The slope-intercept form of a linear equation is $y = mx + b$, where m is the slope and b is the y-intercept.	**forma de pendiente-intersección** La forma de pendiente-intersección de una ecuación lineal es $y = mx + b$, donde m es la pendiente y b es la intersección con el eje y.	$y = -2x + 4$ The slope is -2. The y-intercept is 4.
solid A three-dimensional figure.	**cuerpo geométrico** Figura tridimensional.	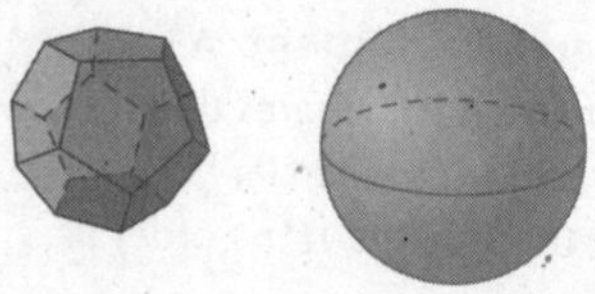
solving a triangle Using given measures to find unknown angle measures or side lengths of a triangle.	**resolución de un triángulo** Utilizar medidas dadas para hallar las medidas desconocidas de los ángulos o las longitudes de los lados de un triángulo.	

ENGLISH	SPANISH	EXAMPLES
special right triangle A 45°—45°—90° triangle or a 30°—60°—90° triangle.	**triángulo rectángulo especial** Triángulo de 45°—45°—90° o triángulo de 30°—60°—90°.	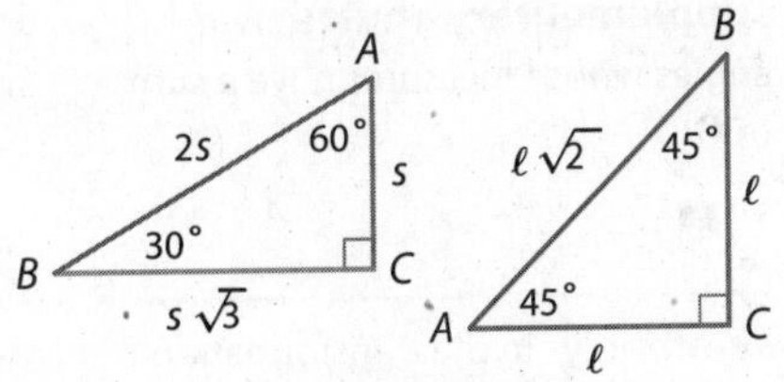
sphere The set of points in space that are a fixed distance from a given point called the center of the sphere.	**esfera** Conjunto de puntos en el espacio que se encuentran a una distancia fija de un punto determinado denominado centro de la esfera.	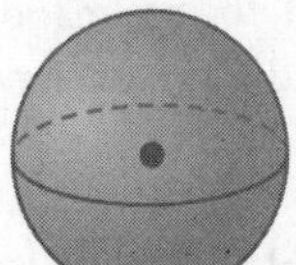
square A quadrilateral with four congruent sides and four right angles.	**cuadrado** Cuadrilátero con cuatro lados congruentes y cuatro ángulos rectos.	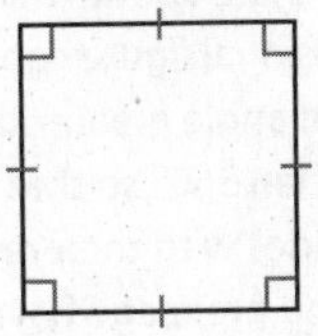
square root A number that is multiplied by itself to form a product is called a square root of that product.	**raíz cuadrada** El número que se multiplica por sí mismo para formar un producto se denomina la raíz cuadrada de ese producto.	A square root of 16 is 4, because $4^2 = 4 \cdot 4 = 16$. Another square root of 16 is -4 because $(-4)^2 = (-4)(-4) = 16$.
square root function A function whose rule contains a variable under a square root sign.	**función de raíz cuadrada** Función cuya regla contiene una variable bajo un signo de raíz cuadrada.	
standard form of a linear equation $Ax + By = C$, where A, B, and C are real numbers and A and B are not both 0.	**forma estándar de una ecuación lineal** $Ax + By = C$, donde A, B y C son números reales y A y B no son ambos cero.	$2x + 3y = 6$
standard form of a polynomial A polynomial in one variable is written in standard form when the terms are in order from greatest degree to least degree.	**forma estándar de un polinomio** Un polinomio de una variable se expresa en forma estándar cuando los términos se ordenan de mayor a menor grado.	$4x^5 - 2x^4 + x^2 - x + 1$
straight angle A 180° angle.	**ángulo llano** Ángulo que mide 180°.	
subset A set that is contained entirely within another set. Set B is a subset of set A if every element of B is contained in A, denoted $B \subset A$.	**subconjunto** Conjunto que se encuentra dentro de otro conjunto. El conjunto B es un subconjunto del conjunto A si todos los elementos de B son elementos de A; se expresa $B \subset A$.	The set of integers is a subset of the set of rational numbers.

Glossary/Glosario

ENGLISH	SPANISH	EXAMPLES
supplementary angles Two angles whose measures have a sum of 180°.	**ángulos suplementarios** Dos ángulos cuyas medidas suman 180°.	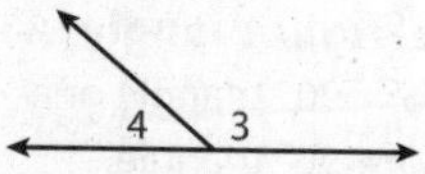 $\angle 3$ and $\angle 4$ are supplementary angles.
symmetry In the transformation of a figure such that the image coincides with the preimage, the image and preimage have symmetry.	**simetría** En la transformación de una figura tal que la imagen coincide con la imagen original, la imagen y la imagen original tienen simetría.	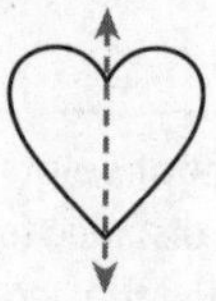
symmetry about an axis In the transformation of a figure such that there is a line about which a three-dimensional figure can be rotated by an angle greater than 0° and less than 360° so that the image coincides with the preimage, the image and preimage have symmetry about an axis.	**simetría axial** En la transformación de una figura tal que existe una línea sobre la cual se puede rotar una figura tridimensional a un ángulo mayor que 0° y menor que 360° de forma que la imagen coincida con la imagen original, la imagen y la imagen original tienen simetría axial.	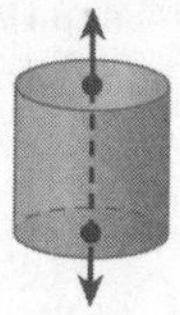
system of equations A set of two or more equations that have two or more variables.	**sistema de ecuaciones** Conjunto de dos o más ecuaciones que contienen dos o más variables.	$2x + 3y = -1$ $3x - 3y = 4$
system of linear inequalities A system of inequalities in two or more variables in which all of the inequalities are linear.	**sistema de desigualdades lineales** Sistema de desigualdades en dos o más variables en el que todas las desigualdades son lineales.	$\begin{cases} 2x + 3y \geq -1 \\ x - 3y < 4 \end{cases}$

T

ENGLISH	SPANISH	EXAMPLES
tangent circles Two coplanar circles that intersect at exactly one point. If one circle is contained inside the other, they are *internally tangent*. If not, they are *externally tangent*.	**círculos tangentes** Dos círculos coplanares que se cruzan únicamente en un punto. Si un círculo contiene a otro, son *tangentes internamente*. De lo contrario, son *tangentes externamente*.	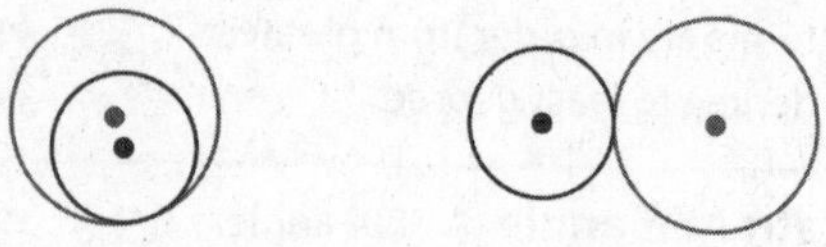
tangent of an angle In a right triangle, the ratio of the length of the leg opposite $\angle A$ to the length of the leg adjacent to $\angle A$.	**tangente de un ángulo** En un triángulo rectángulo, razón entre la longitud del cateto opuesto a $\angle A$ y la longitud del cateto adyacente a $\angle A$.	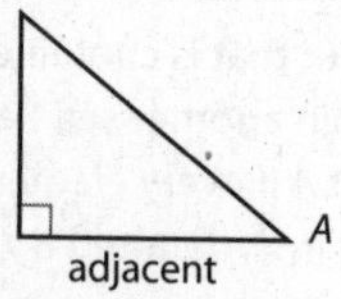 $\tan A = \dfrac{\text{opposite}}{\text{adjacent}}$

ENGLISH	SPANISH	EXAMPLES

tangent segment A segment of a tangent with one endpoint on the circle.

segmento tangente Segmento de una tangente con un extremo en el círculo.

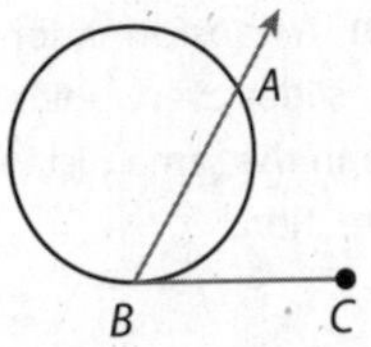

$\overline{BC}$ is a tangent segment.

tangent of a circle A line that is in the same plane as a circle and intersects the circle at exactly one point.

tangente de un círculo Línea que se encuentra en el mismo plano que un círculo y lo cruza únicamente en un punto.

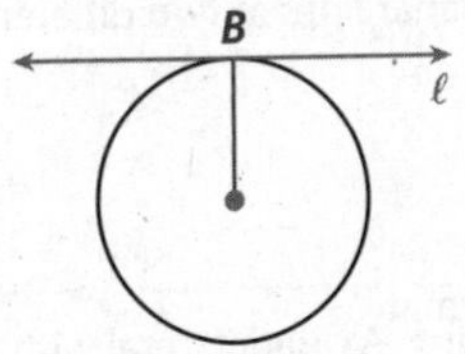

terminal point of a vector The endpoint of a vector.

punto terminal de un vector Extremo de un vector.

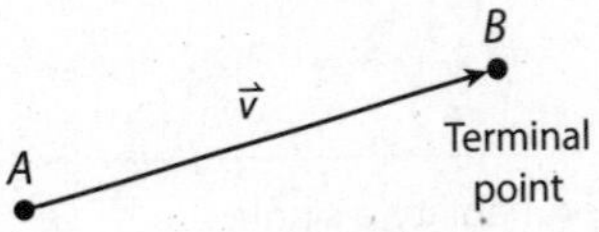

tetrahedron A polyhedron with four faces. A regular tetrahedron has equilateral triangles as faces, with three faces meeting at each vertex.

tetraedro Poliedro con cuatro caras. Las caras de un tetraedro regular son triángulos equiláteros y cada vértice es compartido por tres caras.

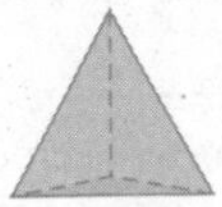

theorem A statement that has been proven.

teorema Enunciado que ha sido demostrado.

theoretical probability The ratio of the number of equally likely outcomes in an event to the total number of possible outcomes.

probabilidad teórica Razón entre el número de resultados igualmente probables de un suceso y el número total de resultados posibles.

In the experiment of rolling a number cube, the theoretical probability of rolling an odd number is $\frac{3}{6} = \frac{1}{2}$.

three-dimensional coordinate system A space that is divided into eight regions by an *x*-axis, a *y*-axis, and a *z*-axis. The locations, or coordinates, of points are given by ordered triples

sistema de coordenadas tridimensional Espacio dividido en ocho regiones por un eje *x*, un eje *y* un eje *z*. Las ubicaciones, o coordenadas, de los puntos son dadas por tripletas ordenadas.

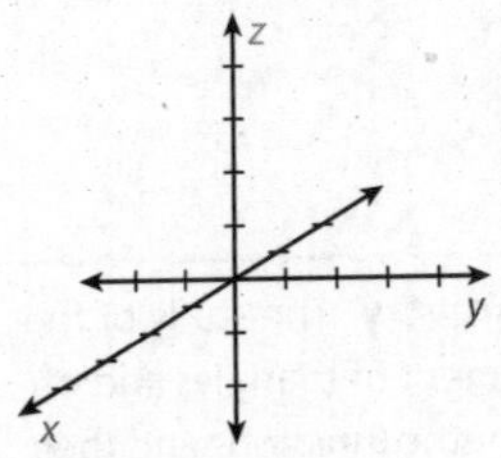

tick marks Marks used on a figure to indicate congruent segments.

marcas "|" Marcas utilizadas en una figura para indicar segmentos congruentes.

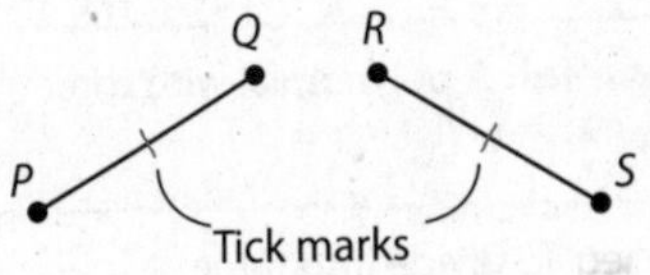

transformation A change in the position, size, or shape of a figure or graph.

transformación Cambio en la posición, tamaño o forma de una figura o gráfica.

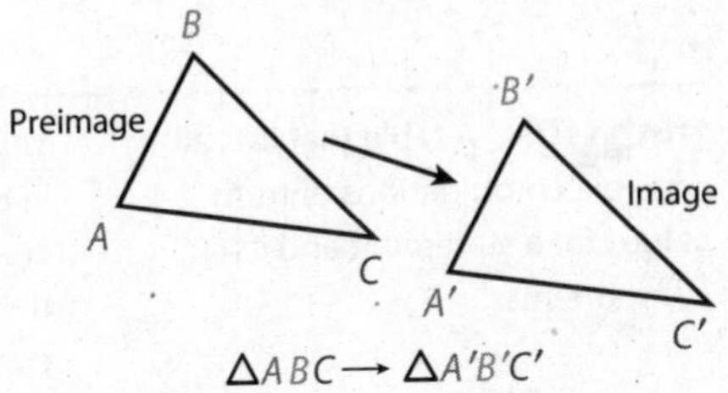

$\triangle ABC \rightarrow \triangle A'B'C'$

Glossary/Glosario

ENGLISH	SPANISH	EXAMPLES
translation A transformation that shifts or slides every point of a figure or graph the same distance in the same direction.	**traslación** Transformación en la que todos los puntos de una figura o gráfica se mueven la misma distancia en la misma dirección.	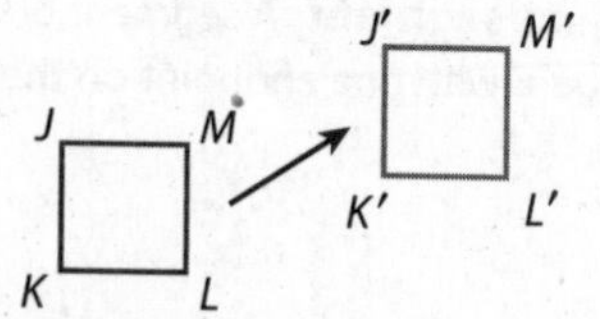
transversal A line that intersects two coplanar lines at two different points.	**transversal** Línea que corta dos líneas coplanares en dos puntos diferentes.	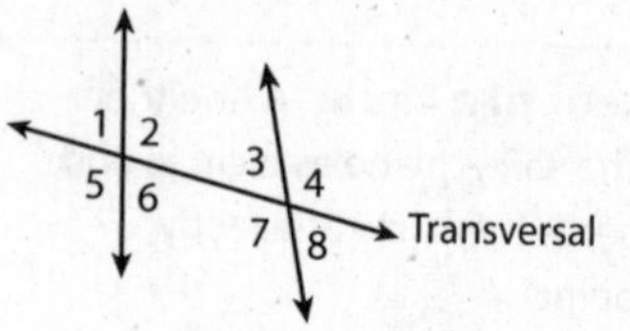
trapezoid A quadrilateral with at least one pair of parallel sides.	**trapecio** Cuadrilátero con al menos un par de lados paralelos.	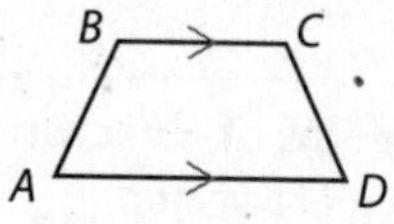
trial In probability, a single repetition or observation of an experiment.	**prueba** En probabilidad, una sola repetición u observación de un experimento.	In the experiment of rolling a number cube, each roll is one trial.
triangle A three-sided polygon.	**triángulo** Polígono de tres lados.	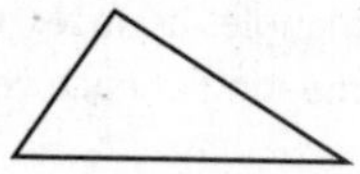
triangle rigidity A property of triangles that states that if the side lengths of a triangle are fixed, the triangle can have only one shape.	**rigidez del triángulo** Propiedad de los triángulos que establece que, si las longitudes de los lados de un triángulo son fijas, el triángulo puede tener sólo una forma.	
trigonometric ratio A ratio of two sides of a right triangle.	**razón trigonométrica** Razón entre dos lados de un triángulo rectángulo.	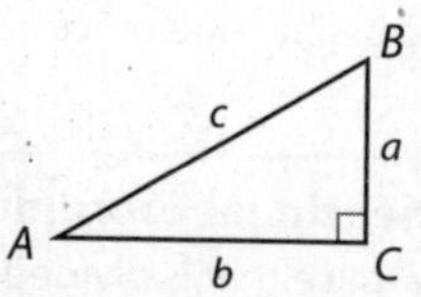 $\sin A = \frac{a}{c}$; $\cos A = \frac{b}{c}$; $\tan A = \frac{a}{b}$
trigonometry The study of the measurement of triangles and of trigonometric functions and their applications.	**trigonometría** Estudio de la medición de los triángulos y de las funciones trigonométricas y sus aplicaciones.	
trinomial A polynomial with three terms.	**trinomio** Polinomio con tres términos.	$4x^2 + 3xy - 5y^2$
trisect To divide into three equal parts.	**trisecar** Dividir en tres partes iguales.	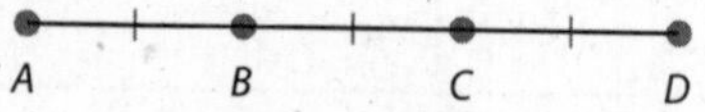 $\overline{AD}$ is trisected.
truth table A table that lists all possible combinations of truth values for a statement and its components.	**tabla de verdad** Tabla en la que se enumeran todas las combinaciones posibles de valores de verdad para un enunciado y sus componentes.	

ENGLISH	SPANISH	EXAMPLES
truth value A statement can have a truth value of true (T) or false (F).	**valor de verdad** Un enunciado puede tener un valor de verdad verdadero (V) o falso (F):	

U

ENGLISH	SPANISH	EXAMPLES
undefined term A basic figure that is not defined in terms of other figures. The undefined terms in geometry are point, line, and plane.	**término indefinido** Figura básica que no está definida en función de otras figuras. Los términos indefinidos en geometría son el punto, la línea y el plano.	
union The union of two sets is the set of all elements that are in either set, denoted by ∪.	**unión** La unión de dos conjuntos es el conjunto de todos los elementos que se encuentran en ambos conjuntos, expresado por ∪.	$A = \left\{1, 2, 3, 4\right\}$ $B = \left\{1, 3, 5, 7, 9\right\}$ $A \cup B = \left\{1, 2, 3, 4, 5, 7, 9\right\}$
universal set The set of all elements in a particular context.	**conjunto universal** Conjunto de todos los elementos de un contexto determinado.	

V

ENGLISH	SPANISH	EXAMPLES
vector A quantity that has both magnitude and direction.	**vector** Cantidad que tiene magnitud y dirección.	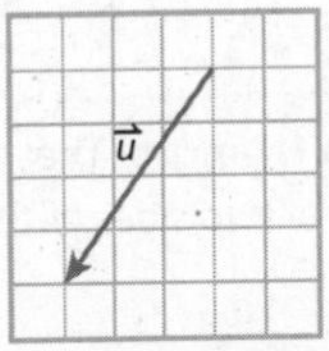
Venn diagram A diagram used to show relationships between sets.	**diagrama de Venn** Diagrama utilizado para mostrar la relación entre conjuntos.	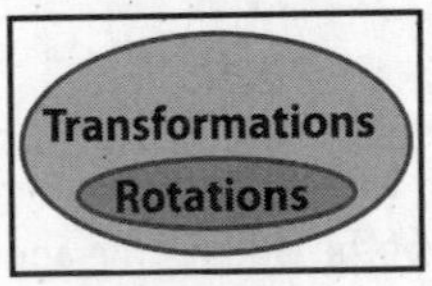
vertex angle of an isosceles triangle The angle formed by the legs of an isosceles triangle.	**ángulo del vértice de un triángulo isósceles** Ángulo formado por los catetos de un triángulo isósceles.	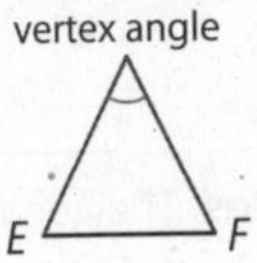
vertex form of a quadratic function A quadratic function written in the form $f(x) = a(x - h)^2 + k$, where a, h, and k are constants and (h, k) is the vertex.	**forma en vértice de una función cuadrática** Una function cuadrática expresada en la forma $f(x) = a(x - h)^2 + k$, donde a, h y k son constantes y (h, k) es el vértice.	

Glossary/Glosario

ENGLISH	SPANISH	EXAMPLES
vertex of a cone The point opposite the base of the cone.	**vértice de un cono** Punto opuesto a la base del cono.	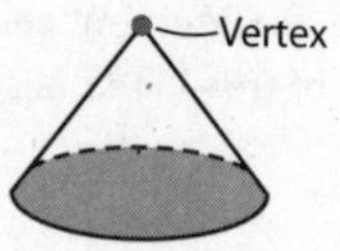
vertex of a parabola The highest or lowest point on the parabola.	**vértice de una parábola** Punto más alto o más bajo de una parábola.	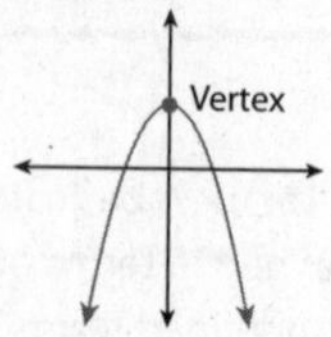
vertex of a polygon The intersection of two sides of the polygon.	**vértice de un polígono** La intersección de dos lados del polígono.	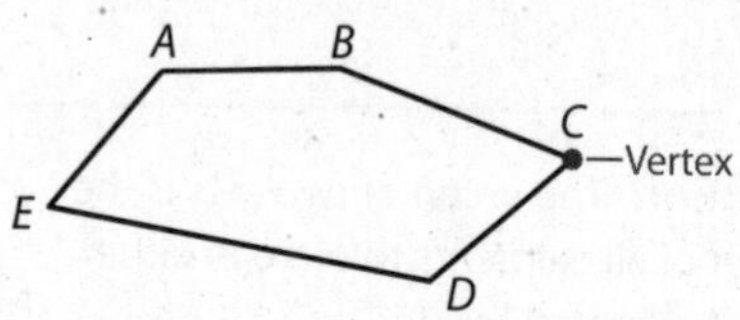 *A*, *B*, *C*, *D*, and *E* are vertices of the polygon.
vertex of a pyramid The point opposite the base of the pyramid.	**vértice de una pirámide** Punto opuesto a la base de la pirámide.	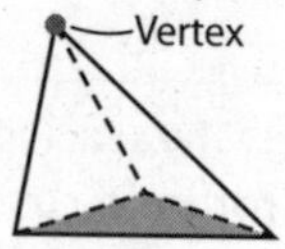
vertex of a three-dimensional figure The point that is the intersection of three or more faces of the figure.	**vértice de una figura tridimensional** Punto que representa la intersección de tres o más caras de la figura.	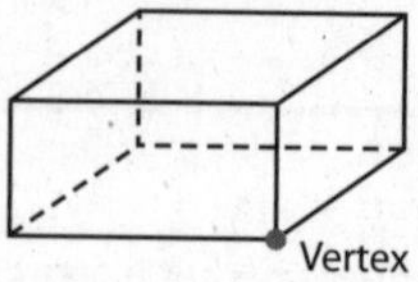
vertex of a triangle The intersection of two sides of the triangle.	**vértice de un triángulo** Intersección de dos lados del triángulo.	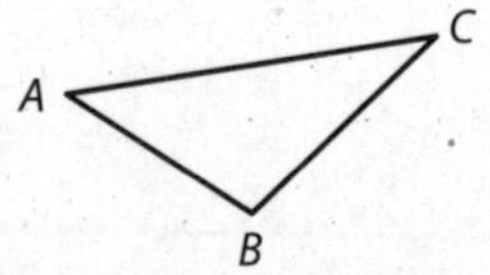 *A*, *B*, and *C* are vertices of $\triangle ABC$.
vertex of an angle The common endpoint of the sides of the angle.	**vértice de un ángulo** Extremo común de los lados del ángulo.	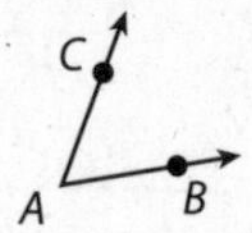 *A* is the vertex of $\angle CAB$.
vertical angles The nonadjacent angles formed by two intersecting lines.	**ángulos opuestos por el vértice** Ángulos no adyacentes formados por dos rectas que se cruzan.	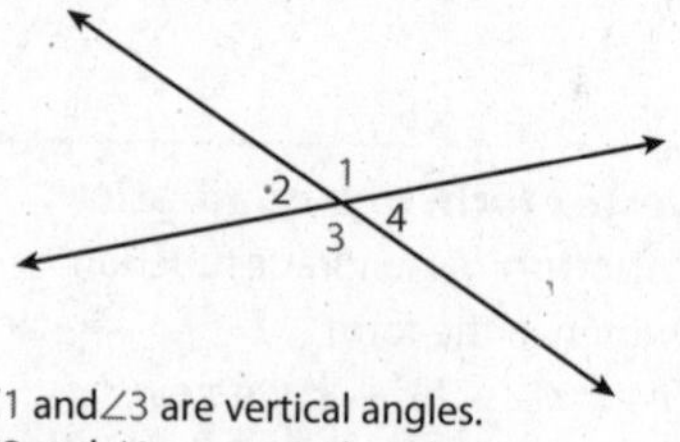 $\angle 1$ and $\angle 3$ are vertical angles. $\angle 2$ and $\angle 4$ are vertical angles.

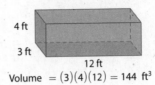

ENGLISH	SPANISH	EXAMPLES
volume The number of nonoverlapping unit cubes of a given size that will exactly fill the interior of a three-dimensional figure.	**volumen** Cantidad de cubos unitarios no superpuestos de un determinado tamaño que llenan exactamente el interior de una figura tridimensional.	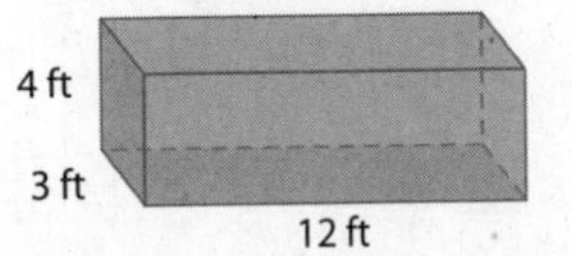 Volume $= (3)(4)(12) = 144\ \text{ft}^3$

X

***x*-axis** The horizontal axis in a coordinate plane.	**eje *x*** Eje horizontal en un plano cartesiano.	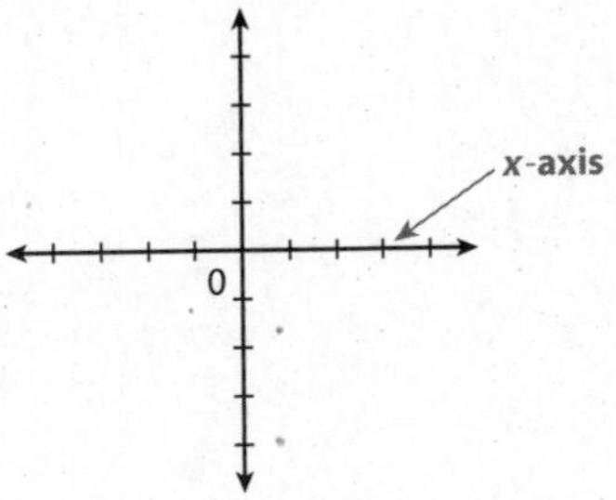

Y

***y*-axis** The vertical axis in a coordinate plane.	**eje *y*** Eje vertical en un plano cartesiano.	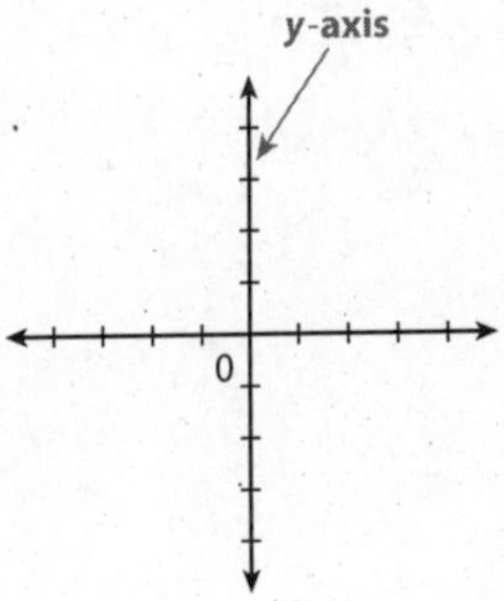

Z

zero exponent For any nonzero real number x, $x^0 = 1$.	**exponente cero** Dado un número real distinto de cero x, $x^0 = 1$.	$5^0 = 1$
zero of a function For the function f, any number x such that $f(x) = 0$.	**cero de una función** Dada la función f, todo número x tal que $f(x) = 0$.	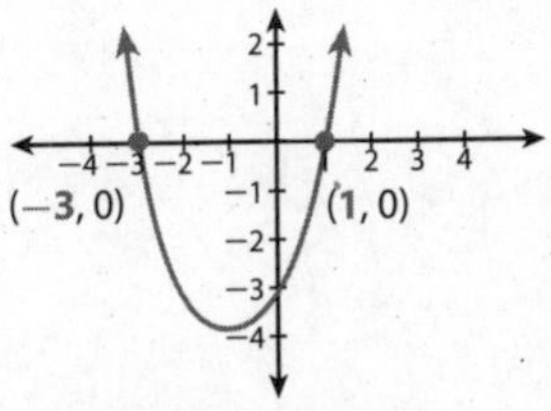 The zeros are −3 and 1.
Zero Product Property For real numbers p and q, if $pq = 0$, then $p = 0$ or $q = 0$.	**Propiedad del producto cero** Dados los números reales p y q, si $pq = 0$, entonces $p = 0$ o $q = 0$.	If $(x - 1)(x + 2) = 0$, then $x - 1 = 0$ or $x + 2 = 0$, so $x = 1$ or $x = -2$.

Index

Index locator numbers are in Module. Lesson form. For example, 2.1 indicates Module 2, Lesson 1 as listed in the Table of Contents.

A

B

C

Index

D

E

F

G

H

I

L

M

Index

N

O

P

Q

R

S

T

U

V

X

Z

Index

Table of Measures

LENGTH

1 inch = 2.54 centimeters
1 meter = 39.37 inches
1 mile = 5,280 feet
1 mile = 1760 yards
1 mile = 1.609 kilometers
1 kilometer = 0.62 mile

CAPACITY

1 cup = 8 fluid ounces
1 pint = 2 cups
1 quart = 2 pints
1 gallon = 4 quarts
1 gallon = 3.785 liters
1 liter = 0.264 gallons
1 liter = 1000 cubic centimeters

MASS/WEIGHT

1 pound = 16 ounces
1 pound = 0.454 kilograms
1 kilogram = 2.2 pounds
1 ton = 2000 pounds

Symbols

$\neq$	is not equal to
$\approx$	is approximately equal to
10^2	ten squared; ten to the second power
$2.\overline{6}$	repeating decimal 2.66666...
$\lvert -4 \rvert$	the absolute value of negative 4
$\sqrt{}$	square root
π	pi: (about 3.14)
$\perp$	is perpendicular to
$\parallel$	is parallel to
$\overleftrightarrow{AB}$	line *AB*
$\overrightarrow{AB}$	ray *AB*
$\overline{AB}$	line segment *AB*
$m\angle A$	measure of $\angle A$

Formulas

FACTORING

Perfect square trinomials	$a^2 + 2ab + b^2 = (a + b)^2$
	$a^2 - 2ab + b^2 = (a - b)^2$
Difference of squares	$a^2 - b^2 = (a - b)(a + b)$

PROPERTIES OF EXPONENTS

Product of powers	$a^m a^n = a^{(m+n)}$
Quotient of powers	$\frac{a^m}{a^n} = a^{(m-n)}$
Power of a power	$(a^m)^n = a^{mn}$
Rational exponent	$a^{\frac{m}{n}} = \sqrt[n]{a^m}$
Negative exponent	$a^{-n} = \frac{1}{a^n}$

QUADRATIC EQUATIONS

Standard form	$f(x) = ax^2 + bx + c$
Vertex form	$f(x) = a(x - h)^2 + k$
Quadratic formula	$x = \frac{-b \pm \sqrt{b^2 - 4ac}}{2a}$
Axis of symmetry	$x = \frac{-b}{2a}$

VOLUME

General Prisms	$V = Bh$
Cylinder	$V = \pi r^2 h$
Sphere	$V = \frac{4}{3}\pi r^3$
Cone	$V = \frac{1}{3}\pi r^2 h$
Pyramid	$V = \frac{1}{3}Bh$